EUROPEAN COMPETITION LAW ANNUAL
1998
Regulating Telecommunications

Claus Dieter Ehlermann
Louisa Gosling
European University Institute

editors

·HART·
PUBLISHING

OXFORD AND PORTLAND OREGON
2000

Hart Publishing
Oxford and Portland, Oregon

Published in North America (US and Canada) by
Hart Publishing
c/o International Specialized Book Services
5804 NE Hassalo Street
Portland, Oregon
97213-3644
USA

Distributed in Netherlands, Belgium and Luxembourg by
Intersentia, Churchillaan 108
B2900 Schoten
Antwerpen
Belgium

Hart Publishing is a specialist legal publisher based in Oxford, England. To order
further copies of this book or to request a list of other publications please write to:

Hart Publishing, Salters Boatyard, Folly Bridge, Abingdon Rd, Oxford, OX1 4LB
Telephone: +44 (0)1865 245533 or Fax: +44 (0)1865 794882
e-mail: mail@hartpub.co.uk
www.hartpub.co.uk

British Library Cataloguing in Publication Data
Data Available

ISBN 1–84113–099–00 (cloth)

Typeset in 10pt Times NR
by Hope Services, Clifton Hampden, Abingdon
Printed in Great Britain by Page Bros, Norwich

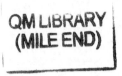

CONTENTS

LIST OF SPONSORS

Allen & Overy: Brussels

Baker & Miller: Washington, DC

British Telecommunications PLC: London

Cable and Wireless: London

Clearly, Gottlieb, Steen & Hamilton: Brussels

Collier, Shannon, Rill & Scott: Washington DC

Coudert Brothers: London

Deutsche Telekom AG: Bonn

Baker & Mckenzie: Frankfurt

ENEL stc/Wind: Rome

Jones, Day, Beavis & Pogue: Brussels

Martinez-Lage & Associates: Madrid

MCI Communications Corp: Washington DC

Skadden, Arps, Slate, Meagher and Flom LLP: New York

Telecom Italia: Rome

White and Case: Brussels

TABLE OF CASES

European Cases

Cases of the European Court of Justice and Court of First Instance

TABLE OF TREATIES AND LEGISLATION

European Union

Articles of the European Treaties

Consolidated Treaties (Amsterdam)	*EC Treaty Article*
Article 3	[ex 3]
Article 10	[ex 5]
Article 28	[ex 30]
Article 49	[ex 30]
Article 81	[ex 85]
Article 82	[ex 86]
Article 86	[ex 90]
Article 95	[ex 100a]
Article 99	[ex 103]
Article 226	[ex 169]
Article 249	[ex 189]

Directives

1987: Directive 87/372/EEC of the Commission on the frequency bands to be reserved for the co-ordinated introduction of public pan-European cellular digital land-based mobile communications in the European Community, OJ L 196/85 (1987).

1990: Directive 90/387/EEC of the Council on the establishment of the internal market for telecommunications services through the implementation of the open network provision (ONP Framework Directive), OJ L 192/1 (1990).

1990: Directive 90/388/EEC of the Commission on competition in the markets for telecommunications services, OJ L 192/10 (1990).

1991: Directive 91/440/EEC of the Council on the development of the Community's railways, OJ L 237/25 (1991).

1992: Directive 92/44 of the Council on the application of open network provision to leased lines, OJ L 165/27 (1992).

1993: Directive 93/38/EEC of the Council co-ordinating the procurement procedures of entities operating in the water, energy, transport and telecommunications sectors, OJ L 199/84 (1993).

1993: Directive 93/97/EEC of the Commission supplementing Directive 91/263/EEC in respect of satellite earth station equipment, OJ L 290/01 (1993).

1994: Directive 94/46/EEC, of the Commission amending Directive 88/301/EEC and Directive 90/388/EEC in particular with regard to satellite communications, OJ L 268/15 (1994).

1995: Directive 95/47/EC of the European Parliament and of the Council on the use of standards for the transmission of television signals, OJ L 281/51 (1995).

1995: Directive 95/51/EC of the Commission amending Directive 09/388/EEC with regard to the abolition of the restrictions on the use of cable television networks for the provision of already liberalised telecommunications service, OJ L 256/49 (1995).

1995: Directive 95/62/EC of the European Parliament and Council on the application of open network provision to voice telephony services, OJ L 321/6 (1995).

1996: Directive 96/2/EC of the Commission amending Directive 90/388/EEC with regard to mobile and personal communications, OJ L 20/59 (1996).

1996: Directive 96/19/EC of the Commission amending Directiv e90/388/EEC with regard to the implementation of full competition in telecommunications markets, OJ L 74/13 (1996).

1997: Directive 97/13/EC of the European Parliament and of the Council on a common framework for general authorisations and individual licences in the field of telecommunications services, OJ L117/15 (1997).

1997: Directive 97/33/EC of the European Parliament and of the Council on interconnection in telecommunications with regard to ensuring universal service and interoperability through the application of the principles of open network provision (ONP), OJ L199/32 (1997).

1997: Directive 97/51/EC of the European Parliament and Council amending Council Directives 90/387/EEC and 92/44/EEC for the purpose of adaptation to a competitive environment in telecommunications (ONP leased lines Directive), OJ L 295/23 (1997).

1998: Directive 98/10/EC of the Council on the application of open network provision to voice telephony, OJ L 101/24 (1998).

1998: Directive 98/301/EC of the Council on competition in the markets in telecommunications equipment, OJ L 131/73 (1998).

1998: Draft Commission Directive amending Directive 98/388/EC in order to ensure that telecommunications networks and cable TV networks owned by a single operator are separate legal entities, OJ C 71/23 (1998).

Regulations

1962: Council Regulation 17/62, implementing Articles 85 and 86 of the Treaty, OJ 13, 21.2.1962, p.204.

1983/84: Commission Regulation on exclusive purchasing agreements, OJ L 173/5 (1983).

1990: Council Regulation 4064/89 on the control of concentrations between undertakings, OJ L257/14 (1990).

1997: Council Regulation 1310/97 amending Council Regulation 4064/89 on the control of concentrations between undertakings, OJ L 180/1 (1992).

General Notices

1998: Commission Notice on the application of the competition rules to access agreements in the telecommunications sector, OJ C 265/02 (1998).

1997: Commission Notice on the definition of the relevant market for the purposes of Community competition law, OJ C 372/5 (1997).

1997: Commission Notice on co-operation between national competition authorities and the Commission in handling cases falling within the scope of Articles 85 and 86 of the OJ C 313/3 (1997).

1995: Commission Notice on the application of EC Competition rules to cross-border credit transfers, OJ C 251/3 (1995).

1990: Commission Notice concerning the status of voice communications on internet under Community law and, in particular, pursuant to Directive 90/388/EC, OJ C 6 (1990).

Communications, Recommendations and Guidelines

1998: Commission Communication on the review under competition rules of the joint provision of telecommunications and cable TV networks by a single operator and the abolition of restrictions on the provision of cable TV capacity over telecommunications, OJ C71/4 (1998).

1998: Commission Recommendation on interconnection in a liberalised telecommunications market, OJ L 73/42 (1998).

1998: Commission Recommendation amending Recommendation 98/195/EC (Part 1—interconnection pricing), OJ L 228/30 (1998).

1998: Commission Recommendation on interconnection in a liberalised telecommunications market (Part 2—accounting separation and cost accounting), OJ L 141/6 (1998).

1998: Commission Guidelines on the method of setting fines imposed pursuan to Article 15(2) of Regulation No 17, OJ C 9/3 (1998).

1998: Commission Communication (Cable Review) concerning the review under competition rules of the joint provision of telecommunications and cable TV networks by a single operator and the abolition of restrictions on the pro vision of cable TV capacity over telecommunications networks, OJ C 71/4 (1998).

United States

1890: Sherman Antitrust Act of 2 July 1890, c. 617, 25 Stat. 209.

1914: Clayton Antitrust Act of 15 October, c. 323, 38 Stat. 730.

1934: Communications Act of 1934, Pub. L. No. 73–416, 48 Stat. 1064 (codi fied as amended in scattered sections of 47 USC).

1938: Robinson-Patman Act (15 USC §§13–14).

1976: Hart-Scott-Rodino Antitrust Improvement Act of 1976, Pub. L. No. 94–435, tit. II §201, 90 Stat. 1380 (codified as amended at 15 USC. §18a (1994).

1982: Foreign Trade Antitrust Improvements Act of 1982 (FTAIA), 15 USC. §6a (1988); *International Guidelines* at §3.12.

1992: US Dept. of Justice & Federal Trade Commission, Horizontal Merger Guidelines (1992), reprinted in 4 Trade Reg. Rep (CCH) 13, 194.

1996: Telecommunications Act of 1996, Pub. L. No. 104–104, 110 Stat. 56 (1996) (codified at 47 USC §§151 *et seq*).

TABLE OF ABBREVIATIONS

AA	American Airlines
AA	Antitrust Authority
ARC	Act Against Restraints of Competition (Germany)
ACA	Australian Communications Authority
ACCC	Australian Competition and Consumer Commission
ADC	Access Deficit Contribution
AP	Associated Press
ART	French Telecoms Authority
ATC	American TV and Communications
ATM	Asynchronous Transfer Mode
AUSTEL	Australian Telecommunications Authority
BA	British Airways
BBC	British Broadcasting Corporation
BIB	British Interactive Broadcasting
BMPT	Federal Ministry of Posts and Telecommunications (Germany)
BR	British Rail
BSB	British Satellite Broadcasting
BT	British Telecom
CAL	Customer Access Lines
CAN	Customer Access Network
CAN	Customer Access Network
CCA	Current Cost Accounting
CFI	Court of First Instance
CRS	Computerised Reservation System
CSD	Spanish Canal Satélite Digital
DAB	Digital Audio Broadcasting
DOJ	Department of Justice
DSL	Digital Subscriber Line Technology .
DT	Deutsche Telekom
DVB	Digital Video Broadcasting
EC	European Community
ECU	European Currency Unit
EEA	European Economic Area
EEC	European Economic Community
ETSI	European Telecommunications Standards Institute
EU	European Union
FCC	Federal Communications Commission
FMI	Fixed-Mobile Integration
FT	France Telecom

FTAIA	Foreign Trade Antitrust Improvements Act (US)
FTC	Federal Trade Commission
GATS	General Agreement on Trade in Services
GSM	Global System for Mobile Communications
HBO	Home Box Office
HCA	Historical Cost Accounting
IAA	Italian Antitrust Authority
IAEAA	International Antitrust Enforcement Assistance Act
ICPAC	International Competition Policy Advisory Committee
ICT	Information and Communication Technologies
IDC	International Data Corporation
IN	Intelligent Network
INMARSAT	International Maritime Satellite Organisation
INS	International News Service
IP	Internet Protocol
IPLCs	International Private Leased Circuits
IPR	Intellectual Property Right
ISDN	Integrated Services Digital Network,
ISOs	Independent Service Organisations
ISPs	Internet Service Providers.
IT	Information Technology
ITC	Independent Television Commission
ITP	Independent Television Publications
JVN	Joint Venture Network
LEC	Local Exchange Carrier
LECOM	Local Exchange Cost Optimisation Model
LH	Lufthansa
LRIC	Long-run Incremental Costs
MDF	Main Distribution Frame
MFJ	Modified Final Judgement
MMC	Monopolies and Mergers Commission
MSG	Media Service Group
MSOs	Multiple System Operators
MSPs	Mobile Service Providers
MTF	Merger Task Force
NERA	National Economic Research Associates
NRA	National Regulatory Authority
NSFI	Non-Shareholding Financial Institution
NTIA	National Telecommunications and Information Administration
NVOD	Near Video on Demand
NZV	Ordinance Concerning Special Network Access (Germany)
O&M	Operating and Maintenance
ODV	Optimised Deprival Value
OFT	Office of Fair Trading (UK)

OFTEL	Office of Telecommunications (UK)
ONP	Open Network Provision
OPTA	Telecommunication Regulatory Authority (Netherlands)
PCMs	Plug-compatible with IBM mainframe
PSTN	Public Switched Telecommunications Networks
PTS	National Post and Telecom Agency (Sweden)
PTTs	Post, Telecommunications and Telegraph
QoS	Quality-of-Service
RBOC	Regional Bell Operating Company
RD	Royal Decree (Spain)
RegTP	Authority for the Regulation of Telecommunications and Posts (Germany)
RFP	Request for Proposal
RTE	Radio Telefis Eireann
SEC	Securities and Exchange Commission
SFN	Single Firm Network
SIM-card	Subscriber Identity Module
SMP	Significant Market Power
SMS	Short Message Services
SPCS	Satellite Personal Communications Systems
SROs	Self-regulatory Organisations
STB	Surface Transportation Board
SWIFT	Society for Worldwide Interbank Telecommunications
T+E	Technology and Economics, Inc.
TCP/IP	Suite of Internet Protocols
TDC	Antitrust Authority (Spain)
TELRIC	Total Element Long-run Incremental Cost
TIM	Telecom Italia Mobile
TKG	Telecommunications Act (Germany)
TMC	Competition Authority (Spain)
TMN	Telecommunications Management Networks
TOs	Telecommunication Organisations
TSLRIC	Total Service Long-run Incremental Cost
UA	United Airlines
ULL	Unbundling of Local Loops
UMTS	Universal Mobile Telecommunications System
UP	United Press
VLSI	Very Large Scale Integrated Microelectronics
VNOs	Virtual Network Operators
WTO	World Trade Organisation
xDSL	Digital Broadband Access

BIOGRAPHICAL NOTES ON
THE PARTICIPANTS

JENS ARNBAK
was born in 1943. He received MSc and PhD degrees from the Technical University of Denmark and worked on international communications for NATO from 1972 until 1980. He held the Chair of Wireless Communications at Eindhoven from 1980 until 1986, when he took up his present assignment as Professor of Tele-information Techniques at Delft University of Technology. Between 1994 and 1997, he was also Part Time Professor in Systems Engineering and Policy Analysis in Delft. He served the Dutch Government in various advisory committees on telecommunications policy from 1984 until 1997, when he was appointed Chairmen of the independent National Regulatory Authority for Post and Telecommunications (OPTA).

MARK ARMSTRONG
is a fellow in economics at Nuffield College, University of Oxford. University of Oxford. His research interests within the sphere of economic policy lie in the regulation of firms with market power and in competition policy, with a special focus on telecommunications and broadcasting markets. He is the author, with Simon Cowan and John Vickers, of *Regulatory Reform: Economic Analysis and British Experience* (1994). He regularly acts an economic advisor to OFTEL. He is currently Managing Editor of the *Review of Economic Studies*.

DONALD I. BAKER
is Senior Partner in the Washington DC law firm of Baker & Miller PLC. He is a former Assistant Attorney General in charge of the Antitrust Division of the US Department of Justice (1976-77) and is the only member of the career staff at the Antitrust Division to have been elevated to that post. He was Professor of Law at the Cornell Law School (1975-76 and 1977-78) and a partner in two major law firms (1978-1994), before founding Baker & Miller. He is author of the treatise, Baker & Brandel, The Law of Electronic Funds Transfer Systems (1980, 1998, 1996, 1999), the article, 'Compulsory Access to Network Joint Ventures under the Sherman Act: Rules or Roulette?' [1993] *Utah Law Review* 999-1133, as well as many other works.

FOD BARNES
was the UK Director General of Telecommunications Policy Advice from 1989 to 1998. In that period, he was closely involved with the transformation of the UK telecommunications sector from effective monopoly supply to effective

competition in most markets. This involvement included the development of the accounting separation structure to be applied to BT and the development of the element based interconnection structure to be applied to BT, as well as the more routine retail price caps and similar issues. He was also very closely involved with the development of OFTEL's approach to the regulatory implementation of convergence. He is currently the Chairmen's Adviser on the Independent Review of the UK Banking Sector (the Cruickshank Review).

HELMUT BROKELMANN

graduated in law from the University of Munich (1994) and obtained a masters degree (LLM) in European Law at the London School of Economics (1994). From 1998 to 1993, he was research and teaching assistant at the Institute of Public International Law at the University of Munich. In 1995, he was admitted to the Madrid Bar and joined Martín Lage & Asociados, one of the foremost European Law Frims in Spain, where he has been a partner since 1999. He specialises in competition law, EU law and telecommunications and media law. He has co-authored, *Telecommunicaciones y Televisión: La nueva regulación en España* (Telecommunications and Television: the New Spanish Regulatory Regime), as well as numerous articles on national and EC competition law.

STUART N. BROTMAN

is President of Stuart N. Brotman Communications, a world-wide management consulting firm from communications, information and entertainment of industry clients. He also teaches at Harvard Law School, where he serves as a Research Fellow. He served as Chairman of the International Communications Committee of the American Bar Association and as a special assistant to President Carter's principal policy advisor on communications at the National Telecommunications and Information Administration in Washington DC. He is also author of four books, including Communications Law and Practice, the leading comprehensive treatise on electronic mass media and common carrier regulation.

CLAUS DIETER EHLERMANN

is Professor of Economic Law at the European University Institute in Florence, and a member of the Appellate Body of the WTO in Geneva. In 1961, he joined the Legal Service of the European Commission, where he was Director General from 1977-1987. He served as spokesman of the Commission from 1987-1990, and then as Director General for Competition from 1990-995. He has lectured at the Colleges of Europe in Bruges, at the Free University of Brussels and at the University of Hamburg, where he became Honorary Professor in 1983. His publications focus on European Community Law and, in particular, on institutional and competition law issues.

HENRY ERGAS

Studied and taught economics before joining the OECD in 1978. At the OECD, he reported on areas as diverse as regulation, industry policy, international trade, competition policy and labour market policies. He was Director of the OECD Secretary-General's Task Force on Structural Adjustment from 1986-87, and OECD Counsellor for Structural Policy from 1991-2. At the same time, prepared a report for the Australian Department of Communications (*Telecommunications and the Australian Economy* 1987) and was a Professor at Monash University and the Ecole Nationale de la Statistique et de l'Administration Economique in Paris. On leaving the OECD in 1992, he taught first at the Kennedy School of Government at Harvad University and then at the University of Auckland. He has advised the Rand Corporation and the Australian Trade Practices Commission and was also a member of the Editorial Boards of *Information Economics and Policy* and of *Telecommunications Policy*. Since 1998 he has advised Telecom Italia and is now Managing Director of the Network Economics Consulting Group in Canberra. Most recently, he was appointed by the Attorney-General of Australia and the Ministry for Industry, Science and Resources to chair a review of Australian intellectual property laws under the terms of national competition policy.

ALLAN FELS

has been Chairman of the Australian Competition and Consumer Commission since 1995. He has a five year appointment. Allan Fels was Chairman of the former Trade Practices Commission from July 1991 until November 1995. He was also Chairman of the Prices Surveillance Authority from March 1989 until October 1992. Allan Fels was formerly the Director of the Graduate School of Management, Monash University from 1985 until 1990, and is now Honorary Professor in the Faculty of Business and economics at Monash University. Professor Fels is the Co-Chairman of the Joint Group in Trade and Competition at the OECD.

IAN FORRESTER

is a Queen's Counsel and practices European law in Brussels with White & Case and Forrester, Norall & Sutton. He also practices as an advocate in Scotland and, as a barrister, is a member of Blackstone Chambers in London. He has participated in many cases before the European Courts, and the European Commission. He represented the European Commission before the European Courts in the *Magill* case about refusals to license by dominant companies, and UEFA in the *Bosman* case about professional football. He specialises in the fields of competition, trade, sport, broadcasting and pharmaceutical regulation. He has lectured on EC legal and policy topics to academic and private bodies in many countries, and has published extensively on these themes. He was appointed Queen's Counsel in 1988 and Visiting Professor in European Law at Glasgow University in 1991.

ELEANOR M. FOX

is the Walter J. Derenberg Professor of Trade Regulation at New York University School of Law. She was a partner and is counsel at the New York law firm Simpson, Thacher & Bartlett. She is a member of the International Competition Policy Advisory Committtee to the Attorney general and the Assistant Attorney General for Antitrust of the United States Department of Justice. She is a member of the Board of Directors and the Executive Committee for Civil Rights Under Law and is a Vice President of the American Law Association. Professor Fox has served as a member of the National Commission for the Review of Antitrust Laws and Procedures, as Chair of the Section of Antitrust and Economic regulation of the Association of American Law Schools, as Chair of the New York Bar Association's Section on Antitrust Law, as Vice President of the Association of the Bar of the City of New York , as Vice Chair of the ABA Antitrust Section, and as Trustee of New York University Law Center Foundation. She frequently visits and lectures at the European Commission's Competition Directorate. Her publications include an antitrust casebook, an EU casebook, a merger treatise, an analysis of competition policy in Central Europe (all co-authored), as well as many articles.

LOUISA KATHERINE GOSLING

is a specialist consultant in telecommunications policy and its effects on market development. Over the past ten years of rapid technological and regulatory change, she has worked as an expert for market players, regulators, think-tanks and academic institutions alike. While a large part of her recent research and work experience has been concentrated within the EU, Louisa Gosling has also worked as a policy consultant in Australia and the United States. Her recent posts include in-house expert for DG IV of the European Commission and internal consultant with the OECD (Telecom and Information Services Policy). Commercial clients have included Sprint, Bellcore, Telstra, Kingston Communications and Cable & Wireless PLC. Louisa Gosling was born in the UK in 1968. She was at school in Melbourne, Australia (1976-85), and is a graduate of Cambridge University.

BARRY HAWK

is a partner at Skadden, Arps, Slate, Meagher & Flom LLP and Director of the Fordham Corporate Law Institute in New York. From 1968-1990, he was Professor at Fordham Law School in New York. He has lectured at, among other institutions, Michigan Law School, New York University Law School and the University of Paris. He has published numerous books and articles focused primarily on competition law and EC law and he has edited the annual volumes of the proceedings of the Fordham Corporate Law Institute since 1974.

HERBERT HOVENKAMP
is the Ben V. & Dorothy Willie Professor of Law and History at the University of Iowa. He is the author of Antitrust Law (formerly with Areeda and Turner, now both deceased), which is published in 18 volumes and is the leading treatise on United States Antitrust Law. He has also written numerous other books and articles in the general area of United States antitrust law. In addition to antitrust, he teaches in the fields of American legal history and real property.

ULTICH IMMEGA
Is Professor of Law at the University of Göttingen, where he has been the Director of the Institute of International Economic Law since 1974. From 1986-89, he was a member and Chairman of the German Monopolies Commission. He was also Professor of Law at Bielefeld (1970-1) and Lausanne (1971-74). He has been Visiting Professor at Georgetown University (USA), Kobe University (Japan), Nanking University (People's Republic of China) and several universities in France. His publications focus on competition law, corporate law and European law, with reference to comparative and international aspects.

FRÉDÉRIC JENNY
is Vice Chairman of the Conseil de la Concurrence. Since 1997, he has chaired the WTO Working Group on the Interaction between Trade and Competition Policy. In 1996, he was appointed special advisor, he was appointed special advisor to the French Minister of International Trade and Competition on international and competition issues. In 1994, he was elected Chairman of the OECD Competition Law and Policy Committee. He was General Counsel (Rapporteur General) of the Conseil de la Concurrence from 1985-1992. Professor Jenny served as a special assistant to the French Minister for Consumer Affairs in 1977, where he was in charge of the revision of French antitrust law. He has taught as Visiting Professor at Northwestern University (USA), Keio University (Japan), and the University of Capetown (South Africa).

GÜNTER KNIEPS
was born in 1950. From 1988-1992, he was Professor of Micro-Economics at the University of Groningen (Netherlands). Since October 1992, he has been Professor of Economics and Director of the Institute of Transportation Science and Regional Policy at the University of Freiburg (Germany). He has published widely on network economics, (de)regulation, competition policy, industrial economics and has undertaken sector studies on telecommunications and transportation.

COLIN D. LONG
is Partner and Joint Director of the Telecommunications Group of Olswang Solicitors, London.

SANTIAGO MARTÍNEZ LAGE

is a supernumerary member of the Spanish diplomatic corps and was Chief
Legal Counsel at the Office of the Secretary for State for Relations with the
European Community during the negotiations for Spanish accession; he also
founded Martínez Lage & Aociados, a law specialising in European
Community Law and Competition Law, in 1985. Santiago Martínez Lage also
edits *the Gaceta Jurídica de la CE y de la Competencia* (EC and Competition
Law Gazette), is Secretary General of the Spanish Association for the Study of
European Law (FIDE), is a former arbitratoe on the Intellectual Property
Arbitration Commission, and is a member of the Royal Spanish Academy for
Jurisprudence and legislation.

BRUNO LASSERRE

undertook postgraduate legal and political studies at the University of
Bordeaux and the Institute d'Etude Politiques de Bordeaux and graduated
from the Ecole National d'Administration. In 1978 he was appointed to the
Conseil d'Etat, in which he served for eight years. He was also a Rapporteur
General of the National Commission on the Right of Reply on Television and
in the Radio. In 1986, he was appointed Director of Legal Affairs at the
Directorate General of Telecommunications and thereafter became Head of
the French National Regulatory Authority for Telecommunications: first, as
Director of Regulatory Affairs at the Ministry of Posts and telecommunica-
tions (1989-1993), then as Director General for Posts and telecommunications.
In this period, he implemented the reform and liberalisation of the French regulatory framework for telecoms and oversaw the privatisation of France
Telecom and the establishment of an independent regulatory authority. He
returned to the Conseil d'Etat in 1988 and was appointed Conseiller d'Etat in
1995. He now heads a Government Commission on 'Government and
Information Technologies', is a Vice Chairman of the National Commission
on Freedom of Information, and is a member of the Conseil de la Concurrence.
He is also a Chevalier de la Legion d'Honneur and has published *Open
Government* (1987).

JAMES F. RILL

graduated from Harvard Law School and is a partner with Collier, Shannon,
Rill & Scott. He frequently appears before the US Department of Justice's
Antitrust Division and the Federal Trade Commission. He also has an active
competition and merger law practice before the US courts and regularly
appears before the competition agencies of foreign jurisdictions. James F. Rill
was Chair of the American Bar Association's Antitrust Section (1987-9) and
the Assistant Attorney General of the Department of Justice's Antitrust
Division (1989-1992). In this capacity, he was the architect of the 1992
Horizontal Merger Guidelines. He is currently Vice Chair of the Business
Advisory Committee to the OECD and advises the OECD on issues involving
competition and trade, including market access and the role of WTO policy

convergence. In 1997, he was appointed Joint Chair of the International Competition Policy Advisory Committee which tackles modern, international antitrust problems. He has published widely and serves on the editorial boards of *Antitrust and Trade Regulation,* The *Antitrust Bulletin* and the *Antitrust Report.*

DANIEL RUBINFELD (ROBERT MAJURE)

is Robert L. Bridges Professor of Law and Professor of Economics at the University of California, Berkeley. He has served as Deputy Assistant Attorney General at the Antitrust Division of the US Department of Justice (1997-8) and is currently a consultant to the Division. He is currently Assistant Chief of the Economic Regulatory Section at the Antitrust Division of the Depratment of Justice.

ALEXANDER SCHAUB

has served as Director general for Competition of the European Commission since May 1995. From 1990-95, he was Deputy Director General for Industry. Alexander Schaub previously served in the cabinets of Ralf Dahrendorf, Guido Brunner, Viscount Etienne Davignin, President gaston Thorn and William de Clerq. In 1998, he was appointed Director at the Directorate General for External Relations and Trade Policy.

JOACHIM SCHERER

is a partner in the Frankfurt office of Baker & McKenzie and a member of Baker & McKenzie's European Law Center in Brussels. He chairs Baker & McKenzie's Telecommunications Law Practice Group on telecommunications law, media law, administrative law, constitutional law and EU law. He advises national, European and international telecommunications enterprises and governmental entities on telecommunications law, media law and data protection law. He is a professor at the Law Faculty of Johann-Wolfgang Goethe University in Frankfurt. He has edited *Telecommunications Laws in Europe,* (4th edition, Butterworth 1998) and is the author of numerous publications.

KLAUS-DIETER SCHEURLE

graduated in Law from Würzburg University in 1980, and completed his practical legal studies in Bavaria (1983). From 1983 to 1985, he worked at the German Federal Ministry of Justice. From 1985 to 1989, he worked at the Bavarian State Ministry for Federal and European Affairs and was subsequently a member of the CDU/CSU parliamentary group. In 1993, Klaus-Dieter Scheurle became Personal Secretary to the Federal Minister of Posts and Telecommunications. In 1995, he became Director of the Basic Policy and International Affairs department at the Federal Ministry of Postst and telecommunications (BMPT). In 1997, he became the Director of the Regulation Department at the BMPT and progressed to the post of President of the BMPT in 1998.

MARIO SIRAGUSA

is a partner at the firm Cleary, Gottlieb, Steen & Hamilton. He is engaged in corporate and commercial practice and specialises in EC competition law. Mr Siragusa began work at the firm in 1973. He is Professor at the Colleges of Europe, Bruges and at the Catholic University, Milan. He lectures on EC law at conferences in various European countries and in the US and has also published numerous articles on EC law.

JAMES S. VENIT

is Joint Chair of the Antitrust Group of Wimer, Cutler & Pickering. He specialises in EU competition law and has had extensive experience in representing multinational companies before the EU Commission in proceedings under Articles 81, 82 (ex 85, 86) and the Merger regulation. James S. Venit has written extensively on various subjects concerning EU competition law, including intellectual property, joint ventures and mergers. He was educated at Yale (BA), Columbia (PhD) and New York (JD) Universities.

ROBERT VERRUE

Has been the Director General of the European Commission responsible for the Information Society (Telecommunications, Markets, Technologies: Innovation and Exploitation Research) since 1996. He studied at the Ecole Supérieure de Commerce et d'Administration des Enterprises (Lille), at the College of Europe (Bruges) and at INSEAD (Fontainbleau), where he was also an assistant. After working in the private sector as a financial manager for SSIH (Switzerland) he joined the European Commission as a member of the DG for Economic and Financial Affairs in 1973. In 1981 he became a member of Vice President Ortoli's cabinet and was responsible for financial and economic affairs, borrowing and lending and restructuring in the coal and steel industry. In 1985, he returned to the DG for Economic and Financial Affairs, becoming head of Division for the Co-ordination of Monetary Policies within the Community. In 1988, he joined the DG for Internal Market and Industrial Affairs as the Director responsible for the co-ordination of the internal market programme. In 1993, he became Deputy Director general responsible for relations wuth Central European countries and CIS republics within the Directorate General for External Relations.

PETER WATERS (DAVID STEWART AND ANDREW SIMPSON)

Peter Waters is a Partner and David Stewart and Andrew Simpson are lawyers of the communications' and technology' law firm, Gilbert & Tobin Lawyers. David Stewart and Andrew Simpson are currently on secondment to Cable & Wireless in London.

DIETER WOLF
Has been president of the German Bundeskartellamt, Berlin, since 1972. Previously, he was employed by the federal Ministry of Economics, where he headed the Industrial Policy Subdivision and the Competition Policy Section.

DIMITRI YPSILANTI
is Head of the telecommunications and Information Policy Section at the Organisation for Economic Co-operation and Development (OECD). Dimitri Ypsilanti's work has included economic and policy analysis in a range of areas, including trade in telecommunication services, international telecommunication tariff-setting and accounting rate issues, the analysis of regulatory issues and the comparative analysis of telecommunications performance among the OECD member countries. Dimitri Ypsilanti has authored numerous articles and books published by the OECD. He studied economics at Bristol University (UK) and at the Memorial and Queens Universities in Canada.

INTRODUCTION

This volume comprises the collected written works prepared for, as well as the edited transcripts of debates held at, the Third Workshop on European Competition Law, which was hosted by the Robert Schuman Centre of the European University Institute, in Florence, in November 1998. Following the successful examples of the First and Second Workshops on European Competition Law, held in April 1996 and June 1997, the Third Workshop brought together a group of around forty leading administrative officials, renowned scholars, private practitioners and representatives from the telecommunications industry. Once again, participants mainly came from the European Union and its Member States, although, Australia, New Zealand and the United States were also represented. With an eye to the particular problems to be discussed, however, the participants at the Third Workshop were not limited to the representatives of the major competition enforcement authorities or academics and private practitioners specialising in competition law. Instead, the group also comprised present and past telecommunications regulators, commercial and academic experts in telecommunications and leading members of the communications industry. Over two days, broken down into three panels, the Workshop discussed the question of how to ensure effective competition in the rapidly evolving telecommunications markets.

In particular, the Workshop was designed to tackle the question of whether, when and how governments should intervene to prevent increasingly powerful firms from abusing their control of the critical 'gateways', or 'bottlenecks', between consumers and the communication information services that underpin our so-called 'information society'. Both service providers and consumers must have access to communications networks, but, while the liberalisation of the telecommunications industry throughout the European Union has opened up the market for the provision of telecommunications networks, this liberalisation alone has not ensured the elimination of established concentrations of market power, nor can it prevent the emergence of new ones.

Market liberalisation and privatisation is replacing traditional government control of the (wired and wireless) communications infrastructure with private ownership. At the same time, technological advances in digitisation and the co-ordination of telephone, audio-visual and computer connected data services (such as internet), determine that one communications network will soon be able to provide customers with access to all these services. The risk of monopoly control over such access is, therefore, an increasingly real one. One obvious solution to the problem of monopoly over access is investment in new and alternative networks that bypass the monopoly structure. However, access bottlenecks remain where duplication is neither technically, nor economically, feasible.

The three panels were designed to address the following three groups of questions:

(1) Panel One was given the task of addressing the question of how efficient access to existing bottleneck network facilities, which are controlled by a dominant company, can be guaranteed. How might competitive access to these network gateways between the providers of, and the potential customers for, services be ensured?

(2) Panel Two was asked to discuss the issues arising in relation to changes in the market structure that have been brought about by co-operative or concentrative interaction between two or more enterprises. How are we to approach strategic alliances, joint ventures, mergers and acquisitions that involve access facilities?

(3) Panel Three was set up to address institutional problems, in particular, the problem of who should be responsible for such issues and for making sure that the rules of fair play and effective competition are effective.

Since the Annual Workshops held at the Robert Schuman Centre of the European University Institute are, at core, workshops on competition law and policy, one of the foremost aims of the organisers was to pinpoint the role which competition law principles play—or could play—in the addressing of the three challenges outlined above. The working hypothesis which formed the basis for the distinction between Panel One and Panel Two was, therefore, directly drawn from differentiation made by EU competition law between the form of anti-competitive behaviour which falls under Article 82 [ex 86] (Panel One) and that which falls under Article 81 [ex 85] (Panel Two) of the Consolidated European Treaties.

Although undoubtedly closely linked to the substantive issues tackled by Panels One and Two, institutional issues were nonetheless dealt with in a separate forum. All too often, the question of 'who does what', is confused with the issue of 'what is to be done', and the further question of 'how is it to be done'. While the issue of 'who does what' is, in theory at least, a second order concern, it is also, in practice, characterised by the strongest political overtones. Institutional issues tend to become the implicit, if not explicit, focus of contention between policy makers within the debate about the application of competition law to the telecommunications sector, since it impacts upon the powers, competence and, indeed, career interests of those involved. Our aim, therefore, was to distance the 'turf war' from the substantive issues of law and policy discussed in Panels One and Two.

The division of labour between the three panels may also be incidentally advantageous to any reader wishing to concentrate his or her attentions on one single aspect of the debate. However, readers should nonetheless take care not to overlook important contributions to the workshop. To take but one striking example, the papers and oral interventions by the competition law experts gathered together in Panel One concentrated, naturally enough, on the 'essential facilities' doctrine. This doctrine was examined in depth, both as regards its origins and developments in the United States and with respect to its recent appearance within EU competition policy and jurisprudence. However, this doctrine was also tackled by contributors to Panel Two, and was even referred to during the discussions within Panel Three. In other words, readers are advised to peruse the entire proceedings for important insights on any one issue and not to be seduced by what may, in fact, be a somewhat artificial distinction between the three panels.

As was the case with the two prior volumes in this series, the transcripts of the panel discussions precede the working papers, prepared in advance for each of the three panels. Naturally, it is for the individual reader to decide in which order he or she wishes to approach the material; nonetheless, the edited transcripts may serve as a useful introduction to the issues examined by each of the panels.

It is not possible to summarise the multitude of insights which the reader will gain through the study of this volume in a few pages. Equally, we do not wish to compete with the expert conclusions of our General Rapporteurs. Thus, the following introductory remarks are limited to a few salient points, which will, we hope, stimulate the curiosity of our readers and incite them to read the major parts or–better still–the whole of this volume.

I. Access to Bottleneck Facilities

Panel One addressed the general problem of access to the resources which market entrants must have disposed of in order to compete in service provision, but which are controlled by their most powerful competitor; a competitor, moreover, who normally has both the incentive and the ability to frustrate the new entrants' competitive efforts. What are (or should be) the obligations of dominant market players to grant access to their network facilities to other, often competing, service providers?

Where are the critical bottlenecks? Can existing competition law, in particular, the 'essential facility' doctrine, satisfactorily guarantee access to these bottlenecks, or are sector-specific regulations either necessary or desirable? These questions arise, in particular, with regard to access pricing, technical interfaces, non-discrimination and structural solutions. Should access rates be negotiated commercially and controlled (*ex post*) through the application of general competition law. Alternatively, should they be regulated (*ex ante*) by special rules? How are these rates to be determined? What are the problems raised by technical rules with regard to transparency and the licensing of IPR at technical interfaces? How 'unbundled', or free from additional packaged services, should access to the facility be? What does non-discriminatory access mean? Should it be defined, and if so, how? To what extent are structural regulatory solutions— *i.e.* enforced unbundling of the access control function from the integrated services business—necessary or desirable? Should unbundling simply be limited to separate accounting or should it extend to the establishment of different legal entities or even total divestiture? How is any putative friction between consumer welfare and the encouragement of competitive entry to be overcome?

These questions were comprehensively examined in the working papers and in the panel discussion. With regard to these issues, the representatives of the 'competition law family' tended to be more in agreement than their 'telecommunications regulation relatives'. However, the views of the latter group proved to be better attuned to the need to find solutions to the problems which arose in Panel One discussions.

There was general consensus among the participants on the identification of the main network bottlenecks of current concern. In particular, bottlenecks are found at: the final network connection or interface with the customer, *i.e.* the fixed 'local loop' (the stretch of dedicated cable reaching the user's own premises); the 'set-top box' (which will increasingly control access to pay TV services); and the navigation software or 'browser' which represents the essential interface between a single computer terminal and the private or public network linking it with other computers and network services. Other current bottlenecks that were mentioned were radio frequencies, radio sites, rights of way and undersea cable. Some bottlenecks will diminish in significance or disappear, while others will become even more critical than they are today. New bottlenecks will emerge in the future.

There was general consensus that the principles of competition law furnish us with an adequate tool to define and to identify where and what the competition problems are, *i.e.* to locate the main bottlenecks and to describe the associated risks of an abuse of market power. All participants confirmed that bottlenecks must be identified with the utmost caution and precision.

By contrast, however, there was also general agreement that competition law, acting alone, cannot establish and implement the 'behavioural' solutions for current structural problems, *i.e.* the cases where bottlenecks exist and persist in the (tele)communications markets. In general, sector-specific solutions were perceived to be necessary in order to allow for the placing of obligations on the gatekeeper of the bottleneck as regards reasonable terms and price of access to a monopoly network resource where such access is essential for other service providers who wish to compete on the market.

The main instrument offered by competition law to ensure access to network bottlenecks is the 'essential facility' doctrine. Developed in the United States, this doctrine is increasingly being used in EU competition law and its principles underlie the 'Access Notice', published by the Commission in 1998. However, although the doctrine has proved to be extremely useful from a conceptual point of view, most participants nonetheless felt that, in practice, the application of this doctrine could not guarantee satisfactory access to network bottlenecks. In particular, the participants were concerned that the doctrine is not precise or certain enough for immediate application and, thus, that the competition authorities, notably DG IV, would not be able to apply it within the relatively short time-frame demanded with regard to the rapidly evolving communication markets.

Recourse to the 'essential facility' doctrine is particularly troublesome with regard to bottlenecks resulting from intellectual property rights, since application of the doctrine could cancel rights intentionally granted by the legislator. By contrast, the abuse of dominant positions which directly result from personal (intellectual property) rights can be tackled through structural remedies (such as the granting of non-exclusive licenses) which are not, or are less easily, available in other circumstances.

The Access Notice recognises, with certain caveats, the priority of sector specific rules. One of the reasons for DG IV's modesty is probably the difficulties which any competition enforcement agency will face if it attempts to determine the appropriate access price with reference to competition law principles.

The difficulties faced by regulators (and, particularly, sector-specific regulators) in their attempts to determine access prices occupy a substantial part of the written and oral contributions to Panel One. Not being sufficiently

familiar with highly technical problems of cost analysis and accounting principles, we prefer not to comment on these aspects of the workshop and to leave
them to the expert participants and the readers.

These difficulties notwithstanding, the EU's directives and recommendations for sector-specific (tele)communications rules, as well as national implementing regulations, were felt, by some at least, to have laid an adequate basis
for the liberalisation of the European (tele)communications market and was
generally considered to be satisfactory and successful. Although the debate did
not fully examine the question of whether the European regulatory framework
should be strengthened and widened, certain warnings were nonetheless voiced
in this regard. Despite the clearly apparent limitations of competition law in
general, and the 'essential facility' doctrine in particular, representatives of the
'competition law family' seemed to be more inclined to rely on traditional competition law instruments than were their 'telecommunication regulation relatives' and the representatives of industry. The latter groups, however, conceded
that sector-specific rules should be informed by the principles of competition
law.

One of the major differences of opinion between participants concerned the
nature of sector-specific regulation. Should this regulation be symmetric for
incumbents and newcomers? Or should it be asymmetric, applying only, or
more intensely, to incumbents? Should incumbents be restricted with respect to
certain business activities and to what extent? Should structural solutions be
imposed upon them and how far should these solutions extend? These questions were not only posed with an eye to economic efficiency, but also derived
from a legal perspective which emphasised dominant positions which had
resulted from exclusive rights historically granted by national governments (see
Article 86 [ex 90] of the Consolidated Treaty).

II. Changes in Market Structure, Brought About by Strategic Alliances, Joint Ventures, Mergers and Acquisitions

Panel Two was asked to discuss the issues resulting from changes in market
structure, which create or reinforce a network access bottleneck, and which are
brought about by co-operative or concentrative interaction between two or
more enterprises. Which regulatory approach should be applied to strategic
alliances, joint ventures, mergers and acquisitions that involve access facilities?
Does it make a difference whether these operations are of a horizontal (*e.g.* the
formation of Global One by Deutsche Telekom, France Telecom and Sprint) or
of a vertical nature (*e.g.* the joint venture between Bertelsmann, Kirch and

Deutsche Telekom)? Does existing competition law provide the appropriate answers? What are the main challenges regarding the application of antitrust rules to agreements involving communications networks? Are these problems particular to this sector? How are the relevant market(s) to be defined in the face of rapid technological development and related globalisation and convergence trends? How are the traditional concepts of dominance and contestability to be applied? Are antitrust decisions in these areas affected by policy considerations—such as the fostering of investment and innovation in new technology and services, even at the price of market foreclosure in the short and medium term—that are different from the traditional objectives of competition policy? Is the development of one (dominant) integrated network and service operator, providing broadband access and interactive services, better than no development at all? Are national or regional competition authorities (such as the EU) suitably placed and equipped to evaluate and to decide upon strategic alliances, joint ventures and mergers that are increasingly international in nature?

The discussions were characterised by a high degree of consensus upon most issues. The most important point of agreement among participants, however, was not even explicitly addressed: the starting assumption in this sector is that general antitrust law *should* be sufficient to prevent the establishment or reinforcement of bottlenecks—and thereby dominant positions—through strategic alliances, joint ventures, mergers and acquisitions. While, as Panel Three demonstrated, sectoral rules do exist and are generally considered to be justified if they deal with the content of information and are designed to protect the plurality of opinions, the underlying contention was that sector-specific rules should not address the problems of co-operation and concentration in the (tele)communications industries. A further implicit area of agreement seemed to exist in that no arguments were made in favour of the adjustment of traditional competition policy objectives in order to take account of industrial policy concerns. On the contrary, such considerations were explicitly rejected by high-ranking antitrust officials.

Normally, horizontal agreements among competitors are considered to be much more dangerous than vertical agreements among companies operating at different levels of the production chain. It was generally agreed that this traditional wisdom does not apply to communications industries. In this sector, vertical agreements can be as dangerous as—if not more dangerous than—horizontal alliances, joint ventures or concentrations. The proceedings of Panel Two and, in particular, the analysis of recent decisions taken by the European Commission, both under Article 81 [ex 85] and under the Merger Regulation, offer ample illustration for this finding. One of the best examples is agreements made between content providers, distributors and network owners in an effort to gain a firm hold over the so-called 'set-top box' which controls access to pay TV services. In this respect, participants were not drawn to criticise the European Commission's widely reported decisions in the *Bertelsmann/Kirch/Deutsche Telekom* and the *British Interactive Broadcasting* cases.

However, the analysis of effects of co-operation and concentration in the field of information technologies is complicated by at least three factors that, although also present in other sectors of the economy, are unusually powerful in this area. The most important is certainly: (1) the extraordinarily rapid process of technological change that has led to convergence between hitherto distinct activities, followed by (2) the liberalisation of traditionally monopolised markets, and (3) globalisation. The use of fundamental economic antitrust analysis tools, such as the determination of the relevant product and geographic market, is, therefore, very difficult, while the risk of errors might be higher than in other sectors. An oft-cited example of unforeseen technological change was the unexpected predominance of the internet.

Participants agreed that, in evaluating the effects of co-operation and concentration in the field of information technologies, antitrust authorities must take into account the present status and the future evolution of the de-monopolisation process and, more generally, of the regulatory situation in the countries which constitute, jointly or severally, the relevant geographic market. Cited examples of contrasting situations included the BT/MCI 'Concert' project in juxtaposition with the DT/FT 'Atlas' operation and the DT/FT/Sprint 'Global One' undertaking. The fact that the decisions in these cases, whether based on Article 81(3) [ex 85(3)] or on the Merger Regulation, might have a considerable influence on the regulatory process was noted, but not criticised.

The emergence or reinforcement of anti-competitive bottlenecks can often be avoided through the appropriate remedies. Participants broadly agreed that these remedies should be structural in nature, so that the regulation or the control of behavioural obligations or conditions is not necessary. While this has been the traditional policy of the European Commission under the Merger Regulation, practice under Article 81(3) [ex 85(3)] has been much more varied. Some participants queried whether the recent reform of the Merger Regulation, equating co-operative behaviour with concentrative joint ventures, will really lead the Commission to take a more flexible attitude towards the implementation of behavioural remedies under the Merger Regulation, thus facilitating the approval of operations which are difficult to evaluate because of the rapidly changing market structures.

These questions about appropriate remedies are part of a wider—and somewhat surprising—concern. Since the early 1990s, both the Merger Regulation and the Commission have been praised with regard to the speed, efficiency and, thus, legal certainty that Merger Regulation decisions provide. Some participants, however, expressed regret that the flexibility found under of the old Article 81(3) [ex 85(3)] procedure for co-operative joint ventures (no deadlines, possibility of review at the expiry of the individual exemption decisions, and behavioural remedies) has been lost. It is possible that similar—and even more serious—regrets will be voiced if the Commission proceeds with its plans to reform Regulation No. 17/62, and abandons the system of prior notification and administrative authorisation under Article 81(3) [ex 85(3)]. Although these instruments are not specific to the communications industries, they may be of particular relevance in this area because of the enormous investments involved and the overwhelming need for legal security.

The rather surprising considerations about the merits of an examination under Article 81 [ex 85] were paralleled by the requests made by some participants that alliances and joint ventures falling under this Article should not be disadvantaged—with respect to access to bottlenecks—as compared with dominant operators who are judged according to Article 82 [ex 86], or with operations to be evaluated under the Merger Regulation. More precisely, the essential facility doctrine should not be more extensively applied under Article 81(3) [ex 85(3)] than under Article 82 [ex 86].

This is only one—although, perhaps, the most important—aspect of a wider debate about the merits of joint ventures, in general, and joint venture networks, in particular, as compared to single firm dominance and single firm networks. One participant forcefully argued that differences in the treatment of joint ventures and single operators, notably in the US, are not justified, and that the creation of networks, as well as competition among networks at network level, should be encouraged. In this view, the EU approach to joint ventures is better balanced and, therefore, preferable. Other participants, however, disagreed. They emphasised the objective differences between co-operation between actual or potential competitors and the behaviour of a single—even dominant—market player. They, therefore, consider that differences in treatment under existing competition law are justified, and further argue that there is little evidence that EU competition rules and practice are more favourable to joint ventures than their American counterparts.

That the latter point of view is correct is borne out by the remarkable similarities in the approach of antitrust authorities on both sides of the Atlantic to co-operative and concentrative operations in the field of information technologies. Contrary to the divergences of views seen with respect to the Boeing/McDouglas merger, discussions among the DOJ, the FTC and the European Commission in information technology cases have been remarkably intense, productive and harmonious, and have led to the same—or, at least, fully compatible—results. These cases clearly demonstrate the need for further co-operation between antitrust authorities around the world. For some participants, at least, these cases were further proof for the contention that some binding basic antitrust principles, applicable at a multilateral level, must be agreed upon worldwide.

A final point, which is worthy of note, leads us back to the beginning of our review of the proceedings of Panel Two. The participants' analysis of recently decided cases not only demonstrated the great degree of confidence in the capacity of the competition authorities to deal with the challenges resulting from the restructuring of markets through alliances, joint-ventures and mergers satisfactorily, they also showed that, in Europe, the European Commission and DG IV have a clear and leading role, in that they establish the precedents which the antitrust authorities of the EU Member States are drawn to follow.

III. Institutional Issues

Whereas Panels One and Two tackled issues of substantive law (answering the question, 'what has to be done under which type of law?'), Panel Three was invited to discuss institutional issues (and answer the question of ' how it is to be done and by who?'). Such institutional issues arise at every level of regulation, be it sub-national, national or supranational. However, they are particularly complex in the context of an EU that must establish a level playing field among its Member States, the internal market, but must also respect the principle of subsidiarity.

The key questions which must be addressed by every legislator concern: (1) the need for, or desirability of, sector-specific regulation in addition to general and traditional competition law; (2) the issue of whether the implementation of the applicable rules are, or should be, entrusted to one or several authorities, and; (3) the question of the division of responsibilities and the mode of co-operation between these (regulatory and competition) authorities. In addition to these 'horizontal' problems, regional integration and globalisation raise the 'vertical' issue of the distribution of responsibilities between Nation States, regional groupings and worldwide organisations.

The discussion on institutional issues was marked by more consensus than had been expected. Yet, significant divergences of views also emerged on a number of important issues. One important—if not the most important—area of broad agreement among the participants had already emerged in Panel One, and found an echo in a general sentiment that general competition law, acting alone, cannot solve the problems of the newly deregulated (telecommunications) markets. Special rules are required to introduce competition and competitive structures into markets which were, up until recently, reserved *de jure* to monopolists, and which will, *de facto*, continue to be dominated by incumbents for some time to come, even after the elimination of exclusive legal rights. Sector-specific rules, normally applied *ex ante*, were considered to be required, in particular, for reasons of predictability, speed and cost. Such rules should, as far as is possible, be informed by the underlying principles of competition law, but might also pursue additional objectives and provide new remedies, not generally available under general competition law. These special rules should not be considered to be antagonistic, but instead should be seen as complementary to existing competition law.

Participants agreed that, in view of rapid technological change, sector-specific regulation should remain lean and flexible. Detailed and rigid rules would be quickly overtaken by events and would hinder the evolution of new products, markets and structures. Competition law must, in any case, fill in the gaps and operate as a security net where the appropriate sector-specific rules do not exist.

A degree of consensus was also apparent with regard to the transitional character of sector-specific rules. The underlying assumption of current debate is that such rules should be phased if and when the specific problems that they are intended to address are solved. Certainly, it became clear that certain technological areas, such as frequency allocation and numbering, will always require special rules. The same is true for regulations that deal with the content of information and which are designed to protect non-economic values, such as plurality of opinions, individual privacy, public morality and public security. However, the convergence of technologies will require a review of the existing media regulations and, in this case at least, the existence of sector-specific regulations was considered to have the potential to complicate the streamlining of the future institutional framework.

Participants held nuanced views about the speed with which sector-specific rules intended to introduce competition and competitive structures into formerly monopolised markets could be phased out. A number of techniques, designed to ensure the transitional character of these rules, were outlined. The vast majority of solutions focused on the abolition of the sector specific regulator, rather than on the elimination of sector specific regulation; yet, it still proves fruitful to differentiate between the abolition of the regulator and the abolition of the rules.

The proceedings of Panel Three give a good overview of the variety of institutional solutions which different countries have chosen in order to administer sector-specific regulations, in addition to general competition law. The problem does not arise if—as in the case of New Zealand—sector-specific regulation is considered to be inappropriate. In such a situation, it makes clear sense to limit the institutional framework to one body, the Antitrust Authority (AA). However, once sector-specific regulation has been adopted, a decision must be made as to whether to entrust its implementation to a distinct sector-specific regulator or to a traditional competition agency which might be adjusted, to a greater or lesser degree, in order to enhance its ability to tackle regulatory tasks. An outstanding example of this second solution is offered by the Australian Competition Authority (ACCC). It is interesting to note that this example has not been followed in the EU, where all Member States have opted, like the US, for a separate national regulatory agency (NRA).

Not all European participants agreed with the choice made by their national legislator. Some would have preferred the adoption of the Australian model. Others clearly approved of the separation of functions between the AA and the NRA, arguing that, in this manner, the danger that an AA's thinking would be contaminated by 'regulatory' policy considerations could be avoided.

The existence of two distinct authorities inevitably creates problems if both are competent to address the same issues. Even where the legislature has made a clear distinction between the competences of the AA and the NRA in relation to their final decisions, (*e.g.* the decision on prices for end-users), both authorities must still interpret identical notions used in statutes or regulations. Both must apply the same policy instruments, both being called upon to engage in the delimiting of relevant markets, in the assessment of market power and in the establishment of fixed and variable costs. The more that sector-specific regulations are inspired by general competition law concepts, the more these notions and instruments will belong to the traditional tool kit of antitrust authorities. How can we avoid differing interpretations by AAs and NRAs? How can we ensure methodological coherence in the application of legal instruments? How can we ensure that both authorities come to the same results?

Panel Three furnished us with a particularly good picture of the reasons which led to Australia's decision to stick with one (expanded) competition authority, and of the different situations which exist in France, Germany, Italy, Spain and the US. The participants largely agreed that overlapping jurisdictions should be avoided. Where an NRA was established, the AA should retain responsibility for antitrust issues, while the NRA should concentrate on the new regulatory tasks entrusted it. New regulatory tasks should not encroach upon traditional antitrust issues, such as the control of mergers and acquisitions. If, however, overlapping jurisdictions have been established and different decisions are reached, the reasons for the differing results should be clearly indicated (*e.g.* the statutory objectives pursued by the NRA differ from those pursued by the AA).

Close co-operation between the NRA and the AA can serve to minimise differences in regulatory approach that are not objectively justifiable. Such co-operation is, in any case, highly desirable so that the general economic experience of the AA may be merged with the special technical knowledge of the NRA. Co-operation can be formal, mandatory and binding for one or the other agency; it may also be informal, facultative and purely voluntary. Modalities of co-operation vary according to subject matters within individual countries and even more so from one country to another. The importance of formal and informal 'bridges' between NRAs and AAs was underlined by all of the participants; their efficiency, however, was sometimes evaluated differently. Conflicts and differences of approach between the NRA and the AA can be avoided, or at least attenuated, where a unified system of judicial control is provided for. However, not all countries have chosen this solution.

Returning to an earlier issue, a broad assumption exists that NRAs, like sector-specific regulations, should, as far as is possible, have a transitional character and should be phased out over time. National legislation has not established fixed dates for the passing of NRAs, while such time-limits would, in any case, be difficult to determine *ex ante* and in view of the uncertain speed with which effective competition and competitive structures are being introduced. Sunset clauses, therefore, take the form of review provisions, the most stringent of which require a review at a pre-established date. However, only a small number of statutes expressly contain such provisions; the majority of them are silent. Participants agreed that reviews should not be entrusted to the NRAs themselves, but to other independent bodies instead. One—audacious—suggestion even favoured a decision to be taken by the European Commission.

While the European situation at Member State level is characterised by the co-existence of NRAs and AAs, the situation at EU level is less clear. The European Commission undoubtedly has all the responsibilities of an antitrust authority, yet it only partially assumes the functions of a regulatory agency. According to European competition law, the European Commission is entitled to take individual decisions, which are binding on enterprises. It does not, however, possess such powers in other economic areas. The Commission is generally confined to the supervision of the behaviour of the Member States and of their legislative, administrative and judicial acts; it, thus, also controls the activities of NRAs.

All the participants agreed that the supervisory functions of the Commission are of enormous importance. Positions differed, however, with regard to the need for, or desirability of, an European Regulatory Agency (ERA). Some participants considered that the establishment of such an Agency was necessary, in order to assure a level playing field in the EU and to give the EU telecommunications regime credibility at global level. Other participants were sceptical about, or even opposed to, such an initiative. They drew attention to the existing powers of the Commission, the progress in the implementation of the existing EU rules and the results achieved, and the length of time that would be necessary to agree upon and to set up a new agency. They also noted that the establishment of a European Regulatory Agency could be perceived as contrary to the principle of subsidiarity.

Some participants emphasised the need for greater co-operation among NRAs, as well as between NRAs and the European Commission. Such co-operation can, indeed, attenuate the absence of an EU regulatory competence outside of the area of competition law. In the absence of reinforced co-operation among NRAs and the Commission, it seems to us to be highly doubtful that the Commission will be able to assure a level playing field within the EU through the use of the unwieldy and slow instruments of control over national action. We arrive at this conclusion in spite of the conviction that sector-specific regulations and the NRAs should be phased out as quickly as possible. We share the scepticism of those who warned against overly optimistic assumptions about the speed with which sufficiently competitive market structures would be established and who emphasised that certain regulatory functions would remain even after the introduction of such market structures.

NRAs should, therefore, compete among themselves, in order to promote the best regulatory practices, but they should also engage in intensive co-operation with a view to eliminating inconsistencies and contradictions among their approaches, and should further improve co-operation with the Commission so that the need for the establishment of an ERA does not arise.

Although the issue of an ERA was vividly discussed, less was said about regulation at world level. The Agreement on Telecommunications recently negotiated within the framework of the World Trade Organisation (WTO) is so new that practical experience is still lacking. It will be implemented under the supervision of the WTO and WTO rules on dispute settlement. These rules are clearly more efficient and better suited to the commercial and competitive global telecommunications market than those of the International Telecommunications Union (ITU). Whether they will prove to be sufficient remains to be seen. A conflict with an antitrust agency acting at world level will not arise, since such an agency and internationally applicable antitrust rules do not exist. It would, however, be surprising if the process of globalisation did not lead to a more intense debate about world-wide rules for the information technology industries and their implementation through institutions acting at world level.

Claus D. Ehlermann

REGULATING ACCESS TO BOTTLENECKS

1

PANEL DISCUSSION

GENERAL RAPPORTEUR:

Tod Barnes
Policy Advisor, OFTEL, United Kingdom

PARTICIPANTS:

Mark Armstrong
Professor, Nuffield College, Oxford, UK

J.C. Arnbak
Professor, Chairman OPTA, the Netherlands

Mr Boettcher
Regulierungsbehörde für Telekommunikation und Post, Bonn, Germany

Henry Ergas
Professor, University of Auckland, Australia

Alan Fels
Professor, Chairman ACCC, Australia

Ian S. Forrester
QC, Professor White and Case, Brussels, Belgium

Herbert Hovenkamp
Professor, University of Iowa, Iowa, US

Günter Knieps
Professor, Dr., Institut für Verkehrswissenschaften und Regionalpolitik, Freiburg, Germany

Bruno Lasserre
Conseiller d'Etat, Secretariat d'Etat à l'Industrie, Paris, France

Colin Long
Partner, Olswang, London, United Kingdom

Vincenzo Monaci
Autorità per la Garanzia nelle Comunicazione, Rome, Italy

Daniel L. Rubinfeld
Professor of Law and Economics, University of California, US

Michael Salsbury
MCI Commuications Corporation, Washington, United States

Alexander Schaub
Dr., Director General, DGIV, Brussels, Belgium

Joachim Scherer
Professor, Dr., University of Frankfurt, Partner, Baker & McKenzie Frankfurt a, M., Germany

Mario Siragusa
Professor, Avv., Cleary, Gottlieb, Steen & Hamilton, Brussels, Belgium

Herbet Ungerer
Dr., Head of Unit, DG-IV, Brussels, Belgium

Alexandre Verheyden
Jones, Day, Beavis and Pogue, Brussels, Belgium

Peter Waters
Partner, Gilbert and Tobin Lawyers, Brussels/Sydney, Belgium/Australia

Panel One: Competitive Access to 'Bottleneck' Network Facilities

▶ EHLERMANN—First, a welcome to all of you, those who have been here on prior occasions, and those who are here for the very first time. I extend this welcome also in the name of Giuliano Amato who has become a member of the new Italian government and is, therefore, obliged to sit this morning at the regular meeting in Rome. He will, however, join us in the course of the afternoon.

At the outset, I would like to thank those of you who have generously sponsored this workshop, which is a premier for us. I refer to the representatives of industry and law firms who join us here. Without your support, this workshop could not have taken place in its present scope and depth.

This is the third, and indeed most difficult, of this form of meeting to take place. It raises more difficulties than its two predecessors, due to the variety of subjects tackled, the technicality of the subjects and by virtue of the fact that very many disciplines are represented at this table, giving rise to the danger that, although we use the same words, we might not be speaking the same language. I hope that we can overcome this difficulty this morning and establish a real exchange of views and a real dialogue.

This workshop is distinguished from all others which I have experienced in the course of my professional activities since everyone around this table is 'active' and will be making his or her contribution as an equal participant. The only special status is that of the three general rapporteurs.

The meeting will not take the traditional course of presentations followed by a discussion. Instead, we mean to have a roundtable discussion; each session will be half presentation and half discussion, and not three-quarters presentation and a quarter discussion. Each subject will be briefly introduced by the general rapporteur. The panellists will make a brief statement, and we shall then turn to the general discussion. I think it appropriate that we give the floor first to the regulators, then to the academic experts and then, to a third group, the lawyers.

The success of this enterprise will greatly depend on discipline, and I will try my best to impose this discipline. I would have liked Giuliano Amato to have been here, since he has more authority than I. In his absence, however, we must all revert to a degree of self-discipline. In this vein, no further introduction is required. Rather, Mr Barnes, you now have the floor as our first general rapporteur.

▶ BARNES—May I start by saying what an honour it is to be here. Let me also reinforce what Claus has just said: this conference deals with an area of extreme difficulty. In OFTEL, we have been discussing most of these issues rather heatedly for the last 9 months.

I have circulated a list of 'aid memoirs' on why the issue of bottlenecks in telecommunications markets may be troublesome. This list includes the current issues facing regulators and competition authorities in the real world. I think that the more productive discussions that can be had between policy-makers, experts and the industry, the more likely it is that these regulation and competition authorities will come up with the right, as opposed to the wrong, answers.

I will try to frame the discussion to encourage a more productive discussion. I think an understanding of why some of these problems arise in this area will help us to focus in a useful way.

One of the problems we face in dealing with this issue is the considerable uncertainty about what competition law, as a concept, or as it is applied, could actually achieve under the particular circumstances that we find in relation to bottlenecks in telecommunications networks. One challenge is the problem of 'small numbers'. We are now in the era where network bottlenecks are usually not pure monopolies; however, though there is generally more than one supplier, there are not very many suppliers. Arguably, there are not enough suppliers to produce a normally competitive market. On the other hand, we are not dealing with a simple monopoly supply. Equally, even if there are small numbers, there is a problem of switching costs—customers may face very high switching costs relative to the values of any particular service that is flowing through the bottleneck. So, again, there is a structural issue which indicates the existence of market failure, even where consumers—the engine of competition—exercise choice.

The normal kinds of structural remedies that are available under competition law may not work under these circumstances. It may not be possible to create a structural solution which deals with the underlying bottleneck. Now, some of the papers have addressed this problem and have suggested that there may be novel ways of dealing with these issues. If these structural, or semi-structural, remedies are available, then, clearly they should be considered. But, in the absence of such remedies, we are pushed back onto behavioural rules; a set of rules which competition law may have difficulty in conceptualising.

Fourthly, bottlenecks in telecommunications networks may be troublesome, since the bottleneck itself may only be an economic bottleneck for certain of the services that pass through that gateway. A very good example is presented by conditional access set-top boxes for digital TV. Almost certainly, they, too, will soon be a bottleneck for pay-TV. They may never become a bottleneck for the provision of banking services, since 'the object' (home banking), is controlled by the alternative suppliers of that service to end-users who do not use telecommunications networks. If you are going to regulate the bottleneck, do you just regulate for TV and not for banking, or do you assume that the bottleneck has market power over all the services passing through it?

Finally, we are also in a situation in which a bottleneck controller can do very strange things. They can change the character of the bottleneck without altering its physical nature. For example, downloading a completely new application interface into a set-top box completely changes its technical characteristics and completely disrupts the operations of any other party who is using the box to supply services. There is, however, no change in the physical nature of the box.

These are a few of the rather serious problems facing regulators and competition authorities. My experience (9-12 months of discussions within OFTEL) allows me to identify issues which, since they tend to be rather unproductive, we should not deal with here.

Discussions about the principle of whether you should use competition law or, alternatively, regulation to deal with these issues does not go very far, due to the uncertainty about exactly what competition law would actually do. Discussions about whether or not competition law would deal with a particular issue at a particular time are also unproductive. To highlight this, we need only consider the current Microsoft case—depending on the outcome of this case, you could answer the question of whether competition law can adequately deal with the issue of Microsoft dominance in the positive (yes, its wonderful, it has solved all the issues) or, in the negative (competition law is useless since it has not addressed the threat that Microsoft poses to society as a whole).

What is much more useful, though more demanding, is the debate about what the substantive set of rules ought to be. What is their nature? What are the right rules of conduct? What structural rules are called for? Which forms of semi-structural remedies might be most effectively applied to these network bottlenecks? We need to enquire as to which remedies should be available; are they just about behaviour or do they include real structural solutions wherever possible? Also, what role can semi-structural remedies, such as accounting separation or IPR, play, and are they effective?

Questions may be raised about the type of remedies which can actually address the underlying problem. They may also be raised about the circumstances in which the rules are to be applied. One world view says they should only apply if dominance can be proven. However, if we remember the problem of the small number of suppliers, we may feel that some other test—with a lesser dominance quotient—might be more appropriate.

There is also the question of whether the rules should be applied just because the bottleneck has been created, or only after the owner has abused the power deriving from ownership.

And finally, what entity should the rules be applied to? Should we apply the rules to the smallest entity possible to try and isolate the bottleneck into the smallest possible problem area or into some sensible notion which contains the bottleneck? Alternatively, should we apply them to the whole of the entity that owns the bottleneck, irrespective of the nature of its other activities?

These issues represent a very broad area for discussion. There are, I think, some ways of structuring discussion to reduce the breadth of debate by (1) identifying what is actually happening when a bottleneck is created, and (2) by pinpointing when regulatory or competition rules then apply to it. What, in fact, happens is that a competition authority, or a regulator, creates some entity which contains the bottleneck. To do this, it creates a regulatory boundary of one form or another. It applies a rule designed to deal with what is inside the boundary, or with behaviour within the boundary, which is not considered to be in the public interest. These are the rules dealing with monopoly pricing and the exploitation of consumers.

A second set of rules deals with downstream markets. They concern the impact of the ownership of the bottleneck on final product markets, where the bottleneck is a necessary input.

These two forms of rules address separate problems. Equally, different remedies are used to address the different problems. Indeed, it is possible to address them independently. A rule may deal with either the downstream markets and not with the bottleneck itself, or with the upstream market; the rules being developed in relation to indirect access to the loop—wireless or fixed—are of this variety.

Within this framework, I think that there are considerable areas of agreement between the papers. One is that the definition of the bottleneck ought to be an economic one—*i.e.* it must have something to do with dominance and market power. Agreement is less clear on whether the test is correctly applied to the bottleneck itself, as well as to the downstream markets. There is also less agreement on whether the test should be restricted to the identification of dominance, or whether it also needs to the capture certain lesser forms of abusive market power. There is agreement that where the owner of the bottleneck can distort competition in a downstream market in which it is itself active, then the rules should apply. However, there is also less agreement about the application of the rules, where the owner has no motivation to distort competition in a market in which he has no interest. What should be done is similarly unclear in cases where the owner is active in only some of the downstream markets— which is, in fact, the likeliest scenario.

There is general agreement that the overall set of rules which should be applied should resemble the set of rules available to combat the abuse of a dominant position. Again, however, there is less agreement on the individual rules which make up the complete set.

Finally, I would like to put one more gloss on the discussion. Namely, whatever regulatory or competition authorities come up with, in the final analysis, the application of these rules to bottlenecks in telecommunications must satisfy a dynamic test: investors must invest over more than one cycle in order to build infrastructure. Where they fail to do so, the short-term benefits identified by regulatory and competition authorities should nonetheless be subsidiary to the greater benefit brought by high levels of investment. Telecommunications is an area of very rapid technological change and an area in need of high investment. Against this background, we can begin to look at one of the issues which is raised by the papers and which I characterise as follows: is there a question to which TELRIC is the correct answer?

At this level, I think, the answer is probably no—but this answer is set against the background of a dynamic industry and area of investment which is vital for the health of the economy at large.

▶ ARNBAK—Before I begin, I would just like to mention that, while I am a lawyer and an academic by training, I am now deeply immersed in practical problems. Based on this experience, I wish to raise some constructive problems which show that, sometimes, our general notions about network services do not really correspond to reality in this specific sector.

Some of the general notions that we might try to impose in this specific sector lead to problems. I would like to draw your attention to a list of particular characteristics that apply to telecommunications and differentiate it from other network sectors. These differences reveal that analogies with classical network sectors should be made with reticence.

First, unlike pipelines, rails, roads and other traditional network services, telecommunications is characterised by transport at the speed of light.

Second, while both telecommunications signals and electricity are transmitted at the speed of light, in the telecommunications sector, unlike the electricity sector, this transport takes place without loss of quality and value. That is, a portion of the electrical power is lost over the course of transmission. This factor restricts the market definition in the electricity sector. Thus, the electricity sector is characterised by rather confined geographical markets, larger than France, but smaller than Europe.

In the telecommunications sector, unlike the printing and publishing sector, we can copy, we can broadcast, we can bundle and unbundle, we can reroute and we can re-file information. This means that, although both publishing and telecommunications are information businesses, telecommunications is free of some of the restrictive notions that apply to the printed medium.

Further more, in telecommunications, we have a choice concerning the method of service provision. Operators can approach customers in two fundamentally different ways. On the one hand, we have wired service, characterised by strong economies of scale, scope and density. On the other hand, we have wireless services, where it is cheap to cover an area and becomes cheaper the more thinly populated an area is. Thus, wireless service reverses the classical anomalies that give rise to arguments in favour of natural monopolies. Consequently, there is a choice between the methods of service provision which we foresee for the years to come.

And finally, unlike sea, air, and rail terminals, telecommunications services can be provided using lightweight or even portable terminals. So, all of the classical arguments regarding terminal bottlenecks—about which we are concerned in normal network economies—are no longer relevant in telecommunications, because terminals were the first thing that we liberalised.

Moreover, as Mr. Barnes said, we have an extremely dynamic sector. Figure 1 in my paper shows exponential increases in performance/price ratios in three different branches of industry: consumer electronics, large-scale computing, and telecommunications electronics.

The most impressive growth has undoubtedly been in consumer electronics. Just recall how much CD players or PCs have improved in performance and gone down in price over the past ten years and you will agree with me.

The second industrial sector included in the statistics is the large-scale computing sector. This sector has seen somewhat slow, but still very impressive with increases in performance and performance/price ratios.

The telecommunications electronics sector has seen the slowest growth of the three. Big, classical telecommunications switches have improved. In fact, they have improved faster since EU procurement rules were brought to bear upon them, meaning that a certain degree of competition was introduced. But still, they are under-performing compared to the other sectors.

These three different branches, then, lead to crossovers. We saw such a crossover with the PC, which was invented by IBM as an intelligent terminal to feed their mainframes. It soon developed into a much more Faustian device, able to do, in private homes, all of the things that mainframes could do earlier on. We have also seen crossovers to the hand-held mobile, which today has as much processing power as a PC had five years ago. And there have also been spin-offs from the computer sector into consumer electronics. Most importantly, with regard to service delivery, we have seen the intelligent network develop. This intelligent network is not really a product of telecommunications services, but rather, of the computing sector, which has furnished us with computer platforms, which, alongside the switches, provide all of the smart applications of modern service delivery. Perhaps most impressively, looming ahead of us—as a threat to some and a very important opportunity for others, is the increase in use of the internet, and how it will affect telecommunications. Obviously, this is also a crossover which may even lead to a convergence of the three industrial branches noted above.

In discussing technology crossovers, we could also add a fourth sector, defence electronics. But I will not discuss this sector today.

If you look at the tables and the classical economic evidence, there is no doubt that the telecommunications service sector is the largest of all of the sectors, and that the ITC market is dominated by telecommunications services. Thus, we are discussing something of enormous economic importance. I have tried, as a simple-minded man, to order this sector in Figure 2 of my paper. This Figure shows four layers, each of which comprises inherent problems and challenges which are different from the challenges present in the other layers. The four areas are the following:

(1) First, shown at the bottom, we have the network infrastructure, providing for transmission passing through interfaces to terminals. Transmission through such interfaces and terminals can lead to bottlenecks.

(2) The next layer is general transport and network services. In this second layer, factors, such as routing of information, mobility management and quality of services, are important, but, as yet, there is no value-added.

(3) The third layer contains value-added services. For example, the 'Kiosk France function', which we have in the French Teletel system.

(4) And finally, there is the fourth layer: the provision of information content.

All of these layers have distinct problems that we must treat differently. If we fail to do so, we will have difficulties, not only in regulating, but also in discussing what we are dealing with.

Now, it becomes intricate. If you examine Figure 3 in the paper, you will see that there is a rather complicated extension of this four-layer model. Of course, at each layer, there can be different competitors. Thus, at each layer, there can, if you like, be horizontal competition and horizontal bundling.

Furthermore, there can also be vertical integration and/or vertical disintegration, which is indicated along the up-down axis in this Figure. As a consequence, the daily problem that we are now facing in regulation is how to deal with access to critical facilities at these different layers—where access should be enforced, where we should consider things to be bottlenecks, and where we should not.

The complexity of the issues is readily apparent, since there are four different layers with four different sets of rules. There are different economic rules, and different dynamics. For example, the lower layers generally develop more slowly than the upper layers. This, in turn, raises issues of whether we should differentiate between *ex ante* and *ex post* regulation on the basis of the different effects they will have upon the different layers.

Finally, the very dynamic sector of mobile, or wireless, access to users leads to new economic considerations at the lowest layer. Consequently, we might anticipate some very fascinating—but also very complicated—issues of fixed-mobile convergence in the first layer.

If we can examine the three-dimensional space in this figure, I suggest that one of the issues that we will have to discuss is whether it is justified, or necessary, to impose strict business-line restrictions in that space. Must we really forbid incumbents from participating in business-lines that others may enter?

For example, I refer to the big differences between the degree of success of cellular communications in the United States and Europe. Cellular communication was developed in the US, but was smothered by structural and business-line restrictions which were imposed, first, on AT&T and, later, upon the BOCs (Bell Operating Companies). These companies were not allowed to run mobile communications in their own coverage regions.

In Europe, by contrast, we never imposed that restraint on incumbents. Instead, we allowed them to develop GSM. I, therefore, submit to you—the exact arguments are in the paper—that this is one of the reasons for the business success of GSM not only in Europe but also throughout the world.

I have personal misgivings about any business-line restrictions which are imposed *a priori* on anybody, however big he, or she, may be. Yet, conversely, I believe that if somebody with significant market power—let alone economic market power in competition terms—is allowed to enter new sectors, such as mobile communications, rules will be required, and they will have to be asymmetric rules. I think this should be one of the critical points for discussion.

▶ MONACI—I believe that this is one of the first presentations of the Italian telecommunications regulatory agency in an international academic forum. As you know, we are very new to this task. From the outset, we had to deal with substantive problems while we were still constructing our own technical structure. In fact, we faced many urgent problems immediately after our establishment in July 1998. This means that we are currently very busy responding to the demand for increased competition in our marketplace.

In particular, the first three issues we faced were (1) the reassessment plan for television, (2) the approval of interconnection rates and, (3) the re-balancing of voice tariffs. The frequency plan or reassessment plan for television, which is a new, special plan, was issued a few days ago.

The second issue was the approval or denial of the interconnection tariff that was presented by Telecom Italia at the end of July. Our decision has already been made and we are currently waiting for the opinions of DG IV, DG XIII and the Italian Antitrust Authority. These opinions will be issued soon. I believe the setting of this interconnection tariff will be a great step forward in the achievement of a new, competitive environment in our country.

The third, and most important, issue was the response to Telecom Italia's requests for the re-balancing of voice telecommunication tariffs. This has required us to analyse our dominant company's declaration concerning the access deficit. We are in the middle of this analysis and the decision will be made by the end of November (1998).

In the process, the redefinition of tariffs will be divided into three phases. The first phase will be completed by November, the second by March, and the third by the end of July. By that time, the total realignment will be completed.

I wish, in the following, to stress various issues which touch upon competitive access to bottleneck network facilities.

First, the regulation of access to essential facilities in the initial phase of competition is, undoubtedly, one of the most important roles for the regulatory authority. This regulation is mainly based upon the establishment of rules and principles for interconnection and access to the incumbent's network. The structure of the interconnection regime and the charges imposed for the interconnection services have an immediate influence upon the investment decisions of the operators, both in terms of the make-or-buy decision, and in terms of network architecture.

Extensive regulation is needed with regard to the network facilities that can influence the competitive process. However, it is also important to identify these facilities, and to establish the conditions to be used to untie the bottlenecks, by creating, wherever possible, commercial incentives for their elimination and for the sharing of the resources between all market players.

For example, in the long distance network, long distance infrastructures can be created relatively quickly thanks, in part, to the fact that alternative structures already exist in most countries. As soon as operators establish long distance infrastructure, competition increases with regard to interconnection services to other operators in the segment, thereby creating a competitive market and reducing the need for regulation and intervention. Thus, it can be assumed that, in the first phase of competition at least, most of the incumbent's network structure will be considered an essential facility, but that, as competition develops, some parts of the infrastructure will lose this quality and the regulatory authority's role will be lessened accordingly.

Secondly, however, new technologies will also play an important role in reducing bottlenecks. Wireless, for example, due to the minor economies of scale and sunk costs, could allow the duplication of some of today's bottleneck services. This could also be the reason why the term 'essential facility' does not itself denote a particular, or 'natural', component or service in each country. Instead, each national market identification would take into account the level of competition, the regulatory framework and the market structure in the country. Certain of the attributes of an essential facility which represent a competitive disadvantage for competing operators and consumers—such as control by a monopoly operator, no access for other operators, the monopoly operator's interest in denying access, discrimination between operators and failure to update access to resources—may apply to different network elements in different countries.

Finally, because of the characteristics of today's telecommunications market and the rapid technological evolution surrounding it, it is also important to structure the market in a manner that does not allow monopolies to take advantage of the new technologies and restrain the development of new services. This risk must be minimised.

With these issues in mind, the following key concepts have guided the work of the Italian national regulatory authority in setting the rules for interconnection: independence from the incumbent, the promotion of infrastructure, a high-level of flexibility concerning the choice of points of interconnection, and an extensive range of interconnection services. Furthermore, the national regulatory authority has not made an *a priori* choice as regards network competition and services competition, and has, instead, left this decision to the operators and to the market.

Given unbalanced tariffs, the presence of a price margin in the long distance market could create a short-term incentive for service providers to use the incumbent's network at a cost to the enterprises. Thereafter, new entrants could offer a discount with respect to the incumbent's unbalanced everyday prices. Some argue that this situation could create a disincentive for investment.

It must be considered, however, that as developments occur, these margins will disappear. An operator's market position will increasingly depend on its ability to innovate, either through the creation of new services or through the provision of better quality services. This will create an incentive to invest in new infrastructure and transmission technologies with lower network costs.

▶ RUBINFELD—When I first came to the Antitrust Division of the US Department of Justice about two years ago, I thought that network industries and bottlenecks might be an interesting area and it has, in fact, turned out that I have spent almost all of my time thinking about these issues.

I wanted to mention four areas of investigation that I have been involved in during my time at the Division, which, I think, fit in with the subject matter we are talking about today. First of all, we filed suit, about two months ago, at the end of a long-standing investigation of VISA and Mastercard. This suit involves our claim that there are substantial issues surrounding bottlenecks created by control over credit cards through the banking system. This case is scheduled to go to trial sometime next year (1999).

Second, we filed suit, about nine months ago, to block the acquisition of the Direct Broadcasting Satellite assets owned by a combination of MCI and Newscorp. This acquisition was to be made by Primestar, which was a consortium of some of the major US cable television companies. An issue in our Primestar case had to do with access to the 110 degree satellite, which was a key bottleneck for potential competition in Direct Broadcast Satellite television. We brought suit and the deal was abandoned about two months ago.

Third, as most of you know, we brought suit, about nine months ago, against the Microsoft Corporation for violation of Section 1 and Section 2 of the Sherman Act. Among the key issues in our Microsoft investigation was our concern about Microsoft's ability to create and misuse access to the internet. We viewed internet access as a potential major bottleneck and we are very concerned about Microsoft's behaviour in that case.

Now, as most of you all know, the ways in which we look at bottlenecks under US Competition policy depend heavily on the nature of the particular antitrust laws that we are enforcing. In the case of VISA, Mastercard and Microsoft, we were focusing on Section 1 and Section 2 of the Sherman Act. Section 2 probably comes closest to some of the issues we are talking about here, because under Section 2 we need to show not simply a dominant position but also abusive practices that have either foreclosed competition or have the potential to foreclose competition. In the case of Primestar, we were operating under the Clayton Act, which provides a slightly different standard for looking at problems of competition. In this case, the concern was potential competition, since the assets of the Direct Broadcast Satellite acquisition had not actually been brought into use and still have not been. Consequently, we are, in fact, concerned about potential competition in the future.

Finally, the area which I have written about in my submission to the group today, involves our continuing analysis and investigation of potential bottle-necks in the telecommunications sector. The authority that we are using here came to us through the long process that resulted from the 1982 consent decree, which itself led to deregulation of telecommunications. Under this decree, we are authorised to give the Federal Communications' Commission substantial advice, which will be given substantial weight in their determinations about entry of competitors into long distance markets. Thus, what I have described in my submission is the Division's continuing position as to what we believe are the appropriate rules for dealing with local bottlenecks under Article 271 of the Telecommunications Act of 1996.

Under Article 271, the conditions are different from what I have described above, because we have the general opportunity to limit, or regulate, entry into long distance markets. Our goal in doing so is to make sure that there is a *quid pro quo*: that the entrants who are allowed to enter into long distance markets must respond by making a commitment to allow competition in local markets. We view this local competition as extremely significant.

For those of you who are not aware of how our Article 271 process works, let me describe very briefly some of the highlights of how we view this competition and why we have taken, as some see it, a pretty tough stance, requiring a substantial *quid pro quo* before we encourage long distance entry. As we see it, there are three major methods to gain entry into local markets. One is resale of an incumbent's existing services. The second is the building of new facilities. The third is the leasing of some mixture of network elements.

We are concerned about local competition because the local market is around double the size of the long distance market. And while we do not think either market has reached—not even the long distance market—our goals of what competition ought to be, we think there are particular problems at local level, because the local exchange carriers have very substantial market power. Consequently, we are concerned about ways to achieve co-operation on the part of the entrants into long distance markets, in order to make sure that they allow others to compete in their local markets. We think it is important that these markets be opened and that these openings be irreversible, not simple initial openings, which could then be closed later on.

There are strategic issues here that trouble us quite a bit. We realise that, through the tougher stance that we are taking under these Article 271 rules in order to allow access into local markets, we are delaying the possibility of initial competition. We realise that, by delaying that access into distance competition, we are foregoing certain short-run costs. However, we believe that our standard of requiring full and irreversibly open entry into local markets is an important stance to maintain and that the potential long-run benefits make it worthwhile. So, while we are aware of, and sensitive to the criticism that we have maintained the bottleneck longer than it should be maintained, we believe that the short-run costs are worth it.

We do not believe, and we have not seen any evidence, that there is a conspiracy of any kind, on the part of the long distance providers, to delay BOC entry. Rather, we are hoping that we can encourage these firms that want to enter into long distance markets to put together plans that will really provide serious long-run solutions for eliminating bottlenecks. Consequently, in our responses to the 271 applications, we focus on what the potential bottlenecks may be and we are aware of the dynamics of the industry and the difficulties of actually determining where these bottlenecks lie.

In the case of resale competition at local level, we see some potential problems but we think that these barriers are likely to be transitory. With respect to wholesale pricing of local telecommunications services, we do not yet see evidence of any major scale economies, or other bottlenecks, that should not make the wholesale market competitive over time as we deregulate. And we think that, with appropriate monitoring, we can also get efficient interconnections at local level. Our concern with certain types of interconnections is part of what led us to be active in encouraging the divestiture of the internet backbone in the MCI/ Worldcom deal last year.

Finally, we think that there is real benefit to be achieved by encouraging un- bundling of local elements. We think that, by doing this we can encourage competitors to design ways of having access to the local loops of bottlenecks, either by having direct access to them, or by providing their own wiring, or by getting their own local loops and having access to existing switches. And, in our treatment of Article 271 applications, we spell out, in some detail, the ways in which we think unbundling of elements at local level can lead to more effective competition. We hope to see that happening in the future.

▶ UNGERER—This is the first time that I have seen a seminar that really brings competition and sector-specific regulators together. It is, particularly interesting for me to see the international context from different perspectives. I am intrigued by this dual dynamic, and hope to benefit from these two types of regulatory and international experience.

My purpose is to compare sector-specific regulation with general regulation through competition law. My suggestion is that we take another look at these two systems of regulation, simply judging them against the criteria of that which we want to achieve. I suggest that we apply three major tests to both systems: sector-specific and competition. And, let us face it, in most countries, particularly in the EU, we now have a dual system, comprised of sector-specific regulation (largely derived from the European and international law), and general competition law.

The first test to be applied to each system should be its ability to ensure efficiency of access in the current market situation. The second test relates to access to 'converging markets'—markets with rapidly changing market definitions—and the third test relates to access to 'innovation markets', which is by far the most difficult and, probably, also the most important, criterion.

I do not wish to go into extensive detail at this moment. What I would like to provide is a very quick balance sheet based upon the current European situation, where we have made, as you know, substantial progress.

First of all, regarding efficiency of access, a brief word on the efficiency of the system. I would take price—or the pricing of interconnection—as the single most important indicator. Sector specific, ONP-type regulation in Europe has been a very substantial success over the last twelve months, bringing interconnection prices down to an extremely reasonable level; basically 0.5 to 1 cent per minute in local markets, and about five times that in long distance markets. That success is, of course, thanks to the national regulatory authorities (NRAs). This is a major factor in bringing competition quickly to the marketplace.

According to its mandate under EC Treaty Article 82 [ex 86], EU Competition law basically deals with extreme situations of predatory pricing and excessive pricing. We have been very successful in excessive pricing situations; the Deutsche Telekom case in 1997 is a case in point. We are now applying this method in the mobile sector and also in accounting situations. But, we are doing so together with sector-specific regulators. In fact, the access notice which the Commission has issued defines the relationship between sector-specific regulators and the Commission in more detail. That relationship is, of course, a topic for Panel III.

I will not go into the major competition cases because, again, this is an issue for Panel II. At this point, I just want to sketch out the efficiency of access which we have already achieved. Yes, sector-specific regulation in Europe has been extremely successful and we *need* it. But, one must also realise that a price may have to be paid for this 'deep' regulation and intervention into market mechanisms. Deep intervention into market mechanisms, with all the risks of the setting of wrong prices, the wrong investment indicators and the wrong signposts for investment, may be costly in general economic terms. I would suggest that we discuss this issue.

This leads me on to the second test, which deals with access in a converging market situation. Here, the balance sheet is less positive. First, we have yet to experience this period. Second, we all realise, as the rapporteur's report has shown, that we find ourselves in a situation of rapidly changing market definitions. This is the difficult point. It will be extremely difficult—and I very much liked what the rapporteur said;—it will be very difficult for a pure sector-specific regulator to be totally correct on this issue, because he or she is called upon to outguess future market developments. This is an interesting issue for future discussion.

The third point involved innovation. Now this is an interesting point because it is, of course, the point which distinguishes this sector from other traditional utilities sectors. When I say innovation, I am not talking about forcing open access in an uncertain market definition environment, such as, for example, the market for set-top boxes. Rather, I am concerned much more about non-existing means of service provision, which only the market dominating operator could reasonably produce. For example, general open access for the internet or general access to broadband signals through the telephone network and the cable network.

This investigation of access within Europe was carried out for different reasons, yet, I think the tests that were applied, in 1997, in the cable review, are also relevant for this meeting. One issue was whether it was possible simply to expand sector-specific type ONP regulation to develop cable networks and telephone networks into broadband networks? The second option concerned the form of competition which should be created as a minimum condition. Here, the answer required legal separation in cases of cross-ownership of cable and telephone operators in order to get at least two identifiable actors into this field of local access. The third option was pure divestiture.

Now, to cut all of this short, the Commission has decided to take the second option, the cautious one. However, it has also noted the arguments of our investigators that only full-scale divestiture, *i.e.* a full structural solution, would resolve the issue. The argument is that, without full divestiture, the necessary investment dynamics are simply not there.

To conclude. What I have noted derives from Member State/EU experience and regulation, and without drawing too heavily on US philosophies, it is apparent that we have required sector-specific regulation to create access quickly and to transmit the benefits of open access to the consumer. Nobody doubts this. It could not have been done without sector-specific regulation. Competition law, alone, would have been insufficient. We have given preference to sector-specific regulatory solutions in so far as they can resolve competition issues.

However, one must also say very clearly that it is doubtful that the same methods can apply in converging market situations and, particularly, in innovation situations. Look at what this really means: the upgrading of cable lines or telephone lines into broadband internet—which could happen over the next three to five years—would mean the investment of 40 billion Euro in Europe, just for the cable network. Which sector-specific regulator could mandate deployment of this type of investment? Who may require this type of investment from an incumbent? Who can say that he does not believe in the market opportunity or that there is no demand? Who may require an incumbent to take this risk in a situation of very large scale market uncertainty? Probably, only a structural solution will suffice. Can regulation be that sector-specific, or competition law cope with such big issues in the future, or must we opt for structural solutions?

▶ ERGAS—The fact that the issues we face are difficult and complex is perhaps the only things on the agenda circulated here that is not extremely controversial. It might be useful to say at the outset that, in my field, many of these difficulties come not from the inherent characteristics of telecommunications networks as such, but rather from the impact of pre-existing regulatory distortion. In particular, regulatory controls over end-user prices in telecommunications—notably, policies that mandate extensive cross-subsidies between territories and between groups of users—seriously distort our market outcomes. I am not convinced that there would be any real bottleneck if these distortions were removed and, in particular, if prices better reflected costs.

Take the local loop, for example. In Australia, the cost of providing the local loop is somewhere between 300 and 400 Australian dollars a year per service operation, that is, per lot. At the moment, regulation prevents residential consumers from being charged more than $11.65 a month for the service, *i.e.* less than 50% of the economic cost of its provision. It is hardly surprising that, under these circumstances, there are not many firms clamouring to compete in the market, and that the incumbent supplier has a market share which is only marginally less than 100%.

Moreover, in addition to distorting current market outcomes, the price distortions also distort the incentives for entry. If competitors can escape the burden of providing the subsidised services, they can make hay in the areas from which the subsidies are being extracted, even if their costs are much higher than the costs of the incumbents. Incumbents rightly say that if you liberalise on this basis, society risks being made worse, rather than better, off.

When retail prices are so distorted, there is, in my view, only one way of precluding inefficient entry. That is to price any alleged bottleneck service on the basis of 'retail minus unavoidable costs', the so-called 'efficient opponent pricing rule'. The problem with this rule is that the resulting prices not only discourage inefficient entry, but also, at least it is claimed by some, may make efficient entry difficult.

The now standard solution to this problem is twofold. It is to charge for the bottleneck service on the basis of cost, and then to mark up these costs so as to reflect the burden of any regulatory pricing obligations. But this is easier said than done. First, it requires determining costs. And second, it involves designing a system of mark-ups that is not, in and of itself, merely an additional distortion.

All of which brings me to my paper. What my paper does is look at these tasks, and, in particular, it asks 'do we know how to measure the costs of bottleneck services?' The answer is that, in theory, we sort of know how to measure them. In practice,—at least on the basis of my experience, having just spent six months working in an incumbent telecommunications operator and trying to measure real costs—the answer is that you do not actually do so well.

The theory is easily summarised. It basically talks about the stand-alone costs of an optimised replacement network. The difficulties in implementing this theory are basically fourfold: (1) We do not know what an optimised replacement network would look like. (2) We do not know what resources are needed to build, upgrade and maintain the network; we can only guess at that. (3) We do not know what the return investors would really require to build such a network. (4) Finally, there is no simple, economically justifiable way of going from an aggregate regulatory revenue requirement associated with the costs of an optimised replacement network to individual prices for particular units of the bottleneck service.

My paper looks at how cost modellers have dealt with these difficulties in constructing what are called Total Service Long-run Incremental Cost (TSLRIC) or Total Element Long-run Incremental Cost (TELRIC) models, which are total service, long run, incremental cost models. And the conclusion the paper comes to is that cost models have not dealt particularly well with these difficulties. As a result, we are in an environment in which our ability to access costs correctly and set prices on that basis is strictly limited.

In such an environment, there is enormous scope for rent-seeking and for special interests to manipulate the regulatory system. As a result, this is an area where regulators play 'God' or social engineer at their peril. The risk is that of being manipulated into decisions which have no efficiency properties whatsoever by the contending parties.

Given these difficulties, the question, to my mind, is whether it really is the case that regulators operating subject to industry-specific rules will do better than general competition policy enforced largely through the courts. In essence, this question needs to be analysed in terms of the vulnerability of each of these modes of social control to rent-seeking and to manipulation by special interests. I work in New Zealand where there is no industry-specific regulation, and in Australia, where there is. In fact, I am at my peril, since the 'Tsar' of Australian telecommunications is sitting next to me. And I would say that life for new entrants is doubtless very much easier in Australia than in New Zealand. But at least the work I have done—and I will admit that there are different views about it, although it is confirmed by some more recent work by Lou Evans—finds that consumer outcomes are, or may well be, superior in New Zealand to those that we have observed in Australia.

Now it would be wrong to try to draw too many conclusions from any one case. But what I think one can say—and I will end on this—is that the choice of regulatory regimes is one between highly imperfect alternatives. The strong claims on behalf of simple regulatory rules, such as 'price bottleneck services on TSLRIC', or however you might want to phrase it, are, at least in my experience, as impractical in operation as they are weak in theory.

▶ HOVENKAMP—I am going to focus my comments on bottlenecks caused by intellectual property laws, focusing mainly on the Microsoft litigation, although I will have to discuss some other US decisions that do not involve telecommunications in getting to this problem. Intellectual property, of course, presents some unique problems in that, first of all, the power to exclude is generally protected by the law in such a way that it is not protected with respect to some hard assets. Secondly, the problems of economies of scale and scope are quite different with respect to pure intellectual property rights than with respect to hard assets. This second factor makes more creative judicial remedies possible, although not necessarily desirable.

I want to emphasise three points. The first is that, in cases of intellectual property bottlenecks, it is absolutely essential that power, or the existence of the bottleneck, be unambiguously proven. I think this amounts to one of the most serious problems in United States antitrust law today, that is, the willingness of courts to accept overly narrow market definitions, or the existence of significant power, on insufficient proof. In particular, where competing technologies exist—and I mean viable, competing technologies at roughly equivalent costs—to find market power on the basis of consumer lock-in, as the Supreme Court approved in the US in its 1992 Kodak decision, is very precarious. And the subsequent Ninth Circuit decision in this case showed the absurd extremes to which this could be taken, in finding that a firm with roughly 22 or 23% of the primary market, in this case in large photocopiers, could be a monopolist in a single market made up, in fact, of complementary, rather than substitutable, parts. And this result was reached simply by virtue of the fact that customers, or certain classes of customers, were found to be locked in.

I do believe, however, that one of the consequences of overly aggressive findings of market power in the US has been a reluctance to apply significantly aggressive remedies. That is to say, the courts find power very quickly, but end up compensating by then being reluctant to impose appropriate remedies, with the optimal remedy being destruction of the monopoly, where it is technically or economically feasible.

Secondly, on conduct, I want to make a point that, first of all, under US law, you must distinguish between Sherman Act applications and applications of the Telecommunications Act. The Telecommunications Act creates what amounts to a no-fault duty to deal. That is, the right of interconnection under the Telecommunications Act does not depend upon the existence of any kind of exclusionary practice. The Sherman Act, however—setting aside for a second the essential facilities doctrine—requires some kind of anti-competitive practice, and, generally speaking, the refusal to deal, in and of itself, cannot be considered to be the unacceptable practice. This is where the essential facilities doctrine comes in, and, in my opinion, typically steps over the line. But, more importantly, the essential facilities doctrine grants access without doing anything about the underlying monopoly structure.

Finally, with respect to conduct, there are many types of exclusionary conduct that can give rise to bottleneck access even under the Sherman Act. These, of course, include many of the substantive claims in the Microsoft case, only some of which involve the internet. Examples of such exclusionary conduct involve tying, in particular, the claim that Microsoft ties its Windows platform—Windows 95, or, in the current litigation, Windows 98—to Internet

Explorer, which is its internet access software. They also include exclusive dealing, or the allegation that Microsoft—or Intel in the litigation before the Federal Trade Commission—enters into contracts conditioned on exclusivity. And they include reciprocity, particularly in the Intel litigation, where there is the allegation that, in some cases, Intel licenses its technology to other firms on the condition that the firm is willing to give, in return, royalty-free licences of its own technology to Intel. They also include market division, which, under our law, can, in fact, be a criminal offence if the offer to divide markets is accepted. The current litigation in the Microsoft case really involves proposals to divide markets, which would be criminal offences only if they had been accepted. It appears, in the current case, that they were not accepted and this places the case into the area of civil, rather than criminal, offences.

Finally, I want to say a few words about optimal decrees with respect to intellectual property rights. The first point is that the primary goal of antitrust ought to be to break up monopolies where the breaking up of the monopoly is technically feasible and can be done without undue economic cost. One of the problems with the 1995 Microsoft decree is that the government was willing to accept a kind of 'duty to deal' on the part of Microsoft, together with an injunction against certain kinds of exclusionary practices. I am largely opposed to this because I think that if breaking up the monopoly is feasible, and, in this particular case, I believe it is, then this is the kind of decree that the government should look for.

Instead, we have a long history in the United States of giving relief, particularly structural relief, which is ineffective at breaking up the monopoly because the scissors are pointed in the wrong direction. Probably the best example is the 1966 Grinnel decree. Grinnel had a series of city-wide monopolies for hard-wired alarm services. The government condemned the monopoly and ordered Grinnel to divest some of its city-wide monopolies while retaining others. The result was that Grinnel simply held on to half as many monopolies as it had had previously. Others owned the other monopolies, but each of the cities was, in fact, still a monopoly and still subject to the same kinds of pricing and output restraints.

For this reason, I think that forcing Microsoft to give up Internet Explorer, a widely discussed possible remedy in the Microsoft case, is wrong-headed. As long as Microsoft retains a Windows monopoly, it will have an incentive to degrade competition in the collateral markets in which it also operates. First it will be internet, later it will be streaming technology or other technologies that are employed in the internet or elsewhere. But the fact that the Windows monopoly is an intellectual property monopoly makes alternative types of remedies feasible. In this case, I think the optimal remedy ought to consist of a type of auction bidding in which both the Windows name and the Windows software are sold to 4, 5 or 6 competitors, each of whom would then be able to issue its own version of Windows—say IBM Windows or Dell Windows, or Hewlett Packard Windows.

Once Windows is offered to separate, non-dominant firms, then the bundling problem basically goes away. One of them can bundle Netscape if it wishes, another can bundle Internet Explorer if it wishes. But this is a solution that is fully authorised by Section 2 of the Sherman Act, and I believe the one that has the greatest potential, not merely for regulating a bottleneck—something to which American courts are very poorly suited—but for actually eliminating the monopoly which causes the bottleneck in the first place.

▶ EHLERMANN—Now, I pass the floor not to Mr. Amory, because DG IV is keeping him very busy in Brussels, but to the co-author of his paper, Mr. Verheyden.

▶ VERHEYDEN—The substance of my presentation today will be to try to highlight the ambiguity in the application of Article 82 [ex 86] and the essential facilities doctrine in the telecommunications sector. It can be summarised in two points. On the one hand, as it currently stands, the essential facility test may prove to be quite narrow when it is applied to different types of access situations. On the other hand, and this has links with what Mr. Barnes said earlier, the desirability of lowering the test of dominance to determine whether we could try to apply general competition rules and Article 82 [ex 86] in a larger number of instances, may have undesired effects, in the sense that it may constitute a disincentive for developing new networks.

With regard to the first aspect of my presentation, I will spare you the various requirements of the essential facility test, but I will highlight one condition, which is that the facility to which access is requested on these grounds must be considered as 'generally' essential. This means that the facility must not be needed by only one particular operator or new entrant, but must be generally needed by all new entrants.

This test may well be useful in our current situation, that is, a short time after liberalisation. At this stage, you still have largely dominant operators with some new entrants. But one can wonder whether this test, as it is currently applied, will still be applicable in the future, when there will be some degree of competition in the market.

I will take a very specific example relating to the nation-wide backbone networks. These types of networks are the first type of networks in which we will see competition developing over the coming years. A number of licences to this effect have already been granted in various Member States. In fact, although the development and the establishment of these networks is very complicated, there are easy ways of developing them, in the sense that you can pull resources together with utility companies, railways, highways, and you can lay cables along these natural paths. You can also rent dark fibre. Alternatively, some degree of competition can be achieved in this market.

On the other hand, the possibilities of rolling out these networks are not unlimited. You usually have only one railroad company in each country, and a limited number of highways and canals. This means that, in the coming years, we will have new entrants who will need access to nation-wide backbone networks but who will not have such a network. In these circumstances, one can wonder whether the generality of the essential facility test should be applicable, since it will be hard to argue that, for example, the national long distance network of an incumbent is 'generally' essential when you already have four or five competing network operators.

In fact, this issue was implicitly dealt with at national level when the national regulatory authorities had to approve the standard interconnection rates of the various incumbents. What we have seen happening in a number of Member States, is that in relation to the collecting service, *i.e.*, the service that enables the users of the local loop to access the network of a new entrant, you do not have a nation-wide collecting service with only one termination point. The incumbents require that operators establish points of interconnection in the various access areas. This basically means that they must have their own backbone network. National regulatory authorities had good reasons to allow such practices at the current stage, but it also reveals the limitations of competition rules because, in the market, we can already see instances where regulators have approved situations in which national incumbents are restricting access to their national network, at least for the purpose of collecting calls.

So that is one side of it: the essential facility test may be too restrictive in some instances. Now, does this, in fact, mean that we must lower the requirements of dominance in order to benefit from Article 82 [ex 86]? That is another question, and this very much ties into the debate about whether we should encourage vertical competition or horizontal competition. Certainly, if you encourage vertical competition, you will secure and maximise the use of existing facilities. On the other hand, however, you may create undesirable effects.

From a legal point of view, competition rules must be applied in a neutral way. This means that you must foster competition regardless of whether it is horizontal or vertical. Yet, one of the particularities of the telecommunications sector is that, beyond a certain stage, if you foster vertical competition beyond desirable levels, then you may create a disincentive for investment in alternative networks. This ties into what Mr. Ungerer said this morning when he referred to the very high investments in data networks. Now, from a telecommunications policy of point of view, it is desirable to have these high capacity data networks, but an incumbent (or any operator well-positioned to develop these networks) may not have the incentive to develop them if he knows that, after he has invested the large amount of resources necessary to have such a network, he will be required to allow unlimited access.

To sum up and summarise: it is questionable whether the current competition rules will be appropriate in the future to ensure access in a largely liberalised environment. On the other hand, it is, perhaps, not really desirable to change the rules to that effect. And this is where, maybe, there is room for sector-specific regulation.

▶ SCHERER—The topic of my presentation was going to be access to bottlenecks in local loops and submarine cables. But, under the current constraints of time and space, I do not think I am going to dive as deep as submarine cables. Instead, I will stay somewhat on the surface and talk about access to local loops.

Before I begin, I will add a few remarks about the essential facilities doctrine and its relationship to sector-specific regulation in the EU. In particular, based upon reactions to the Commission's access notice, it would appear that the essential facilities doctrine is some kind of a magic wand. This 'magic wand' enables the European Commission, in its increasing role as a European super-regulator, to open up telecommunications markets by providing new entrants with access to facilities controlled by incumbents.

I would like to set a certain counterpoint to this impression by arguing that both national telecommunications law and secondary Community law—which often forms the basis for national telecommunication law provisions—have already incorporated many of the elements of the essential facilities doctrine, and have adapted these elements to the needs of the re-regulated telecommunications markets. Thus, it is my view that access to telecommunications networks can, and should, primarily be assured by the application of the *lex specialis* (sector-specific regulation) rather than by the application of the essential facilities doctrine.

To turn to the specifics, I understand that, in providing telecommunications services to their customers, new entrants feel a need to obtain access to the local loop. This can be ensured in various manners. Thus, regarding access to the local loop, what would be the main shortcomings of the essential facilities doctrine? Well, despite the conceptual clarity of the Commission's access notice it is obvious, particularly in the light of the ECCJ's Bronner decision, that the scope of applicability of the essential facilities doctrine is fairly limited.

I will only cite three points of this limitation. The first limitation is the requirement that access to the facility in question be, in the words of the Commission, 'generally essential' for companies desiring to compete with the provider of the facility on a related downstream market. This criterion of 'general essentialness' is opaque and fraught with uncertainty. In particular, it provides little guidance related to the time dimension. In today's discussion, it has been mentioned, time and time again, that the telecommunications market is extremely dynamic.

Consequently, in the short and medium term, almost any refusal of access to the various segments of the network infrastructure will make the provision of competitive services seriously and unavoidably uneconomic. Once the establishment of alternative infrastructures has begun, however, this may change rapidly. Does this mean that a facility may be considered essential only as long as no satisfactory alternative to the facilities of the incumbent exists? Or does it mean that the facility is not essential at all, because, given the fact that amortisation of alternative infrastructure will occur over the medium term, the refusal of access does not make the proposed activity unavoidably uneconomic?

Another ambiguity of the essential facilities doctrine test lies in the criteria which allows for objective justifications of the refusal to provide access. To date, these objective justifications have not been specified.

Furthermore,—and this may be its major shortcoming—the essential facilities test does not address the un-bundling of facilities. Let me define what I mean by un-bundling. Un-bundling is the separation or segregation of services, service features, or capabilities, each of which can be installed, provided, accessed, measured, and purchased separately from other services, service features, and capabilities. If the incumbent is obliged to un-bundle its facilities, then new entrants and other users can freely choose and buy only those services, service features, and facilities which they want—without being obliged to buy those that they neither want nor need. The essential facilities doctrine, either in its classic form under competition law, or in the form of the Commission's access notice, does not establish sector-specific un-bundling requirements. Rather, it relies on Article 82(d) [ex 86(d)]. And I would submit that answers to many of these shortcomings are provided by the EU's ONP concept.

On this subject, I wish to stress three brief points. The first point is that the ONP directives define, as a matter of law, which telecommunications related facilities are to be considered as essential. That is, essentiality is defined by operation of law. The second point is that the ONP concept also provides very detailed justifications for the refusal of access. These justifications are the so-called 'essential requirements,' 'no harm to the network,' 'maintenance of network integrity,' 'inter-operability of services' and 'data protection' requirements. These reasons, and only these reasons, justify the refusal of access to essential facilities. The third point is that another difference between the application of the essential facilities doctrine under Article 82 [ex 86] on the one hand, and the inter-connection rules on the other hand, relates to enhanced procedural efficiency.

I realise that this third point is the topic of the third panel, but allow me, Mr. Chairman, to just say one or two words at the present time. The procedures before the Commission under the competition rules of the Treaty are not subject to deadlines, and, as everybody around this table knows, it takes, on average, about 2 years until a decision is reached. The interconnection obligation, however, obliges the national regulatory authorities, at the request of either party, to resolve certain disputes within 6 months after an application has been made. The ONP directive establishes other, similar, deadlines.

For example, I turn to the specific case of the bottleneck in the local loop in Germany, one of the most controversial country-specific decisions. I should, in the interest of full disclosure, state that I may not be the most objective person on this case, because I represented the regulatory authority before the courts. In this case, the German regulatory authority decided to oblige Deutsche Telekom A.G. to provide new entrants with access to so-called 'customer access lines,' or what we call the 'local loop'.

Without going into excessive detail here, I believe the case illustrates that sector-specific national legislation, which is based on EC telecommunications law, provides a very useful and, for what it is worth, reasonably efficient tool to ensure un-bundled access to the local loop. In fact, recourse to the essential facilities doctrine in this particular case was not required.

As far as procedural efficiency goes, this was a reasonably efficient method to obtain access to the local loop. It started in November of 1996, with the beginning of negotiations between the new entrants and Deutsche Telekom. An order of the regulatory authority instructing Deutsche Telekom to open its network was issued in May of 1997. The Administrative Court of Cologne took its preliminary decision in August of 1997, almost a year after the negotiations had started, and only gave its 'first-instance' decision a week ago. My conservative estimate is that, if Deutsche Telekom avails itself of all the legal remedies available, this court procedure will take at least another five to eight years. So much for procedural efficiency and so much for the essential facilities doctrine and sector-specific regulation.

▶ MONACI—However, I understand that the order of the administrative authority has not been suspended in this case.

▶ SCHERER—That is correct. Consequently, in the interim, access is being granted. The fight is now about pricing, but that is another story altogether.

▶ BARNES—I do not want to structure the discussion, but I think it is worth pointing out that the last intervention has indicated an interesting point, which may reveal the core problem that we face. The essential facilities doctrine does not appear to produce the right rule for telecommunications. Indeed, if you look at the ONP and Information and Communication Technologies (ICT) directives, what is being created is a mechanism by which telecommunications operators have both an obligation to provide access and a right to interconnection, *i.e.*, a right of access.

These obligations and rights raise a question which may link competition law with this kind of regulation which is unavailable under competition law. That is, if a network operator has a motivation not to interconnect, could we conclude that it has market power in this instance and, therefore, should be required to interconnect? If the answer to this is 'yes', then we may wish to apply general rules like access and interconnection to all operators. Each of these operators will be in one of two states. Either it will have no motivation to refuse access or it will be motivated to use market power and refuse access. In the former case, a rule requiring access is redundant but will not distort behaviour. In the latter case, you have identified that the operator in question has market power. Consequently, it is in the public interest to apply this obligation to them.

This conclusion might just marry competition rules, at one extreme, with regulation, at the other, in this area where we have only a few operators.

▶ LASSERE—Thank you, I was deeply interested by this morning's presentations, and I would like to come back to an issue which has been addressed by nearly all the speakers. This is the classical dilemma between access, on the one hand, and investment and innovation, on the other. I think this is a crucial question to the telecommunications industry. Every national regulatory authority faces it. Should they favour access to what exists, in an effort to prompt initial competition, or should they encourage new entrants to develop their own infrastructure, to invest by their own means. It is a classical dilemma, and there have been different answers brought to the equation. I would like to ask this question not solely from an academic standpoint. Rather, I would like to have precise answers from regulators who may have taken different views on the subject. More precisely, this is the issue of local loop un-bundling.

The UK's OFTEL has had a real policy objective which was, first, to encourage local competition and, second, to encourage investment by favouring network operators above services operators; or, at least, that is the assessment often made about OFTEL. Is this policy also considered as having favoured innovation in the telecommunication industry?

Others have taken different views. For example, in the US, the FCC and local regulators have made local loop un-bundling one condition for allowing local carriers to invest in long distance markets. What is the assessment in the US?

Among the European countries, Germany has taken one of the firmest views on the subject, making access to local loop something which is precisely mandated in telecommunications legislation.

Ideally, I would like to have quick answers from OFTEL, from the German Regulator and from the US experience. After some months, or years, of competition, what assessment can these different regulators make about the economic effects of allowing, or not allowing, access to the local loop, and of un-bundling?

▶ ARMSTRONG—Some of this morning's interventions seem to me to be a bit too optimistic about the benefits of competition in overcoming bottleneck problems. And, although it is sometimes overlooked, it is a pretty point of common sense that once someone has signed up with a telecommunications firm, that firm has a monopoly over telnet calls to that subscriber, whether fixed or mobile. This fact has nothing to do with fixed costs or anything like that. It's just that, once someone has signed up with a particular firm, that firm controls access to that subscriber. So if a country has got 30,000,000 lines, I would say that there are 30,000,000 separate bottlenecks in that country.

Consequently, it doesn't matter very much how those lines are divided up between competing networks. It is a little bit like Professor Herbert Hovenkamp's regional security monopoly problem. It does not matter whether there are four monopolies or one combined monopoly. In the long run, competition is not going to do away with control over bottleneck services unless there are some major technological developments.

We have seen a little example of this recently in Britain, where there are four mobile companies. At the moment, there is a major dispute about call termination rates. Equally, the mobile firms may or may not be competitive at the retail level, but there is no question that they are not competitive in providing call termination services. So, I will just add a note of pessimism about competition in telecommunications infrastructure.

▶ SALSBURY—I would like to make a few observations, some of which may be relatively controversial. No one has spoken from the business community as of yet, and listening to the various comments this morning, I was struck with how many times MCI has been involved in some of these issues. We view ourselves as a competitor, but we have had a bite taken out of us in the internet backbone area and we were even an entrant in New Zealand. Thus, I speak with some experience.

First of all, there is only one bottleneck in the telecommunications industry and that is the local loop. The internet backbone is not a bottleneck. The recent decision to the contrary, which comes out of the European Commission, was unfortunate. At the time, MCI acquiesced in that decision because it took place in a merger setting where time was of the essence. But it is a bad decision, and should not be extended. It is not true that the internet backbone is a bottleneck of any sort. And I will add that if there had been a right of appeal in Europe from that decision, we might very well have challenged it. But the timing might have still driven us to acquiesce.

Wireless is not a bottleneck, obviously. Undersea cables are not a bottleneck. And local switching is not a bottleneck. It is only the local loop that is a bottleneck. And I say this from the perspective of a businessman, from the perspective of a competitor, as well as from that of a lawyer.

In fact, wireless can only influence the pricing of competitive wired 'services'. It is not an access substitute; therefore, it cannot influence access pricing.

Furthermore, there was a comment this morning concerning how one should determine the right price for access, given the fact that TELRIC or TSLRIC is an academic sort of amorphous standard. I do not know the answer to this; we have obviously struggled with trying to apply these standards. I will just say that if the result comes out anywhere other than at least 40 or 50% below retail cost, then you have got the wrong answer. You simply need that margin in order to enter the business in competition with the incumbent.

My second observation is that where there is a bottleneck there is dominance. It is very simple. It is sort of a tautology in my view. If there are three or more suppliers, however, that dominance will be short-lived.

If I were a regulator, I would not concern myself with trying to encourage us, the competitors, to build infrastructure. That is our business; it is not your business. If there are at least three competitors, we will make the right decision. Trust us.

As far as regulating, there are really two possibilities. You can either have a structural solution—the line of business separation between the bottleneck supplier and the downstream market—or you can have behavioural solutions. The structural solutions work; the behavioural solutions do not. But it is a policy choice. You can have something that works or something that does not work.

With respect to the behavioural solutions that have been proposed in the United States with regard to the local loop, I would observe that these solutions require time-tested experience. The issues are technical—interconnection and pricing. If you have several years of experience in service provision and pricing, then you can generally rely on that experience for allowing the incumbent into the downstream market. That is, your experience will provide a benchmark with which to judge the incumbent's behaviour. If their behaviour shifts, then you will know that they are deviating in favour of trying to use their influence, their dominance, in the downstream market.

There were several comments this morning asking whether our business assessment would be different in converging or new markets. I think the answer, generally speaking, is no. Monopolists argue that you need to allow them to develop downstream markets, otherwise there will be no entry. But there generally is not a shortage of capital. We can raise the money to invest if there is a market in which to invest. That is, if there is a consumer demand and we can make a decent profit, we will invest. You can, again, rely on us to make that choice.

What we have difficulty with, is the rules. In the United States, we are currently facing fifty different sets of rules. I hope you will not make the same mistake in Europe, because we are trying to enter the market in Europe, and if we end up with fifteen different sets of rules, it will be a difficult problem for us. This is particularly true when you have non-privatised competitors, as well as incumbents. In these situations, in our view, our competitor is also making the rules.

I think time is a major problem. It is a major issue because so much of our decision-making is based on investing money. We need to get the return, that is, we need to get the cash-flow back, in a particular period of time. Therefore, if we face a long-scale delay, we probably will not invest.

There has been a lot of talk about the essential facilities doctrine this morning. Based upon MCI's experience, I think, clearly, it is a very useful tool in exposing the problem, but it is not particularly good at suggesting solutions. Antitrust courts are not good at pricing decisions. It is not in their area of expertise.

However, the essential facilities doctrine is clearly something that has a place in the sector in terms of identifying the problem, the bottleneck. And I hope we know that the bottleneck is, as I have said, the local loop.

In closing, I will just add two comments. First, I would encourage the regulators to consider the choice between urban markets and rural markets. This will be very important. It is important to us in terms of our customer base because, obviously, it is much easier to justify an investment in an urban setting where there are many concentrated users. You may think about things that would encourage us to go into rural areas, and you may consider whether different rules should apply.

For example, in the United States, we have been involved in an experiment where we have a local municipality actually providing the local loop, and encouraging people to come in and use it. It is overbidding the incumbent. It has been a remarkable success in one or two rural markets. I would be pleased to talk further with some of you about this project, perhaps outside of this seminar.

I wish to stress once more that structural separation is the key. If you have the will, you clearly can divorce the local loop business from the rest of the network. Otherwise, you have a line of business restriction. It does work. Good fences make good neighbours.

▶ WATERS—I have also been working in the new entrant in Australia for the last several months. In fact, I have been battling against Henry Ergas who has been working for the incumbent. Since the Australian regulator is here, we could probably have a mock mediation or arbitration of our interconnection charge.

I would like to say something about the problem of TSLRIC or TELRIC, whichever version you want to use. Costing the optimal network can seem very seductive to a new entrant. Once you have grabbed on to TSLRIC for this purpose, you think that you have made a significant advance in evaluating start-up costs.

However, the outcome in Australia so far shows that there can be serious distortions caused by a slavish application of TSLRIC across the whole network. To borrow an American movie title, I would call this 'The Groundhog Day Syndrome.'

The problem arises from the sequential application of the TSLRIC model of building optimal networks. Consequently, Nero is currently calculating the interconnection price that should apply in Australia today for the year in progress. For this purpose, it pretends that the network was built on 30 June 1997. If the parties have a dispute in three years time, then, I suppose, logically Nero, would say: 'We pretend that we built the network on 30 June 2001, for traffic in 2002.'

That assumption is sensible for a lot of the equipment in the network, like switches, because it operates somewhat like a compulsory retirement scheme for that equipment. Consequently, new entrants do not get stuck paying for equipment of the incumbent which is capable of being replaced.

However, when you use an optimal network model, you also require rebuilding from scratch of the duct system. This sounds very boring, but the duct system, according to Nero, accounts for 40-50% of the total fixed costs in the customer access network. And this is why I call it a Groundhog Day syndrome, because every time that you come to recalculate TSLRIC, you pretend that the streets are dug up again by the incumbent in order to install a new network. And each time it does that, if you like, it gets to reboot the capital base of that duct system. So, you get a terrible distortion caused by the ducts.

Now, there is no new technology in ducts. They have been there for 40 or 50 years. So, you get this enormous lump every time you recalculate and apply TSLRIC to the duct costs. It causes a double distortion if you do not have re-balancing in your system, such as we have in Australia. Without rebalancing, you get an absolutely enormous Access Deficit Contribution (ADC). This ADC bubble is created each time and reappears in the interconnection charge because the incumbent does not recoup those rebooted costs through tariffs on access line.

This shows that, as a new entrant, you can sometimes start with an economic theory that you think is going to deliver a superb outcome on historic costs. But you can get a situation, such as in Australia, where the interconnection charge actually started at about 3.1 cent in 1991 and Telstar is now claiming close to 5 cents per minute. So, we have actually seen an inter-connection charge go up.

▶ FELS—You will have to await until early next year for our wisdom on this subject. On a couple of the questions that have been asked, I think it is a little early to settle the controversy about investment. That is my impression. And secondly, on the question about distortions affecting the degree of market power, yes, they clearly do, as Professor Ergas has said. However, there are, arguably, other sources of market power once the distortions have been removed, including the strong position that the incumbent starts from.

I just wanted very quickly to outline the Australian approach, as part of my answer to some of the questions this morning. There is also a tiny spill-over to tomorrow morning. In Australia, we decided that competition law was not quite good enough to deal with access problems.

In particular, we noted the New Zealand experience, where access for Cleo was left to the courts and it took six years to get a decision. Thereafter, that decision was not accepted by the government, who insisted upon another solution. Problems like these led us to conclude that it is not quite feasible to settle the questions in terms of antitrust law offences. The courts also have big problems coming up with remedies regarding costs. You need something a bit more than antitrust alone.

Consequently, because we think this access problem will arise in numerous public utility areas, we have passed a general law about access. This general access provision is now part of our competition law. In principle, it applies to all sectors of the economy, and it relates to the service arising from a facility, rather than to the facility itself. If you cannot get access, the first step is to go through a process in which an independent body declares whether or not there should be access to the service from the facility. The main tests are whether such access would promote competition in at least one market (other than the market for the service itself) and whether it would be uneconomical for anyone to develop another facility to provide the service. There are also some other tests, including public interest and safety tests.

This is but a brief summary of a long law, and there are several other mechanisms besides this access declaration provision. Nevertheless, I believe this is the most interesting provision for today's discussion.

If an access declaration is granted, there is a further process. If the parties cannot agree upon the terms and conditions of access, then the regulator, which would be the competition agency in this case, acts as an arbitrator. In reaching this decision, the regulator uses a number of general criteria to balance the investment considerations we heard about this morning, with the competition considerations.

Moving from the general access law to the telecommunication sector, we have a couple of additional complications. Until 1997, we had a system not totally unlike the UK's OFTEL system. We had AUSTEL, a managed duopoly system in the reserved services. But, in 1997, we decided to absorb all of this within the competition law structure. Consequently, the competition regulator does the main economic and competition regulation in telecommunications. The old AUSTEL has therefore been abolished.

Meanwhile, the relevant access laws have been written into the competition law with a specific regime concerning telecommunications. This regime is similar to the generic law that I just described, but it takes account of a few special features about telecommunications, including the desirability of interconnection.

Of course, there are also some general laws passed by the Parliament about cross-subsidies and so on, which must be taken into account. So, once again, there is an entire law defining when we declare access for carriage services. Under this law, there are a number of criteria, of which the key criterion is the interest of end-users.

Also, there is explicit reference to the desirability of promoting investment in infrastructure. Consequently, the regulator must weigh these points and must listen to all of the feverish arguments about the terms and conditions of access, which you have all heard this morning.

In my view, the access issue is the fundamental provision in the law, but the question of abuse of market power also arises and plays a supplemental role.

My other point concerns the factors associated with such abuse. With regard to these factors—abuse of market power, abuse of dominance, monopolisation, and Section 2 of the Sherman Act—the law has been strengthened. That is, in recognition of what is regarded as a high degree of market power held by the telecommunications incumbent, the law has been beefed up.

Consequently, for most Australian businesses, we had a concept of dominance or abuse of market power that had a few soft edges. Some of these soft edges have now been taken out of our law. It is a little bit stronger. Yet, the concepts are still competition ones.

In addition, the processes are a little different. Normally, if you are conducting a case about abuse of dominance, you go to court and wait several years for the results. In this case, by contrast, the regulator can very quickly decree that certain behaviour is, in fact, an abuse of market power. Thereafter, if the operator continues with that behaviour, it can be fined 10,000,000 Australian Dollars, a million a day after that, providing that the regulator's original decision is ultimately upheld by the court. So, you must go back to the court to collect damages, but there is a slightly different incentive there.

In summary, the philosophy in Australia has been to try to shift the economic and competition regulation into the general competition policy area, but to create an expanded competition law, with some extra provisions for telecommunications in recognition of its very special characteristics.

Very briefly. One of the major topics that was mentioned by many of the panellists this morning concerned whether we needed somehow to change the essential facilities doctrine. That is: is the essential facilities doctrine insufficient to cope with the problems that we have and, if so, must we lower the threshold of applicability of that doctrine?

I would be very concerned about any such trend. Why? The essential facilities doctrine is typically a concept of competition law, an antitrust doctrine. It therefore applies to all markets, even to developing markets, which are not really very integral to what we are talking about today. So, if we lower the threshold of the essential facility test, we will lower it not only in telecommunications, but in all sectors of industry. This is inappropriate because we have specific problems in telecommunications, which may not be generalised to other industries.

In particular, at least in Europe, we are going from state monopolies to markets. So, what we need are transitional rules in order to bring us from legal monopoly to market. I think that this is what the Commission has done in its directives, but my sincere hope is that once this is done, we will forget about telecommunications regulation, because I already see a contrary trend in Europe. That is, once the market has been established, these authorities—which have been organised in order to police the market—may, following a typical European tendency, start re-regulating the industry, bringing us back to square one. The result would be that we would not have a true market system, but we would have a regulated industry once again.

Consequently, I would be very much in favour of maintaining the essential facilities doctrine as a remedy which should no longer be applicable once the market has been established, that is, once we have successfully gone from legal monopoly to market. Otherwise, I see the danger that Mr. Salsbury was mentioning.

As an aside, I am happy to inform Mr. Salsbury that the decisions of the European Commission are subject to appeal. Of course, it is a bit difficult in a merger case, where time is of the essence, but, fortunately, we have a system of law in Europe. Therefore, it is possible to appeal.

Going back to what some of the regulators were saying, I still prefer a legal system. I like the regulators, but I prefer judges. Consequently, I think that we must revert as quickly as possible to a system where the judges decide what an essential facility is and whether it is at issue in a particular case. I think a regulator can undertake this task on a provisional basis, but he must be subject to strict judicial control.

▶ ARNBAK—I agree with much of what has been said here. I believe that sector-specific regulation has a transitional role to play. We do need it for the reasons pointed out here. And the Australian experience shows that there is more to it than just the initial general application of competition law. But, of course, you can let the particular rules that you add to competition law be exercised by a competition authority. This is not at all at issue.

I would just like to mention the Dutch experience about investment in proper pricing and un-bundling the local loop. This relates a little bit to what Mr. Salsbury said about the dichotomy between rural and urban areas. Holland, by contrast, is basically urban throughout its territory. Thus, the dichotomy we face is between big business uses and small uses, be they small business uses or domestic consumers.

We see that most businesses—and they do not have to be very big—take the local loop from two different suppliers, or try to get it from two different suppliers. They try to organise themselves so that they will have a choice. They allow themselves to choose. Consequently, we do not have to worry so much about the business users; they already have a choice and will ensure that choice because they are powerful enough in the market to ask competitors to provide two local loops. The public policy issue is really: how do you provide general consumers with that choice?

And there, the unfortunate message, which is partly an answer to Mr. Lassere's question, is that it is very difficult to provide small users with that choice unless you re-balance tariffs so that you pay the proper price. This is similar to what Mr. Ergas argued. If you continue to have access deficits on the local loop and if you do not actually allow (or even force) incumbents to re-balance, we will not have alternative local loops for the consumers. And that is a public policy which is difficult to swallow. This is particularly true in a cultural setting, such as Europe, where we have concepts of universal service and distorted pricing. In summary, this is a public policy problem that cannot be solved by the operator unless he is mandated to re-balance tariffs.

We have mandated such re-balancing in the Netherlands. That is, we have used the non-discrimination rules to argue that the incumbent is forced to un-bundle his local loop. What we are not yet clear about is how the pricing should be structured. We are studying that now.

► BOETTCHER—I would also like to come back to Mr. Lassere's question. He pointed out the dilemma between low prices, on the one hand, and lack of investment, on the other. Generally speaking, we also focus upon this question. However, we must apply the Telecommunications Act, which does not focus particularly on that dilemma.

For example, when we resolve interconnection disputes, we must decide on prices for interconnection. When we determine these prices, we must simply apply the appropriate rules. These rules dictate that our decision must focus on cost efficiency. Consequently, decisions under the Telecommunications Act do not depend on whether our decision furthers investment, we simply look at cost efficiency in pricing.

This was the process we followed when we decided on interconnection prices ten months ago. The interconnection price we decided upon was a rather low price. It led to very fierce competition, which led to very low prices in a very short period of time. The end-result was a rather large number of competitors. Therefore, I really cannot answer Mr. Lassere's question, because we simply apply the Telecommunications Act, which focuses on cost efficiency.

The question Mr. Baker posed, regarding improper and proper pricing is the most difficult question we must solve. This is especially true given the time frames involved. First, it is very difficult to get the right data to prove the prices of the applicant. Once we have the appropriate data, we enter into the situation we heard about this morning: whatever way we decide, it is very difficult to say that we have chosen the right price. This is all the more difficult given the fact that we must decide within ten months.

As I described just seconds ago, we found a proper price for interconnection. Therefore, I would say, Mr. Lassere, that it is important to ask whether the prices we set in interconnection disputes may lead to a situation in which there is little investment in bottleneck infrastructure. Deutsche Telekom will cut prices by 60%, beginning next year. This price cut may mean that the incumbent's competitors will have little chance of surviving on the market. Therefore, we could say that it will encourage the renewal of Telekom's dominance, so that it will be able to create markets. It will be able to make the necessary investments. Consequently, you could argue that price regulation ultimately leads to a situation where investment is made.

▶ HOVENKAMP—Two very brief comments. The first is in response to Mr. Salsbury's very interesting observation that bottleneck and monopoly go hand and hand. As an empirical matter, this is true most of the time. However, the one set of cases where it is clearly not true is where the bottleneck is subject to multiple ownership.

Indeed, many inputs in many markets are shared by multiple firms. You might think differently about the bottleneck problem if, for example, the Bell Atlantic/Nynex loop were owned by Bell Atlantic, MCI, AT&T, Sprint, Westinghouse and several other firms, all of whom operated it as a joint venture. To be sure, different kinds of antitrust problems would arise with respect to duties to deal with other parties, price fixing, standard setting, etc. Nevertheless, these are different, and frequently more manageable, problems.

Indeed, what I suggested in my earlier comment about compulsory licencing in the Microsoft case begins with the premise that the basic Windows platform is a bottleneck. One way to solve the monopoly problem is to recognise the fact that it is bottleneck and then compel multiple ownership of the bottleneck. Thereafter, one can rely on the laws of competition plus antitrust oversight to manage the facility.

My second point concerns the essential facilities doctrine as it has developed in the United States and why I remain extremely pessimistic about its use. The first point is that access does not improve the situation unless it is linked to some kind of decision about output or pricing. That is to say, if you compel access and do nothing else, the owner of the essential facility will sell to the plaintiff at the monopoly price. Output will not increase. There will be two sellers sharing this essential facility, but overall output will be the same. As a result, prices will be the same and, at least in the short run, consumer welfare will not be noticeably improved.

Consequently, access must almost always be accompanied by some kind of pricing or output order. Unfortunately, the United States federal district courts are woefully inadequate for this task. Therefore, all deregulation has accomplished is to transfer a great deal of oversight away from the specialised agencies toward courts of general jurisdiction, where, in many circumstances, decisions are subject to fact-finding by a jury under US law.

One of the best signs of this problem is the fact that the most common type of pricing regulation that the courts give is a non-discrimination order. Non-discrimination orders have an intuitive appeal to fairness, but they are not necessarily optimal pricing rules. In fact, many regulatory agencies have adopted alternatives to non-discrimination pricing policies, such as Ramsey pricing policies and two-part pricing policies, which yield much more efficient results than simple non-discrimination orders.

In summary, if the end result is price control and decisions made by courts of general jurisdiction, then the deregulation process has not been an improvement at all.

▶ Long—Well, I have heard many very stimulating, provocative and also controversial comments. I am afraid my remarks may add to the latter group.

Telecommunications in Europe was the domain of state-owned operators (known in Europe as the TOs) until the 1990's. It seems to me dubious that when these firms were released onto the competitive market, they were released with what were essentially inherited assets. This is something that we should not forget when considering the role of regulation. That is, one of the fundamental purposes of regulation is to try to deal with the consequences of that inheritance.

In our discussion of local loops, there is a risk of our being somewhat distracted into thinking that the local loop is the only important inherited asset. Believe me, it is not. They are many inherited assets that could be deemed to be essential. In physical infrastructure, local loop is a prime example, but other inherited assets include rights of way, strategically located sites and even radio frequencies. You may argue that, in the new order, many of these inherited advantages have been replaced by the granting of new licences to replace those that were effectively inherited. Nonetheless, the vestiges of this inheritance remain with us today, and I think that regulation has only recently begun to scratch the surface of the implications of this problem.

To be particularly provocative, I think that, when it comes to the availability of these assets, interconnection was the very first manifestation of an attempt by the regulators to make the assets available, on a shared basis, to the rest of the sector. And, if you think about it, perhaps a very clever trick was played upon the new entrants to the industry, if not upon the regulators themselves. That is, the extent to which interconnection was pushed as a solution can be seen to benefit the incumbents, because interconnection presents the provision of a service by the incumbent, rather than a true sharing of assets. If these assets were originally national assets, they should have been shared for national benefit. Therefore, you could argue that they should be made available in a much more un-bundled way.

The local loop debate is just the beginning of an understanding that we need to get below the structural surface. The concept of interconnection is a temporary arrangement which got the market entrants into play but it is not the ultimate solution.

Moving on, I would take issue with Tod Barnes here, when he made, I think, a stunning assertion. If I understood him correctly, he argued that if a party refuses to interconnect, such refusal could indicate a bottleneck, a dominant position, an essential facility or, something along these lines. In my country, such an assertion would result in many cable operators immediately grabbing the microphone to suggest that, although they own their customers, they certainly do not have anything approaching an essential facility.

The important thing is to look at all these facilities in their context. What other means of access are available to the customer? Already, just to take my early example, I have three means of access available to me and to other operators. I have a mobile phone, I have a cable line, and I have my traditional BT line (wire line). All these are providing means of access to me as a consumer. Are any of them an essential facility? The answer must depend on the context and what alternatives are available to reach the customer.

My final point is that somebody has quite rightly raised the point that the UK has been at the forefront of encouraging the building of network infrastructure as a means of providing the platform for effective choice. This was always the fundamental tenet of UK liberalisation: that you provide choice of operators through alternative infrastructure. And I think—just a cautionary word—that regulators must be very careful to avoid selecting technologies in this field. In a sense, however, by choosing to protect and promote infrastructure, there is an element of choosing technology. We already have examples of market failure in this regard, because, only the other week, Ionica, which is an alternative local loop wireless provider, went out of business. This was a company that had chosen to take on the incumbent in providing the local loop service. Now, I know the regulators would say that their job is to provide all available means of access or to assist in providing all the possible means of access. In their view, since this network infrastructure is one of the primary platforms to meet that access goal, infrastructure building should be encouraged. Otherwise, you are left to pure service competition.

However, provided the pricing is correct, service competition can equally provide a viable means for securing customer benefit.

▶ SCHAUB—I want to underline that, as often as I agree with Mario Siragusa about the absolute need to maintain the transitional character of the sector-specific rules which we are now struggling with, Herbert Ungerer and Allan Fels have made it clear that such rules were absolutely necessary. It would have been a mistake–as we have seen in the New Zealand examples and others—to try to solve all the problems just on the basis of the general competition rules.

But, of course, there is a serious danger that once sector-specific regulation has been launched, it will be difficult to dismantle. For example, in Germany, it has always been said that the special regulator is only of transitional nature, and at some stage, if they do the job well, they should disappear. There is, however, a danger that things, once created, do not easily disappear.

Therefore, we must be very careful that this process does not become a permanent feature; because, if we take half-cooked, undeveloped decisions into the future, we are in danger of remaining in a permanent transition. It is so beautiful to use the toys we have, why should those who have the toys in their hands give them up?

There is also the fact that you often have so many people working on the task. What should you do with them? In Germany, one reason (not the only reason) for which a new, specific regulator was created, rather than giving the task to the Bundeskartellamt (which could have done it), was that something had to be done with the thousands of officials who had worked in the Ministry of Post and Telecommunication. I am sure that heads of the German regulatory agency are not particularly delighted about the crowds that have joined them—many without the right expertise. However, they are there and we all hope that, somehow, the problem will be controlled.

Further, I agree with all of those who have very mixed feelings about pricing decisions taken by regulators or competition authorities. I can tell you that we hope to be involved as little as possible in such individual pricing decisions, but the initial dirty-work must be done by someone. Consequently, we may also have to do it at some stage, but, certainly, our objective would be to get away from this as quickly as possible. We hope to establish clear and convincing general rules so that individual pricing decisions become obsolete. Maybe, that's an exaggerated optimism, but in the world in which we live, we must sometimes be optimists.

On the point Mario Siragusa made about judges, I must say I would not have any problem with an increased role for judges in competition policy enforcement. Maybe, we should also consider this with regard to the EU regime. It could usefully enrich the overall landscape; yet, I think one also has to avoid any naïveté in this regard. We have just heard Professor Hovenkamp talking about US experience with the courts. In fact, if you talk to Americans, you are struck by contradictory impressions of the role of the federal judiciary.

Finally, I would like to make one remark on Mr. Salsbury's comment concerning Worldcom/MCI. Of course, we would have been delighted if that case could have gone to court. We are always grateful if there is a critical examination of what we are doing. Consequently, we deeply regret that MCI thought it would be preferable to live with what was decided.

Moreover, this decision was reached not just by some crazy Europeans, but jointly with American and European competition authorities. That is, this was one case where the American and European case-handlers worked closely together from the first to the last day, and where the remedies were negotiated by a joint team. Therefore, in the Worldcom/MCI case you were confronted with the combined trans-Atlantic wisdom of competition authorities and, indeed, it would be useful to expose this wisdom, from time to time, to jurisdictional control. We hope that, on another occasion, MCI will be more helpful.

▶ KNIEPS—I would like to comment on some of the issues raised in the papers. I would like to start with Mr. Ungerer's conclusions, since he was looking at three possible ways forward for regulation in the telecommunications sector: competition policy, sector-specific regulation, and structural separation. The question that follows is: what could be a realistic future path?

This issue relates to the question as to how realistic the future phasing out of sector-specific regulation will be. I think that this question, in turn, has a lot to do with the issue of how to specify or localise the minimal sector-specific regulatory needs. Let us say, *prima facie,* that there is no future need for sector-specific regulation at all and use it only as long as there is a remaining bottleneck in the local loop. Alternatively, let us identify what the monopolistic bottleneck is.

In the case of telecommunications, the monopolistic bottleneck is now the local network; but consider also airlines, airports, railway and the electricity grids (long distance and local). These are all durable monopolistic bottlenecks. We economists like to identify stable monopolistic bottlenecks which exist over a substantial period. Phasing out of such bottlenecks is possible, but it is not achievable overnight. From this point of view, the durable monopolistic bottleneck in telecommunications, the local loop, can—depending on technological progress—be phased out fairly quickly. Here, however, sector-specific regulation of this monopolistic bottleneck is required. Of course, it is not enough to trust to bargaining, and *ex ante* sector-specific regulation is necessary to discipline access—but only that—to the monopolistic bottleneck.

I agree with Mr. Hovenkamp: it is not enough to say access should be guaranteed without discrimination, you must also discuss the conditions for access. The conditions then lead directly to the question of price and cost regulation. Europe has latterly issued several recommendations with respect to costing and pricing of interconnection services. Here, my argument is, first, that regulation should be limited strictly to the monopolistic bottleneck. Secondly, it should not be price structure regulation, but it should be only be price-gap regulation. That is, it should provide freedom for the active firm to search for innovative price schedules.

For example, the German rail company, Deutsche Bahn A.G., has recently introduced a non-linear, two-part tariff for track access. The question now is: is this tariff discriminatory or not? The argument is that it is not a discriminatory tariff because it applies equally to everyone who offers train services. The situation should be similar in telecommunications, since, here, a lot more potential exists to design innovative price schedules which are Pareto superior, in the sense that they are especially beneficial for the consumers. The established theory of non-linear pricing says that, in order to cover the total cost, and given a price above marginal cost, you can always find a non-linear pricing schedule which is Pareto superior, *i.e.*, which is better for the firms and for the customers. This means that the optimal policy is not price-structure regulation but price-gap regulation, combined with a kind of accounting separation in order to avoid cross-subsidisation between monopolistic bottlenecks and the rest.

This conclusion also provides a good argument on which to base the phasing out of this regulation, because it is a kind of light-handed regulation. It is not that you need analytical cost models. In fact, I oppose them strongly. Analytical cost models are models which try to calculate the costs of the incumbent carrier. Unfortunately, this is an impossible task because the models cannot reflect the true costs of an established firm, and they also cannot reflect the true costs of newcomers. This is true because the cost decisions depend strongly on the expectations which you have of the market and the economic dispositions, etc.. So, my argument is that there is a strong need to go from historical cost-accounting to current cost-accounting, but there is no way to simulate the cost of an active firm on the basis of these simulations.

Therefore, I feel price-gap regulation and accounting separation must be adequate regulatory mechanisms. This, of course, leaves the question of what to do all with all of these regulators, who would like to do some business. That is a difficult question, but, from the consumer point of view, it is important to find a symmetric framework. Such a framework must enable infrastructure and services competition to function without the (final) backing of industrial or technology policy.

Going through all the papers in the first volume, I had the impression that the question of whether a monopolistic bottleneck existed or not, was raised several times. From the economic point of view, it is important that two conditions are met before something can be treated as a monopolistic bottleneck: The first condition is that you need access to this facility in order to compete in the complementary markets. The second condition is that it is not economically feasible to duplicate the facility. These are the two inquiries one must seriously make because it is always strategically attractive for competitors to gain access to a facility for free, or for a very low price: this cannot be acceptable.

▶ RUBINFELD—At the US Department of Justice, we like to think of ourselves as involved in encouraging competition or enforcing antitrust laws, but not so much in regulating. In this regard, in our activity determining conditions for access to long distance under Article 271, we see ourselves as trying to set up conditions under which competition will be encouraged and not need further regulation.

Because we do not yet have enough experience, we are not sure how all of the un-bundling will work at local level, but we do believe that un-bundling can be productive, as long as it is based on some kind of forward-looking prices of the kind that were suggested earlier today. And once we set up the right system for such competition to exist, we believe there will be no need for us to be involved on a regular basis. So we will not have the Groundhog Day problem that was described earlier.

What will probably be necessary in that world down the road is some regulation of the local loop, which is clearly a bottleneck now and probably will be for the foreseeable future. Perhaps this is the right role for the state regulatory authorities. We see our role in that ideal world as simply being one of intervening in, hopefully, what will be a minimal number of cases.

We do use our authority under Section 2 of the Sherman Act when dominant firms behave in a manner that is anti-competitive. But, this intervention is a far cry from regular day-to-day or month-to-month regulation.

In summary, this is our hope and this is why we are being very careful about treating the issue as access into markets. We are also hopeful that there will be continued interest, on the part of local incumbents, to compete in neighbouring or other markets. Therefore, we are also trying to make sure we create the conditions that will allow this to continue.

▶ UNGERER—What I want to say is the following: first, I think perhaps we should make a distinction regarding institutional issues. This is a part of tomorrow's discussion, but I think we ought also to discuss this principle with regard to general regulation. That is, because we have seen different models, we should identify which institution in which country is the source of these systems. I would simply like to make a comment on the previous two points.

There is a kind of broad agreement that sector-specific regulation can provide the power to bring about competition in services rapidly. We have the proof of this in Europe. But there is certainly one thing to keep in mind. In one way or another, one must determine the price to be paid for access, which means that the regulator also determines, to a large extent, investment behaviour. Unfortunately, he will also determine which investment will not take place. And that is a much more difficult choice. So I think whichever system is used, everybody should be clear about the fact that this is a maximal intervention approach.

The second point I wanted to make concerns the essential facilities concept. First of all, I must say, that the access notice is not much focused on the essential facilities doctrine. Rather, it is a decision based on an interpretation of Article 82 [ex 86], including the possibilities left for judging abuse of collective dominance. This concept would also catch those areas which are much more likely to occur in the future with bottlenecks under some type of collective control. For example, collective bottlenecks may be typical in the internet situation.

Now, if one considers this point, I was a bit astonished to hear suggestions that the essential facilities concept is not efficient. If this critique relates to procedural issues, I think that this probably concerns a more general fairness argument. In problems which we refer to judges, there is always a trade-off between the rights of parties and the efficient adjudication of competition. Also, do not forget that, in the end, if there is abuse, it can entail fines. So, this type of behaviour—refusing access or giving it on unfair terms—results in a different kind of penalty.

The other argument was that the essential facilities concept could not apply because there may be alternative possibilities. My naïve impression would be that this is a very welcome effect. Should we even be interfering if we have a near competitive situation? This is exactly what I have always thought to be a merit of the essential facilities doctrine: as soon as you come near to a competitive situation, the government withdraws. For me, this is an advantage. And this is exactly the danger in sector-specific regulation, which would always be prone to being overly active to its own sector.

Finally, I wish to bring attention to one point. At the moment, we are not just speaking theoretically about these models. We have experience in other sectors, such as regulation in electricity, as well as in telecommunications itself. For example, we looked at the possible convergence point between fixed and mobile markets in the year 2005. Because we have always been wrong in our forecasts in the past, it will probably be earlier.

In the interim, we must choose a regulatory system. This morning, we have only been talking about fixed telecoms. Mobile telecoms are regulated differently in Europe, particularly because there is no price regulation either of interconnection in mobile services or final-user access—with some qualifications, of course. Consequently, we have these two different models in fixed network and mobile network services. We have a different development, marked by very low interconnection rates in fixed services, which we think we now need. We also have a mobile interconnect rate that we are currently investigating under competition law in the mobile interconnect proceeding. And we have very substantial investment on the mobile side, which has been attracted by the high rates which are possible in the mobile sector.

Consequently, a big issue for the 1999 review of the ONP is to decide which model will prevail. That is really what is at stake. We must decide whether the current fixed model will be extended, that is, will price regulation be extended to the mobile system in one way or another. Or could we accept—and I find it regrettable that this is not discussed enough—the extension of the current mobile model into the fixed area.

▶ LASSERE—I would join Herbert Ungerer in concluding that we are anticipating tomorrow's debate about the specific roles of sectoral regulators and competition authorities. This observation leads me to two observations.

The first one is that we may tend to overestimate the role of the regulator and to underestimate the role of the legislator. I think it is very important to note that they are a couple. A regulator is nothing if he cannot rely on firm, precise legislation and a political consensus upon what his mandate entails. And perhaps, compared with the competition authority, a regulator's added value is that he has a policy objective, a long term strategy. We agreed this morning that he must manage a transition from monopoly to market competition, so he must have a view about the landscape upon which he wants to build. And his role is certainly to reduce uncertainty in this transition.

The second thing I wanted to highlight, based in part on what Colin Long was saying, is that in continental Europe we are more influenced by the investment model than by the access model. I suspect this is due to the role of legislation. Further, our thinking is shaped by the fact that, in Europe, the idea of competition has been politically sold to the policy makers, who were, in fact, initially reluctant to accept it. It became acceptable only because it was sold with reference to the amount of investment it would generate and how many jobs it would create. This certainly was much more efficient as a marketing strategy than speaking about bottleneck facilities or access to the local loop and un-bundling. So, European legislators and the regulators are more influenced by political packaging of the notion of competition.

▶ ERGAS—I would like to comment on the question of whether there is a bottleneck, and if so, where it is.

To my mind this issue really boils down to your views as to the extent and competitiveness of alternatives to the local loop and, more specifically, to the fixed local loop. There, the prime issue is that of the possible role of the wireless local loop as an alternative means of access. In this regard, my view is that, in those countries where the price of fixed access has been held below cost, it is very unlikely that, at current prices and regulated service quality levels, wireless local loop is, or will in the near future be, a strong alternative to the fixed network.

However, we do have some areas where the wireless local loop is being used by competitors, notably in the form of high capacity or high band-width access to remote sites. For example, the wireless local loop may be a viable alternative when you need to link up an establishment, such as a factory, that is a bit out of the way, out of the central business areas, but to which you can get line of sight access. In such conditions, there is quite a lot of digital microwave and forms of the wireless local loop being deployed. At the moment, we see a lot of this, particularly in New Zealand.

The question then is, if prices were allowed to be brought into closer balance with the avoidable costs of service provision, would the wireless local loop be a feasible alternative? On this issue, the two cost studies with which I have been involved (one in Australia and one in New Zealand) do suggest that, for reasonably significant parts of the current access line population, the wireless local loop either is now, or, on current equipment pricing plans, is expected within five years to be, a quite viable network alternative.

Indeed—and this may be a bit of an indicator of the cost competitiveness— on the South Island of New Zealand, Telecom New Zealand is pulling out fixed links, particularly rather old and very long copper pair lines which have reached or are reaching the end of their useful life, provide relatively low quality, and are quite vulnerable to rain and storms. This local loop is being replaced by wireless access. The cost savings associated with this are sufficient to bring forward the replacement decision by somewhere between one and five years, depending on how you do the sum. Consequently, as matters now stand, I think it is reasonable to conclude that if we had re-balanced prices, the fixed local loop would not be a bottleneck to anywhere near the extent that is currently pled.

Moreover, if you did have re-balanced prices, then you would have stronger incentives for investment to be made in improving wireless local loop technology. And at this point, rather than having to wait five years for the wireless local loop to be a widespread alternative, it might be a viable alternative in the very near future.

▶ FORRESTER—I would like to comment on a remark by Colin Long, who accurately drew our attention to the fact that the incumbents, when they were privatised, enjoyed a number of other assets in addition to the local loop. These were genuine advantages. I would like to point out that the incumbents also came to the private sector, or the semi-private sector burdened with two enormous disadvantages. In many countries at least—I cannot speak for all of them, but I suppose it may be true for most—one disadvantage is their wretched reputation. They reach the market with a miserable standard of service and the hostility that most people feel towards an inefficient, clanking, dinosaur-type monopoly. Now this hostility is difficult to measure, but I suspect it is relevant to how people look and also, probably, to how people regulate.

The second big disadvantage is the fact that the former incumbents were civil-service oriented and they come with huge labour costs. That is, their staff is under-trained, fully pensioned, and imbued with a civil service mentality. Now, these burdens continue to cost the incumbents huge sums of money. I am not speaking up for dinosaurs, but I am joining the three gentlemen from Brussels who said that the deliberately unlevel nature of the playing field, built in order to encourage the arrival of new operators, should not last too long. I warmly support that conclusion.

I make these remarks about the weaknesses of the incumbents to suggest that, although they have very important, very genuine, advantages, nonetheless they may be burdened by a few very serious disadvantages, which may not be so easy to quantify.

▶ SALSBURY—I view my role here as one of promulgating the perspective of business people who operate in the sector, so I am going to try to confine my remarks to that. I just want to make one comment about what Mr. Ergas said about the wireless local loop. I will tell you that in this context we are one of the biggest access customers in the world, and our engineers tell me that the wireless local loop is nowhere on the horizon for us. Now, they are probably looking more in the American market where we have very serious problems of spectrum availability. That is, you just cannot get enough spectrum space in major urban settings

Secondly, there are some quality issues. Although, generally speaking, line of sight microwave can get around the weather problems, you do have privacy problems. Also, where the business is going, which is to broad band, there is again the spectrum issue: can you really get sufficient spectrum to offer wireless broadband services to customers?

As an observation for people here, currently less than half of MCI's traffic is voice. Two or three years from now, it will probably be no more than 10-20% of our business. Data is so overwhelming the market and growing at such a rate that broadband is the future. And, at least in America, we do not currently see a technology that would make the wireless local loop a really feasible alternative for us to provide such services.

The next point concerns the pricing issue. To me, the fundamental question is: will the incumbent be in the downstream market? Pricing is critical if this is the case. However, if we are not viewing the incumbent as a competitor, access pricing is less crucial. I will observe that, in the United States, MCI was in a competitive long distance market and the providers (the BOCs) were not. In this situation, access cost was not that important to us. We did not want it to be too high. That is, we always wanted the price lower because that would lower the overall cost of providing service, but as long as the BOCs were not our competitors in long distance services, their access prices were not that crucial to us.

Thirdly, on Mr. Hovenkamp's point about joint ownership, I absolutely agree, but this is making my point about structural separation.. We have joint ownership today in some areas. For example, all of the undersea cables—or almost all of them—are jointly owned. If there was different ownership of the local loop, obviously there would be less of a problem. Maybe access problems would not be essential. Joint ownership would raise other issues, but clearly you would solve a lot of the problems. If we were an owner, we would be able to control it.

Beyond pricing, part of the problem about ownership is one of innovation, because we have new products and services that we want to offer. Consider the problem of having to share this with our competitors when we go to them and request new ways of access. They may respond that access will take two years. Thereafter, they introduce a competing product on the market in a year. This problem would make it very difficult for us if we were not an owner. If we were an owner, it would be a totally different situation.

With respect to Mr. Arnbak's point about the business consumer, I think the issue is that businesses can afford to buy two or more loops, but most households cannot justify multiple phone lines.

Further, the real issue for the future is: can we come up with a broadband access into the home? The Digital Subscriber Line (DSL) would obviously solve this problem and there you get into the structural separation question. I think DSL is really not here yet. It is something we see on the horizon. It will offer fixed loop broadband access. I think it is the wave of the future. And in this situation, if there were structural separation, consumers would get access to competitors very quickly. The problem that we face when we wish to reach consumers is that we cannot justify building to consumers because they will not pay the cost. And, I think un-bundling ownership of the local loop is the real policy issue in the US, because such un-bundling gives rights back to the consumers who, for heaven's sake, have paid for these loops fifty times over. That is, consumers pay over and over again on a monthly basis, but they do not control it. If they could control who got to use it, that would be a very different situation.

Finally, on this point about the Worldcom situation, let me just say that, obviously, this decision is in the past. It is over with. The point I was trying to make is that, from our perspective, the decision was made in a merger context. At this point, the bottleneck issue was not that critical to our business, so we accepted it. However, I would hope that, from a policy perspective, one does not view the internet backbone as an essential facility, because it is not. I do not think the people in the business look at it that way, and I think it would lead to bad policy results.

From our perspective, I think that the internet is, in a sense, an arbitrage opportunity. This is the reason you will find us fighting all efforts to regulate it. If the internet is sitting out there as an unregulated business, then it is an alternative to us if we do not like the results in the regulated sectors. And it helps force down the pricing. For example, if voice over the internet becomes a reality in a year or two, and we do not like the access charges that the fixed operators are offering, we will just use the internet if it remains unregulated. I think this is the critical issue. While I would say I disagree with the outcome in the MCI/Worldcom case, it's not important anymore; I just say, please do not view the internet as an essential facility.

▶ EHLERMANN—We now call upon Mr. Barnes to close this morning's panel and provide suggestions for the future.

▶ BARNES—Thank you. I am not going to attempt to sum up this morning's panel in the conventional sense. Instead, in the next ten minutes, I hope to identify some underlying positions that have emerged this morning. These underlying themes may explain the disagreements we have had, and may also clarify some points of agreement. Hopefully, I will also be able to suggest a way forward, which may solve some of the more intractable problems that have arisen.

Underlying all of the papers and interventions today, including my own, is a set of implicit objectives. These implicit objectives determine our different answers to a common question: what is the purpose of intervention in the telecommunications market in relation to bottlenecks? In my opinion, differences in the approaches we take toward this market often stem from differences in objectives, implicit though they may be. That is, the disagreement at the level of how our rules ought to operate is not so much a disagreement about whether these rules are efficient or inefficient. Rather, it is basically a disagreement about the objectives of these rules.

In my opinion, there is actually a consensus at the highest level. We probably agree on a high-level objective, such as encouraging the maximum amount of effective and efficient competition. I think the disagreement starts to arise, however, when we translate that high-level objective into operational policy, and therefore operational rules.

There are a number of explanatory factors for this difference. I am going to characterise these as polar extremes to try to illuminate the differences. However, I do not mean to suggest that anyone in the room has adopted either of the polar extremes. Nor am I suggesting that there is no potential for choosing a more realistic position in the middle.

We have two different views of the world. We have the optimist's view: any additional rules that must currently be applied are transitional. These sector-specific rules should sunset at some point, and, at that point, normal competition law should be adequate. That is, there are no specific aspects of the telecommunications industry that would demand different rules in the long run.

On the other hand, there are the pessimists. They agree that there ought to be transitional rules. That is, they also realise that the present situation is not ideal. However, they are not convinced that these rules will only be transitional. At least some of these rules may be permanent. There will be a permanent need for sectoral rules over and above normal competition law.

A related debate concerns whether you achieve these rules by altering competition law to take account of the fact that telecommunications are different, or whether you instead have additional rules, which only apply to telecommunications and may be applied by a sector-specific regulator. In my view, this issue is not a crucial one. Rather, the important point is whether, in the long run, telecommunications require additional rules above and beyond those applied to the rest of the economy. The good news is that there is at least some agreement about the type of transitional rules that should be used.

In my view, the difference between the 'optimists' and the 'pessimists' is partly explained by a philosophical difference. Can you eliminate the bottlenecks from the telecommunications networks? That is, can intervention ultimately eliminate the bottlenecks, or do you have to supervise and control them over the long run? I think there is a high measure of agreement to the effect that we should eliminate bottlenecks if this is possible. There seems to be much less agreement, however, concerning whether or not existing bottlenecks can be eliminated. Further, in areas that we have not really examined because we have concentrated on voice telephony, there are differences of opinion regarding whether or not new bottlenecks will be created in the future.

We have some agreement on the situation in which we must control a bottleneck, either because it is in transition or because it is a permanent bottleneck. The agreement is essentially that some form of rule against price discrimination is required to eliminate distorting effects in the downstream market. There seems to be less agreement regarding whether or not this rule must go so far as to forbid any discrimination. That is, there is not a consensus on the issue of whether everyone who uses the bottleneck must be charged on exactly the same basis, irrespective of whether it distorts competition in the downstream market. Thus, there is more dissension in the audience regarding whether or not we need a strong or weak version of the non-discrimination rule.

Indeed, this is an issue that has lurked in the corner for most of the discussion. However, this is a critical issue, at least for regulators who are trying to make decisions in this area concerning the impact of the rule structure on the ability to discriminate through price. Moreover, the ability to price discriminate may turn out to be quite significant in this sector. This issue has been touched on by a number of papers and interventions, but it has not really been dealt with in a satisfactory way. We have not clearly determined whether the ability to price discriminate is a good or bad thing. One of the fundamental difficulties facing both regulators and competition authorities is whether price discrimination is, in and of itself, a good or bad thing. This determination can be made in theory, but, in practice, it turns out to be quite difficult.

There is a further disagreement, which I suspect is related to the failure to address the price discrimination question properly: what is the right way of dealing with bottlenecks once they have been identified? Do you deal with them by restrictions on lines of business? Do you have an exceptionally rigid rule around them? Do you isolate the bottleneck as far as you can? Or, can you get away with behavioural rules across these sorts of boundaries? Or, potentially, are there other ways forward?

Joint ownership is one way forward that has been suggested. This solution is sort of a mixture between structural and behavioural rules. That is, joint owners face some restrictions on their behaviour, but they are imposed mainly by competition law. It is not a sector-specific regulator who is trying to impose such prescriptive behavioural rules.

This brings me to my final point, which is the way forward. How do we proceed from here? And just so that I cannot be accused of having my own private agenda, because I am going to argue that more regulatory work is needed, let me reveal that at the end of December I will no longer be a regulator. I am leaving OFTEL. So the following comments are without prejudice to my own position.

I think the way forward is to increase the area of analysis. The impact on consumers, on end-users, needs to be taken into account in a much greater way than it has been up to this point. This involves going back to the objectives, and looking at the objectives at the next level down. Effective competition is a statement like 'motherhood and apple pie'. What does it mean? We are really not sure, but we believe it must be good for people.

In the real world, there are sometimes trade-offs between different areas within which competition can take place, different areas within which price discrimination is easy or hard to carry out. This has different impacts on users. So, a fuller analysis of the policy prescriptions for dealing with bottlenecks needs to be done. It must take into account the actual impact different policy prescriptions are likely to have on different end users. Ultimately, I think that both the regulators and the competition authorities need to take account of the existing distortions in the marketplace. We cannot afford to assume that the rest of the world, *i.e.*, the bit we are not currently looking at, is optimal and does not interact with the particular bottleneck that is the focus of the decision. Because one of the thing regulators—and, in my view, competition authorities—need to avoid is reacting to the existing market distortions in a way that does not take their impact into account.

By this, I mean that it is, at best, irresponsible for regulators to encourage competition where this competition is only viable because of a regulatory distortion elsewhere in the marketplace. The obvious examples of this problem are the asymmetric application of access charges in the US and the asymmetric application of similar charges in much of Europe and the UK. We have to take these interactions into account when making decisions on bottlenecks. In summary, my plea is for fuller analysis of the actual impact of policy prescriptions on bottlenecks, whether this means eliminating bottlenecks or confining the bottleneck into as small an area of activity as possible.

I think I was asked a couple of specific questions to which I will give one word answers. Has the UK experiment been a success? I think the answer to this is yes, but it is, actually, still in transition. Therefore, the answer cannot yet be provided, given the extraordinarily long time it takes to invest in new, wire-based infrastructure.

There was also a question about whether price distortions in the price of the local loop are the only problem. I think the answer to this is no. There are more problems than just the local loop, and, indeed, re-balancing the local loop prices has very little impact on the major problems that we face.

Finally, I was accused of saying outrageous things. I do not mind this, because I often do so. In this particular case, however, I do not think I was actually being outrageous, because the obligation to interconnect—even that imposed on people without significant market power—arises from the interconnection directive. It is already here. It is the ONP rule, which, I think, comes into effect in most Member States on 1st January 1999. So, it might be outrageous, but at least it was not me being outrageous. Thank you.

PANEL ONE

REGULATING ACCESS TO BOTTLENECKS

2

WORKING PAPERS

I

Fod Barnes*

Statement by the Rapporteur on Panel One

I. Introduction

The panel focused on two different, but intimately related, types of question under the general framework of the application of Article 82 [ex 86] 'rules'. These were:

1. What rules apply to the conduct of firms owning bottleneck network facilities (largely a legal question); and
2. What 'rules' should apply to these firms (which is a normative question).

Although the first of these questions is essentially a legal question, and one that, at least in theory, has a definitive answer there is, in fact, considerable uncertainty as to the precise behavioural rules that flow from the application of Art 82 [ex 86] to (tele)communications networks. This uncertainty about the precise meaning of the existing rules led to some confusion in the discussion—in particular some apparent disagreements as to the adequacy, or otherwise, of existing competition law to deal effectively with the future changing market place, arose from different interpretations of what the current rules mean, rather than from any disagreement as to which rules are necessary.

However, by no means all divergences of opinion could be traced back to this source. Indeed, amongst the papers presented, and in the wider discussion, serious differences emerge as to what the content of the rules ought to be. It also emerged from the discussion that this is an extremely important question, as the answer will have a significant impact on the commercial operation of the sector.

In particular, there was a range of views as to how many (if any) 'special' competition rules would need to apply to the (tele)communications sector, once the transition had been made from legal monopoly to an open and competitive market.

---

* OFTEL.

II. What is the Objective of Competition Policy?

Because the normative question (what rules should apply?) played a central role to the discussion, the underlying question (what are the objectives?) also needs to be addressed. Although the papers do not address this issue directly, the panel discussion touched on it. In addition, there are important, if indirect, implicit assumptions within a number of the papers. A generally agreed starting point was that there was nothing special about telecommunication networks which would determine that it would be inappropriate for 'normal' competition law to be applied—an implicit acceptance that the objectives of normal competition law are also appropriate.

Yet the telecommunications sector very rapidly raises awkward trade-offs. Does access to the local loop at TELRIC (or similar) reduce the scope for competition in the provision of this service? Even if it increases the scope for competition in the provision of trunk and international circuits (and retail services). Can one kind of competition be traded off against another? If so, who decides which one is 'better'? And on what basis?

These awkward trade-offs may stand at the core of another area where there was no real agreement. Much competition law is primarily concerned with market structures—so that the outcome of intervention is a market structure that ensures that competition can work without further ongoing intervention. (Tele)communications seems to throw up significant areas of activity where such 'self policing' market structures are either difficult or impossible to achieve. Although the model of 'regulated monopoly' has been shown to be significantly flawed, liberalisation has (so far at least) failed, in many cases, to deliver self-sustaining 'normal' competitive markets.

Given these difficulties, the question of whether or not the lack of 'normal' competitive markets is transient is of some considerable importance. If it is transient, then normal competition law (and normal competition institutions) should, in the medium term, be sufficient. The competition problems facing (tele)communications are transient, and stem from the historical starting position—of market dominance by an incumbent based on legal monopoly—rather than being fundamental to the industry. If these problems are not transient, then more difficult problems must be faced. The long-term need for special rules, either behavioural and/or structural, needs to be addressed. What kind of rules? Applied to what market players under what circumstances? Applied by what type of institution?

III. Bottlenecks—Long Term Problem or Transient Phenomena?

There was general agreement that the existing market structures produced significant bottlenecks. In particular the 'copper' (fixed wire/fibre based local connection) local loop represents such a bottleneck, if it is provided by a dominant operator. There was less agreement that such a local loop was a bottleneck if a non-dominant operator (e.g. new entrant) provided it. It was possible that there was a bottleneck only for call termination type services, but not for call origination. The distinction here relates to who is choosing: in the case of call termination, the person making the call very rarely (if ever) has a choice of who provides the call termination service, even though they are (usually) paying for the use of that asset; while, with call origination, the person making the call does have a choice of the supplier of call origination services, by changing local access provider.

However, some doubt was expressed whether this distinction was adequate to achieve an objective of maximising competitive supply across all (tele)communication services. Does limited choice at a high infrastructure level (e.g. choice of local access provider) mean that there is adequate competitive market pressure within the (different) economic markets for services that must use that high level infrastructure? Or, alternatively, does the 'capture' of the customer by one infrastructure supplier mean that that supplier gains market power over the customer for the supply of all services that need to use that infrastructure? If this is the case, what is the appropriate measure to determine at which point such market power (which may or may not be defined as dominance) may be abused, and thus trigger potential intervention by the competition/regulatory authorities?

Because the historic market structure of the telephony business has resulted in the incumbent holding very high proportions of the local loop infrastructure, however measured, the precise definition of 'dominance' and 'significant market power' has not been an issue. Whatever measure is used the incumbent has 'passed' the test and intervention has been legitimised under conventional competition analysis. Yet, this convenient outcome is now breaking down. On the one hand, the spread of new suppliers of local loop access has meant that in some (limited) geographic areas the incumbent's market share has declined to levels where the answer is no longer clear cut. Meanwhile, on the other hand, allegations of distortion of competition in downstream markets are be made against new entrants who, in a conventional analysis, have very low market shares (too low to seem to permit the creation of any market power at all, let alone 'dominance').

Even more troublesome, however, are the particular issues that seem to be arising in markets using new infrastructures. Mobile phone markets do not have the monopoly supplier history—but that has not stopped competition problems arising in relation to services provided over those (multiple supplier) networks. UMTS, with its greater potential range of services that can be supplied over the telecommunications infrastructure, looks like making these issues more important.

Similar issues are arising in relation to the digital broadcasting and the conditional access systems that are necessary to make them work. Do conditional access systems represent a 'bottleneck', even before they have been rolled out to any significant extent? Even if they do, what is the appropriate competition policy response? In particular, at what point in the development of these services (and, critically, the investment cycle in the infrastructure) should intervention take place?

IV. Competition Authority Type Rules and/or Additional Types of Rules?

The discussion identified that the 'easy part' of telecommunications liberalisation may turn out to be the early transition from a single legal monopoly supplier to a market that is open (no legal restrictions on the number of suppliers) and a number (probably a small number) of actual participants. A good justification for regulatory intervention existed—the historic monopoly position of the incumbent—and the major market player clearly satisfied the test of dominance. Under these conditions, the usual controls on dominance were clearly appropriate, as were additional rules to deal with the legacy of the historic legal monopoly.

However, beyond this early stage of the transition and, more problematic, in the areas of new infrastructure and services, the appropriate competition response looked more difficult unless the market very quickly became 'normal'.

Some participants even saw a few potential problems with the application of normal competition rules to dominant operators. In particular, a very strict interpretation of 'non discrimination' could result in all users of a particular infrastructure being charged the average costs of use. This, in turn, could make some services using the infrastructure uneconomic even though they would be viable if they were required only to cover their incremental costs. The result could be higher prices for all users.

Because much of the new (tele)communication infrastructures have low long run incremental costs, but high average costs, sorting out the allowable degree of price discrimination is important for the economy. A number of preferred positions emerged from the discussions:

- tight controls combined with a high dominance test before they are applied;
- flexible tests with a high dominance threshold;
- flexible tests applied to market players who were not necessarily dominant in their own right, but were either 'jointly dominant' or, individually, had 'significant market power'—where 'flexibility' means allowing price discrimination within some pre-defined economic boundaries, as long as that discrimination does not distort competition in a downstream market.

If rules were to be applied to operators not traditionally dominant in their own right, there was general agreement that these rules would look like those applied to dominant undertakings (no margin squeeze in downstream markets, obligation to supply, etc). More problematic, and an issue upon which there was consequently less agreement, was the issue of what, if any, additional types of rules were necessary.

V. Anticipating Dominance/Regulation for Competition

One area where there was little agreement, was the question of the desirability, or otherwise, of 'anticipating' the creation of a new dominant position (or position of significant market power) and applying behavioural, or even structural, rules to undertakings before they were achieved this position. The EC's Advanced TV Directive,[1] has this effect because behaviour rules governing access to conditional access systems (e.g. pricing and non-discrimination rules) are being applied even before services using this infrastructure have been launched.

However, given the fundamental economics of conditional access systems there is a reasonable degree of certainty that, if these services are successful at all, the controller of the set top boxes will acquire significant market power, if not a dominant position. Intervention now could reduce the potential for abuse of dominance in the future (which is likely to be a good thing), but could clearly reduce the incentives to innovate and to make considerable, sunk, investments in infrastructure. On the other hand, the investors face considerable regulatory uncertainty if their business plan relies on establishing a powerful market

---

[1] Directive 95/47/EC of the European Parliament and of the Council on the use of standards for the transmission of television signals, OJ L 281/51 (1995).

position, but they do not know what type of rules will be applied to them when they reach that position. Even if there was no agreement around the panel as to what was the best policy to adopt, there was some agreement that, given the need for very large private sector investment in the new infrastructures, sorting out this issue was important.

At a more general level the panel discussed the need for the general application of structural or behavioural rules to apply to the sector (i.e. to all market players irrespective of their relative market position). Such a suggestion expands competition policy far beyond its normal application, even where the 'rules' that are to be applied have the same substance as rules that would apply to a dominant operator. Although there was general agreement that the sector did have economic characteristics that made it significantly different from the normal economy—in particular, the need to interconnect with competitors and the need for system-wide interoperability—there was no agreement that this divergence was great enough to justify a significantly different application of competition rules.

VI. Additional Rules of Substance

Finally, the need for additional rules, over and above those available under general competition law, was discussed. 'Special rules' were required to deal with the transition from legal monopoly to competitive market. These special rules were particularly required where the move away from a legal monopoly had not been accompanied by any restructuring of the undertaking. (Indeed, restructuring at the time of transition could itself be seen as the application of a special competition rule.)

There was a general recognition that some additional rules were required to deal with issues such as numbering and interoperability. Whether these were really competition rules, rather than industry wide 'technical regulation', was not agreed, and this disagreement impacted on the institutional issues dealt with in Panel Three. However, more important, was the general recognition that these 'technical rules' could have an impact on competition and that, at the very least, this impact needs to be taken into account in their application and, indeed, the application of any competition rules, if and when they are applied to the market players. A particular issue that highlights this problem is the way in which technical standards, intellectual property rights and competition law come together in ensuring end-to-end-interoperability for services across networks provided by different undertakings in competition with each other.

VII. Conclusion

In some ways, the application of competition law in the early transition phase from incumbent legal monopoly to multiple suppliers is the easy part. The issue of dominance is clear cut, and controlling that entity through the application of competition rules de facto provides for a measure of control over the industry. The next phase of development is more difficult—either where the market structure is characterised by a 'few', equally sized, entities (e.g. providers of mobile infrastructure), or where the incumbent has lost a significant section of its market(s) (so is no longer dominant?), but is still bigger than any other individual player. In either case, dominance is less obviously present, so that abuse of dominance is more difficult to establish, even if it is agreed that something is wrong with the behaviour of one or more market participants. But, at least, the broad range of solutions for this problem are now clear.

The trickiest area of public policy relates to the anticipation of market power in new markets. Conventional competition law relating to an abuse of a dominant position clearly does not apply, but the advantages of creating new competitive market structures is likely to be significant, if this can be done without dampening the incentives to innovate. Thus, both the legal and economic framework need to be developed to ensure that, if action is taken, it leads to better outcomes than waiting for concrete evidence of market failure before taking action to then try to correct the uncompetitive market structure.

II

Bernard Amory and Alexandre Verheyden*

Article 82 [ex 86]: Fair and Efficient Terms of Access to
'Bottleneck' Network Facilities?

I. Introduction

This paper contains practical considerations on the legal issues identified as the substance of the Panel One discussion on how to ensure fair and efficient terms of access to 'bottleneck' network facilities when the gatekeeper has no incentive to grant them.

II. Main Bottlenecks in Communication and Information Networks

For the purpose of the panel discussions, six main bottlenecks in the telecommunications sector have been identified: the local loop; frequencies; appropriate sites for radio networks; internet backbone; undersea and terrestrial cable capacity; and rights of way.

1. The Local Loop

The term local loop generally refers to the part of a telecommunications network (generally made of copper wires) between the local exchanges and the network termination point at customer premises. In order to offer services to customers, operators must use, in a way or another, the local loop. It is often suggested that the local loop cannot be duplicated economically. As an example, in France, duplication of France Telecom's network is estimated at FF 150 billion (ECU 22.5 billion) for which the local loop accounts for the most parts.

However, in the future, utilisation of wireless technology may constitute an acceptable substitute to wireline local loop. Therefore, provided the scarcity problems affecting both frequencies and adequate sites for radio network are resolved, a local loop may become, in the future, less of a bottleneck. Similarly, in certain countries existing infrastructure, such as cable TV network, may constitute an alternative to access to the end users via the traditional telecommunications network.

---

* Jones, Day, Reavis and Pogue, Brussels.

2. Frequencies

Spectrum is, in essence, limited. Each Member State of the EU has identified and reserved a portion of the frequency spectrum to certain types of services or purposes, in accordance with its national frequency plan. Frequencies are limited because of the purpose for which they can be used (e.g. 900MHz bandwidth is reserved for GSM) and due to the number of channels available for each service or purpose.

Such limitations have even greater effects in small countries with neighbouring countries since the assignment of frequencies is subject to international co-ordination in order to avoid interferences with the frequencies used in neighbouring countries (e.g. this is particularly the case for Luxembourg, Belgium and The Netherlands).

Notwithstanding the opportunities to establish a more efficient use of the spectrum due to technological developments (compression, digitisation, cellular technology), and as a result of better frequencies management (e.g. through the pan-European reservation of frequencies), it is unlikely that such improvements will permit that frequencies no longer constitute a bottleneck.

3. Appropriate Sites for Radio Networks

Radio sites can also be bottlenecks. In cities, radio sites are limited by the limitation of tall buildings. In the country, radio sites are often limited as a result of the difficulty of obtaining the necessary planning permissions for the establishment of appropriate masts.

A possible answer to the scarcity of adequate sites is the sharing of these sites between operators. This solution has been encouraged by the European Commission which has mandated that all restrictions with regard to the sharing of sites be removed[1]. In light of the multiplication of radio networks, one may wonder if site-sharing may constitute a permanent solution[2].

---

[1] See Article 3c of the Commission Directive 96/2/EEC amending Directive 90/388/EEC with regard to mobile and personal communications (OJ L 20/59 (1996)).

[2] The development of wireless local loop is going to increase the demand of adequate sites for radio networks, at least in city or metropolitan areas.

4. Internet Backbone

The internet is a conglomerate of many interconnected data networks. Although internet is usually presented as an illustration of a decentralised network, it nonetheless constitutes a bottleneck. In its *WorldCom/MCI* decision, the Commission identified the main internet backbones as bottlenecks (i.e. the networks of WorldCom, AT&T, Sprint and MCI). The Commission's findings were based on the fact that in order to provide the internet access service, internet service providers (ISPs) must offer global reach. Global reach cannot be attained without a direct or indirect connection to one of these backbones. Consequently, these backbones must be considered as bottlenecks in relation to the provision of internet access services.

5. Undersea and Terrestrial Cable Capacity

According to the European Commission, undersea and terrestrial cable capacity may be considered as a bottleneck[3] because there is no fully adequate substitute for undersea cables, since the same level of quality and security cannot be achieved through satellite connections.[4] In *BT/MCI (II)*, the Commission demanded divestiture of BT's circuits, corresponding to MCI's overlap capacity to which BT was given access as a result of its merger with MCI.

Undersea cable capacity is a good example of the fact that bottleneck situations are ever changing. Approximately two years ago, undersea cable capacity could have been considered a bottleneck, but today this is no longer the case.

6. Rights of Way

Access to large real plots of land (e.g. ducts placed along highways, railways or gas pipes etc.) provides significant advantages for the establishment of backbone telecommunications networks. In the absence of such rights of way, operators are required to obtain planning permission all along the path followed by their cables which is often required from and in respect of the territory of each municipality which is being crossed.

---

[3] *BT/MCI (II)*, Case No IV/M.856, OJ L 336 (1997).
[4] In its *BT/MCI II* decision, the Commission concluded that transatlantic satellite and cable routes were not substitutable.

III Competition Law Doctrines and Access to Bottlenecks

The Commission has recently published a notice on the application of the competition rules to access agreements in the telecommunications sector (the 'Access Notice').[5] The purpose of this notice is to provide guidance on the various competition law issues applicable to access requests and agreements. The Access Notice provides a test inspired from the US essential facilities doctrine which can be used to assess whether access to a particular network must be granted pursuant to Article 82 [ex 86] of the Consolidated Treaty. What follows is a discussion of if and how the 'essential facilities test' of the Access Notice relates to the existing case law of the European Court of Justice or the administrative practice of the European Commission; whether such test addresses all possible access issues; and how it articulates with ONP rules on interconnection and access.

1. The Essential Facilities Test as Derived from Current Case Law or Administrative Practice

a) The Essential Facilities Test
The Access Notice identifies five cumulative criteria to assess under Article 82 [ex 86] of the Consolidated Treaty access requests to an essential facility, the so-called 'essential facilities test'. At the outset, it should be noted that no Court cases or Commission decisions have identified or applied the criteria proposed by the Commission. To date, the only cases identifying a particular bottleneck as constituting an 'essential facility' are the Commission's harbour decision on Holyhead.[6] However, these decisions did not contain any reference to the 'essential facilities test'.

The first part of the test requires that the access to the facility be 'generally essential'[7] in order to allow companies to compete on a market related to the

---

[5] Commission Notice on the application of the competition rules to access agreements in the telecommunication sector: framework, relevant markets and principles, OJ C 265/2 (1998).

[6] See, *B&I/Sealink*, [1992] 5 CMLR 255, recital; *Sea Containers/Stena Link*, 94/19/EEC OJ L 15/88 (1994), recital 66; *Port of Rødby*, 95/119/1994, OJ L55/52 (1994), recital 12.

[7] According to recital 91 (a) of the Access Notice, *essential* means that 'it will not be sufficient that the position of the company requesting access would be more advantageous if access were granted, but refusal of access must lead to the proposed activities

market affected by an essential facility. This condition was already present, at least implicitly, in *Commercial Solvents*.[8] In this case, Commercial Solvents was the only producer of a raw material, necessary for the production of the derivative chemical, ethambutol, and refused to supply it to a competitor manufacturing ethambutol. The Court of Justice held that Commercial Solvents abused its dominant position when it decided to stop supplying raw materials to its competitor and to start producing ethambutol on its own.

In *Radio Telefis Eireann (RTE)*,[9] RTE published its own TV weekly guides listing its own broadcasting programmes. The other broadcaster, the BBC, also published its own weekly TV and radio guide pertaining to its own programmes. A new entrant requested access to the listings containing the programmes of both RTE and BBC with a view to publishing a comprehensive weekly guide containing the programmes of both RTE and the BBC. RTE and BBC refused to provide access to the detailed list of their programmes, arguing amongst other reasons that they were protected by intellectual property rights. The Court of Justice held that RTE and BBC's refusal to provide access constituted an abuse of dominant position since they prevented the emergence of a new product (a comprehensive weekly TV magazine), thereby implicitly recognising that RTE and BBC's advance programmes listings were generally essential for any company wanting to compete on the market for TV guides. Therefore, the requirement that the facility be regarded as generally essential is contained in the case law of the European Court of Justice.

b) Sufficient Capacity Available to Provide Access
Pursuant to the European Court of Justice case law, refusals to supply, or decisions to suspend, the supply of certain products by a dominant undertaking constitutes a violation of Article 82 [ex 86] of the Consolidated Treaty, unless it is justified by an objective reason.

In *Commercial Solvents*,[10] the Court indicated that in view of the company production capability and the probable size of the customer's requirements,

---

being made either impossible or services by and unavoidably uneconomic'. 'Generally' means that 'it would be insufficient to demonstrate that one competitor needed access to a facility in order to compete in the downstream market. It would be necessary to demonstrate that access is necessary for all except exceptional competitors in order for access to be made compulsory'. See Access Notice, n. 67.

[8] *Commercial Solvents Corp.* v *Commission*, Joined Cases 6–7/73, [1974] ECR 223.
[9] *Radio Telefis Eireann* v *Commission*, Case T–69/89, [1991] ECR II 485; see also the *British Broadcasting Corp.* v *Commission*, Case T–70/89 [1991] ECR II 535. Both cases have been affirmed by the Court of Justice.
[10] *Commercial Solvents Corp.* v *Commission*, Joined Cases 6–7/73, [1974] ECR 223.

there should be no difficulty in meeting its needs. The Court of First Instance made a similar holding in *Hilti*.[11]

In its *Sea Containers/Stena Sealink* interim decision, the Commission observed that there was enough capacity in the Holyhead Harbour (the essential facility) to satisfy the request of Sea Container to use the harbour to operate a new ferry service.[12]

Conversely, in instances where there was a capacity problem, the Court has considered that the refusal to supply was justified. For instance, in *BP-ABG*[13] the Court held that, given the situation of oil shortage (during the 1973 oil crisis), the refusal to supply an occasional customer was justified.

It follows from the above that, again, the second criteria of the 'essential facilities test' derives from established case law of the European Court of Justice or the Commission's administrative practice.

c) The Facility Owner Fails to Satisfy Demand on an Existing Service or Product Market, Blocks the Emergence of a New Service or Product, or Impedes Competition on an Existing or Potential Service or Product Market

All Court cases or Commission decisions where a refusal to supply was held abusive had an effect on the satisfaction of an existing service or product market, the emergence of a new service or product, or competition on an existing or potential service or product.

In both *Maxicar* v *Renault*[14] and *Volvo* v *Veng*,[15] car manufacturers were held to have abused their dominant position (obtained through intellectual property rights) notably because of their decision no longer to produce spare parts for particular models while there was an existing demand for these parts, thereby affecting an *existing* service or product.

In *Radio Telefis Eireann (RTE)*[16] the finding of an abuse of dominant position was based on the prevention of the emergence of a *new product* (a comprehensive weekly TV guide) as a result of RTE and BBC's refusals to grant access to essential information (advance listings of its television programmes).

---

[11] *Hilti* v *Commission*, Case T–30/89, [1991] ECR II 1439.
[12] *Sea Containers/Stena Sealink,* 94/19/EEC, OJ L 15/88 (1994).
[13] *BP* v *Commission*, Case 77/77, [1978] ECR 1513.
[14] *Maxicar* v *Renault*, Case 53/87, [1988] ECR 6039.
[15] *Volvo* v *Veng*, Case 238/87, [1988] ECR 6211.
[16] *Radio Telefis Eireann* v *Commission*, Case T–69/89, [1991] ECR II 485; see also the *British Broadcasting Corp.* v *Commission*, Case T–70/89 [1991] ECR II 535. Both cases have been affirmed by the Court of Justice.

Several cases illustrate the condition that in order to be abusive, a refusal to grant access impedes *competition*. For instance, in *Commercial Solvents*, the Court made clear that Commercial Solvent could not, just because it decided to start manufacturing ethambutol on its own (in competition with its former customers), act in such a way as to eliminate competition.[17]

In *United Brand*,[18] the Court noted that the termination of supplies to a distributor by a producer of bananas holding a dominant position was designed to have a serious adverse effect on competition on the relevant banana market by only allowing firms dependent upon a dominant undertaking to stay in business.

In *London European/Sabena*,[19] the Commission declared that the refusal by Sabena to allow London European access to its computer reservation service was an abuse of dominant position. In its decision the Commission observed that Sabena's refusal to allow access to its computer reservation service was designed to force London European to raise fares on the London-Brussels route or to withdraw from this route.

d) Readiness to Pay a Reasonable and Non-Discriminatory Price

The Access Notice provides that the company seeking access is prepared to pay a reasonable and non-discriminatory price. This requirement is a logical application of the conditions relating to the absence of valid justifications. The circumstance that the undertaking requesting access to a bottleneck would not be prepared to pay a reasonable and non discriminatory price would constitute an objective justification for refusing access.

e) The Absence of Objective Justifications

The existing case law admits objective justification to refusal to supply. Obviously, the objective justifications referred to below are different from those relating to capacity. Amongst other possible objective justifications, the Court held in *Commercial Solvents*[20] that a dominant undertaking is permitted to take reasonable steps to protect its own commercial interests. The Court, however, concluded that the sanction consisting of a refusal to supply by an undertaking in a dominant position was in excess of what might reasonably be contemplated as a sanction in similar circumstances. In its *BBI/Boosey &*

---

[17] *Commercial Solvents Corp.* v *Commission*, Joined Cases 6–7/73, [1974] ECR 223.

[18] *United Brand* v *Commission*, Case 27/76, [1978] ECR 207.

[19] *London European/Sabena*, OJ L 317/47 (1988).

[20] *Commercial Solvents Corp.* v *Commission,* Joined Cases 6–7/73, [1974] ECR 223

Hawkes decision, the Commission stated that a dominant undertaking may always take reasonable steps to protect its commercial interests.[21]

2. Is the Essential Facilities Test Sufficient to Address all Access Requests?

a) The Purpose of the 'Essential Facilities Test'

The 'essential facilities test' in the Access Notice serves two main purposes. First, the Commission is rearranging a number of legal concepts (contained in the case law of the European Court of Justice or the administrative practice of the Commission) to assess the validity of a refusal to provide access or interconnection, thereby facilitating the task of establishing an abuse of dominant position.

Second, since the Commission has indicated that access requests were to be addressed primarily at the national level, the Access Notice provides useful guidance to competent national authorities for the assessment under Article 82 [ex 86] of the Consolidated Treaty of a particular access request, thereby facilitating the mission of such national authorities having to assess the compatibility with Article 82 [ex 86] of the Consolidated Treaty of a particular access refusal. In addition, it maximises the chances of a uniform application of competition rules in the Community.

b) The Limitations of the Access Notice

In spite of the benefits associated with the 'essential facilities test', such a test carries the following limitations: it is narrow; and it is likely to affect national authorities' ability to expand upon it.

3. The Narrowness of the Essential Facilities Test

The narrowness of the 'essential facilities test' mainly results from the requirement that the essential facility to which access is sought be 'generally essential'. While it can be assumed that all network components of an incumbent operator are likely to be regarded as generally essential shortly after network liberalisation, this may rapidly no longer be the case after some degree of competition has been achieved in the market. This is illustrated by the following examples.

---

[21] *BBI/Boosey&Hawkes*, 87/500/EEC, OJ L 286/36 (1987).

a) Backbone Telecommunications Networks
In most Member States, several operators have obtained licences to built pan-European or national backbone telecommunications networks. Once these networks become operational, it would seem difficult to continue to consider that particular backbone networks (presumably the ones of incumbent operators) are generally essential. Furthermore, even before such networks become operational, the fact that many operators have committed themselves to invest in the establishment of such networks suggests that, even in the absence of any effective alternative, such networks are not 'generally essential', since they can be duplicated in a short period of time. This issue will be important in the future, in particular in relation to access to high speed data networks which are likely to be established in the future.

b) GSM Networks
Since two or more GSM networks are now in operation in each Member State, it is questionable whether each network can be regarded as 'generally essential' for service providers, given the existence of the other networks. This is likely to affect Virtual Network Operators' (VNOs)[22] ability to use the 'essential facilities test' as a way of obtaining access to mobile networks. This issue is particularly true with respect to mobile operators. Indeed even in cases where two GSM operators have, for instance, market shares of respectively 70 percent and 30 percent, it is arguable that none of them could be deemed to hold a dominant position. Indeed, a dominant position is defined as a position of economic strength which enables an undertaking to behave, to an appreciable extent, independently of its competitors, customers and ultimately of consumers.[23] Since GSM networks in the same country tend to be of comparable quality (because of the fact that they are subject to basically the same network quality and coverage obligations), none could in effect behave irrespective of its customers without suffering from a significant churn rate.

d) The Local Loop
Wireline local loop is likely to remain 'generally essential' over the coming years. However, National Regulatory Authorities (NRAs) in most Member

---

[22] A VNO is a provider of mobile telecommunications services with its own SIM cards, mobile numbers and network control centre which requests access to a GSM network at reduced tariffs since it only uses the transmission/radio portion of GSM networks.

[23] *United Branch*, [1978] ECR 207, at 65; *Hoffman-La Roche v Commission* [1979] ECR 461, at 38; *Michelin v Commission* [1983] ECR 3461, at 30.

States have initiated public consultations on the award of wireless local loop licences and have announced their intentions of granting such licences. In such a case, to the extent that wireless local loop would technically constitute an equivalent alternative to a wireline local loop and that licences are available, the issue of whether local loop as a whole would be regarded as 'generally essential' would be open for debate.

In conclusion, the 'essential facilities test' is not likely to be of significant use if and when a certain level of competition is achieved in respect of various telecommunications services and networks.

The fact that an undertaking can avoid giving access to its network or facilities by providing reasonable justifications can also limit the ability to address access issues under Article 82 [ex 86] of the Consolidated Treaty. This is illustrated by situations relating to site sharing. In some countries, the roll-out of mobile networks was facilitated by agreements with companies/authorities which already had existing masts. As is often the case, such masts were established at times where mast-sharing was not even envisaged. As a result, they are of a relatively small size and are not engineered to support more than 2 antennae. Accordingly, the owner of a mast could legitimately refuse access to a new operator, to the extent that such masts cannot physically support more than two antennae. Therefore, again, competition law would not constitute an appropriate tool for permitting access to an essential facility.

e) The Limited Ability of National Authorities to Expand on the Essential Facilities Test

In spite of the fact that notices such as the Access Notice do not have any binding nature, the Access Notice is likely to remain, at the level of Member States, a reference for the test to be applied for the assessment of the validity of a particular decision refusing access. As such, it may limit Member States' ability or willingness to find alternative means of encouraging access to bottleneck facilities.

3. The ONP and Competition Rules

a) The Advantages of Directive 97/33/EC

In view of the limited scope of application of the Access Notice, ONP rules and regulations, Directive 97/33/EC has an important role to play. Indeed, this Directive provides for a right to interconnection or access to certain types of networks. This Directive further indicates the criteria which must be taken into account by National Regulatory Authorities when exercising their responsibility of ensuring adequate interconnection (e.g. the need to ensure satisfactory end-to-end communications, the need to stimulate the market, the need to ensure the proper development of an harmonised European telecommunications market etc.). Similarly, this Directive also contains some of the principles on which National Regulatory Authorities must base their decisions relating to interconnection disputes (e.g. users interest, regulatory obligations imposed on the parties, the desirability of stimulating innovative market offerings, the availability of technically and commercially viable alternatives, the nature of the request in relation to the resources available to meet interconnection requests etc.).

Some of the criteria provided for in Directive 97/33/EC are similar to those provided for in the Access Notice. This is the case of:

(1) the desirability of stimulating innovative market offerings;
(2) the availability of technically and commercially viable alternatives to the interconnection requested;
(3) the nature of the request in relation to the resources available to meet the request; and
(4) the relative market position of the parties.'

However, Directive 97/33/EC does not require the existence of a 'generally essential' facility and enables greater flexibility as a result of the application of additional criteria (e.g. the user interest; regulatory obligations or constraints placed on any of the parties; the desirability of ensuring equal access arrangements; the public interest (for example the protection of the environment); the promotion of competition; the need to maintain a universal service). Accordingly, interconnection requests or disputes are more likely to be addressable pursuant to Directive 97/33/EC than pursuant to Article 82 [ex 86] of the Treaty as highlighted in the Access Notice.

b) The Shortcomings of Directive 97/33/EC
Article 9 of Directive 97/33/EC which provides for the criteria used by National Regulatory Authorities for the assessment of interconnection applications or disputes is limited to interconnection and does not include the criteria used in relation to access. Such a limitation may be of significance. Indeed, interconnection is defined as 'the physical and logical linking of telecommunications networks'. Telecommunications networks are defined as 'transmission systems and, where applicable, switching equipment . . . which permit the conveyance of signals between defined termination points. . .'. This means, arguably, that requests for interconnection other than between telecommunications networks

(i.e. comprising transmission systems) would not constitute an interconnection request in the meaning of Directive 97/33/EC. As an example, VNOs requests of interconnection to mobile network operators would not constitute a request for interconnection pursuant to Directive 97/33/EC since VNOs do not operate transmission systems. It would only constitute an access request, falling outside the scope of Article 9 above-mentioned.

IV. Access Issues: Horizontal and Vertical Dimension

Access is a means of promoting both horizontal and vertical competition. It promotes horizontal competition insofar as it permits competition between various network operators (e.g. ability for a customer of operator A to call a customer of operator B). It promotes vertical competition since access enables service providers to access the network of an operator in order to distribute or resell its services (e.g. service providers of a mobile network).

It is generally recognised, from a legal point of view, that competition rules must be applied in such a way that they improve competition as a whole, irrespective of whether a more competitive market is achieved as a result of vertical or horizontal competition. This is the reason why the Access Notice does not address the issue of whether horizontal or vertical competition is more desirable.

From a telecommunications policy point of view, it is a fact that the promotion of vertical competition could limit the development of horizontal competition. Indeed, the telecommunications sector is characterised by various barriers to entry amongst which are the high investments required in order to establish a network. It is submitted that the extent to which network operators are required to give to their competitors access to their networks could create an disincentive to making high investments in the establishment of competing telecommunications networks as is illustrated below.

New entrant GSM operators (as opposed to Telecommunications Organisations (TOs)[24] were required to develop comprehensive high quality GSM networks. In addition to the common difficulties associated with the

---

[24] While the same reasoning should, in principle, apply to GSM subsidiaries of TOs, different conclusions may be reached as a result of the fact that such subsidiaries enjoyed additional benefits because, for example, they were usually the first GSM operator in their country, they benefited from the economies of scales of their TO, they were originally often able to operate without any formal interconnection agreement being in place etc.

development of such networks (competitive bidding for obtaining the licence, granting of planning permissions, high interconnect rates with the incumbent as the first interconnection agreement entered into by TOs), new entrant GSM operators were often required to pay high licence fees. VNOs are now requiring access to GSM network operators, in such a way that they can use GSM operators' transmission capacity, without having to use their network control centres and switches. These types of access are currently under review by DGIV. The scope of the access given to VNOs will affect operators' desire to invest in the development of new mobile networks. Such an effect will be even greater, as time goes by, because of the gradual reduction of margins on mobile telecommunications services.

In relation to fixed telecommunications networks, certain operators have decided to invest in the establishment of high speed data networks. The establishment of such networks will enable them to offer better services at lower costs. Again, if such operators are required to provide unlimited access to their networks, such a policy may affect operators' willingness to establish such networks.

In conclusion, the promotion of horizontal and vertical competition is equally desirable from a legal point of view. However, from a telecommunications policy point of view, since horizontal competition provides a greater availability of telecommunications capacity, vertical competition must be encouraged, only to the extent that it does not affect horizontal competition.

V. Easiness and the Prospects of Anti-competitive Behaviour

1. The Cost-orientation of Tariffs

Competition law is not an appropriate tool for ensuring cost orientation of tariffs for the following reasons:

a) The Uncertainty of Action by the Commission
On a number of occasions, the Commission did not pursue cases which were clearly of Community interest and which constituted an abuse of dominant position. For instance, during the year 1994–1995, certain TOs had developed tariff policies which were conditioning the level of discounts granted for national traffic (in which there was no or less competition) on the level of discounts granted for international traffic (in which there was competition). This meant that customers had an incentive to concentrate all their telecommunications requirements with TOs and not to use alternative providers for

their international traffic. The Commission failed, to a large extent, to take a position on these matters, thereby creating a feeling of legal insecurity in the market.

b) The Sluggishness of Procedures

If and when the Commission has decided to pursue a case, it takes, on average, a minimum of two years to take a decision. It is customary for the Commission to take one year to prepare a statement of objections pursuant to Article 2 of Regulation 99/63/EEC.[25] Pursuant to Article 4 of such Regulation, the Commission is required in its decision to deal only with the objections for which the concerned undertakings have been given an opportunity to comment upon. In practice, this means that the Commission is not likely to base any decision on facts which were not addressed in the statement of objections. Since it takes usually a year between the statement of objections and the adoption of a decision, this gives ample opportunity for the undertaking which is said to have abused its dominant position to adapt its behaviour making it extremely difficult, if not impossible, for the Commission to apprehend anti-competitive behaviours in their entirety.

The inadequacies of procedures are further increased in relation to inter-connection or access issues, since operators' interconnection needs tend to evolve rapidly. As an illustration, in 1996, operator's interconnection needs were limited to non reserved voice and data services. After January 1, 1998, operators' needs have expanded to included C7-based interconnection neces-sary for the provision of voice telephony services and are now expected to include interconnection with data networks over the next few months. This means that any interconnection complaints which may have been filed in 1996 (with a decision in 1998) do not address the interconnection issues which oper-ators are facing today.

c) The Absence of Evidence

Evidence of non cost-oriented tariffs must be based on data held by the under-taking responsible for such non-cost-orientation. Therefore, it is virtually impossible for a third party to submit to the Commission evidence that certain tariffs are not cost-oriented. Such cases can only be initiated and prosecuted by the Commission under its own initiative.

---

[25] Commission Regulation No 99/63/EEC of 25 July 1963 on the hearing provided for in Article 19(1) and (2) of Council Regulation No 17.

d) The Absence of Subsequent Monitoring
Unlike standard refusal to deal cases where the issue of monitoring does not arise, interconnection issues are recurrent. Therefore, any decision of the Commission would have to be followed upon and monitored by the Commission in order to ensure that, in the event of abuse, the grounds for abuse would no longer arise. There is no specific unit within the Commission which is in charge for ensuring compliance with the conditions provided for in a decision.

2. Intellectual Property Rights Issues

IPR have so far not raised any significant issues in the telecommunications sector. Indeed, standards are usually open, precisely in order to facilitate interconnection.

3. Non-discrimination Issues

Existing case law and administration practice on discrimination is fully applicable to the telecommunications sector.

4. Unbundling Issues

Again, the existing case law and administrative practice on bundling is fully applicable in the telecommunications sector. In practice, bundling issues have, in the past, mainly pertained to the combined offer (through rebates) of national and international telecommunications services. Bundling issues are now arising in relation to local loop access (i.e. interconnection at the local level excluding the use of switching capacity) or to access to mobile operators (i.e. interconnection with mobile network operators' transmission capacity to the exclusion of their switches and network control centres).

The reason why unbundled local loop access issues have not arisen so far is because it requires a point of presence of competing network operators at the local level which takes time to achieve in terms of network development. However, such issues will undoubtedly appear as alternative networks develop and as alternative network operators establish points of presence at the local levels.

5. Consumer Welfare and Competition

To date, consumer welfare has been served by competition. Indeed, the liberalisation of the telecommunications sector has triggered a significant reduction
of tariffs for long distance and a greater availability of telecommunications
capacity and services.

However, Telecommunications Organisations carry out missions of general
economic interest,[26] insofar as they guarantee the provision of a minimum set
of services to everyone at an affordable price. When Directive 90/388/EEC was
originally adopted, it was agreed that TOs would still be in a position to secure
their missions of general economic interest, in spite of a partial liberalisation of
telecommunications services, because they derived most of their revenues from
the provision of voice telephony services which were not liberalised.[27] After the
full liberalisation of telecommunications networks and services, through the
subsequent amendments to Directive 90/388/EEC, alternative means of ensuring the proper accomplishment of missions of general economic interest had to
be secured. This gave rise to the possibility for Member States of adopting a
special regime aiming at ensuring the provision of universal service.

Such regulations may give to TOs an opportunity of being compensated for
the costs associated with the provision of universal service (through a fund
and/or access deficit charges). While such regimes can secure the provision of
universal service, they can also have anti-competitive effects insofar as the costs
taken into account for the purpose of determining the level of contribution of
new entrants are exaggerated.

---

[26] Telecommunications activities are regarded, pursuant to a well established case
law as activities of general economic interest referred to in Article 86(20) [ex 90(2)] of
the Consolidated Treaty (see, for example, *Italian Republic* v *Commission*, Case 41/83,
[1985] ECR 873).

[27] See Recital 18 to Directive 90/388/EEC as originally adopted: 'Article 86(2) [ex
90(2)] of the Treaty allows derogations from the application of Articles 49 and 82 [ex 59
and 86] of the Treaty where such application would obstruct the performance, in law or
in fact, of the particular task assigned to the telecommunications organisations. This
task consists in the provision and exploitation of a universal network, i.e. one having
general geographical coverage, and being provided to any service provider or user upon
request within a reasonable period of time. The financial resources for the development
of the network still derive mainly from the operation of the telephone service.
Consequently, the opening-up of voice telephony to competition could threaten the
financial stability of the telecommunications organisations [. . .].'

VI. Conclusion

Competition rules currently provide sufficient legal grounds to ensure access to bottlenecks in the telecommunications sector. It is likely, however, that the requirement of dominant position, implemented under the Access Notice as a requirement that a particular facility be 'generally essential' may limit the prospect of applying the 'essential facilities test' as the telecommunications sector becomes more competitive and the dominance of TOs diminishes. Furthermore, procedurally, the relatively long time necessary to adopt a decision and the lack of monitoring capability by the Commission are additional obstacles to the proper handling of access issues under competition rules. This is mainly because access issues in the telecommunications sector are recurrent and not occasional.

III

Jens Arnbak*

The Dynamics of Access, Entry and Costs in Electronic
Communications Markets

I. Introduction

After the formal liberalisation of the telecommunications market in the
European Union (EU) on 1 January 1998, a number of questions still have to
be answered about the best way to ensure the rapid replacement of regulated
monopoly providers by a sufficient number of competitive firms. The diamet-
rically opposite virtues, issues and legal foundations of the initial monopoly
and the (ultimate ideal of a) competitive telecommunications market have been
studied and debated by academics for decades. Now more practical problems
posed by dynamic, but uncertain, markets in transition are upon us. Like parents of eager adolescents, the national and European authorities overseeing the
communication markets are faced with the unpredictable turbulence of vigorous new forces, loudly voiced ambitions and angry complaints. And just as
some parents in such circumstances, authorities may be more inclined to argue
about each others' role and responsibility, than to develop a joint view on the
growth of what they wish to foster: networked competition.

I am not entitled to the punishing role of the father leading the way to the
promised land of effective competition with Arts. 85 and 86 inscribed in stone
tablets, descending on abusive dancers around golden calves. Moreover, I
choose not to speak for the independent National Regulatory Authority (NRA)
required by Community law to mother its young communications market(s)
through the transition from (state-owned) monopoly to effective competition,
but about the technological and economic dynamics in the liberalised communication sector(s). My central thesis is that these forces should be better observed
and acknowledged in policies and rulings. Digital information and communications technologies (ICT) offer a combination of features and options with great
economic significance: transport with the speed of light (unlike pipelines,
railtrack, roads, etc.); massive transport at vanishing unit cost, without loss
of quality (unlike electric power): instant copying/broadcasting, bundling and

---

* Chairman OPTA (Dutch Independent Post & Telecommunications Authority)
and Delft University of Technology. I gratefully acknowledge suggestions made by
Charlotte Betlem of DDV, and Mirjam van Bergen and Wolf Sauter of OPTA.

re-routing/refiling of information (unlike the mail, printing and publishing sectors); complementary customer-access options: choice between wired access (with strong economies of scale, scope and/or density) and wireless networks (with area-coverage abilities, e.g. cellular mobile networks; broadcasting with or without conditional access); and lightweight/portable terminal devices (unlike sea, air and rail networks).

In competition terms, these five properties will increasingly affect the relevant geographical markets (which can be much larger than a national or even European jurisdiction) and product markets (e.g. by the ability to bundle products or services in converging sectors). Digital communications differ substantially from other networked services, such as power distribution or airline transport, as illustrated by the ease of arranging either call-back or 'tromboning' via third countries to allow arbitrage between inconsistent national prices for delivery of traffic.

This analysis is an attempt to stimulate discussion about the regulatory challenges resulting from the five properties of digital communications listed above. Section II outlines the rapid changes in ICT economies. The layered structure of network and service markets is reviewed in Section III, as a prelude to the definition, in Section IV, of an 'open space' for competitive provision of communications. Section V cites two topical examples of regulatory challenges due to convergence of imperfect communication markets in this open space. Related dilemmas for public policy are sketched in Section VI. The concluding section outlines some key competition issues and the author's tentative proposals for analysing them in the increasingly dynamic setting of ICT, seen from the perspective of a communications systems engineer who happens to work as a regulator in the Netherlands NRA, and to serve as a member of an Appeals Board dealing with complaints lodged against decisions of the NRA in another EU Member State.

II. The Significance of (Understanding) the Dynamics of Production Costs

The relative importance of technological innovation and regulatory reform as drivers of successful delivery of services is a permanent subject of debate. Recall the anecdotal minister who tasked his legal staff to write a White Paper on airline regulation just after World War II. In the spirit of international cooperation in those days, the legal experts' draft set out as follows: 'Civil aviation is based on international law established by modern nations in order to regulate international traffic'. But when the ministry's technical staff got wind of this, a counter-proposal was tabled with the following opening statement: 'Civil aviation is based on the aerodynamic laws of nature which permit man to fly in vessels heavier than air'.

Certainly, a purely engineering approach to public telecommunications arrangements is no longer appropriate. Such approaches dominated virtually all of the incumbent operators in Europe (and former European colonies), as well as the 'Bell System' in North America. Still, I submit that neither legislators nor NRAs can neglect the (im)potencies of relevant technologies, when considering rights and obligations of telecommunication operators and 'their' customers. In particular, the cost dynamics introduced by novel approaches to transmission and switching, such as Asynchronous Transfer Mode (ATM) and the suite of Internet Protocols (TCP/IP), must be allowed for. Where sufficient economies of scale can be achieved with optical cables, the cost of long-distance transmission tends to zero. This 'death of distance', in turn, exposes the increasingly dominant cost of the local networks providing access to individual customers. When traditional benefits and costs are shifted to different user communities, or to other (parts of) communication networks, requirements for modifications of the regulatory framework for public control of tariffs and access obligations are likely to arise.

The ongoing innovation of information and communication technologies only seldom decides the resulting products and services in the market place unilaterally. I became highly sceptical about technological determinism as a young member of the international service of NATO during the 1970s, when working on the development of integrated networks[1] for joint political command and control of the allied forces. The individual Member States and their incumbent telecom operators all considered the same technological options, but for various reasons, and to our professional despair, often preferred very divergent solutions. However, did we innovative system engineers involved in developing and testing of survivable, flexible and secure computer communications then ourselves foresee the present challenges to the plain old telephone system by the resulting Internet protocols and cellular mobile networks, invented in the 1970s? To be honest, I cannot recall any indication of such a recognition. In those days orthodox telephone engineers were outspoken about the infant principles of mobile telephones and non-hierarchical computer networking: clearly inefficient and an obvious threat to quality of service! Yet in the second half of the 1990s, telephone companies and switch manufacturers scramble to

---

[1] Based on a mix of network facilities leased from incumbent operators in the fifteen Member States, and NATO-owned international infrastructure (satellite networks and troposcatter radio links).

include many of the so-called 'inefficiencies' and 'threats' in their commercial offerings.

1. The Role of New Technology Options

In hindsight, the missing link in the engineering picture twenty years ago was the subsequent advent of cheap computing power in terminals, both in offices and homes (the PC) and underway (the hand-held mobile telephone terminal). In due course, this missing link was to be discovered and ascertained on liberalised terminal markets. These emerged slowly, first in the United States following the Carterphone decision[2] by the FCC in 1968, and some twenty years later in the European Community. Since then, the most impressive *network* growth rates occurred for Internet and mobile communications, spurred by the cost reductions and performance improvements of the corresponding *user terminals*, namely, the *personal* computer and the *personal* mobile telephone. The buyers of these terminal devices have benefited from the periodic improvements of each successive generation of very large scale integrated (VLSI) microelectronics,[3] combined with the fierce competition in consumer electronics markets. Thus affordable, yet highly advanced professional equipment features have come within direct reach of consumers, as evidenced by the rapid entry of the PC and the standardised fax terminal into private homes.

Another example is the use of 'smart-card' technology in the pan-European GSM-system.[4] This particular mobile telephone system introduced highly personalised, professional security and service features programmed in a low-cost standardised chip card (known as the subscriber identity module, or SIM-card), which can be inserted into any GSM-terminal. Most economic dynamics were brought about where mobile markets liberalised,[5] and service providers were allowed by regulators to provide attractive package deals, including 'free' terminals, as part of their marketing efforts. Evidently, such package deals should not stifle competition by foreclosure of a new market by

---

[2] The FCC held that blanket prohibitions by the network operator against attachment of customer-provided terminals to the telephone network were unreasonable, discriminatory and unlawful.

[3] Arnbak (1997: 67–72).

[4] Jens Arnbak, The European (R)evolution of Wireless Digital Networks, *IEEE Communications Magazine*, September 1993, at 75.

[5] During the early GSM introduction in Europe, it did not pay to move terminal production to world regions with lower labour costs, as long as much greater demands for terminals existed in the liberalised European market.

dominant players, for instance by locking a mobile terminal to a particular SIM card in order to prevent the subscriber to exploit any better choices offered by number portability. If the SIM-card were to evolve into a general credit card, which can be used for payments in conjunction with the mobile terminal, additional regulatory issues may arise.

Figure 1 indicates the emergence of some significant cross-over paths between previously separate branches of the electronics industry in the past two decades.[6] Such paths allow the extension of the professional performance of more costly proprietary products to much cheaper equipment produced by a different industry. Where new paths ('confluences') between traditional industry branches can emerge, the capacity of terminals and networks rise faster, and at less unit cost, than along the three beaten tracks of industrial products in Figure 1.

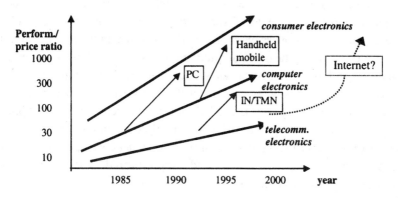

Fig. 1. *Performance trajectories of electronic products (indicative)*

2. The Role of Standardisation

The market introduction of 'cellular data cards' for connecting a laptop computer to a GSM terminal (in order to support international mobile computing, Group III fax, short message services (SMS) and wireless access to the Internet), illustrates the rapid emergence of proprietary 'standardisation' on liberalised markets. This particular product innovation combines two of the most successful cross-over branches shown in Figure 1: the PC and the mobile

---

[6] This type of representation was proposed by O. Martikainen, 'Trends in Telecommunications and the Role of IN', (manuscript) paper presented at the IFIP/TC–6 and ICCC Joint Meeting, Funchal, Madeira, 1994.

telephone. Evidently, such a data card adds more *value* for those professional mobile users prepared to pay the price for its novel features, than would any periodical update of a standard consumer product; nevertheless, the manufacturing *cost* can be kept within the normal range of consumer electronics. Accordingly, manufacturers may reap higher unit profits from such upgraded products with a premium price.

The commercial success of cross-over paths between what used to be strictly separate market segments has been enforced by standardisation and liberalisation of terminals. The acceptance of the price mechanism for terminals meant that they were withdrawn from the classical monopoly game of distributing internal subsidies between different groups of network subscribers, so the true cost benefits of modern technology could be discovered on a consumer market. A minimum set of regulations and standards to ensure compatible interfaces with, and integrity of, public networks now suffice. Moreover, European procurement rules[7] have exposed telecommunications switch manufacturers, who had long enjoyed the protection of national procurement procedures, to competition levels more similar to those prevailing in the much younger computer industry. Computer manufacturers, whose faster innovation cycles and lower unit costs can accelerate upgrading of conventional telephone networks and services with novel ICT platforms, have recently opened the cross-over path between the lower industry branches shown in Figure 1. This confluence between two different capital-goods industries now streamlines the internal business processes of traditional network operators by 'intelligent network' (IN) features and sophisticated telecommunications management networks (TMN).

3. Services Competition

Despite these positive effects of competition in the communications hardware sectors (including terminals) and the computer sector, these hardware sectors lag far behind the largest and fastest growing business sector based on ICT: telecommunication *services*. Table 1 illustrates this fact in the Netherlands. Just as in other Member States, the core markets of network-based services were, for the larger part, protected from competition. The gross revenues in 1997 of the Dutch incumbent, KPN Telecom, from previous monopoly activi-

---

[7] Council Directive 93/38/EEC coordinating the procurement procedures of entities operating in the water, energy, transport and telecommunications sectors, OJ L 199/84 (1993).

ties—since mid-1997 falling under Open Network Provision (ONP) regulation by OPTA—were 5.7 milliard ECU; its additional revenues in mobile communications were about 1 milliard ECU. Less than 10% of the service revenues in 1997 accrued to national competitors of KPN Telecom.

Table 1 illustrates the heterogeneous structure and different growth of the various ICT market sectors, and suggests the need for a suitably structured market model.

Table 1: Size of ICT market sectors in the Netherlands, 1994–1997 in milliard ECU (1996 & 1997 are estimates)[1]

	1994	*1995*	*1996*	*1997*
Computer hardware	3.011	3.347	3.616	3.876
Software products	1.613	1.789	2.019	2.275
IT services	2.590	2.751	2.920	3.102
Telecom hardware	1.166	1.568	1.442	1.561
Telecom services	5.156	5.685	6.430	7.297
TOTAL	13.486	15.140	16.427	18.111

[1] *Ministerie van Economische Zaken, ICT en de Economie* (Netherlands Ministry of Economic Affairs, *ICT and the Economy*, in Dutch), 14 (1998).

III. A Layered Market Model for Networks and Services

Figure 2 presents a generic model of the market provision of telecommunications,[8] divided according to horizontal layers of services and underlying network facilities.[9] Its conceptual use in the present discussion can best be illustrated by mobile networks, as mobile users are more likely to demand the higher-layer services with added value, than are the majority of subscribers to

[8] Adapted from, Arnbak, van Cuilenburg *et al* (1990: 58).

[9] An alternative layered model, reflecting manufacturers' supply of different products, would contain the following four levels: intelligent network (IN) level (services/network control technology); transport network level (transmission and switching products for core networks); access network level (subscriber loops or air interfaces in wireless networks); terminal level (user transmit/receive technology). Evidently, these four layers do not map uniquely onto those in Figure 2. Either model may be more useful, depending on whether the emphasis is on evolution of personal integrated *service* provision to network users, or on the dynamics of *technology*, which opens new possibilities for media convergence and for transport-service substitution.

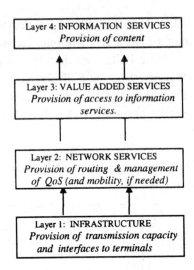

Fig. 2. *Generic telecommunications model for the provision of transmission capacity and services to (fixed and mobile) terminals*

a fixed public switched telephone network (PSTN). This difference is not merely caused by the early adoption of wireless services by more demanding or affluent ('leading-edge') customers: The typical circumstances of users on the move, away from their facilities in the office and at home, generate additional requirements for more extensive, personalised service and support features.

Layer 1, the lowest layer in Figure 2, would in a mobile market typically comprise the access link between a customer moving in a specific service area and the corresponding radio (base)-station or low-earth orbiting satellite covering that area, in which various customers are active from time to time. Layer 1 also includes the (fixed) transmission links connecting the base stations or satellites to their corresponding controllers and switching and service centres, which are linked by high-capacity transport networks (in which impressive economies of scale can now reaped with optical technologies).

Layer 2 comprises the switching centres, other fixed network nodes and the associated intelligence to control, route and tariff the traffic to and from the appropriate user terminals. In the future, competitive provision of an adequate quality-of-service (QoS) will become decisive for the commercial choice between routing over classical telecommunication facilities, new networks with customer-negotiated performance based on ATM, and networks based on IP which may provide a (less demanding) 'best-effort' performance. Mobility management, where required to identify and serve mobile users, is also exercised at this layer, both for the network operator's own subscribing customers moving across the service area, and for roaming visitors from other operators' service areas.

Generally, interconnection between networks of competing operators and with foreign networks takes place at Layer 2. This is a focus of much attention in the present work of NRAs in the EU. So increasingly are the issues surrounding (unbundled) access to the local loop of incumbents at Layer 1. However, it is the two uppermost layers (3&4) which are now becoming pivotal in the regulatory studies of and commercial plans for convergence with two adjacent sectors: information technology (IT) and (multi-)media content. These layers are perceived to 'add value'; often, this business perception results in vertically integrated firms or market offerings. Most public telecommunications network operators offer additional specialised communication services at Layer 3, provided either by the network operator itself or by value-added service providers selected by the individual user via the lower-layer facilities of the network. Typical examples are voice mail boxes and fax gateways. The EC Interconnection Directive[10] provides a framework of rules for special access to the network (generally at layer 1 or 2) by service providers, depending on the market power of the network operator. Layer 4 provides information content, such as travel information, news and other on-line data services of a narrowband or, where broadcast regulations and/or technology so allow, broad-band nature. The next section will consider the implications of the technological and economic dynamics discussed earlier, when acting on these different layers, for creation or protection of competition in the future communications sector.

IV. Competitive Development of New Networks and Services

In order to maximise competition in ICT-based markets by safeguarding the ability of new players to discover and deliver the most competitive technology and service concepts in a network sector with such inherent economies of scale and scope, guarantees for access to bottleneck facilities of competitors may be required even in a fully liberalised market.[11] It may be prudent to retain such guarantees in Community law in the future by (more generic) ONP rules,

---

[10] Directive 97/33/EC of the European Parliament and of the Council interconnection in telecommunications with regard to ensuring universal service and interoperability through application of the principles of open network provision (ONP), OJ L 199/32 (1997).

[11] Jens Arnbak *et al*, *Network interconnection in the domain of ONP*, Study for DG XIII of the European Commission, 10 (WIK/EAC, final report, 1994).

rather than relying on application of the 'essential facilities doctrine' as developed in US law. New players are particularly vulnerable to the extra delays of such *ex post* procedures. In any event, barriers to accessing end users and/or various new elements of the value chain in a converging environment will offer regulatory challenges, which can be illustrated in an 'open interconnection and access space', as depicted in Figure 3. This figure is the extension of the model in Figure 2, at each of the four horizontal layers, into the two additional dimensions of alternative providers and hierarchical level in their networks. Obviously, the resulting three-dimensional space contains an abundance of internal interfaces where network elements belonging to a single telecommunications firm are connected. Selecting the most profitable path through this space is a classical economic problem faced by all network operators and service providers in their ongoing engineering response to market needs.

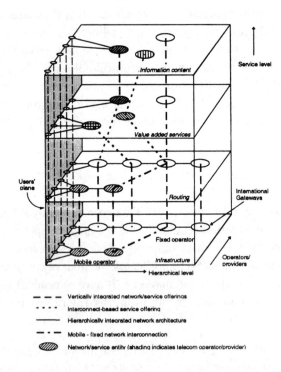

Fig. 3. *Open space for communication*[12]

---

[12] Arnbak et al., *supra* n 11.

1. The Past: Horizontal and Vertical Integration

Under the classical condition of monopolistic supply of telecommunications services, the incumbent national operator used to be *horizontally integrated*: it supplied all network elements between the international gateway(s), located at the far right at layers 1 and 2, and down to (or even including) the end user's terminal equipment connected at the far left in Figure 3. So only a few, external interfaces were open to access by other parties: foreign operators were given access through transit exchanges (international gateways) at the highest hierarchical level to the right in the figure; later, when the terminal markets were liberalised, subscribers were given more individual freedom in their choice of access means. As a result, the extreme left and right interfaces have become the most widely standardised access points. In a similar way, the national incumbent was also *vertically integrated:* it supplied not only most or all transmission, switching and routing capabilities, but also value-added services (such as operator assistance) and information content (directory assistance, weather, stock exchanges, etc.) in the upper planes of Figure 3.

2. The Present: the Transition Phase

On the other hand, in a modern competitive networked market, contenders require—and should on reasonable terms be entitled—to enter the Open Space in Figure 3 at the access points where they can best interface to an existing dominant provider, presenting them with a bottleneck. It would seem rather unlikely that the multitude of potential issues related to (arbitration of) any conflicts of interest in this complex space could always be resolved in a timely manner without recourse, if necessary, to an impartial regulator, clothed with the authority of the public interest. Typical conflicts would involve the determination of the appropriate rights to and reasonable costs of access to—sufficiently unbundled—facilities, in the event that commercial negotiations fail or protract indefinitely. Costs, in particular, are notoriously difficult to determine in a timely manner by competition law. Interestingly, the EU Commission recently acknowledged the benefits for competition authorities of the cost models established under present ONP rules for players with significant market power.[13]

---

[13] Commission Notice on the application of the competition rules to access agreements in the telecommunications sector, OJ C 265/02 (1998).

Alternatively, imposing restrictions on dominant players of their lines of business inside an otherwise Open Space may be deemed necessary to prevent dominant players from stifling competition. It is the author's opinion that such business restrictions have, in the past, tended to affect market dynamics in a counterproductive way. Thus, the unequalled progress of mobile cellular telephone markets in the Nordic countries was led by incumbents, subjected to the discipline of vigorous competition from new entrants. On the other hand, the US, where cellular technology was invented in the Bell Laboratories,[14] lost its competitive advantage when AT&T was barred from operating mobile networks in its own area of operation. Similarly, neither the UK/North-European teletext system nor the French Minitel/Télétel system would have come about without the involvement, experience and resources of incumbents, whereas the structural separation of basic and enhanced services imposed by the FCC hardly proved conducive to development of public higher-layer (telematic) services in the US. Is there perhaps a question here about the consequences of rigorous *structural* restrictions as proposed by the European Commission in its draft Cable Directive?[15] Would *behavioural* rules (e.g. non-discriminatory access of competitors) suffice in certain circumstances?

V. Future Network Developments: Two Examples of New Regulatory Challenges

Early in the new millennium, the results of the 1999 ONP Review will be implemented in the EU. This section illustrates some of the likely network developments that should be catered for in this process.

1. Fixed-mobile Integration (FMI)

In the foreseeable future, the majority of mobile calls will continue to originate or terminate in a PSTN, generally with proprietary national interfaces. Accordingly, the classical fixed-network applications and management practices of the PSTN layers in Figure 2 may still exercise relatively strong constraints on mobile networking and services. It was the design requirement for

---

[14] Arnbak, *supra* n 4.

[15] Draft Commission Directive amending Directive 90/388/EC in order to ensure that telecommunications networks and cable TV networks owned by a single operator are separate legal entities, OJ C 71/23 (1998).

a Europe-wide mobile telephone system interoperating with many different national fixed telephone networks, and for managing the roaming of users across this (technically and operationally) fragmented region, which gave rise to the engineering effort between 1982 and the resulting mandatory GSM standard for the EU over ten years later.[16] However, the transaction costs of this effort have been earned back with ample interest, namely, the proven ability to deploy and integrate GSM-based systems fast in most countries throughout the world. The key success factor for the world-wide commercial acceptance and continued evolution of the GSM standard would appear to be the practical fact that only this standard extends well beyond to the radio subsystem and its air interface with mobile user terminals: The standard includes the crucial aspects of access to, and interworking with, the diverse fixed national analogue networks in Europe (PSTN) as well as the ISDN. Arguably, this challenge was absent in North America, where mobile networks could simply be grafted on the interfaces of the ubiquitous Bell System, which continued to exist after divestiture of AT&T.[17]

Service convergence on a larger scale between public fixed and mobile networks will most likely be based on innovative use of Intelligent-Network (IN) or Telecommunication Management Network (TMN) facilities.[18] Such facilities are becoming easy to implement, thanks to lower costs of adding new computer platforms to the comparatively inflexible and costly switching architecture of a traditional PSTN, as shown in Figure 1. The recent success of prepaid cards for subscription-free access to GSM networks in several European countries relies on IN-facilities, and shows their ability to introduce new business.

Mobile telephony started as a premium service, offering voice transmission with mobility. Propagated by the technology and cost dynamics, mobile telephony now evolves into a more mature offering of voice and data services, which—given adequate public policies for pricing and unbundling of local loops (ULL), access to the IN of competitors, etc.,—will obviate the need for

---

[16] Commission Decision 94/12/EC of 21 Dec. 1993 on a common technical regulation for the telephony application requirements for public pan-European cellular digital land-based mobile communications, OJ L 8/23(1994).

[17] Arnbak, *supra* n 4.

[18] In facilities which allow routing and tariffing of international mobile calls across borders in a fixed—rather than international roaming—mode, and hence may expose the high revenues presently enjoyed by signatories to the GSM MoU. Other possibilities for FMI are at the switching level (Layer 2 in Figure 2), often in conjunction with unbundled local loops of the incumbent, and at the terminal level (Layer 1 in Figure 2), e.g. for wireless extensions of corporate networks.

separate subscriptions to the PSTN and a mobile network. Services offered with fixed-mobile integration already available in some EU Member States and giving rise to regulatory issues, are the following:

Home zone tariffing, allowing subscribers to make (and receive?) wireless calls at lower rates, when located in the immediate proximity of their homes. The rate charged could be close to that for fixed-line calls and hence would allow substitution of the PSTN, as already experienced in Scandinavia. Thus the clear regulatory distinction in the ONP regime between fixed and mobile telephony will no longer fit the actual situation.

Personal numbering, making fixed and mobile terminal connections 'melt' together. When calling such a number, it is uncertain where the call will be picked up. In existing personal numbering-based services, the subscriber can set personal preferences, i.e., determine what the 'priority call pick-up' should be, the home (fixed), the office (fixed) or a mobile terminal . Thus different pricing options exist: should the extra costs be charged to the caller, or to the called party? Should fixed tariff principles apply (as set out in the recent ONP Directive on to voice telephony),[19] or would the present, more commercial mobile pricing practice suffice? Different policy choices could lead to different behaviour of the future telephone market.

Value-added services, such as voice mail and forwarding of messages, as part of both fixed and mobile service packages. For instance, a mobile terminal could serve as a remote control for re-routing overly demanding or costly wireless traffic (graphical fax messages, video conferences, etc.) via a subscriber line to a nearby fixed terminal capable of handling the necessary higher capacity faster and/or cheaper. The commercial viability of this scenario will depend on the local coverage and pricing of broadband third-generation mobile networks, such as the Universal Mobile Telecommunication System (UMTS), and on interconnection at intelligent-network (IN) level.

2. UMTS Licensing Conditions

UMTS provides a second example of the regulatory challenges arising from a new technological trajectory through the Open Space for Communication in Figure 3. Obviously, the European ambition is to safeguard the inheritance and

---

[19] Directive 98/10/EC of the European Parliament and of the Council of 26 February 1998 on the application of open network provision (ONP) to voice telephony and on universal service for telecommunications in a competitive environment (replacing European Parliament and Council Directive 95/62/EC), OJ L 101/24 (1998).

international success of GSM, by contributing to a flexible, upwards compatible third-generation air interface standard with world-wide acceptance in the next century. If this ambition is to be realised, yet another type of confluence will be required, namely that of regional mobile standards. In Hong Kong and Singapore, where the world's different regional second-generation mobile standards now compete directly with each other, the recent experience of the local telecom regulators is that business users show a clear preference for the ability to roam globally and/or to 'personalise' mobile terminals by a smart card. Accordingly, GSM subscriptions sell at much higher (premium) prices than the subscriptions to mobile networks based on the other regional standards available. Unlike GSM, standardisation and introduction of UMTS will therefore hardly be confined to Europe initially.

The globalisation of third-generation mobile communications will require a timely regulatory framework for UMTS licensing in Europe, with due regard for leading-edge markets as influenced by emerging global mobile satellite networks and mobile multimedia. But at the same time, further expansion of personal communications must be based increasingly on the larger subscriber numbers on broader consumer markets, which inherently are more locally defined. Consumers are less inclined to pay a high mark-up for innovative service value, as they cannot claim reimbursement of communication costs as a business expense. Moreover, they have stronger expectations of equitable treatment in terms of non-discriminatory (e.g. geographically averaged) pricing. Public policy choices about such issues are likely to decide the (time to) market for new systems such as UMTS. Licensing procedures and any related mandatory standardisation should reflect this.

Thus, given the present high penetration of mobile telephony and the scarce spectrum available for the future (high-capacity) systems, the licensing conditions for domestic roaming between *national* competitors could become a matter of crucial importance for the future position of third-generation mobile networking and multimedia. Should a few active multimedia users be prioritised above some hundreds of mobile telephone conversations, occupying the same total bandwidth? Even if the saying is true that 'a picture says more than a thousand words', would most customers be prepared to pay a thousand times more for the picture on a mobile screen? This commercial question will have to be answered by a UMTS-operator who may have obtained a license in an expensive frequency auction. Evidently, the type of public policy adopted, its ability to differentiate (discriminate?) between market segments, and the related regulatory conditions for market entry and access to networks of (incumbent) national competitors, will all play significant roles in determining the type and speed of market growth in the UMTS time frame.

VI. Emerging Dilemmas for Communications Policy

The examples of regulatory challenges in the communication sector(s) given above suggest that change is becoming imperative. Note that the increased dynamics and global importance of a key business sector do not, *per se,* provide a logical justification for regulating it *less,* but only for regulating it *differently.* A topical example of this is the vital—but at critical times highly volatile—converging financial services offered by banks, insurance companies, building societies, etc. Although increasingly competitive and international by nature—or perhaps exactly for that reason—the underlying institutional networks would not continue to enjoy sufficient confidence from clients at home and abroad without internationally accepted principles for impartial monitoring of commercial arrangements and public control of, say, rates of interest and exchange in financial transactions. Trade and other business transactions have not become less, but much more dependent on impartial monitoring and regulation of the present international financial system. Arguably, national shortcomings in this field lie at the roots of the recent severe financial crises in some world regions.

Seamless (tele-)communications networks and services are becoming as important for international trade as the seamless financial networks and services markets now monitored by the central banks. Indeed, banking markets are increasingly based on advanced telecommunications. How then should telecommunication services be monitored, and regulated in the future, given their rapidly growing dynamics and global economic impact? In addressing this question we need to weigh the likely consequences of different options for regulatory intervention to correct market imperfections, at each of the four levels in Figure 2. As for economic dilemmas, it must be decided how the increasingly complicated bottleneck issues in the future will be resolved in a timely manner: What are the transaction costs of relying on commercial negotiations with dominant gatekeepers or between peer (IP) competitors, without recourse to validated cost information from the dominant players? Alternatively, should such players be forced *a priori* to certain (behavioural) terms of trade, or even to (structural) divestiture of horizontal ownership of communication networks? These dilemmas relate to the elimination of negative externalities. It is equally necessary to address the positive externalities of networks and to ask whether global communications and information services develop satisfactorily without *ex ante* safeguards for consistent numbering/domain names, standardised roaming parameters, directories and other matters determining the ability to identify or address a growing number of users in the general public?

VII. Conclusion: Horizontal and Vertical Competition Issues in the Open Communications Space

It would be foolhardy to conclude this analysis with detailed predictions of the appropriate future regulatory regime for competitive provision of (tele)communication networks and services in the EU Member States. However, on the basis of the foregoing, I believe there is a case for extending ONP rules in the direction of competition law, for at least two related reasons. First, the compelling cost trends of modern information and communication technologies (ICT), which will erode the economic principles of classical networks by 'the death of distance' and by the increasing processing power of terminals and switching (Figure 1) in liberalised markets, and will as a consequence further *increase* the relative burden of the cost of network access. Secondly, as recognised by the recent WTO agreements,[20] the increasingly global nature and impact of basic telecommunications services, which—much like the international financial system did in the latter half of the 1990s—will reveal any anomalies and shortcomings of national monitoring and regulation, with potentially harmful effects on regional economies.

This conjugate pair of observations indicates the need for, on the one hand, internationally agreed and enforced principles of global liberalisation, and, on the other hand, closer monitoring of local gatekeepers controlling bottleneck facilities for access to networks and/or customers. A paradox would appear to emerge: even though market discipline can now be relied upon for core/long-distance networks, the benefits of a direct choice between such networks are hardly enjoyed by the majority of individual users or new entrants. How should such market imperfections be addressed?

I tentatively propose the following items for an agenda of inquiry into potential networked-market failures or significant imperfections of electronic communications markets, adding my own more or less preconceived opinions:

(1) Where are the future bottlenecks in the Open Space for Communications (Figure 3), other than conditional access systems and local loops/radio interfaces of individual network subscribers?
I expect that the recurrent terminating-access issues will increasingly include network and service *control facilities* such as intelligent-network (IN) interfaces—not to be confused with the proprietor's IN databases—and must

---

[20] Annex to the Fourth Protocol of the General Agreement on Trade in Services, February 1997.

be addressed by public policy, or by appropriate commercial MoUs subject to adequate monitoring. Unless the European Court of Justice upholds the 'Essential Facilities Doctrine' developed in US antitrust law[21] in a sufficiently general communications case in a liberalised market, I remain sceptical that this doctrine will be an adequate substitute for more explicit access obligations laid down in Community law. (For the separate issue of pricing access to bottlenecks, see item 5 below).

(2) Should specific vertical and/or horizontal business-line restrictions or demands for complete divestiture of activities be imposed on players with significant market power in the Open Space for Competition?

In the past it has indeed been counterproductive to bar incumbents or other players with substantial resources and experience from innovating networks or services. However, whatever dominant network players grant themselves in a bottleneck area should, on reasonable terms, also be opened to their competitors. Examples in this area are the use of the incumbent's—unbundled—local loop for competitive introduction of fixed-mobile integration or digital broadband access (xDSL) to telephone subscribers. If granted a UMTS license, a GSM/DCS1800 operator with significant market power in the area of mobile telephone services might be required to accept national roaming from any UMTS operator without a previous mobile telephone licence, in order to give the latter an equivalent room to develop broadband applications.

(3) Should network operators with significant market power on the telephony market in the Open Space for Communication (Figure 3) be allowed to engage in Internet activities?

Yes. This question is related to the previous issue, but is complicated by the European Commission's current view that Internet activities should, in principle, continue to be unregulated.[22] Any such *technologically* defined service market (i.e., linking different layers in Figure 2) encourages incumbents to study evasive scenarios with code words such as 'Escape ONP' or 'Beyond Universal Service Obligations'. As suggested by the rightmost cross-over path in Figure 1, the next confluence between the telecommunications and computer

---

[21] For more informed discussions of the applicability of this doctrine in Europe, see the contributions elsewhere in this volume by Bernard Amory, Joachim Scherer, and James S. Venit.

[22] Commission Notice of 10 January 1998 concerning the status of voice communications on internet under Community Law and, in particular, pursuant to Directive 90/388/EC, OJ C 6/ (1998).

manufacturing sectors might well be a rapid introduction of low-cost TCP/IP computer platforms in lieu of key telephone exchanges in the national network. If such computer platforms were connected by a high-speed ATM backbone network, all that would be needed to lift most telephone users to the—entirely unregulated?—Internet, is unbundling their local loop at the main distribution frame (MDF) and terminating it at the nearest computer platform. The key policy question is not whether an incumbent should be allowed to do this, if finding the TCP/IP-technology to be cheaper and/or more capable of broad-banding than conventional circuit switching, but whether that should auto-matically rescind the incumbent's various obligations under ONP regulations.

(4) How should interconnection between Internet providers be ensured in the future?

Voluntary peering between Internet providers is unlikely to guarantee any-to-any communication, if the present market consolidation continues to enhance the emerging differences in market power between these providers. This would become particularly objectionable, if IP telephony were to develop, for instance in the way considered above in item 3.

(5) How should 'reasonable' prices (or profits) of suppliers with significant market power be determined in future regulations, if at all?

Present ONP regulations speak of 'cost orientation' and so require much more detail in price setting than the bluntly defined, huge range between 'excessive' and 'predatory' prices as understood for *ex post* application of competition law. This level of detail is in accordance with the intervening, *ex ante* regula-tion required for the present, still highly imperfect markets emerging in the wake of monopoly. On the other hand, the detail of pricing models based on network costs is difficult to maintain in the climate of rapid change of the price/performance ratios of ICT (see Figure 1), notably if forward-looking cost models are deemed appropriate.[23] Moreover, pricing may have to ensure more generous incentives for future investments, as competition develops. Such con-siderations justify price setting by price caps, *once* the return on investments on the various activities offered by the regulated firm has been initially calibrated (re-balanced) by a 'cost-plus' approach in order to reduce the risk of anti-competitive cross subsidies between the dominant firm's different activities. However, setting reasonable price caps has to be based on a good judgement of the firm's future efficiency and so entails a much closer (negotiating?) relation

---

[23] For a thorough discussion on cost accounting theories, see Prof. Henry Ergas' contribution to this volume.

with the regulated firm than in the 'cost-plus' approach, which can be based on standard accounting and external controlling practices. The greater regulatory 'intimacy' required in setting price caps for a regulated firm should be adequately balanced by broad public consultations about the appropriate principles. I am not convinced that this is always done in the EU Member States, but believe it will become necessary to increase public understanding of the profit margins that could be required to innovate networks and services at greater pace than in the past. Fortunately, such higher profits may be offset by the lower costs of modern ICT.

By way of conclusion I would like to recall the following recipe for developing a light(er) regulatory regime, first suggested in an essay by Prof. E.C.M. Jurgens.[24] In order to reduce public intervention in communication markets to the level which is strictly necessary, the following sequence of escalating questions should be answered:

- Is there a public interest to be satisfied? If yes,
- Does that public interest call for a specific service to be offered? If yes,
- Can the commercial (market) sector provide that service without public intervention? If not,
- Is the market failure satisfactorily discovered and repaired by the general rule of (*inter alia*, competition) law? If not,
- Can the market failure be removed by imposing appropriate *ex ante* sector-specific rules and regulations on relevant players? If not,
- Can (and should) government itself provide the desired public service?

Clearly, the answers to this progression of questions will become less far-reaching as communications markets liberalise effectively, meaning that customers are given a choice. Only in the few instances of derogation in EU Member States after January 1998 can the ultimate question still be reached and answered in the affirmative. We should now be searching for the right answers to the two penultimate questions, so as to determine the appropriate mix between reliance on general competition law and the Community law specific to one of the most dynamic sectors of the economy.

---

[24] Jurgens (1995).

IV

*Henry Ergas**

TSLRIC, TELRIC and Other Forms of Forward-Looking Cost Models in Telecommunications: A Curmudgeon's Guide

I. Introduction

Regulators in North America, the EU and Australia have mandated the use of forward-looking cost models as the basis for interconnection charging. This paper sets out some of the major issues involved in the construction and use of these models.

II. The Background

Accounting systems structure the collection, analysis and disclosure of cost and revenue information. By so doing, they serve to reduce the transactions costs involved in designing and implementing the explicit and implicit contracts that regulate relations between suppliers and users of resources.[1] Given that this is their purpose, it is not surprising that somewhat differing accounting systems are needed to support differing types of transactions. For example, in most countries, tax accounting differs in important respects from the financial accounting systems used to provide information to the suppliers of firms' financial resources. Equally, it is common for governments to impose special accounting requirements as part of the public procurement process.

In the control of public utilities, *regulatory accounting* serves to support the design and implementation of the regulatory contract—that is, the complex of more or less formalised understandings between regulatory authorities and regulated entities as to the terms and conditions on which services will be

* Director Network Economics Consulting Group Pty Ltd/Centre for Research in Network Economics and Communications, the University of Auckland. This paper reflects work and discussions with Alexis Hardin, John Small and Bridger Mitchell, and I am grateful to them, and to my other colleagues at NECG for their assistance. It also reflects work and discussions with Paul Paterson at Telstra Corporation, and I am grateful to him and his colleagues for the input they have provided. However, the views expressed are strictly my own, as is responsibility for any errors.

1 Sunder (1997).

provided. Twenty years ago, telecommunications regulation, in most OECD countries, was not separated from service provision; it therefore made little sense to talk of a 'regulatory contract'. Since then, this separation has been effected in virtually all OECD countries. As a result of this separation, the design of regulatory processes, and of the accounting systems needed to support them, has become an issue of obvious importance.

The United States has, of course, long had a clear formal separation between regulatory entities and telecommunications service providers. Issues of regulatory accounting, therefore, emerged early on in the US, with complex systems being designed to supply the regulatory authorities with cost and revenue information.[2] These systems formed a natural point of reference when similar needs arose elsewhere.

The systems of regulatory accounting developed in the United States had two salient features.[3] First, they were based on historical costs, which were generally viewed as reflecting (1) the resources investors had devoted to the utilities at issue and hence (2) the claim these investors had on the revenues the systems generated. Second, they relied on exhaustive systems of cost allocation, often referred to as 'fully distributed costing', to allocate costs to individual products and services. Both of these features have been heavily criticised.

As regards the historical cost convention, economists,[4] as well as economically minded accountants,[5] have long held the view that the outlays incurred in past periods provide a poor guide to decisions involving resource allocation. In particular, it has been argued that historical costs:

(1) are merely a collection of variously dated outlays, to which no clear meaning can be attached;[6]
(2) need not reflect the costs,[7]

---

[2] On the early evolution of regulatory accounting for the telephone system. see Danielian (1939: 334); Weinhaus and Oettinger (1988).

[3] A clear formulation of the philosophy underpinning conventional US regulatory accounting, as well as some of the major criticisms levelled against it, can be found Bonbright, Danielsen and Kamerschen (1988).

[4] See e.g., Wicksteed's dictum that a man setting his selling price by reference to past costs of production 'is either allowing an irrelevant consideration to affect his judgement or else is deliberately taking a commercial risk to gratify a personal feeling', Wicksteed (1933: 386).

[5] MacNeal (1939); Chambers (1983): 12–22; Whittington (1983: 39–59).

[6] Chambers and Wolnizer (1990: 353–68).

[7] In the sense of the resources a supplier would need to forego to supply the service at issue.

(3) consequently bear no direct relation to the revenue a supplier of such a service would need to obtain in order to maintain intact either its service capability or its financial capital;[8] and

(4) when used as the basis for pricing decisions can therefore distort consumption and investment decisions.[9]

As for fully distributed costing, scholars of accounting have long argued that the exhaustive allocation of costs relies on judgements that do not reflect cost-causality and, hence, are essentially arbitrary.[10] Relying on such allocations to determine prices for individual services may not be consistent with preserving the financial viability of the service provider and, in any event, can seriously distort resource allocation.[11]

Accounting systems based on current costing have been advocated as providing a superior alternative to the approaches criticised above. While the term 'current cost accounting' covers a wide range of differing approaches,[12] recent interest in telecommunications regulation has focussed on approaches which have two characteristics: they rely on measuring the costs that a hypothetical efficient supplier would incur in the longer term; and they define the relevant costs as those that would be incurred by such a supplier in the provision of a specified increment of output. They thereby combine the optimisation emphasis that characterises the Optimised Deprival Value (ODV) approach to valuation of the asset base[13] with the marginal approach, and the resulting emphasis on the relevant output increment, characteristic of economic decision analysis.[14]

TSLRIC (total service long run incremental cost) and TELRIC (total element long run incremental cost) are the main practical forms this approach takes in telecommunications. In essence, these concepts involve three elements: the relevant increment is defined as the total volume of the service at issue; the decision at issue is taken to be whether the increment is supplied over the longer run—so that the capital stock is variable and, hence, is included in the cost pool; and the concern is with the resources that would be needed to provide this service with current technology and management practices, as against those that may have been inherited from earlier periods.

---

[8] Solomons (1995: 42–51).

[9] Coase (1973: 97–132).

[10] Thomas (1969); Thomas (1974).

[11] Baumol, Koehn and Willig (1987): 16–21; Kaplan and Cooper (1998).

[12] A particularly useful taxonomy can be found in, Ma and Mathews (1979: 478).

[13] Whittington (1983: 131–136).

[14] Fabrycky, Thuesen and Verma (1998).

A number of strong claims are typically made in support of such an approach. First, it is argued that by focussing on the costs an efficient supplier would incur over the time period stretching out from the present, the approach sets aside the errors or distorted decisions the supplier may have made in the past and, hence, reflects the opportunity cost of the services to be provided. Second, these opportunity costs, if they are used to set the regulated supplier's revenue target, should provide an indicator of the income the supplier requires for the maintenance of operating capability (that is, service potential). Third, by focussing on the costs incurred as a result of supplying some increment of output, arbitrary cost allocations are avoided.

From an analytical point of view, these claims are over-stated. As a general matter, there is no meaningful sense in which replacement costs, even of a hypothetical efficient supplier, measure the opportunity cost of using existing assets.[15] Rather, analysis of replacement costs is merely capable of providing the answer to the following thought experiment: what resources would be required to replace the assets that now provide the entirety of the service if, for some reason, those assets disappeared?

It is not easy to give a strong normative interpretation to this thought experiment. Two related interpretations are nonetheless worth mentioning.

First, the answer to this thought experiment may provide an indicator of the stand-alone cost a consumer would face in opting out of the existing system. In a contestable market, no consumer (including a competitor purchasing the service as an intermediate input) or coalition of consumers could be charged more than its stand-alone cost. Hence, this indicator can be used to define a ceiling to the revenue that an incumbent supplier could secure in a contestable market.

Second, assume the regulator put out to tender a contract for the supply, on an indefinite basis, of the service at issue. The thought experiment set out above could be structured so as to provide an indicator of the greatest amount the regulator should expect to pay so as to make the incumbent indifferent between entering and not entering into such a contract.[16] Again, the cost measured in

---

[15] Bromwich (1977: 242–49).

[16] Note, however, that it will not do so if it does not allow the regulated supplier to recover its joint and common costs. As a result, the thought experiment needs to capture the stand-alone costs involved in providing the service, including in these the joint and common costs. Moreover, the costs measured in the thought experiment need to allow the maintenance of the financial capital of the supplier (as against solely providing for the maintenance of physical capital), Sterling (1982: 3–58). Whether or not they do so will depend on the determination of the cost of capital, on the depreciation policy adopted, and on whether costs include the option value associated with deferring investment.

this thought experiment suggests a ceiling price, rather than unambiguously defining a revenue requirement.

The first of these interpretations simulates competition 'in the market', while the second simulates competition 'for the market'. In each case, approaches based on forward-looking costing can be viewed as providing an indicator of the ceiling revenue requirement associated with the provision of a regulated service.

Seen in this light, estimates of forward-looking costs would seem to be of interest, though they could not be said to be determinative. However, as a practical matter, deriving such estimates involves a significant number of difficulties. As will be seen in the following section, these difficulties may be such as to reduce the usefulness of the resulting estimates severely.

III. Implementing Forward-Looking Costing Approaches

Given a decision to build a forward-looking cost model, nine key issues need to be faced. These are:

(1) determining the relevant increment;
(2) specifying the technology to be used to supply that increment;
(3) determining the time frame in which a network corresponding to that technology will be built;
(4) determining the base of existing assets and services to which this new network is to be added;
(5) specifying provisioning rules with respect to the capacity/demand balance;
(6) determining the appropriate level and time path of operating and maintenance outlays;
(7) identifying the level of indirect costs;
(8) determining the treatment of capital charges, including with respect to depreciation, the opportunity cost of capital and the cost of not deferring investment;
(9) validating the model through appropriate sensitivity testing, and determining confidence intervals around the estimates.

Once these issues have been addressed, further questions arise before the results can be used as a basis for charging. In particular, consideration needs to be given to:

(1) determining whether costs will be expressed with respect to a particular year or as a levelled amount—that is, as an annuity factor;

(2) translating these estimates into units useable for regulatory purposes—that is, taking the pool of costs and decomposing it into a cost per line, per peak call attempt, or per call duration.

These issues can, for the sake of simplicity, be roughly grouped under three broad headings: definition and design of the hypothetical network; assessment of the costs of that network; and interpretation of the results for regulatory purposes. Each of these is addressed below.

IV. Definition and Design of the Hypothetical Network

1. The Relevant Increment

A first step in constructing a forward looking cost model is to define the outputs being incremented—that is, to specify what it is that is being costed. This involves determining the service, or grouping of services, being incremented and the relevant volume of that increment. At least in an interconnection context, this typically centres on three questions. First, is the relevant increment only the service volume being supplied to one or more competitors, or does it include the volume the incumbent supplies to itself? Second, what base volume should be used in the modelling? And third, when this volume of services is being supplied, are other services being provided as well?

With respect to the first of these questions, it is apparent that an increment defined in terms of, say, the minutes of carriage supplied to one or more competitors will provide a very different answer compared to an increment defined in terms of the minutes of carriage supplied both to competitors and by the incumbent to itself. The 'competitor only' approach imputes to the competitor all of the scale economies involved in the service's provision. Any charge based on such a calculation can only be a floor price, and when the outputs of the incumbent and of competitors are direct substitutes, may well be below any sensible price floor.[17] As a result, it is not apparent that any normative implication can be drawn from analysing an increment so defined. Rather, it seems

---

[17] When the outputs are direct substitutes, the marginal cost to the incumbent of supplying interconnection includes the foregone revenue in the downstream market. If the downstream services are not priced at cost (because of the need to fund joint and common costs), (1) the incumbent would never use marginal resource costs as a floor price for the sale of interconnection services and (2) a regulator which required these to be used for that purpose would threaten the supplier's financial viability.

reasonable that the increment be defined in terms of the *total volume* of the service, including both sales to competitors and the incumbent's supply to itself. This total volume is, however, itself uncertain. In principle, a regulator seeking to replicate the outcomes associated with a contestable market should seek to cost the output level that would prevail in such a market (as against using the output level that happens to prevail in the 'real world'). Where prices are marked up above the contestable market benchmark, the actual output may be lower than the output level that should be costed. Using this lower level as the relevant increment will overstate costs whenever there are unexploited scale economies.

In practice, the difference between actual and hypothetical output will be small, at least in most mature networks. In these networks, access and local calls account for the largest share of the output to be modelled, and demand for these is extremely inelastic.[18] As a result, in the typical mature network, moving prices to the contestable market level will have little effect on the aggregate load, and hence on costs. It is, therefore, reasonable to use actual loads, and their projected growth, as the basis for determining the volume change being modelled.

Assuming the volume change is determined in this manner, there is still the issue of whether the increment only encompasses the service directly at issue. For example, in an interconnection context, the primary concern will typically be with originating and terminating PSTN access.[19] The relevant increment would then be the PSTN Customer Access Network, as well as the switching and transmission networks used to carry PSTN traffic to and from points of interconnection.[20]

---

[18] For example, it is reasonable to suppose that the price elasticity of demand in Australia is in the order of –0.05 for residential access, –0.06 for business access, and -0.06 for local calls (which are untimed). The elasticities may be slightly higher for corporate customers, as these face a broader range of substitution possibilities.

[19] The PSTN is the Public Switched Telecommunications Network. 'Originating and terminating PSTN access' refers to the provision of the facility of transporting calls between customer premises and the points of presence of the incumbent and/or competitors, as well as the actual conveyance of those calls between customer premises and these points of presence.

[20] The Customer Access Network (CAN) links customers' premises to points of traffic concentration, which may be either local exchanges or sub-units such as Remote Integrated Multiplexors and Remote Switching Units. The nodes at which the CAN terminates, together with the transport facilities linking these nodes to each other and to higher level exchanges (generally, trunk network exchanges), form the Inter-Exchange Network (IEN).

However, it might be argued that the facilities used by the PSTN are also used by other services, such as leased lines, and by other networks, such as the ISDN and the IN.[21] The services provided by these other networks and facilities, it is then argued, should also be included in the relevant increment so as to capture the cost sharing that occurs in the network. Reflecting this argument, the model built by NERA for the Australian Consumer and Competition Commission (the industry regulator) defines the relevant increment as originating and terminating PSTN access *and* originating and terminating ISDN access *and* leased line services.

It is difficult to know what to make of this approach. To begin with, it seems fairly arbitrary. Thus, the relevant increment, as NERA defined it in Australia, includes some services which share significant facilities with the PSTN but excludes others. At the same time, since costs now need to be distributed among the services sharing the facilities at issue, it re-introduces the allocation difficulties that an incremental cost standard was supposed to avoid. Unless the services are perfect substitutes, resolving these difficulties by apportioning costs on the basis of usage factors (as NERA does) is not economically defensible.[22] The resulting estimates cannot be given an economic interpretation either as a price ceiling or as a price floor. Rather, if the outcome of the exercise is to be interpreted as a price ceiling, then the relevant increment should be PSTN originating and terminating access, and that alone. Unfortunately, none of the major TSLRIC models take this approach.[23]

2. Specifying the Technology to be Used

Given the increment being modelled, the next task is to specify the technology by which it will be supplied. 'Technology' here is to be interpreted broadly, as comprising the facilities to be used and the manner in which they will be maintained and operated.

---

[21] The ISDN is the Integrated Services Digital Network, which is an end-to-end digital circuit-switched network that (in ETSI systems) provides capacity in bearer units of 64kbit/s. The IN is the Intelligent Network, which is a network that uses the signalling network to supply enhanced control capabilities to local and trunk exchanges.

[22] This is because the services will face different demand elasticities, and hence should bear a differing share of any joint and common costs: 'When economies or diseconomies of scale are present, both the state of demand and the structure of costs must be taken into account in the setting of efficient [access] prices' Sidak and Baumol (1994: 50).

[23] The major US and UK models include leased lines, but exclude ISDN and data networks. The Australian model is unique in including ISDN.

The major issue that arises in this respect is that of the extent and nature of optimisation. In practice, telecommunications networks are extremely complex systems linking many millions of terminal and intermediate nodes. Moreover, they are multi-purpose systems, comprised of inter-dependent but distinct sub-systems. Re-optimising an entire existing network would be an extremely demanding task—indeed, it is questionable whether the task could even be carried out to any acceptable level of accuracy. So as to make this complexity tractable, forward-looking cost models typically adopt three important simplifications.

First, they keep certain key features of the existing network constant. In particular, they usually assume that the location of local exchanges is not changed—that is, that the broad geography of local switching nodes is kept intact. For this reason, they are often referred to as 'scorched node' models (that is, models in which everything other than the location of the nodes is treated as scorched) as against 'scorched earth' models (in which the location of nodes is also treated as variable).

Second, rather than using the 'best available technology', they generally seek to embody the 'best technology in widespread use'. This reflects two considerations:

- To the extent to which the cost estimate is used to set a revenue cap for a carrier, modelling 'best available technology' would penalise carriers for not constantly adopting the most recent breakthrough. Such a standard seems unreasonable, and might well have a range of undesirable consequences.[24]
- No less importantly, the cost properties of recently developed technologies are only poorly known, and the optimisation tools available for modelling their application are often experimental. As a result, cost estimates for networks embodying such technologies would be highly sensitive to the precise assumptions made and would have very wide confidence intervals.[25]

Third, while the modelling is based on the assets corresponding to the 'best technology in widespread use', substantial parts of the rules according to which these assets are deployed and operated are not re-optimised. For example, it is usual to scale switching capacity by using Erlang processors that correspond to the conventional distribution of voice telephony. However, it is well known

---

[24] For example, a carrier which did develop and adopt a breakthrough would, under such a standard, not earn any innovator's rents.

[25] Ims (1997: 51–57).

that these do not do a good job of representing the traffic patterns and switching needs now emerging from the growing use of the Internet or more generally, of mixed voice/data networks.[26]

Combined, these assumptions mean that the networks embodied in 'forward-looking' cost models are not terribly forward-looking. They do not, in
fact, reflect the network that would be built today, were the assets used to provide existing services to disappear. Rather, they involve a limited optimisation
in which clearly obsolete vintages are scrapped in favour of the vintages more
recently placed into service. This makes it difficult to interpret the results as
reflecting the outcomes that would prevail under contestability.

The difficulties associated with either building the model or interpreting the
results are compounded when the service increment is defined too broadly. For
example, the NERA model in Australia involves some optimisation of the
PSTN, notably in terms of greater use of distributed multiplexing and switching. However, although it includes leased lines and ISDN in the service increment, no optimisation has been done of these services. The result is an uneasy
amalgam, in which a hypothetically re-engineered PSTN shares capacity with
the inherited leased line and ISDN services.

3. The Time Frame for Network Construction

Having specified the network facilities that need to be constructed, the next
task is to define the manner and timing of their construction. From a practical
point of view, there are very substantial cost differences between building a network 'in one bang' and building it over a long period of time.[27] The Australian
experience in telecommunications is that construction costs are highest for very
fast and very slow roll-out speeds, reflecting a mixture of factors that includes
the availability of skilled personnel, the cost of stock-piling materials and the
extent of volume discounts for aggregated purchases.

In practice, forward-looking cost models are generally based on build costs
that reflect the recent experience of network service providers. This implies that
they embody a relatively slow roll-out speed, characteristic of the pace of
replacement and expansion investment in mature networks. However, this
means, as a logical matter, that costs should include a substantial amount for

---

[26] Minoli (1993: 99).

[27] This point, and its implications for cost modelling, were emphasised by A. Alchian
in his masterly essay on 'Costs and Outputs', (1997: 273–300).

capitalised interest during construction. This is almost universally over-looked, adding to the difficulty involved in interpreting the results.

4. The Base of Existing Assets and Services

Whatever the time-frame adopted, the cost of building capacity to handle the relevant increment will clearly depend on the assumptions made about the base to which the increment is to be added. If other telecommunications services are being provided, or other assets which can be used already exist, costs will be lower than they would be for construction from scratch.

As a practical matter, it is unlikely that other telecommunications services would be provided in the absence of originating and terminating PSTN access. Moreover, even if they were, the asset base and resulting cost structure associated with their provision is difficult to model with any accuracy.[28] As a result, the best assumption that can be made is that the relevant increment is the first service to be provided.

Even so, there are still choices to be made as between modelling on a 'green-field' versus 'brownfield' basis. In brownfield modelling, conventionally used for systems such as railway networks, it is assumed that perpetual structures, such as embankments, landfills, tunnels and other corridor formation assets, do not need to be reproduced. In contrast, in greenfield models, all structures are modelled as needing replacement or reproduction. The cost differences between these modelling approaches can be very substantial.

The choice between these boils down to the treatment of sunk costs. As a matter of theory, forward looking cost models are intended to act 'as if' sunk costs did not exist. As a result, it seems inconsistent with the purpose to assume that some sunk costs (say, those associated with trenching) should be treated as sunk, while others (say, those associated with cabling) are not. Moreover, the line drawn between these would seem to be arbitrary, and would hence reduce the significance of the results.[29]

---

[28] For example, it is conceivable that leased lines would be provided in the absence of originating and terminating PSTN access. However, it is unlikely that they would be ducted, except in CBDs. Rather, more extensive use would be made of fixed radio technologies.

[29] Additionally, a regulator who mandates that certain costs are to be treated as sunk signals a risk that a similar writing-off of costs may be carried out in the future, perhaps with a wider coverage. This increases regulatory risk and hence will increase the required rate of return.

Consequently, it seems best to adopt consistently a greenfield approach. However, this has not always been the approach adopted. For example, the NERA model developed for the ACCC treats the existing stock of connections (that is, the cost associated with actually linking premises to the distribution network and activating service) as pre-existing, as well as assuming that all the links from the Network Termination Point to the Property Entry Point do not need to be costed. It is not apparent for what reason these network elements have been treated as sunk, while others are not.

5. Specifying Provisioning Rules and the Capacity/Demand Balance

In practice, networks are built to handle demand that varies over time according to a pattern that has both stationary and non-stationary elements. The former typically reflect the pattern of traffic over the time of day/day of week/ week of year, while the latter reflect long run changes in the structure and level of demand.

Given this variability, the efficient provision of network facilities involves building capacity that both handles peak demand at some reference date (say, in the year being modelled) and caters for continuing growth in demand. *The margin over average load provided to handle the peakiness of demand* should reflect a grade of service target (for example, in terms of how long customers may have to wait before securing a second line, or how many calls are blocked at peak). *The margin provided for growth* should reflect optimisation for a given degree of lumpiness of investment—as a general matter, it is more costly to make frequent additions to capacity than to provision somewhat ahead of demand.[30]

Forward-looking cost models can generally cater for the first of these needs. Thus, information on traffic distributions is used to dimension traffic-sensitive facilities such as multiplexers, exchanges and transmission paths to meet a specified grade of service targets. However, greater difficulties arise in providing for the continuing growth of demand.

Thus, none of the major models makes any attempt directly to model growth over time and on that basis minimise costs on an explicitly intertemporal basis. Rather, growth is typically handled by using the standard provisioning rules employed by major carriers and by adopting fill factors for

---

[30] For example, in designing a new network, it is generally cheaper to provide 2 pairs per anticipated year 1 service in operation than to have to add small pair gain systems so as to cope with increased demand some years down the track.

equipment that reflect a certain degree of sparing (that is, provision in excess of instantaneous demand). However, the standard provisioning rules and fill factors are generally designed to optimise the costs of incrementally expanding an existing network;[31] using them to capture the efficient structure of inter-temporal provision in a greenfields network is inappropriate.

V. Determining the Costs of that Network

1. The Level of Operating and Maintenance (O&M) Outlays

Given the design of the hypothetical replacement network, the cost of operating and maintaining it needs to be determined. This will generally differ from that of the existing network, as the asset base has changed, work practices may be subject to some degree of optimisation and input prices may also be varied.

In principle, the O&M outlays associated with the new network should be modelled explicitly. This can be done by examining O&M outlays in the carrier being modelled for the 'best in widespread use' assets, and then grossing these outlays up to reflect the prevalence of these assets in the hypothetical network. However, this assumes that these outlays reflect efficient work practices and input prices.

Whether this is viewed as a drawback depends on an assessment of the appropriate degree of optimisation. 'Inefficient' work practices or input prices above those paid elsewhere may simply reflect differing factor endowments and policy distortions across jurisdictions — for example, many materials costs are higher in Australia than in the United States because of differences in the structure and level of taxes. In other instances, they may reflect the extraction of monopoly rents by input suppliers, with consequent income transfers. In either case, it is by no means apparent that they are under the control of the network service provider. As a result, merely making the market in which that network provider operates contestable would not necessarily alter the level of these costs.[32] To the extent to which this is the case, they should not be changed in the calculation of costs for the hypothetical replacement network. Rather, the best option seems that proposed above — that is, to set O&M charges on the basis of the best in use in the carrier being modelled, taking account of likely productivity improvements genuinely within the operator's control.

---

[31] Carroll (1977); Freidenfelds (1981).

[32] Though it would arguably increase the pressure on the network service provider to achieve any efficiencies that were within its control.

What is done in practice can differ greatly from this recommendation. For example, the NERA model developed for the ACCC calculates O&M charges as a percentage of the total capital cost, based on estimates provided by various operators in Australia and NERA's experience elsewhere. However, this approach raises a number of problems, most of which were identified by NERA themselves in their assessment of the UK bottom-up model of BT's costs.

First, operating to capital cost ratios are, by way construction, specific to a particular mix of capital and operating expenditure and will, therefore, vary significantly among different operators.[33] Unless capital costs estimates and operating to capital cost ratios are estimated from the same source, as recommended above, then the results produced by applying operating to capital cost ratios will be misleading.

Even with the same level of efficiency, operating to capital cost ratios may differ between operators. At least to some extent, this reflects the trade-off that exists for operators between capital and O&M expenses. NERA identified a number of other reasons why the ratios may differ significantly. These include the different ways in which operators categorise their operating costs, different assumptions used by operators in their estimates of incremental costs of network components and different methods of splitting costs into network and retail components. Therefore, using an average ratio estimated across a number of operators will not be consistent with the choice of capital expenditure adopted in the model.

Second, the operating to capital cost ratios used by NERA are calculated for existing operators. In practice, operators' networks are not entirely new and the operating cost information that they submit will reflect the maintenance requirements of both new and old assets. This will mean that the operating cost information is not consistent with the annual capital cost which is estimated on a forward-looking, best-in-use basis.

2. The Level of Indirect Costs

The forward looking cost models being surveyed are essentially engineering models and do not pretend to measure the level of many indirect costs—going from those associated with personnel functions through to those of corporate

---

[33] In their review of the UK bottom-up model of BT's costs, NERA found a large degree of difference between BT and other operators for the estimated ratio of aggregate operating to capital cost for exchanges.

governance. However, it is apparent that these costs need to be factored into any estimate of the price ceiling associated with stand-alone supply.

Where indirect costs are causally related to the service increment, they should be modelled explicitly. For example, vehicle fleet costs should be related to the output being provided within the framework of an activity based costing model, and the extent of these costs required to provide the service increment determined. Where costs are not attributable, such as the costs associated with corporate governance, the actual costs incurred by the operator should be used (at least in the absence of tangible proof of inefficiency).

As a general matter, the costs being modelled in an interconnection setting are those of a wholesale service provider—that is, of an operator supplying PSTN terminating and originating access to competing retail service providers (including its own such operation) which then market services to end-customers. The indirect costs associated with the retailing function (such as advertising and promotion, end-user billing and end-user revenue collection) should therefore generally be excluded. However, this does not justify excluding *all* retail costs; rather, the only retail costs that should be excluded are those that a hypothetical wholesale service provider would avoid.

For example, the models universally assume that customers have been supplied with access lines, and hence can use these lines to place and receive traffic. This implies that the hypothetical wholesale service provider is carrying out the functions involved in the retail supply of access lines. The costs associated with these retail functions ought, therefore, to be included.

In short, it would seem desirable to (1) model indirect costs explicitly; and (2) include in these the retail costs the network service provider would not avoid when it supplies service to downstream competitors.

Practice often departs from these recommendations in significant respects. For example, there are a number of models in which indirect costs are determined by using ratios relative to direct costs. For example, in the model built for the ACCC, NERA estimated indirect capital and operating costs as a percentage of total direct network capital costs and total direct network operating costs, respectively. Data from the US, as well as data for BT, were used to construct these ratios to which two 'adjustments' were then made. First, the ratios were adjusted to take into account any differences in the Australian environment.[34] The relevance of the cost item to interconnection charges was then estimated and the figures were again 'adjusted' to ensure only relevant costs were

---

[34] In the NERA model only one environmental adjustment was made to the operating cost category titled 'Legal' which was adjusted downward by 50 per cent.

included. While NERA noted that these adjustments involved a degree of judgement, no indication was provided on how these judgements were made.

3. Reliance on these ratios is flawed for a number of reasons

First, the valuation base, according to which the ratio is calculated, may, and often does, differ from that being used in the model. Thus, in the NERA model referred to, the ratios for indirect capital costs were calculated using historical costs in the numerator; the assumption that this provides any indication of the 'right' level of outlays relative to assets valued at replacement cost seems entirely arbitrary.

Second, the ratios are typically calculated for each line item over a sample of operators—for example, by looking at the ratio of vehicle fleet expenses to network expenses for a range of US local exchange carriers. Some average of the values of this ratio in the sample is then taken as reflecting the appropriate level of this item of outlay. However, whether this is reasonable depends on the assumptions being made about the relation between the various items. If they are substitutes, that is, if greater expenditure in one category is associated, for an efficient operator, with lower expenditure in another, then taking averages across disparate carriers may be inappropriate as it would not capture these substitution effects.

Rather, the conventional approach in economics would be to use Stochastic Frontier Models or the non-parametric Data Envelopment Analysis method to estimate a production function, and then derive a reasonable configuration of the relevant costs from the function so estimated.

Last but by no means least, there is no obvious rationale for assuming that the ratios derived from one country (the United States) are applicable to another (Australia), even when these ratios are correctly measured. Rather, it is obvious that adjustments need to be made—but there is no simple or reliable way in which to do this. As a result, adjustments, when they are made, tend to be highly arbitrary, and undermine the credibility of the overall results.

It has, for example, been noted above that the NERA model developed for the ACCC makes an adjustment to US ratios for legal expenses, presumably on the basis that Australia is less litigious than the United States. The amount of the adjustment is not explained. However, NERA does not increase the estimate of vehicle fleet costs, despite the far stronger argument for doing so (Australian tariffs on vehicles being relatively high, increasing Australian prices for vehicles relative to those in the US).

4. The Level and Treatment of Capital Costs

Three complex issues are involved in determining the level of capital costs: the required rate of return on capital; the role of option values; and the treatment of depreciation.

For most purposes, it can be assumed that the required rate of return will be modelled using the framework of conventional finance theory. In this approach, a weighted average cost of capital is calculated, based on the estimated costs of debt, the cost of equity and the firm's optimal capital structure. Typically, the most contentious element in this process, the cost of equity, is derived through application of the Capital Asset Pricing Model (CAPM).

Without reviewing the merits and demerits of the CAPM, it is clear that it can only be used if the cash flows being discounted correspond to the model's assumptions. In particular, the expected future cash flows being discounted must come from a stationary normal distribution. Where there is some net present value to the option of delaying investment,[35] then the resulting expected cash flows need not be so distributed.[36] The problems this creates are especially acute when the CAPM is being applied in a context where regulation makes the distribution of risks one-sided (the firm can incur losses on some investments, while being prevented from earning supra-normal returns on others[37]).

In these circumstances, the expected cash flows need to be transformed to be consistent with the CAPM. This is best done by including, as an outlay in

---

[35] In practice, an investment in new assets can almost always be delayed. Furthermore, under some conditions, an investor will prefer to delay the project while demand evolves, because immediate investment incurs a risk that the project will fail to earn the cost of capital. If the expected value of delaying investment is positive, the ability to delay has the same advantages as a call option in finance. Because it is defined over a real asset, however, it is referred to as a real option. The value of a real option is simply the expected additional profit from delaying the investment. Equivalently, it is the expected value of the profit that would be lost by investing immediately. The source of this loss is the risk that the asset will be incapable of earning the cost of the capital employed. In other words, an appropriately calculated real option value is also the expected cost of the asset becoming stranded. See, Ergas and Small (1998).

[36] For option values to be positive, the earnings series must display first-order stochastic dominance. The series may be stationary but autocorrelated. The inconsistency with the underlying CAPM assumptions arise when the series is not stationary, Ehrhardt (1994: 212).

[37] The use of TSLRIC to set interconnection prices may itself have this effect. Thus, the regulated firm will take a loss whenever best-in-use equipment costs fall more rapidly than expected, but (if regulatory reviews are sufficiently frequent) will not earn supranormal profits when costs fall less rapidly than expected.

the cash flows being modelled, the actuarial value corresponding to the risk of stranding. In practice, this is equivalent to assuming that the firm needs to self-insure against the risks whose cash flow consequences are not normally distributed, and that the costs of this self-insurance need to be included in the relevant cost base.[38] Equivalently, the required grossing-up of outlays can be expressed as a mark-up over the weighted average cost of capital.[39]

Given corrected cash flows, the CAPM-based required rate of return can be used to measure the return on capital for a given value of assets. To obtain the total capital charge for the period, the depreciation charge must be added to this amount.

Economic, rather than accounting, depreciation should be used in this calculation. In essence, accounting depreciation allocates the historical cost of assets to the time periods in which these assets are used.[40] In contrast, economic depreciation measures, in each period, the holding cost associated with using that asset in that period, this cost being assessed as the change in the value of the asset in that period.[41]

Viewed in an *ex ante* sense, economic depreciation can be regarded as a contract between future periods that is established when a non-current asset is acquired.[42] The terms of this contract ensure that, if capacity can be adjusted in an accounting period, that period bears a charge equal to the *ex ante* (anticipated) change in replacement cost during that period, with the total charge across such periods 'adding up' to the capacity's original cost.[43] If capacity

---

[38] For example, under a TSLRIC rule, firms would need to insure against stranded asset risk, since (in a TSLRIC world) this is not a risk that investors can diversify. However, there is no market for third-party provided insurance against asset stranding, and any instruments which attempted to provide such insurance would be vulnerable to moral hazard. As a result of these transactions costs considerations, efficiency requires that firms self-insure.

[39] It is sometimes claimed that the same effect can be achieved by accelerating the depreciation schedule. Even in the circumstances in which this can be done (and it depends on accelerated depreciation increasing the net present value of the firm—which it does not always do), the correct amount of the acceleration needs to be determined by calculating the charge referred to in the text. In other words, the cost associated with the option value (the value of the ability to defer investment) needs to be computed explicitly.

[40] Peirson and Ramsey (1994).

[41] That is, the amount that must be added to the balance sheet in order to keep wealth intact Hulten and Wykoff (1996: 10–23)

[42] This view of economic depreciation as an implicit contract can be traced back to Ladelle in 1890, Brief (1967: 27–38).

[43] Note that the replacement concept must itself be interpreted in an *ex ante* sense: that is, replacement cost in the future as anticipated in the firm's optimal plan.

cannot be adjusted within accounting periods, then replacement costs are not relevant and the depreciation charge, while continuing to 'add up', is imputed to each period based on the asset's value-in-use.[44]

As a general matter, the pattern of charges generated by accounting depreciation need not be sustainable in a contestable market, even when changes in asset values are correctly anticipated.[45] As a result, it the *ex ante* concept of economic depreciation that should be used in forward-looking cost models.

In short, the return on capital should be calculated correcting the cash flows so as to make them consistent with the CAPM (if the cost of equity is being calculated on a CAPM basis); while the return of capital should be based on anticipated economic depreciation.

The practice of forward looking cost models departs substantially from these recommendations.

Thus, none of the major models explicitly corrects the level of cash flows before applying a CAPM-based weighted average cost of capital. As a result, they misstate, and probably understate, the return an investor would require to finance the facilities at issue.

At the same time, they do not use economic depreciation to calculate the return of capital. The main US models default to straight-line depreciation, as do the WIK model of the German network and the NERA model developed for the ACCC. A more complex approach has been adopted in the UK. In BT's top-down model, straight-line depreciation was used in addition to a factor to account for price changes which resulted in a slight forward tilting of the depreciation profile. In the initial version of the UK bottom-up model a tilted annuity method was used to allocate capital costs. In their assessment of these models NERA correctly concluded that the depreciation methods used would not provide a good approximation of economic depreciation. Subsequent to NERA's review, model developers estimated economic depreciation profiles for each of the main categories of assets in the bottom-up model so that the depreciation charge in each period would reflect economic depreciation. However, no change was made to the treatment of depreciation in the top-down model and the 1994/95 version of this model still uses straight-line rather than economic depreciation.

---

[44] Atkinson and Scott (1982: 19–42).
[45] Zajac (1995: 240–42); Panzar (1998).

5. Model Testing and Validation

Forward looking cost models are inevitably based on important simplifications. Typically, even in the most detailed models, crucial parameters are based on summary statistics derived from samples of complex distributions. For example, the highly detailed model developed by Bellcore of the costs of providing service in high-cost areas in Australia relies on a one per cent stratified sample to estimate summary statistics for loop length distributions.[46] Further uncertainties are introduced by the process of analysis, including, in terms of the assumptions made about such matters as the extent of trench sharing, the degree of sparing, the level of indirect costs and the pace and pattern of depreciation.

Given these uncertainties, the resulting estimates are no more than that— estimates. Before they can be relied on, some sense is needed of the likely margin of error.

In principle, the risk of error should be assessed using formal tools for model validation. In essence, this requires making explicit the confidence intervals associated with the sampling used to derive input data. It also requires testing the sensitivity of the outcomes to changes first, in the input data and second, in the key functional relations.

What is done in practice falls well short of this. For example, NERA, in its Report to the ACCC, carried out sensitivity tests by varying some individual parameters; however, it did so holding everything else in the model constant. This can only be justified when the parameters being varied are independent of those being held constant. While this is true for some parameters, a properly built model should have quite significant interdependencies. When this is the case, model validation requires that these linkages be accounted for in the sensitivity analysis.[47] This can be done through a Monte Carlo analysis that traces out the response plane of the estimate to changes in sets of input values and in functional relationships.

---

[46] According to the documentation, the goal was to divide PNLAs into sets based on cost drivers and then to measure the variability of the sample by selecting several ESAs from each set. Costs for each of the selected ESAs were to be estimated so the variance of the distribution of costs within each set and hence the required number of sample exchanges needed to achieve the desired level of precision could be calculated. Bellcore recommended a 95% confidence interval at 10% variance. The 1% sample actually used is intended to approximate the recommended Bellcore method.

[47] Thuesen and Fabryky (1993: 503).

When such an analysis is not carried out, the best that can be done is to gross up the estimate so as to account for the risk of error. Thus, in engineering economics, it is standard to use contingency factors which vary with the degree of project completion. For a typical major project—e.g. construction of a new port facility—it is assumed that the likely error range in the initial cost estimate (that is, a cost estimate made before 2 per cent of the project has been completed) is plus or minus 40 per cent. Investors funding such a project would generally require a contingency allowance of some 30 per cent to be added to costs—in other words, costs would be grossed up to 130 per cent of the original estimate to insure against the risk that that estimate was unsustainably low.

VI. Making Use of the Results

1. Levelisation and the Choice of a Reference Year

The result of the steps outlined above should be a stream of annual costs, consisting of year-on-year capital charges and expenses arising from operations and maintenance. This stream will start in year 1 (the first period in which the network is in operation) and stretch out over the network's useful life.[48]

As a general matter, the costs associated with each year will vary—that is, the values associated with year 1 will not be same as those in year 2, which in turn will differ from those in year 3 (and so on). As a result, the choice of which year is taken as a base will matter—in other words, the revenue ceiling arising from the estimate will be different depending on whether it is assumed that we are in year 1 (the network has just been built) or in year 10 (the network is now 10 years old).

This proposition—that the choice of reference year matters—is, at times, disputed on the basis of the following argument. Let us suppose that the regulator requires the capital charge to be calculated on a year 1 basis, namely, at the end of the first year. If we are in 1998, then the network was built in 1998. The capital charge will be the sum of economic depreciation over 1998 and the cost of capital on the average written down value of the assets in that year. Now assume that the regulator specifies that the capital charge should be calculated on a year 10 basis. Then, still in 1998, this means the network was built in 1988, and hence built at 1988 prices. With economic depreciation being applied, the annual capital charge today on a network built ten years ago should be no

---

[48] If the stream is truncated before that time, there will be a terminal value capitalising the stream of costs to be incurred subsequent to the end-date.

different from the annual charge today on a network built one year ago. As a result, the choice of reference year does not matter.

However, this argument is flawed. To see this, let us assume that the cost K of constructing a network falls at the constant rate α per annum. The relationship between the costs of constructing a network in 1988 and 1998 is, therefore, given by $K_{98} = K_{88}(1 - \alpha)^{10}$. Given a construction date, the connection between written down values in various years is simply $w_t = w_0(1 - \delta)^t$ and assuming that the rate[49] of depreciation is also constant at δ, we can, therefore, see that the 1998 capital charge for a network constructed in 1988 is:

$$C_{98,88} = (\delta + r)K_{88}(1 - \delta)^{10}$$

whereas the corresponding charge for a network constructed in 1998 is:

$$C_{98,98} = (\delta + r)K_{98}(1 - \delta)$$
$$= (\delta + r)K_{88}(1 - \delta)^9 (1 - \delta)$$

Thus, unless the rate of decline in construction costs α is exactly equal to the depreciation rate δ, the capital charge will be different for networks of different ages.

For the economic depreciation rate and the rate of decline in construction costs to be identical economic depreciation, would therefore, have to reflect technological obsolescence *only*. However, in practice, assets are replaced for a range of different reasons, including capacity constraints, physical deterioration and technological obsolescence. A depreciation method that is consistent with economically efficient decision making will take account of these replacement characteristics. Therefore, in addition to technological obsolescence, economic depreciation reflects physical deterioration and capacity constraints in which case today's annual capital charge on a network built ten years ago is likely to be substantially different from today's annual capital charge on a network built one year ago.[50]

An alternative to calculating the capital charge for a particular year is to levelise the capital charge such that its value is equal in each year of the asset's life. Adopting this approach, the annual capital charge would be calculated as:

---

[49] Note that the implied connection between d_t and δ is simply $d_t = \delta w_t$.

[50] A year 1 charge may also involve double counting. This is because the price of new capital goods usually include an element of pre-paid maintenance—that is, that they can be viewed as 'steady state' assets which have just had a comprehensive overhaul. If the maintenance costs typical for a steady state asset are added to the annualised cost of an entirely new asset, actual year 1 costs will be over-estimated.

$$C_l = \frac{r}{1-(1+r)^{-n}} \bullet \sum_{t=1}^{n} \frac{(\overline{w}_t \times r + d_t)}{(1+r)^t}$$

where C_l is the levelised capital charge;
r is the WACC;
n is the useful life of the asset;
w is the written down value of the asset; and
d is economic depreciation.

Unlike the year 1 approach, a levelised capital charge is consistent with the contestable market standard. In a contestable market in which long-term contracting could occur, a firm could only charge the year 1 price in year 1 if it could credibly commit itself to charging the year 2 price in year 2 and so on. Since any higher price would induce entry (by firms offering a levelised charge on a long-term contract basis), the firm would have to accept an expectation of price defined by the levelised charge.

The levelised charge, therefore, corresponds most closely to the thought experiment discussed at the outset—namely, how much revenue would the regulator need to commit to allowing the service provider to earn to make that firm indifferent to entering into an indefinite term contract for the supply of the services at issue? It consequently seems the most reasonable way of translating the estimated stream of costs into annual terms.[51]

Here, too, however, practice often departs from the approach that the theory suggests. In the UK, the bottom-up model annualises BT's estimated capital costs by simply taking the first year capital charge, even though substantial efforts were made to estimate economic depreciation profiles over the entire useful lives of each asset group. Similarly, in the model developed by NERA for the ACCC, the annual capital charge was calculated as the sum of depreciation and the cost of the capital in the first year of the network's life.

---

[51] The claim is sometimes made that use of the year 1 charge is desirable because (like accelerated depreciation) it provides some insurance against the regulator acting opportunistically. This argument is unconvincing. To begin with, with very long lived assets, use of the year 1 charge would only have a slight effect in terms of insuring against regulatory opportunism. As a result, the year 1 approach is a poor instrument for dealing with the problem. Rather, to the extent to which there is such a risk, it ought to be reflected in the weighted average cost of capital. If it is not, then it is the cost of capital that should be adjusted.

2. Unitisation

The main output of a TSLRIC model is an amount of costs—that is, a dollar total. This total amount can be viewed as the ceiling revenue requirement described above. In practice, this total is almost always re-expressed in more disaggregated terms, both as a series of sub-totals and ultimately as a cost per physical unit.

A typical first step in this respect is to decompose total direct costs into 'line related' and 'traffic related' costs, where the line-related costs are those that do not vary with traffic. There are two problems with what is done in this respect.

First, the purported allocations may bear little relation to cost sensitivities within the model at issue. For example, using the Hatfield model for seven US States, the percentage of the dominant local exchange carrier's total costs which is traffic sensitive can be calculated as ranging from 15.0% to 21.1% (see Table 1).[52]

However, increasing traffic by 30 per cent above the default level specified in the model increases total costs in each of these States by less than 1 per cent.

Table 1: Share of Traffic Sensitive Costs in Total Costs

Hatfield Model 5.0a	
State	Traffic Sensitive Costs
California	19.4%
Florida	17.1
Montana	18.4
New York	21.1
Georgia	15.0
Missouri	15.4
Maryland	17.9

---

[52] The percentage of total costs in the Hatfield model that is usage sensitive is estimated by assuming that all loop and switch port costs are NTS, and all remaining switch costs, all signalling, and all transport costs are TS. Note that the model computes the costs of the UNEs inclusive of attributed common and overhead costs, including the costs that are shared with the private line services provided by the network. However, dedicated transport has been excluded from the calculations reported.

The split between traffic and non-traffic sensitive costs, therefore, maps very poorly into incremental, and even less so, marginal, costs. As a result, using this split to set unit charges, 'as if' the split reflected cost causality, could be seriously distorting.

Secondly, decomposition into sub-totals creates issues about the allocation of common costs. Thus, in practice, costs do not fall neatly into 'traffic' and 'non-traffic' sensitive categories as line elements share many costs with traffic systems. As a result, there are substantial common costs between these component parts.

The standard practice is to distribute these common costs through a proportionate mark-up on the attributable costs. However, there is no obvious economic justification for this practice. References are, at times, made to Shapley values as being consistent with such an equi-proportionate mark-up.[53] However, it is not apparent why the Shapley value is the appropriate standard for this purpose. As with all cost-allocation rules based purely on costs, the Shapley value will not yield an economically efficient mark-up. No less importantly, there is no *a priori* reason to assume that the Shapley value is sustainable—that is, that the regulated firm could actually secure the revenue patterns and levels determined by the Shapley rule.[54] When by-pass is a possibility, the use of equi-proportionate mark-ups may result in revenue targets for each subcomponent that cannot be achieved. As with Fully Distributed Costs, the use of this allocation rule may, therefore, undermine the network providers' financial viability.

These issues of cost allocation are exacerbated by the allocation to subpools of indirect costs. Here, too, equi-proportionate mark-ups are generally used, raising the same issues as those discussed above.

Rather than such essentially arbitrary unitisations, it may be preferable simply to view the cost estimate generated by the models as an aggregate revenue cap. It would then be up to the network service provider to ensure that the relevant revenues did not exceed this cap, subject only to the constraint that the charges through which this is achieved are broadly competitively neutral.

---

[53] The Shapley value is a solution concept in cooperative games. Formulated loosely, it is the expected value of the pay-off to each player when the game is played an infinite number of times, so that each possible sequence of play is fairly represented.

[54] The Shapley value need not, in other words, be in the core of the cost allocation game. This is because it takes no account of the opt-out possibilities open to subcoalitions within the game.

VII. Conclusions

Properly constructed forward-looking cost models can be viewed as providing an indication of the revenue requirement associated with the provision of a regulated service. When the service at issue is modelled as including the joint and common costs of service provision, this amount defines a ceiling to the revenues a regulator would need to allow the network provider to earn. However, in the absence of special assumptions, replacement cost modelling will not provide more information than that.

Whether it even provides that information depends on the reliability of the estimates generated. The practice of forward-looking costing departs in many respects from the theory: as has been shown above, the models reviewed are littered with short cuts and assumptions that limit their validity. The authors of the models often justify these assumptions by asserting that each assumption's consequences are small. However, what matters is the cumulative error range the sequence of assumptions creates. With minor exceptions, the models at issue do not provide estimates of this range and in some cases cannot be used to do so.

It is well known that attempts to introduce forward-looking costing into statutory financial accounts have generally been unsuccessful because investors have had little confidence in the accuracy of the resulting estimates.[55] Regulators are of course better placed than individual investors to audit the information they require. Even so, there is a clear need for realism about the results of models such as those reviewed above, and for the results of these models to be compared with those of other approaches to determining regulatory revenue requirements.

---

[55] Thuesen and Fabryky (1993: 503).

V

*Herbert Hovenkamp**

Antitrust Remedies for 'Private Intellectual Property Bottlenecks'

I. Introduction

Many industry bottlenecks result from two interrelated necessities found in networked markets: interconnection and compatibility. Significantly, one can have both interconnection and compatibility without bottlenecks, and many joint ventures, particularly in the computer industry, are designed to facilitate both whilst maintaining the participants' status as viable, and sometimes even aggressive, competitors. Once bottlenecks exist, however, identifying the least costly way of getting rid of them can be extraordinarily difficult.

Bottlenecks based on intellectual property rights can differ significantly from those based on hard technology, and optimal remedies may differ too. Structural remedies are often difficult to manage in the case of hard technology bottlenecks, because sharing often works poorly, and because the division of facilities either imposes significant diseconomies of scale or fails to break up the monopoly. By contrast, intellectual property bottlenecks can often be broken up through the simple device of compulsory licensing.

Good examples of hardware bottlenecks are the hardware loop that continues to form the core of the local telephone companies' monopolies, and to which nearly all general access communications services must have interconnection access;[1] and the system of terminals, or gates, at airports. In many cases a single carrier, or sometimes two carriers, dominate the gates, and airfares are often significantly higher into and out of airports that are controlled by one or two carriers. The telecommunications loop is a facility that is very difficult to break up and make competitive, at least by court decree. The gate structure at airports could perhaps be broken up more easily should an appropriate antitrust violation be found.

---

* University of Iowa.
[1] By general access I mean services that wish to hook into the world-wide voice and data interconnection network. Of course, one can have such things as 'two way' or even many party communications systems via radio, but if general access is desired, at some point one must be hooked into the loop, or at least hooked into someone else who is hooked into the loop.

The most prominent example of a software bottleneck today is Microsoft, whose market dominance rests entirely on its intellectual property rights in the Windows name and software, plus complementary rights. Intel can also be regarded as a bottleneck. According to the FTC's 1998 antitrust complaint against that firm,[2] Intel accounts for approximately 80 percent of a worldwide market for general purpose computer processors, and has held that position for more than five years. Although technologically complex production facilities and expertise certainly make entry barriers into this market high, this is undoubtedly not the true source of Intel's control, since many other firms either have, or could readily obtain, production capability. Instead, the key to Intel's market dominance is its numerous patents covering the various aspects of its microprocessor and related technology.

While the breaking up of intellectual property bottlenecks poses fewer management problems than the dissolution of hardware bottlenecks, the difficulties should not be underestimated. Furthermore, in the United States neither the Patent nor Copyright statutes provide any basis for compulsory licensing against the intellectual property owner who has not 'misused' his rights.[3] The whole point of the intellectual property grant is to create a right not to share the article, process, or expression protected by it, and the courts have consistently recognised that right.[4] Contrary formulations, such as the

---

[2] In *re Intel Corp.*, FTC Docket #9288 (June 8, 1998).

[3] On 'misuse', see Areeda and Hovenkamp (1996: paras. 704–705, 709); Hovenkamp (1998: para. 1803e) (exclusive dealing).

[4] See *Cygnus Therapeutic Sys.* v *Alza Corp.*, 92 F.3d 1153, 1160 (Fed. Cir. 1996) (patentee 'under no obligation to license;' antitrust claim dismissed); *Genentech* v *Eli Lilly & Co.*, 998 F.2d 931, 949 (Fed. Cir. 1993), cert. denied, 510 U.S. 1140 (1994) (same; patentee's 'right to select its licensees, to grant exclusive or non-exclusive licenses or to sue for infringement and the pursuit of optimum royalty income, are not of themselves acts in restraint of trade'); *Data General Corp.* v *Grumman Systems Support Corp.*, 36 F.3d 1147 (1st Cir. 1994); *Patlex Corp.* v *Mossinghoff*, 758 F.2d 594, 599–600 (Fed. Cir.), modified on other grounds, 771 F.2d 480 (Fed. Cir. 1985); *Axis* v *Micafil*, 870 F.2d 1105 (9th Cir.), cert. denied, 493 U.S. 823 (1989) (no antitrust claim for refusal to license patents); *USM Corp.* v *SPS Techs.*, 694 F.2d 505, 513 (9th Cir. 1982), cert. denied, 462 U.S. 1107 (1983) (may license 'only on such terms as [the patentee] sees fit'); *United States* v *Studiengesellschaft Kohle, m.b.H.*, 670 F.2d 1122, 1131 (D.C.Cir. 1981) (finding no cases imposing a duty to license, and refusing to create one); *W.L. Gore & Assocs.* v *Carlisle Corp.*, 529 F.2d 614, 623 (3d Cir. 1976) (lawful for patentee to charge any royalty it pleased, since it could also refuse to license altogether); *Boston Scientific Co.* v *Schneider*, 1997 W.L. 677855 (D.Mass. 1997) (while concerted agreement among patentees to refuse to license might be unlawful, unilateral refusal is not; here, no allegation that defendant patentees who had entered cross-licensing agreement had actually agreed with each other not to license to third parties); *Wahpeton Canvas Co.* v *Bremer*,

one given in the Ninth Circuit's 1997 Kodak decision,[5] linking compulsory licensing to the patentee's state of mind, are not only incapable of administration, but are also inconsistent with a recent Supreme Court opinion,[6] and with the express language in the Patent Act, which provides that:

> No patent owner otherwise entitled to relief for infringement . . . of a patent shall be denied relief or deemed guilty of misuse or illegal extension of the patent right by reason of [their] refusal to license or use any rights to the patent.[7]

Furthermore, the Ninth Circuit's decision rests on a serious misunderstanding of the nature of the patent grant. The court reasoned that a patent must be understood as creating a protected right in a single market, but not in two. In this case, the patents covered various parts installed in Kodak brand photocopiers, and Kodak was refusing to sell these parts to independent repair technicians or to license to them copyrighted diagnostics software to identify copy machine problems. The court concluded that if Kodak's subjective intent was to protect its intellectual property rights in parts and diagnostic software, then the intellectual property regime protected Kodak from antitrust liability. But if its motive in refusing to sell the parts and software was to create a monopoly in the service market, then it had a duty to license which could be enforced via the Sherman Act.

---

958 F.supp. 1347 (N.D.Ia 1997) (summary judgment for patentee who selectively refused to sell patented aftermarket parts); *Crucible* v *Stora Kopparbergs Bergslags AB*, 701 f.supp. 1157, 1162 (W.D.Pa. 1988) (refusal to license lawfully acquired patents cannot be antitrust violation); *G.A.F. Corp.* v *Eastman Kodak Co.*, 519 F.Supp. 1203, 1233 (S.D.N.Y. 1981) (unilateral refusal to license lawful); *Gates Learjet Corp.* v *Magnasync Craig Corp.,* 339 F.Supp. 587, 601 (D.Colo. 1972) ('A patentee need not license anyone'). The copyright cases are similar: *Tricom* v *Electronic Data Systems Corp.*, 902 F.supp. 741, 743 (E.D.Mi. 1995) (owner of copyrighted software may not be compelled to license); *Advanced Computer Services* v *MAI Sys. Corp.*, 845 F.Supp. 356 (E.D. Va. 1994) (unilateral copyright licensing policies cannot be antitrust violation); *Corsearch* v *Thomson & Thomson*, 792 F.Supp. 305, 322 (S.D.N.Y. 1992) ('Under the copyright laws, the copyright owner has a right to license the use of its intellectual property and to terminate or limit that use in such manner as it deems appropriate. . . .').

[5] *Image Technical Services* v *Eastman Kodak Co.*, 125 F.3d 1195 (9th Cir. 1997), cert. denied, 118 S.Ct. 1560 (1998).

[6] *Professional Real Estate Investors* v *Columbia Pictures Indus.*, 508 U.S. 49 (1993) (right of copyright owner to enforce its claim in court depends on objective validity of copyright claim, not on anti-competitive state of mind).

[7] 35 U.S.C. §271(d).

A subsequent decision in a case brought against Xerox[8] expressed far greater familiarity with the nature of a patent grant:[9]

The scope of a 'patent monopoly' is defined by the claims of the patent, not by the limits of what a court determines is the most analogous antitrust market.

We believe that the Ninth Circuit in Kodak, in reaching its conclusion, implicitly assumed that a single patent can create, at most, a single 'inherent' economic monopoly.[10] In the case of Kodak, the Supreme Court certainly did not reach this conclusion but stated that it 'has held many times that power gained through some natural and legal advantage such as a patent, copyright, or business acumen can give rise to [antitrust] liability if 'a seller exploits his dominant position in one market to expand his empire into the next [market].'[11] The Court's statement is simply not applicable where a patent holder, exercising his unilateral right to refuse to license or use his invention, acquires a monopoly in two separate relevant antitrust markets. There is no unlawful leveraging of monopoly power when a patent holder merely exercises his or her rights inherent in the patent grant. In other words, to the extent Xerox gained its monopoly power in any market by unilaterally refusing to license its patents, such conduct is permissible under the antitrust laws. Xerox's legal right to exclude ISOs in the service markets from using Xerox's patented inventions arose from its patents, not from an unlawful leveraging of its monopoly power in the parts market.

Patents only claim inventions. Because each use of that invention may be prevented by the patent holder, the patent may have some anti-competitive effect in each market in which it is used or not used. The patent statute expressly grants patent holders the right to exclude others from manufacturing, selling, or using their inventions.[12] Manufacturing, retail, and service markets all fall within this statutory grant of power to patent holders. Thus, Congress, by enacting the patent statute, apparently contemplated that a single patent could implicate more than one market.

The reward for a patented invention is the right to exploit the entire field of the 'invention', and not the right to exploit the single most analogous antitrust market.

---

[8] *Independent Service Organisations Antitrust Litigation*, 964 F.Supp. 1454, 1479 (D. Kan. 1997), 1997 W.L. 805237 (D. Kan. 1997).

[9] Citing several decisions, including *Dawson Chem. Co.* v *Rohm & Haas*, 448 U.S. 176, 221 (1980) ('[T]he boundary of a patent monopoly is to be limited by the literal scope of the patent claims.

[10] Citing *Kodak*, n. 5, 125 F.3d at 1215–16.

[11] Quoting *Eastman Kodak Co.* v *Image Tech,. Servs.*, 504 U.S., 451, 479 n. 29 (1992), which was in turn quoting *Times-Picayune Pub. Co.* v *United States*, 345 U.S. 594, 611 (1953).

[12] Citing and quoting 35 U.S.C. ss. 154, 271(d).

Setting aside the Ninth Circuit's misunderstanding of patents, judicial management of compulsory licensing claims under the Ninth Circuit's test would create a litigation nightmare, particularly under the United States jury system. The fact finder would effectively be asked to consider whether, in refusing to license a patented article such as an aftermarket part, the defendant's 'intention' was to protect its intellectual property right in the part or to exclude others from servicing Kodak photocopiers. For example, if a firm refused to license its copyrighted (or patented) diagnostics software to others, that refusal is permissible if the firm's intent is to protect any monopoly it might have in the diagnostics software market. But it is not permissible if the firm's intent is to create or maintain a monopoly in the servicing market. This question is not even coherent, if only because the only reason anyone would want diagnostics software for a particular machine would be to analyse problems and conduct repairs on the machine. Presumably, Kodak could lawfully refuse to license its software or aftermarket parts to the actual owners of its photocopiers, because then no service market would be threatened, but no one would ever want to refuse to license aftermarket parts to one's own primary market customers.

Notwithstanding the inadequacies of the Kodak formulation, there are cases in which antitrust can legitimately be brought to bear on intellectual property bottlenecks. The prerequisites are that:

(1) market dominance requirements must be taken seriously or the intellectual property owner must have engaged in a 'naked' restraint of trade not requiring proof of power;
(2) the challenged conduct must be something that is not authorised by the intellectual property provisions and it must constitute a substantial antitrust violation;
(3) with the first two conditions established, the antitrust remedy should be tailored so as to further innovation, or at least not restrain it unnecessarily.

II. Dominance Requirements Must be Taken Seriously

Effective identification of market dominance in the United States is hampered by the combination of private antitrust enforcement, jury trials, and judges who are poorly trained in economics or antitrust and willing to give too much credence to strained or idiosyncratic theories about market power. The result is that we have so many decisions identifying firms as market dominating when in fact they are not, that courts are invited to compensate by issuing anaemic forms of relief. The result is that when a truly market dominating firm (or joint venture) comes along, the same rather anaemic remedies are applied.

The Kodak case once again provides an example. Kodak produced some 22 percent of the market's photocopiers (the dominant firm is Xerox), but the Supreme Court had already held in 1992 that a firm such as Kodak could be found to have market power in its own aftermarket parts *vis-à-vis* consumers who are 'locked in' by their previous purchase of a Kodak photocopier. These consumers cannot readily switch to another brand merely to avoid high after-market prices. According to the Supreme Court, this allows the primary market manufacturer to take advantage of the fact that some customers are poorly informed about aftermarket prices and trade the gains from higher prices *vis-à-vis* these poorly informed customers against the losses that accrue when well-informed customers decide not to buy a Kodak copier because of high repair part prices.[13]

Whatever one may think of the merits of this argument,[14] the Ninth Circuit then seriously compounded the error by confusing substitutes and complements. It held that a single relevant market could exist for 'Kodak parts', even though the parts themselves are not interchangeable, reasoning:

> The 'commercial reality' faced by service providers and equipment owners is that a service provider must have ready access to all parts to compete in the service market. As the relevant market for service 'from the Kodak equipment owner's perspective is composed of only those companies that service Kodak machines', the relevant market for parts from the equipment owners' and service providers' perspective is composed of 'all parts' that are designed to meet Kodak photocopier and micrographics equipment specifications.[15]

It is certainly a 'commercial reality' that a service provider needs 'all the parts'—just as a driver needs both a car and petrol, a computer user needs both hardware and software, and cooling requires both a refrigerator and electricity. But that hardly creates an 'car/petrol' market, a 'computer/software' market or a 'refrigerator/electricity' market. Indeed, when we say that four shoe sellers located in the same area are in the same 'market' it is manifestly not because the shoe buyer must purchase shoes from all four of them. Rather, it is

---

[13] *Kodak*, 504 U.S. 451 (1992).
[14] For my own criticisms, see Hovenkamp and Areeda (1996: n. 3, para. 1740); and Hovenkamp (1993).
[15] *Kodak*, n. 5, 125 F.3d at 1203.

because the buyer need purchase shoes from only one of them, and this forces the sellers to compete on price and other elements.

More seriously, while the price of goods in the same market move in the same direction (every farmer's wheat, or every refiner's petrol), the prices of complements move in opposite directions. For example, less petrol will be consumed in response to increased petrol prices, leading to less car use. This will reduce the demand for cars, whose price will then fall. Or in response to a refrigerator price increase people will use them less, thus using less electricity and reducing the demand for it.

Because it confused complements and substitutes, thereby creating a 'relevant market' of complementary goods, there was never any fact finding that could be taken seriously that Kodak had significant market power in any particular part, whether patented or unpatented.[16] This effectively meant that the Ninth Circuit imposed compulsory licensing on a non-monopolist.

The court then exacerbated the problem by holding, without any analysis of the problem, that once a relevant market had been defined, the duty to deal extends to everything within that market, and not simply to things that are not capable of being duplicated or are not readily available from other sources. For example, among the 5000 parts that Kodak used in a photocopier were a small number that were patented and technologically sophisticated. The great majority consisted of such things as a flat glass plate, nuts, bolts, washers, wires, metal doors, wheels, handles and other common products. Some of these were 'off the shelf' items that could be purchased from numerous alternative suppliers. Some could be readily duplicated by any metal or glass shop. The duty to deal was found to extend to all.

While the court did not rely on the 'essential facility' doctrine, its compulsory dealing order went far beyond even the most aggressive essential facility decisions, depriving the word 'essential' of any meaning. The most far-reaching Supreme Court decision prior Kodak was Aspen Skiing.[17] In that decision the relevant market had been defined as 'downhill skiing in Aspen, Colorado.' The inputs into that market would presumably include ski slopes, a ski lodge, chair lifts, a shop that sells or rents equipment, instruction, and

---

[16] Even in this idiosyncratically engineered market of non-substitutable goods, the court was able to get Kodak's market share up to 55 percent only by aggregating parts that Kodak made with parts that were made for it under contract by other firms, and the fact that Kodak 'discouraged' some of its suppliers from selling to independents. Apparently realising that this was scant evidence of monopoly power, the court hastened to add that it was sufficient for an attempt to monopolise claim (125 F.3d at 1207).

[17] *Aspen Skiing Co.* v *Aspen Highlands Skiing Corp.*, 472 U.S. 585 (1985). See (Areeda and Hovenkamp 1996: para. 772).

the like. The plaintiff in Aspen was only requesting the right to continue participation in a marketing and promotion joint venture. But under the Kodak reasoning the plaintiff could just as well have requested that the defendant share all of its inputs except labour, whether or not these inputs were available from alternative sources or could be created by the plaintiff itself.

When the dominance question is handled so ineptly, courts end up treating truly dominant and non-dominant holders of intellectual property rights in exactly the same fashion. The result is to make them less inclined to do anything of significance. Instead, bottlenecks need to be defined with much greater care, and if that is done, only a small number of firms will pass the test. However, once the bottleneck is properly defined, close scrutiny over conduct is in order, and aggressive remedies are appropriate when a significant violation is found.

III. 'Essential Facility' and Other 'No Fault' Approaches Rejected

As developed under United States law, the essential facility doctrine would require a firm to provide access under the following, rigorously defined circumstances:

(1) the claimed essential facility must be an 'essential' input for production in the market for which access is claimed;
(2) the claimed facility must be practicably incapable of duplication and have no adequate substitutes under existing technology;
(3) a *sine qua non* for the first two conditions is that the facility must dominate or identify a properly defined relevant antitrust market;
(4) sharing of the facility must be technologically feasible and must not strain the facility's capacity;
(5) the firm requesting access must be a competitor at either the primary or else in a vertically related market.[18]

As defined, the essential facility doctrine comes as close as United States antitrust law ever comes to a doctrine of 'no fault' monopoly—that is, it condemns the mere refusal to share a legally owned facility, notwithstanding a strong common law tradition that permits the owners of property to refuse to share it with others.

One of the most serious problems with the essential facility doctrine is that

---

[18] For full development of the doctrine under United States antitrust law, see Areeda and Hovenkamp (1996: paras. 771–74).

in the absence of judicial control of price and terms of sharing the defendant[19] compelled to share will charge the monopoly price. The result is that two or more persons will have access to the bottleneck, but throughput will be no larger than prior to sharing, prices will be no lower, and thus consumers will not be better off.[20]

As a result, sharing orders must always be coupled with orders administering the terms of sale. This can take the form of price regulation, non-discrimination provisions,[21] royalty-free licensing, and the like. While in a proper case a United States Federal Court is capable of administering a non-discrimination rule or compelling royalty-free licensing, it is certainly not capable of administering prices. For that reason, the essential facility doctrine should generally be limited to situations where some other agency or disinterested agent is available to determine the price and terms of the sharing.[22] Antitrust's purpose is to seek out 'market' solutions that restore competition to the degree possible. A decree such as the one in the Ninth Circuit's Kodak case is anti-competitive because it destroys competitive incentives to produce things that are readily capable of being produced under competitive conditions. That is to say, the goal of the antitrust laws should be to achieve the competitive provision of aftermarket parts insofar as possible. It should not be to turn a firm such as Kodak into a price regulated utility. If 'regulatory' solutions are necessary, they generally fall outside of antitrust's domain, although antitrust can be of some assistance in controlling residual, or unregulated, conduct on the part of the regulated firm.

Another significant problem in using the essential facility doctrine as an antitrust vehicle when the defendant has substantial intellectual property rights is that the intellectual property statutes expressly permit refusals to license. Once again, it must be borne in mind that the essential facility doctrine is a kind of 'no fault' antitrust provision: it deduces the antitrust obligation to share entirely from the structural characteristics of the facility. In the typical case involving property that does not enjoy intellectual property protection the essential facility doctrine serves to abrogate the common law rule ordinarily applied in the United States that a firm may deal or refuse to deal without

---

[19] This paper uses the term 'defendant' to describe the firm whose conduct is in question, even though it is purely hypothetical or has not been sued

[20] See Areeda and Hovenkamp (1996: para.771b).

[21] In *Kodak*, the Ninth Circuit required the defendant to sell its parts at the same price charged to a large buyer that Kodak had already engaged to take over its repair business (*Kodak*, n. 5, 125 F.3d at 1227).

[22] Areeda and Hovenkamp (1996: paras. 771c, 772).

giving its reasons for doing so. The federal antitrust laws naturally pre-empt inconsistent conclusions that might be reached by common law. But in the case of patents and copyrights, the source of the right to refuse to deal are the federal Patent and Copyright Acts themselves, which expressly permit intellectual property owners to refuse to deal.

A recent decision illustrating the problem is *Intergraph* v *Intel*.[23] Without discussing the Patent Act at all, the District Court declared that Intel's advanced computer processors and related technology were essential facilities, and issued a preliminary injunction compelling Intel to continue to license this technology to the plaintiff. In assessing this requirement the Court noted that Intel's refusal to share its technology with downstream rivals such as Intergraph imposed a 'severe handicap' upon such companies, and that '[r]easonable and timely access to critical business information that is necessary to compete is an essential facility'.[24] The Court then concluded that Intel's refusal to supply advanced CPUs and essential technical information to Intergraph was likely to violate Section 2 of the Sherman Act, because they are not available from alternative sources and cannot be feasibly duplicated, and because competitors cannot effectively compete in the relevant markets without access to them. Moreover, the court concluded that Intel has no legitimate business reason to refuse to deal with Intergraph.

But all of this appears to be inconsistent with the provisions of the Patent Act quoted previously entitling the patentee to refuse to license its product, irrespective of whether or not the product is available from alternative sources and essential to competition, and without giving any justification whatsoever. The court apparently concluded that the Patent Act's right not to license only applied to patents that could readily be duplicated and protected only those refusals to license that were not supported by a 'legitimate business reason.'

Indeed, the court's only mention of patents was in its conclusion that Intel's ownership of patents in CPUs 'does not confer upon it a privilege or immunity to violate the antitrust laws',[25] and that '[a] monopolist cannot use the pretext of protecting intellectual property in order to violate the antitrust laws'.[26] Of course, these rather generic assertions of policy state the obvious point that one can use patents to violate the antitrust laws—for example, by filing baseless

---

[23] *Intergraph Corp.* v *Intel Corp.*, 3 F.Supp.2d 1255, (N.D.Ala. April 10 1998): rev'd F. 3d (Fed Cir 1999).

[24] *Ibid,* citing *Bellsouth Adver. & Publ'g Corp.* v *Donnelley Info. Publ'g*, 719 F.Supp. 1551, 1566 (S.D.Fla.1988), aff'd, 933 F.2d 952 (11th Cir. 1991).

[25] *Intergraph,* see n.23.

[26] *Ibid,* citing the Ninth Circuit Kodak decision, 125 F.3d at 1218–1219.

patent infringement suits,[27] or by various licensing practices that are not authorised by the Patent Act, such as the tying of non-patented goods,[28] the attempt to use contracts to extend royalty periods beyond the patent's expiration date,[29] and perhaps a few other practices.

But a mere refusal to license a patent, when unaccompanied by any of these unauthorised practices, must be regarded as statutorily protected. This means that if a broader duty to license must be assessed in the case of 'essential', or 'market dominating' patents, that duty must be declared by Congress. The United States Patent Act is a frequently amended statute, and Congress has been quite willing to tinker with it in order to expand or contract its protections. Indeed, the strong refusal to license language stated in §271(d) of the Patent Act was added in 1988.

In any event, the essential facility conclusion stated by the Intergraph court was completely unnecessary, because Intel had (according to the complaint as well as one subsequently filed by the Federal Trade Commission)[30] misused its patent rights. In this case Intel badly wanted to have access to patented technology for a reduced instruction set (RISC) microprocessor developed by the plaintiff. It conditioned further sales of its own patented technology to Intergraph on Intergraph's willingness to give Intel a royalty free license in Intergraph's RISC technology. As the District Court noted, this was a claim of reciprocity—generally analogised to tying,[31] and unlawful when the defendant has market dominance, as Intel very likely does, and when not supported by a legitimate business justification.[32] In any event, the Appellate Court properly reversed the District Court.

IV. 'Misuse' Defined by Antitrust Principles and not Authorised by Patent or Copyright Statute

The significance of the requirement of patent or copyright 'misuse'—an anticompetitive act that is not expressly sanctioned by the relevant statute—is that the Patent and Copyright Acts grant only a limited power to exclude. Were it

---

[27] See, Areeda and Hovenkamp (1996: par 709).

[28] See, Areeda and Hovenkamp (1996: para. 1782).

[29] *Ibid,* para. 1782c.

[30] See, n. 23.

[31] See, Areeda and Hovenkamp (1996: paras. 1775–1779).

[32] See, *Brokerage Concepts* v U.S. *Healthcare,* 140 F.3d 494 (3d Cir. 1998) (concluding that reciprocity ought to be illegal *per se* where market power requirements are met, but finding insufficient power in this case).

not for the intellectual property provisions, firms would be able to copy and sell the inventions or expressions of others without penalty. When the patentee or copyright holder simply asserts its rights as granted to it under those statutes, then the owner of the right is protected from copying as well as from liability under the antitrust laws or a conflicting state law.

But once the intellectual property holder asserts an exclusionary power that is not protected by the Patent or Copyright Act, or commits a potentially anti-competitive act that those statutes do not authorise, then the firm loses the protection of those provisions. In the presence of sufficient power or a 'naked' restraint not requiring power, antitrust can be brought to bear.

In determining whether anti-competitive 'misuse' exists, we suggest the following set of queries. Is the practice under examination, narrowly defined, explicitly authorised by the Patent or Copyright Act? If so, antitrust can proceed no further.[33] If the practice is not expressly authorised, then (a) does the patentee or copyright holder have significant market power in the market(s) affected by the challenged restraint; or (b) is the restraint at issue a 'naked' one not requiring a power inquiry. If the answer to both questions is no, then antitrust has no role to play. Examples of restraints requiring proof of power are the bringing of unjustified patent infringement suits, where the improperly brought suit establishes the conduct element of the monopolisation claim, but power must still be shown;[34] or, tying, reciprocity and other practices that are not expressly permitted by the Patent Act and that can be found unlawful under the Sherman Act.[35] An example of a 'naked' restraint not requiring proof of power is market division, such as is alleged in the Antitrust Division's complaint against Microsoft—namely, that Microsoft propose to Netscape

---

[33] This was one of the most significant errors of the Kodak decision, n. 5, which condemned under the antitrust laws a practice (refusal to licence) expressly authorised by Section 271(d) of the Patent Act..

[34] See Areeda and Hovenkamp (1996: para. 208).

[35] The arrangement can be condemned. See Areeda and Hovenkamp (996: n 3, at Chapter 17C). Furthermore, the US Patent Act makes this requirement explicit where the tying product is patented. See, 35 U.S.C. §271(d). No patent owner otherwise entitled to relief for infringement or contributory infringement of a patent shall be denied relief or deemed guilty of misuse or illegal extension of the patent right by reason of his having done one or more of the following: . . . conditioned the license of any rights to the patent or the sale of the patented product on the acquisition of a license to rights in another patent or purchase of a separate product, unless, in view of the circumstances, the patent owner has market power in the relevant market for the patent or patented product on which the license or sale is conditioned.

that MS develop a web browsers only for Windows machines, while Netscape develop its browser only for non-Windows machines.[36]

V. Antitrust Remedies

1. Preferred Goal is Destruction of Monopoly or Bottleneck

Once a monopolist, or dominant firm, has committed a substantial antitrust violation the optimal solution is to break up the monopoly and make the market structurally more competitive without losing any of the efficiencies made possible by the monopolist's size and scope. Such remedies are difficult to fashion, and due regard must be given to two possible pitfalls. First, many monopolists owe their size to significant economies of scale or scope, and breaking up the monopoly in the wrong way could produce significant diseconomies. In such cases the welfare losses from small scale production could easily exceed any gains from increased competition.[37]

Second, any judicially created structural remedy must break up the monopoly and not merely separate two monopolies from each other or the monopoly from non-monopolised elements. For example, if Microsoft was found to have abused its dominant position in the Windows 98 platform by tying its web browser, in which it does not have a monopoly, it would do little good to force Microsoft to divest its browser. It would still retain the Windows monopoly. By way of illustration, in its 1966 *Grinnell* decision the US Supreme Court condemned the defendant's monopoly of hard-wired security systems in which fire, entry and other alarms were connected to a central station. The defendant held a dominant position in such systems in several United States cities, and the relief forced the defendant to sell the systems in some cities whilst retaining them in others.[38] But such relief did nothing to reduce monopoly power in any

---

[36] See, Complaint, *United States* v *Microsoft* (D.D.C., filed May 18 1998).

[37] If, for example, the monopolist's price was 25 percent above its costs, but breaking it up imposed costs of 40 percent, then the post-breakup competitive price would be higher than the pre-breakup monopoly price, even assuming that the post-breakup firms behaved perfectly competitively.

[38] The premise of the relief was the conclusion—almost certainly factually incorrect—that the relevant market was nation-wide rather than city-by-city. *United States* v *Grinnell*, 384 U.S. 563 (1966). Subsequently the lower court (Wyzanski, J.) ordered Grinnell to spin off its holdings in some cities while retaining others. See *Grinnell*, 495 F.2d 448, 452 (2d Cir. 1974) (describing District Court's divestiture decree). See also Grinnell, 384 U.S. at 590 (Fortas, J., dissenting, objecting to the way the firm was to be broken up); and see (Areeda and Hovenkamp 1996: 653c2).

single city. It simply created a situation where the defendant continued to own their monopolies in some cities, while others acquired monopolies in other cities.

While forcing Microsoft to divest Internet Explorer does deny Microsoft the opportunity to distort the browser market, it is unacceptable for two reasons. First, the development of integrated platform/browser programmes is almost certainly efficient and in consumers' best interests; indeed, we may soon see the day when the platform itself will be principally a window into the internet (or other remote computers) for which browser functionality is essential. Furthermore, as noted earlier, many browser functions are already essential to the platform itself. In sum, simply separating the platform from the browser could interfere significantly with the efficient development of technology in this area—much like a decree forbidding a car manufacturer from developing its own engines.

Second, a remedy that divests Internet Explorer whilst leaving the Windows monopoly intact is simply myopic. Today's secondary market subject to distortion is that for browsers, but tomorrow it is likely to be the streaming technology necessary for high-speed, high-resolution motion video. The day after tomorrow it will be some other collateral technology. The occasion for abuse in this case is market dominance, and in the case of a pure software monopoly, market dominance can be remedied through a modified form of structural relief.

2. Remedies Must Promote Future Innovation or not Restrain it Unnecessarily.

Existing case law makes clear that divestiture is an appropriate remedy for dominant firms found guilty of substantial acts of monopolisation.[39] Unfortunately, structural remedies have fallen out of fashion in recent years except in merger cases. Instead, remedies have tended to be conduct injunctions which leave the defendant's market share largely intact, but are designed to open avenues of new entry by rivals. In the process, such remedies pose a significant threat of hobbling the defendant's ability to innovate aggressively itself whilst doing little to mitigate its power, at least in the short run.

---

[39] See *Grinnell*, n. 38, 384 U.S. at 577 (antitrust decree should 'break up or render impotent the monopoly power found to be in violation of the Act. . . .'); see also *United States* v *AT&T*, 552 F. Supp. 131 (D.D.C. 1982), aff'd mem. sub nom. *Maryland* v *United States*, 460 U.S. 1001 (1983) (approving decree breaking up telephone company).

The consent decree negotiated with Microsoft in 1995 illustrates the problem. Section IV(E) of that consent decree provided that:

> Microsoft shall not enter into any License Agreement in which the terms of that agreement are expressly or implicitly conditioned upon: (i) the licensing of any other Covered Product, Operating System Software product or other product (provided, however, that this provision in and of itself shall not be construed to prohibit Microsoft from developing integrated products); or (ii) the OEM not licensing, purchasing, using or distributing any non-Microsoft product.

The gist of this provision was that Microsoft was forbidden from licensing Windows 95 upon the condition that the licensee also agree to license a separate product. However, Microsoft was permitted to develop 'integrated' products. The crux of the subsequent dispute which went to the Circuit Court was Microsoft's practice of bundling, or including, the programme for Microsoft's web browser, Internet Explorer, in the Windows 95 package and refusing to license Windows 95 without the browser.[40] Significantly, some of the software code necessary to run Internet Explorer was within the basic Windows 95 operating system and could not be removed at all—and certainly not by a novice— without impairing the functionality of Windows 95.[41] However, the desktop icon or Programme Designations for Internet Explorer could readily be removed by any knowledgeable user of Windows 95, and some of the code files for Internet Explorer could be designated as 'hidden', which means that they would not be visible to the ordinary user. In brief, while much of the code for Internet Explorer contained in Windows 95 could not be effectively removed from the latter programme, a sophisticated licensee, such as an OEM, could make Internet Explorer invisible to the user and could then install an alternative browser such as Netscape.

In deciding that the inclusion of Internet Explorer into the Windows system constituted 'integration' rather than the mere bundling of separate products,

---

[40] See *United States* v *Microsoft*, 147 F.3d 935 (D.C.Cir. June 23, 1998) (finding that this bundling did not violate the 1995 consent decree). Microsoft's Windows 95 license agreements have required OEMs to accept and install the software package as sent to them by Microsoft, including IE, and have prohibited OEMs from removing any features or functionality, i.e., capacity to perform functions such as browsing.

[41] Of course, a Windows 95 version of Internet Explorer cannot run without Windows 95; so in one sense Windows 95 contains code for Internet Explorer just as it contains Code for MS Word, Corel Wordperfect, Myst, or thousands of other programmes. The significant difference here is that Windows 95 contained code designed exclusively for Internet Explorer

the court relied on the conclusions of the Antitrust Law treatise[42] that goods consolidated into a single product offering should ordinarily be considered a 'single product' for antitrust purposes when the two work better together when fitted by the manufacturer than when fitted together by the purchaser.[43] By contrast, if the goods are merely bolted together—something the customer could presumably do as easily as the manufacturer—then they should be counted as separate.[44] The significant amount of Internet Explorer code in Windows 95 that was necessary to full Windows 95 functionality would seem to suggest a decision in favour of Microsoft. Superficially, one could separate the Windows platform from the browsers and install a different browser, but it would be extraordinarily difficult for most users to rewrite Windows 95 so as to exclude the code while permitting it to function normally in other respects. If one could not install Windows 95 without installing at least a portion of the Internet Explorer code, then the two should probably be characterised as a single product.

Presumably, Windows 95 could have been written in a different way, without any Internet Explorer code,[45] but as Microsoft pointed out, putting some of the Internet Explorer code into the platform served the highly useful purpose of enabling the user to perform certain browser-related functions without actually invoking the browser.[46] The Antitrust Division responded to these concerns by insisting that, while the browser code need not be removed entirely from the platform, OEMs must be allowed to conceal the code by designating its files as hidden. The court equated this to permitting the defendant to tie, but the purchaser to discard, the tied product.

In sum, the form of relief manifested by the Microsoft consent decree—prohibiting the bundling of 'separate' software products—is an invitation to endless litigation about when software aggregations constitute a single product, and when they constitute a bundling of separate products. Perhaps this problem would be less serious were it confined to instances of truly dominant firms with very substantial market power. But as Part II indicates, the courts have not taken the power requirement nearly as seriously as they should, and private plaintiffs will not be as restrained as the Antitrust Division. Soon we will have

---

[42] Areeda, Elhauge and Hovenkamp (1996: para. 174b at 229).

[43] See para. 1746b, speaking of 'physical or technological interlinkage that the customer cannot perform', quoted in *Microsoft,* n. 40.

[43] *Microsoft,* 147 F.3d at 942 n. 3.

[44] *Ibid.*

[45] Indeed, earlier versions were so written.

[46] *Microsoft,* 147 F.3d at 942 n. 3.

numerous private plaintiffs claiming that software bundles which displace their formerly independent, but now collateral, product constitute unlawful tying.

Furthermore, such rules are socially harmful to the extent that they force firms to innovate around them. For example, the D.C. Circuit appeared to be leaning toward a rule that two different software applications are integrated if one of them contains code that is necessary for the other and the code in the first is designed exclusively for incorporating the other. But with such an antitrust rule in place, future software developers in Microsoft's position will respond by spreading their code over both components, with the result that the laws treats them as 'integrated' rather than the bundling of separate products. Furthermore, this will be done irrespective of whether or not it is efficient or sensible as a matter of software design, but only to comply with the antitrust mandate. At that point, however, plaintiffs will rightfully object that the spreading of the code was unnecessary and the court will be enmeshed in regulation of the contents of computer software.

In the same way, if the standard is that each product works better when combined with the other, software developers will find it easy to comply. Indeed, by redistributing software code, Microsoft could easily design a version of Windows and a version of Internet Explorer such that neither would work at all unless the other were present as well. That is to say, software design is almost infinitely 'plastic' in the sense that code can be grouped into different files (or placed on different diskettes) largely at the developer's will. If Microsoft chose to do so it could place all the Windows and Internet Explorer code on a single computer file, divide up files in such a way that code for both was on each file, or divide them so that Windows code was in one set and Explorer code in another.

But the real problem of unbundling remedies is that they do nothing, at least in the short run, to diminish the defendant's power. They simply restrain future product development by imposing limitations that are not imposed on non-dominant firms. The track record of such remedies in dislodging monopoly power has not been very promising to date. For example, the 1995 consent decree also restrained Microsoft from employing 'per processor' licensing on computer manufacturers. Under the prohibited licensing schemes, a manufacturer paid Microsoft's Windows license fee for every computer it made, irrespective of whether any Windows product was actually installed on that computer. The result is that if the computer manufacturer wished to install a non-Microsoft operating system on some of its computers, two license fees would have to be paid: one to Microsoft and one to the licensor of the alternative system. The impact of per processor licensing was that computer manufacturers had very little incentive to offer their systems with alternative

Microsoft or non-Microsoft operating systems. But by the time the Microsoft consent decree was issued the damage had been done. Although the decree has been in place nearly four years, this observer still does not see manufacturers of general IBM-compatible computer systems advertising Microsoft and non-Microsoft systems in the alternative.

3. 'Structural' Remedies More Readily Adapted to Intellectual Property Bottlenecks

As noted previously, structural remedies have not been in favour in the United States in recent years except in the area of mergers, and even then they are generally limited to cutting up firms along the lines of acquisition or ordering firms to divest certain assets before a merger will be approved. Despite this, structural remedies have unique possibilities in situations where the principal source of the bottleneck is intellectual property rights. First, breaking up a set of intellectual property rights is, structurally speaking, much less intrusive than forcing a firm to divest a portion of its plants or other hardware assets. Secondly, auctions can be conducted that predefine the number of buyers and make them actual head-to-head competitors (this is frequently not the case where a firm is forced to divest some of its plants, which may differ from one another in significant respects). Third, judicially compelled transfers of intellectual property rights can serve the all important purpose of hastening rather than retarding innovation. They can create a situation in which a number of competitive firms produce precisely the same product or their own unique variations, and each bundles, integrates, or innovates without restraint.

Consider the Microsoft case, and assume that substantial antitrust violations in the form of tying, exclusive dealing, reciprocity, or naked market division arrangements have been found. Simply enjoining these practices without attacking the structural monopoly does no more than encourage the monopolist to look for some new way of exercising its dominance that is not covered by the current injunction. Furthermore, the injunctions themselves may help force future innovation down less-than-optimal avenues.

A better solution is a limited 'divestiture' decree, which in this case takes the form of a judicially supervised auction in which Microsoft is required to give non-exclusive licences in all of its Windows software and the 'Windows' name to a predesignated number of winning bidders—say, five. The five highest bidders would bid a price representing the value of such a licence to them, which would be the value of Windows when sold in a moderately competitive market. That is to say, the price of Microsoft's abuse of its monopoly would be to force t to be a competitor rather than a monopolist; but entitle it to compensation for the competitive value (or something slightly higher)[47] of its monopolised assets. The result would be that Microsoft itself would be able to offer whatever package it wished to sell under the 'MS Windows' name, but there would also be five other firms, perhaps offering 'IBM Windows', 'Compaq Windows', 'Corel Windows', and the like, depending on the identity of the winning bidders. This scheme would probably have to contemplate the existence of a joint venture among the six firms to enable them to maintain compatibility without unnecessarily restraining their competitive offerings. Because no single firm would be dominant, each would from that point be able to bundle as it pleased—for example, Microsoft itself could offer computer manufacturers and end users a Windows package including Internet Explorer and MS Office. By contrast, Compaq Windows might offer a package including Netscape plus Corel Office Suite, and so on.

Lest this sound draconian, one must bear in mind that a court would offer such a remedy only in the presence of significant market dominance and a legal conclusion that there has been a significant antitrust violation. Moreover, the goal of antitrust remedies is general deterrence, and not simply the destruction of a single monopoly for whatever social good that in itself might impose. Future dominant firms would know that anti-competitive practices not authorised by the intellectual property laws would subject them to similar types of relief.

---

[47] The value might be higher because even after the auction Windows would not be sold in a perfectly competitive market.

VI

Günter Knieps*

Access to Networks and Interconnection:
A Disaggregated Approach

I. Introduction

By virtue of recent deregulatory trends and the consequent vertical disintegration of networks, problems of network access and network interconnection are gaining in importance. The purpose of this paper is to analyse the vertical and horizontal interconnection problems within networks in a conceptual manner.[1] This conceptual approach involves raising two related questions: to what extent can problems of interconnection and access be solved by contractual agreements between private parties and to what extent should government and EC interventions be implemented? The basic idea behind this disaggregated approach to network regulation is to identify the parts of networks where market power, which may be abused in the interconnection process, remains. The key concept is the identification of monopolistic bottlenecks and the application of the 'essential facilities doctrine', which is an established feature of US antitrust law. In the context of networks, this principle, which is traditionally applied on a case by case basis, can also be generalised and applied to a class of cases, where the localisation of market power may be argued to be based on the same factors.

In the final analysis, government regulation of interconnection and access conditions (tariffs, quality of access, etc.) is only justified in those network areas where market power can be identified *ex ante*. In all other network areas, government regulation of interconnection and access conditions is not only superfluous, but also acts as a barrier to efficient negotiations between the private parties involved. Furthermore, the fallacies within other regulatory interventions (e.g. prescribing inadequate price-setting rules, extending regulatory basis) may also be highlighted.

---

* Albert-Ludwigs-Universität Freiburg in Breslau. The author thanks Tod Barnes for very helpful comments on an earlier draft.

[1] See, for case studies focussing on railway systems and airlines, Knieps (1996); for the new regulatory framework for telecommunications in Germany is analysed Knieps (1995).

II. Localisation of Monopolistic Bottlenecks

The characteristics of network structures are an insufficient reason to guarantee market power. The markets for network services are far from the ideal picture of perfect atomistic markets. For example, an essential characteristic with respect to supply of train services is its network structure. Incentives may exist for train companies to bundle traffic either on a given line (economies of scale) or onto serving several lines jointly (economies of scope). However, a possible lack of competition between active firms in the market in a specific area with low population density could be replaced by efficient potential competition. The same argument also holds true for other network service providers, for example, airline companies, bus companies, telecommunications and postal service providers. If the incumbent companies produce inefficiently or make excessive profits, newcomers will enter the market.

The pressure of potential competition can create incentives for the active supplier to improve the quality and variety of services as well as to produce more efficiently. These networks are, therefore, described as contestable.[2] An essential condition for the functioning of potential competition, in order to discipline firms already providing network services, is that the incumbent firms do not have asymmetric cost advantages with respect to potential entrants. In fact, trains, like aeroplanes or buses, do not need to be considered as sunk costs; they can be used to serve other networks in different locations once demand in the former network has dropped too far to keep up a profitable train service. Another example for contestable networks are the markets for telecommunications services (*infra* IV).

An important condition for the effectiveness of potential competition is that all (active and potential) suppliers of service networks have equal (symmetric) access to the complementary infrastructures. As long as a train company has preferred access to rails and stations (e.g. if there is congestion) or has advantages with respect to scheduling procedures, it possesses competitive advantages with respect to potential entrants and active competitors. The same holds true for airline companies that have preferred access to landing rights, or telecommunication service providers that enjoy preferred access to local telephone networks.

When economies of scale arise (due to indivisibilities) in combination with sunk costs so that entry and, in particular, exit are not free, we can expect that network specific market power will emerge. Whilst sunk costs no longer repre-

---

[2] Baumol, Panzar, Willig (1982).

sent a relevant consideration for the incumbent monopoly, a potential entrant is confronted with the decision of whether or not to build network infrastructure and thereby incur irreversible costs. The incumbent firm, therefore, has lower decision-relevant costs than the potential entrants. This creates scope for strategic behaviour by the incumbent firm to ensure that inefficient production or excessive profits do not automatically result in market entry. Economies of scale, together with irreversible costs, are characteristic of the construction of transportation infrastructures such as railroads and airports. Consider, for a moment, a domestic railroad operator simultaneously supplying rail capacities and rail transport services as all national railroad companies do. The railroad operator may exploit its monopoly position vis-à-vis a foreign rail transport company and thereby restrict access to its own market. Non-contestable networks can also be observed in local infrastructures for gas, water and electricity.

Network infrastructure, however, need not necessarily lead to the creation of network-specific market power. In the first place, economies of scale may become exhausted as, for example, in long-distance telecommunications transmission. Secondly, technological change may provide alternative network infrastructures, so that monopolistic bottlenecks assume less importance. Examples are the increasing relevance of cableless local mobile communications and the increasing relevance of cable television networks for telecommunication purposes.[3] Consequently, a clear-cut distinction between network infrastructures as monopolistic bottlenecks and contestable networks is not always easy to find. Comprehensive sectoral studies must, it seems, be undertaken.

III. The Necessity for a Symmetric Regulatory Approach

Symmetric regulatory conditions should neither advantage nor disadvantage the former network monopolist. On the one hand, all monopoly privileges must be abandoned; on the other, all one-sided regulatory obligations (e.g. cross-subsidising of universal services) must be terminated. In general terms, symmetric regulation means providing all suppliers, incumbents and new entrants alike, a level playing field on which to compete: the same price signals, the same restrictions, and the same obligations. Yet, as Shankerman has indicated, all forms of asymmetric regulation contain an intrinsic bias toward some firms or technology.[4]

---

[3] Knieps (1997a).
[4] Shankerman (1996: 5).

Even if one accepts criteria such as relative market share, financial strength, access to input and service markets, as a starting point in the evaluation of the existence of market power, the development of an *ex ante* regulatory criterion nevertheless creates a need for a more clear-cut definition of market power. This is even more important, because rough indicators based on market shares can lead to incorrect criteria for government intervention in network industries.

It is important, therefore, to develop and apply a disaggregated approach of market power regulation. Furthermore, it is necessary to differentiate between the areas in which active and potential competition can work and other areas, so-called monopolistic bottleneck areas, where a natural monopoly situation (due to economies of bundling), in combination with irreversible costs, exists. The regulation of market power is only justified in monopolistic bottleneck areas. In all other cases, the existence of active and potential competition will lead to efficient market results (see Figure 1).

sub-market	with sunk costs	without sunk costs
natural monopoly (bundling advantages)	(1) regulation of market power (non-contestable networks)	(2) potential competition (contestable networks)
no natural monopoly (bundling advantages exhausted)	(3) competition among active providers	(4) competition among active providers

Fig. 1. *A disaggregated approach to market power regulation*

The pressure of potential competition can create incentives for the active supplier to improve the quality and variety of services as well as to produce more efficiently (*infra* IV). An essential condition for the functioning of potential competition in order to discipline firms already providing network services, is that the incumbent firms do not have asymmetric cost advantages in comparison with potential entrants.

An interesting question is the relation between 'pure economic' analysis and real-life networks (and the services that run over them). What about the reality of 'contestable networks'? It seems obvious that the behaviour of markets for network services, as soon as competition works, becomes more complex than assumed in the 'simple' models of the theory of contestable markets. Examples may be strategies of product differentiation, price differentiation and goodwill. However, even strategic behaviour in competitive markets for network services should not lead to the opposite conclusion to re-regulate these markets again. In contrast, the very point of the disaggregated approach is the development of the *preconditions* for competition on the markets for network services. The only purpose of the theory of contestable markets is, therefore, to localise the stable network specific market power, which systematically hampers the development of competition on the markets for network services. Whereas strategic behaviour and informational problems do not lead to stable market power on the markets for network services, monopolistic bottlenecks— due to sunk costs—do create stable market power even if all the market participants are well informed. The development of a set of rules to deal with transactions across the boundary between contestable networks and (non-contestable) monopolistic bottlenecks is, therefore, important in order to guarantee the preconditions for competition of the markets for network services (*infra* VI).

IV. The Case of Telecommunications

An example of contestable networks are the markets for telecommunications services that are often provided via service networks. Even the market for public telephone services is contestable, because suppliers of value added services are also prepared to offer telephone services. An important condition, however, is the guarantee of number portability. The term 'number portability' means the ability of users of telecommunications services to retain, at the same location, existing telecommunications numbers without impairment of quality, reliability or convenience when switching from one telecommunications carrier to another. Even if the market shares of incumbent firms are large, inefficient suppliers would then be immediately confronted with rapidly decreasing market shares.[5] But contestable sub-areas can also be localised in the area of telecommunications infrastructure. The pressure of potential competition in wireless networks, for example, satellite, microwave systems and mobile communication, is guaranteed as long as symmetric access to complementary inputs—e.g. to rights of way and the radio spectrum—is ensured. More generally, an important condition for the effectiveness of actual and potential competition is that all (active and potential) suppliers have equal (symmetric) access to the complementary monopolistic bottleneck.

---

[5] Knieps (1995).

In contrast, in local cable-based networks, where sunk costs are relevant, consumers, who would intrinsically be willing to switch immediately to less costly firms, cannot do this. Market entry is unlikely where sunk costs are both sufficiently high and very relevant. It can, therefore, be concluded that sector specific *ex ante* regulatory intervention in order to discipline market power can only be justified in non-contestable networks (monopolistic bottleneck areas), that is, where bundling in combination with irreversible costs is relevant. Sunk costs are no longer decision-relevant for the incumbent monopoly, whereas the potential entrant is confronted with the decision of whether or not to build network infrastructure and thus incur irreversible costs. The incumbent firms, therefore, have lower decision-relevant costs than the potential entrants. This creates scope for strategic behaviour by the incumbent firms, so that inefficient production and monopoly profits do not necessarily result in market entry.

The aim of future regulatory policy should not be the global regulation of markets. Instead, only a disaggregated regulation of non-contestable networks is justified. The aim of policy is, then, to localise the market power in monopolistic bottleneck areas and discipline this market power by regulatory intervention. The asymmetry of market power due to monopolistic bottleneck facilities does not necessarily require asymmetric regulation. Instead, the symmetry principle requires that all firms have access to local telecommunications networks on terms identical to those of the incumbent (non-discriminatory access). The symmetry principle demands that only bottleneck facilities are regulated, irrespective of whether the owner is the incumbent or a newcomer. The disaggregated location of market power is summarised by Figure 2.

V. Unregulated Interconnection among Contestable Networks

Consider the case where interconnection and access requirements arise among contestable networks. Let us consider a local community operating a mobile radio network, which is considering the various opportunities to establish a long distance connection by microwaves, or of two specialised satellite networks to be connected. Other examples are the horizontal interconnection among different specialised value added service networks of telecommunications or the (vertical) interconnection of a value added service network into a microwave long distance network.

	Competitive/ contestable	Non-contestable (monopolistic bottleneck)
Terminal equipment	X	———
Telecommunications services (including voice telephone services)	X	———
Satellite/mobile networks	X	———
Long-distance cable based networks	X	———
Local cable based networks	———	X

Fig. 2. *A disaggregated location of market power in telecommunications systems*

1. Efficient Private Bargaining of Interconnection and Access Conditions

Potential competition fulfils the function of mitigating market power. It can be expected that private bargaining of interconnection and access conditions between the different network owners will lead to economically efficient solutions. Strategic behaviour can be excluded because every bargaining partner can easily be substituted by an alternative (potential) network carrier (due to the contestability of networks).

Private bargaining solutions on interconnection conditions among contestable network carriers are not only beneficial for the carriers themselves but, in particular, improve the market performance of the network services provided to the customers. Independent of the market size of the carriers involved, inefficient suppliers of interconnection services are rapidly confronted with strongly decreasing market shares due to the strong pressure of alternative (potential) network service providers. The rapidly changing computer and telecommunications equipment market during the 1960s and 1970s in the US already indicates the enormous switching potential of consumers.[6] Government regulation of such private bargaining processes would artificially disturb the bargaining process and automatically lead to inferior solutions.

---

[6] Fisher *et al.* (1983).

2. Unregulated Interconnection and Access Tariffs

Carriers of contestable networks do not possess market power due to the (potential) competition of alternative network carriers. Excessive interconnection and access charges which allow monopoly rents or insufficient network service qualities would immediately initiate switching to an alternative network carrier. There is no need for government interventions aiming to discipline the market power of active network carriers where the underlying networks are contestable.

The question arises, therefore, whether interconnection tariffs which result from private bargaining can guarantee the viability of efficient providers of network capacities. Price regulations with the aim of achieving interconnection tariffs according to long-run incremental costs (including fixed costs of capacity), would either be superfluous or would reduce the viability of the incumbent carrier. Where the long-run incremental costs to private interconnection capacity are equal to stand-alone costs of interconnection facilities, cost-covering interconnection tariffs would be the result of private bargaining.[7] If common costs (overhead costs) between the interconnecting networks play a significant role, then the problem arises of how to cover the difference between stand-alone costs and incremental costs, because the sum of the incremental costs does not cover total costs. Consequently, the network providers must have flexibility to raise interconnection tariffs so that the total cost covering constraint (viability condition) is fulfilled. In particular, they must be free to allocate common costs depending on the price elasticities of the relevant demand schedules. *Ex ante* allocations of overhead costs according to fully allocated cost principles, however, would be detrimental,[8] since they would neither be based on economically justified cost-causality nor take into account demand side considerations. As a consequence, regulators who set interconnection rates on the basis of fully allocated costs may encourage inefficient bypass activities, even when efficient (viable) market solutions exist.

Pricing rules enforced by regulatory agencies in order to allocate overhead costs cannot solve the problem. The most popular methods of pricing access follow the principle of fully distributed costs. For example, a proportional

---

[7] Since the focus of this paper is on analysing regulatory problems of residual market power once legal entry barriers within networks are abolished, we ignore the problem of cream-skimming (unsustainability) and the related discussion on the re-establishing of legal entry barriers, Faulhaber (1975); Holler (1990).

[8] Owen and Braeutigam (1978: 212–220).

sharing rule distributing the common costs (among the complementary networks) in proportion to the incremental costs, so that the relative mark-up is equal,[9] may create incentives for the inefficient bypassing of interconnection facilities. If, for example, the stand-alone costs of a specialised entrant for building a separate network are lower than the incremental costs of interconnection capacities plus the symmetrically allocated common costs, then private bargaining will result in lower mark-up requirements for the entrant. Nevertheless, the bargaining result would be efficient because the competitor also contributes to cover common costs. In contrast, a proportional sharing rule induces inefficient cost duplications because it creates incentives for inefficient bypass of the entrant. Similarly, it can be shown that many other possible fully distributed cost principles may induce inefficient bypass activities as well.

In the context of unbundling of networks, Baumol has proposed an access pricing rule, called the 'efficient component pricing rule'.[10] Let us suppose that entrants supply a component in competition with the incumbent, for which they need access to the incumbent's facility. This rule states that the efficient interconnection and access charges to the single-supplier's component cover the incremental costs of this component plus the opportunity costs, which include any foregone revenues from a concomitant reduction in the single-supplier's sales of the complementary component. The basic idea behind this rule is that an entrant on the competitive market segment should only enter if he is more efficient. However, where the networks are contestable, any enforcement of the 'efficient component pricing rule' is superfluous. Since excessive profits on the competitive part of the network do not exist, 'opportunity costs' in the sense of foregone profits are zero and, consequently, interconnection and access tariffs automatically reflect the real opportunity costs of network access, including congestion costs to use the single-supplier's component (irrespective of the question of by whom this facility is used). Where common costs between different networks must also be covered, the 'efficient component pricing rule' may be interpreted to argue in favour of the *pre-entry* allocation of common costs. As a consequence, incentives for inefficient bypass could be created, especially in situations where the stand-alone costs of a specialised entrant would be below the sum of the incremental costs and the portion of the common costs attributed by the 'efficient component pricing rule'. In contrast, under such circumstances, private bargaining would result in lower mark-up requirements for the entrant. Again, the bargaining result would be efficient,

---

[9] Tye (1993: 46).
[10] Baumol (1983); Baumol and Sidak (1994).

because the competitor also contributes to cover common costs without creating incentives for inefficient bypass.

VI. Regulation of Interconnection to Monopolistic Bottlenecks

1. The impact of Market Power on Bargaining of Interconnection and Access Conditions

Interconnection among contestable networks may play an increasing role in the future, especially in the telecommunication sector. Nevertheless, there still remains the problem that non-contestable network infrastructures may be involved. Let us take, for example, railway systems, where competitive suppliers of transportation services still need access to the tracks and railway stations. In contrast to rail services, railway tracks must be regarded as sunk costs, which cannot be shifted to another market. Therefore, if a potential competitor plans to enter with a parallel track, the incumbent railway owner could reasonably claim to reduce his tariffs on short-run variable costs. As soon as a railway network is completed, one cannot expect further entries with additional tracks. The relevant-decision costs of entry include the costs of tracks, which could not be covered by tariffs based on short-run variable costs. In contrast to the supplier of rail services, the track owner in question has obtained market power.[11] Similarities exist (at least so long as current technology persists) within cable based local telecommunication networks, airports, and electricity and gas networks.

In contrast to interconnection among contestable networks, the market power involved in non-contestable network infrastructures fundamentally disturbs private bargaining processes. One extreme alternative could be (vertical) foreclosure of competitors on a complementary service market. Such tying can be used as a method of price discrimination, enabling a monopolist to earn higher profits[12]. Another way of abusing market power within the bargaining process on interconnection and access conditions is to provide insufficient network access quality or excessive interconnection charges. Examples of insufficient interconnection and access quality may vary within the network sectors under consideration. An example of inferior access conditions is lower quality access to local telephone networks offered to competitive long distance carri-

---

[11] Fremdling and Knieps (1993: 148–152).

[12] Posner (1976: 171–184); for the case of railroads, see, Fremdling and Knieps (1993: 150–152).

ers. A central argument in favour of the Antitrust Divestiture Case in the US has been to guarantee non-discriminatory equal access conditions (equal quality and tariffs) for all interstate long distance competitors.[13] Monopolistic interconnection and access charges are another danger when market power caused by non-contestable networks is involved.

Because of these different obstacles to interconnection processes caused by non-contestable network infrastructures, it may be possible to argue in favour of the traditional vertically integrated networks. Interconnection and access problems could again be solved internally without creating problems of strategic behaviour among the different parties involved. This paper, however, recommends an opposite course of action for several reasons. In the first place, the avoidance of strategic interaction among different bargaining partners would not solve the problem of disciplining the market power of vertically integrated networks to the extent that subparts of the infrastructure networks are non-contestable. Secondly, vertically integrated systems are less capable of exhausting the advantage of horizontal integration of specific functions within networks. For example, traffic control systems possess an intrinsic potential for European-wide co-ordination and co-operation. This advantage of horizontal integration cannot only be illustrated by the case of air traffic control in Europe but also for the case of an integrated European-wide train traffic control system, involving the harmonisation of train schedules and co-ordination of train movements on a European-wide scale.[14] It seems obvious that such a process of horizontal integration can be implemented more easily after vertical disintegration. Thirdly, the benefits of competition among different suppliers of network services can only be gained after vertical disintegration. Instead of concentrating on the developments towards vertical disintegration, we shall analyse the role of regulatory interventions in order to restrict the degrees of disturbance to private bargaining when non-contestable network infrastructures are involved.

2. Regulatory Instruments to Discipline Market Power

The essential facilities doctrine offers a good starting point for any attempt to structure government interventions into interconnection and access processes. Well known and often applied in US antitrust law, the essential facilities

---

[13] See CC Docket 78–72, Phase III, May 31, 1983.
[14] Knieps (1993: 204–205).

doctrine has also gained importance in European competition law .[15] The doctrine focuses on the creation of access upon equal terms for all competitors to
what is known as a 'monopolistic bottleneck'. The essential facilities doctrine
developed in the US through the application of the Sherman Act 1890.[16]

Liability, under the essential facilities doctrine, is based on the following
criteria:[17]

1. control of an 'essential facility' by a monopolist (endowing monopoly
   power);
2. a competitor's inability practically or reasonably to duplicate the facility;
3. the denial of the use of the facility to a competitor; and
4. the feasibility of providing the facility.

It is obvious that the preconditions of the essential facilities doctrine are not
fulfilled in the case of interconnection and access among contestable networks
because competitors always possess access to alternative (potential) networks.
There is simply no case of market power. If an incumbent carrier were to foreclose access or behave in a non-competitive way in other aspects, new network
providers would arise automatically (independent of the market share of the
incumbent carrier). The application of the essential facilities doctrine to interconnection and access among contestable networks would even be detrimental
because it would artificially restrict degrees of freedom in the search for Pareto-
optimal bargaining solutions among the market participants.

The 'essential facility' concept should only be applied, in a limited manner,
to those interconnection and access cases where market power (at least on one
side) is involved. In US antitrust law, the essential facilities doctrine has been
applied to specific infrastructures (terminal railroads, municipal electricity networks etc.) on a case-by-case basis. Accordingly, the key purpose of the doctrine, the restriction of monopoly power, has been subject to interpretational
variations in different courts over time. One particularly vexed issue was the
question of whether the feasibility of providing the facility to a competitor

---

[15] Glasl (1994).

[16] The Act has two major provisions: *Section 1.* Every contract, combination in the
form of a trust or otherwise, or conspiracy, in restraint of trade or commerce among the
several States, or with foreign nations, is hereby declared to be illegal; *Section 2.* Every
person who shall monopolise, or attempt to monopolise, or combine or conspire with
any other person or persons to monopolise any part of the trade or commerce among
the several States, or with foreign nations, shall be guilty of a misdemeanor . . .

[17] *City of Anaheim* v *Southern California Edison Co.*, 995 F. 2d 1373, 1380 (9th Cir.
1992).

would be an absolute criterion, or whether 'valid business reasons' could be a legitimate rationale for a refusal to deal. This, somewhat elusive, latter interpretation can easily be criticised because the fact that granting access would obviously reduce the profit of the owner of the facility cannot by itself constitute a 'valid business reason'.[18]

The enforcement of the essential facilities doctrine cannot be seen in isolation from the terms of access provided to the competitors. Clearly, where the terms are so onerous as to foreclose the competition, the effect of the terms is equivalent to a complete refusal to offer a bundled and an unbundled rate.[19] An effective application of the essential facilities doctrine must, therefore, be combined with an adequate regulation of access conditions (quality and tariffs). This requirement has been partly incorporated in the criteria of the essential facilities doctrine itself. Not only the denial of the use of the facility, but also the imposition of restrictive terms for the use of the facility, with the result that competition is substantially harmed, has been considered in earlier case law as a criterion for the essential facilities doctrine.[20] Nevertheless, a significant scope for interpretation remains, especially given the historical fact that antitrust lawyers are not normally specialised in dealing with complex matters of access conditions.

As a consequence, the enforcement of the essential facilities doctrine should be combined with the application of regulatory instruments, which focus on access conditions (especially regulation of interconnection and access charges). One advantage of the explicit combination of regulatory concepts with the antitrust concept of the essential facilities doctrine is the shift from case-to-case applications to the definition of a class of cases characterised by non-contestable network infrastructures. Thus, whilst the rather global concept of the abuse of market power by dominant firms requires that the relevant market be established (in a narrow sense) and that the meaning of dominance be clarified,[21] a generalisation of the essential facilities doctrine would enable the formation of a class of cases where market power is based on the same reasons. Within networks, this leads to the non-contestable network infrastructures.

Similar to the case of interconnection among contestable networks, access charges must not only cover long-run incremental costs but also the total costs of the monopolistic bottlenecks. Common costs of providing contestable and

---

[18] Tye (1987: 346).
[19] *Ibid*, at 359.
[20] *Ibid*, at 346.
[21] George and Jacquemin (1990: 228).

non-contestable networks must be covered by access/interconnection charges, without the owner of an 'essential facility' being accused of abusing market power. If, however, the 'efficient component pricing rule' was applied in such a manner that the monopolist's 'opportunity costs' of providing access also included monopoly profits as part of its foregone opportunities in the contestable segment, the market power of the non-contestable network carrier would be cemented. The application of the 'efficient component pricing rule' in this context would be anticompetitive because the (potential) entrants in the complementary contestable networks would have to reimburse incumbents for their foregone monopoly rents. Such artificial 'opportunity' costs should not be confused with the real opportunity costs for the usage of the scarce capacities of bottleneck facilities.[22]

The reference point for the regulatory rules concerning interconnection and access charges should be the coverage of the full costs of the monopolistic bottleneck (in order to guarantee the viability of the facility). In particular, when alternatives to bypass 'essential facilities' are absent, the cost-covering constraint may not be sufficient to forestall excessive profits. Therefore, price-cap regulation should be introduced.[23] The primary purpose of price-capping is to regulate the level of prices, taking into account the inflation rate (consumer price index) minus a percentage for expected productivity increase. It seems important to restrict such price-cap regulation to the non-contestable parts of networks, where market power caused by monopolistic bottleneck is, in fact, creating a regulatory problem. In other sub-parts of networks price-setting should be left to the competitive markets.

The question therefore remains as to whether regulators should also be allowed to prescribe pricing rules that focus on the tariff structures within monopolistic bottlenecks. There are compelling arguments for regulators to refrain from detailed tariff regulation. In the first place, firms should have the flexibility to design (Pareto superior) optional tariff schemes.[24] Pricing rules prescribed by the regulator could induce inefficient bypass activities. For example, a first pricing rule could be access tariffs according to long run average costs of the 'essential facility'. Since in such a case a differentiation among different user groups according to different price-elasticities is impossible, incentives for inefficient bypassing of the bottleneck facility may be created for certain user groups. A second pricing rule would be access pricing according to

---

[22] Economides and White (1995).

[23] Beesley and Littlechild (1989).

[24] Willig (1978).

the Ramsey pricing principle.[25] Mark-ups on the marginal costs of access to the monopolistic bottlenecks are chosen according to the elasticities of demand for network access in order to maximise social welfare given the cost-covering constraint. However, Ramsey prices could become unsustainable even if strictly applied to monopolistic bottlenecks. The technological trend towards the unbundling of monopolistic bottleneck components increases the possibilities for inefficient bypass. Secondly, the danger arises of regulators extending the regulatory basis to such a degree that they include the contestable sub-parts of networks. From the point of view of increasing static (short-run) efficiency such behaviour could even be justified by welfare theory. It is well known, that efficiency distortions applying Ramsey pricing can be reduced by extending the regulatory basis.[26] Nevertheless, such an endeavour would in fact mean a return to fully regulated networks, including price- and entry-regulation of the contestable subparts. As such, this would not be a suitable response to deregulation.[27]

In any case, regulators should not be allowed to intervene in the competitive price-setting process within the contestable sub-parts of networks, since otherwise the competition process within the contestable networks would be severely hampered. Any regulation of interconnection and access conditions should be strictly limited to the parts of networks where market power has been localised. The design of pricing rules should be within the decision-making process of the firms.

VII. Unbundling and the Proper Role of the Essential Facilities Doctrine

The essential facilities doctrine is the tailor-made answer to a specific competition problem: the vertical integration between a competitive market and a complementary, monopolistic bottleneck area. The provision has two elements: localisation of the monopolistic bottleneck as a factual finding and the right to access as a legal consequence.

It has been shown (*supra* IV) that, from the point of view of competition in the long-distance network, the local networks still have to be considered as a monopolistic bottleneck. In other words, in order for a long-distance network operator to conduct his own business, he needs to have access not just to a few

---

[25] Baumol and Bradford (1970).

[26] Laffont and Tirole (1994).

[27] Damus (1984).

local networks but to all local networks. The essential facilities doctrine can, in principle, be applied to substantiate a claim made by long-distance network competitors to be allowed to have access to the local networks of the established carrier.

The purpose of the essential facilities doctrine is to overcome the structural market entry barrier caused by vertical integration with a monopolistic bottleneck. A claim to access merely *elements* of the monopolistic bottleneck ('demand-oriented' unbundling) can, therefore, not be derived from the essential facilities doctrine. Moreover long-distance competitors must accept the established carrier's local network as it is, including the disadvantages and problems that have evolved historically. They cannot bypass this by simply selecting elements from the local networks that a network set up today would ideally contain.[28]

VIII. Costing and Pricing of Interconnection Services: The case of Telecommunications[29]

1. The Role of Long-run Incremental Costs (LRIC) in Determining Interconnection Prices

It is well-known that, even after complete entry deregulation, economies of scale and economies of scope create common costs which cannot be directly attributed to the individual network services. Although activity-based costing can help to identify the directly attributable costs to specific products, it is still impossible to declare all costs as incremental costs without applying economically unjustified allocation of common costs. Provided that the established network carrier is determining the incremental costs based on decision-oriented accounting methods, it immediately becomes clear that the sum of the incremental costs does not permit survival. In fact, the established firm must also cover its product-group specific costs as well as the firm-specific overhead costs by means of mark-ups on the LRIC. In order to avoid inefficient bypass activities of entrants, market-driven mark-ups should be raised by the established carriers. An obligation to provide the services according to LRIC, however, would disturb the symmetric treatment of the infrastructure owner and service provider. The incentives to be the owner of the infrastructure supplying interconnection and network access

---

[28] For a detailed analysis of this topical issue with special emphasis on the German Telecommunication Act, Engel and Knieps (1998).

[29] For more extensive analysis, Knieps (1997b).

would disappear because it would be cheaper to use the infrastructure of the competitors and thereby avoid a contribution to the common costs. A symmetric treatment of the owners and the users of infrastructure, therefore, requires that the stand-alone costs of network infrastructure must be covered.

2. Management Accounting Versus Pseudo Data Models

a) The Obsoleteness of Historical Cost Accounting
In competitive industries, the value of a firm's productive assets is equal to the discounted (present) value of the anticipated net cash flows earned by the assets over their remaining useful life. These net cash flows are determined both by competitive market forces and by the firm's actions, but are not influenced by the book asset value. In regulated industries, however, the value of the firm's assets that are in place—the rate base—has been strongly influenced by regulated depreciation charges. Since the regulatory agencies were under political pressure to keep the local rates down, and therefore also the capital costs of local networks, artificially low depreciation charges and an excessively long life time were prescribed (not sufficiently taking into account technical progress and changed substitution possibilities).

Although it is true that historical cost accounting is obsolete, the reform towards desiam-relevant costing should still be based on management and financial accounting data. Management accounting approaches are based on real costing data, observing the relationship between input-prices, outputs and the costs of production. In contrast, engineering-economic models (process analysis approaches) develop pseudo cost data. After describing the production function from engineering data, the cost-output relationship is then derived as a result of assumed global optimisation behaviour. The following section suggests that, rather than engineering-economic models, an adequate reform of management accounting is needed, based on forward-looking cost accounting methods. Moreover, it should become clear that the concept of an efficient network needs much further elaboration. Whereas current-cost accounting methods, by their very nature, take into account the path-dependency of network evolution (as long as it is efficient from a forward-looking perspective), engineering-economic models usually ignore the strategy of successive upgrading of networks.

b) The Fallacies of Pseudo Data Models in Determining LRIC
Engineering-economic models are inadequate for determining the long-run incremental interconnection costs of interconnection services of established

carriers. Process analysis is placed on simulating the production function from engineering data. After describing the production function, the cost-output relationship is then derived as a result of assumed optimisation behaviour. Instead of real accounting data, the cost-data developed by engineering-economic models are simulated (pseudo) data, their informational value is strongly dependent on the quality and the characteristics of the underlying process model. Although the process analysis approach was not very popular for a long time,[30] it has been applied in the field of telecommunications.[31] Gabel and Kennet developed the so-called LECOM (Local Exchange Cost Optimisation Model) in order to generate data to address the issue of economies of scope in local telephone networks. With LECOM, it became possible to solve the problem of selecting the combination and location of facilities that minimised the costs of satisfying varying levels of demand.[32] The three types of facilities within the local exchange carrier's network are the local loop, switching and trunking. The local loop is composed of facilities that provide signalling and voice transmission path between a central office and the customer's station. The central office houses the switching computer that connects a customer's line to either another customer who is served by the same switch, or to an inter-office trunk. Calls between central offices are carried on trunks. The model takes as data a city's dimensions and customer usage level. LECOM then searches for the technological mix, capacity and location of switches that minimises the annual cost of production. The location of the switches are optimised by the non-linear optimisation model. In principle, there are an infinite number of possible configurations to be considered. For each economically and technically feasible combination of switches, a certain number of possible iterations are allowed. An iteration involves the calculation of the cost of service at one or more alternative locations for the switches. For each market, and a given level of demand, LECOM evaluates a number of different switch combinations. In other words, LECOM has been designed to develop a green-field approach. Gabel and Kennet[33] have pointed out some important limitations to engineering optimisation models. In the first place, optimisation models are not normally designed to quantify the less tangible costs of providing service (administrative costs). Secondly, LECOM is limited by bounded rationality. Since global optimisation is not feasible, only a reasonable number of possible solutions are examined. It is obvious that a great degree of freedom exists in the

---

[30] Griffin (1972: 47).
[31] Gabel and Kennet (1991).
[32] Gabel and Kennet (1994: 386ff).
[33] *Ibid*, at 390ff.

search for 'plausible' solutions. Thirdly, the value of the pseudo-data approach ultimately rests on the quality and completeness of the underlying process models. Measurement errors and behavioural errors still persist, even in the best model.[34]

Beyond this serious critique of engineering-economic models, the most important point to remember is that they are simply the wrong tool for deriving the LRIC of established carriers. Even if the analysis is based on a 'scorched node' assumption, which implies that the incremental cost estimate reflects the current network topology, engineering-economic models—by their very nature—are not able to derive the LRIC of the efficient network of the established carrier. The reason is the path-dependency of networks. This means that the gradual upgrading is efficient (given the network history), if the additional costs of upgrading are lower than the costs of building new network facilities. This implies that the economically efficient incremental costs must be calculated on the basis of the factual costs of the incumbent's network in place (including its history of upgrading). As long as the incremental costs of upgrading of the established carrier are lower than the stand-alone costs of a hypothetical new network of an entrant, the required network capacity should be provided by the historically grown network of the established carrier. This is true because entry would replace the service of the incumbent firm over its existing network, not the service of a hypothetical efficient provider. Path-dependent costs of gradual upgrading are then economically efficient and are also relevant from a forward-looking costing perspective.[35] Furthermore, they should also not be confused with sunk costs, because the upgrading strategy is then incentive-compatible even if all investments could easily be shifted to another market (perfect 'second-hand' market). Under efficient upgrading strategies, the economic value of the existing network components is the only decision basis. It is simply not in the spirit of the engineering-economic models to take into consideration this network history. Even under the scorched node assumption engineering-economic models use the high degree of freedom of simulation models to find cost-minimising solutions by ignoring the historically grown network infrastructure that is already in existence.

Beyond this fundamental critique of the usefulness of engineering-economic models for determining the LRIC of the established carriers, other

---

[34] Griffin (1977): 125.

[35] As long as upgrading is an efficient strategy, its costs should not be confused with phantom costs due to overvaluation of installed investment (based on differences between economic and historical depreciation patterns).

points of criticism have already been indicated in NERA's studies for OFTEL.[36] In particular, the insufficient determination of the factual usage of network capacities, and of the factual routing patterns have been identified.

c) The Necessity of Reforming Management Accounting: From Historical Cost Accounting to Current Cost Accounting

It is often argued, that the necessary and overdue departure from historical cost accounting (HCA) in a competitive environment can only be accomplished by introducing engineering-economic models. This is, however, particularly misleading because the necessary reform should still be based on management accounting. In the following we shall argue that a transition from historical cost accounting to forward looking current cost accounting (CCA) is unavoidable. Under competitive conditions the valuation of the assets and the depreciation-charges must reflect their economic values. The true economic value of any productive asset is the discounted present value of the anticipated stream of net earnings it is capable of producing. Thus, the economic depreciation of a productive asset during a time period is the decrease in its economic value during the period. It should be noted that historical book values and historical depreciation patterns typically reflect neither capital market valuation of assets in place nor economic depreciation. A transition from historical cost accounting to current cost accounting thus necessarily poses the problem of phantom costs due to overvaluation of existing network equipment.[37] However, phantom costs should not be confused with economically efficient forward looking costs of upgrading existing network (path-dependency). A periodical re-evaluation of the assets as well as an adaptation of economic depreciation rates seems unavoidable, especially in such dynamic markets as telecommunications.

---

[36] The reader is referred to a series of studies that NERA provided to OFTEL: The Methodology to Calculate Long-Run Incremental Costs, March 1996; Reconciliation and Integration of Top Down and Bottom Up Models of Incremental Costs, June 1996; Reconciliation and Integration of Top Down and Bottom Up Models of Incremental Costs, Final Report, December 1996.

[37] Albach and Knieps (1997: 31).

VII

*Daniel L. Rubinfeld and Robert Majure**

Ensuring Fair and Efficient Access to the
Telecommunications 'Bottleneck'

I. The Local Bottlenecks

The history of telecommunications deregulation in the United States can be seen as an effort to identify those parts of the telephone network that, in an economic sense, constitute real bottlenecks and to minimise the anti-competitive impact of such bottlenecks. In the 1982 consent decree that broke up the old Bell system, the US Department of Justice acted on the presumption that while the entire local network appeared to be a bottleneck, the anti-competitive effects of that bottleneck could be confined to the local network.[1] By separating ownership of local telephone service and long-distance service, the consent decree sought to open the long-distance market to competition. The Bell Operating Companies (BOCs) were to continue to provide local service essentially as regulated monopolies. The expectation was that by divesting the bottlenecks in local service from AT&T's long-distance business, regulators could more effectively enforce rules for fair and efficient access to the local network. Removing the bottleneck holder's incentive to favour its long-distance affiliate over non-integrated competitors would ease the regulatory task of ensuring no undue influence from the local bottleneck on long-distance competition. Without that distorting influence, competitors would face a more level playing field in the long-distance market. Note, however, that the consent decree was not designed to ease the task of regulating the local bottleneck by ensuring efficient local telephone services or by ensuring that the non-discriminatory price of access paid by all long-distance competitors was efficient.[2]

---

* Daniel L. Rubinfeld is Robert L. Bridges Professor of Law and Economics at the University of California. At the time this article was written Robert Majure was Deputy Assistant Attorney General at the Antitrust Division of the US Department of Justice: he is currently Assistant Chief, Economic Regulatory Section, of the same organisation.

[1] See generally the Antitrust Division's Competitive Impact Statement in Connection with Proposed Modification of Final Judgement; *United States* v *Western Electric and American Telephone & Telegraph* (Federal Register Vol. 47, No. 32 Feb. 17, 1982).

[2] A different consent decree might have imposed a separation between the ownership of the local loop (or some other set of facilities) and all retail services. Such a separation would leave fewer incentives to misuse the bottleneck, but would involve increased risk of anti-competitive harm if the bottleneck arose outside of the local loop.

Today, almost twenty years later, the presumption that long-distance could become competitive appears to have been an appropriate one. AT&T's share of long-distance revenues, which has constantly been declining since the break-up, has recently dropped to below 50 percent.[3] In addition to the major facilities-based competitors, MCI-Worldcom and Sprint, hundreds of new companies have entered the business using their own facilities in some cases and by reselling in others. At least two start-up companies, Qwest and Level3, are building fibre-optic networks to carry traffic nation-wide. There is an almost constant unveiling of new promotional packages each offering lower rates than the last, and certainly no indication that the lower prices have meant a drop in quality.[4]

The 1996 Telecommunications Act attempts to introduce competition in *all* industry segments, including the largely monopolised local networks. The purpose of the Act is both to increase the competitiveness of markets dependent on access to local networks (such as long distance), and to improve performance and ultimately reduce regulation in the local networks themselves. As one Congressional Committee put it, the purpose of the Act is:

> to provide for a pro-competitive, de-regulatory national policy framework designed to accelerate rapidly private sector deployment of advanced telecommunications and information technologies and services to all Americans by opening all telecommunications markets to competition.[5]

II. Means of Local Entry: Securing the Cooperation of Incumbents

Recognising that the key remaining bottleneck is somewhere in the local networks, the Act imposes a number of obligations on the incumbents in local markets to share their networks with entrants. These obligations are designed to create three possible avenues for entry into local telecommunications markets: resale of the incumbent's existing services; building new facilities to reach the customer; and leasing some mixture of the network elements of the incum-

---

[3] The FCC report 'Long-Distance Market Shares—First Quarter 1998' (June 1998) puts AT&T's share of toll revenue at 44.5 percent in 1997, down from 90 percent in 1984.

[4] The FCC tracks numerous measures of quality (*see, for example* the FCC report '1997 Common Carrier Scorecard') and has not identified any significant adverse trends in the quality of service.

[5] S. Conf. Rep. No. 104–230, 104th Cong., 2d Sess. 113 (1996) (Joint Explanatory Statement of the Committee of Conference).

bent (possibly in combination with some of the entrant's own facilities). Each of these new avenues will require some cooperation from the incumbent.

If an entrant is reselling the incumbent's services, it not only needs the incumbent to establish a wholesale offering at an appropriate discount (reflecting the incumbent's ability to save retailing costs); it also needs the incumbent to develop all of the back-office systems and procedures to support that wholesale offering. An entrant that is selling services using part of the incumbent's network needs to establish (with the incumbent) how the network will be unbundled and the terms and conditions that are needed to acquire various parts. This new entrant will have an even greater need to coordinate with the incumbent to ensure that the transition to the new provision of service is a smooth one and that customers do not experience a significant loss of service. Even an entrant building its own facilities needs to work out how its customers will send and receive calls with the incumbent's customers, that is, the terms of interconnection.

Any entrant has to have some way to communicate effectively with the incumbent. Pure resellers and entrants using elements of the incumbent's network need to be able to send orders for the inputs they are buying from the incumbent. All entrants will need effective communication to confirm that customers' accounts and telephone numbers are properly recorded and to provide effective maintenance and repair.[6]

Since the incumbent, on account of its position, has most of the customers initially, any delay in establishing the framework for facilitating the switching of customers to entrants would appear to be in the incumbent's best interest. The less effective the incumbent's wholesale offerings[7] at any point in time (either because the prices are too high or because the systems and procedures needed to deliver offerings to a competitive market do not exist or do not work well), the less competitive the new entry faced by the incumbent. A strategy that raises the cost of those entry avenues that rely most on the incumbent's wholesale offerings has the potential to discourage entry generally, or to divert entrants' efforts into inefficiently duplicating the incumbent's network.

---

[6] The FCC's August 8, 1996 order *In re Implementation of Local Competition Provisions in the Telecommunications Act of 1996, First Report and Order* evaluates in detail the importance to entrants of obtaining particular inputs from the incumbent. *See also,* the Department of Justice's evaluation of Southwestern Bell Telephone's application to provide long-distance service in Oklahoma ('Oklahoma evaluation') for a discussion of the need for effective wholesale support systems and procedures.

[7] The term 'wholesale offerings' includes not only service for resale, but everything an incumbent is now required to offer at wholesale, including unbundled network elements and interconnection.

Incumbents are also in a unique position to affect the speed at which the mandates of the 1996 Act are achieved by delaying efficient entry. Only the incumbent knows the true costs associated with key aspects of its operation. Moreover, the incumbent has the ability, if it chooses to exercise it, to impair the regulators' efforts to establish reasonably priced wholesale offerings. In much the same way, the incumbent can 'slow roll' the development of its own systems and procedures for supporting any such offering. Thus, the creation of effective and realistically supported wholesale offerings itself represents a potential bottleneck.

The 1996 Act recognises that there may be a divergence between the incentives of incumbents and the public interest in the creation of wholesale offerings for entrants. For the BOCs created in the AT&T break-up (the largest incumbents with the most contiguous territories), the 1996 Act requires that the incumbent has to have made a showing to the regulators with respect to the openness of markets before these local incumbents are allowed into the long-distance market for calls originating in their home regions. In part, this requirement serves to motivate the incumbents to not unduly delay entry by providing a reward for good behaviour. This regulatory 'carrot' (as opposed to the 'stick' of regulatory fiat), is an interesting approach to the central question posed to this panel: how to ensure fair and efficient terms of access to 'bottleneck' network facilities when the gatekeeper has no incentive to grant them.

III. BOC Entry into Long-Distance

The FCC reviews an application by a BOC to enter the long-distance market on the basis of statutory criteria that include satisfaction of a checklist of market opening measures and a determination that entry would be in the public interest. The Act requires the FCC to give the Department of Justice's evaluation 'substantial weight' in making its determination and allows the Department to use any standard in making its evaluation. How does the Department fulfil its role in this process?

After soliciting and reviewing comments from all interested parties,[8] the Department decided that it would evaluate applications based on whether the incumbent had demonstrated the market to be 'fully and irreversibly open to

---

[8] In addition to meeting with virtually all of the affected players, the Department reviewed almost seventy five responses to an open letter in November of 1996 from Assistant Attorney General Joel Klein soliciting comments from all interested parties.

competition.'[9] The Department examines whether the incumbent has demonstrated that its wholesale support is adequate to provide competitive entrants with a functionality on a par with what the incumbent provides to its own retail operations. The Department also looks at whether the appropriate wholesale offerings are available at prices that seem reasonably designed to produce efficient entry decisions.[10]

The Department of Justice believes that the best evidence that local markets are fully open is to see widespread and substantial entry using all three entry alternatives. At the same time the Department has stated that 'we do not regard competitors' small market shares, or even the absence of entry, standing alone, as conclusive evidence that a market remains closed to competition. . .'[11] Taking the middle ground, the Department has chosen to consider evidence 'that significant barriers are not impeding the growth of competition. . . .'[12] Obviously, the less that current conditions approximate to the substantial entry that seems likely if markets are fully open, the more the burden falls on the incumbent to provide a factual showing of why, if the market is open, entry is not occurring.

As the 'irreversible' part of the test would imply, the Department looks not only to today's circumstances, but also at the likelihood that these offerings and this level of support will be available after an approval is granted. A credible commitment to post-approval performance, reporting requirements needed for regulators to evaluate post-approval performance, and a baseline of satisfactory pre-approval performance to serve as a regulatory benchmark, is the kind of irreversibility evidence the Department looks for.

The 'fully and irreversibly open' standard balances the benefits of expediting entry into local markets against the costs of foregoing entry by the BOCs into the long-distance market. The standard establishes a clear set of criteria for when the 'carrot' will be awarded while leaving it to the companies with (superior) information to determine the best way to achieve those criteria. The standard also commits the regulators not to give in to the kind of time-inconsistency problems that could crop up if the 'carrot' could potentially be used to motivate implementation of one regulation after another. A more detailed discussion analysing the reasonableness of this standard can be found

---

[9] This standard is explained more fully in the Oklahoma evaluation and is discussed in each of the Department's evaluations to date.

[10] See, in particular, the Department's evaluation of Bell South's application for long-distance entry in South Carolina ('South Carolina evaluation').

[11] South Carolina evaluation, p.3.

[12] South Carolina evaluation, p.3.

in an expert affidavit that the Department has submitted with each of its evaluations to date.[13]

A number of the BOCs desiring to enter long-distance have questioned whether the Department's standard is an effective way to motivate the gatekeepers to provide fair and efficient access to bottleneck facilities. One criticism claims that by making the BOCs' entry into the long-distance market subject to the decisions on local market entry of the current long-distance incumbents, the criteria for long-distance entry tends to deter rather than promote entry.[14] Another criticism argues that this 'carrot' is particularly costly. The Department has acknowledged that, at least in the short-term, BOC entry into the long-distance market is likely to provide some benefit to that market. Some studies of cases where the incumbent local carrier has been allowed into long-distance have estimated that the costs of foregoing these benefits is large. This suggests that a standard that defers these benefits in order to obtain faster local market competition may not be cost-effective.[15] To date, the Department has not found either criticism to be significant.

The argument that the Department's criteria for BOC long-distance entry is an unnecessary bar to entry raises an interesting question. Some critics argue that BOC entry into the long-distance market has the potential to be significantly pro-competitive; the result is that firms currently competing in that market have a strong incentive to delay that entry. The argument further assumes the long-distance companies have, at least tacitly, agreed not to enter the local market in order to prevent the BOCs from satisfying the Department's criteria. The conclusion of this line of thinking is that the Department should waive its criteria so that the long-distance companies will enter the local market and the BOCs can enter the long-distance market.

The Department has not been persuaded by this line of argumentation, in part because it believes that incentives to enter should be distinguished from the ability to enter.[16] The conclusion that long-distance competitors would quickly enter the local market once the local incumbent's application to enter long-distance had been granted does not appear entirely consistent with experience in other locales. Not all of the incumbent local telephone companies are

---

[13] Affidavit of Marius Schwartz May 14, 1997, originally filed with Oklahoma evaluation.

[14] See, for example, Bell South's brief in support of its second application to provide long-distance in Louisiana.

[15] See, for example, Declaration of Jerry A. Haussman filed with Bell South's second application to provide long-distance in Louisiana.

[16] For a more detailed evaluation of this argument, see Supplemental Affidavit of Marius Schwartz (3 November 1997) originally filed with South Carolina evaluation.

subject to the entry restriction. At least one fourth of all local telephone customers are served by companies that are already free to provide them with long-distance service. One of these, GTE, serves about as many customers as one of the BOCs, although these customers are spread across the entire country. Another, SNET, serves almost the entire state of Connecticut and looks like a small BOC. Both of these companies are offering long-distance service today, but local entry to compete for their customers has been no faster than it has been for any of the BOCs.

In addition, the companies in the long-distance market are not the only companies whose entry would be relevant under the Department's criteria. There are a number of firms that have begun operations since 1996 with the sole intent of providing competitive local services. None of these firms seem to have been significantly more successful in entering the residential local market than the long-distance incumbents.[17] Moreover, their very existence calls into question whether there would be any incentive to agree not to enter the local market among long-distance competitors only.

The argument that the Department's standard is not cost-effective is also troubling. However, while initial studies appeared to show substantial foregone benefits, the Department remains concerned that the benefits of motivating faster local market entry will be outweighed by the costs. The Department of Justice believes, for several reasons, that estimates of the effect on long-distance prices of BOC may be overstated. For example, the estimates rely heavily on a comparison of AT&T's rates with the rates SNET offered in Connecticut when it added long-distance to its local service offering there. That comparison has been called into question for its treatment of differences in the menu of price plans offered by AT&T and for not acknowledging the existence of other competitors with even lower price plans than those of SNET for important groups of customers.[18] Nevertheless, the Department does acknowledge that there can be benefits from BOC entry into long-distance. The Department recognises that any costs associated with increasing the risk that these benefits of long-distance entry may be delayed have to be weighed against the benefits of earlier local market competition where the incumbent is motivated to comply with market opening measures.

---

[17] See the assessment's of local competitive conditions attached to each of the Department's evaluations for details on the entry of companies such as E.spire, KMC Telecom, American MetroComm, and many others. For more general information, *see* the FCC's 'Responses to the First CCB Survey on the State of Local Competition'.

[18] For a more detailed discussion of this and other flaws in the numerical analyses, *see* Marius Schwartz' Supplemental Affidavit.

The benefits from stimulating local competition can be expected to be relatively large compared to the foregone benefits in long-distance for two important reasons: the local market is starting with far less competition than long-distance and the local market is much larger (about twice as large in terms of revenues). There is some indication that the incumbents who do not have the incentive of long-distance entry are more resistant to local market entry than the BOCs. Thus, the appropriate question is not just whether the costs of delaying BOC entry into long-distance are large, but whether they outweigh the benefits.[19]

IV. Local Competition Looking Forward

Regardless of one's views on these implementation issues, one might question the objective of this latest de-regulation. In a nutshell the question is: 'Which of today's barriers to entry are transitory and which will require continuing regulatory oversight to safeguard competition?' Some have imputed to the Telecom Act of 1996 the goal of fostering facilities-based competition everywhere with resale and unbundled network elements seen as only transitory measures.[20] While facilities-based competition may require the least amount of regulatory oversight, it simply may not be efficient to duplicate the functionality of the incumbents' networks in all instances. The Act does not appear to favour one of the entry paths over another. It is possible that each wholesale offering will be used in some circumstances—indeed, all three have been observed—so the future bottlenecks associated with each entry strategy will need to be evaluated.

In terms of resale competition, it seems likely that all of today's barriers to entry will be transitory. Retail operations are not typically a big bottleneck to competition. Underlying today's barriers is the need for entrants to find an effective way for their operational support systems (the computer systems that govern ordering, billing, maintenance, etc.) to communicate with the incumbent's systems. Another potential barrier is the wholesale price of the service. The Telecom Act requires that services be made available for resale at a dis-

---

[19] See Marius Schwarz' Supplemental Affidavit for a more detailed comparison of the likely costs and benefits.

[20] In a recent appellate court filing, for example, GTE argued that prices which encouraged entrants to use unbundled network elements were inappropriate because such prices would discourage the entrants from building their own facilities. See, *GTE South Incorporated* v *Morrison*, No. 98–1887 (4th Cir.).

count from retail rates computed on the basis of the retailing costs a wholesaler can avoid. Some incumbents have claimed that very few of their retailing costs are actually avoided unless they get out of retailing altogether. At this point, however, most regulators have not found this argument persuasive—presumably, they have not found there to be significant economies of scale in retailing.[21] It is certainly possible that such scale economies exist and that the competitive inroads available through resale are not viable, but at this point it seems more likely that the bottleneck in telecommunications will not be found in the retail operations.

The question of which of today's barriers to facilities-based entry are transitory depends quite heavily on one's optimism about new technologies for local access. At the time that the Act was being drafted there was a good deal of speculation that cable television facilities would quickly be converted to carry telephone traffic. The reality has been that the job of converting an existing coaxial cable network into something that can carry two-way traffic and, in particular, voice traffic, requires substantial capital upgrades. Many cable companies have been making the investment in their networks in order to get into the telecommunications business, however, and now are beginning to offer telephone service to some of their residential customers over their own facilities at some locations.

Duplicating the functionality of the incumbent's network is only one of the barriers faced by facilities-based entrants. Signing up some customers for their new facilities will not be sufficient to keep those customers if entrants cannot provide efficient interconnection to the incumbent's customers. While degrading the interconnection might disadvantage just as much of the incumbent's traffic as it does the entrant's, the fact that the incumbent has a much larger share of all customers means that the effect of a degradation would be much greater for an entrant's customers than for the incumbent's and may be a profitable strategy in the long term. The interconnection today between Internet backbone providers is an example of a similar situation. With the Internet there is virtually no regulation of interconnection; furthermore, no single network has been so large that it has had such an incentive to degrade interconnection quality. The requirement for MCI to divest its Internet backbone business before being acquired by WorldCom illustrates the Antitrust Division's awareness that incentives to degrade interconnection could grow if, through the merger, one provider came to command a significantly larger share of the

---

[21] See, for example, the arguments made by GTE in its recent appeal of the Virginia State Corporations Commission's arbitration of GTE's interconnection agreement with entrants (*GTE South Incorporated* v *Morrison*, No. 98–1887 (4th Cir.)).

market. Thus, the structural relief provided by the divestiture will help reduce the need for interconnection conduct regulation, by reducing incentives for misconduct. In the case of local telephone networks, where incumbency is an advantage, direct regulation may be needed to ensure that one firm cannot manipulate the network externalities to protect its monopoly.

Finally, consider the future of unbundled elements. It is important that competitors be able to enter either by using the local loops from the incumbent's switches and connecting those loops to their own switches or by connecting their own loops to the incumbent's switches. Alternatively, they could combine the two, thereby providing service over a network 'platform' composed entirely of elements of the incumbent's network. In retrospect, it is hardly surprising that the future of unbundled elements is more clouded than the Act's other entry avenues. The requirement that incumbents make the elements of their network efficiently available at wholesale to competitors is one of the most striking innovations of the Act. In theory, unbundling would make regulation easier: if the bottlenecks are to be found in the inputs to production; then regulation can focus on the inputs and leave it to competition to pass the benefits on to consumers. In practice, however, the questions of what network components (and in what combinations) will be considered elements, how those elements will be priced, how competitors will obtain access to the elements, and what the competitors can do with the elements, have been subject to numerous legal challenges.

If we were to be optimistic, we would hope to see a relatively clear articulation of the rules that will govern competitors' use of unbundled network elements in a relatively short time. Ideally, those rules will allow competitors flexibility and provide them with the correct incentives to identify which elements of the network are really bottlenecks in serving particular customers and which can be provided by competitors. The more that entrants see the real economic cost of the network elements (including the economies of scale and scope which the incumbent enjoys merely as a by-product of its incumbency), and the less that prices are based on accounting costs, the more efficient the entrants' choice between building and renting particular elements. Moreover, if entrants are not artificially penalised for using existing combinations of elements, but have the option to use any or all elements at prices based on forward-looking costs, they will have appropriate incentives to make efficient decisions as to when to use all or part of an existing network and when to construct some or all of their own facilities. For example, the cost of an unbundled local loop might efficiently include the real costs of disconnecting that loop from the incumbent's switch, but if the entrant wants to purchase that same loop with the unbundled switching element, the incumbent should be discouraged from creating artificial costs associated with performing a needless disconnect and re-connect.[22]

In summary, the 1996 Telecommunications Act has substantial promise. It could ultimately be a positive move in the direction of deregulation, in the process focusing regulation directly on bottlenecks and increasing reliance on competition to protect consumers. The Act's ability to fulfil that promise, however, depends on how effectively the spirit of the Act successfully survives the current phase of transition. The Department of Justice is working hard to give the Act that chance.

---

[22] While this may seem like an obvious requirement for the system to perform efficiently, some of the resistance to this kind of requirement may, in fact, be due to a political concern that this particular part of the Act would motivate quicker implementation of other parts (i.e., the Act's requirement that implicit subsidies be eliminated and that where policy requires some form of subsidies those be made explicit and competitively neutral).

VIII

Joachim Scherer*

Access to Bottleneck Facilities, Local Loop and Submarine Cables: the German Experience

I. Introduction

After a long and 'twisted journey'[1] through and from the United States, the 'essential facilities doctrine' has reached European shores.[2] The Commission first made reference to the essential facilities doctrine in the *Holyhead Harbour Cases*[3] and it has since been applied and refined in the *Port of Rødby Case*.[4] In its recent 'Notice on the application of the competition rules to access agreements in the telecommunications sector'[5] (the Access Notice), the Commission has attempted a sector-specific restatement of its own essential facilities doctrine for the access to bottlenecks in the telecommunications sector. The ECJ has, for the first time, explicitly addressed the doctrine and has construed it quite narrowly in its *Bronner* judgement.[6]

Various academic comments on the Access Notice view the essential facilities doctrine as a 'magic wand', which will enable the Commission, in its role as a European 'super-regulator', to open up telecommunications markets by enabling new entrants to obtain access to facilities controlled by incumbent operators;[7] others, on the contrary, suggest its application will have the opposite effect.[8]

The purpose of this paper is to illustrate (using two specific bottleneck situations as an example) that both national telecommunications law, and the

---

* Partner, Baker & McKenzie Frankfurt a.M. and Brussels; Professor of Law at Johann Wolfgang Goethe University, Frankfurt a.M.

[1] Kezsbom and Goldman (1996)

[2] For a comparative analysis, Venit and Kallaugher (1994).

[3] *B & I Line plc.* v *Sealink Harbours Ltd.*, Commission Decision of 11 June 1992, [1992] 5 CMLR 255; *Sea Containers* v *Stena Sealink*, Commission Decision 94/19/EC, pursuant to Article 82 [ex 86] of the Consolidated Treaty, OJ L 15/8 (1994).

[4] Commission Decision, 94/119/EEC, OJ L 55/52 (1994).

[5] Access Notice 98/C 265/02, OJ C 265/2 (1998).

[6] *Oscar Bronner GmbH & Co.KG*, Case C-7/97, [1998] ECR I–7791.

[7] Riehmer (1998) and John Kallaugher and Sven B. Völcker, 'The Application of the 'Essential Facilities' Doctrine', (manuscript), paper presented to the IBC Conference on European Telecommunications Law, Brussels 1991.

[8] See, for example, Engel and Knieps (1998).

secondary Community law which provides its basis, have already taken up many elements of the essential facilities doctrine and have specified and adapted them to the particular needs of the re-regulated telecommunications markets. Therefore, access to bottleneck facilities can and should primarily be ensured through the application of the *lex specialis*, rather than by application of the essential facilities doctrine, which, in Europe as well as in the US, still is an epithet in need of clearly defined limiting principles[9].

Among the main bottlenecks that have been identified in the telecommunications sector are the network infrastructures provided by the incumbent telecommunication organisations (TOs). As the Commission states in its Access Notice:

> Although [. . .] alternative infrastructure may, from 1 July 1996, be used for liberalised services, it will be some time before this is, in many cases, a satisfactory alternative to the facilities of the incumbent operator. Such alternative infrastructure does not, at present, offer the same dense geographic coverage as that of the incumbent TO's network.[10]

The two specific infrastructure bottlenecks tackled by this paper are the local loop and the international submarine cable system. The term 'local loop' denotes the part of the telecommunications network lying between the local exchange (or switching installation) and the network termination point at the customer's premises. In order to provide telecommunications services to their customers, new entrants need to obtain 'access' to the local loop, which can be ensured in various manners. International seacables are either copper or optical fibre cables, which provide transmission capacity, mainly on international routes. In the Commission's view, undersea cable capacity may be considered as a bottleneck because no technologically adequate substitute exists, since satellite connections do not provide the same level of transmission quality and network security.[11]

---

⁹ Areeda (1990); for a discussion of the concept of 'essentiality' with regard to competitive access in the telecommunications sector see, Larson, Kovacic and Douglas (1998).

¹⁰ Access Notice, *supra*, n 5, para 91.

¹¹ See, European Commission, *BT/MCI (II)* Decision, OJ L 336/1 (1997); see also European Commission Press Release IP/97/406 of May 14, 1997.

II. The Essential Facilities Doctrine and EC Telecommunications Law

1. Development of the Case Law

The first case in which the Commission explicitly addressed the essential facilities doctrine was *Stena Sealink*. The case concerned the refusal by Stena Sealink, which owns and operates port and ferry facilities at Holyhead in Wales, to provide access to those facilities, on a non-discriminatory basis, to competing enterprises that intended to provide competitive ferry services. The Commission found that:

> [an] undertaking which occupies a dominant position in the provision of an essential facility and itself uses that facility, i.e. a facility or infrastructure without access to which competitors cannot provide services to their customers, and which refuses other companies access to that facility without objective justification, or grants access to competitors only on terms less favourable than those which it gives to its own services, infringes Article 82 [ex 86] if the other conditions for applying that Article are met. A company in a dominant position may not discriminate in favour of its own activities in a related market . . . [T]he owner of an essential facility which uses its power in one market in order to strengthen its position in another related market, in particular, by granting its competitor access to that related market on less favourable terms than those of its own services, infringes Article 82 [ex 86], where a competitive disadvantage is imposed upon its competitor without objective justification.[12]

This ruling was explicitly based on the case law of the ECJ developed in the *Commercial Solvents* line of cases[13]. In Commercial Solvents, the Court had held that:

> an undertaking which has a dominant position in the market in raw materials and which, with the objective of reserving such raw material for manufacturing its own derivatives, refuses to supply a customer, which is itself a manufacturer of these derivatives, and therefore risks eliminating all competition on the part of its customer, is abusing its dominant position within the meaning of Article 82 [ex 86].[14]

---

[12] *Sealink, supra*, n 3, para 66.
[13] *Istituto Chemioterapico Italiano SpA and Commercial Solvents Corp.* v *Commission*, Joined Cases 6-7/73, [1974] ECR. 223; see also *United Brands*, [1978] ECR at 217 and *Benzine en Petroleum Handelsmaatschappij: B.V.* v *Commission*, Case 77/77, [1978] ECR. 1513. For a succinct analysis of the case law of the Court and of the Commission, Temple Lang (1994).
[14] *Commercial Solvents*, [1974] ECR at 250–251.

The Commission's 1992 *Sea Containers* decision re-states the general essential facilities principle in almost the same words as the B&I/Sealink decision, but adds:

> This principle applies when the competitor, seeking access to the essential facility is a new entrant into the relevant market.[15]

The *Port of Rødby* decision,[16] which was based on Article 86 [ex 90] Consolidated Treaty, concerned a refusal by the Danish Ministry of Transport to allow Stena to build a private commercial port near Rødby harbour and to operate a new ferry service from Rødby itself.[17] The Commission found that it would be an abuse of a dominant position, were the port authority to refuse to allow a competitor access to the port. It was, therefore, a violation of Article 86 [ex 90] for the state to refuse to authorise use of the port facility by the new entrant. The Commission found no evidence that the capacity limitations that had been claimed by the Danish government actually existed. Furthermore, it was clear that Stena was willing to finance any necessary alterations at the port facility.[18]

In the *Magill* case, which is often seen as an (implicit) confirmation, by the Court, of the essential facilities doctrine,[19] the ECJ confirmed the Commission's decision that the refusal by television broadcasting companies, which were the only source of programming information, to allow a competitor to publish comprehensive programming information in their copyrighted weekly program listings, constituted an abuse of a dominant position.[20] The Court found that, although a refusal to license does not of itself—in the absence of other factors—constitute an abuse, dominant firms may, 'in exceptional circumstances', be obliged to license competitors to use their intellectual property.[21]

In the *Bronner* case,[22] Advocate General Jacobs took a restrictive view of

---

[15] Commission Decision, 94/19/EEC, OJ L 15/8 (1994), at para 67 (hereinafter: *Sea Containers*).

[16] *Port of Rødby, supra,* n 4.

[17] *Ibid,* at 52.

[18] *Ibid,* at 54.

[19] Deselaers (1995: 565).

[20] Commission Decision, 89/205/EEC, *Magill TV Guide/ITP, BBC and RTE,* 89/205/EEC, OJ L 78/43 (1989); Case T-69/89, *RTE* v *Commission,* [1991] ERC II–485; Case T–70/89, *BBC* v *Commission,* [1991] ERC II–535; Case T–76/89, *ITP* v *Commission,* [1991] ERC II–575; Joined Cases C–241/91 P and C 242/91 P, *RTE and ITP* v *Commission,* [1995] ERC I–743.

[21] *Magill, ibid,* at 743.

[22] *Oscar Bronner GmbH & Co.KG,* Opinion of Advocate General Jacobs, *supra,* 6.

the essential facilities—which was adopted by the Court—and pointed out three of the doctrine's general limitations:

> First, it is apparent that the right to choose one's trading partners and freely to dispose of one's property are generally recognised principles in the laws of the Member States, in some cases with constitutional status. Incursions on those rights require careful justifications . . . .
>
> Secondly, the justification in terms of competition policy for interfering with a dominant undertaking's freedom to contract often requires a careful balancing of conflicting considerations. In the long term, it is generally pro-competitive and in the interest of consumers to allow a company to retain for its own use facilities which it has developed for the purpose of its business. For example, if access to a production, purchasing or distribution facility were allowed too easily, there would be no incentive for a competitor to develop competing facilities. Thus, while competition was increased in the short term it would be reduced in the long term. Moreover, the incentive for a dominant undertaking to invest in efficient facilities would be reduced if its competitors were, upon request, able to share the benefits. Thus the mere fact that by retaining a facility for its own use a dominant undertaking retains an advantage over a competitor cannot justify requiring access to it.
>
> Thirdly, in assessing this issue, it is important not to lose sight of the fact that the primary purpose of Article 82 [ex 86] is to prevent distortion of competition—and in particular to safeguard the interests of consumers—rather than to protect the position of particular competitors. It may therefore, for example, be unsatisfactory, in a case in which a competitor demands access to a raw material in order to be able to compete with the dominant undertaking on a downstream market in a final product, to focus solely on the latter's market power on the upstream market, and conclude that its conduct is reserving to itself the downstream market and is automatically an abuse. Such conduct will not have an adverse impact on consumers unless the dominant undertaking's final product is sufficiently insulated from competition to give it market power.[23]

On this basis, the Advocate General suggested that the essential facilities doctrine should not be applied to a dominant Austrian newspaper group, which refused the publishers of a competing newspaper access to its home-delivery network. The decisive criterion, in the Advocate General's opinion, was the 'essentiality' of the facility in question, i.e. the nation-wide home-delivery network: Advocate General Jacobs pointed out that:

---

[23] *Ibid*, para. 56–58.

it is not sufficient that the undertaking's control over a facility should give it a competitive advantage . . . [rather, the dominant undertaking must have] . . . a genuine stranglehold on the related markets. That might be the case for example where duplication of the facility is impossible or extremely difficult owing to physical, geographical or legal constraints or is highly undesirable for reasons of public policy.[24]

In particular, the Advocate General proposed a high threshold which must be met, so that only the restrictive cost of duplicating the facility may constitute an insuperable barrier:

[If] the cost of duplicating the facility alone is the barrier to entry, it must be such as to deter any prudent undertaking from entering the market. In that regard . . . it will be necessary to consider all the circumstances, including the extent to which the dominant undertaking, having regard to the degree of amortisation of its investment and the cost of upkeep, must pass on investment or maintenance costs in the prices charged on the related market . . . .[25]

The Court followed the Advocate General's restrictive interpretation of the essential facilities doctrine and pointed to the limitations established in *Commercial Solvents*[26] and in *Magill:*[27]

Although in *Commercial Solvents v Commission* and *CBEM* . . . the Court of Justice held the refusal by an undertaking holding a dominant position in a given market to supply an undertaking with which it was in competition in a neighbouring market with raw materials and services respectively, which were indispensable to carrying on the rival's business, to constitute an abuse, it should be noted, first, that the Court did so to the extent that the conduct in question was likely to eliminate all competition on the part of that undertaking.

Secondly, in *Magill*

the Court held that refusal by the owner of an intellectual property right to grant a licence, even if it is the act of the undertaking holding a dominant position, cannot in itself constitute abuse of a dominant position, but that the exercise of an exclusive right by the proprietor may, in exceptional circumstances, involve an abuse.
    In *Magill*, the Court found such exceptional circumstances in the fact that the refusal in question concerned a product (information on the weekly schedules of

---

24 *Ibid*, para. 65.
25 *Ibid*, para. 66.
26 *Supra*, n 14.
27 *Supra*, n 20.

certain television channels), the supply of which was indispensable for carrying on the business in question (the publishing of a general television guide).

It should be emphasised in that respect that, in order to demonstrate that the creation of [an alternative] . . . system is not a realistic potential alternative and that access to the existing system is therefore indispensable, it is not enough to argue that it is not economically viable by reason of the small circulation of the daily newspaper or newspapers to be distributed.[28]

It follows, both from the Advocate General's analysis, and from the Court's own interpretation of its precedents, that two criteria must be met before a facility (or service) can be qualified as 'essential':

(1) Refusal to provide the facility (or service) must be 'likely to eliminate all competition' on the part of the undertaking requiring access to the facility (or provision of the service).[29]
(2) Access to the facility (or provision of the service) must be 'indispensable for carrying on the business in question',[30] insofar as there is 'no actual or potential substitute in existence'.[31] Furthermore, the refusal to grant access to the facility (or to provide the service) must be objectively justified.[32]

The Court's *Bronner* decision has reduced the essential facilities doctrine to its core: it is an instrument that can (only) be used in cases where an undertaking holding a dominant position on a vertically integrated market fails to grant access to a facility (or to a service) which meets the 'essentiality' test set out above.[33]

2. The Commission's Access Notice

In its Access Notice of August 1998,[34] the Commission, for the first time, expanded the scope of the applicability of its essential facilities concept from the transport sector to the telecommunications sector. The Commission

---

[28] *Supra*, n 6, paras 38, 39, 45.
[29] *Ibid*, para. 38; see also, Opinion of Advocate General Jacobs, para. 65.
[30] *Ibid*, para. 40.
[31] *Ibid,* also Opinion of Advocate General para 41 and 66.
[32] *Ibid* para. 41.
[33] See, in particular, Areeda (1994).
[34] *Supra*, n 5.

describes the essential facilities doctrine fairly broadly as the principle 'that a firm controlling an essential facility must give access in certain circumstances'.[35]

These circumstances include a case in which the absence of commercially-feasible access alternatives means that the party requesting access would not be able to operate on the service market:

> '[R]efusal in this case would therefore limit the development of new markets, or new products on those markets, contrary to Article 82(b) [ex 86b], or impede the development of competition on existing markets'.[36]

The Commission states that, in order to determine whether access should be ordered under the competition rules, it will take into account the following five cumulative criteria:

(1) access to the facility in question is generally essential in order for companies to compete on an existing or potential market for which access is being requested;
(2) there is sufficient capacity available to provide access;
(3) the facility owner fails to satisfy demand on an existing service product market, blocks the emergence of a potential new service or product, or impedes competition on an existing or potential service or product market;
(4) the company seeking access is prepared to pay the reasonable and non-discriminatory price and will otherwise, in all respects, accept non-discriminatory access terms and conditions;
(5) there is no objective justification for refusing to provide access.[37]

3. Shortcomings of the Essential Facilities Doctrine

Despite the conceptual clarity of the essential facilities test as set forth in the Access Notice, it is obvious (particularly in the light of *Magill* and *Bronner*

---

[35] Access Notice, *ibid*, para 88 with further references.

[36] *Ibid.*

[37] *Ibid* para. 91. It is interesting to note that these elements are almost identical with those articulated by the United States Court of Appeals (7th Circuit) in the MCI Case. Based upon an analysis of the case law, the MCI Court found the following four elements necessary to establish liability under the Essential Facility Doctrine: (1) control of the essential facility by a monopolist, (2) competitor's inability practically or reasonably to duplicate the essential facility, (3) the denial of the use of the facility to a competitor and (4) the feasibility of providing the facility, *MCI Communications Corporation and MCI Telecommunications Corporation v American Telephone and Telegraph* Company, 708 F. 2d 1081, 1132–1133 (7th Cir. 1983).

cases) that the scope of applicability of the essential facilities doctrine is fairly limited:

First, the requirement that access to the facility in question must be 'generally essential' (or, in the terminology of *Bronner*, 'indispensable'), in order for companies to compete with the provider of the facility on a related (downstream) market, is both opaque and fraught with uncertainty: The Commission's proposed test—refusal of access must lead to the proposed activities being made either impossible or seriously and unavoidably uneconomic[38]—does not provide much guidance since it does not address the time dimension. In the short and medium term, almost any refusal to grant access to the different segments of a telecommunications infrastructure, will make the provision of competitive services 'seriously and unavoidably uneconomic'. Once the establishment of alternative infrastructures has begun, this may rapidly change. Does that mean that a facility may be considered 'essential' (only) as long as no 'satisfactory alternative' to the facilities of the incumbent operator exists?[39] Or, does it mean that the facility is not 'essential' because the refusal to grant access does not make the proposed activities 'unavoidably' uneconomic, since amortisation will occur over time?

A further ambiguity in the essential facilities test is apparent in its fifth criterion, which allows for 'objective justifications' for the refusal to provide access; but does not specify the reasons in any detail. Equally, the essential facilities test does not address the 'unbundling' of facilities: Unbundling—the separation or segregation of services, service features or capabilities which can be installed, provided, accessed, measured and purchased separately from other services, service features or capabilities—is a crucial instrument to promote competition in telecommunications markets. If the incumbent is forced to 'unbundle' its facilities, entrants and other users can freely choose and buy only those (unbundled) facilities or components of facilities which they require or need. Seen in this light, the Commission's Access Notice does not establish sector-specific unbundling guidelines, but appears, instead, to rely on the general prohibition of tying arrangements found in Article 82(d) [ex 86(d)].

---

[38] Access Notice, *supra*, n 5, para 91 (a).
[39] This appears to be the Commission's view, *ibid.*

4. Sector-specific Legislation: The Interconnection Directive

Competitive access is one of the primary objectives of the EC's Open Network Provision (ONP) concept. The ONP Framework Directive[40] establishes harmonised principles for open access to, and use of, public telecommunications networks and, where applicable, public telecommunications services. It thus defines, for specific facilities, the rules under which fair and open access must be granted and establishes, as a matter of law, that such facilities are 'essential'.

Based on the ONP principles, the Interconnection Directive[41] has established a regulatory framework to ensure the interconnection of telecommunications networks as an instrument to foster competition, both with regard to the services to be provided to end users, and in relation to the access to those facilities necessary to provide that service to end users.[42] The Interconnection Directive provides for two types of access to essential facilities: interconnection and (special) network access. Interconnection is defined, in Article 2(1a) of the Directive, as:

> the physical and logical linking of telecommunications networks used by the same or a different organisation in order to allow the user of one organisation to communicate with users of the same or another organisation, or to access services provided by another organisation. Services may be provided by the parties involved or other parties who have access to the network.

In addition to 'open and efficient interconnection', the Interconnection Directive, in Article 1, also provides for 'open and efficient . . . access to public telecommunications networks and publicly available telecommunications services'.

'Interconnection', and the other forms of (special) 'access' addressed in the Interconnection Directive, differ with regard to: (1) the party that is obliged to grant access; (2) the means with which access is to be granted; (3) the justification for a refusal to provide access, and; (4) the available remedies.

---

[40] Council Directive 90/387/ECC of 28 June 1990 on the establishment of the internal market for telecommunications services through the implementation of open network provision, OJ L 192/1 (1990) as amended by Directive 97/51/EC, OJ L 295/23 (1997).

[41] Directive 97/33/EC of the European Parliament and of the Council of 30 June 1997 on interconnection in Telecommunications with regard to ensuring universal services and interoperability through application of the principles of Open Network Provision (ONP), OJ L 199/32 (1997).

[42] For this distinction see the Access Notice, *supra*, n 5, para. 45.

(1) The right and the obligation to negotiate interconnection applies to: (i) organisations which provide fixed and/or mobile switched telecommunications networks, and/or publicly available telecommunications services, and which, in so doing, control the means of access to one or more network termination points identified by one or more unique numbers in the national numbering plan; (ii) organisations which provide leased lines to users' premises, (iii) organisations which are authorised in a Member State to provide international circuits between the Community and third countries, and to which have been granted exclusive and special rights, and; (iv) organisations providing telecommunications services which are permitted to interconnect in accordance with relevant national licensing or authorisation schemes.

The obligation to interconnect, which is not explicitly established in the Directive, but which follows from the 'obligation . . . to negotiate' and from the powers of the NRAs (National Regulatory Authorities) to order interconnection, does not depend upon the market position of the interconnecting parties, but merely upon their role as providers of 'switched and unswitched bearer capabilities to users upon which other telecommunications services depend' (Article 4(1) Interconnection Directive). By contrast, the obligation to 'meet all reasonable requests for access to the network, including access at points other than the network termination points offered to the majority of end users', (Article 4(2) Interconnection Directive), applies only to organisations that are authorised to provide certain public telecommunications networks and services,[43] and that have significant market power.[44]

(2) The second difference between 'interconnection' and other forms of (special) network 'access' lies in the mode of technical implementation. 'Interconnection' denotes the physical and logical linking of networks, with a view to allow end-to-end interoperability of services for users. Network 'access', by contrast, is a much broader concept, which has been further specified for the fixed telephone network in Article 16 of the ONP Voice Telephony Directive. Article 16(1) provides that:

---

[43] The relevant telecommunications networks and services are listed in Annex I and include the fixed public telephone network, leased lines services, public mobile telephone networks and public mobile telephone services.

[44] Under Article 4(2), para. 2, 'an organisation shall be presumed to have significant market power when it has a share of more than 25% of a particular telecommunications market in the geographical area in a Member State within which it is authorised to operate'. NRAs may determine that an organisation with a market share of less than 25% in the relevant markets has significant market power or that an organisation with the market share of more than 25% in the relevant market does not have such power.

national regulatory authorities shall ensure that the organisation with significant market power in the provision of fixed public telephone networks deals with reasonable requests from organisations providing telecommunications services for access to the fixed public telephone network at network termination points other than the commonly provided network termination points referred to in Part 1 of Annex II. This obligation may only be limited on a case-by-case basis and on the grounds that there are technically and commercially viable alternatives to the special access requested, and if the requested access is inappropriate in relation to the resources available to meet the request.

Similarly, Article 6 of the ONP Leased Lines Directive, provides for open access to and usage of leased lines.

(3) The justifications for a refusal to grant interconnection differ significantly from the justifications under the essential facilities doctrine, in that they are characterised by a high degree of specificity: interconnection may only be restricted in order to safeguard the 'essential requirements' set forth in the ONP Framework Directive,[45] and further specified in Article 10 Interconnection Directive. These 'essential requirements' are: (i) security of network operations; (ii) maintenance of network integrity; (iii) interoperability of services, and; (iv) data protection. The Interconnection Directive makes it clear that none of these 'essential requirements', *per se*, justifies a refusal to negotiate terms of interconnection. Rather, the NRAs are obliged to impose, where necessary, proportionate and non-discriminatory conditions that ensure compliance with the essential requirements.

A refusal to interconnect may be justified on a case-by-case basis, if the national regulatory authority agrees to limit the interconnection obligation on a temporary basis. Here, however, certain caveats still apply by virtue of Article 4(1) of the Interconnection Directive. Accordingly there must be technically and commercially viable alternatives to the interconnection requested; meanwhile, the requested interconnection must be inappropriate in relation to the resources available to meet the request.

The justifications for a refusal to provide network access are slightly broader, in that requests for special networks access must be 'reasonable'.[46] This 'rule of reason' is not further specified in the ONP Directives, but is subject to (technical) specification: the Commission may, in consultation with the ONP Committee, request the European Telecommunications Standards

---

[45] Article 3(2) Directive 90/387/EEC; see also Article 6(1) ONP Leased Lines Directive.

[46] Article 4 para. 2 Interconnection Directive; see also Article 16 para. 1 ONP Voice Telephony Directive.

Institute (ETSI) to draw up standards for new types of national access (Article 16(8) ONP Voice Telephony Directive).

(4) Another difference between the application of the essential facilities doctrine under Article 82 [ex 86] on the one hand, and the interconnection rules under the ONP Interconnection Directive on the other, relates to procedural efficiency. Whereas Commission investigations under competition rules are not subject to time-limits and take, on average, two to four years, the Interconnection Directive requires NRAs to resolve 'interconnection disputes' between organisations in a single Member State, at the request of either party, within six months of the request.[47] No such deadlines exist for the NRAs' decisions on disputes relating to special network access. Article 16(4) ONP Voice Telephony Directive, merely provides that national regulatory authorities:

> may intervene on their own initiative at any time, where justified, in order to ensure effective competition and/or interoperability of services and shall do so, if requested by either party, in order to set conditions which are non-discriminatory, fair and reasonable for both parties and offer the greatest benefit to all users.

Summarising briefly, the ONP Directives have established a regulatory framework which provides for access to specific 'essential' telecommunications facilities (including telecommunications services), subject to narrowly defined exceptions and to regulatory oversight both at national and at EC level.

III. Bottleneck in the Local Loop: The German Customer Access Line Case

One of the most controversial country-specific regulatory decisions relating to 'bottleneck' situations in Germany, was the 1997 decision of the Federal Ministry of Posts and Telecommunications (*Bundesministerium für Post und Telekommunikation,* BMPT) and the German NRA (*Regulierungsbehörde für Telekommunikation und Post,* RegTP), to grant the competitors of Deutsche Telekom AG (DT) access to DT's customer access lines (CAL).

In the Customer Access Line Case, which was brought before the German administrative courts,[48] DT's obligation to provide its competitors with

---

[47] Article 9 (5), sentence 1 Interconnection Directive.

[48] Following its decision in the preliminary court procedure refusing, DT's application for a stay order, the Administrative Court of Cologne, as the court of first instance, gave its preliminary judgment on 5 November 1998 and dismissed DT's court action as unfounded.

unbundled access to CAL in the local loop, was established and clarified. The case illustrates how sector-specific national legislation, based upon EC telecommunications law, may provide a useful and efficient tool to ensure 'unbundled' access to the local loop. Recourse to the essential facilities doctrine under Article 82 [ex 86] was not necessary.

1. The Bottleneck

CAL are lines running from the network termination point at the customer's premises to the local switch. The provision of 'unbundled' CAL means that neither switching nor transmission functions are provided.[49] In order to provide voice telephony services to end customers, competitive carriers need to connect the customer's terminal equipment to their telecommunications networks. From a technical point of view, this can be achieved in various ways, including the installation of new customer access lines by the competitive carrier, or the provision of an alternative local network access infrastructure (e.g. a radio link or 'wireless local loop'). Equally, access to the customer can be achieved through the interconnection of the competitive carrier's (long distance) telecommunication network to the incumbent's local network, through the provision of customer access services (including certain transmission functions) by the incumbent to the competitive carrier, and through the provision of (unbundled) customer access lines by the incumbent to the competitive carrier.

Under present circumstances, both the establishment of alternative CAL or the use of alternative local network infrastructures, such as the wireless local loop, would not merely seem—in the terminology of the Commission's Access Notice—to be 'seriously and unavoidably uneconomic', but might, rather, be described as—in the terms of the *Bronner* Case—'impossible'.[50] Similarly, interconnection to the incumbent's local network, as well as the provision of carrier access services by the incumbent, would leave the provision of numerous service functions in the hands of the incumbent and would thus prevent competitive carriers from competing with the incumbent in downstream customer markets.

---

[49] For a more detailed description see Superior Administrative Court of Northrhine Westphalia, hearing protocol of 29 September 1997, published in, MMR 1998, 98.

[50] Access Notice, *supra* n 5, para. 91: '. . . Refusal of access must lead to the proposed activities being made either impossible or seriously and unavoidably uneconomic'.

In conclusion, therefore, under present technical and market conditions, access to the 'unbundled' CAL is necessary, if competitive carriers are to be allowed to compete with an incumbent in downstream market.

2. The Regulatory Framework

The German Telecommunications Act (*Telekommunikationsgesetz*, TKG),[51] does not establish specific rules regarding access to CAL. However, Section 33 TKG, provides both for the 'special control of abusive practices', and for the imposition upon dominant operators of an obligation to grant competitors access to its internal and external services—on a non-discriminatory basis and on the same conditions applying to itself—where such services are 'essential' in order to provide other telecommunications services, and where there are no objective justifications for less favourable treatment. Section 33 TKG, aims to ensure competitors' non-discriminatory to a dominant provider's 'essential' services, which may include 'essential' facilities.

3. Practical Implementation: The *Teilnehmeranschlußleitung* Case

a) Procedural background
In 1997, three of DT's competitors—Mannesmann Arcor, o.tel.o and NetCologne—began proceedings before the German NRA; at that time the BMPT. The new entrants had been attempting to negotiate access to DT's CAL since November 1996. DT, however, was not prepared to offer access to the 'bare copper wire', but, instead, offered a form of carrier customer access that included certain transmission functions which the new entrants did not require.

In the absence of an agreement, the BMPT issued an order instructing DT to make an offer, in accordance with the competitors' demand, for the provision of unbundled access to DT's CAL. According to the order, DT was not allowed to include, within its offer, service features which its competitors had not requested. DT could only avoid the interconnection obligation where it could show, in each individual case, that granting access to the customer line was factually impossible.

---

[51] Of 25 July, 1996, Bundesgesetzblatt [Federal Law Gazette] I, p. 1120 as amended by the Act Accompanying the Telecommunications Act of December 16, 1997, Bundesgesetzblatt I, p. 3108.

The BMPT's order had immediate effect and DT applied to the Administrative Court of Cologne for a preliminary stay of action. This was refused,[52] and DT then appealed to the Superior Administrative Court of the state of Northrhine Westphalia. In a preliminary decision, the Court made it clear that it would reject DT's motion and gave a detailed statement of reasons for its judgment. As a consequence, DT withdrew its motion and agreed to submit to its competitors, a detailed offer for access to CAL within two weeks. The offer was submitted and, in a subsequent procedure, the price for the provision of CAL services was set, by the BMPT, at DM 20,65 (DT had requested that the price be set at DM 28), pending a final decision.

b) Main issues and Arguments

In the Customer Access Line Case, the German courts were faced with four main issues,[53] which mirror, in part, the elements of the essential facilities doctrine, as laid down by the Commission in its Access Notice:

(1) What are the 'services' to which the dominant operator must provide access?
(2) What is an 'essential' facility?
(3) Which reasons justify a refusal to provide access to the CAL.
(4) How much unbundling may be required? In this case, the Court had to decide whether the dominant operator, DT, could be obliged to 'unbundle' its services in the local loop to such an extent that only the bare customer access line (without any transmission or switching functions) would be provided.

What is a 'Facility'?

With regard to the issue of the definition of a facility, DT took the position that the 'services' to which it is obliged to grant access are limited to 'telecommunication services'. In other words, DT argued that it was only obliged to grant fair and non-discriminatory access to 'telecommunications services' and not to other types of services, such as CAL. The Administrative Court held that this interpretation was neither in accordance with the wording of Section 33(1) TKG, nor fitted with its purpose. Both terms (telecommunications services and

---

[52] Judgment confirmed on the 5th November 1998.

[53] In addition, DT had argued that the administrative order lacked the required specificity and that the Regulatory Authority had failed to exercise its discretion.

services) are found within the same sentence in Section 33(1) TKG, while , 'services', addressed by Section 33(1) and Section 33(2) TKG are identified as the 'precondition' for the competitive provision of telecommunication services. The Administrative Court therefore concluded:

> The term 'service' is, therefore, by necessity broader than the term 'telecommunication services' and includes, in any event, those internal elements of the applicant's infrastructure which are required for the provision of telecommunication services on the market.[54]

The Superior Administrative Court concurred with this view and pointed out that only a broad interpretation of the term 'services' would allow the legislative objective of creating and enhancing workable competition to be achieved:

> If the new entrants were restricted to using the existing service offerings of the dominant provider or, if they were restricted, in the case of network access to the bandwidths or bit rates offered by the dominant provider, to the transmission technology used by him, the true competition envisaged by the legislator would not be achievable.[55]

What is 'Essential'?

As regards the essential nature of the CAL and the burden of proof, DT argued that new entrants must demonstrate that a particular service—such as the provision of CAL—was 'essential' in order to satisfy a concrete demand in an individual case. Under this standard, the new entrants would have been required to disclose their detailed product and service plans to DT, in order to demonstrate that the provision of an individual CAL was actually required to satisfy a specific consumer's needs.

Again, the Court demurred and opted for a pro-competitive interpretation. The Court held that a service is 'essential' if 'the competitor is, in fact, precluded from the provision of the telecommunications services which it intends to provide, unless the required service is provided.[56]

The Court also implicitly addressed the requirement, laid down in the Commission's Access Notice, that it is not sufficient that the position of the

---

[54] Administrative Court of Cologne, Court Order of 18 August 1997, MMR 1998, p. 98, 99 MMR, 1998, p. 102, 103.

[55] Superior Administrative Court of Northrhine Westphalia, Hearing Protocol of 29 September 1997.

[56] Administrative Court of Cologne, *supra*, n 54, at 103.

company requesting access would be more advantageous if access were granted and that the refusal of access 'must lead to the proposed activities being made either impossible or seriously and unavoidably uneconomic'.[57]

The Administrative Court found that:

> the intervenor [the new entrant] does not possess the required lines and cannot establish them with reasonable effort on a nation-wide basis. The intervenor, who intends to provide voice telephony services through fixed lines, would, therefore, be precluded from reaching the approximately 40 million end users that are presently using the services of the applicant, unless it is granted access to the customer access lines, irrespective of the technical conditions under which such access is granted. The intervenor would, therefore, be precluded from providing such service offerings on this market.[58]

Justifications for a Refusal to Grant Access

DT had claimed, during the administrative procedure, that its network security would be jeopardised if competitors were allowed to access CAL because 'areas of responsibility' for the proper functioning of the network could no longer be clearly delineated. This argument, however, was not raised before the Courts. Instead, DT's main justification of its refusal to provide access to its CALs was based upon a capacity argument. An obligation to provide CALs to a competitor would preclude DT: (1) from providing these CAL to its own customers; (2) from providing telecommunication services to the customer, and; (3) from using the CAL for the provision of services to several customers (e.g. the use of multiplexing equipment) in the case of scarcity.

Though rebutting these claims, the Court noted that:

> [Section 2 (3) NZV . . .] specifies the statutory basis for the ordinance in Section 35(5) TKG . . . [by providing] . . . that no obligation for unbundling and therefore no obligation to make a corresponding offer exists, if the (network) operator can provide evidence that such a requirement is not objectively justified in a given instance. With regard to the customer access line, unbundled access can, therefore, not be demanded if the operator is, due to an existing overloading of the line, already using transmission systems allowing the multiple use of the medium, and if

---

[57] Access Notice, n 5, para. 91.

[58] Administrative Court of Cologne, *supra*, n 54, at 103; 'The . . . essentiality criterion is fulfilled . . . if the competitor is, in the absence of the requested service, in fact prevented from rendering the telecommunications services which it intends to provide, whereby . . . the court must 'examine whether such services are objectively essential for the provision of telecommunications services'.

such line is also to be used in the future for the provision of services to end customers other than those of the competitor who is seeking access. In this case, the
competitor can only demand 'bundled' access, i.e. the competitor will, where necessary, be obliged to share the transmission systems and to pay for such usage. The
same applies if, due to the demand of a competitor, a need to install such systems
arises where end customers remaining with the dominant provider will not be able
to receive services without such systems. In this case, 'bundled' access to the line is
justified; [the operator] is not obliged to cede a line to the requesting party and to
provide service to its own customers through cost-intensive new installations.[59]

The crucial issue to be determined by the Court was whether or not DT was
obliged to 'unbundle' its services in such a manner that only the 'bare' CAL—
without any transmission or switching functions—would be provided to DT's
competitors. In this context, Section 2(2) of the Ordinance on Network Access
provides that '[T]he carrier shall provide unbundled access to all network elements, including unbundled access to the customer access line'.[60]

Both DT's competitors and the regulator had assumed that DT would be
obliged to unbundle this 'essential service' in accordance with requests received
from its competitors, insofar as this was technically possibile. In their view, the
only 'objective' limitation to the unbundling obligation was its technical feasibility. With regard to the specific case of the CAL, the competitors and the
NRA found support for their position in Section 2(3) NZV, which provides
explicitly that '[T]he unbundling requirement shall not apply where the carrier
can provide evidence that such requirement is not objectively justified in a
given instance'.

This provision was viewed by the NRA and the new entrants, as a specification of the general 'unbundling' obligation which underlined the obligation
of the dominant enterprise to provide non-discriminatory access to essential
services (Section 33(1) TKG), as a specification of the particular obligation to
provide non-discriminatory network access (Section 35(2) TKG) and as a specification of the unbundling requirement which applies to all forms of access to
networks or services.

Both the Administrative Court and the Superior Administrative Court
found that the unbundling requirement of Section 2(2) NZV applied. The
Administrative Court did not conclude, however, from the unbundling
requirement, 'that the technical feasibility alone provides a yardstick for the

---

[59] Superior Administrative Court of Northrhine Westphalia, *supra*, n 55, at 100.
[60] Verordnung über besondere Netzzugänge (Netzzugangsverordnung—NZV)—
Ordinance concerning special network access, of 23 October 1996, BGBl. I, p. 1568.

service packages that are to be provided in conjunction with the unbundled access to the customer access line'.[61]

Instead, the Administrative Court viewed the unbundling requirement in Section 2 NZV as a 'sector-specific version of Article 82(2)(d) [ex 82(2)(d)] Consolidated Treaty'. Under this analysis, the degree to which DT's 'essential services' must be unbundled, is not determined by (demand and) technical feasibility alone, but by 'the relation that exists between the main service and the alleged additional services'.[62] The decisive criterion for determining the required degree of unbundling was, in the Administrative Court's view, 'whether or not a relationship exists in such a manner that technical or economic reasons justify the combination of the services concerned in a single offer'.[63]

By contrast, the Superior Administrative Court found a clear guideline for the degree of unbundling required in Section 2(2) NZV. This provision grants to DT's competitors a right of access to the CAL and imposes a corresponding obligation upon DT to unbundle its services, so that only the CAL is provided.[64]

IV. Bottlenecks in International Facilities: Access to Submarine Cable Systems

International submarine cable systems are generally considered as bottlenecks because they were historically constructed and operated exclusively by incumbent telecommunications organisations; the establishment of a seacable system is a time-consuming process, taking, on average, two to four years from the conclusion of the constituting agreement to the 'ready for service date'. There is, currently, no substitute for submarine cable systems, because international satellite links are less secure and do not provide for the same degree of transmission quality.[65]

1. The Bottleneck Situations

International submarine cables are copper cables, or optical fibre cables, with transmission capacities that range between 1.5 GBit/s and 40 GBit/s. An inter-

---

[61] Administrative Court, *supra*, n 54, 104.

[62] *Ibid.*

[63] Administrative Court, *supra*, n 54, 104.

[64] Superior Administrative Court, *supra*, n 55, at. 99.

[65] For a comprehensive analysis of the international law and practice relating to submarine cables see Smits (1991: 93 and 101); Hitchings (1998).

national submarine cable system consists of the following components and segments:

- the terminal station (or cable station), which is a building near the coastline where the seacable is physically connected to the land-based cable system;
- the connection between the seacable landing point (also known as 'beach joint') to the cable station; and
- the seacable between two beach joints.

Access to seacable capacity has become a 'bottleneck' issue in two ways: first, with regard to the cable stations and; secondly, with regard to the provision of 'unbundled' transmission capacity on the seacable.

a) Bottleneck in the Cable Stations

Competitive carriers who have already established or are in the process of establishing their own land-based fixed telecommunications network infrastructures are seeking access to cable stations in order to connect their land-based communications lines with submarine cable systems. Typically, these competitive carriers have leased (or bought) transmission capacity on the seacable. By connecting their own land-based cables to the seacable, these competitive carriers have direct access to seacable capacity, which generally makes better economic sense than use of 'backhaul' services that are offered the incumbent operators.

In Germany, DT owns and operates all of the cable stations. It has, on occasion, refused its competitors access to such cable stations on the grounds that:

(1) certain cable stations are not sufficiently large to allow for third party access;

(2) certain cable stations do not allow for the necessary network security measures; and

(3) certain cable stations do not have the technical capacity to break down the 155 MBit/s transmission capacity of the seacable into smaller transmission capacities.

b) Bottleneck in the Seacable

The second 'bottleneck' issue in this sector is that of access to seacable capacity. Traditionally, seacable systems were built by consortia of telecommunications operators on the basis of Construction and Maintenance Agreements (C&MA). Prior to the liberalisation of the telecommunications markets, the parties to the C&MA were the telecommunications organisations of those countries where the seacable was landed. On the basis of the C&MA, each contracting party acquired part of the transmission capacity of the seacable. To this end, the total transmission capacity is divided into 'Minimum Investment Units (MIUs) which are equivalent to a defined transmission capacity (e.g. 2 MBit/s). By acquiring one or more MIUs, the contracting party obtains:

(1) a corresponding share of the ownership of the seacable segment between two landing points;
(2) the corresponding voting rights in the administrative bodies which are established under the C&MA, and which are in charge of the management and administration of the seacable system's operations;
(3) the right to use the transmission capacity which corresponds to the MIUs that have been acquired, and;
(4) the right to acquire additional transmission capacity if the design capacity of the seacable system is subsequently extended.

Under most C&MAs, the parties' rights to use transmission capacity are limited to one half of the seacable, i.e. from the landing point on their territories to the nominal mid-point of the seacable. This usage right is sometimes referred to as a 'half-interest'. The other half-interest may be owned by the same contracting party; and, in this case, the contracting party owns two 'half-interests' or a 'whole interest'. By contrast, the other half-interest may be owned by another contracting party on the basis of an MIU. The other half-interest may also be owned by a third party (i.e. an operator which is not a party to the C&MA) on the basis of an 'Indefeasible Right of Use' (IRU).

The contracting parties may 'sell' the usage rights (which they have acquired in the form of MIUs) to third parties. The object of such 'sale' is typically an IRU, i.e. the indefeasible right of the purchaser to use a specific part of the seacable's transmission capacity (e.g. 2 MBit/s) for the lifetime of the seacable system.

At first glance, the provision of an international private leased circuit (IPLC) would seem to be a viable alternative to the 'sale' of an IRU. Like the owner of an IRU, the lessee of an IPLC has the right to use a defined capacity of a seacable system. Upon closer scrutiny, however, it becomes clear that substantial economic differences exist between an IRU and an IPLC; they relate to:

(1) Usage time: Whereas an IRU grants an *indefeasible* right to use seacable capacity for the lifetime of the seacable system, lease agreements regarding

IPLCs can be terminated (i.e. they are not indefeasible), and they are typically limited, in time, to several weeks or months.

(2) Scope of usage: An IRU typically grants a right to use seacable capacity between the two termination points of a seacable. By contrast, the lessee of an IPLC is normally also obliged to use transmission capacity between the termination point and the next available international switch; in other words, the lessee of an IPLC will not only receive transmission services between seacable landing points, but also 'backhaul' services.

(3) Scope of services: Normally, the lessor of an IPLC will guarantee, to the lessee, a certain quality of service. By contrast, the owner of an IRU is in a position to set its own service quality standards.

(4) Price: The price of an IRU is considerably lower than the price of an IPLC.

2. Access Provisions under EC Telecommunications Law

a) Access to Cable Stations

Among the organisations which are obliged, under Article 4(1) of the Interconnection Directive, to enter into interconnection agreements, are:

> organisations which are authorised in a Member State to provide international telecommunications circuits between the Community and third countries, for which purpose they have exclusive or special rights (Annex II Interconnection Directive).

These organisations are obliged to interconnect their international telecommunications circuits with the networks of other organisations authorised to provide public telecommunications networks and/or publicly available telecommunications services.

The location of the point of interconnection is subject to agreement between the parties; if the party seeking interconnection wishes to interconnect in a cable station, the party providing interconnection can restrict access only with specific reference to one of the 'essential requirements'.

It follows, from the wording of Annex II of the Interconnection Directive, that organisations which operate international telecommunications circuits, without having been granted exclusive or special rights, are not obliged to interconnect their submarine cable systems to the networks of other operators.

However, such operators are subject to the obligation to provide special network access,[66] provided that they have 'significant market power'. Such

---

[66] Article 4(2) Interconnection Directive, *supra*, at n 41.

access may reasonably be requested at cable stations, which are 'points other than the network termination points offered to the majority of end-users' (Article 4(2) Interconnection Directive).

a) Access to Submarine Cable Capacity

The European Commission made it clear in the *BT-MCI* case[67] that it considers direct access by international telecommunications service providers to 'unbundled' submarine cable capacity as an important element of competition on international routes. Specifically, the Commission cleared the BT/MCI merger on the basis, *inter alia*, of the parties' undertaking:

> to make available to new international facilities operators in the UK, without delay and at prices corresponding to BT's true cost of purchasing capacity from the cable consortium, all of their current and prospective overlapping capacity on the UK-US route resulting from the merger on the transatlantic cable TAT 12/13 . . . [and] . . . to sell to other operators, at their request and without delay, Eastern end matched half circuits currently owned by BT in order for them to be able to provide international voice telephony services on the UK-US route on an end-to-end basis.[68]

Since its decision fell under the Merger Regulation,[69] the Commission did not have to find a legal basis in European telecommunications law for its demand for 'unbundled' provision of access to submarine cable capacity. However, where one needs to determine whether or not secondary EC telecommunications law provides a legal basis for the imposition of a duty to provide access to submarine cable capacity upon an operator of a cable station, it is important to determine the object of the access right.

Normally, new entrants are seeking access to 'unbundled' transmission capacity on submarine cable systems between the beach joints. Such transmission capacity is usually 'sold' in terms of contractually-defined bit rates. As noted above, IRUs are property rights: they convey upon their owner a permanent right to use a defined 'unbundled' transmission capacity during the lifetime of the seacable. The placing of an obligation upon an operator to grant access to IRUs or to sell IRUs would, therefore, be tantamount to the seizure of an property right. The constitutional difficulties which such an expropriation would present in most, if not all, EU Member States might easily be avoided through the adoption of a narrower definition of the 'facility' to which

---

[67] European Commission, Press Release IP/97/406 of 14 May 1997.
[68] European Commission, Press Release IP/97/406 of 14 May 1997.
[69] Council Regulation 406–4/89 of December 21, 1989, O.J.L 257/14.

access is sought. Normally, new international facilities operators are seeking access to 'unbundled' transmission capacity on a long-term basis. Such a long term lease can be distinguished from an IRU, in that it would not preclude the 'owner' of the transmission capacity from reclaiming such capacity, if and when he can establish that the capacity was needed for the requirements of his own customers.

An obligation to provide unbundled (or transparent) transmission capacity is set forth in the ONP Leased Lines Directive:[70] The Directive defines leased lines as:

> the telecommunications facilities which provide for transparent transmission capacity between network termination points and which do not include on-demand switching (switching functions which the user can control as part of the leased lines provision), (Article 2(2)).

'Network termination points' are defined in the ONP Framework Directive as:

> the physical point at which a user is provided with access to a public telecommunications network (Article 2 No. 5 ONP Framework 5 Directive).

Read in conjunction with the special access obligation set forth in Article 4(2) Interconnection Directive, the duty placed on NRAs to establish 'network termination points' (Article 2 No. 5 ONP Framework Directive), would seem to require that submarine cable stations be designated, for regulatory purposes, the boundaries of the public telecoms network.

Summarising briefly, EC telecommunications law obliges telecommunications organisations with significant market power to provide access to the 'unbundled' transparent transmission capacity of international submarine cables.

3. Access Provision under National Telecommunications Law: The German Case

German telecommunications law does not establish a specific regulatory regime for submarine cable systems. Rather, access to submarine cables is

---

[70] Directive 92/44/EEC, OJ L 165/27, as amended by Directive 97/51/EC, OJ L 295/23 (1997).

governed by the general provisions on interconnection, special network access and by the provisions of Section 33 TKG on the special control of abusive practices.

a) Access to Cable Stations

As regards access to cable stations, new entrants in Germany have a right of access under the special network provisions of Section 35(1) TKG in conjunction with Section 3 NZV. In particular, the Network Access Ordinance obliges dominant carriers to provide unbundled access:

> at the location of the transmission, switching or operational interface in a non-discriminatory manner and on the same conditions which such carrier applies to itself for use of the said offering.

This collocation obligation can be fulfilled either in the form of a 'physical collocation' or by providing use of the facilities on equal economic, technical and operational conditions, i.e. in the form of 'virtual collocation' (Section 3(2) NZV).

b) Access to Submarine Cable Capacity

On the basis of the Customer Access Line Case, new entrants have a right of access to 'unbundled' transmission capacity on international submarine links under Section 33(1) TKG. The provision of such unbundled transmission capacity is an 'essential service' within the meaning of this provision. If there are concerns that a dominant operator may be permanently precluded from using sea-cable capacity for his own purposes, these can be addressed in contractual arrangements: If and when the dominant operator can establish that the requires the transmission capacity is required for his own purposes, the lease arrangements with the new entrant can be terminated.

IV. Conclusions

The essential facilities doctrine , which has been spelled out by the European Commission in its Access Notice and which has been narrowly construed in the ECJ's *Bronner* judgement, is not a magic wand that will easily open the doors to telecommunications facilities. The criteria of the essential facilities test are too vague and the procedures before the Commission are too slow to ensure the speedy access to bottleneck facilities that is required in a marketplace as dynamic as the telecommunications sector. EC telecommunications directives and national telecommunications laws have established sector-specific rules governing access to those 'bottleneck facilities', which are considered essential for a competitive telecommunications market. The essential facilities doctrine may provide a theoretical background for these sector-specific rules and their limitations, but it cannot and should not replace, restrict or alter them.

IX

*Herbert Ungerer**

The Case of Telecommunication in the EU

I. Introduction

Access to bottleneck facilities has become a theme of central interest, not only for the future evolution and interpretation of EC competition law, but also for a market and economic development that extends far beyond the EU. With the current economic transformation and the growing importance of the 'networked' sectors, a number of similar situations[1] have emerged across these sectors.

Nevertheless, it is safely to assume that the issue of access to bottleneck network facilities in the EU has so far been most clearly developed in the telecommunications sector, particularly since the full liberalisation of the sector in January 1998.

Indeed, a comprehensive framework of sector specific regulation is now developing at both Member State and EU level (the EU Open Network Provision framework). Furthermore, it is the sector where the European Commission has developed the most consistent position concerning the application of EC competition law to bottleneck access, with the adoption of the 'Access Notice'.[2]

Besides displaying the characteristics of a traditional utility sector, and therefore showing certain similarities with other sectors, such as gas and electricity, the situation in the telecoms sector may allow the Commission to work out the most critical issues most clearly, mainly due to two characteristics:

Firstly, apart from the air transport sector, the telecoms sector is the only one of the traditional utility sectors where full liberalisation has already been implemented in the EU—complete liberalisation was also achieved within a

---

* Visiting Fellow, Harvard University. Adviser, European Commission. The statements put forward in this paper are the author's sole responsibility and do not represent positions by the European Commission.

[1] Reference is made to the developments in the EU concerning sectors such as air transport, rail transport, electricity, gas, post, and certain financial services

[2] Commission Notice on the application of the competition rules to access agreements in the telecommunications sector, OJ C 265/02 (1998), hereafter referred to as the Access Notice.

very short time period. This has resulted in the creation of a comprehensive scheme of sector-specific access regulation, and at the same time liberalisation has led to a number of landmark cases in the application of EC competition rules to such situations, both of which allow the discussion of the main issues in concrete terms.

Secondly, the telecoms sector is characterised by a rate of innovation that is amongst the highest experienced in human history. Equally, it is faced with the phenomenon of convergence with major neighbouring sectors. This means that the sector requires the application of new tests to the strength of the methods employed for securing access to bottleneck facilities. In turn, these new tests may be fundamental for the measurement of the impact of such measures on economic structures and markets in the future.

As will be set out in this paper, it is proposed to apply three critical tests to the regimes used in the sector for ensuring access to bottleneck facilities:

- *Test 1* : achievement of efficient access in a relatively stable market environment;
- *Test 2* : suitability in a situation of convergence, i.e. inherently unstable market definitions;
- *Test 3*: suitability of a regime in a market characterised by the requirement to develop innovative ways of access which may not even exist, but may be required by markets with a high innovation rate.

The discussion in this paper requires substantial simplification. The paper will, therefore, set out the framework, and then concentrate on a few, critical, case studies.

II. Background

It is useful to begin with a brief historical account to explain the context to the current regime now governing the development of the telecommunications sector in the EU.

Since this history has been extensively documented elsewhere,[3] it is sufficient to explain here how the main trends of development have led to the basic framework which now determines access to bottleneck situations in the sector in the EU: a dual regime based on sector specific regulation *and* the application of EC competition rules.

---

[3] See, e.g. Ungerer (1996).

EC telecommunications liberalisation developed mainly as a consequence of three factors. First, by the end of the eighties, the growing digitalisation of European telecommunications networks began to transform telecommunications networks into multipurpose information infrastructures. The opportunities offered by telecommunications networks and services began to extend into markets substantially beyond the traditional telephone service, particularly the so-called 'value-added-services'—the precursors of today's internet services and ISPs (Internet Service Providers). As a result, the access to the traditional monopoly networks in the telecommunications sectors became a major issue in all EU Member States, and there was a growing conviction that without a loosening of monopoly rights—*and* a consequential definition of access conditions—it could neither be assured that new markets could develop, nor that the new services offered could be made available to consumers. Secondly, in *British Telecommunications*,[4] the ECJ confirmed that EC competition rules applied to the telecommunications sector. The third factor was the impact of developments in the United States, in particular the AT&T divestiture consent decree and the resulting transformation of the US market that also began to be felt in Europe. At the same time, the progressive deregulation of the UK telecommunications sector and the privatisation of British Telecom made Europe more receptive to the concept of market deregulation.

The combination of these factors led the Commission to issue, in 1987, its Telecommunications Green Paper which set forth a comprehensive policy framework for EU action in the telecommunications sector.[5] The Green Paper envisaged a number of changes in EU telecommunications:

* full liberalisation of markets and progressive introduction of competition for services,[6] in order to allow rapid opening for value-added-services;
* the separation of regulation and operations,[7] a pre-requisite for the

---

[4] Commission Decision, 82/861/EEC, OJ L 41/83 (1985), [1983] 1 CMLR 457 (*British Telecommunications*). The issue was presented on appeal in *Italy* v *Commission*, Case C–41/83 [1985] ECR 873, [1985] 2 CMLR 382.

[5] *Green Paper on the Development of the Common Market for Telecommunications Services and Equipment* COM(87)290, 30. 6. 1987.

[6] At that time still with the exception of public voice telephony, and public network infrastructure.

[7] This progressively led to profound organisational reform in all Member States, resulting, first, in a transformation of telecommunications monopolies (the traditional PTTs, now referred to as TOs for Telecommunications Organisation) into normal companies, and second, to privatisation. Besides the privatisation of BT, the privatisation of Deutsche Telekom (DT), France Telecom (FT) and Telecom Italia were among the

development of an open market but also the base for the development of a
sector specific regulatory regime ; and

- most notably, in the context of this debate, simultaneously with the Green
  Paper, definition of harmonised access conditions (the Open Network
  Provision, or ONP concept)[8]

An EU Telecom review led, by 1993, to an agreement on the full liberalisation of the EU telecommunications market by 1st January 1998,[9] including the
remaining public voice telephony and telecommunications network infrastruc-
ture/facilities monopolies.

The review led, *inter alia*, to an agreement by the EC Council to adjust the
ONP framework to fully liberalised market conditions and to establish a regulatory framework for interconnection and access to services and networks.[10]

Without going into further detail, two comments should be made. First, the
development of the telecommunications policy framework was, from its incep-
tion, based on a sector specific policy approach; the Green Papers published by
the European Commission, setting forth the proposed overall concept and
promoting broad consultations and the subsequent adoption of the basic principles—such as, liberalisation, market opening and universal service—by successive resolutions of the EU Council of Ministers and the European
Parliament. These resolutions also established the framework for the general
competitive conditions.[11]

---

largest transactions ever to take place on the European stock markets. Telecom stocks
are now leading stocks in all major European stock indices.

   [8] Formalised by the adoption of the ONP Framework Directive, Council Directive
90/387/EEC, OJ L 192/1 (1990).

   [9] Formalised by the adoption of Full Competition Directive, Commission Directive
96/19/EEC, full competition in telecommunications markets, OJ L 74/13 (1996).

   [10] This was implemented by the adoption of the ONP Interconnection Directive,
Directive 97/33/EC of the European Parliament and of the Council on interconnection
in telecommunications with regard to ensuring universal service and interoperability
through application of the principles of open network provision (ONP), OJ L 199/32
(1997). It should also be mentioned that the Full Competition Directive set general
requirements for interconnection and interconnection offerings by the incumbents.

   [11] The telecommunications sector was, with the exception of the television sector, the
first sector in which this method of proposing comprehensive policy blueprints, i.e.
Green Papers, and broad sector consultation were used extensively. Subsequent to the
problems encountered by the EC during the ratification of the Maastricht Treaty, the
Commission emphasised transparency in policy formulation and broad consultation.
The method is now widely employed in all areas of EU policy.

Secondly, throughout the implementation of the telecommunications policy concept, the application of EC competition law was of primary importance.[12] Access and its relationship to competition law figured centrally on the sector agenda as early as the *BT* case, often viewed as a legal cornerstone of the EU telecommunications framework. In *British Telecommunications*, the Court hinted at a number of key issues in access which have only been fully elaborated over the past few years.

The Court confirmed the requirement to give access to a 'value-added' service provider.[13] The Court implied that it would have been in BT's interest to allow the operation of the services offered by private message-forwarding

---

[12] In December 1989, a basic policy compromise defined the respective role of measures based on EC competition law (Article 86 [ex 90], associated with application of Articles 81 and 82 [ex 85 and 86], as well as other Treaty Articles), and harmonisation through internal market legislation based on Article 95 [ex 100a] of the EC Treaty. The compromise reached between the Commission and the Member States on the occasion of the adoption of the Telecommunications Services Directive and the ONP framework Directive established the principle of a complementary role of liberalisation under Article 86 [ex 90], EC competition law, and harmonisation under Article 95 [ex 100a]. The Full Competition Directive is based on Article 86 [ex 90] and the associated competition law principles. The ONP Interconnection Directive is based on Article 100(a), internal market legislation.

[13] The case concerned the activities of certain private messaging forwarding agencies via the BT network at the time (1982). In its Decision, the Commission found that British Telecom (at that time still in a monopoly position and in public ownership) had abused its dominant position in the telecommunications systems market by taking measures to prevent certain private messaging agencies from offering a given type of service. The service permitted telex messages to be received and forwarded on behalf of third parties at prices lower than those charged by BT for its international telex service. It should be mentioned that one of the main issues in that case was how far Article 86(2) [ex 90(2)] of the EU Treaty could be applied to exempt BT's abuse of its dominant position on the telecommunications system market by preventing access and the forwarding of the messages in question. First, the Court made clear that it was for the Commission to decide (subject to review by the Court) on any derogation to be granted from the application of the Competition rules on the basis of Article 86(2) [ex 90(2)]. Article 86(2) [ex 90(2)] stipulates that 'undertakings entrusted with the operation of services of general economic interest . . . shall be subject to the rules contained in this Treaty, *in particular to the rules on competition*, in so far as the application of such rules does not obstruct the performance, in law or in fact, of the particular tasks assigned to them. The development of trade must not be affected to such an extent as would be contrary to the interests of the Community' (emphasis added). Second, the Court made it clear that it would favour a narrow interpretation of the scope of a derogation under Article 86(2) [ex 90(2)] from obligations under competition law, in particular taking into account possible resulting delays in the development of new technologies.

agencies which accessed its network because it would have attracted international telex traffic onto BT's network. The Court specifically addressed the issue that development of new technologies in this context was in the public interest.

It should therefore be noted that, as early as *British Telecommunications*, three elements emerged which are also relevant to today's debate on access :

- the key role of access to the network of the incumbent;
- the issue of non-discriminatory access; and
- the issue of the development of new technology markets/new services.

As value added services were progressively liberalised in Europe, access to bottleneck network facilities started to become a recurrent theme and a central issue in the telecommunications, media, and information technology markets.

Competition law cases emerged first in the case of agreements and co-operation between companies, in the context of notifications under Article 81 [ex 85].[14] The *Infonet* case, an early case right after the start of liberalisation, is a good example of this.[15]

In *Infonet*, the Commission required, *inter alia*, undertakings from the parties relating to non-discrimination, 'to eliminate the risk that [Infonet] is granted more favourable treatment in relation to access and use of the public telecommunications network or reserved services [than other service suppliers]'.

Infonet inaugurated a line of a number of cases of similar nature.[16] The

---

[14] Notifications and other basic procedures are governed by Council Regulation No 17 of 6.2.1962, implementing Articles 85 and 86 of the Treaty, OJ 13, 21.2.1962, p.204, generally referred to as Regulation 17.

[15] See *Infonet*, Case IV/33.361, OJ C 7/3 (1992). Infonet's data communications services, the largest part of its business, were operated on the basis of an international packet-switched network, constructed with lines leased from the telecommunications organisations and other operators, and nodes belonging to Infonet. At the time, a number of its shareholders had exclusive or special rights for the leasing of lines to telecommunications services suppliers. Replace monopoly rights with dominant position and international leased lines with Internet backbone, and the reader may find certain similarities with current situations emerging in the internet context. In fact, the liberalisation of value added services in the start up phase of EU telecom liberalisation in the early nineties was the very basis for the introduction of the internet in Europe, the first link-ups with the US internet backbone and the appearance of the first private ISPs (Internet Service Providers) in Europe by that time.

[16] The Commission published, in 1991, *Guidelines on the Application of Competition Rules in the Telecommunications Sector,* outlining potential case situations, OJ C 233/2 (1991).

issue of access and interconnection acquired a key role in the big alliances cases which started to dominate legal attention in the application of EU competition law (and more generally at global level in antitrust) from the mid-nineties, as a prelude to full liberalisation of telecoms in the EU with the Full Competition Directive of 1996, in the United States with the adoption of the 1996 Telecom Act, and, at a global level, with the 1997 WTO agreement on basic telecom services.

In relation to liberalisation, two aspects should be emphasised. First, with full EC liberalisation, and the emerging sector specific EU regulatory framework, the definition of access and interconnection within the ONP framework acquired increasing importance. This was refined with the adoption of the ONP Interconnection Directive of 1997. At the same time, originally due to developments in other sectors, the concept of access to bottleneck facilities started to be defined more explicitly as an 'essential facilities concept' in the context of EU competition law, in particular under Article 82 [ex 86]. The concept found its current and clearest formulation in the Access Notice, which drew its conclusions from a broad range of Commission decisions on access to bottlenecks under competition rules, as well as from court rulings in this context.

III. EU ONP Regulation and the Access Notice—Sector Specific Regulation and Competition law

The current framework for access in the telecommunications field in Europe is characterised by the EU's ONP Directives and their transposition into national laws[17]—which provide now the legal basis in the EU for sector specific regulation of access—and by the Access Notice which contains the Commission's interpretation of general EC competition law as it applies to access issues.

It is worthwhile taking a brief look at the relationship between the working of sector-specific regulation under the ONP framework and general competition rules. This relationship is defined in substantial detail in the Access Notice.

The Access Notice states that a party concerned with access to a telecommunications network, or another critical bottleneck network resource in the EU, faces two main choices, namely:

---

[17] All Member States have by now set up the sector specific regimes required by the ONP Directives and established sector specific regulators. The UK had already established sector specific regimes and OFTEL long before the Directives. See, *Commission Communication on Transposition of the EU Telecom Reform package into Member States Law*, COM(1998)594, for details of ONP implementation.

- following specific national regulatory procedures now established in accordance with Community law and harmonised under Open Network Provision, or;
- bringing an action under national and/or EC law, in particular competition rules, before the Commission, a national court or a national competition authority.

In the Access Notice, the Commission recognises that EC competition rules are not sufficient to remedy all of the various problems in the telecommunications sector. The (sector-specific) NRAs (National Regulatory Authorities) thus have a significantly wider ambit and a far-reaching role in the regulation of the telecommunications sector.

The ONP Directives impose on the TOs (Telecommunications Operators) that enjoy significant market power, certain obligations of transparency and non-discrimination that go beyond those that would normally apply under Article 82 [ex 86] of the Treaty. ONP Directives lay down obligations relating to transparency, obligations to supply and pricing practices. These obligations are enforced by the NRAs, which also have jurisdiction to take steps to ensure effective competition.

This is, however, subject to important caveats :

(1) Under Community law, national authorities, including regulatory authorities and competition authorities, have a duty not to approve any practice or agreement contrary to Community competition law.[18]

(2) An *efficient* procedure must be in place. According to the Access Notice, an access dispute before a NRA should be resolved within six months of the matter first being drawn to the attention of that authority. This resolution should take the form of either a final determination of the action or another form of relief that would safeguard the rights of the complainant.

(3) There must be availability of, and criteria for, interim injunctive relief. The Notice states that 'if interim injunctive relief were not available, or if such relief was not adequate to protect the complainant's right under Community law, the Commission could consider that the national proceedings did not remove the risk of harm, and could therefore commence its examination of the case'.

(4) The Commission may, nevertheless, intervene if, for example, the issue is of sufficient pan-European interest to justify immediate action. More gener-

---

[18] See Case 66/86, *Ahmed Saeed* [1989] ECR 838.

ally, if it appears necessary, the Commission can also open own-initiative investigations or launch sector inquiries where it considers this necessary.[19]

To summarise, therefore, it can been seen that within the European framework a *dual* system of intervention has developed concerning treatment of access to bottleneck situations. Within the framework of sector-specific regulation of access—the ONP framework and the specific regulations at the national levels—the NRAs can act in a substantial *ex-ante* manner and mandate, in substantial detail, interconnect provisions concerning pricing, accounting, and the technical details of access.

The application of competition rules to access issues is limited—in the current interpretation of EU competition law—to dealing *ex-post* with the abuse of a dominant position, and the measures taken to terminate such abuse.

According to the Access Notice, sector specific regulation will generally take precedence with regard to action under competition law, if such sector specific action is pro-competitive and efficient. This is to avoid undue duplication of procedures.

IV. Test One: Creation of Efficient Access to Bottleneck Facilities in a Stable Market Environment—the Current Approach

The experience in the European telecoms sector of the success of the dual regime, with a priority role for the sector specific regulation under the ONP framework, is interesting but complex. The analysis will, therefore, concentrate only on the most prominent aspect in access regulation: the pricing of interconnection and the working of the mechanism to date in this respect at the European level.

A few general remarks on the ONP framework are required, as it has been revised over the last two years, with a particular focus on the Interconnection Directive.

---

[19] Under Regulation 17, the Commission could be seized of an issue relating to access agreements by way of a notification of an access agreement by one or more of the parties involved, by way of a complaint against a restrictive access agreement or against the behaviour of a dominant company in granting or refusing access, by way of a Commission own-initiative procedure into such a grant or refusal, or by way of a sector inquiry. In addition, a complainant may request that the Commission take interim measures in circumstances where there is an urgent risk of serious and irreparable harm to the complainant or to the public interest.

As stated, the (sector specific) ONP framework had originally been developed to secure access for value-added services to the monopolists' networks. With the Interconnection Directive, the framework was adjusted to a competitive market situation and a multi-operator environment:[20]

(1) ONP became the general framework for the definition of the basic principles of the regulation of access to public telecommunications networks in the EU.

(2) The concept of the 'public telecommunications network operator' replaced the role of the monopoly network provider. The Directive defines a number of categories of operators.[21] Each category has rights and obligations which are defined in the Directive.

(3) Rights of public network operators concern, in particular, the right to interconnect with competitors of the same category.

A general obligation to supply access is imposed on public network operators with Significant Market Power, the SMP operators, principally defined as operators with more than 25% market share.[22] This makes the SMP concept—besides the 'category' approach—the central one in the new framework.[23] It

---

[20] Since January First 1998 a substantial number of licences have been allocated. By mid-1998, in the fixed network sector, more than 500 local loop network licences, together with a substantial number of long distance and international licences had been allocated; in the mobile sector, more than 30 GSM licences and some 50 DCS 1800 (PCS) licences. However, more than 90% of the telecoms network market across the Community remains with the incumbents, in particular in the local loop.

[21] Annex I of the Directive defines four networks/services as 'Specific Public Telecommunications Networks and Publicly Available Telecommunications Services': the fixed public telephone network; the leased lines service; public mobile telephone networks; public mobile telephone services.

[22] According to the ONP Interconnection Directive the notification (by the NRA) of an organisation as having significant market power depends on a number of factors, but the starting presumption is that an organisation with a market share of more than 25% will normally be considered to have significant market power. Other factors which can be taken into account by the NRA are turnover relative to the size of the market, ability to influence market conditions, control of the means of access to end-user, international links, access to financial resources and experience in providing products and services in the market, as well as the situation of the relevant market. In practice, the traditional telephone incumbents have been notified as having SMP. Some Member States have notified certain public mobile operators as having SMP, or are considering this.

[23] Essential articles of the Interconnection Directive in this context are: Article 4(2): obligation to supply access; Article 6 : non-discrimination; Article 7: cost orientation; Article 8: accounting separation for 'interconnection services'.

should be added that, according to the general line taken in the Directive, details of interconnection should be fixed, as far as possible, by commercial negotiations between the parties supplying and seeking interconnection. However, the sector specific regulator acquires substantial powers of regulation.

With regard to the pricing of interconnection, the Interconnection Directive:

(1) Establishes the principle of 'cost orientation'. The national regulators 'ensure'[24] the implementation of this principle. The Directive defines substantial powers of rate review and the rate approval for interconnection pricing, associated with requirements concerning transparency, accounting practice and non-discrimination.

(2) Defines two major markets, a retail market and an interconnection and access market.

(3) However, it also limits price regulation to the two areas of public network operators with significant market power (SMP), and public fixed telephony.

Apart from setting the general framework in the fifteen EU Member States, the Interconnection Directive also gained in immediate effect since it is applied in combination with a number of Recommendations issued by the Commission after its adoption.[25] The Recommendation on Interconnection Pricing, for example, established price ranges for interconnection rates across the EU, based on the 'best practice' of the three Member States with the lowest interconnect rates at the time of issuing the Recommendation.

These ranges have largely determined the interconnection offerings submitted and approved by the national regulators in the Member States. This benchmarking of interconnection pricing against 'best practice' has made the EU an area with some of the lowest interconnection rates in the world market, with local access in the range of 0.5–1 Eurocents per minute.[26]

---

[24] According to Article 7(1) and 7(2), ONP Interconnection Directive, Member States 'shall ensure' for organisations 'operating the public telecommunications networks and/or publicly available telecommunications services' that 'charges for interconnection shall follow the principles of transparency and cost orientation'.

[25] Commission Recommendation, 98/195/EC, on interconnection in a liberalised telecommunications market on Interconnection Pricing, OJ L 73/42 (1998): Commission Recommendation of 29.7.1998 amending Recommendation 98/195/EC (Part 1—Interconnection pricing), OJ L 228/30 (1998); 98/322/EC: Commission Recommendation of 8.4.1998 on interconnection in a liberalised telecommunications market (Part 2—Accounting separation and cost accounting), OJ L 141/6 (1998).

[26] According to Recommendation 98/195/EC, *supra*, set in close conjunction with the NRAs.

Thus, it seems that sector specific regulation, based on the ONP framework, has been highly effective in rapidly achieving low priced access to the incumbents' local telephone networks across the EU.

Let us now turn to the application of competition law to the pricing of access to telecommunications networks. The principles and the possibilities for action are set out in the Access Notice.[27]

The approach is principally based on Article 82 [ex 86], EU competition law, and the Access Notice addresses in particular :

(1) The issue of market definition of the access market under competition law, where the Access Notice explicitly states that it does not define markets—market definition under competition law can only be undertaken in the context of an individual case. The Notice does, however, refer to two types of essential product markets, i.e. the provision of services and the provision of access to facilities to provide those services.[28]

(2) The geographic market is defined as the area in which the objective conditions of competition are similar, while regard will also be had to the economic structure of the market, as well as regulatory conditions such as the terms of licences. Given the former monopolisation of telecoms within individual Member States, and the regulatory regime in Europe, markets will often be national.

(3) Abusive pricing. In line with the basic orientation of Article 82 [ex 86] (which does not intend to regulate prices, but addresses the issue of unfair pricing only), the Notice limits itself to addressing the issues of excessive pricing and of predatory pricing.

To tackle the issue of excessive pricing first, the Access Notice indicates a number of methods, which can be used to determine excessive prices:

(1) by reference to the costs of providing the service, which requires a comprehensive cost analysis, together with a decision on the appropriate cost allocation method to be used;[29] and

---

[27] For a general overview, see also, Coates (1998).

[28] The Commission has published a Notice on the definition of the relevant market for the purposes of Community competition law, OJ C 372/5 (1997).

[29] It should be noted that the ONP framework emphasises the use of 'current cost accounting' (CCA) methodology, and evaluation of network assets at forward-looking or current value of an *efficient* operator. The ONP Interconnection Directive states that 'charges for interconnection based on a price level closely linked to the long-run incremental costs for providing access to interconnection are appropriate for encouraging the rapid development of an open and competitive market'.

(2) by reference to prices charged in other geographic areas.

The Notice states that a comparison with other geographic areas can be used as an indicator of an excessive price: the ECJ held that, if possible, a comparison could be made between the prices charged by a dominant company, and those charged on markets which are open to competition. Such a comparison could provide a basis for assessing whether or not the prices charged by the dominant company were fair. In certain circumstances, where comparative data were not available, regulatory authorities have sought to determine what would have been the competitive price were a competitive market to exist. In an appropriate case, such an analysis may be taken into account by the Commission in its determination of an excessive price.[30]

It is this method of comparative analysis, which has been principally used to date in the cases dealt with under competition law as regards excessive pricing in the sector.[31]

Another method of assessing excessive prices is to refer to calculations undertaken by regulatory authorities to determine prices which would be charged were a competitive market to exist. Here, the Court has indicated that account may be taken of Community legislation setting out price principles for the particular sector, i.e. in the current case sector specific regulation of access prices.[32] The Notice refers explicitly to the ONP context:

---

[30] The Court has said—Joined Cases 110/88, 241/88 and 242/88, *Lucazeau a.o./SACEM*, ECR [1989] 2811 (paragraph 25): 'when an undertaking holding a dominant position imposes scales of fees for its services which are appreciably higher than those charged by other Member States and where a comparison of the fee levels has been made on a consistent basis, that difference must be regarded as indicative of an abuse of a dominant position. In such a case it is for the undertaking in question to justify the difference by reference to objective dissimilarities between the situation in the Member State concerned and the situation prevailing in all the other Member States'.

[31] *DT* case, press release IP/96/975, 4.11.1996. See Haag and Klotz (1998). In this case, the Commission dealt with the problem of access to the network of Deutsche Telekom (DT). A comparative market analysis commissioned by the Commission showed that the proposed prices were likely to be excessive. It was assumed that a price is highly likely to be abusive if it exceeds by more than 100% the ones found on comparable competitive markets. As a result, DT declared itself willing to substantially reduce its access tariffs. The method of comparative market analysis was subsequently applied in the 'best practice' approach for access pricing.

[32] In *Ahmed Saeed, supra*, the Court held that pricing principles set out in sector specific regulation could be used to determine whether a price was excessive.

if a case arises, the ONP rules and Commission Recommendations concerning accounting requirements and transparency will help to ensure the effective application of Article 82 [ex 86] in this context.

On the issue of predatory pricing, it is important to realise that while excessive pricing in interconnection is still the dominant issue in the current transition from monopoly to a competitive environment in the EU, predatory pricing issues are becoming a common denominator of a number of cases currently before the Commission and that this issue is probably going to develop into a major issue in the long term. The Notice makes reference to the *AKZO* doctrine [33] that a price is abusive if it is below the dominant company's average variable costs or it is below average total costs and part of an anti-competitive plan. However, it also states that 'in network industries a simple application of the above rule would not reflect the economic reality of network industries'.

As the Notice sets out, in the case of the provision of telecommunications services, a price that equates the variable cost of a service may be substantially lower than the price the operator needs in order to cover the cost of providing the service. The Notice states that:

> to apply the AKZO test to prices which are to be applied over time by an operator, and which will form the basis of that operator's decisions to invest, the costs considered should include the total costs which are incremental to the provision of the service. In analysing the situation, consideration will have to be given to the appropriate time frame over which costs should be analysed.[34]

The Commission has applied the principles set forth on pricing with substantial success in the DT case and is proceeding on certain cases still pending. Without going into further detail, some conclusions may be drawn at this stage on the question as to how far the dual approach has ensured efficient access to the incumbents' telecom networks in Europe to date, particularly with regard to the pricing of access.

Ex-ante sector specific (ONP) regulation goes far beyond general competition law when regulating access. Within the EU, NRA intervention has gener-

---

[33] Case C–62/86, *Akzo* v *Commission* [1991] ECR I–3359 (paragraphs 71–72).

[34] The context of predatory pricing also requires a comment on discounting. If a dominant operator were to target its discount at particular customers where it was facing competition, this *could* constitute discrimination as it would tend to have an effect on its competitors. Particularly substantial discounts could have the effect of constituting predatory pricing on the retail level, or could contribute to a price squeeze.

ally proven, during recent months, to be a very efficient means to secure access to the incumbent's bottleneck network, particularly as regards pricing of interconnection and access. General competition law must concentrate on the two extreme situations in pricing: excessive pricing and predatory pricing. *Ex-post* action in these areas is based on the establishment of abuse, and is subject to the (still relatively slow) procedures of Regulation 17.[35] In many instances, the case law to which reference can be made is limited. The principles set forth in the Access Notice will be helpful in this context.

The Commission, therefore, has, in major recent cases where procedures had been opened under competition rules, tended to stay procedures where sector-specific proceedings under ONP or derived national regulations were likely to resolve the issue (see the *Mobile Interconnect*[36] proceeding and the *Accounting Rate*[37] proceeding). This confirms the Commission's basic position

---

[35] However, it should also be kept in mind that the establishment of anti-competitive behaviour such as unfair pricing can entail substantial fines under EC competition law for the bottleneck holder concerned. The Commission has recently published guidelines on the method of setting fines imposed pursuant to Article 15(2) of Regulation No 17, OJ C 9/3 (1998).

[36] *Mobile Interconnect* proceedings: Press Release IP/98/707, 27/7/1998. In January 1998, the Commission launched an inquiry into interconnection charges between fixed and mobile operators opening 15 cases, i.e. one for each Member State due to growing concern about persistently high prices for mobile communications particularly for fixed to mobile calls. The objective of the Commission's Inquiry was to check whether: prices charged by the incumbent fixed network operator for terminating mobile calls into its fixed network were excessive or discriminatory; termination fees charged by mobile operators, which have joint control among themselves over call termination in their networks, were excessive, and; the revenues retained by the incumbent fixed network operator on fixed to mobile calls were excessive. In the Press Release, the Commission concluded that at least 14 cases warranted in-depth investigation given preliminary indications of possibly excessive or discriminatory prices. The fourteen cases comprised: 4 cases of mobile-to-fixed termination charges by Deutsche Telekom, Telefónica, KPN Telekom (Netherlands) and Telecom Italia respectively, which would be suspended for 6 months in favour of action by national regulators; 2 cases of termination fees charges by mobile operators in Italy and Germany; 8 cases regarding the retention on fixed-to-mobile calls by public switched telecommunications networks (PSTN) operators Belgacom, Telecom Éireann, BT, P&T Austria, Telefónica, KPN Telekom (Netherlands), Telecom Italia and Deutsche Telekom. The Commission would suspend the case involving BT given an on-going inquiry by the UK Monopolies and Mergers Commission (MMC) on this issue.

[37] *Accounting Rate* proceeding: Press Release IP/98/763, 13/08/1998. The Commission opened procedures in the Autumn of 1997 concerning European operators with a potentially dominant position, regarding the accounting rates (transfer prices) charged to terminate international calls. Following a preliminary assessment, the

that sector-specific regulation should take precedence where *efficient* procedures exist which can terminate the abuse.

However, there remain a number of caveats. Firstly, sector specific regulation, particularly as regards price regulation, is a deep intervention in market mechanisms, with a high risk and responsibility for the regulator. Pushed too far, it can substantially reduce investment incentives in facilities, both for the bottleneck holder, as well as for the party seeking access. [38]

Second, the ONP regime and the derived national sector specific regimes have become highly dependent on definitions, which imply a high degree of technicality, and therefore have a high potential of legal conflict. The regime depends largely on two concepts for its impact: the 'category' within which the party seeking access and the bottleneck holder falls; and the SMP (Significant Market Power) determination. In a number of Member States, major conflicts concerning the interpretation of these concepts loom. The questions of who qualifies as public network operator (and therefore for the low network interconnect rates), and who should be designated as a SMP operator (and therefore become subject to substantial regulatory scrutiny and to regulatory rate approval) have become central.

Thirdly, the regulatory approval of interconnect rates (and the associated approvals of costing and accounting systems) inevitably lead to a substantial intervention by the regulator in the day-to-day business practices and strategies of the bottleneck holder, with the danger of a heavy-handed regulatory approach. The difficulties become even more apparent when one considers the issue of unbundling the 'dark' access wire/fibre. Again, there is a danger that the European telecommunications sector could be drawn into protracted legal conflicts between the incumbent and the NRA, as has happened, for different reasons, elsewhere.

Commission announced in the press release that it appeared that 'the international accounting rates charged within the EU by 7 operators may result in excessive margins'. The 7 operators were: OTE of Greece, Post & Telekom Austria, Postes et Télécommunications Luxembourg, SONERA (formerly Telecom Finland), Telecom Eireann, Telecom Italia, Telecom Portugal. The Commission concluded that it would further investigate the prices for international phone calls paid to these operators. On this occasion, the Commission stated that 'the issue may also be tackled under the ONP rules (Open Network Provision). The Commission has informed the NRAs of its findings. Where the NRAs institute proceedings, the Commission will defer its decision on its own investigation for six months.

[38] For example, in the EU telecoms sector, a current question is how far access regulation should be extended from the fixed to the mobile sector (which has grown in an environment where prices were generally not subject to approval by a sector regulator).

Therefore, while sector specific intervention can, without doubt, assure efficient intervention for opening access and interconnection to the incumbent bottleneck provider in a relatively stable environment, not all issues are resolved. The limitations of a sector-specific approach become all the more apparent when rapidly developing markets begin to converge.

V. Test Two: Securing Access in Converging Markets—Rapid Market Change

Since the mid-nineties, the telecommunications sector has undergone a phase of rapid convergence with neighbouring sectors. While attention is generally fixed on the convergence of telecoms and media[39]—and a number of major merger cases have resulted from this convergence that have been examined under EC competition law—the impact of this phenomenon is also being felt in other fields. The convergence of mobile/fixed markets is an obvious example, but convergence between telecoms and financial services, as well as between telecoms and certain distribution services, could also become major issues—all of them with their own sectoral regulations and regulators.

For the issue of access to bottlenecks, two major consequences seem to emerge :

(1) New types of Service Providers will require new types of resources and access to new types of bottlenecks and bottleneck holders, ranging from sophisticated network resources to access to set-top boxes, conditional access systems, navigator software, APIs,[40] and content rights.
(2) Convergence also threatens to outpace existing sector-specific regimes. Additionally, in many instances, sectoral regimes for ensuring access to bottlenecks in the neighbouring sectors are far less developed than in the telecoms sector.

The growing complexity of requirements in relation to resources is shown in Table One.[41] The Table sets out requirements for four types of Service

---

[39] The Commission has published a Green Paper on the convergence of the telecom and media sectors which examines this situation in substantial detail. See *Green Paper on the convergence of the telecommunications, media and information technology sectors, and the implications for regulation,* COM(97)623, 3.12.1997

[40] APIs: Application Programme Interfaces, notably relevant for the programming of set-top boxes.

[41] Taken from Wilmer, Cutler & Pickering, *Competition Aspects of Access by Service*

Providers: service providers acting as resellers, providers of mobile services, providers of multi-media services, and providers of Internet services—(the ISPs). The complexity of requirements—and of access to be secured—is bound to grow further, as the Internet develops.

Imagine an internet with 100 times the current performance/cost levels in throughput and speed to the final user. The telephone would become a by-product. Nearly unlimited distribution capability for television or other video products from distributed video servers via the Internet could become available—not just for national but for world-wide distribution. E-commerce would become a reality in every household.

Such possibilities may seem remote at the current levels of internet performance and use, but there are some indications: cable access to the internet, internet telephony, and high performance video streaming techniques. Bandwidth requirements within the internet have started to double every six months. We could be faced with such a situation in three to four years from now, unlikely as it may sound. If this happens, market definitions will have to change radically. Actors will be faced with a plethora of new access issues—such as those now discussed in the internet domain name arena.

One likely reaction is to seek convergence of sector-specific regulatory regimes, in order to parallel market convergence—such as between telecoms and media.[42] But, there will also be a growing number of cases which will not be covered by any—even extended—sector specific regime (by nature, *ex-ante*, and, thus, unable to plan for all conceivable cases of innovation).

It can, therefore, be safely expected that general competition law (which by definition is cross-sector) will be increasingly faced with bottleneck situations, which cannot be covered by any sector-specific regime. This will inevitably emphasise the treatment of bottleneck situations under general competition law.

The further development of the 'essential facility' concept under competition law will be a natural consequence and a response to the challenge of convergence. It is therefore worthwhile examining the principles concerning that concept in the Access Notice in some detail.[43]

Providers to the Resources of Telecommunications Network Operators, Report to the European Commission (DGIV), Dec 1995.

[42] In the US and Canada, a single regulator carries the responsibility for both telecoms and media, as does the newly created NRA in Italy.

[43] The 'essential facility' concept is at the centre of the approach taken in the Access Notice. While the Notice relates explicitly to the application of EC competition rules to the telecoms sector, it also states, in its preamble, the objective 'to create greater market certainty and more stable conditions for investment and commercial initiative in the

The Notice uses the expression 'essential facilities' to describe a facility or infrastructure which is essential for reaching customers and/or enabling competitors to carry out their business, and which cannot be replicated by any reasonable means.[44] The Commission:

> must ensure that the control over facilities enjoyed by incumbent operators is not used to hamper the development of a competitive telecommunications environment. A company which is dominant on a market for services and which commits an abuse contrary to Article 82 [ex 86] on that market *may be required*, in order to put an end to the abuse, to *supply access to its facility* to one or more competitors on that market. In particular, a company may abuse its dominant position if, by its actions, it *prevents the emergence of a new product or service* (emphasis added).

The Notice addresses the balance to be drawn between the rights of those requesting access and those who have to give access, the crucial point in any essential facility concept.
The main principles are (to be taken cumulatively):
(1) It will not be sufficient that the position of the company requesting access would be more advantageous if access were granted. Refusal of access must lead to the proposed activities being made 'either impossible or seriously and unavoidably uneconomic'.

(2) There is sufficient capacity available to provide access

---

telecoms *and* multimedia sectors. . .' and 'to explain how competition rules will be applied in a consistent way across the sectors involved in the provision of new services, and, in particular, to access issues and *gateways in this context.'* (emphasis added).

[44] See also the definition included in the 'Additional commitments on regulatory principles by the European Communities and their Member States' (often referred as the 'Regulatory Annex') used by the Group on basic telecommunications in the context of the World Trade Organisation (WTO) negotiations (the 'basic telecoms liberalisations agreement'): '[E]ssential facilities mean facilities of a public telecommunications transport network and service that: (a) are exclusively or predominantly provided by a single or limited number of suppliers and; (b) cannot *feasibly be economically or technically substituted* in order to provide a service (emphasis added). The essential facilities is a relatively recent concept under EC competition law. It derives from a line of cases, originally in sectors other than telecommunications. See in particular: Joined Cases 6/73 and 7/73 *Commercial Solvents* v *Commission* [1974] ECR 223 (chemicals); Commission Decision 94/19/EEC, *Sea Containers* v *Stena Sealink*, OJ L 15/8 (1994); Commission Decision 94/119/EEC, *Port of Rodby (Denmark)*, OJ L 55/52 (1994) (transport); Joined Cases C–241/91P & C–242/91P, *Radio Telefis Eireann* v *Commission*, (*Magill*), [1995] ECR, I–743. See also Temple Lang (1994).

(3) The facility owner 'fails to satisfy demand on an existing service or product market, blocks the emergence of a potential new service or product, o impedes competition on an existing or potential service or product market.

(4) The company seeking access is prepared to pay a reasonable and non discriminatory price and will otherwise in all respects accept non discriminatory access terms and conditions.

(5) There is no objective justification for refusing to provide access, 'such as an overriding difficulty of providing access to the requesting company, or the need for a facility owner who has undertaken investment aimed at the intro duction of a new product or service to have sufficient time and opportunity to use the facility in order to place that new product or service on the market.[45]

This last point expresses the delicate balance which must be found between the interest of the party seeking access (who will generally want to achieve access at low rates and according to his own requirements), and the rights of the bottleneck holder (who will focus on obtaining benefits from the investment undertaken for the development of his own product).

However, the basic principle to be kept in mind is that the bottleneck holder—given his dominant position—must not act to prevent competition from emerging.

Without going into further detail, it is sufficient for present purposes to note that competition law—in the form of a developed essential facilities concept—can adjust, in a flexible manner, to situations of convergence, by adjusting the market definitions used and without changing either the regulatory framework or its basic principles.

It would, therefore, seem that this second test—securing access in a converging environment—could give a certain advantage to general competition law in the handling of access to bottleneck situations, as compared to the sector-specific regimes which, due to their intrinsic *ex-ante* and more interventionist nature, must, to some extent, 'outguess' the future (market and social) development if they want to ensure efficient access in such a situation of rapid market change.

---

[45] However, the Notice also states that 'although any justification will have to be examined carefully on a case-by-case basis, it is particularly important in the telecommunications sector that the benefits to end-users which will arise from a competitive environment are not undermined by the actions of the former state monopolists in preventing competition from emerging and developing.

VI. Test Three: Development of New Ways of Access

The most demanding situation in terms of both sector-specific regulation and general competition law will be the situation where new markets can only develop if the bottleneck holder develops new ways of access and makes the necessary investment.

The discussion of this situation will be focused on one single case, which, however, is crucial for the future development of the EU telecoms sector and, more generally, the development of the future internet, e-commerce and media markets in the EU.

The future development of the local access market in telecoms in Europe is likely to be determined by its capability to develop the multi-functional capabilities which are required to support the converging telecoms, multi-media and internet markets. Leaving aside satellites and wireless access means,[46] there are two mass distribution systems available in the local loop, both of which have the capability to develop the multifunctional broadband access likely to be required: the public telephone network (now connecting some 190 million lines in the EU, with a household penetration of almost 100%), and the cable TV networks (with a total of now more than 40 million and a household penetration near 30%, but reaching penetrations of 50% and over 90% in some Member States).

The telephone network could be upgraded via the new xDSL[47] technologies to carry broadband access. The (broadband) cable networks could be upgraded also to carry two way (including narrow-band telephone) traffic. Both will require, however, substantial investments.

By 1997, cable networks were 'cross-owned' in more than half of the Member States by the incumbent telephone operator. In fact, nearly 60% of cable customers were served by a cable operator wholly or partly owned by the main telecommunications provider. As a consequence, in 1997, the Commission launched a review to investigate if, under these conditions, any of the two

---

[46] Which still have intrinsically limited technological capabilities for meeting all (interactive) multi-media requirements; see Arthur D. Little Int., 'Study on the competition implications in telecommunications and multimedia markets of (a) joint provision of cable and telecoms networks by a single dominant operator and (b) restrictions on the use of telecommunications networks for the provision of cable television services', Report to the European Commission, 1997.

[47] Various modes of Digital Subscriber Lines.

networks was likely to be upgraded to a full multi-functional access capability
It published the Review (and proposals) in March 1998.[48]

The Review was based on substantial legal and market analysis.[49] The mar
ket analysis was focused on examining the incentive for a local bottleneck
provider to upgrade the local network under these conditions. Some of the
main options investigated were :

(1) extend the (sector specific) ONP regime to cover the new situation;
(2) legal separation, to establish a minimum separate development base for
    both networks; and
(3) full-scale divestiture of the cable network by the incumbent telephone oper
    ator, to establish a business case for both networks to develop full future
    capabilities.

As regards option (1), it was found that the (sector specific) regulator would
face a substantial challenge to implement an ONP regime efficiently in the new
environment; yet, this alone would still not resolve the investment issue. It
would require the regulator to order the incumbent to undertake a very high
investment under conditions of relatively high market uncertainty.[50]

As regards option (2), this was found to be the main condition for establishing effective surveillance of competitive behaviour. However, only option
(3) could establish the conditions for the required full-scale development of the
local access market, by eliminating any conflict of interest of the owners and
establishing full competition between the two networks in the local access
market.

---

[48] Commission communication concerning the review under competition rules of the
joint provision of telecommunications and cable TV networks by a single operator and
the abolition of restrictions on the provision of cable TV capacity over telecommunications networks (OJ C 71, 7.3.1998, p.4); referred to as the Cable Review.

[49] The Commission commissioned two studies. (Market) see Arthur D. Little, *supra*;
(Legal), see Coudert, 'Study on the Scope of the Legal Instruments under EC competition law available to the European Commission to implement the Results of the ongoing review of certain situations in the telecommunications and cable television sectors',
1997.

[50] It should however be mentioned that the options should not necessarily be considered as exclusive of each other. Facing complaints by service providers, the French
NRA (the ART) has in fact ordered France Telecom (owner of the basic network cable
infrastructure in the Paris area) to upgrade the cable network to a certain two way capability by a given date.

In fact, the Commission chose option (2) as a minimal solution for the EU as a whole.[51] However, it also made clear that:

Article 82 [ex 86] should be applied *a fortio*ri to an undertaking which is the owner of both a telecommunications and a cable network, in particular when it is dominant on both markets. Where companies enjoy a dominant position on two markets, they must take particular care not to allow their cond*uct to impair genuine undistorted competition*. In particular, that dominance cannot be leveraged into neighbouring markets*, impede the emergence of new services* or strengthen their dominance through acquisitions or co-operative ventures either horizontally or vertically (emphasis added).

The Commission went on to state that:

in certain circumstances it might be that the only means which would allow the creation of a competitive environment consists in the divestment of the cable television network by the telecommunications operator. Other solutions may also be explored depending on the precise circumstances of the case (emphasis added)

Thus, while it is difficult to see that sector specific regulation could be used to force an incumbent bottleneck holder to upgrade the access facilities into new technologies where massive investment are required (such as for widespread deployment of xDSL, or advanced two way capability for cable networks[52]), it may be possible to resolve the issue by creating a competitive access to open a new market opportunity.

The Commission has made it clear that it strongly favours this perspective in the cable TV market. In the Cable Review, it said that:

from a competition policy point of view, convergence must build on the development of a broad base of pro-competitive infrastructures of telecommunications and

---

[51] The Commission found in its Cable Review that joint ownership of both telecommunications networks and cable TV networks 'limits the development of the telecommunications and multimedia market in the Member States in four main ways by: delaying the upgrading of cable networks to have bi-directional capability; blocking the development of competing infrastructures; limiting service competition, and; constraining innovation. It stated that 'the mere separation of accounts will only render financial flows more transparent, whereas legal separation will lead to more transparency of assets and costs and will facilitate monitoring of the profitability and the management of the cable network operations.

[52] Estimates for investment requirements for upgrading Europe's *existing* cable networks alone to advanced two way capability total some 20–40 billion Euros, depending on technologies used.

cable TV networks. Therefore this review is central to the success of convergence in building pro-competitive structures, and complementary to the Convergence Green Paper.

How far a divestiture of bottleneck facilities could be enforced under EU competition rules will be an issue for future case law. The Commission has, however, made it clear that for notifications of co-operative joint ventures or mergers in the field:

> the Commission will assess such a notification in the light of the facts underlying the case. It can be expected that an extension of an operator dominant in both telecommunications and cable television networks into related fields could raise serious competition concerns.[53]

VII. Conclusion

The EU's experience of regulation to secure access to network bottleneck facilities is still in its early stage. It seems that the current approach to interconnection and access is shaped by a three pillar approach, based on the interplay of 'hands-on' sector-specific *ex-ante* regulation of access, an *ex-post* use of EU competition rules, and, to some extent, the search for structural solutions aimed at the development of competitive access markets.

All of these approaches have been applied, to varying degrees, in other countries, such as, the United States and Canada, Japan, Australia and New Zealand. While the first group of countries seems to emphasise a sector-specific regulatory approach (but has also not hesitated to use antitrust to achieve radical structural solutions, such as the ATT divestiture), Australia, and especially New Zealand have latterly given a greater role to competition law.

The EU and its Member States, in the current phase of full market opening, clearly emphasise the sector-specific approach based on *ex-ante* regulation of the bottleneck holder. The three tests employed (efficiency of access in the current market situation, access in converging markets and access in innovation markets) tend to demonstrate that this choice is likely to be the right approach in the phase of transition to full competition in the telephone market. However, the tests also show that the more the convergence of markets becomes the dominant feature, and the more rapidly innovation proceeds and innovative invest-

---

[53] See Alexander Schaub's paper in this Volume.

Table One: Network Access requirements of Service Providers

Network Resource	Reseller	International GSM Service	ISP	Multimedia
Telephone Networks:				
Public switched services	X		X	X
Leased circuits, VPN	X		X	
Caller identification	X		X	
Inward dialling	X		X	
Numbering schemes	X		X	
Tariff discount schemes	X		X	
Operator assistance	X			
Customer directories	X			
Telephone cards	X			
Billing data	X		X	X
Billing services			X	X
Network management data	X		X	
Videotex/gateways-system			X	X
Mobile Networks:				
Subscriber numbers		X		
Air time		X	X	
Billing data		X	X	
CATV/Satellite Networks:				
Channels	X		X	X
Conditional access systems			X	X
Billing data	X		X	X
Billing services			X	X

ments by the bottleneck holders are needed, the more necessary an approach that is based on general competition law principles will become.[54]

The need for the application of general competition principles becomes all the more evident when analysing the global market developments. As the current events surrounding the internet have shown, given the global nature of the internet—and of e-commerce—it is unlikely that any detailed sector-specific global framework for regulating access can—or even should— be established. However, the very concept of private sector self-regulation of the Internet will

---

[54] See Panel Three in this Volume for the institutional issue of who (sector-specific regulators or antitrust authorities) will apply competition law principles.

make strict application of antitrust and competition rules indispensable, as well as the search for structural solutions for securing competitive access markets, in order to avoid the emergence of new bottleneck holders at the level of the global communications market: be it at network level, at internet domain name level, at navigation level, or at the level of the organisations which will provide global trust and certification services.

This context puts new requirements on the interaction between competition authorities worldwide and their specific counterparts in the telecoms sector.[55] Accordingly, given that important bottlenecks continue to exist in the core telephone market which could frustrate the effects of the market liberalisation, the primary task in the EU will be to ensure the efficient development of the system of sector regulation. However, EU competition law can—and will—support this operation, whenever the pro-competitive results cannot be achieved otherwise.

Equally, it will also be important to avoid the danger of over-regulation, and of a too deep an intervention, particularly in the field of pricing where the wrong investment signals could be set. The underlying development philosophy, should be that of a competitive regime, which is characterised by competitive access markets, and the application of general competition rules.

---

[55] See Panels Two and Three within this Volume for a fuller analysis.

X

James S. Venit*

The 'Essential Facilities' Doctrine:
Its Role in EC Competition Law

I. Introduction

The so-called 'essential facilities' doctrine, which has its origins in US antitrust law,[1] requires monopolists to allow competitors to benefit from a 'facility' owned, operated, licensed to or developed by the monopolist under a narrow set of strictly limited circumstances.[2] Under EC competition law, the obligation of dominant companies to deal with competitors is already so broad that one can question whether the 'essential facilities' doctrine, as applied in the US, is either required or has a role to play in EC law—at least, if one is thinking of the doctrine as one that might increase, rather than limit, the obligation of a dominant company to supply. This paper will review (i) the 'essential facilities' doctrine that has emerged in US law; (ii) the obligations to deal imposed on dominant companies under EC competition law; (iii) the use of the 'essential

---

* Partner, Wilmer, Cutler & Pickering, Brussels. The introductory sections of this paper are based on an article written by the author and John Kallaugher in connection with the Fordham Annual Corporate Law Conference held in New York in 1994, see Venit and Kallaugher (1994).

[1] Cases applying the doctrine include *City of Malden* v *Union Elec. Co.*, 887 F.2d 157, 160 (8th Cir. 1989); *Ferguson* v *Greater Pocatello Chamber of Commerce*, 848 F.2d 976; 983 (9th Cir. 1988); *Interface Group* v *Massachusetts Port Auth.*, 816 F.2d 9, 12 (1st Cir. 1987); *Aspen Highlands Skiing Corp.* v *Aspen Skiing Co.*, 738 F.2d 1509, 1520 (10th Cir. 1984), *aff'd on other grounds*, 472 US 585 (1985); *City of Chanute* v *Williams Natural Gas Co.*, 743 F. Supp. 1437 (D. Kan. 1990); *Monarch Entertainment Bureau* v *New Jersey Highway Auth.*, 715 F. Supp. 1290, 1300 (D.N.J.), *aff'd*, 893 F.2d 1331 (3d Cir. 1989); *Consolidated Gas Co.* v *City Gas Co.*, 665 F. Supp. 1493, 1533 (S.D. Fla. 1987), *aff'd*, 880 F.2d 297 (11th Cir. 1989), *reinstated on reh'g*, 912 F.2d 1262 (11th Cir. 1990) (en banc; per curiam), *vacated as moot*, 111 S. Ct. 1300 (1991); *Beverage Mgmt.* v *Coca-Cola Bottling Corp.*, 653 F. Supp. 1144, 1156 (S.D. Oh. 1986); *see also Hecht* v *Pro-Football, Inc.*, 570 F.2d 982, 992–93 (D.C. Cir. 1977), *cert. denied*, 436 US 956 (1978).

[2] The nature and utility of the *essential* facilities doctrine in US law has inspired a mass of academic commentary: Areeda and Hovenkamp (1992); Sullivan (1991); Hylton (1991); Areeda (1990); Blumenthal (1990); Ratner (1988); Werden (1987); Easterbrook (1986).

facilities' doctrine under EC law;[3] and (iv) the potential role of this doctrine in the area of telecommunications.

II. The Legal Context for the Essential Facilities Doctrine under Section 2 of the Sherman Act

The essential facilities doctrine under US law is an exception to the basic rule set out in *U.S.* v *Colgate & Co.* that 'in the absence of any purpose to create or maintain a monopoly' even a monopolist can 'exercise his own independent discretion as to the parties with whom he will deal'.[4] To appreciate the role of the essential facilities doctrine in this context, it is useful to consider and distinguish the other two lines of cases establishing exceptions to this rule: the intent test and the monopoly leveraging test.

The intent test is based on the initial limitation on the *Colgate* rule that the right to choose customers does not apply where that right is exercised with the purpose of creating or strengthening a monopoly. As articulated by the Supreme Court in *Aspen Skiing Co.* v *Aspen Highlands Skiing Corp.*,[5] the intent test relies on determining the 'objective' intent of the would-be monopolist. In effect, to prove monopolisation under the intent test, a plaintiff must show both exclusionary effects in the monopolised market, resulting from the challenged conduct, and a lack of business justification for that conduct. In contrast to the situation under EC law,[6] US courts have recognised a wide variety of circumstances where legitimate business justifications may defeat an allega-

---

[3] Commission Decision 94/19/EEC, *Sea Containers* v *Stena Sealink*, OJ L 15/8 (1994); Commission Decision 94/119/EEC, *Re Access to Facilities of Port of Rødby*, OJ L 55/52 (1994).

[4] 250 US 300, 307 (1919).

[5] 472 US 585 (1985).

[6] There are few, if any, published cases in which a legitimate business justification for a refusal to supply has been accepted by the Courts or the Commission, although in *United Brands* (Case 27/76, *United Brands* v *Commission*, [1978] ECR 207), the Court did outline a proportionality test linking the proportionality of the decision not to supply to the need to defend the dominant company's legitimate interests. See also, *ABG Oil*, Commission Decision 77/327/EEC, OJ L 117/1(1997). For cases in which the Commission has justified refusals to deal, see *Filtrona/Tabacalera*, Nineteenth Report on Competition Policy, Point 61 (1990) (termination of purchases of cigarette filters by cigarette manufacturer justified where manufacturer has vertically integrated downstream to its own production of filters, and *Boosey & Hawkes*, Commission Decision 87/500/EEC, OJ L 286/36 (1987) (obligation to supply limited in time and conditioned on purchaser not using goods as a loss leader).

tion of anti-competitive intent. In particular, a showing by the monopolist that a refusal to co-operate with a rival tends to increase economic efficiency (such as by achieving economies of scale or maintaining greater control over distribution) would generally be regarded as constituting a legitimate business justification under US law.[7]

The monopoly leveraging test derives from the ruling of the Second Circuit in *Berkey Photo v Eastman Kodak Co.*[8] *Berkey* rests on the Supreme Court's dictum in *United States v Griffith*[9] that 'the use of monopoly power, however lawfully acquired, to foreclose competition to gain a competitive advantage, or to destroy a competitor, is unlawful'. The *Berkey* court focuses on the second part of this dictum, finding that 'a firm violates §2 by using its monopoly power in one market to gain a competitive advantage in another, albeit without an attempt to monopolise the second market'. The *Berkey* court went on to observe:

> We accept the proposition that it is improper, in the absence of a valid business policy, for a firm with monopoly power in one market to gain a competitive advantage in another by refusing to sell a rival the monopolised goods or services he needs to compete effectively in the second market.

Like the intent cases, the monopoly leveraging cases, typified by *Berkey*, recognise an absolute defence where a valid business justification exists. The difference between these two lines of cases lies in the nature of the anti-competitive effects required to constitute an antitrust violation. Whereas cases under the intent test look to exclusionary effects in the market where the defendant firm possesses market power, the leveraging cases look to advantages obtained by the monopolist in a second related market.[10]

---

[7] For an up-to-date discussion of US decisions finding business justifications under the *Aspen* rule, see Ahern (1994).

[8] 603 F.2d 263 (2d Cir. 1979), *cert. denied* 444 US 1093 (1980).

[9] 334 US 100.

[10] The validity of the leveraging theory as a basis for applying Section Two is under attack. A number of circuits have rejected the leveraging analysis, observing that the language in *Griffith* relied on in *Berkey* comes from a case where leveraging did not in fact play a role, e.g. *Fineman v Armstrong World Industries*, F2d (3d Cir 1992). See also, *Alaska Airlines, Inc. v United Airlines, Inc.*, 948 F2d 536 (9th Cir. 1991) *cert. denied*, 112 S.Ct. 1603 (1992) in which the Court ruled control of a CRS by the two defendant airlines, which had only a 14% market share of the air transportation market, did not give the airlines the power to monopolise any market vertically related to the CRS itself. Since the Court declined to apply an essential facilities analysis in *Alaska Airlines* that case should probably not be understood as a stricter application of a market leveraging

1. The Relationship of the 'Intent' and 'Monopoly-Leveraging' Cases to
the 'Essential Facilities' Cases

The line of cases establishing a special duty under Section Two of the Sherman
Act regarding access to an 'essential facility' overlap to a considerable extent
with cases addressing 'intent' or 'monopoly leveraging' issues. *Aspen Skiing*, for
example, was treated by the Tenth Circuit Court of Appeal as an essential facilities case. *Otter Tail Power*, often regarded as a proto-essential facilities case,
has elements of both leveraging and anticompetitive intent. Likewise, the products denied the plaintiffs in *Berkey Kodak* could be described as essential facilities although, since the legal test stated in this case only required that refusal
give a comparative advantage, it is not clear that they need have been 'essential',
in the way that the term has been defined in the essential facilities cases.

Despite this overlap, the cases invoking the essential facilities rule appear to
differ from the approach in the intent and monopoly leveraging cases,
described above in two ways that are important for putting the rule in a comparative law context. First, whereas in both the monopoly-leveraging and
intent cases substantial scope is given to business justifications as a defence
legitimising a refusal to deal, the business justification for refusing access to an
essential facility appears limited to cases where access would disrupt the
monopolist's own business. Thus, while a showing that a refusal to share access
might be justified in an 'intent' case by showing that the monopolist will maximise short term profitability by not co-operating with its rival, such a showing
would presumably not be sufficient to justify a refusal to grant access to an
essential facility. Second, in contrast to the monopoly-leveraging cases, the
essential facilities rule only comes into play where denial of access to the facility has its effects in a market *where the defendant has market power*. This follows from the nature of the requirement that the facility be 'essential'. As the
Court of Appeals for the Ninth Circuit ruled in *Alaska Airlines, Inc. v United
Airlines, Inc.*, '[a] facility that is controlled by a single firm will be considered
essential only if control of the facility carries with it the power to *eliminate* competition in the downstream market'.[11]

---

approach but rather as indicative of the requirement under the essential facilities
approach that there already be monopoly power in the downstream market. In the
recent, highly publicised, settlement of the case against Microsoft, Inc. it was noteworthy that the US Department of Justice did not press the monopoly-leveraging charges
that apparently featured in the complaints regarding the behavior of Microsoft.

[11] 948 F2d at 544 (emphasis in original). The Court goes on to observe that where
a refusal to provide access does create the power to eliminate competition in the

2. The Rationale for an Essential Facilities Rule

Neither the courts nor the commentators have always articulated the reason for this doctrine, and there has been considerable analytic inconsistency in its application in the United States.[12] Historically, the essential facilities concept seems to have emerged from nineteenth century cases involving the common law duty of persons holding a local monopoly to deal fairly with potential customers. (Thus, for example, millers could not unreasonably refuse to grind a local farmer's grain).[13] Seen from this perspective, the essential facilities doctrine could have become a type of 'public carrier' doctrine, subject only to limits on the capacity of the essential facility, and there have been several cases

---

downstream market 'there is little need to engage in the usual lengthy analysis of factors such as intent', *ibidem* at 546.

[12] The first case in which the doctrine is explicitly denominated as such in a Section 2 case is *Hecht v Pro-Football, Inc.*, 570 F2d. 982, 992–93, *cert denied*, US 956 (1978). In *Hecht* a potential franchisee in a rival football league had sought to challenge a restrictive covenant in the stadium lease of an established league's team. The covenant in question prohibited leasing the stadium to any other professional football team. The Court of Appeals ruled that the District Court had erred in failing to give a jury instruction on the essential facilities doctrine, stating that, that doctrine 'would also support an allegation that the Redskins' refusal to waive the restrictive covenant constituted illegal monopolization under Section Two. In defining the doctrine, which it also referred to as the 'bottleneck principle' the Court traced its origins back to *United States v Terminal Railroad, supra*, note. See also *Otter Tail Power Co. v United States*, 410 US 366 (1973) (upholding liability of wholesale supplier of electricity that refused to supply power to power system that competed with it for retail customers where other power system had no other source of supply). In *Otter Tail*, the Supreme Court did not indicate whether it was applying the intent test or the essential facilities doctrine, both of which appeared to have been applied by the Eighth Circuit. In its brief, the US government, as plaintiff, had argued that the refusal by Otter Tail, an integrated public utility, to sell or transmit electric power to municipalities in its service area who had sought to enter the market for the supply of electric power was also illegal under 'the antitrust principle that a firm may not use its strategic dominance over a facility controlling access to a market for the purpose of maintaining its monopoly by shutting out potential competitors'. *Brief for the United States at 74–75 (citations omitted)*. From the formulation of the issues in *Hecht* and *Otter Tail Power*, it seems clear that the essential facilities doctrine, as applied to Section 2 cases requires not only control over access to an essential facility but also, in contrast at least to the monopoly leveraging cases, dominance on the downstream market. It is this latter factor that appears to distinguish the essential facilities doctrine from the monopoly leveraging cases.

[13] Sullivan (1997).

where a principle of fairness, rather than the type of economic analysis appropriate to antitrust law, appear to have predominated.[14]

Academic commentary on the development of the essential facilities doctrine has been largely unfavourable. Indeed, some authors have challenged the validity of the essential facilities concept as distinct from the general, intent-based test for monopolisation. Insofar as commentators have recognised a policy basis for preserving a separate essential facilities infringement under Section 2, they have focused on the possible efficiency-enhancing impact of an obligation to share access to essential facilities, particularly where the market for providing the facility is subject to price regulation.[15]

Despite the silence of the commentators, a coherent rationale may be identified for treating a refusal to provide access to an essential facility differently from other refusals to co-operate with a competitor. Such a rationale may be based on the central distinction in Section 2 between monopoly power lawfully attained and maintained, through the application of skill, foresight and indus-

---

[14] *See, Fishman v Estate of Wirtz*, 807 F.2d 550, 574 (Easterbook, J. dissenting). In this case, which has been criticised by Areeda, the doctrine was applied to the refusal of the defendant, which controlled a sports arena in Chicago and which was also bidding for the franchise in question, to lease the latter to the plaintiff who was therefore denied approval as a purchaser of a professional basketball franchise. Areeda argues that the case involves a misuse of the essential facilities doctrine since competition among basketball teams would not be affected by whether the plaintiff or the defendant owned the team in question, see Areeda and Hoverkamp (1992). Curiously, there may be some hints of an approach similar to the public carrier approach in the Advocate General Gullman's proposed resolution of the *Magill* cases (Case T–69/89, *RTE v Commission*, Case T–70/89, *BBC v Commission*, and Case T–76/89, *ITP v Commission*, [1991] ECR II–485, 534, and 575). In his opinion, the Advocate General appears to seek a result that would limit the obligation to grant licenses to situations involving non-competitors, leaving the patentee's monopoly rights intact vis-à-vis his competitors. This approach, which would impose an obligation to license only in respect of fields in which the patentee is not itself active, appears to derive from the doctrine of non-use applied under some Member State compulsory license legislation.

[15] The economic analysis of most commentators starts with the premise that a monopolist's denial of access to an essential facility will normally not affect consumer welfare because the monopolist already has a right to demand a monopoly rent in the market for providing the facility. Areeda notes that '[I]n all events the key point is that a monopolist cannot earn double profits by monopolising a second, vertically integrated, market' and suggests that a case like *Otter Tail,* where prices for use of the facility were controlled, provided a rare example of a case where a duty to deal might benefit consumers, see Areeda and Hovenkamp (1992). Interestingly from a comparative law point of view, Professor Areeda also suggested that this analysis might not apply in a legal system where excessive pricing by dominant firms was subject to control, making specific reference to Article 82 [ex 86], at 846–47.

try, which is not prohibited by Section 2, and monopoly power maintained through other means, which is.

First, where a firm refuses to deal with rivals in cases where no essential facility is involved, the existence of a business justification normally means that effective exercise of market power is the result of the firm's skill, foresight, and industry. Where an essential facility exists, however, it may be argued that the firm's continued exercise of market power is not attributable to the firm's own efforts, but rather to the externalities that make it impossible for rivals to duplicate the facility. This argument is most compelling where the existence of the essential facility results from natural causes or the grant of a franchise by the state.[16]

Second, since in essential facilities cases the owner of the facility already has market power on the market downstream of the facility, the refusal to grant access to the essential facility constitutes a virtual *per se* infringement in the absence a justification concerning the capacity of the facility and the interference

---

[16] The argument is perhaps even more compelling in Section I cases where the essential facility results from the pooling of resources of a number of competitors. The essential facilities doctrine may also apply in cases in which the original creation of the facility may have involved exemplary competitive behavior. In cases where the essential facility results from the innovativeness or investment of the defendant, there may be important prudential considerations that weigh heavily against regulatory interference in the decisions of firms with market power with respect to their dealings with rivals that are absent in the case where the market power results from external factors, see Areeda and Hovenkamp (1992). This distinction reflects the jurisprudential differentiation between these incidents of property that reflect the achievements of an individual and those external to a person's own merit (such as those made available by accident of birth). As John Rawls has argued in developing a theory of a just society: Rawls (1971: 73–74 and 100), allowing 'the distribution of wealth and income to be determined by the natural distribution of abilities and talents . . . is arbitrary from a moral perspective' . . . while 'inequalities of birth and natural endowment are undeserved'. On the other hand, a much stronger claim can be made for inequalities resulting from achievement: 'given a just system of cooperation as a scheme of public rules and the expectations set up by it, those who, with the prospect of improving their condition, have done what the system announces that it will reward are entitled to their advantages. In this sense, the more fortunate have a claim to their better situation . . . .' (103). To be sure, Rawls goes on to subject the claim based on achievement to important limitations; nevertheless, its superiority to the claim based on the 'natural lottery' is clear. Balancing the competing interests of rewarding a competitor for its legitimate creative efforts and preserving competition becomes considerably more difficult, and may tilt against the imposition of a duty to deal where the essential facility has resulted from efforts either encouraged by statute—as in the case of patents—or regarded as socially beneficial—as in the case of R&D.

(other than competition from a rival) with the owner's ability to conduct its own business that would result from the granting of access to the facility.

3. Applying the Essential Facilities Doctrine

In its current form, the US courts apply a four-part test for determining whether a refusal to deal in respect of an essential facility constitutes actionable monopolisation:

(1) Control of an 'essential facility' by the monopolist;
(2) Inability on the part of a competitor practically or reasonably to duplicate the essential facility;
(3) Denial of the use of the facility to the competitor; and
(4) Feasibility of providing the facility.[17]

In reviewing the cases and commentary, the following points emerge regarding the application of the essential facilities concept in practice that could inform a discussion of possible future developments in the EC:

The facility must be essential. It is clear that to give rise to a duty the facility must be truly essential, i.e., it must be vital to the competitive viability of the monopolist's competitors. It is therefore not sufficient that the facility provides the monopolist with a competitive advantage of some sort.[18]

---

[17] *MCI Communications Corp.* v *ATCT*, 708 F.2d 1081, 1032 (7th Cir.), *cert. denied*, 464 US 891 (1983). Areeda suggests a somewhat more refined approach designed to limit the scope of the requirement to grant access. In particular, Areeda takes the view that: (i) the essential facilities doctrine should only be applied exceptionally; there being no general duty to share one's resources; (ii) a monopolist's facility should be treated as 'essential' only where it is vital to rivals' competitive viability; it must therefore be critical (as opposed to desirable) and it must not be capable of duplication; (iii) the case for access is strongest in the case of a regulated monopolist whose denial of access enables him to evade rate regulation: in contrast, where the monopolist is free to charge a market price for his resources, denial of access will seldom reduce output or increase price; (iv) no one should be forced to deal unless this is likely to improve substantially competition in the marketplace; (v) only actual or potential competitors may claim access to an essential facility; (vi) denial of access can never be *per se* unlawful; (vii) the defendant's intentions are not relevant; (viii) access should not be required if this will force the Court into a supervisory role in ensuring implementations of the remedy; and (ix) in private damage suits, the plaintiff must show that he has been injured by the allegedly illegal conduct.

[18] For example, in a number of cases, courts have found that use of a hospital's facilities was not essential for a doctor to compete for patients, *e.g. McKenzie* v *Mercy*

The facility must be needed for competition in a market where the defendant has market power. In contrast to the monopoly leveraging cases, the essential facilities doctrine does not concern effects in a separate, related market. Even where there may be said to be a 'market' for the facility in question, the essential facilities doctrine, if it is to be meaningfully distinguished from the monopoly leveraging cases, always involves monopolisation by the defendant firm in a market where that firm enjoys market power due to its control over the essential facility.

A 'facility' is a resource. Courts have also noted, however, that the facility need not be a 'facility' in the physical sense. Rather, the cases support Professor Areeda's suggestion that an essential facility is 'a resource possessed by the defendant that is vital to the plaintiff's competitive liability'.[19]

The facility must not be 'reasonably' capable of duplication. The cases do not require that it be physically or financially impossible to duplicate a facility.[20] It

---

Hospital 854 F2d 365 (10th Cir. 1988)(suggesting that a doctor could see many patients at a clinic or in his office). One District Court rejected the argument that access to advertising in a specific magazine was an essential facility, observing that some of the plaintiff's competitors did not advertise in that magazine and that alternative ways existed to reach the intended audience, *Soap Opera Now, Inc.* v *Network Publishing Co.*, 737 F.Supp. 1338 (SDNY 1990).

[19] In at least one case an intangible asset has been described as an essential facility, *Bellsouth Advertising & Publishing Corp.* v *Donnelly Information Publishing*, 719 F.Supp. 1551 (S.D. Fla. 1988), *aff'd* 933 F2d 952 (11th Cir. 1991)(describing information belonging to a party as an essential facility).

[20] In applying the essential facility doctrine in a 'same market' dominance context, strong policy reasons suggest that the Commission (or a national court) should follow the strict approach adopted in similar cases in the United States concerning the 'essentialness' of the facility. In particular, a more interventionist approach inspired by the monopoly-leveraging cases could risk inhibiting legitimate competitive behavior. To avoid this danger, the essential facilities doctrine should arguably only apply where the facility is (i) incapable of duplication and (ii) truly essential (i.e., does more than give the dominant firm a competitive advantage). On its face, the Commission's *Aer Lingus/British Midland* decision (*Aer Lingus/British Midland*, 92/213/EEC, OJ L 96/34 (1992)), which is sometimes described as an essential facilities case, would appear to meet neither of these tests inasmuch as: (i) the Commission did not examine whether the facility was truly essential for entry by British Midland. Rather it found that the refusal by Aer Lingus to interline put British Midland at a competitive disadvantage; and (ii) the Commission did not examine whether British Midland could duplicate the facility by building up sufficient frequencies to make interlining unnecessary. In fact, the only constraint on British Midland's ability to do so was the scarcity of slots at London Heathrow and the consequent need to shift slots from other profitable uses in order to expand Dublin services. British Midland did have slots that it used for other services. Shifting those slots to Dublin services was, however, a less valuable economic use of

is sufficient that the cost of duplication would be unreasonable in light of the size of the transaction for such duplication to have been facilitated. The fact that creating or using an alternative facility would impose an additional cost or inconvenience on competitors, does not, however, suffice to show that the facility cannot be duplicated.[21]

The defendant need only offer a reasonable alternative. Whether the defendant has actually refused access to the facility is a question of fact. It is clear that offering access to a facility only on unreasonable terms constitutes a constructive denial of access to the facility.[22] It is equally clear, however, that as long as the terms offered to the applicant are reasonable, they need not be identical to the terms or access enjoyed by the owner of the facility or by other users.[23]

The defendant is entitled to reasonable compensation for use of the facility. The requirement that access be allowed on reasonable terms implies that the monopolist may still expect payment for use of the facility. Indeed, Professor Areeda assumes that the defendant is entitled to charge the 'market price', i.e., a price reflecting monopoly power in the market for provision of the service in question.

'Feasibility' in providing the facility is linked to possible disruption of the defendant's own operations. The principle that making a facility available must be feasible has two applications in practice. First, there are clearly cases where capacity or supply in respect of an essential facility is limited. In such cases, the defendant is not required to ration access to the facility.[24] Second, and more

---

those slots for British Midland. Where entering a market efficiently may require a new entrant to re-assign inputs used in other markets to the new market and the entrant decides not to shift those inputs for commercial reasons, it is difficult to characterise a substitute for those inputs controlled by a competitor as an essential facility.

[21] *Alaska Airlines* v *United Airlines*, 948 F.2d 536 (9th Cir. 1991); *Twin Labs* v *Weider Health & Fitness*, 900 F.2d 566 (2d Cir. 1990).

[22] *Laurel Sand & Gravel, Inc.* v *CSX Transportation,* 924 F.2d 539 (4th Cir.), *cert. denied,* 112 S.Ct. 64 (1991).

[23] *Southern Pacific Communications Co.* v *American Tel. & Tel. Co.*, 740 F.2d 980, 1009 (D.C. Cir. 1984), *cert. denied* 470 US 1005 (1985) ('Absolute equality of access to essential facilities . . . is not mandated by the antitrust laws').

[24] For example in *Illinois ex rel Burris* v *Panhandle Eastern Pipeline Co.*, 935 F.2d 1469 (7th Cir. 1991), the Court found that the pipeline was not required to transport gas for others where that would reduce its ability to transport its own gas, which it was legally bound to purchase. Also, *Hecht* v *Pro-Football*, 570 F.2d 982, 993 (D.C. Cir. 1977). *cert. denied* 436 US 956 (1978) ('antitrust laws do not require that an essential facility be shared or would inhibit the defendant's ability to serve its customers adequately'.).

difficult, are cases where making access available would disrupt the defendant's legitimate conduct of its own business. Where a defendant has been able to make such a showing, the courts have been willing to view the granting of access as unfeasible.[25]

III. The Essential Facilities Doctrine in Community Law

1. Refusals to Deal Under Article 82 [ex 86]

The obligation under Article 82 [ex 86] of the Consolidated Treaties that is placed on dominant firms to deal with customers would appear to go far beyond that recognised under Section 2 of the Sherman Act. Indeed, the European Commission has asserted that, as 'a general principle an objectively unjustifiable refusal to supply by an undertaking holding a dominant position on a market constitutes an infringement of Article 82 [ex 86]'.[26] Although the Community courts have not articulated this obligation as a 'general principle', they have confirmed the obligation on dominant firms to deal in a number of cases. These cases fall into two categories: (i) cases involving termination of existing customers; and (ii) cases involving vertically integrated companies.

United Brands—Termination of Supplies to a Dependent Firm
The leading case involving a 'dependency' analysis is *United Brands*. Following complaints from a banana ripener regarding the activities of United Brands Co., the Commission issued a decision finding that UBC held a dominant position and had been involved in four types of abusive conduct.[27] The Court of Justice affirmed the Commission decision insofar as it found an abuse based on

---

[25] Thus, the courts have accepted that utilities may refuse to provide access to lines providing low cost power where to do so would reduce the ability of the utility to provide such power to other customers *Cities of Anaheim* v *Southern Cal Edison Co.*, 1990–2 Trade Cas. (CCH) Para. 69,246 (C.D. Cal. 1990). In cases involving AT&T, the courts reached differing views as to whether interconnectivity was feasible in a given case without disrupting AT&T's other operations, *compare MCI* (finding refusal unjustified) and *Southern Pacific Communications Co.* v *AT&T*, 740 F.2d 980 (D.C. Cir. 1984), *cert. denied*, 464 US 891 (1985) (finding refusal could be justified if decision made in good faith based on conditions at that time).

[26] *Polaroid/SSI Europe*, Thirteenth Report on Competition Policy, point 157 (1983).

[27] The four abuses were: excessive pricing, discriminatory pricing, termination of a distributor and a restriction on trade in unripened bananas. Commission Decision 76/353, *Chiquita*, OJ L 95/1 (1976).

termination of supplies. The refusal to supply aspect of the case involved the termination by United Brands of banana deliveries to Olesen, a Danish banana ripener. United Brands alleged that Olesen had associated itself with the attempt of the Standard Fruit Company, United Brand's largest competitor, to supplant United Brands as the leading supplier of bananas. United Brands maintained that Olesen had consequently failed to use the proper amount of care in ripening and distributing its bananas.

The Court began its assessment of this claim by stating:

> [I]t is advisable to assert positively from the outset that an undertaking that is in a dominant position for the purpose of marketing a product—which cashes in on the reputation of a brand name known and valued by the consumers—cannot stop supplying a long-standing customer who abides by normal commercial practice, if the orders placed by this customer are in no way out of the ordinary. Such conduct is inconsistent with the objectives laid out in Article 3(f) [ex Article 3(f)] of the Treaty, which are set out in detail in Article 82 [ex 86], especially in paragraphs (b) and (c) since the refusal to sell would limit markets to the prejudice of consumers and would amount to discrimination which might in the end eliminate a trading party from the relevant market.

The Court recognised that in some cases even a dominant firm was entitled to take action to defend its legitimate commercial interests. The Court ruled, however, that any such action must be 'proportionate' to the interests served. The Court concluded that Olesen's conduct did not justify the extreme remedy of termination.

The analysis in *United Brands* appears to focus on the relationship between the dominant firm and its dependent customer. United Brands itself was not in competition with its customer; nevertheless, the impact of termination on that customer was deemed abusive since it was found to be disproportionate to the justifications for termination proffered by United Brands. Although the Commission decision had considered the possible impact that terminating Olesen could have on the willingness of other customers to deal with United Brands' rivals, the Court's judgment focuses on preserving the 'independence of small and medium sized firms in their commercial relations with the firm in a dominant position'.[28] The Court's emphasis is highlighted by its reliance on

---

[28] See, however, Temple Lang (1994), in which it is argued that the obligation to deal was imposed in *United Brands* because the refusal was designed to force a customer to purchase exclusively from UBC. While such a narrowing of the rule established in *United Brands* would be welcome, doubts remain, in light of the language cited above, as to whether the Court's ruling can be limited in this way.

paragraph (c) of Article 82 [ex 86], which focuses on the impact of conduct on customers of the dominant company in downstream markets regardless of whether the dominant firm is vertically integrated. This kind of obligation, which requires the dominant firm to deal with parties with whom it is not itself in competition, appears to have no parallel in US antitrust law.[29] Both German[30] and French law[31] do, however, incorporate far-reaching requirements on dominant firms to sell, even where the dominant firm is not in competition with the customer. These requirements are usually justified either on the basis of protecting the customers involved from exploitation or on promoting access to the downstream markets.

Commercial Solvents—Gaining Competitive Advantage in Related Markets
The leading case involving vertical integration and indeed the first major case involving a refusal to deal is *Commercial Solvents* v *Commission*.[32] In this case, the defendant held a dominant position in the market for supply of raw materials used for manufacturing ethambutanol, a drug used for treating tuberculosis. Although it had supplied these raw materials to the complainant company for five years, it refused to supply further orders. After attempting without success to find alternative sources, the customer complained to the Commission, which adopted a decision finding that the refusal to supply was an abuse of a dominant position, and ordered the defendant to reinstate supplies.[33]
The Court affirmed the Commission finding of abuse, ruling that:

> an undertaking being in a dominant position as regards the production of raw material and therefore able to control the supply to manufacturers of derivatives, cannot, just because it decides to start manufacturing those derivatives (in competition with its former customers) act in such a way as to eliminate competition which, in

---

[29] In *Official Airline Guides* v *FTC*, 630 F.2d 920 (2d Cir. 1980), *cert. denied*, 450 US 917 (1981), the Court of Appeals for the Second Circuit reversed a Federal Trade Commission ruling that the publisher of the Official Airline Guide was obliged under Section 5 of the Federal Trade Commission Act to publish listings including commuter flights. The court ruled that, although it accepted the findings that the refusal damaged the commuter carriers and the proffered justification was insufficient, the defendant was under no obligation absent a showing that its purpose was to restrain competition or extend its monopoly.

[30] Gesetz gegen Wettbewerbsbeschränkungen, Para. 26(2).

[31] Ordonnance No. 861243 du 1er décembre 1986 relative à la liberté des prix et de la concurrence' (J.O. 9 déc. 1986), Articles 8, 30, 36(2).

[32] Cases 6 & 7/73, [1974] ECR 223.

[33] Commission Decision 72/457/EEC, *ZOJA/CSC-ICI*, OJ L 299/51 (1972).

the case in question, would amount to eliminating one of the principal manufactur‐
ers of ethambutanol in the common market.[34]

The Court observed that Commercial Solvents did not seriously dispute
that in view of its production capability and the probable size of the customer's
requirements, there should be no difficulty in meeting its needs.

It should be noted that in finding this refusal to supply abusive, the Court
did not examine the competitive situation on the downstream market for
ethambutanol. Indeed, in an earlier portion of the judgment, it was suggested
that rival therapies competed with ethambutanol as treatments for tuberculo‐
sis, making it unlikely that Commercial Solvents would have achieved a dom‐
inant position in the downstream market, even if it became the sole supplier of
ethambutanol. Thus, *Commercial Solvents* and the cases that follow it appear
analogous to the *Berkey* 'monopoly leveraging' line of cases under US law,
because they focus on the use of dominance in an upstream market to forge a
competitive advantage in a related market without any requirement that there
be market power in the downstream market.[35]

2. The Refusal to Deal Cases in the Context of the General Principles of Article 82 [ex 86]

The *United Brands* and *Commercial Solvents* lines of cases reflect two distinct
strands in the theory of abuse under Article 82 [ex 86]. As interpreted by the
Court of Justice, Article 82 [ex 86] incorporates a general rule, first clearly artic‐
ulated in *Hoffmann-LaRoche* v *Commission*, which focuses on conduct by a
dominant firm that affects competition in markets where competition has been
weakened by the presence of the dominant firm. Under this rule, a dominant
firm abuses its position if its conduct either reduces residual competition or
prevents development of new competition and if the conduct is not 'normal
competition based on traders' performance'.[36] Article 82 [ex 86] also incorpo‐

---

[34] *Commercial Solvents* at 250/251.

[35] Also, Case 311/84, *Télémarketing* v *CLT*, [1985] ECR 3261; Case 22/78, *Hugin* v
Commission, [1979] ECR 1869; and Commission Decision 88/589, *LEA\Sabena*, OJ L
317/47 (1998).

[36] In the English translation of *Hoffmann-LaRoche* (Case 85/76, [1979] ECR 461) the
crucial concept of 'performance' was lost because the word 'performance' ('Leistung' in
German and 'prestation' in French) was mistranslated as 'transaction'. This error was
corrected in subsequent cases applying the concept (*see*, Case 322/81, *Michelin* v
Commission, [1983] ECR 3461; and *Perfume*). It is clear from other cases notably *Hag*

rates a series of examples (82(a) to 82(d)) that focus on conduct that affect a dominant firm's customers or the ultimate consumers of its products. Thus, irrespective of whether a dominant firm is itself active in a downstream market, it may be an abuse for a dominant firm to charge excessive prices, to refuse to satisfy a significant consumer demand for a product, to discriminate among customers in ways that put them at a commercial disadvantage vis-à-vis their competitors, or to tie sales of unrelated products or services.[37]

In many cases, both strands of abuse theory will be present. Thus, in *United Brands*, the Commission was clearly concerned with the fact that a refusal to supply a dependent customer would not only limit that customer's independence but would also foreclose the options of United Brands' rivals. Similarly, in *Commercial Solvents* the fact that the customer was dependent on supplies from the dominant firm and would therefore go out of business in the absence of supplies may have influenced the Commission's treatment of the case, quite apart from the competitive advantages that Commercial Solvents would have gained by eliminating a competitor in the downstream market.

A feature common to both types of cases that is particularly important for analysing refusals to deal under Article 82 [ex 86] is the possibility that a dominant firm may legitimise its conduct through objective justifications. In cases where abuse is based upon the general test, however, it is not clear whether the 'business justification' relates to the requirement of 'competition on the basis of performance' or is, instead, a special defence based on general principles of Community law. Although there is clearly a relationship between business

---

11 (Case C–10/89, *CNL-Sucal* v *Hag*, [1990] ECR I–3711) and *AKZO* (Case C-62/86, *AKZO* v *Commission*, [1991] ECR I–3359) that the emphasis is on whether competition is 'performance-based' rather than on whether it is 'normal'. Indeed the word 'normal' may be viewed as defining the class of conduct which is performance-based. In other words, normal competition *is* competition based on performance and competition based on performance cannot be abnormal.

[37] In the historical development of Article 82 [ex 86], at least until the Court of Justice judgment in *Continental Can* (Case 6/72, *Continental Can* v *Commission*, [1973] ECR 215), there was substantial doubt as to whether Article 82 [ex 86] applied to conduct directed at a firm's competitors as opposed to conduct that affected the dominant firm's customers, see generally Joliet (1970). There was in contrast general agreement that a function of Article 82 [ex 86] was to protect the customers of dominant firm from exploitation and from limits on their economic autonomy: Deringer (1968:166–7), '[T]he purpose of the competition rules is to preserve the freedom of choice of those who transact business in the market, as the free interplay of supply and demand in competition. The exploitation is therefore an abuse where the dominant position is used to restrain or eliminate the freedom of decision in competition either of competitors or of the consumers.'

justifications and performance-based competition, the better view would prob ably be that the concepts are distinct. That is, the burden is on the dominan firm to prove a business justification, while the burden of proving abuse including proof that conduct is not performance-based, should rest with th Commission (or the plaintiff in a private action). This conclusion is supporter by the fact that the objective justification test appears to be based upon a pro portionality analysis (i.e. do the interests of the dominant firm justify th impact of its conduct on third parties and is there a less restrictive alternativ for protecting those interests) while the criterion of 'normal methods of com petition based on performance' looks to a categorisation of types of conduc without regard for the effect of that conduct in a particular case.[38]

From a comparative law perspective it may be observed that, while th 'fairness/dependency' strand of Article 82 [ex 86] cases apparently find no (o only little) application in modern US Section 2 law, the 'performance-base competition' test appears, at least superficially similar, to the 'skill, foresight and industry' encouraged under Section 2. It is important to recognise, how ever, that the concept of performance-based competition in Article 82 [ex 86] i considerably narrower than the 'competition on the merits' test sometime articulated under US law. It may be questioned whether the conduct con demned in cases like *Hoffmann-LaRoche* or *British Gypsum*[39] (granting o rebates to customers who purchase exclusively from the dominant firm) woul be regarded as lacking a business justification under Section 2 (although wher the arrangements foreclosed substantial parts of the market they might be sub ject to other provisions of the Sherman or Clayton Act).

3. The Commission's Essential Facilities Cases

Although a number of earlier cases may be susceptible to an essential facilitie analysis, the first case in which the Commission explicitly articulated an essen tial facilities theory was *Sea Containers* v *Stena Sealink*.[40] This case involved

---

[38] Case C–62/86, *AKZO* v *Commission*, [1991] ECR I–3539. It could be argued, how ever, that there is a legitimate presumption that a dominant firm will supply any cus tomer that is willing and able to pay the purchase price for its goods or services. Thus, in the special case of refusals to supply, a burden could be put on the dominant firm to rebut the presumption by showing that it had a good reason for its refusal.

[39] Case T–65/89, *BPB Industries Plc. and British Gypsum* v *Commission* [1993] ECR II–389.

[40] Commission Decision 94/19/EEC, OJ L 15/8 (1994). The fact that the Commission chose to adopt and publish a formal decision in a case in which it had rejected the

access to the port facilities at Holyhead in Wales that are used for ferry services to Ireland. The Commission found that Stena Sealink, which owns the facilities, had declined to provide access to the facilities on a non-discriminatory basis to a rival firm that wished to operate an innovative service to Ireland using high-speed catamarans. The Commission ruled that an:

> undertaking which occupies a dominant position in the provision of an essential facility and itself uses that facility (i.e. facility or infrastructure without access to which competitors cannot provide services to their customers) and which refuses other companies access to that facility without objective justification or grants access to competitors only on terms less favourable than those which it gives to its own services, infringes Article 82 [ex 86] if the other conditions for applying that Article are met.[41]

The Commission went on to suggest that Sealink's rejection of proposals made by the applicant and its failure to make any counter offers or engage in negotiations 'was not consistent with the obligations of an undertaking which enjoys a dominant position in relation to an essential facility. Nor was it the conduct which would have been expected from an independent port authority'. The Commission also emphasised that Sealink never consulted with the other ferry operators in Holyhead and set up no procedures for dealing with its responsibilities as a ferry operator. The Commission observed further that

> 'an independent harbour authority, which would, of course, have had an interest in increasing revenue at the port, would have, at least, considered whether the interests of existing and proposed users of the port could best be reconciled by a solution involving modest changes in the allocated slot times or in any plans for the development of the harbour.'[42]

The Commission then concluded that Sealink had not offered access to its competitor on non-discriminatory terms.

It may be observed that the *Sealink* decision falls squarely within the tradition of monopoly-leveraging/refusal to deal cases under Article 82 [ex 86]. Although it appears that Sealink may have held a dominant position for purposes of Article 82 [ex 86] in the market for ferry services, the Commission based its Article 82 [ex 86] analysis on dominance in the market for providing

---

complainant's request for interim measures can be taken as an indication that, in the Commission's view, the case represents a significant development of the law.

[41] *Ibid* para. 66.
[42] *Ibid* para. 75.

harbour services. Indeed, the Commission probably could have found an abuse based on the unjustified refusal to allow access to the port without invoking the essential facilities concept given the probable effects of its conduct on the downstream market where it appears that Sealink was also dominant.

Nevertheless, there appear to be two related differences between *Sealink* and cases like *Commercial Solvents* or *Télémarketing*. First, the Commission's decision in *Sealink* appears to suggest that, where a firm controls an essential facility, it is under a strict duty not to discriminate. This may go beyond the prohibition of discrimination in respect of equivalent transactions covered by Article 82(c) [ex 86(c)]. It is possible that the notion that a firm controlling an essential facility is under greater obligations than generally apply to dominant firms may reflect the dependency/fairness rationale that sometimes underlies Article 82 [ex 86] analysis. However, as discussed below, the more stringent obligations imposed on a firm controlling an essential facility may stem from its dual role as both an administrator of an infrastructure and as an operator on a market utilising the infrastructure.

The second difference between *Sealink* and previous cases involves the standard of the independent harbour operator imposed on the operator of the essential facility, i.e. the suggestion that Article 82 [ex 86] imposes special procedural obligations on firms that control an essential facility. The Commission found it unnecessary, at least at the interim measures phase, to consider whether there were factual justifications for refusing access. The fact that Sealink had failed to negotiate and consult with its customers as an independent operator sufficed to create at least a presumption of abuse.

The second case invoking the essential facility concept is *Re Access to Facilities of Port of Rødby*.[43] Like *Sealink*, *Port of Rødby* involved access to a ferry terminal, in this case used for ferry services across the Baltic sea from Denmark to Germany. Unlike the *Sealink* case, however, *Port of Rødby* involved the outright denial of access to port facilities to a competing ferry company. Also unlike *Sealink*, this case involved the refusal of the Danish government to authorise the new services. Using language similar to that used in *Sealink*, the Commission asserted that it would be an abuse of a dominant position for the ferry company that controlled the port facilities to refuse to allow a rival access to those facilities. Applying the *effet utile* concept developed under Article 86 [ex 90], the Commission further found that the government's refusal to authorise use of the facility to the new entrant put the ferry company in a position that it could only have achieved by violating Article 82 [ex 86]. As a result, the government action also violated Article 86 [ex 90].

---

[43] Commission Decision 94/119/EEC, OJ No. L 55/52 (1994).

Leaving aside the issues raised by the application of Article 86 [ex 90] in this case,[44] the *Port of Rødby* decision provides an insight into the Commission's views on the justifications necessary to justify limiting access to an essential facility. The Danish government had argued that allowing a new ferry operator to use the facilities was not acceptable because there was no unmet demand for additional services and because access for a new entrant would limit increased use of the port by incumbent operators. In a subsequent response, the government suggested that technical reasons made access for an additional ferry operator impractical.

The Commission found, as a factual matter, that the projections of the government regarding future demand and the capacity limitations of the port were invalid. The Commission also indicated, however, that even if the existing facilities were 'saturated' so that they could not accommodate additional sailings, it would be desirable to introduce competition by providing access to the new entrant. This suggests that the inability to accommodate a new entrant on the basis of existing capacity would not be a sufficient justification for refusing access to an essential facility.[45]

IV. Limitations on the Essential Facilities Doctrine

The recent opinion of Advocate General Jacobs in *Bronner* v *Mediaprint*[46] illustrates a more cautious approach to the essential facilities doctrine outside the transport sector. In this case, Oscar Bronner GmbH. & Co. KG ('Bronner'), the publisher of the Austrian daily newspaper *Der Standard*, with 3.6% of circulation and around 6% of advertising revenues of the national daily newspaper market in 1994 sought an order from the Austrian Kartellgericht

---

[44] The Commission's Article 86 [ex 90] analysis is based on an expansive reading of the judgment of the Court of Justice in Case C-18/88 *RTT* v *GB-Inno-BM SA*, [1991] ECR I–5941. That case involved the grant to the state telephone monopoly of powers to establish the technical specifications for products used on its networks, allowing the telephone monopoly to obtain competitive advantages in the market for providing equipment. *RTT* thus constituted a genuine monopoly-leveraging case where the monopolist's control of the downstream market was facilitated by the State measure. In *Port of Rødby*, the status of the ferry company as operator of the port is irrelevant to the position of the parties, because the government retained the right to determine who operated from the port.

[45] It is conceivable that in this situation the Commission may be tempted to require the dominant firm to share the rare resource, perhaps even on a rotating basis.

[46] Case C–7/97 *Oscar Bronner GmbH & Co. KG* v *Mediaprint Zeitungs- und Zeitschriftenverlag GmbH. & Co. KG and other*, [1998] ECR I–7791.

requiring Mediaprint Zeitungs- und Zeitschriftenverlag GmbH & Co. KG and its subsidiaries (together 'Mediaprint') to allow Bronner access to its nation-wide home delivery service for daily newspapers against payment of reasonable remuneration. Mediaprint publishes, markets and collects advertising revenues from the daily newspapers *Neue Kronen Zeitung* and *Kurier*, whose combined 1994 market share was 46.8% of total circulation and 42% by total advertising revenues. These newspapers reach 53.3% of the population over the age of 14 in private households and 71% of all newspaper readers.

Relevant market. The Advocate General accepted the submission by Bronner and the Commission, which had intervened, that the relevant market was that of newspaper distribution, and not the market for the sale of daily newspapers. The claim, therefore, related to an alleged abuse by Mediaprint of its market power in the area of newspaper distribution with a view to eliminating competition on the connected newspaper market.

Dominant position and abuse. Bronner relied on the essential facilities doctrine to frame its contention that Mediaprint was obliged to grant access to newspaper distribution as a prerequisite for effective competition on the daily newspaper market. The Advocate General noted that in the long term it is generally pro-competitive and in the interests of consumers to allow a company to retain for its own use facilities which it has developed for the purposes of its own business. He recalled that the primary purpose of Article 82 [ex 86] is to prevent distortions of competition and, in particular, to safeguard the interests of consumers, rather than to protect the position of particular competitors. The Advocate General further suggested that intervention, whether understood as an application of the essential facilities doctrine or, more traditionally, as a response to refusal to supply goods or services, can be justified on competition grounds only in cases in which the dominant undertaking has a genuine stranglehold on the related market. He noted that such might be the case where duplication of the facility is impossible or extremely difficult owing to physical, geographical or legal constraints, or is highly undesirable on public policy grounds. It is insufficient that the undertaking's control over a facility gives it a competitive advantage.

The Advocate General conceded that the costs of duplicating a facility alone might constitute an insuperable barrier to entry. However, he suggested that, for an abuse to arise, the refusal of access must make it extremely difficult for not only the undertaking demanding access, but also any other undertaking, to compete. Thus, if the cost of duplicating the facility alone is the barrier to entry, it must be such as to deter any prudent undertaking from entering the market. In the present case, the Advocate General considered that although Bronner itself may be unable to duplicate Mediaprint's network, it has numerous alternative, albeit less convenient, means of distribution open to it. In this context, the Advocate General noted that claims made by *Der Standard* that it was enjoying spectacular growth were hardly consistent with its claim that access to Mediaprint's home delivery system was essential. He further observed that, although it may well be uneconomic and involve short term losses for Bronner to establish its own competing nationwide network, an independent network would allow it to compete on equal terms with Mediaprint's newspaper and to increase its geographical coverage and circulation substantially.

Lastly, the Advocate General noted that to accept Bronner's contention would lead to detailed regulatory fixing of prices and conditions by regulators in large sectors of the Community economy—not only an unworkable, but also an anticompetitive result in the longer term and incompatible with a free market economy. Accordingly, he concluded that the case fell well short of the type of situation where it would be appropriate to impose an obligation requiring access to a facility which a dominant undertaking had developed for its own use.

V. Comparing the Cases Under Section 2 and Article 82 [ex 86]— What Is the Role for An Essential Facilities Doctrine in Community Law?

In comparing the cases applying the essential facility principle under US and EC law, several points emerge that raise questions as to whether the essential facilities doctrine, as understood in the United States, can or should play a role under Article 82 [ex 86]. In the United States, the essential facilities doctrine creates an exception to a broad general rule that allows firms to deal with whom they choose, even if that choice limits competition, provided that their choice has some business justification. Article 82 [ex 86], in contrast, imposes broad duties to deal on dominant firms. In the United States, the essential facilities doctrine focuses on effects in markets where a firm holds market power subject to control under Section 2. The Article 82 [ex 86] cases, in contrast, appear to apply the concept in a monopoly-leveraging context without extensive consideration of the extent to which the dominant firm holds a dominant position in a downstream market.

This comparison is well illustrated by the example of cases involving access to CRS distribution facilities for airlines. In *LEA/Sabena*,[47] (often discussed as a proto essential facilities case) the Commission found that Sabena had a

---

[47] Commission Decision 88/589/EEC, OJ L 317/47 (1998).

dominant position in the market for providing CRS services and thus had an obligation to provide such services to its airline competitors, without any consideration of whether Sabena had a dominant position in the airline market.[48] In *Alaska Airlines*,[49] in contrast, the Ninth Circuit found that even if an airline had market power in the CRS market, it could only be required to allow access to its CRS under an essential facilities test if refusal would allow that airline to create or maintain market power in a market for airline services.[50]

Insofar as the role of the essential facilities concept under Article 82 [ex 86] is to impose a greater duty on a dominant firm to justify its refusal, the ferry port cases do perhaps reflect an approach similar to the US cases insofar as US law applies a stricter standard to reliance on legitimate business justification in an essential facility context. Here again, however, it may be argued that the ferry port cases come within the tradition of the proportionality analysis for justifying refusals to deal under *United Brands*. If this is the case, it is not clear how the essential facility label adds to the analysis.

Insofar as the principal role of the essential facilities doctrine as articulated in *Sealink* is to impose a stricter requirement of non-discrimination and certain procedural obligations (the independent operator standard) on the company controlling the essential facility, the emerging EC doctrine may be at odds with the essential facilities doctrine as it has developed in the United States since there is no suggestion in the US cases that a firm controlling an essential facility is under any obligation other than to provide a facility, where feasible, on reasonable terms. Seen from this perspective, use of the term 'essential facilities', with its unavoidable invocation of the US doctrine, may give rise to some confusion if, under EC law, the doctrine gives rise to strict duties regarding a dominant firm's ongoing conduct.

---

[48] In airline cases, the Commission has also treated slots and ground facilities as essential facilities without, however, referring to the term. As a result, it has required the cession of slots where their unavailability would preclude market entry. Commission Decision 96/180/EC *Lufthansa/SAS*, OJ L 54/28 (1996).

[49] *Alaska Airlines, Inc.* v *United Airlines, Inc.*, 948 F2d 536 (9th Cir. 1991) *cert. denied* 112 US 1603 (1992).

[50] The need for market power in the airline market to support an essential facilities analysis is emphasised in Areeda and Hovenkamp (1992: 846–47).

VI. The Role of the Essential Facilities Doctrine under EC Law

1. The 'Special Duties' in Dual Monopoly, Dual Role Cases: Limitation of the Doctrine to Cases of Dual Monopoly

The special duties imposed on Stena Sealink in *Sealink* would appear to go considerably beyond the type of obligation to deal imposed on dominant companies in cases like *Commercial Solvents* and *United Brands* in that there does not appear to be any scope for taking into account the dominant companies' legitimate business interests in the downstream market.[51] The justification for this approach would appear to lie in the fact that in a case like *Stena/Sealink*, one is dealing with what can be characterised as a double monopoly, i.e. monopoly control over the essential facility *and* the resulting monopoly it confers in a downstream market. Where this situation exists and where the double monopolist plays a dual role as both operator of the essential facility of infrastructure *and* competitor on a market downstream of that facility or exploiting that infrastructure, it can be argued that the doubly dominant company can be held accountable to a strict code of conduct requiring it to act, in its role as owner of the essential facility, as if it were a neutral operator without interests in the downstream market.

In the absence of this unique situation, it would appear that Article 82 [ex 86] would not countenance the strict approach applied in *Stena/Sealink*. This conclusion is suggested by the judgment of the Court of Justice in *BP v Commission*[52] which suggests that, at least in a context where there is no monopoly power downstream and the dominant position results from customer dependence in a time of shortage, the role of Article 82 [ex 86] is not to impose regulatory patterns of conduct on dominant firms. In *BP v Commission*, the Court of Justice overturned a Commission decision finding that an oil company had violated Article 82 [ex 86] when, during the first oil crisis, it had refused to supply fuel to a former occasional customer, favouring its regular customers instead. The Commission had asserted that the oil company

---

[51] In *United Brands*, the Court accepted that there would be situations under which a dominant company could legitimately terminate a distributor or refuse to supply in order to protect its legitimate commercial interests. In contrast, in the port cases, presumably the only legitimate justification for a refusal to provide access would be the limited capacity of the port and even here it has been suggested the appropriate approach is not to deny access but rather to make capacity available, if need be on a rotating basis to all comers.

[52] Case 77/77, [1978] ECR 1513.

was obliged to ration fuel according to a formula based on purchases by all customers during the period preceding the crisis. The Court, however, found that
the oil company had no such duty, because the complainant was not comparable to the oil company's regular customers who received priority on supplies.
Noting that any increase in supplies to the complainant would have resulted in
a decrease of supplies for the regular customers, the Court concluded that a
duty to apply a formula such as that proposed by the Commission 'could only
flow from measures adopted in the framework of the Treaty, in particular
Article 99 [ex 103], or in default of that, by the national authorities'.[53]

Advocate General Warner's Opinion in *BP* helps to elucidate the significance of the Court's ruling. Advocate General Warner characterised the
Commission's position in this case as amounting to the view that 'where there
is a *lacuna* in whatever government measures may have been taken, Article 82
[ex 86] may be invoked to fill it'.[54] The Advocate General went on to suggest,
however, that if there was such a lacuna, it was not 'a lacuna of a kind that
Article 82 [ex 86] is designed to fill or is appropriate to fill'.[55] After challenging
the Commission's approach to dominance, which, as noted above, was alleged
on the basis of customer dependence, Advocate General Warner suggested that,
for Article 82 [ex 86] to apply 'there must be found in the terms of that Article
some rule, either express or implicit, that suppliers are required to observe in
such a situation'. Since Article 82(c) [ex 86(2)] (an explicit rule) did not apply,
the rule must be implicit. He then concluded that an implicit standard could
only be the basis for abuse if it were 'equitable, practical, and generally
accepted'.[56] The Court's finding that the standard proposed by the Commission
could only be imposed by legislation appears to follow this analysis.

The analysis of the Commission in *Stena Sealink* (the dominant firm should
have behaved like an independent port operator and negotiated, proposed,
etc.), seems very close to the analysis rejected in *BP* (the dominant firm should
have rationed according to a formula treating all customers fairly). Seen from
this perspective, it could be argued, in light of the approach in *BP*, that there is
no scope under Article 82 [ex 86] for the use of the essential facilities concept to
create a special duty imposed on a dominant firm beyond that recognised in
Commercial Solvents or *United Brands*, either to put competitors in the same
position as the dominant firm, or to organise its business so as to separate the
provision of the essential facility and act as an independent operator would.

---

[53] *Ibid* para. 34
[54] *Ibid* at 1537.
[55] *Ibid* at 1538
[56] *Ibid* at 1539.

Under this analysis, the standard for determining whether a dominant firm has abused its dominant position in limiting access to its essential facility would be one of reasonableness, and thus very similar, in the end, to the standard applied under US law.

On the other hand, it should be recognised that the dual role/dual monopoly cases involve situations far more extreme than those in *United Brands* and *Commercial Solvents*, let alone *BP*. As a result, it may well be that the very extensive obligations imposed in *Stena/Sealink* will withstand scrutiny.[57] In any event, even if a Court-made limitation were imposed on the scope of the dominant firm's obligations in dual role/dual dominance cases, the independent operator standard could well be a useful criterion where the Commission exercises its legislative function. It could also, conceivably, be relied on under appropriate circumstances in exemption decisions under Article 81(3) [ex 85(3)], and it might also define the proper scope of a behavioural remedy in cases in which the operator of the essential facility has a well-established history of refusing to provide access on reasonable terms.

2. Essential Facilities Analysis and Intellectual Property

One area which has often been described as lending itself to an essential facilities analysis is the Article 82 [ex 86] intellectual property interface. Yet, consideration of the *Magill* case[58] demonstrates that an essential facilities analysis

---

[57] This issue may come up in the appeal by Deutsche Bundesbahn of the Commission's decision imposing a substantial fine for DBV's alleged attempts to discriminate in favor of traffic originating from or to German ports. Commission Decision 94/210, *HOV-SVZ/MCN*, 23 April 1994, OJ No L 104/34 (1994), However, the DB case is considerably more complicated than either of the port cases, in particular because (i) depending on how the downstream market is defined, there may not have been a second dominant position; and (ii) it is not clear that DB's dominant position as a provider of traction in Germany can be viewed as an essential facility.

[58] Commission Decision, 89/205/EEC, *Magill TV Guide* v *ITP, BBC and RTE*, OJ L 78/43 (1989); Judgment of the Court of First Instance in Case T–69/89, *RTE* v *Commission*, [1991] ECR II–485; Judgment of the Court of First Instance in Case T–70/89 *BBC* v *Commission*, [1991] ECR II–535; Judgment of the Court of First Instance in Case T–76/89 *ITP* v *Commission*, [1991] ECR II–575; Judgment of the Court of Justice in Joined Cases C–241/91P and C–242/91P, *RTE and ITP* v *Commission*, [1995] ECR I–743. In two earlier cases, Case 63/87 *Consorzio italiano della componentistica di ricambio per autoveicoli and Maxicar* v *Régie nationale des usines Renault* [1988] ECR 6039 and Case 238/87 *AB Volvo* v *Erik Veng (UK) Ltd.* [1988] ECR 6211, the Court had acknowledged the possibility that the assertion of industrial property rights to prevent the marketing of infringing products (in this case side panels for the repair of

does not really assist in dealing with the difficult issues that arise at the patent antitrust interface.

Magill concerned the refusal by two television broadcasters, Radio Telefis Eireann (RTE) and the British Broadcasting Corporation (the BBC) which published its own weekly television program listing, Independent Television Publications (ITP), to allow use of their copyrighted weekly broadcast listings by an independent publisher (Magill) wishing to produce a comprehensive weekly television guide. The Commission ruled that this constituted an abuse of a dominant position, and ordered RTE and ITP to license their program list-ing information. This decision was upheld by both the Court of First Instance and, subsequently, the Court of Justice, notwithstanding the weighty opinion of Advocate General Gulmann, who recommended the annulment of the Commission's decision on the basis that it amounted to a compulsory licensing order. On the question of dominance, the Court confirmed the position of the CFI that the two broadcasters had a dominant position in respect of their own weekly program listings since, by virtue of their *de facto* monopoly on the information concerning their own TV programming, they could prevent effec-tive competition on the downstream market for weekly TV magazines. The broadcasters' refusal to license, even though an exercise of their intellectual property rights, constituted an abuse of this dominant position because of the 'exceptional circumstances' of the case. These 'exceptional circumstances' were as follows. First, the refusal to license prevented the emergence of a new prod-uct (i.e., a comprehensive weekly TV guide listing both broadcasters program-ming) in violation of Article 82(b) [ex 86(b)]. As a result of this 'exceptional circumstance,' the Court rejected the approach of its Advocate General, who had considered that while the prevention of the production of a new *non-com-peting* product could have been an abusive use of the broadcasters' right to refuse licences, they were entitled to use their copyright to prevent development of a product which would compete with their own, albeit more limited, TV guides. Second, the refusal to license was not justified. Third, RTE and ITP reserved to themselves the secondary market for comprehensive weekly TV guides, by denying access to the basic information which was the raw material indispensable for the compilation of such a guide.

---

automobiles) could constitute an abuse under Article 82 [ex 86] where one of three con-ditions relating to exploitative abuses (output restrictions or excessive pricing) were pre-sent. However, these cases involved responses to references to questions from national courts not, as in the case of *Magill*, a judgment upholding a Commission decision which amounted to an order to grant a license.

While the Court of Justice in *Magill* does not explicitly characterise the broadcasters' monopoly rights as 'essential facilities', the judgment appears to be based implicitly on an essential facilities analysis[59] inasmuch as the broadcasters' weekly program listings were an indispensable input for the production of a comprehensive TV guide and, because of the combination of the broadcasters' control over their own programming, its advance dissemination and their copyrights were also not susceptible to economically meaningful duplication by a third party. Thus, the crucial points in the Court's reasoning were that the broadcasters enjoyed an effective monopoly position in the market for TV magazines, and controlled the program information which was necessary for a competitor to establish itself on that market.

Two observations concerning the potential impact of *Magill* are warranted.

First, the scope and potential impact of the judgment depends upon the interpretation given to the three factors identified by the Court as constituting the 'exceptional circumstances' which justified the application of Article 82 [ex 86]. It is unclear from the judgment whether the Court regarded these factors as cumulative, or whether any one of them would have been sufficient. If all factors were necessary, the application of the case is extremely narrow; if any of the factors would suffice to make the broadcasters' conduct 'exceptional', then the case has potentially broader application.

Second, like the harbour authorities in the *Stena Sealink* case, the broadcasters in *Magill* were effectively in a position of dual dominance, i.e. they were dominant both in respect of the possession of program information, and in the market for the provision of a product incorporating that information. The case does not, therefore, provide a strong basis for the application of Article 82 [ex 86] in a situation where a dominant operator does not have monopoly power in the downstream market.[60]

Subject to these qualifications, *Magill* does illustrate a possible use of essential facilities doctrine in a market other than transport. However, it also illustrates why the essential facilities label may not add anything to the analysis of the difficult issues arising out the application of Article 82 [ex 86] to intellectual property rights. The principal difficulty with using an essential facilities

---

[59] This is the conclusion, also, of Ridyard (1996).

[60] Where other competitors are successfully contesting the downstream market with the holder of the IP right, the characterization of the IP as an essential facility would appear to be a contradiction in terms and the application of the essential facilities doctrine would both appear to be excluded ipso facto. In the more likely case where the IP owner is not active on the downstream market, the failure to exploit and license the IP could well be treated as an output restriction proscribed by Article 82(c) [ex 86(c)] without any need for reference to the essential facilities doctrine.

analysis to justify the application of Article 82 [ex 86] is that it presupposes the answer to a difficult institutional and societal question concerning the balanc-ing of interests at the patent antitrust interface.[61] There will be far too many cases where the use of technology protected by intellectual property rights may be viewed as a 'necessary input' in order to compete with an incumbent that controls the rights and enjoys market power.[62] Yet, as the Advocate General has recognised in his opinion in *Magill*, it is exactly this ability to exclude rivals and gain a competitive advantage that is the essence of the intellectual property right protected by both national law and the EC Treaty.[63] In light of this situ-ation, there is a strong argument that the essential facilities analysis is not appropriate in the case of intellectual property rights, because such an analysis would, in every case, automatically override the essential nature of the prop-erty right in the interests of the competing claims of antitrust law, thereby, dis-regarding or limiting by regulatory fiat, the scope of the property right and the monopoly that it confers.

3. Role of the Essential Facilities Doctrine in 'Same Market' Abuse Cases

a) The 'Same Market' Problem
The essential facilities doctrine may be of assistance as a formal matter of antitrust analysis with respect to cases in which the essential facility comprises something that cannot be characterised as a market. In such cases, invocation of the essential facilities doctrine can correct an analytic anomaly that has resulted from the treatment of these cases as market leveraging cases. In *Decca Navigator System*,[64] for example, the Commission identified a separate market

---

[61] The institutional issue, discussed by the Advocate General in his *Magill* opinion, is whether, in light of the legislative character of the patent or other intellectual prop-erty monopolies, an antitrust authority should adopt a regulatory stance that effectively negates the essential character of the property right. The societal issue involves the determination of the proper way to balance the conflicting interests represented by intel-lectual property rights and antitrust law.

[62] For example, it could be said that access to rights to copy Volvo body panels was an 'essential facility' for anyone wishing to enter the market for manufacture of such panels in competition with Volvo, but that factor did not disturb the Court's rejection of any abuse in *Volvo* v *Veng* (Case 238/87, [1988] ECR 6211).

[63] The Advocate General rejected the argument put forward by the Commission and accepted by the Court of First Instance that the use of intellectual property rights to exclude rivals in a market 'ancillary' to the one where the rights were developed some-how changed the position.

[64] Commission Decision, 89/113/EEC, OJ L 43/27 (1989).

for the provision of the DNS signals used in conjunction with a navigational aid, despite the fact that the rights to receive these signals were not normally purchased or sold on the market.[65] The Commission then concluded that by making reception of these signals more difficult for receivers manufactured by its rivals, the dominant firm strengthened its position in the market for selling receivers, where it also held a dominant position. Likewise in *Magill*, the Commission identified a separate market for the provision by television broadcasters of the information used to produce published television listings, even though where publication was authorised, the broadcasters did not usually charge for this information. The Commission then alleged that the broadcasters had used their dominant positions in these 'markets' to exclude competition in the separate market for publishing television guides. In both of these cases, the Commission had to strain, or ignore, the economic facts in order to fit them into a market leveraging analysis.

As explained above, the essential facilities doctrine in US law does not concern effects in a separate, related market. Even where these may be said to be a 'market' for the facility in question, the essential facilities doctrine always involves monopolisation by the defendant firm in the downstream market where that firm enjoys market power due to its control over the essential facility. A similar approach under Community law would provide a useful tool for

---

[65] It might also be tempting to apply the same approach to type cases such as the *Langnese/Schöller* cases, Commission Decisions 93/405, *'Schöller'* and 93/406, *'Langnese,'* OJ L 183/1 and L 183/19 (1993), which involve access to freezers used for impulse ice cream in small retail outlets. It has been suggested that where ice cream manufacturers provide freezers either free or at concessionary rates on the condition that the freezers be used exclusively for that manufacturer's products, such a condition would be an abuse of a dominant position. Postulating a separate market in the provision of freezers to retail outlets that is dominated by each supplier simply does not reflect the economic reality. If dominance exists in the ice cream market, however, the possession of a substantial estate of installed freezers often in premises where installation of a second freezer may be impractical, might be regarded as an essential facility. If this approach were taken, the denial of access to competitors could be characterised as an abuse. There is, however, an argument *against* applying an essential facility analysis in cases such as these where the facility in question has been furnished by, and at the expense of, the supplier of a 'downstream' product. In such cases, application of an essential facility analysis will extend that doctrine beyond cases in which the facility in question has nothing to do with the skill, wisdom and foresight of the dominant company to encompass cases where it does. In cases involving effort, investment or marketing acumen, it is arguably preferable to apply more conventional antitrust principles (e.g. a prohibition on entering into long-term exclusive contracts or on tying) rather than invoking the essential facilities doctrine with the particularly onerous obligations that it imposes on the dominant company.

dealing with cases where a firm is dominant in the market downstream of an essential facility. If the Commission had applied this approach in *Decca* where the defendant held a dominant position in the receiver market, the beacon signals could legitimately have been regarded as an essential facility for competitors in that market. The dominant firm's actions in depriving competitors of access to that facility could then be viewed as abusive, without any need for an 'artificial' market leveraging approach.[66]

b) Relationship of a 'Same Market' Essential Facility Test to General Rules under Article 82 [ex 86]

Application of an essential facility concept in 'same market' cases would be entirely consistent with the general concepts underlying Article 82 [ex 86]. As already noted, under the general rule articulated in *Hoffmann-LaRoche*, a dominant firm may abuse its dominant position where its conduct has exclusionary effects and is not 'normal competition based on 'performance''. Denial of access to an essential facility in a concentrated market will usually have exclusionary effects satisfying the first part of the test.

The second part of the test, however, poses more difficult issues. Usually, the construction by a manufacturing firm of a more efficient plant would be regarded as a form of 'normal, performance based, competition'. Likewise, development of an efficient facility to ensure a dependable supply of inputs for the business of a dominant firm would also normally be regarded as enhancing the firm's internal efficiency and thus as a form of competition based on performance. The fundamental question raised by the essential facility doctrine is if, and under what, if any, circumstances this analysis should change if the contribution of the facility to the firm's competitiveness vis-à-vis its rivals, does not derive solely from the more efficient nature of the facility itself, but rather from the fact that for objective reasons unrelated to their own skill, industry or foresight, it is impossible for the rivals to duplicate the facility. In other words, while the dominant firm's original foresight in developing the facility may have involved a form of superior economic performance that should normally be recognised and protected under consumer-welfare oriented antitrust law, should the analysis shift if the dominant firm's continued advantages over the medium term derive not from that foresight but rather from the external factors that prevent duplication? If this question is to be answered in the affirmative, retaining these advantages for itself will no longer be regarded as a

---

[66] If access to the beacons were an essential facility, US precedent suggests that Racal was entitled to payment from its competitors, something that the Commission found to be unjustified in that case.

performance-based method of competition. As a consequence of this shift, a refusal to grant access to an essential facility will constitute an abuse under Article 82 [ex 86]. The difficult question is whether, and if so, under what specific set of circumstances, such an approach is appropriate.[67]

c) A Possible Basis for Imposing Restrictions on Conduct
The difficulties with using the essential facility analysis to require a dominant firm to adhere to an 'independent operator' standard have been discussed above. Arguably at least, this standard of conduct cannot be reconciled with the general line of cases applying Article 82 [ex 86] to refusals to deal. However, a strong argument can be made that the objections become considerably less cogent where the application of Article 82 [ex 86] is based on a dominant position in the market for which access to the essential facility is required and where the dominant company is also charged with the management and operation of the essential facility. Indeed, it is no coincidence that both *Sealink* and *Port of Rødby* were cases where the dominant firm was dominant in the downstream market. Once the focus is on the ability of a dominant firm to exclude rivals in the dominated market, it might well be regarded as reasonable to require that firm to adhere to a higher conduct standard than might apply if the firm did not dominate the downstream market.

The Port Authority cases suggest that the essential facilities doctrine may be translatable to the area of telecommunications especially as the telecoms authorities seek to enter downstream markets in order to recoup the revenues lost as a result of their having lost their monopoly rights in certain service areas.

4. Essential Facilities and Article 86 [ex 90]

Ultimately, the area where an essential facilities analysis may prove to be of greatest value concerns cases under Article 86 [ex 90]. As a practical matter, many facilities in Europe that are, at least arguably, 'essential' are either controlled by the state or state-owned undertakings or are operated subject to regulation by the state. As a result, many of the general points made above

---

[67] To cite just one example, Areeda has argued that it is not appropriate to apply an essential facilities analysis to cases involving intellectual property rights or research and development because doing so would be inconsistent with the policy and goals underlying the intellectual property rights system or, in the case of research and development, contrary to the societal interests in encouraging such activity.

regarding the application of the essential facilities doctrine may have direct application in Article 86 [ex 90] cases, particularly in respect of telecommunications or transport infrastructure. Moreover, since, in the case of state-owned monopolies or monopolies conferred by the state without regard to the performance or competitiveness of the monopolist, the application of the essential facilities doctrine to deregulate and open up markets may prove to be considerably less controversial than application of that doctrine to private company conduct.

The Court's judgment in the case *ERT* v *Commission*[68] would appear to provide a basis for the application of an essential facilities analysis in cases involving Article 86 [ex 90]. In this case, the Court affirmed a Commission ruling that the granting of exclusive rights both for terrestrial broadcast and retransmission of television programs by Greece over cable violated Article 86 [ex 90], because the dual grant facilitated discrimination by the grantee as a cable operator in favour of the programs it produced as a broadcaster. It would, therefore, appear from *ERT* v *Commission*, that there is an obligation on a Member State where it grants special or exclusive rights, not to grant those rights in such a way as to facilitate eventual abuse.

In the context of essential facility cases, application of the *ERT* rule could mean that where an undertaking is allowed to control an essential facility, it should, if possible, not be allowed to compete in the market where the facility is used. Furthermore, it could be argued that although the type of conduct obligations imposed in *Sealink* may not be justified as obligations of a dominant firm under Article 82 [ex 86], a Member State may be obliged under Article 86 [ex 90] to impose such obligations in cases where it grants control over an essential facility to a vertically integrated company.

VII. The Essential Facilities Doctrine in the Context of Telecommunications

The liberalisation of the EC telecommunications sector may offer a potentially fertile field for the application (and perhaps misapplication) of the essential facilities doctrine given the relationship between infrastructure and service provision and the high costs of duplicating infrastructure. In particular, although most Member State markets for basic voice telephony services were opened to competition as of 1 January 1998, competition in downstream markets will

---

[68] Case C–260/89, [1991] ECR I–2925

continue to depend on access to upstream network services which are still controlled by the Zorma TO monopolists.

The foundation for the Commission's development of essential facilities principles in the field of telecommunications was laid down in the 1987 Green Paper on Telecommunications,[69] which was followed in 1990 by the Telecommunications Services Directive.[70] The latest amendment to the Services Directive[71] provided for the implementation of full competition in telecommunications markets, and, for the first time, contained a statement in the recitals that 'pursuant to Article 82 [ex 86], all public telecommunications network operators having essential resources for which competitors do not have economic alternatives are to provide open and non-discriminatory access to those resources'. The Commission also explicitly addressed the essential facilities principle in its Notice on the application of the competition rules to access agreements in the telecommunications sector, where it considered the question of whether an access provider should be obliged to contract with a service provider, to allow the latter to operate on a new service market. On this question, the Commission noted that the essential facilities principle hitherto applied in the transport sector applied likewise to the telecommunications sector since, in the absence of commercially feasible alternatives to the access requested, a refusal to grant access would be sufficient to prevent the requesting party from operating on a service market. According to the Commission, such a refusal was therefore likely to have abusive effects contrary to Article 82 [ex 86]. In particular, the essential facilities principle may be used to require a dominant operator to provide access if the following conditions are satisfied:[72]

(1) access to the facility is 'essential' in order for all but exceptional companies to compete on the downstream market. It is not sufficient that access would be advantageous to the requesting company. Refusal of access must lead to the proposed activities being made either impossible, or seriously and unavoidably uneconomic;

(2) there is sufficient capacity available to provide access;

---

[69] *Green Paper on the Development of the Common Market for Telecommunications Services and Equipment*, COM(87)290, 30 June 1987.

[70] Council Directive 90/388, OJ L 192/10 (1990).

[71] Council Directive 96/19, OJ L 74/13 (1996).

[72] The Commission notes that the starting point for its analysis will be 'the identification of an existing or potential market for which access is being requested', thus suggesting that the Commission plans to continue its broad approach to identifying markets even where there has hitherto been no demand for access.

(3) the facility owner fails to satisfy demand on an existing service or product market, blocks the emergence of a potential new service or product, or impedes competition on an existing or potential service or product market;
(4) the company seeking access is prepared to accept reasonable and non-discriminatory price and access terms;
(5) there is no objective justification for refusing to provide access. Relevant justifications could include the difficulties of providing access, or the need for a facility owner who has undertaken investment to introduce a new product or service to have sufficient opportunity to use the facility in order to place that product or service on the market.

In considering whether the behaviour of a dominant firm amounts to a refusal to provide access contrary to these principles, the Commission will take into account not only the existence of an agreement or refusal *per se*, but also the timing of any response to a request for access and the price for access. Unjustified delays in responding to a request, and excessive pricing for access may, according to the Commission, in themselves amount to an effective refusal to grant access.

The essential facilities doctrine has begun to emerge in some recent cases concerning the exemption of telecoms joint ventures under Article 81(3) [ex 85(3)]. In the *Atlas* decision,[73] the Commission considered the application of Article 81 [ex 85] to a joint-venture (Atlas) between France Telecom (FT) and Deutsche Telekom (DT), principally to target the market for customised packages of corporate telecoms services, and the market for packet-switched data communications services. The Commission noted that DT and FT owned the only existing nation-wide packet-switched data communications networks in their respective home countries. Accordingly, in order to prevent the elimination of effective competition, the Article 81(3) [ex 85(3)] exemption was granted subject to the condition that (*inter alia*) (i) DT and FT would not discriminate in favour of Atlas in respect of decisions to modify technical interfaces for access to essential facilities; (ii) DT and FT establish standard interfaces to access their national public packet-switch data networks, offer access on non-discriminatory terms, and publish standard terms and conditions for the interface standards. On the same day as the *Atlas* decision, the Commission adopted a decision exempting the GlobalOne joint venture between FT, DT and Sprint, and imposing similar conditions regarding non-discrimination and access to essential facilities.[74] Similarly in *BT-MCI II*, the Commission required under-

---

[73] Commission Decision 96/546/EEC, *Atlas*, OJ L 239/23 (1996).
[74] Commission Decision 96/547/EEC, *Phoenix/GlobalOne*, OJ L 239/57.

takings with regards to the availability of transatlantic undersea capacity, given the strong position held by BT and MCI on the UK to US route. Although the Commission did not identify such capacity as an essential facility (and although given the ease and rapidity with which transatlantic capacity is being expanded, it might be difficult to do so, at least if one takes a two to three-year time frame), the Commission's approach suggests that it was treating the need for access to transatlantic submarine cable capacity as an essential input.[75]

The Commission has, yet to apply the essential facilities doctrine in Article 82 [ex 86] telecoms cases. Nevertheless, the essential facilities analysis may be relevant in a number of situations involving relations between network operators and service providers including the following two:

Resale. Resellers may optimise customer prices for network communications by using flat-rate leased lines or volume-discounted circuits; they may also route calls through third countries, or use call-back equipment to reverse the direction of a call where it is cheaper from one country than from the other. A number of facilities could be described as essential facilities in reseller markets, including the public switched telephone service, leased circuits, directories, numbering schemes and tariff discount schemes. In any event, as noted above, in *BT-MCI II* the Commission approached cable capacity as an essential facility.

International GSM mobile services. On this market, GSM operators provide numbers, SIM cards and air time; mobile service providers (MSPs) provide customer services and equipment sales or rental. The essential facilities doctrine could apply to require a GSM operator to allow a new MSP to resell its services, by making available facilities such as blocks of numbers and air time on terms that are available to other comparable customers.

VIII. Conclusion

Use of the term 'essential facility' in recent Commission decisions tends to justify the validity of the approach taken by the Commission in those cases by reference to an established line of cases under US antitrust law. For this reason, it is important to consider whether the cases invoking the concept in the EC label really reflect the doctrine as applied in the United States.

---

[75] Commission Decision 97/815/EEC, *British Telecom/MCI (II)*, OJ No. L 336/1 (1997).

As explained above, the essential facilities doctrine, as developed under US law, is a narrowly applied exception to the general rule that even monopolists are not required to deal with their rivals. In essence, this doctrine has been applied under US law only where the company in question dominates a market downstream from the essential facility. It is this factor that distinguishes essential facilities cases under US law from other Section 2 cases where the obligation to deal is imposed either because it has been established that the monopolist's refusal to deal has been motivated solely by exclusionary intent or where the refusal to deal will extend the monopolist's market power to a related market.

Given the very broad obligations to deal that are already imposed on dominant companies under Article 82 [ex 86], there may be some question as to the role to be played in EC law by the essential facilities doctrine which, under US law, limits the obligation to deal to a narrowly defined set of facts where the facility in question is truly indispensable and where the firm in question is already dominant on the market downstream of that facility. Similarly, there may be some doubt as to the utility or wisdom of applying the US doctrine in EC law in a manner that would go beyond the controls imposed by the US courts when applying the essential facilities rule inasmuch as Article 82 [ex 86] seeks to protect normal, performance-based competition, a factor that may strongly argue in favour of limiting the obligation of dominant companies to extend to their competitors the benefits of their own skill, foresight and effort.

The essential facilities doctrine could have an important role to play in the context of so-called 'dual role' cases, normally involving Article 86 [ex 90], in which, as a result of the granting of a state monopoly over an essential facility or infrastructure, a company is charged at once with both the operation of that facility or infrastructure and is, at the same time, a dominant operator on the market downstream of that facility. In addition, the essential facilities doctrine may also provide a useful analytic tool in other cases where there is no real relevant market for provision of the facility. However, the application of the doctrine is likely to pose greater problems in the case of the former telecommunications operator monopolies post liberalisation, since once the statutory monopoly has been eliminated and the competition introduced there will be a stronger justification for a stricter assessment of the indispensability of the alleged essential facility, and, arguably, greater scope for an efficiency defence. However, where dominance persists in the downstream market, there is a strong likelihood that the essential facilities doctrine will come into play.

AGREEMENTS, INTEGRATION AND STRUCTURAL
REMEDIES

1

PANEL DISCUSSION

GENERAL RAPPORTEUR:

Alan Fels
Professor, Chairman ACCC, Australia

PARTICIPANTS:

Mark Armstrong
Professor, Nuffield College, Oxford, United Kingdom

Donald I. Baker
Partner, Baker & Millar PLLC, Washinton, United States

Eleanor Fox
Professor, School of Law, New York University, New York, United States

Herbert Hovenkamp
Professor, University of Iowa, Iowa, United States

Günter Knieps
Professor, Dr., Institut für Verkehrswissenschaften und Regionalpolitik, Freiburg, Germany.

Michael Reynolds
Partner, Allen & Overy, Brussels, Belgium

James F. Rill
Partner, Collier, Shannon, Rill & Scott, Washington, United States

Alexander Schaub
Dr., Director General, DGIV, Brussels, Belgium

Mario Siragusa
Professor, Avv., Cleary, Gottlieb, Steen & Hamilton, Brussels, Belgium

Peter Waters
Partner, Gilbert and Tobin Lawyers, Brussels/Sydney, Belgium/Australia

Panel Two

▶ EHLERMANN—We now move into Panel II. Alan, please, your introduction.

▶ FELS—Thank you. Well, I will be a good deal briefer in my opening. I have an interconnection role to play, connecting this morning and this afternoon. In talking about mergers, joint venture agreements and so on, the decisions we will discuss this afternoon are largely the decisions of competition authorities, not sector-specific regulators. There are some exceptions to this, especially in the broadcasting area. Furthermore, in Europe, quite a high proportion of the decisions rest with the Commission. Consequently, this afternoon, we will become more involved in some standard competition law issues, approaches and procedures. However, given the fact that we have competition law questions in front of us, I would like the speakers to question whether, in the area of telecommunications, the answers might be a bit different from the conventional competition law solutions.

We will discuss structural, rather than behavioural, solutions this afternoon. This morning, by contrast, we analysed a number of behavioural approaches and solutions. Of course, structural questions arise in making decisions about whether to approve mergers and joint ventures. The questions tend to be structural and sometimes structural conditions are proposed, but this afternoon, I think we could explore the viability of some of the structural solutions that were mentioned this morning more fully. It is useful to probe deeper: what are the limits of structural solutions? What are their advantages and disadvantages? Could we have more straightforward divestiture, for example, in Europe? What about simple divestiture solutions outside merger decisions; is this an area worth considering? Does not divestiture give you much cleaner structural outcomes without the need to rely upon regulatory solutions?

Naturally, although divestitures looks attractive on paper, there are some concerns about the lost efficiency gains that could result from the integration that divestiture prevents. Furthermore, there are some questions about how well divestiture actually works in practice.

We also heard this morning quite a lot about access matters. Obligatory access provisions are behavioural solutions but, typically in mergers in competition law, we look to structural, rather than behavioural, remedies. We shun behavioural solutions, and are hesitant to allow mergers on the condition that there is price control imposed on the resulting monopolist. However, we may have a new issue in this sector, namely, should we allow mergers because we think that access arrangements can overcome potential bottleneck problems?

There are a number of issues built into this question. How does the existence of regulation affect our analysis of market power? Does it alter our perception of the state of market power? Can we permit certain mergers we would otherwise not, if we are confident that our access rules would work well? Or, should we just forbid mergers that would create such bottlenecks, notwithstanding the availability of access arrangements?

Just a couple of other points. We are now more in the province of competition law and policy, and within that field we have certain conventional wisdom. How well does this wisdom apply in telecommunications? For example, in competition law, we are typically very concerned about horizontal arrangements, agreements and mergers. On the whole, we are less concerned about vertical arrangements. In telecommunications, however, based upon the talk around the table, our concerns are about vertical relationships. This might be a distinction we should address a bit more.

It is also conventional for merger law to be relatively permissive of socalled 'conglomerate' mergers between people involved in quite different activities. I note this issue in one or two of the papers. For example, with the telecommunications and pay-television mergers and links, we may ask: is this another area where things are different from the rest of competition law?

We also have a paper from Don Baker that raises another question about the treatment of joint ventures and single firm networks. He argues that there seem to be different standards, at least in the United States, on this question. In his view, joint ventures establishing network arrangements, often tend to encounter more trouble than a single firm which happens to have a network. Is this true? If this is a true statement of policy, should we be concerned?

In our discussion this afternoon, we cannot ignore the pressure for international mergers, alliances and joint ventures. Perhaps we could hear one or two comments on what is causing these pressures, but I wanted to just ask a particular question about international link-ups. In most areas of competition law, international mergers and alliances are caused by conventional factors: the need for scale, dealing with global customers and so on. However, are there, in this case, any links here with the regulatory regime and, in particular, with what I perceive to be a breakdown in the international regulatory field—a breakdown of accounting rule approaches and so on? Is regulatory failure a factor promoting mergers? That is, are these new forms of international linkage a reaction to the breakdown of this system?

Moreover, there are several papers that raise various international questions. For example, they discuss questions about the opening of markets to foreign participants and various international co-ordination issues.

Finally, there are some very challenging issues of market definition in this field, which seem to stand out in the papers. One such issue concerns markets that are very new or practically non-existent. These markets are not fully developed, but we still have to make decisions about them. Some of these decisions may even prevent these new markets from developing. Consequently, there is the question of the impact of rapid technological change in this area. Does this make the task of market definition especially challenging?

Further, on what basis do we approach market definition in the telecommunications sector? Do we examine the physical network of the operator, or do we, in the context of mergers, look more at the customer base and think of the firms' linkages with people in different areas? There are certainly quite a few new, and challenging, questions in market definition that I think are being confronted by agencies around the world.

▶ SCHAUB—My paper develops a number of case studies of restrictive agreements and mergers to explain the types of issues, difficulties and solutions that have emerged. I would like to highlight here a limited number of issues and comment upon them in the light of practical cases.

One of the most controversial issues we have experienced, in the cases I have examined, is the problem of 'access versus investment in new technologies'. The innovation issue was mentioned this morning, but one can also express the problem in a much less sophisticated way. For example, in the *Bertelsmann Kirch-Deutsche Telekom* case, we were told that we competition people should not fiddle around so much with access questions. It was argued that these access arrangements destroy the incentives for technological progress. Therefore, we were told that we should—at least in the start up period for new technologies—forget about competition issues and let courageous investors do their job. I think that this was the most concentrated objection to what we were doing in that case. Instead of focusing on access, our critics argued that we should let them develop into strong international competitors who could stand up to the Americans and Japanese. Thereafter, in the second phase, we could examine the competition questions more thoroughly.

In particular, our critics claimed that the restrictions imposed in this case would destroy any prospects for the development of digital television in Germany. They argued that development would be retarded for several years. I believe that this is a totally mistaken approach, and I would strongly warn against giving in to such a form of propaganda, because it is not a new argument. We have seen it in other areas. We hear it in the car, aircraft and shipbuilding sectors: why are you so tough on these companies who are making such an effort to compete with the Americans and Japanese?

I think this is basically the old-fashioned industrial policy approach. There is, however, no reason to believe that this worked in the past, and there is even less reason to believe that it will work in the future. Despite the Bundeskartellamt's and the EC Commission's negative appraisal of *Bertelsmann Kirch-Deutsche Telekom* case, digital television will still develop in Germany, and it may come earlier rather than later. In my view, the negative appraisal in this case has linked to the particular qualities, abilities and cultures of the two main partners: we have rarely seen two such ill-matched partners in a multi-billion investment operation. Given their constant quarrelling throughout the authorisation process, the modest, down-to-earth observer had to wonder how they were going to be able to co-operate with one another in business.

There was also another peculiarity, which is important to keep in mind: when you discuss remedies in such a high-risk, high-investment sector, each partner, naturally, has to evaluate whether certain remedies would still be acceptable or whether they would reduce the economic attractiveness of the operation. This is what they normally do, and this is why MCI went ahead with the transaction in spite of our not-so-welcome remedy in the Worldcom merger. Clearly, you can have such a situation with merger partners who are in a very strong economic situation, or who are starting with zero debt, and you can have a similar merger project between partners who are in a difficult financial position from the outset. If they have already lost more than a billion Dollars investing in the sectors and are then examining whether certain remedies are digestible or not, the answer is not necessarily the same as if they were starting with zero debt in the operation. Should we then consider this as a specific circumstance that would allow us to forget about certain remedies because one partner is weak or has financial problems? I do not think that this would be the right solution. I believe that, in the future, there will be quite a number of comparable cases of this sort, where competition authorities will be under strong pressure to be more favourable to modern technologies and to the dramatic pace of innovation in a system of global competition. As in the past, the competition authorities will have to keep cool and carefully analyse the competition problems.

This is important because experience teaches us that if you let these giants go ahead and then, after a number of years, try to correct the situation, it is much harder. It is not impossible to impose *ex post* rules, but the practical problems involved render this solution much more difficult. Moreover, I believe that, by taking negative decisions in such situations, you sometimes protect investors from being exposed to harmful competition.

The second issue I wish to tackle is that of market definition. In a sense, market definition in telecommunications is particularly difficult. On the other hand, this problem is not a new one. For as long as we have been talking about market definition, we have realised that such definitions are not static concepts. Market definitions can be moving targets. For example, when we examine periods of integration in the European Union, any competition authority is obliged to examine and analyse markets that were once local or regional, but are now becoming national, European, or international.

In telecommunications, we have an additional ingredient: new or unusual factors of development, in particular, rapid technological change. Unanticipated technologies are quickly emerging. Furthermore, we are faced with convergence among once disjointed markets. Such convergence creates new problems.

Consequently, I think we have to keep in mind that the problem of market definition is not fundamentally new, but still poses difficulties. It may be particularly risky to make a prognosis on what may happen in this sector in 1–4 years. Market definition is always difficult, and one can make mistakes, but telecommunications are trickier.

This means that competition authorities and regulators are, more than ever, obliged to follow economic and technological, as well as legal developments in the field. In the 'good old days', it was sufficient to have a number of reasonably intelligent lawyers. This is no longer adequate. You may also need intelligent engineers, physicists and scientists, who can give you a feel of what is possible and what is to be expected in the future.

Because I believe this is very important, I will mention two practical examples. We have faced problems related to market definition of cable and satellite transmission services. In an earlier case, in 1984, we concluded that these were distinct markets. I suppose that, at that time, they were distinct. In the *Bertelsmann Kirch-Deutsche Telekom* case, however, we concluded that it is better to treat them as a single market. Similarly, there is a dispute on whether mobile and fixed telephony already constitute a single market or are still separate markets.

These issues are not just academic questions. Rather, they have very important consequences. For example, as soon as fixed and mobile telephony can be considered a single market, the mobile providers should also participate in the financing of public service commitments. This is an aspect that would be warmly welcomed by fixed service providers, who, until now, have had to finance public service commitments alone.

Remedies also raise interesting issues. The Commission has special expertise in this area, because it is not only a case handler, but also a regulator. Moreover, it deals not only with companies but also with national governments who enact legislation.

► ARMSTRONG—I am going to be talking about Article 81 [ex 85] issues in the pay-television market. In this context, I am interpreting Article 82 [ex 86] broadly to encompass various alliances or agreements among firms. I will not be talking about mergers. I should also define what I mean by the pay-television market. Everything is really pay television. Viewers pay, either by the inefficient means of watching advertisements, or through subscription fees. My intervention focuses only on this latter type of service, that is, conditional access technology, where the company can switch you off if you do not pay your monthly bill. This type of pay television is becoming an increasingly important—and increasingly competitive—industry.

For instance, in the US, I believe about three quarters of all television households watch pay television. Most of these use the local cable company, but about 15% of the market in pay television is made up of satellite provision. Furthermore, as a result of the 1986 Telecommunications Act, the regional telecommunications companies are entering into the cable television market in pay television. We use the over-pejorative term 'overbuilding' to refer to this development. This name seems to give it the wrong flavour, but, in any case, there is increasing competition. Consequently, many people now have a choice of three kinds of operators.

Another thing to bear in mind is that there is widespread vertical integration between cable infrastructure and cable programming. A lot of networks have alliances there.

In Britain, on the other hand, there are three main platforms. There are satellites, where Sky is the main company. Sky also has a large share of the premium programming rights since it buys sports' rights and Hollywood films. Moreover, it also makes quite important in-house programming. It also has close links with BT, the telecommunications company, which is banned, at the moment, from providing television over its network. I will return to these links in a second.

The UK also has cable companies and a large number of regional and monopoly cable franchises. They neither produce significant in-house programming, nor have rights to premium programming produced elsewhere. Consequently, they mainly buy their programming from Sky. They almost invariably offer telephony in addition to their pay television services.

Finally, a new terrestrial television company will be launched the day after tomorrow. They will offer about 14 channels, and will produce several important in-house channels, which are already in production. But, again, because they have little in the way of premium services, they will buy these from Sky.

Just a brief word about the connections between BT and Sky, which fits directly into the topic for this afternoon. It seems clear that BT has an interest in helping Sky get as many subscribers as possible. The reason is that Sky does not operate in telephony and BT does not operate in pay television, but they have a common enemy in the cable operators who offer both television and telephony. Moreover, almost everyone who signs up for telephony or television with the cable companies, also buys the other service.

It follows that if BT can arrange for Sky to have more subscribers, each of these new subscribers is one less subscriber for the pay television cable companies. This means there will be more subscribers for BT due to the interaction with the telephony link. Thus, it is obvious that BT has an interest in helping Sky at the expense of the cable operators.

BT tried to do so a couple of years ago through a joint marketing plan. The net effect of the arrangement was that any person who had a joint subscription between BT and Sky had about a 100 Pound Sterling discount on their annual bill. This was ruled illegal by OFTEL, on the grounds that it was unwarranted discrimination. This decision was slightly controversial, but it was clear that BT and Sky had a questionable arrangement.

The second way in which BT and Sky have co-operated is a joint venture of which they are the major stake holders. BT and Sky each have about a one third interest in this joint venture, which provides a new, interactive service called British Interactive Broadcasting. In the short term, the main objective of this company is to provide, develop and subsidise the set-up box and digital access technology. It is been announced that they will sell these boxes at half price funded out of this joint venture. Thus, in effect, BT is subsidising user access to the digital access technology that is used by Sky.

Clearly, there are competition issues here. For example, how long will we permit the joint venture to operate at a loss. They will run at a loss in the beginning, but is this seen as a predatory action? Or, is it, instead, viewed as a new standard service for which you allow loss-making at the outset, in the expectation that the losses will be recouped once the business is up and running?

This is one issue to do with Article 81 [ex 85]. The second issue looks slightly toward the future, examining the possibly collusive nature of agreements between competing pay television operators. As I have already said, there are various platforms offered even now—three in Britain. Naturally, most subscribers will only use one of them. Most subscribers will not buy both a cable and a satellite for their home. So, even though there is competition for providing infrastructure, each customer is only going to buy one infrastructure system. Therefore, the issue is whether it is desirable for each subscriber to be able to watch the programmes produced or obtained by competing infrastructure providers. That is, given vertical integration, should someone who subscribes to the cable company be able to watch the programmes produced by Sky and vice versa (should that day arrive)?

This problem is similar to the issue of inter-connectivity in telecommunications. It would be desirable for each subscriber to be able to watch all programmes. This might be viewed the same way as in any other industry, but vertical integration poses some additional issues.

There are two obvious ways you can deal with this issue. Imagine you have two vertically integrated networks. They each produce their own programming and they each operate a network infrastructure. They are competing for subscribers and you want to see to it that the subscribers of each firm will have access to the programming of the other.

There are two ways you might go about this. You might call the first method 'wholesale interconnection.' Wholesale interconnection would be when one firm sells its programmes to the other firm. The latter firm then sells both sets of programmes to its customers. So, the second firm controls the retail prices, and bundles them together as it wishes, but it pays the producer for the right to show its programmes. This is more or less the current situation in the UK, with cable operators who buy programming from Sky. This is the wholesale model.

The other way of doing it, which is favoured more and more by the regulatory authorities, might be called 'customer service interconnection'. Under this model, a firm is allowed to sell its programmes directly to the competing firm's subscribers by paying a delivery fee to the other firm. This is more like the telecommunications way of doing it. This solution gives the programme producer full control over its own retail prices. Therefore, there is a big difference.

In the first case, with wholesale interconnection, a firm controls all of the prices charged to its connected customers. With customer service interconnection, a firm controls the prices of all of its programmes shown to all people in the country. These are two possible ways of organising the market, and I would argue that both of them have major problems in terms of collusion.

This is a major issue for the future. With wholesale interconnection, each firm offers its programmes to the other firm at some cost, and this has the effect of raising customers' retail prices. This is the same with interconnecting phone companies: if they charge each other a high rate for terminating calls, that feeds through into a high retail price. This acts as a kind of anti-competitive device raising each other's costs in the way that anti-competitive joint ventures might do. The result is a kind of collusive or semi-collusive outcome in terms of raising each other's costs.

In the second case, customer interconnection, I would argue that there is very weak competition in infrastructure. One firm controls the price of its programmes to its own customers and to its competing firm's customers. If it raises both prices equally, that price increase does not affect its competitive position vis-à-vis the other firm. The effect is merely to raise prices for its programming, let us say by 10 Pounds on each network, but this does not affect its relative position in attracting subscribers to its own network. I would say the infrastructure competition is very weak in this case, and this means we could have collusion. Moreover, that collusive result could even occur in a simple model, even if you had a zero cost of delivering each other's programs. Therefore, even if each of the programmes is priced at its marginal cost, you are going to get very ineffective competition between infrastructures.

▶ Fox—My intervention focuses on joint ventures and mergers under US law, in particular, with regard to access questions. I want to start first, however, by taking a lead from Mr. Salsbury who gave us a line from Robert Frost: '[G]ood fences make good neighbours.' And I am sure you will agree with me if I add another line from the poem, which says: '[B]efore I build the wall, I would like to know what I was walling in and walling out'.

In preparing my remarks, I decided to provide a perspective on the evolution of the treatment, under United States law, of joint ventures with access problems. In the process, I realised that I did not always want to make a distinction between the joint venture case and the single firm case. This distinction sometimes seemed inappropriate because I think that there are some overriding themes that interconnect access problems, whether they involve access to a single firm network or to a jointly owned one. Therefore, as I trace this legal evolution, I will sometimes analogise access issues to a monopoly problem and sometimes to a joint venture problem.

First, I would like to mention two legal guideposts that existed in the pre-Reagan era. Then, I want to say a word about what happened in the 1980's in the United States, which was very important. Finally, I will examine the new themes that affect our problem since the Reagan era.

My two guideposts start with our most famous case on bottleneck access. It is a joint venture case known as the *St. Louis Railroad Terminal* case, which may be familiar even for those who are not well-acquainted with US law. The case dealt with a railroad consortium, which controlled access over an area that spanned across the Mississippi River, over mountains where no one else can build the access route and the turntable. Faced with such facts, the Supreme Court decided that it was necessary for the joint venture to be inclusive. It was required to provide access to other railroads who could easily use the facility of the joint venture without degrading its facility. In modern terms, you would say that the joint ventures had no incentive to deny access except for the fact that they would get a big jump on their competitors.

The rule that has come out of this in the US applies to both single firm behaviour and joint firm behaviour. It is our essential facilities doctrine, and it is a very narrow doctrine. That is, it is hard to meet the tests of the doctrine: (1) that a facility be truly essential, (2) that it cannot be feasibly duplicated, and (3) that access can be given without degrading the facility.

This, of course, is a first point of reference. I agree with what Mr. Salsbury said on this issue: the essential facilities doctrine is a good way of analysing the problem, but it does not necessarily identify what the best solutions are. We know that we did not like the railroad consortium's exclusionary conduct, and, indeed, it was very inefficient. However, if we can not require an easy break-up, we must resort to arduous regulatory solutions, which entail difficult problems of their own.

The second guidepost I want to mention is the *Associated Press* case. At the end of the 1940's, and certainly throughout the 1950's and 60's, US law began to take a point of view geared toward inclusiveness. For example, if you had competitors with a very valuable joint venture and another competitor wanted to enter, there was a period of time when US law said: why not provide a level playing field for the competitor who wants to enter? After all, we ought to have equality of opportunities for those who want to enter.

Thus, by the end of the 1950's and certainly in the 1960's, the US seemed to be developing a rule under which a highly successful joint venture might find itself saddled with a duty to provide services to others. Indeed, the 1977 guidelines represent a typical US analysis. Under these guidelines, you looked to see whether a joint venture was overly exclusive and you looked to see whether it had unreasonable restrictions, but you also looked to see whether the competitor was entitled to have access to the joint venture.

Now, I will fast forward to the early 1980's, when Assistant Attorney General Bill Baxter drew on the work that Don Baker did concerning AT&T. 1981 is really a turning point in US antitrust policy. Baxter gave very important speeches about antitrust being about efficiency, not equality and inclusiveness. Consequently, he said that there was a fallacy to this inclusiveness model of joint venture analysis; it led to fuzzy thinking and it helped competitors for the sake of helping competitors. He also said that one should think not about whether the competitors should have access, but about whether alternatives would be feasible. Perhaps, through collaboration between those excluded from the initial joint venture, you could have further joint ventures. That would be a far superior way of achieving effective competition than simply requiring everyone to be included in the single existing joint venture.

Of course, with respect to the over-inclusiveness rule, Baxter realised that there were competitive problems associated with collaboration among too many competitors. Perhaps, they would like to collaborate effectively to raise price and lower output. A joint venture could provide a wonderful forum for their collaboration, in effect, cartelisation.

Furthermore, there is another problem involved with collaboration among the major players in an entire industry, especially if they own a facility essential for other competitors who wish to enter the market. Such collaboration could be a highly effective barrier to entry. That is, new entrants may be blocked from a market or no longer have the incentives to enter it because of their competitors' collaboration.

This, of course, did not cause Bill Baxter to reject the essential facilities doctrine as it was. In fact, our AT&T case and the local loop problem it presented involved clear essential facilities problems. We not only saw the problem in theory, but we saw it working. That is, AT&T, which did many wonderful things, also had strong incentives to exclude MCI, the developer of the great microwave technology. In fact, the case law reveals many examples of AT&T's exclusionary practices. It denied MCI connections to the local loops for no other reason than the fact that MCI was becoming an effective and challenging competitor.

A question was raised earlier concerning the proper point at which you force your companies to form a new network, rather than allow them access to an essential facility. I am sure that, in the period up to and including 1981, a court would not have denied MCI access to the local loop on the grounds that it was the best positioned of anyone to find a new technology to manoeuvre around the tight hold of the local loop. Forcing MCI to build its own infrastructure to enter the local market would not have been feasible for many years. Therefore, at some point, there was going to be access to a bottleneck. As technology develops, however, alternative networks might become feasible and it might no longer be appropriate to require access.

Let us move on to the post-Reagan era. Three things happened, slightly changing the tilt of our law and enforcement efforts. First, there was a political economy change, moving from a very strong presumption that what business did was right and efficient, toward a more sceptical view of business power. This also involved arrival at where we are today, which is a presumption that access is good, rather than a presumption that what business does is fine.

The second thing that happened is that, in the wake of global competition, the idea that firms ought to have access to foreign markets began to effect our cases. The third thing that happened involved the technology issue and the question of how technology is advanced and retarded.

Today, we have a huge debate, for example, as to whether we should leave Microsoft alone. This is the same argument that Mr. Schaub mentioned a moment ago. It is the argument that Microsoft is doing wonderful things, and if you intervene you are going to kill its incentives and kill the goose that lays the golden eggs.

On the other side, the question about these technology issues is whether we should be pushing toward more open access. Will we have more incentives if those who are on the outside can come in? Will we facilitate technology in this way? I think that the overarching technology issue is one of the most significant issues we are facing. Peoples' perceptions about this issue, and hopefully research about this issue, will be a most important point for solving our future problems.

▶ BAKER—I can not resist saying that when I started my career at the Justice Department, I was involved in bringing the AT&T case. After I left, the government won the case and broke up AT&T. My wife was then a senior official at the Federal Communications Commission, so we have sector-specific regulators and competition people in the same family. Someone said at a party, 'what do you do?' She replied, 'Oh, it is the same old stuff. Cleaning up Don's broken crockery on the kitchen floor'.

Anyway, what I want to discuss is what I call a 'trans-Atlantic disconnect' on how we deal with access to established networks. I also want to disagree a bit with some of what Eleanor Fox just said. The subject is intellectually interesting and it is practically important because as networking becomes global, the rule anywhere is likely to be the rule everywhere. This is the message of the IBM interface dispute from the early 80's, and it may also be the message of Boeing McDonnell Douglas.

My paper deals with rules for access to established joint ventures. I am not arguing that Europe treats joint ventures and single firm networks roughly the same way for access, while the US has quite different rules for compelling access. I am also not talking about the creation of a new joint venture or the creation of a new merger. In both of these cases, the regulators on both sides of the Atlantic feel much freer to compel access for disadvantaged competitors. I think that the symmetry of results between the Justice Department and DG IV in cases such as GlobalOne, flows from looking at them in the same way.

What I suggest here, however, is that we have started off with what Eleanor Fox rightly describes as the St. Louis Terminal case position, and assume that the Associated Press case is the root of the evil. We had three networks in the news business at the time, of which the Associated Press was the biggest. The Court compelled access and the other two networks sort of withered away. We ended up with, pretty much, a single news network.

I want to clarify that, around the table, we are using the word network to mean a lot of different things. The way I use it in my paper is, however, quite limited. For the purposes of my paper, a network is a device by which primary market competitors exchange traffic, transactions or business. They do so because it enhances their value to their primary market customers. You can pick a whole range of examples: banks forming payment networks, for example.

The policy question behind this is the following: when you are starting something new, a joint venture may be a very good way to do it, because it assures that there will be traffic on the network, and it allows risk-sharing. We have, therefore, seen a variety of cases where this has been done, including, most notably, the payments networks. When we face these issues, *i.e.*, once we have a large, successful network such as Associated Press, the question is whether we want to encourage competition at network level. Or, instead, is it sufficient to have a large, inclusive network so that no primary market competitor is left behind? It seems to me that the answer to this question depends on the facts. There is no one-size-fits-all rule. In general, if there is enough potential traffic to support competing networks, we probably want them, because competing networks will bring value to the primary market competitors in terms of competition on the terms on which network business is transacted.

There really are risks of being overly inclusive in creating access rules. I was struck by Advocate General Jacob's points in the Oscar Bronner case, where he speaks about this very issue. It is really an issue of incentives and risks: if the network creator knows that latecomers can always enter on favourable terms, then the initial incentives to create the network are weakened.

The worse problems come when the network develops something of a public franchise, as with a payments network, or as we have also got in a variety of other kinds of business: flowers by wire, etc.. This was not really an issue in the Oscar Bronner case, which dealt with an invisible delivery mechanism. But the problem comes when the network enables its partners, the participants, to obtain something special. The Associated Press case was such a wonderful example because the creators wanted to have an especially good press service. When they were compelled to take everyone in, however, the leaders of the Associated Press service—The New York Times, The Chicago Times and The Los Angeles Tribune—formed their own syndicate. We ended up having one national news service, and the United Press and International News Service folded out.

Now, when you have a public franchise, this question of access to the network becomes a question of compulsory licencing of the network trademark, going back to Professor Hovenkamp's point on that issue. Are we really going to compel access not only to the backbone of the network, *i.e.*, the switching facilities, but also to the network's trademarks? It seems to me that this entire analysis must depend on monopoly power, and the problem with *Associated Press* was that, instead of focusing on market power, the Court relied upon loose notions of boycott. The Court said that the collaborators were boycotters, boycotting those who they did not want in the system.

Therefore, we got away from monopoly power. It seems to me that where the network has pretty much complete monopoly power, even where it has a franchise, we probably should compel access. But when it does not have monopoly power, then requiring access blunts the incentives to create the network.

Two quick points, the first being addressed to Eleanor Fox. One, I do not think the world changed as much in Professor Baxter's time as you think, because in my opinion, at the practical level, people who were running networks and were threatened with boycott suits gave in. Secondly, I would ask you to examine his business review clearance denying an exclusivity rule for financial interchange. I know it well because I filed it.

My final thought is that the disconnection between Europe and the US on joint ventures and single firm networks can probably be substantially eliminated if two things happen (maybe neither of which will ever happen). First, if the Court of Justice follows Advocate General Jacob's view in *Oscar Bronner*, the European treatment of single firm networks will come a lot closer to that of the US. Secondly, if the Justice Department loses the *Visa* case, which Mr. Rubinfeld talked about, we may bring the American approach to joint ventures a little closer to that of the Europeans. I have nothing to do with Bronner, but I do work in Visa.

▶ LONG—I have already had some airtime, so I will keep these remarks as brief as possible. First of all, I would like to pick up on the rapporteur's remarks for this session. He asked whether the presence of regulation in the markets under consideration should influence the merger control assessment.

I am a firm believer that the regulatory conditions should influence this decision, because they are a market-affecting mechanism. In fact, there are a number of cases where this has received affirmation at European level. For example, the Commission's merger task force has taken existing regulatory conditions into account in deciding whether to approve a given merger.

In some cases, the Commission has also used conditions imposed on the parties to kick-start regulatory changes. This is a more controversial approach because one can argue that the Commission's role is not to accelerate regulatory change in this area; instead, such change should be the responsibility of legislatures and regulatory agencies themselves. Perhaps this is an issue we may turn to.

In fact, if I may be very topical on this particular point, I learned only the ther day that the agreement filed by the parties in the BT-AT&T venture has condition precedent. Specifically, if the Commission makes its approval conitional on the rapid unbundling of the local loop, then BT will have a right to valk away from the transaction. This is a very interesting and rather conrontational approach which challenges the Commission in order to avoid premature regulation of a market. It will be very interesting to see what impact this has on the hearts and minds of the officials in Brussels.

Anyway, returning to the importance of considering regulatory and echnological conditions in the context of merger review, I wish to revisit an ssue raised by the *Worldcom-MCI* proceedings and Salsbury's contribution his morning. The fact that, under the Merger Regulation, the Commission must consider transactions in a short time-period means that it is under normous pressure to consider the impact of the transaction, particularly egarding new technologies. Therefore, a merger review is not the ideal orum in which to decide upon arrangements that may have a very long-erm impact, not only on competition cases, but perhaps also on regulatory hinking.

Moreover, the Commission is, understandably, not very keen on behavoural remedies in these cases. Instead, it seeks structural remedies because of he policing problems associated with behavioural remedies. In my opinion, his means that you are in for some rough and ready justice in merger control ases. After all, this is a rather pragmatic and expedient context, because you have a very busy regulatory authority which has many other cases to consider and few, but very well educated, resources to deal with them. Meanwhile, you have parties who are under pressure to defuse confusion in the marketplace about whether the transaction will take place, about the impact the transaction will have on customers and, perhaps most importantly, about the effect the transaction will have on share price. This dictates that the parties must reach, somehow, a pragmatic solution. This is not always the best context for a settlement based on the strict legal merits of the matter.

Finally, I wish to move into the world of convergence and discuss its possible implications for regulation and merger control. A lot has been said this morning about how, in the future, fixed and mobile communications will come together. I think we are already in this situation. In fact, we already have, certainly in the developed jurisdictions in which telecommunications infrastructure is relatively mature and licences have been granted, a world where operators are already involved in converged services and in mobile communications services competing at an advanced level with fixed telecommunications services and vice versa.

This process, which has already started, is going to have a significant impact on market definition. On the one hand, people will be arguing that the market is now much larger than it was, because the players in it have come from different sectors to compete in this converged marketplace. On the other hand, it would be naïve to suggest that the regulators are going to fall for this and fail to find separate sub-markets within this converged market. In fact, there are also discrete markets which could have their own discrete competitive effects.

Such convergence will have a big impact on the area of interconnection. We will need to reassess the interconnection models that we have today, which are very much geared toward voice telecommunications. These models are not appropriate for uniform application to converged services.

In this area, my particular hobbyhorse is that the whole interconnection debate seems to be marked by historical thinking about tariff models, and, in particular, usage-based charging. At the moment, we have the usage-based traditional retail tariff model, which is a per-minute or per-second based method of charging. It is time to consider the alternative possibilities of capacity-based pricing.

In particular, I think it is unfortunate that the emphasis on alternative pricing models, particularly Long-run Incremental Costs (LRIC), has distracted the industry from the advantages of capacity-basis pricing. If you subscribe to the view, which I think is generally accepted, that regulation should mimic the effects of competition, you must conclude that per-minute based charging does not have this effect. In fact, the variable costs of telephone calls are a very small component of the costs of interconnection services. Therefore, if you think about it, charging on the basis of the amount of time that customers spend on the network is not a very accurate substitute for costs.

If you want a truly cost-based environment, there is a better way of approaching it. The costs that the incumbent faces are geared toward its fixed and variable costs and the variable costs are a small element. If you want to put the new entrant in a position similar to that of the incumbent, it follows that you should think about replicating the kind of costs that the incumbent faces. Capacity-based charging is one way of achieving this. I am not saying that it is the only way, but it is an option worth considering.

Therefore, let us hope that when we examine interconnection in a conversion environment, we do not wear the strait-jacket of old thinking on interconnection pricing. This pricing question will also raise issues about universal service contributions and regulation of bundling.

▶ REYNOLDS—While I am a practitioner, I wanted to point out that we are not all slaves to time-sheets and clients. Some of us, like Mario Siragusa and myself, do academic work. Nevertheless, as a practitioner, I thought that I would concentrate on some more practical points. In particular, I wanted to focus on procedural points.

I will begin by sketching the way some of the telecommunications alliance cases have been dealt with in Brussels. I will then turn to the changes under the Merger Regulation and the impact that they might have, because this does affect the way that these cases are dealt with, and indeed, the types of remedies that can be offered. Further, I think that, to some extent, the shape of the review procedure taints the way in which the alliances are put together.

First, we should not underestimate the challenges regulators face in making the necessary appraisals, regardless of the regime they are operating under— whether its under Article 81 [ex 85] or the Merger Regulation. This is particularly true in the case of the Merger Regulation, which is a one-off transaction during which difficult assessments have to be made. The Commission must spot what may become a bottleneck and determine how far existing bottlenecks may be used to dominate downstream competition. Likewise, in the context of a very rapidly changing market of shifting alliances (because many of these alliances are made up of partners who are not always faithful), the competitive environment often changes. Finally, as has been mentioned so often, the fast-changing nature of technology makes prognosis difficult.

As an aside, whenever I think of technology, I always think of Bill Gates, and something he said about the fast-moving pace of technology. He was actually comparing the computer industry with the motor industry. He once said that if General Motors had kept up with technology, like the computer industry, we would all be driving $25 cars that do 1,000 miles to the gallon. General Motors was so stunned by this rebuke that they issued a press release that said that if General Motors had developed cars the way Microsoft had developed computers, we would all be driving cars with the following characteristics: (1) for no reason whatsoever, your car would crash twice a day. (2) every time they repainted the lines on the road, you would have to buy a new car. (3) only one person at a time could use the car, unless you bought Car95 or CarNT, but then you would have to buy more seats. (4) the airbag would say 'are you sure?' before going off. (5) occasionally, for no reason whatsoever, your car would lock you out and refuse to let you in until you simultaneously lifted the door handle, inserted the key, and grabbed hold of both mirrors and the radio aerial.

So much for technology. I have always agreed with the late President Pompidou, who said there were three roads to ruin in life. One was women, one was wine, and the third was, certainly, technology.

Returning to the review of telecommunications alliances, we should recall that when they started to happen, these alliances often fell foul of a procedural problem. That is, the complicated European definition of what constituted a merger or concentration made it difficult to determine how these alliances should be treated. This is a decisive issue and should not be underestimated in terms of the remedies that can be offered or the time frame for review. In turn, the remedies available and the time-frame used affect the substantive way in which these things are reviewed, and may help determine the stamp that the regulators in Brussels put on the industry from an antitrust point of view.

For example, the parties in the first *BT-MCI* case tried to present the arrangement as a concentration, because, in many ways, it looked like a merger. The Commission decided, however, that there were so many aspects of co-operation involved that it had to be treated under Article 81 [ex 85], and, therefore, it had to be re-notified.

I wanted to emphasise the important differences this classification has made, which leads to the changes under the new amendments to the Merger Regulation. Under the amended Regulation, more of these alliances will be treated under the Merger Regulation and the competitive aspects will be examined within tight time-limits.

The most important differences are the following. First, if a case is considered under the Merger Regulation, it is a one-off exemption, whereas, if it is dealt with under Article 81 [ex 85], it is subject to review within a certain period of years. The type of review also governs the type of remedy that can be imposed because, under the Merger Regulation, only structural, and not behavioural remedies have been considered. In the Media Service Group (MSG) case, the parties tried to propose behavioural remedies, and were told they would not be accepted in a merger context. The first *BT-MCI* case managed to go through rather easily. I think the Commission was comforted by the fact that the UK market was already fairly liberalised and they had confidence in the local network.

The next case, *Atlas-Global One*, to which Don Baker referred, posed many more difficulties. It involved powerful players, and the Commission was careful to ensure that they were not able to exploit bottlenecks to prevent effective competition downstream. The case was also complicated by the need to use the case in a way that would bring about more rapid liberalisation on the French and German markets. Therefore, the exemption was suspended until two additional licences in the countries had been granted. At the end of the day, the alliances were approved, subject to a raft of quite detailed behavioural conditions. Those conditions were worded so that the breach of any one of them would cause the exemption to fall.

Thereafter, of course, the Commission received cases under the revised Merger Regulation. For example, we have heard about the second *BT-MCI* case and the *Worldcom-MCI* case. Alliance cases, such as the current *BT-*

T&T case, are now analysed under the Merger Regulation, and I wanted to focus on the difference this will make.

The test will now be whether or not the alliance is a full-function joint venture and the aspects of co-operation will be dealt with under that Merger Regulation, rather than under Article 81 [ex 85]. That is, the Article 81 [ex 85] analysis will take place within the context of the merger review, within tight time-limits. On the one hand, it is very encouraging that we have a very harmonious system. It almost seems slightly odd that systems with such different consequences were being applied to similar types of transactions, and that 'co-operative' alliances would be subjected to rather different treatment.

What we do not yet know is how the new regime will work in practice. In fact, I think it will be very interesting to hear the views of the Brussels regulators about how this is going to operate. Clearly, more behavioural remedies will be possible under this new regime. Officials from the Article 81 [ex 85] section of DG IV will also be able to take part in the assessment along with the Merger Task Force, and this should mean that they are able to deal with behavioural undertakings.

So, it does make sense to have a coherent system, but it also makes sense that we have a level playing field. For the alliances that passed under the previous regime, which had a raft of behavioural conditions attached to them, it is important that all the alliances are subjected to the same sort of analysis and rigour. Given the fact that there has been a change in procedure on the review of those previously granted exemptions, or on cases that are now considered under the Merger Regulation, it is important that an attempt be made to ensure the alliances are dealt with even-handedly.

The other point I wanted to make is that none of these cases would really succeed if there were no co-operation between the authorities on both sides of the Atlantic. So far, in these cases, this co-operation has worked well, and I would like to endorse what was said earlier in reference to the Worldcom-MCI case. It really was a good example of close co-operation. One hopes that under the new regime in Brussels—*i.e.,* the amended Merger Regulation, which will impose tight time-limits—that this co-operation works equally well.

How the crystal ball gazing actually works in the context of a very tight time limit remains to be seen. One of the advantages of looking at these arrangements under Article 81 [ex 85], without tight time limits, is that more attention could be focused on submissions made. Moreover, the time-limited exemption gave the regulator an opportunity to review the case in the light of experience. Under the Merger Regulation, by contrast, there is more pressure to get the thing right in the first instance, and this crystal ball gazing may be very difficult.

Of course, as was pointed out, if the Commission gets it really wrong, there is the right of appeal. Regarding this issue, I certainly endorse the comment made by Mario Siragusa, and I was also interested to hear, from Alexande Schaub, that we might have more of a judicial role in this area, and that such a role would be welcomed. On the other hand, of course, this ignores one of the great bottlenecks, which is in the European Court of First Instance in Luxembourg.

Many of these companies have appealed merger cases, not necessarily in the telecommunications field, but in other fields, and companies have ever appealed approval decisions where they felt the market definition was wrong. That is certainly possible. The question that remains to be answered is how practical it is to involve judges in these matters.

Finally, the concern in Europe has always been focused on vertical foreclo- sure. Under the Merger Regulation, this was apparent early on in the *Alcatel- Telectra* case, and, of course, very prominently in the *MSG* cases, and in what I will call the 'son of the *MSG* cases', all of which have led to prohibitions. But these were fairly unique cases, where the parents had a very strong starting position. In addition, there was strong evidence that the new pay television companies would not enter a market if, in so doing, their access would be defined entirely by the new joint venture through its control of the pay televi- sion customers.

Furthermore, I would entirely endorse what Alexander Schaub says, because it is often difficult to correct such problems at a latter stage. The Commission has to get it right the first time around, and exercise its judgement to spot a situation where there may be long-term anti-competitive conse- quences. If you allow something like this to go through, it is going to be very difficult to control it *ex post*, relying on the Article 81 and 82 [ex 85 and 86] behavioural remedies, because, *inter alia*, people are often very reluctant to lodge complaints against major players in the market.

▶ SIRAGUSA—In my paper, I try to establish whether networks are subject to different treatment, under Article 81 [ex 85] and the Merger Regulation, depending upon whether they are controlled by a sole operator or whether they are the result of an agreement between different parties. Following Mr. Reynolds's presentation, it is clear that, with the Merger Regulation, a part of the issue has been solved, because, at least with respect to full-function joint ventures, we now have the same treatment. The treatment, as you know, is the creation and the strengthening of dominant positions. We are, thus, very close to the treatment that is applied to networks that are controlled or created by a sole operator.

Still, I think an area of agreements that will not qualify as full-function joint ventures remains. These agreements will, instead, be subject to Article 81 [ex 85]. Consequently, we can think of examples of networks that exist, or will be created, that will be subject to Article 81 [ex 85]. In these cases, I am afraid that there is a difference.

I think Europe, like the US, treats the two cases—sole operator and joint venture—differently. The difference stems from the fact that these agreements involving networks are often examined by the authorities upon their creation, and are, therefore, subject to an exemption decision. The Commission cannot resist inserting a number of obligations, subjecting the approval to a number of conditions, even in cases where we are very far from an essential facilities situation. In fact, I can think of many cases in which the Commission has imposed a number of obligations on network agreements, even if the market share was very far from the existence of a dominant position. I have given some references in the paper.

This will continue. Furthermore, because of the nature of the exemption, I can imagine that, even after its creation, a network agreement may be subject to access provisions. Its very existence may also be subject to review, for example, once the decision has expired, so that the problem may exist not only at the creation, but also during the life of the agreement.

There is a very interesting development mentioned in my paper, which is the recent decision of the Court of First Instance in the *Night Services* case. It concerns a joint venture between a number of railway operators to provide a night service. The Commission exempted the venture under Article 81(1) [ex 85(1)], but it imposed a number of conditions under Article 81(3) [ex 85(3)]. Thus, the parents had to provide rail services to other operators who wanted to operate between France and the UK.

The Court annulled the decision, concluding that the Commission had not proven the absence of alternatives. That is, the Commission had not shown that the four other operators were unable to obtain the same services from third parties. Therefore, the Court annulled an Art 81(1) [ex 85(1)] decision by using reasoning very similar to the essential facilities doctrine, which I think is a very healthy development in the direction of treating the two situations equally. If the Commission were obliged to apply such a standard in 81(3) [ex 85(3)] cases, then we would reach the point of parallel treatment within these two cases.

Finally, a word on the *Visa* case that was mentioned. As you know, this case has already been decided under European law. I do not consider it to be an access case. The system was that any bank could access the Visa system. The issue in the Visa system is the other way around. It concerns an obligation for the member banks not to use any other computing system. Since 80% of all world banks are part of the Visa system, I think that, under any system, this should be deemed to be exclusionary.

▶ WATERS—In Australia, we had a rather bizarre outcome concerning competition in broadband networks. Telstra and Optus would race each other down the street. One day, Optus began employing the network aerially, and the residents would strap themselves to the trucks to stop the aerial network. The next day, Telstra would go down the street digging the streets up, and the residents would strap themselves to the bulldozers to stop Telstra from digging up the streets. Thus, 40% of Australian homes are passed by three networks. We have one incumbent copper network, one incumbent broadband network, and one new entrant broadband network.

Telstra's strategy clearly was foreclosure. In its prospectus, Telstra's merchant bankers wanted to write down the broadband network on a standard line basis by a very substantial amount of money, hundreds of millions of dollars. But Telstra convinced them not to write it down as such a cost, while the prospectus states that the reason for this is telephony retention on the PSTN network. Thus, by overbuilding the Optus broadband network, Telstra hopes to retain customers on their PSTN network.

The second mistake made was to have exclusive content on pay television. To come back to a point that Mark Armstrong made earlier, exclusive content helps you differentiate infrastructure. In this way, customers can choose infrastructure and services, and this may lead to greater competition in infrastructure. All of this ignores the greed of the American Hollywood studios, however. When competing local broadband providers seek Hollywood programming, Hollywood studios rub their hands together and start an auction. Ultimately, what happened in Australia is that one of the providers, a satellite provider, collapsed under the burden of the payments to the Hollywood studios. In fact, content on the wholesale level in Australia costs twice as much as content in the UK on a per-subscriber basis, and that is no way to run a broadband business.

The third thing that happened in Australia involved the interaction between broadcasting and printed media. There is a moral in the story, which, as usual, involves Mr. Murdoch, a co-national of mine, who we have exported to the rest of you.

Mr. Murdoch has a fascination with the deep pockets of telephony PSTN incumbents. He formed a merger in Australia between himself and Telstra, the national incumbent. He then tried to merge with the satellite operators against the broadband new entrant, Optus. This would have been akin to BSkyB and BT merging together. Professor Fels and the Commission stopped this merger twice. The consequence was that Australis went into liquidation and Professor Fels still bears the injuries from Mr. Murdoch's newspapers. This is a classic example of cross-market leverage, in which an industry player can castigate, in his newspapers, the conduct of a regulator who is dealing with him in other areas. That is not uncommon in these multimedia companies.

▶ SIRAGUSA—It would have been even worse if Mr. Murdoch had been running as Prime Minister of Australia. I wanted to go back to some comments that were made this morning by Dr. Ungerer on the convergence of fixed and mobile telephony. I think interesting issues are emerging, even prior to full convergence.

Currently, some mobile operators can enter the fixed market, but the reverse is not true. I suppose that, in the future, we will see a number of alliances between fixed and mobile operators. It seems that there is a finite number of mobile operators. The interesting issue is what is going to happen. If it is essential to be able to offer a package including both fixed and mobile services, how will the theories we have talked about be applied in such a situation?

This goes back to the essential facilities doctrine: does a mobile operator, whatever market share he has, become an essential facility, because the fixed operator can offer a full package of services only through an alliance with a mobile operator? This would be an undue extension of the essential facilities doctrine to a market structure that is not a traditional one.

▶ HOVENKAMP—I want to comment very briefly on two earlier presentations about the rationale for possible similar treatment of jointly owned, or jointly operated networks, and of networks owned by a single firm. First of all, networks are clearly ancillary restraints within the terminology of US antitrust law. This means they are subject to the rule of reason, which means market power must be proven. Challenged anti-competitive effects must also be proven and the practice at issue must be found to be unreasonable. Finally, less restrictive alternatives must be examined in the case of practices, which are found to be reasonable but which might be conducted in a less restrictive manner. Beyond that, however, I think it is vital that a differentiation be maintained between unilateral and multilateral ownership. I think there are three justifications for this.

First, a single firm acting unilaterally is generally entitled to set its own price. In the absence of abuse, or in the absence of an exclusionary practice under US law, a monopolist is free to set its own price, and an essential corollary of this is that the monopolist is entitled to reduce its own output accordingly; you cannot set your own price without also setting the market clearing output. As a result, if General Motors unilaterally decides to reduce its advertising output, that is a unilateral act not subject to the rule of reason. Indeed, it is normally not even addressable under the antitrust laws. I posit, first, that we do not want a joint venture rule that permits joint venture participants, acting in concert, to reduce their output. In order to maintain this outcome, at least under the current institutional regime we have, we must also distinguish unilateral from multilateral conduct.

Secondly, in the ordinary course of events, monopolies take a very long time to create. They require a very great deal of innovation, predation and aggressive business practices that can be resisted by others. I am setting aside, for a moment, the case of a firm whose monopoly is handed to it, for example in the case of de-nationalisation of a regulated industry. Because monopolies take so long to create and because there is so much give and take in this progress, we are typically quite lenient about unilateral conduct. Joint ventures and cartels, by contrast, can be created in a very short period of time, frequently, simply by agreement. That means the joint venture may have significantly less investment in an output restricting practice, and this means that it may be profitable upon the production of considerably less efficiency. This situation warrants much closer judicial supervision.

Thirdly, and in some ways most important, is the problem of the administration of access decrees. I would like you to compare, in your own minds, the difference between American Express, which is a unitary credit card system, and Visa, which is a multilateral system. In order to guarantee access to American Express, you confront all of the problems of the essential facilities doctrine. The terms of access have to be developed, the price of access would have to be set or judicially administered. In very sharp contrast, when a group of firms acts together in a joint venture, such as, for example, the 6,000 banks that are currently involved in Visa, administration of access requires no more than an injunction against the enforcement of the exclusionary rule. Once this rule is set in place, each one of these 6,000 banks is free to issue a competing card. That is, each of them is free to grant access to a third party. And in that case, we can have a great deal of confidence that the market, via the competition among those 6,000 banks, will determine whether Discover, American Express, or some other third-party credit card company is entitled to have access and on what terms.

In the interest of full disclosure, I should state that I have been consultant at one time or another to Discover and the Justice Department.

▶ KNIEPS—I would like to return to this morning's session. In looking at essential facilities provided under joint ownership or control, one should not forget to apply the necessary access rules. Regarding the telecommunications sector, I think a situation exists whereby there are two or three active competitors and where there is a large amount of competition, so one should then focus on the local loop.

For purposes of analytical comparison, we should consider the electricity sector in Germany, where we had several regional monopolies. Under the new energy law, passed a few months ago, these regional firms are now open to competition. Now the question is how to respond when regional electricity firms want to merge. We know of course, that the long distance, high-wattage electricity transmission network is also a monopolistic bottleneck. I do not agree that horizontal integration should be *a priori* forbidden if the market power of the owner or the essential facility would thereby increase, since there are important network effects, *i.e.,* economies of scale and scope. Therefore, integration is value added. For instance, in electricity, there is a bundling advantage.

Consequently, the crucial question, which Mr. Ungerer also touched upon in his paper, is how to design adequate access rules for this network. When you have a monopolistic bottleneck, in my view, it would be much better to focus on developing the possible conditions of access rather than imposing structural solutions.

Returning to telecommunications, we have a local loop, which is identified as the bottleneck. If you have two firms, should they be allowed to merge? It is not easy simply to forbid such a merger. In fact, though it no longer exists, joint ownership was a feature in the US for a long time. There were several reasons why this joint ownership was dissolved, but mergers and other forms of joint ownership are motivated by economies of scale and scope between different kinds of activities. In the local loop case, I would suggest that we should allow mergers if such motivations also exist, but that we should then focus on an adequate regulation of access charges and conditions.

▶ BAKER—I would like to clarify a couple of things. I think that the full function joint venture idea that the European Community has come up with in the new Merger Regulation, is a great step forward in terms of trying to differentiate between joint ventures. I argue we should distinguish between full and partial joint ventures. Further, I argue that we should apply the same rules on access and exclusivity to the full function joint venture as we apply to mergers.

As Professor Hovenkamp noted, we, in the US, allow for a great deal of leeway for a refuse to deal. There is more room for refusal to deal in the US than exists in Europe. Thus, we get to the situation that Mr. Siragusa identified in relation to the *Visa* case. In the US, Visa has about a 45% market share. We are not going to litigate the *Visa* case here, but my position would be that a company in the US with a 45% market share could pick who it was associated with and to whom it wanted to provide access. My understanding is that in Europe, a company with a 45% market share might well be termed dominant and thus be obliged to deal with others.

There is a relationship between access to the joint venture and the licensing rules. Visa, in fact, fought, in a private case, for the right for it to choose not to deal with American Express and Discover. It won, in line with the theory that this would reduce competition at the network level. The current case involves whether it can have an exclusive licensing rule.

I would like to say one final thing. That is, American networks might well wish for something like the Article 81(3) [ex 85(3)] process, putting aside the full function joint venture issue, because at least under that process you can present something to the authorities. If they accept it, you are then immune, at least for a period. We live in a world in which joint venture networks are constantly doing sub-optimal things because they are threatened with private lawsuits and it is not worth the cost of defending them. The *Visa* case is one of a few cases where the network has defended an exclusivity rule, or an access rule, and not only defended, but won. Thus, it seems to me that one of the big things we are after is some degree of certainty.

Finally, I do not agree with Professor Hovenkamp's point at all: why do we not just let them in? If the founders of the joint venture have invested in developing the system and the mark, you are right back to the price of access. Someone who has spent millions of dollars developing a joint venture network ought to be paid an access fee for entry, and we are back to the 'World Commission of Just Prices.'

▶ RILL—It is, in a way, unfortunate that no one is here from the US Federal Trade Commission, which is in the process of trying to develop joint venture guidelines. They might turn out to be a simple reiteration of the children's crusade, but we will wait to see what they produce.

I wish to attempt to merge the concepts of the First and Second Panels. In the US, I suspect the full function joint venture, in its formulation stage, would, analytically-speaking, be treated as a merger. This would certainly be the case if there were a sufficient joinder of assets and sales to pass the reporting threshold under the Hart-Scott-Rodino Act.

I was struck by Mr. Salsbury's comments on the Worldcom-MCI merger: that the internet backbone is not an essential facility and is not a bottleneck. I do not think that this is a question that needed to be confronted, either by the

Commission or by the Court of Justice, since it arose in a merger context. There was no need to prove monopoly, instead both bodies were concerned with anti-competitive consequences. In the US, a merger can be blocked if there is a substantial likelihood of damage to competition. Particularly in the case of a network market with externalities and a potential tipping effect, it is not difficult to demonstrate that the merger of numbers one and two in a particular segment of the market was enough—at least in the US and perhaps in Europe as well—to force divestiture, without anyone having to look at the issue of whether the particular transaction deals with a bottleneck or an essential facilities market.

My point is simply that there is a degree of latitude, and, I think, an appropriate latitude, when it comes to dealing with the formation of a merger or a full function joint venture, which can produce a reduction in, or a modification of, competition. This latitude is to be seen as being wholly divorced from the question of whether or not an essential facility or a bottleneck exists. I do not think Mr. Salsbury would agree with this premise.

Finally, serious frictional and efficiency loss issues are involved in the divestiture of an existing structure. Fewer issues relate to the prohibition of a merger or a full function joint venture, unless it can be show that the merger or joint venture creates opportunities for efficiencies that will trump the anti-competitive potential of the transaction. In the US, the efficiency 'defence' is very difficult to prove; in the EU, as I understand it, it is non-existent. Perhaps one thing that could be done to improve the entire situation is to give some realistic content at least to a threshold analysis of the efficiency details.

▶ EHLERMANN—A thank you to all participants. We certainly have more to discuss, but time forces us to draw to a close.

AGREEMENTS, INTEGRATION AND STRUCTURAL REMEDIES

2

WORKING PAPERS

I

*Mark Armstrong**

Anti-Competitive Agreements Between Firms in the
Pay-TV Market

I. Introduction: The Pay-TV Industry

Over the past 10 years, pay-TV has played an increasingly important part in the broadcasting industry.[1] Recent advances in digital technology will mean an acceleration of this process, and consumers will shortly have a choice of watching several hundred channels as well as participating in various interactive services. But, as the market grows, the potential for anti-competitive conduct grows with it, and care needs to be taken that the full benefits of the revolution are realised.

1. A Description of the Industry

Over-simplifying somewhat, there are three layers in the pay-TV industry: (i) the production of programming, (ii) the retailing of programming to consumers (together with the possible wholesaling of programming to rival retailers), and (iii) the delivery (or distribution) of programming to consumers. For simplicity, we include within the programme production sector various monopolised inputs such as sports rights and movie rights (these scarce resources being termed 'premium' programming). The retailing sector buys programming from producers, and possibly from rival retailers at wholesale level, and packages these in various ways for sale to consumers (possibly including advertising). Naturally, there may be vertical integration between production and retailing, and a retailer may make some of its programmes 'in-house' (most likely the 'basic' programmes).

The delivery sector provides the transmission system through which retailers supply their services to consumers. Broadband cable, encrypted satellite

---

* Nuffield College, Oxford OX1 1NF.
[1] Viewers always pay for TV services in some form, whether by an annual licence fee, by watching advertising, by monthly subscription or by 'pay-per-view'. In this paper the term 'pay TV' means the situation where TV services can only be viewed in return for money payment.

and terrestrial broadcast are the three current delivery systems.[2] Naturally, there may also be vertical integration between retailing and delivery. A central ingredient to the industry, which is probably best regarded as being part of the retailing sector, is the encryption system together with the 'set-top box' used by consumers to decode the scrambled signal. There are several different encryption systems currently in use throughout Europe, and it is possible that a set-top box designed for one system will not be compatible with another. For convenience, we refer to the encryption/set-top box technology as 'conditional access technology'. As well as the basic encryption software and hardware, associated functions of the conditional access provider might include subscriber billing systems and the electronic programme guide (the latter will be of increasing importance as the multitude of channels grows).

Digital terrestrial television has recently been launched in parts of Europe, and this includes many of the basic free-to-air services currently broadcast using analogue technology together with new subscription channels. Both types of services require a set-top box (or a new integrated digital television), but the former does not require conditional access technology (since viewers make no payment).

2. Economic Features of the Industry

Of most relevance for policy towards the industry are the areas where there are actual or potential bottlenecks. Obvious examples in the production sector include premium programme production (e.g. the football Premier League in the UK, or a newly released film). If these premium programmes are sold using exclusive contracts to retailers, then the bottleneck is extended into the retailing sector.

Unless subscribers are extremely fluid between retailers (unlikely, for the reasons given below), current market shares are an important indicator of future market shares. Therefore, retailers with a high current market share will, in general, be able to bid more for exclusive premium programming in any auction, which will further consolidate their position. However, it is an open question whether an exclusive contract is really the most profitable strategy for premium programme producers (especially for pay-per-view retailing), and it

---

[2] A major difference between satellite and the other delivery technologies is that, roughly speaking, satellite can only deliver a nationwide service whereas cable and terrestrial can tailor programme delivery to local areas.

may be that, as competition in retailing becomes more entrenched, a producer will prefer to offer a programme to all retailers at a fixed price per viewer.[3]

In the delivery sector, there are important resource constraints for each of the three main transmission media. Economies of density mean that it is probably unlikely, at least in the UK, for there to be more than one new cable operator in any local area (although BT may choose to upgrade its telecom network to provide broadcast services when it is permitted by Government to do so). Radio spectrum and transponder capacity on suitable satellites is limited, which puts a ceiling on the number of channels that may be delivered by satellite. Finally, spectrum for terrestrial broadcasting is also limited. However, it is one of the main impacts of the new digital technology that spectrum and transponder constraints are now much less of an issue than they were 10 years ago, and a country like the UK will shortly have hundreds of channels.

A more subtle potential bottleneck is the conditional access technology. Given that the decoding equipment (set-top box) will continue to be a costly item (although retailers may choose to subsidise these to consumers), it seems unlikely and undesirable for a consumer to possess more than one such device. Therefore, if a consumer's retailer controls whether the box is also used to access other retailers' services then the retailer may—if free to do so—choose to forbid rival retailers access to its consumers. The extreme case of this would be if each consumer decided to get all pay-TV services from a single retailer and there was no joint supply. In this case, the retailer has a monopoly over the supply of programmes to its consumers.

Closely related to the above point is the existence of consumer switching costs and the resulting advantages for the first movers in the industry. Thus, if one proprietary conditional access technology is established by an incumbent firm, then new entrants—unless allowed access to the incumbent's set-top boxes—will have to persuade consumers to invest in a new and costly set-top box if they are to switch retailer. This will give the incumbent firm much leeway in setting its retail charges. Another major first-mover advantage is the possibility that an incumbent firm has long term exclusive contracts for much of the premium programming in place, which makes effective entry difficult for new retailers.

---

[3] To take an extreme example, when Hollywood studios make deals with video rental retailers, they do not sign exclusive contracts (e.g. of the form whereby the latest Disney film will be only be available through the Blockbuster chain of video stores). Similarly, while some Internet service providers, such as Microsoft and America Online, have offered exclusive content for their subscribers, this is an insignificant part of the market. See Armstrong (1999) for a formal analysis of this issue.

3 Questions for Policy

Important questions for policy include:

1. The profitability and desirability of exclusive dealing arrangements between premium programme producers and retailers (e.g. exclusive sports rights), and the danger that long-term exclusive contracts might be used as an entry-deterring strategy by incumbent retailers. For instance, should there be an upper time-limit placed on contract length, or should exclusive contracts even be permitted at all? (A prior question is whether it is really practical to ban exclusive contracts by programme producers.)

2. To what extent is it profitable to extend market power in one retailing sector (e.g. for premium programming) to others (e.g. 'basic' programming) which might potentially be more competitive? (One method of doing this, if desired, would be for a retailer to tie the supply of premium programming to that of its own basic programming, at either the retail or wholesale level.)

3. What are the incentives for a dominant conditional access provider (should the market develop in this way) to set desirable charges for access to its set-top box to rival retailers, and is public policy needed to bring about the desirable outcome?

4. If there are several conditional access providers, what are the incentives to offer each other access to their set-top boxes? In particular, is there scope for 'collusion' in the retail market (for instance, by charging each other a high, reciprocal charge for conditional access)?

5. Is there an incentive for a dominant retailer to form an alliance with one of its rivals in order, for instance, to weaken the remaining rivals? For instance, if a minimum number of subscribers is needed to fund a rival bid for premium programming, could the dominant firm try to 'buy off' one rival—maybe by offering it favourable wholesale rates for its premium programmes—in order to keep rival subscriber numbers down, and so maintain its monopoly of premium programming?

6. Could a powerful telecommunications firm, not willing or able to participate in the TV market, have an incentive to form an alliance or joint-venture with a powerful pay-TV retailer? A natural example might be when there are some firms active in both the telecoms and pay-TV sectors. In this case, a telecom-only company might wish to 'help' a TV-only company because this would damage the joint telecom/TV firms, and hence damage the competition to the telecom-only firm.

Questions 1, 2 and 3 are Article 82-type [ex Article 86] issues, and as such are to do with the getting and preservation of market power, which is not discussed in this paper.

II. The Industry Around the World

1. The Industry in Britain

The pay-TV industry in Britain started in 1989 when two satellite-based networks, *Sky* and *British Satellite Broadcasting* (BSB), were licensed. The two companies used different satellites, and hence a separate satellite dish was needed to receive the two signals. Sky managed to launch its initial four channels more than a year earlier than BSB, the latter having a series of delays and not fully launching until mid-1990. Cable TV companies also started in earnest in 1990, these being companies granted regional monopoly franchises, and they provided the early outlet for BSB's programmes while the satellite service was waiting to be launched. In the event, BSB did not manage to make up its lost ground against Sky, and Sky bought up BSB in late 1990, renaming the combined operation *BSkyB*. Thus, by 1991 there were only two providers of pay-TV, BSkyB and the regional cable companies.

There are, of course, important interactions with telephony. Since 1991, the cable companies have been permitted to offer telephony services over their cable TV networks, and virtually all companies do so. BT, on the other hand, is at present not allowed to offer TV services over its telephone network, although it is permitted to own cable TV companies (and does so in a few instances). However, the Government has recently announced that it plans to allow BT to offer TV services over its main network from early in the new millennium. This asymmetric treatment of BT and the cable companies, at least in the short term, is explored in more detail in section IV.

The following table gives basic statistics for the UK pay-TV industry.[4] We see that the number of households taking pay-TV has increased dramatically over the eight years covered, that the market share of satellite has gradually fallen—though still remaining very substantial—as cable networks have expanded their networks, and that cable penetration as a fraction of homes passed has stayed quite constant.

BSkyB is the main provider of programmes in the pay-TV market, and sells its programmes to cable operators as well as broadcasting these itself. BSkyB owns the UK non-terrestrial rights for the output of major Hollywood studios

---

[4] Figures are taken from, An Analysis of the ITC Report into Channel Bundling, NERA (1998), Table 3.1. Note that 'penetration' means percentage of all households with any form of television. Also, the cable companies have only 'passed' (i.e. can feasibly deliver service to) a fraction of households in the country, so we include figures on penetration here.

Table 1: Development of Pay-TV in the UK

	1992	1994	1996	1998
Satellite Penetration (%)	9.5	12.3	15.2	17.8
Cable Pentration (%)	1.5	3.2	6.5	10
Cable Pentration of Homes Passed (%)	21.1	21.2	21.3	22.2
Total Pay-TV Pentration (%)	11.0	15.5	21.7	27.8
Market Share of Sattelite in Pay-TV Homes (%)	86.4	79.5	70.1	64

and many key sporting events, such as the football Premier League. Wholly owned BSkyB channels (Sky 1, Sky News, film and sports channels, and so on) account for 43% of total cable and satellite viewing hours, and all independent channels have a tiny market share.[5] However, the share of viewing hours is not necessarily an accurate measure of power, and there is evidence that premium programming, of which BSkyB has at least a short-run monopoly, is the major driver of subscription. Indeed, a recent survey reported that 79% of subscribers cited premium programming as their original reason for joining.[6]

Throughout 1995–7, there were controversies over the wholesale terms at which BSkyB offered its programmes to its rival cable networks. For instance, BSkyB encouraged cable companies to supply the formers own basic programming to any cable subscriber that wished to have its premium programmes—see Question 2 in Section I.3 above. It was decided that there should not be a reference to the Monopolies and Mergers Commission (MMC), and that BSkyB should be permitted to pursue its bundling (and other discounting) strategies for the time being.[7] Also, in 1998, BSkyB announced that it wished to move further upstream and to purchase Manchester United, probably the most successful Premier League football team. This has now been referred to the MMC to investigate any possible anti-competitive impact of such vertical integration.

Another area of controversy has been the recent co-operation between BSkyB and CWC, the main cable operator.[8] In 1997, cable companies had

---

[5] See NERA (supra, Table 3.4) for more detail.

[6] Source: Television, The Public's View, Independent Television Commission (1997).

[7] For more details see Office of Fair Trading (1997; OFTEL (1997).

[8] According to NERA (supra, table 3.3), CWC has over one third of all homes passed by cable.

been showing signs of increasing independence from BSkyB, and been planning to substitute the BBC's 24-hour news service in place of Sky News, and also to launch an independent movie channel. However, in August 1997, CWC signed a deal with BSkyB, which meant that it would only offer programmes supplied by BSkyB (and at terms that were more generous than those offered to other cable companies).[9] As a result, it appears that the attempt to negotiate terms with Hollywood for a new movie channel by the remaining cable operators has fallen through for the time being. Clearly, this move on the part of BSkyB could be motivated by the issue covered in Question 5 in Section I.3 above, and this is discussed in section V.

New digital television services were offered at the end of 1998 (in the case of BSkyB and the newly-formed OnDigital) and will be offered in 1999 (in the case of cable). In 1997, the Independent Television Commission (ITC) awarded licences to provide terrestrial digital television. The main pay-TV licence, which was for three-quarters of the available new channels, was bid for by British Digital Broadcasting (a consortium of BSkyB and two existing terrestrial companies, Carlton and Granada) and DTN (wholly owned by the cable company NTL). The main worry with the former bid was the major involvement of BSkyB, and the concern that this would mean that the consortium would not compete effectively against BSkyB for premium programming, for instance. In the end, the ITC preferred the bid offered by BDB over that of DTN, but insisted on the removal of BSkyB from the consortium. The resulting entity has been given the brand name 'OnDigital'.[10]

Another major controversy—maybe *the* major controversy—has been the possible future dominance of BSkyB in setting standards for the 'set-top box' once digital TV becomes established, together with the possible need to regulate the terms on which other retailers (for instance, the BBC) can gain access to BSkyB's box (see Question 3 in Section I.3 above). For instance, it would probably be desirable for competition if a BSkyB subscriber who wishes to move to, say, OnDigital's service was able to continue to use the same set-top box to receive the new service. The issue is complicated by BSkyB's plan to subsidise the cost of such boxes, at least in the initial stages, and so public policy needs to ascertain just how much contribution others should make to this access subsidy if they use the box.[11]

---

[9] See the Financial Times, August 30 and September 1, 1997.
[10] For more detail see OFTEL (1997b).
[11] In Britain it is the telecoms regulator, OFTEL, which has responsibility for setting policy in this area—see OFTEL (1998) and earlier documents for more detail.

The entity that will be concerned with BSkyB's conditional access technology, the selling (and subsidy) of the set-top box, together with subsequent interactive services, is *British Interactive Broadcasting* (BIB), a consortium involving BSkyB, BT, Matsushita and the Midland Bank. Both BSkyB and BT each have a 32.5% stake in the joint-venture. Concerns were expressed about the involvement of two powerful players in the UK telecom and pay-TV industries, but the joint-venture has been cleared both in the UK and recently in Europe. It is highly likely that the consortium will run at a loss in its initial stage, mainly because of the substantial subsidy involved in the marketing of the set-top box, which apparently will cost about £400 each to produce but will retail for £200, and so one effect of the joint-venture will be for BT to contribute to the subsidisation of access to BSkyB's digital TV network.[12] This issue (which was Question 6 in Section I.3 above) has obvious concerns for BSkyB's rivals, most notably the cable operators, and this is discussed further in Section IV below.

2. The Industry in the United States

The industry in the United States is perhaps unique in the world for the prevalence of pay-TV subscription in its population.[13] Thus, in 1997, only 23% of television households received television programming entirely from over-the-air broadcast reception. Of the remaining households, 87% received service from their local franchised cable operator, and the great majority of the remaining 13% took their service from satellite providers. The number of households able to obtain cable TV services (i.e. whose homes are 'passed') is very high, at about 97%. However, much of the reason for this high take-up of pay-TV is the often low quality of over-the-air reception, and many people use cable to receive the main over-the-air broadcast television stations. (In 1997 these television stations accounted for 67% of total viewing hours, delivered both over the air and via cable. The largest four broadcast networks, ABC, CBS, Fox and NBC accounted for 59% of all prime-time viewing hours.)

Most cable companies operate as local monopolies, and because of their importance in the overall television market have their non-premium subscription rates regulated (in contrast to virtually all other countries). However, since the 1996 Telecom Act, which permitted cable companies to offer telephony and

---

12 See Financial Times, 14 March 1998.
13 All of the data in this section are taken from Federal Communications Commission (1998).

telephony companies to enter TV markets, there has been a degree of competition for TV subscribers within cable franchise areas, and by 1997 about 5 million people in the United States had a choice of cable operator.[14] Provided that the FCC determines that there is 'effective competition' in these areas, price regulation on incumbent cable companies is lifted. (Premium and pay-per-view programming is not regulated in any event.)

There is a mixed pattern of vertical integration between pay-TV delivery companies and programme suppliers. Thus, in 1997, of the 172 cable channels, 40% were vertically integrated with—i.e. had an ownership stake held by—at least one cable delivery company. (This compares with 53% in 1994.) In particular, TCI, the largest cable delivery company, holds ownership interests in 23% of all national cable programming services.

III. Collusion Between Rival Retailers

In this section, we consider a drastically simplified model of the pay-TV industry, designed to shed some light on Question 4 in Section I.3.[15] Specifically, we suppose that TV networks each produce programmes 'in house', which they may sell to each other, and there is no outside market for programmes (such as sports rights and so on). Thus, the model is one of complete vertical integration between programme supply and production. (An alternative interpretation might be that of a short-run model where exclusive contracts to premium programming have already been secured.)

There are two broadcasters, A and B, who each produce a set of programmes and who deliver programmes to their subscribers. There is a fixed per-subscriber cost k comprising the cost of digital decoders, satellite dishes, cables to the home, and so on. Once programmes have been produced the marginal cost of supplying them to a subscriber is zero (provided that the per-subscriber cost has been incurred). All subscribers have the same tastes for the programmes, and once a subscriber has access to one firm's programmes she has a positive, but decreasing, incremental utility from viewing the second set of programmes. (This implies that the two sets of programmes are imperfect substitutes for each other.) Both firms are symmetric, in the sense that connection

---

[14] The somewhat pejorative term 'overbuilding' is used by the FCC and others for when there is more than one cable network laid in a given local area. See FCC (supra, paragraphs 178–204) for some case studies concerning cable competition.

[15] A formal description of this model, including the assumptions needed to ensure that the following arguments are valid, is contained in Armstrong 1999.

costs are the same and consumers derive the same utility from both sets of programmes.

There are three natural kinds of regime: one where firms supply only their own programmes to subscribers (termed *no interconnection*), and the other two where networks are 'interconnected' in some sense. The two kinds of interconnection considered are *wholesale interconnection*, in which firms supply each other with their programmes at wholesale level (so that each firm retains control over retail pricing decisions to customers), and *customer interconnection*, in which firms are granted access to each other's customers (so that the firm which produces the relevant programmes retains retail pricing control on these programmes to the rival network's customers). In the two cases of interconnection we refer to the charge that one firm makes to the other for (i) rights to its programmes (in the case of wholesale interconnection) or (ii) rights to its customers (in the case of customer interconnection) as the 'access charge'.

Before we discuss these various configurations, however, we note the collusive, joint-maximising outcome, which is for each consumer to be connected to a single firm but to watch both sets of programmes. Subscribers have their entire surplus extracted by the tariff. As all subscribers are identical in this simple model, this also maximises total welfare (even though consumers are left with none of the gains from trade).

No Interconnection: This simple situation is illustrated in Figure 1 below. Here, depending upon parameter values, each subscriber (i) obtains services from only one firm, or (ii) chooses to buy from both firms. In either event, though, there is an inefficiency. In case (i) subscribers view only a single set of programmes even though they gain positive utility from a further set of programmes (which have a zero incremental cost of supply). In case (ii) subscribers

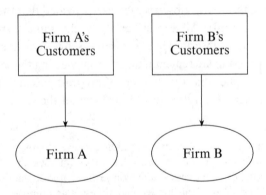

Fig. 1. *No interconnection*

watch both programmes but incur the fixed connection cost twice, which is not necessary.

Wholesale Interconnection: Suppose now that the two firms agree to supply each other with their own programmes—see Figure 2 below. Specifically, suppose that for an 'access charge' of a per subscriber a firm may purchase the other firm's programmes. (Note that we assume that the interconnection contract takes the form of a per-subscriber charge, rather than say a lump-sum payment for the rights to programmes.) Given the symmetry of the industry, it makes sense to suppose that firms agree that the access charge is the same in each direction, i.e. the charge is 'reciprocal'. Given a particular choice of access charge, we assume that prices in the retail sector are chosen without co-operation.

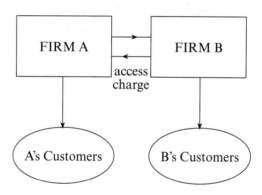

Fig. 2. *Wholesale interconnection*

Then it can be shown that, as long as the access charge is not too high, firms will choose to offer both sets of programmes to subscribers (and subscribers choose to watch both programmes). Moreover, there is a one-to-one relationship between the access charge and the final retail price (for watching both programmes): a higher access charge feeds through into a higher retail price (and higher profits for the two firms).[16] By charging a high (but not too high) reciprocal access charge, each firm is willing to buy the rival firm's programmes, which increases its cost of supply from k to $k + a$. In many cases—roughly speaking, the two sets of programmes cannot be too close substitutes—an access charge can be chosen that sustains the collusive retail price, and all consumer surplus is extracted. Because firms offer identical services at retail level, they make no profits in the retailing sector, and all profits are generated by the

---

[16] We cannot make the access charge too high, for in that case a firm would do better to serve only its own programmes (i.e. to 'bypass' the services of the rival).

wholesaling of programmes to 'rivals'. Note that it is important for the access charge to be levied on a per-subscriber basis, since this affects the marginal cost of serving subscribers—if firms just levied a lump-sum charge for the rights to screen each other's programmes then marginal costs would not be affected and collusion could not be sustained.[17]

Customer Interconnection: Finally, suppose that the two firms agree to grant each other access to their own subscribers. Specifically, suppose that for an access charge of a per subscriber one firm may use the other's delivery system to deliver its own programmes to the rival's customers—see Figure 3 below. Again, given the symmetry it makes sense to suppose that this charge is the same in each direction. Now, each firm chooses *two* retail prices: the price for watching its programmes if the customer connects to its own network, and the price for watching its programmes if the customer is connected to the rival network. Again, we assume that for a given access charge the (four) retail prices are chosen competitively.

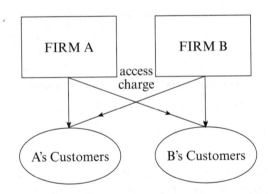

Fig. 3. *Customer interconnection*

Then it can be shown that, for a broad range of parameters (and again provided that a is not too large), equilibrium in the retail market ensures that consumers are indifferent about which firm they connect to and choose to buy both sets of programmes. The access charge affects the balance between a firm's two retail prices but not the sum; since consumers buy both sets of programmes (for a total charge equal to the sum of retail prices), this implies that the effective retail charge faced by consumers (and the profits generated

---

[17] The insight that firms have an incentive to set a high mutual access charge in order to sustain collusion in the retail sector is similar to that obtained in the telecommunications setting by Armstrong (1998); Rey and Tirole (1998).

by each firm) is not affected by a. In some cases this total charge is actually the collusive level. The access charge affects the balance of prices for directly and indirectly supplied programmes, but this has no impact on profits since the *sum* of the prices is all that matters. The collusive mechanism is quite different with customer interconnection than with wholesale interconnection. Here, there is no effect in terms of the raising marginal cost of supply. Rather, by controlling the prices of obtaining its programmes both for its own (directly connected) customers and for its rival's customers, a firm can raise its prices without putting itself at a competitive disadvantage. For instance, if a firm raises both its prices by the same amount it does not affect the relative attraction of connecting to one firm over another—both firms appear less attractive.

Discussion: The model ignores the crucial issue of how programmes are produced or otherwise obtained by firms. For instance, one could extend the model by introducing an initial stage of production where firms could choose the quality of programming at some cost. Once programmes are produced, this cost would then be sunk and the subsequent interactions could be modelled as above, and firms would choose their respective programme qualities taking the resulting returns into account. A more ambitious extension is to introduce an outside market for premium programming, where the suppliers of premium programmes would sign contracts—exclusive or otherwise—with the networks, again taking into account the subsequent interactions between the two firms.

Secondly, the model is symmetric, which may be appropriate for analysing the market in the 'long run', but it ignores important asymmetries in the early stages. For instance, if one firm is able to enter the market before other firms, then it may have an incentive to refuse to serve firms considering entry with its programmes in order to attract subscribers to its own service (who are then 'locked in', to some extent, due to the sunk cost nature of the delivery technology).

Thirdly, the fact that all subscribers were assumed to have identical tastes is unduly strong (and unrealistic). This assumption had the impact that welfare could not be adequately discussed in the model: the collusive outcome also maximised welfare. However, if subscribers differed in their tastes, then setting retail prices above costs causes dead-weight welfare losses. The same mechanisms described here should carry over to the case of differing tastes, and even if full joint profit maximisation is not quite achieved, prices substantially above costs will be induced by suitably chosen interconnection contracts.

These major limitations aside, however, I hope this simple formal model serves to illustrate the potential dangers of pay-TV firms signing mutually advantageous reciprocal contracts to (i) supply each other with pro-grammes or (ii) to give each other access to customers. Those concerned with public policy towards the industry should be prepared to invoke Article 81 [ex 85] or similar powers should such self-serving contracts be observed.

IV. Anti-Competitive Alliances Between Telephone-Only and TV-Only Firms

In this short section, we discuss further Question 6 raised in Section I.3 above. Consider three firms, denoted as *A*, *B* and *C*. Firm *A* is a telephony-only firm (such as BT in Britain), *B* is a pay TV-only firm (such as BSkyB in Britain), and *C* is a firm supplying both telephony and pay-TV services (such as the cable companies in Britain). All three firms incur fixed costs in connecting sub-scribers. Suppose that all consumers wish to purchase telephone services (over the relevant range of prices), so that that market size is fixed. Consumers who wish to purchase pay-TV services have the choice of either obtaining their joint telephony/TV services from *C* alone or by combining the services of *A* and *B*. (For simplicity, we assume that tariffs are such that all telephone-only con-sumers go to firm *A* for their service. Economies of scope between TV and tele-phone services for firm *C* imply that the vast majority of its subscribers obtain both services from it, just as happens for the cable companies in the UK.)

Suppose that firm *A*'s price is fixed by regulation, and that prohibitions on 'undue discrimination' or similar prevent *A* from charging a different telecoms price to pay-TV and non-pay-TV subscribers (as is roughly the case in Britain).[18] Given this price, the remaining two firms compete for subscribers. If competition is quite intense, it is plausible that firm *A* would like to reduce its price below the regulated level selectively to those subscribers interested in pay-TV services, since these are the only people attracted by *C*'s services. However, it is forbidden to do this, and so it has to search for another mechanism with which to achieve a similar aim.

One way to do this is to offer to subsidise *B*'s service. Thus, if *A* offers to pay *B* a certain amount for each subscriber which it signs up, this effectively reduces *B*'s fixed connection cost and causes it to compete more aggressively against its rival *C*. For instance, *A* and *B* could enter into a 'joint-venture', the

---

[18] In 1997 BT was prevented by OFTEL from entering into a marketing campaign with BSkyB to offer discounts to people who subscribed to both BT and BSkyB services as this was held to be 'undue discrimination'.

purpose of which is to subsidise access to *B*'s pay-TV network.[19] If this happens, competition between *B* and *C* will result in more subscribers going to *B* and fewer going to *C*. But fewer subscribers for *C* implies that *A* then has more subscribers (since the total number of telephone subscribers is fixed). Thus, *A* may have an incentive to subsidise *B*'s service. Whether or not it actually does have this incentive depends on how effective the subsidy is: for instance, if it costs firm *A* a subsidy to *B* of £*s* to gain (or retain) one subscriber, this is worthwhile only if *s* is less than the average profit it makes from its subscribers (or at least those subscribers attracted to pay-TV services).

But in any event, it is possible for *A* to circumvent policy restrictions on selective discounts to pay-TV subscribers by means of such joint-ventures. To the extent that such selective discounts are judged to be undesirable—an open question—policy makers should the be alert to the dangers of such joint-ventures.

V. Keeping Rivals Small

In this short section we discuss Question 5 raised in section I.3 above. To make sense of this issue, we need to use a somewhat *ad hoc* model, for reasons discussed at the end. Suppose there are three pay-TV firms bidding for some premium programming rights (such as the year's output of a Hollywood studio), these being denoted *A*, *B* and *C*. Firm *A* has the largest number of subscribers, but may be smaller or larger than the sum of subscribers of *B* and *C*. All subscribers are prepared to pay up to *v* to have access to this premium programming.

We suppose that only exclusive contracts for this premium programming are used, and that the supplier of the programming gives it to the firm (or group of firms) that make it the highest offer. We also suppose that the number of subscribers is fixed in the short term (say, because of the sunk cost nature of the access technology used by each firm), and not affected by which of the three firms obtains the rights to the premium programming. The number of subscribers of the three firms are *a*, *b* and *c* respectively (where *a* is the largest of

---

[19] As mentioned, in the UK, BT and Sky have just such a joint-venture. BT's stake of 32.5% in the joint-venture, which, at least in the short run, reportedly aims to subsidise set-top boxes by £200, could be interpreted as BT giving Sky about £65 per subscriber towards the fixed costs of connecting its subscribers. However, the presence of two other firms in the consortium, Matsushita and the Midland Bank, who do not have the same incentives as BT to damage the cable companies, suggests that other effects are also at work.

these numbers). Because these subscriber numbers are fixed, firm A is prepared to pay up to av for the programming rights (since its subscribers are each prepared to pay v to watch), and similarly for the other firms.

There are two sets of alliances to consider: one where B and C bid against A for the rights, and one where A persuades B to join forces with it to bid against C. Thus, for the purposes of illustration, we could think of A representing BSkyB in the UK and B and C representing the cable companies, with B representing CWC in the UK. (Recall from Section II.1 above that BSkyB may have persuaded CWC to cease participating in the cable companies' bid to offer a new, cable-exclusive film channel in 1997.)

There are two situations to consider. First suppose that A has the majority of subscribers, so that $a > b + c$. Thus, it will win the auction for the rights regardless of whether it has B on its side, but will make higher profits if it does persuade B to join forces. For if it acts alone A will win the rights if it pays $(b + c)v$, since this is the most that B/C can afford to pay. Therefore, by making its subscribers pay v for these programmes, it makes a net profit of $v(a - b - c)$ by winning the bid. The other firms make zero profit from this auction. But suppose now that A offers to combine forces with B. Since B makes no profit without the alliance, A only has to offer it a tiny amount to be willing to participate. Therefore, suppose A offers B the deal whereby if A/B wins the auction it will offer it the rights for v per subscriber (or a bit less to induce it to join). B will then make a tiny profit from joining the alliance. But because its opposition is now diminished, A only has to pay cv for the rights (the most that C acting on its own can pay), and so its total profits, including profits made from selling on the rights to B is $v(a + b - c)$. This is significantly greater than the case when A acted alone, and so the firm does have an incentive to 'buy off' one of its rivals when bidding for programming rights. (This argument is not affected if B secures a more significant share of the proceeds of the deal.)

A similar argument works if A's combined rivals have the majority of subscribers, i.e. when $a < b + c$. In this case, the rivals win the auction when A acts alone, and pay av for the rights (the maximum that A can pay on its own). If, as seems natural, B and C share the cost for the rights in proportion to their subscriber bases, then B's net profits from the bid are $bv(1 - a/(b + c))$. Naturally, firm A gets nothing in this situation. Now suppose A induces B to join it in the bid for the rights. A must compensate B for the profits it would have made if it had acted with C, so suppose A offers B the deal whereby if it wins the auction, it will offer B the rights for a charge of $av/(b + c)$ per subscriber. (Because B can sell on these programmes to its subscribers for v each, this gives it a total profit equal to that it received when acting with C.) A can then win the auction for cv, the most that C can afford acting alone. Therefore,

A's net profit from the deal is $(a - c)v + bv(1 - a/(b + c))$, which is certainly positive given that *A* is the largest firm. Therefore, *A* again has an incentive to pursue this strategy.

While this simple model may help explain the behaviour of BSkyB and CWC in 1997, and the subsequent collapse of a planned cable-exclusive film channel, it has a number of peculiar features which would need justifying in a fuller analysis. First, the assumption that subscriber numbers were fixed is extreme: subscribers are likely to switch supplier if another supplier obtains valuable exclusive rights. However, more puzzling is the behaviour of the original supplier of the premium programming—why does he agree to offer exclusive contracts? By selling to a subset of subscribers he makes strictly less than if he offered the rights to *all* firms for a charge of *v* per subscriber! Until we have a satisfactory explanation for the presence of exclusive contracts in the industry, it is hard to evaluate the pros and cons of a large firm attempting to keep its rivals small when bidding for programme rights.

II

Donald I. Baker*

The US Antitrust Bias Against Joint Venture Networks on Access and Exclusivity Issues

I. Introduction: Networks in our Electronic World

Networks are vital in the modern world and yet their competitive significance and the incentives to create them are frequently misunderstood. As a result, incentive-blunting antitrust policies are too often applied to them—and this is especially so of joint venture networks in the United States. The broader problem may also be present in Europe, but the European Commission and European court in general do not seem to single out a joint venture network for clearly more stringent exclusivity and access rules than those applied to a single firm network with a comparable degree of market power.

Networks can be conveniently (though roughly) categorised as:

a) Interchange networks—which enable market participants to exchange traffic, transactions, and output among themselves. Traditional examples would include a stock exchange floor or a bank-clearing house. More modern examples would include AT&T or MCI (connecting local telephone systems), Visa or MasterCard (connecting banks), or WorldCom (connecting Internet service providers).

b) 'On Us' retail networks—which offer ultimate consumers the ability to communicate with other users of the same network. The classic example would be the traditional local telephone company (such as British Telephone or New York Bell) and a new example would be a proprietary on-line computer service company (such as America Online).

My principal focus here is on interchange networks, which I shall just call 'networks.' Some interchange networks have been competitive entities organised by the natural monopoly firm(s) in different geographic markets (e.g. an international telephone network organised by local monopoly companies). At other times, such networks have been local monopolies organised by

* Baker & Miller PLC, Washington, DC. I owe very special thanks to John Temple Lang (of the European Commission's Directorate General IV), Damian Collins (of McCann Fitzgerald in Brussels), Professor Ernest Gellhorn (of Washington, D.C.) and my partner William Todd Miller for their insightful comments and questions on various aspects of earlier drafts. Needless to say, the final version is my own responsibility.

competitive firms (e.g. a bank clearing house or real estate multiple listing system). Sometimes they have been competitive systems organised by a competitive enterprise (e.g. American Airlines' Sabre reservation system) or a group of them (e.g. Visa). The basic purpose of such networks is to increase the efficiency of each 'primary' market participant or to enable each participant to offer its customers more (or a more valuable) service.

Some networks have been single firm undertakings (e.g. the Sabre reservation system or AT&T), while others have been organised as joint ventures (e.g. VISA or the New York Stock Exchange). Sometimes a joint venture network will compete against a single firm network (as Associated Press does against United Press International in wire service news or MasterCard does against American Express in payments services).

II. The Basic Antitrust Problem

A successful interchange network will often enjoy some degree of market power in the 'network' market because of economies of scope and scale—or what are now called 'network externalities.' In other words, the network becomes more valuable to each participating enterprise or ultimate user to the extent that it connects larger numbers of other users. This reality may be so strong that only one network can survive in a relevant 'network' market, or it may just mean that the number of competitors in the 'network' market are few. In any event, a successful competitor in the 'network' market can be a source of competitive advantage for its users (or owner-users) in the 'primary' market; and this reality generates many of the antitrust disputes over exclusivity and access.

The single firm network (SFN) and the joint venture network (JVN) are subjected to significantly different market power tests under the US antitrust laws. This occurs because the SFN is treated generally under the 'monopolisation' provisions of the Sherman Act §2—which requires a real showing of present or probable monopoly power and, in the absence of such power, gives the SFN a broad right to refuse to deal. Meanwhile, the JVN is subjected to the broader and perhaps less discriminating 'conspiracy,' 'restraint of trade' or 'boycott' rules of Sherman Act §1, where a much more modest showing of *market power* may be sufficient to establish liability, if the court does not accept the Defendant's justification as being legitimate (and sometimes a *per se* antitrust prohibition may even be invoked against a joint venture rule).

Thus, the SFN does not face significant antitrust risks for refusing to deal in the absence of a showing of monopoly power, while the JVN may face a 'boycott' case under Sherman Act §1, even if it has less than half the 'network' market. The broad right of a single enterprise (other than a clear monopolist) to refuse to deal is a core principle of US antitrust law enshrined in the co-called *Colgate* doctrine: it simply has no counterpart where the enterprise is labelled 'joint venture' rather than 'business corporation.'

The practical difference for the affected networks may be large. The JVN with any apparent degree of market power has to run the cost, burden, and risk of factually justifying its refusals to deal or access rules. The SFN does not—unless it is truly a monopolist.

The key question asked in this article is whether (or to what extent) a bias against JVNs represents appropriate competition policy. In asking this question, I assume that networks are becoming ever more important and creation of new networks (including JVNs) ought to be encouraged. Yet, the US approach punishes (or, at least, neutralises) JVN success—and therefore reduces the incentive of primary market participants to create a new network or to invest heavily in network expansion as a source of product differentiation or other competitive advantage vis-à-vis other 'primary' market competitors. It is often a 'competitive equality' doctrine rather than a 'competition based on efficiency' concept.[1]

Europe seems different. Under Articles 81–82 [ex 85–86] of the Consolidated Treaty, the same kind of bias against JVNs does not appear to exist to any significant degree (as discussed in Section 9 *infra*). The 'essential facilities doctrine' in Europe is more stringently applied to a market leader than would be true in the United States and most EU law in the area seems to have developed in the single firm context under Article 82 [ex 86]. It is hard to find Article 81 [ex 85] cases applying much more stringent access rules to JVNs or other joint ventures.

As international networks become ever more common, the US discrimination against JVNs takes on operational significance. It is more than just an interesting intellectual question. Successful international JVNs may be more subject to attack on access and exclusivity in the US, even though the same

---

[1] Sometimes the 'joint venture' label may be invoked to try to justify a thinly veneered cartel that simply 'manages' its members' independent competitive efforts—but a real 'network' almost by definition creates something new and interdependent and hence, generally, a network is not a candidate for 'cartel' rules when it is performing a 'network' function. Thus, when the New York Stock Exchange used to fix its owner-members retail brokerage commissions, it was not performing a 'network' function. It was managing a retail brokers' cartel. By contrast, when it sets charges for using the Exchange Floor, it is performing a 'network' function that any network has to be able to do.

network rule might be permitted in Europe. (Conversely, the European Community's more stringent 'essential facilities' doctrine, discussed in Section 9 *infra*, might result in compulsory access orders against successful international SFNs that would be unlikely to occur in the US[2]). Complainants will go to wherever the best opportunities are.

III. Competitive Relationships and the 'Network' Idea

A 'network' is concerned with both facilities and rules.

The *facilities* side is easily envisioned: big telephone switches, stock exchange floors and railroad classification yards were traditional examples. Today the 'facilities' may largely consist of traffic-handling computer programs and the big-but-ordinary computers on which they run, plus communications links by cable, satellite or microwave. How large, expensive, and long-lasting network 'facilities' are, may vary substantially from system to system and from generation to generation.

The *rules* side is more subtle, but perhaps more important. For a network to operate efficiently, its participants must agree to accept technical and operational standards for 'network' transactions—including non-discrimination rules, interface arrangements, and perhaps predetermined compensation arrangements. Such rules should be designed to avoid opportunism or uncertainty among network users, and thus, to improve the network's efficiency.

The 'network' market for interchanging transactions, traffic, or information can be contrasted in many instances with the 'primary' market, where competitors deal directly with consumers and users. Thus, in a 'primary' market, a stockbroker sells retail transaction services to investors; a bank offers cheque accounts and credit cards to consumers; a railway solicits traffic from shippers; an airline offers scheduled transportation; and an Internet service provider offers E-mail connections and Internet access.

Access to a network may be indispensable to 'primary' market competitors—depending on the nature of the 'primary' market service, and on how strong the need to interchange traffic. Or access may merely be advantageous because it involves some cost advantage over available alternatives. Smaller firms may have a stronger need to interchange traffic than larger ones because

---

[2] We certainly have some examples—most notably the Boeing-McDonnell Douglas merger in 1997—where the European Commission has applied more stringent rules than the US to a proposed integration. At the same point, the same thing is likely to happen to a SFN or a merger creating an SFN.

they generate fewer 'on us' transactions. A stock or real estate broker may be able to get significantly better prices on transactions for its clients where it has access to an efficient network.

The relationship between 'network' market provider(s) and the 'primary' market participants may vary substantially. Thus, 'network' services may be provided by:

a) an independent third party (e.g. WorldCom);
b) a joint venture of 'primary' market competitors (e.g. Visa or the New York Stock Exchange);
c) a single leading 'primary' market competitor offering 'network' services to its competitors (e.g. American Airlines Sabre reservation system);
d) an integrated primary market competitor that operates a 'captive' network (e.g. American Express payments system);
e) an independent third party offering the 'network' service directly to end-users using links provided by the 'primary' market entities (e.g. the AT&T long distance network); or
f) a governmental entity providing a 'network' service, usually on a subsidised basis for the benefit of 'primary' market participants and their customers (e.g. the Federal Reserve cheque clearing system in the US).

Important antitrust issues are most likely to arise where three conditions exist. First, substantial monopoly power exists in the 'network' market. Second, competition is limited (and substantial new entry unlikely) in the 'primary' market. Third, the network monopolist is a leading 'primary' market competitor. By contrast, however, 'antitrust mischief' is most likely to arise where:

g) workable competition exists at the 'network' level;
h) network services are differentiated (i.e. are not perceived to be essentially interchangeable);
i) one network has created a superior franchise in the minds of consumers (or primary market competitors) so that 'good will' must be added to 'facilities' and 'rules' as part of this network's profile; and
j) the network is a joint venture whose owners promote the network's (assumed) superiority in their own 'primary' market offerings.[3]

---

[3] These conditions clearly describe *Associated Press* v *United States* (discussed *infra*) and may describe the justified *United States* v *Visa USA* (*infra*).

Where the network operator does not compete (or seek to compete) in the 'primary' market, the issues fall into a *public utility regulation* model rather than an *antitrust* one.[4] The question is simply whether the government is going to seek to set or supervise the terms on which primary market competitors are going to be given access to the (assumed) network monopoly; or whether just let the parties bargain over terms. (Where the primary market competitors have the capability—and potential traffic—to create a network alternative of their own, they should be encouraged to do so if they are seriously dissatisfied in their dealings with today's non-integrated 'network' market monopolist.)

IV. Network Market Competition

Creating (or enhancing) network market competition is almost always the preferred choice from a competition policy standpoint. Two (or more) competing networks will seek more interchange traffic from 'primary' market competitors—in the absence of capacity constraints—so that supervision problems of the 'essential facilities' doctrine can be avoided. If there is enough actual or potential traffic to support at least two efficient competitors in the 'network' market, then antitrust rules ought to facilitate it—and a joint venture may be the key. By contrast, compelling access to an (assumed) monopoly network can involve difficult, and often uncertain, supervision problems.

Competition in performing the 'network' market function may threaten even the well-entrenched 'network' market monopolist, as we saw in the US in the 1970s, when MCI burst onto the scene to challenge AT&T's long-time monopoly in long-distance communications. It may come from a joint venture of users, an independent network entrepreneur, or a large 'primary' market participant. Or the monopoly network may face some form of 'bypass competition' from some (usually large) members who are able to exchange some of their traffic directly outside the facility. (Bypass competition is generally desirable where the network is a clear monopoly, but it may represent 'free-riding', where effective competition already exists in a 'network' market where product differentiation exists.[5])

The emergence of highly efficient computer and communications systems has created new opportunities for 'network' market competition. Thus, the modern network need not be tied to a particular physical location (e.g. the floor

---

[4] See the discussion of the *Official Airline Guides* decision *infra*.

[5] See *Rothery Storage & Van Co.* v *Atlas Van Lines, Inc.*, 792 F.2d 210 (D.C. Cir. 1986) cert. denied, 479 US 1033 (1987).

of the New York Stock Exchange). Instead, its central function is the inter-change of information over a (virtually) distance-insensitive set of electronic links, based on established rules and sophisticated, expensive-to-create computer programs.

Modern networks based on information-processing capability have gener-ated increased competitive opportunity in 'network' markets (and for each network to differentiate itself from other networks). The successful network competitor may, in turn, enable its user-enterprises (or joint owners) to differ-entiate themselves as 'primary' market competitors. One computer/communi-cations network may differ from another in terms of how it is configured and programmed, how fast and fail-safe it is, what information it transmits and *how it is perceived by its users,* be they 'primary market' competitors or ultimate consumers. The extent to which this type of competition occurs will depend on a variety of factors, including the willingness of network owners to accept the risks and opportunities inherent in competition at 'network' level.

Such familiar interchange networks as VISA and MCI could be called 'product-creating' networks, as opposed to the traditional 'invisible back office' networks (e.g. the New York Clearing House or the Sabre reservation system). A 'product-creating' network occurs when consumers make the affir-mative choice of which network to use (as with credit cards), rather than hav-ing the network choice entirely left to primary market competitors (as with cheque or clearing). Such a 'product creating' network not only has facilities for communications, storage, and sorting for primary market participants—key rules for transactions—but also a trademark and a message to tell the pub-lic where the network service is available. Success may require a lot of advertising and promotion by the network, or its participants, or both.

Various product creating networks have been created over the years. Those organised as joint ventures nearly all have long histories of private antitrust lit-igation. Thus, joint venture networks providing, for example, flowers by wire, one-way truck and trailer rentals, long distance household moving, automatic teller machines and credit cards have been subjected to a few government cases and many private antitrust cases.[6]

Competition in the 'network' markets has many of the same benefits asso-ciated with competition generally: network competition puts continuous cost pressure on network operators (including joint ventures); it drives prices down toward costs; and it encourages innovation and improvements in reliability. In addition, 'network' market competition can pressure the network operator

---

[6] See Robert H. Bork (1978); as a Judge, Professor Bork later decided the *Rothery Storage & Van Co.* case, *supra.*

(including a joint venture) to include features that differentiate it from other networks, thereby offering comparative advantages to 'primary' market participants.

Where networks compete, 'primary' market demand usually drives service design and differentiation at 'network' level. Aggressive 'primary' market participants may see a competitive advantage in being able to offer a differentiated 'network' service on an exclusive or, at least, quasi-exclusive basis in a local market (as the founders of Visa and Associated Press did). Allowing such exclusivity may, in turn, encourage the creation of an alternative network—either as a joint venture or as a proprietary network—to meet this opportunity.

Where the network is a monopolist, the 'network' market is more likely to be driven by paternalism (and politics), as we saw with the US long-distance telephone market prior to 1975. The monopoly network often becomes a source of covert cross-subsidies in aid of 'worthy' causes, such as below-cost service to rural or residential subscribers (which the monopolist can then use legally and politically to justify its continued monopoly status). At the same time, a network monopoly can have the same detriments generally associated with monopolies: high costs, poor service, conservatism, lack of innovation, and special deals for politically favoured users.

Sometimes, though ever less frequently, economies of scope, scale or specialisation may dictate natural monopoly as the only operationally efficient way of handling the potential traffic in a particular 'network' market, and may force regulation as a decidedly second-best solution.

V. Incentives to Create a Joint Venture Network

In an emerging 'network' market context, a joint venture may have some very practical advantages. A JVN provides a way of spreading initial costs and risks. In particular, it gives those with potential network traffic a direct economic stake in the success of the network enterprise. A JVN also allows those with complementary skills or facilities to share them. Thus, an ATM network allows the bank with cardholders in one area to offer their customers cash access at machines elsewhere—perhaps very far away—and to seek out new depositors and cardholders based on this perceived advantage.[7]

Initially, potential network partners must ask themselves whether there is sufficient demand for the potential 'network' service to justify the commercial risks and costs necessary to create the network. 'Primary' market competitors

---

[7] See Baker and Brandel (1996) at paragraphs, 6.04, 24.03[1], and 25.03.

with substantial potential 'network' traffic can use the proposed JVN to reduce their individual risks and provide necessary reassurance to each other in the crucial start-up phase. (Even so, the ultimate success is still likely to depend on how much the new 'network' service improves on existing or likely alternatives, and thereby adds value for participating 'primary' market competitors.)

The joint venture form may be especially desirable and reassuring when establishing a 'network' service of the 'product-creating' type which requires not only potential traffic volume but expensive consumer marketing to generate demand. This is because any advertising to promote a new 'product creating' network is a totally sunk cost that cannot be recovered if the network fails to attract sufficient traffic. The issue has arisen especially with banking interchange networks (for automated teller machines and point-of-sale transactions), some of which have been a lot more successful than others.

VI. The Core Conceptual Issue that Generates Discrimination

The Sherman Antitrust Act differentiates in a fundamental way between agreements and business integration and it is this differentiation that gives rise to the problem for JVNs discussed here.

Section 1 of the Sherman Act (15 USC. §1) deals with a 'contract, combination, or conspiracy . . . in restraint of trade.' The most stringent rules are those against agreements among competitors—particularly pricing agreements, customer and market allocation agreements, and coercive boycotts— and these can be punished without any showing of market power. Even less clear cut agreements (such as standards setting decisions, network rules, patent licenses) are still dealt with under a 'rule of reason' standard that requires extensive factual inquiry and uncertain case outcomes. (The formerly quite stringent approach to vertical agreements has been almost entirely eliminated, except for minimum resale pricing agreements.)

Section 2 of the Sherman Act (15 USC. §2) deals with monopolists and would be monopolists by providing three related offences—attempt to monopolise, conspiracy to monopolise and monopolisation. Attempt to monopolise and monopolisation are single-firm offences: 'a firm with a monopoly position in a market can be punished (or even dismembered) because it takes affirmative acts going beyond skill, foresight, and industry' to exclude or cripple competitors in a market. A firm that is not yet a monopolist but generates a 'dangerous probability' of obtaining a monopoly position can be punished for conduct that is predatory in the sense that it has no apparent purpose other than to injure a competitor.

The two approaches differ substantially in a basic respect. In the Section 2 monopoly area, the jurisprudence has reflected concern than antitrust rules do not punish success and efficiency. Therefore, a real showing of monopoly power (or 'dangerous probability' of same in an attempt case) is required. Moreover, a generally exhaustive inquiry is made into business justifications and efficiency implications of the particular conduct at issue. (This is precisely what is going on in Washington right now in the trial of *US* v *Microsoft* in the US District Court for the District of Columbia.) By contrast, horizontal agreements among competitors are viewed with an Adam Smith-like suspicion that competitors seldom get together for any good reason and many agreements are struck down on modest showings of market power.

For years, the courts had a great deal of difficulty in dealing with partial integration such as joint ventures; and there were a long series of cases in which the courts treated a joint venture sports league, or some other similar group, to the ordinary rules that would be applied to agreements among unintegrated, straight competitors. This produced some bizarre results in which product creating joint venturers had their internal pricing and territorial arrangements struck down *per se* by the Supreme Court, even where the joint venture (or its members) faced much larger or stronger competitors in the relevant market.[8]

The 'contract versus integration' bias runs fairly deeply throughout US law: we regularly allow mergers among parties that could not make agreements with each other over price, output or areas served. The underlying rationale is that integration by merger involves potential efficiencies and, consequently, we have had to develop rules based on market power rather than the categorisation of the agreement.

The practical difference between analysing a joint venture network (JVN) under Sherman Act §1, and a single firm network (SFN) under Sherman Act §2, shows up in the situation where the network faces competition.

a) The JVN—being a network—may well have some degree of 'market power' flowing from economies of scope, scale and/or specialisation. This may be enough to force it to face a rule of reason inquiry under Sherman Act §1, for almost any rule or decision. The outcome of such a case turns on a fact finder's determinations on the rationale for the particular rule. This inquiry involves questions on how necessary the rule is to the joint venture's function and whether it appears designed to disadvantage 'primary market' competitors. At best, the JVN faces a long and perhaps uncertain trial.

---

[8] See, *e.g. United States* v *Sealy, Inc.*, 388 US 350 (1967) and *United States* v *Topco Associates*, 414 US 801 (1973).

b) The SFN, by contrast, really does not face serious antitrust exposure unless it is a monopolist or, at least, an incipient monopolist in the 'network' market and maybe includes the primary market as well.[9]

c) Only then does it face the potential antitrust 'essential facilities' order that it provide service to disadvantaged 'primary market' competitors. The notorious Robinson-Patman Act (15 USC. §§13–14), prohibiting various kinds of pricing and other discrimination, does not apply to sales of 'services' (as opposed to 'goods'), so the monopolistic SFN has a greater ability to discriminate than would a manufacturer holding a similar degree of monopoly power.

There is also a broader issue: a joint venture must operate by 'agreements,' while a single firm operates to a greater extent by the business discretion and the judgement of those responsible for managing the enterprise. Thus, a JVN's membership rules, compulsory ruling rules or strategic decisions are all treated as horizontal 'agreements' among the members and subject to § 1. When the SFN makes a decision not to deal with a particular 'primary' market firm, that is simply a unilateral refusal to deal; and the US law gives an individual firm broad discretion to refusal to deal, even for anti-competitive reasons.[10]

The situation in the European Union is quite different for reasons that we shall see in Section 9 *infra*. First, the EU seems to have a lower market power threshold for applying the abuse provisions of Article 82 [ex 86]—so that a European SFN would be more likely than its American counterpart to be subject to a single firm abuse of dominance remedy under the 'essential facilities' doctrine or otherwise. Second, the 'essential facilities' doctrine in Europe has largely evolved in a single firm context and it does not seem to me that it is more stringently applied in a joint venture context. Third, the European Commission

---

[9] Up until 1984, the line had been sometimes blurred by the so-called 'intra-enterprise conspiracy' doctrine which allowed the parent and subsidiaries of a corporate group be charged with 'conspiracy' under Sherman Act Section 1 on the theory that they were separate legal entities; however, in *Copperweld Corporation* v *Independence Tube Co.*, 467 US 752 (1984), the Supreme Court overruled prior precedent (in a case on which I worked for the successful appellant).

[10] See *United States* v *Colgate & Co.*, 250 US 300 (1919) ('in the absence of any purpose to create or maintain a monopoly, the [Sherman] act does not restrict the long recognised right of trader or manufacturer . . . freely to exercise his own discretion as to parties with whom he will deal'). Even when the SFN enters into agreements with network users over the terms and conditions of service, these are *vertical* agreements and subject to the much more permissive rule on vertical agreements that have emerged since *Continental TV* v *GTE Sylvania*, 433 US 36 (1977) (essentially allowing vertically imposed territorial arrangements by subjecting them to rule of reason analysis).

has more flexibility than its US counterparts because it can grant an Article 81(3) [ex 85(3)] exemption for certain types of joint venture agreements that it deems to be efficiency enhancing. Fourth, the European approach to vertical agreements is generally tougher than the modern US one for a variety of policy reasons, including consideration of market integration, and thus, a European SFN that imposes vertical agreements on users may not be treated substantially differently than a European JVN imposing the same type of agreements.

VII. The Principle Sources of Joint Venture Network Confusion in the United States

The Supreme Court had three opportunities to deal with joint venture network problems in the first half of the Twentieth Century. It got the answer right the first time (in 1913), missed the boat in the second case (in 1918) and created very fundamental errors in the third case (in 1945).[11] We are still suffering— and profoundly at times—from the consequences of these last two decisions. Let us review each in turn.

1. United States v Terminal R.R. Association of St. Louis, 224 US 383 (1912)

The first of these cases involved a monopoly railroad terminal complex in St. Louis, Missouri, owned by 14 out of the 24 railroads that connected at this important railroad hub on the Mississippi River. The joint venture terminal owned the tracks that connected railroads to both the two trans-Mississippi River bridges and the ferry service that were used to interchange traffic among them. The defendant joint venture had been created by the merger of prior rail facilities and ferry owners; and the Justice Department's antitrust case sought to have the Terminal Company broken up. The Supreme Court rejected this approach in favour of a more regulatory remedy to insure that the 10 non-owner railroads could become owners, if they wished, on equal terms or could obtain equal access.

What is so important is how the Court explained its novel remedy. To start with, it emphasised that the joint venture had clear monopoly power:

---

[11] I have reviewed these decisions in detail elsewhere, Baker (1993).

The result of the geographical and topographical situation is that it is, as a practical matter, impossible for any railroad company to pass through, or even enter St. Louis . . . without using the facilities entirely controlled by the Terminal Company.' (224 US at 397.)

This crucial predicate was not always recognised in the later cases imposing compulsory membership or access remedies on joint ventures (as we shall see in discussing the *Associated Press* case *infra*).

Secondly, the Court recognised the importance of the 'network' concept— which is why it rejected the Government's request that the terminal be broken up. '[Terminal systems] are a modern revolution in the doing of railway business and are of the greatest public utility. They, under proper conditions, do not restrain, but promote commerce.'[12]

Essentially, on its own motion, the Court developed the basic concept for the modern 'essential facilities' doctrine. Its remand told the District Court to 'provide for the admissions of any existing or future railway to joint ownership and control of the combined terminal properties, upon such just and reasonable terms as shall place such an applying company upon a plane of equality in respect to benefits *and burdens* with the [14 original owners].' The District Court was also told to provide access to the terminal facilities for the non-owners 'upon such just and reasonable terms and regulations as will in respective use, character, and cost of service, place every such company upon as nearly an equal plane as may be with respect to expenses and charges as that occupied by the [owner] companies.[13] Note that the Court recognised implicitly the 'free-rider' problem, when it sought to assure that new members share the founders' burdens.

Thus, in its first chance, very early in Sherman Act history, the Supreme Court crafted an appropriate remedy predicated on monopoly power at 'network' level. This decision did not create any discrimination against any JVN, because the SFN with the same degree of market power, would be subject to a similar kind of 'reasonable access' remedy (as we shall see in discussing the *Otter Tail Power* in Section 8 *infra*).

2. Chicago Board of Trade v United States, 246 US 231 (1918)

The Supreme Court's second effort, only five years later, was far less insightful. The defendant Board of Trade, a joint venture of grain warehouseman,

---

[12] *Ibid.* at 402.

[13] *Ibid.* 411–12 (emphasis added).

brokers, and traders located in Chicago, was clearly the dominant commodities market in the Mid-West and probably in the whole country. The Justice Department challenged its rule that prevented members from doing trades overnight at any price other than the closing exchange price. This was thus a price fixing rule imposed by those controlling a dominant market.

The District Court struck the rule down without an opinion, while the Supreme Court reversed in a much-quoted opinion by that celebrated American jurist Justice Louis Brandeis. It was here that he spelled out his classic articulation of the rule of reason: 'the true test of reality is whether the restraint imposed is such as merely regulates and perhaps promotes competition or whether it is such as may suppress or even destroy competition. To determine that question the court must ordinarily consider the facts peculiar to the business to which the restraint is applied; the conditions before and after the restraint was imposed; the nature of the restraint and its effect, actual or probable.'[14]

The dictum is fine, but the way that the Court applied it was not. First, the Court essentially ignored the defendant's substantial degree of monopoly power at 'network' level and failed to recognise that the night trading was a form of 'bypass competition' which should generally be allowed in a monopoly network context. Second, the Court, instead, focused on the fact that the night trading was done by a few larger traders and the smaller Board of Trade members did not like it. Justice Brandeis, a classic populist, thought that the competitive disadvantage of the smaller 'primary' market competitors justified the anti-bypass rule.[15] Third, the real harm in Justice Brandeis' opinion was that it completely ignored the monopoly power issue at the 'network' market level and created a rule of reason test that was so unfocussed as to turn Sherman Act §1 investigations and cases against JVNs into long, expensive and often-unstructured proceedings.

3. Associated Press v United States, 326 US 1 (1945)

This case gave the Supreme Court its first chance to deal with modern information-based JVN and the Court got it wrong. It allowed populism to tri-

---

[14] 246 US at 238.

[15] Professor Robert Bork labelled this as 'a most unhappy performance by Justice Brandeis' and 'nothing more or less than judicial subjectivism', *supra*, n . In any event, the result turned out to be quaint: the modern global economy (which has no doubt eroded the market power of the Chicago Board of Trade) has forced it, and its offspring the Chicago Board Options Exchange, to go to round-the-clock electronic trading.

umph over efficiency and product differentiation in a competitive 'network' market.

At the time of the decision, there were three news services in the United States—Associated Press (AP) which was a joint venture of a number of prominent newspapers from around the country, United Press (UP) which, owned by the Hearst Company, was offered to other newspapers on a subscription basis, and International News Service (INS) which was another proprietary organisation. AP was the largest of the three, but was not indisputably dominant. It had about 50% of the 'network' market in wire service news. Some newspapers subscribed to two or more of these services. AP had a rule that allowed a local AP member to veto membership for a competing local paper in the same market. The theory of the AP rule was that AP stories were a source of differentiation in the local market and a member was entitled to preserve that differentiation.

The Justice Department challenged the rule as a horizontal boycott and sought to have it invalidated. The Government prevailed in the Supreme Court in a very populist plurality opinion written by Justice Hugo Black (i.e. no Supreme Court majority agreed on any opinion).

Essentially, AP had started off as a joint venture under which each member got the right to use copyrighted news stories generated by others. In time, it added its own reporting staff and also generated its own AP stories and photographs. It was successful and thought, by a number of the jurists, to be better in quality than its two wire service competitors, and thus to create competitive advantage for its members in their local 'primary' markets.

Justice Black's plurality opinion simply side-stepped the market power issue, and the presence of two substantial (albeit smaller) competitors. Instead, like Justice Brandeis in *Chicago Board of Trade*, he focused on the disadvantage to 'primary' market competitors from a particular form of competition in the 'network' market. In doing so, he articulated some sweeping anti joint venture language:

> The Sherman Act was specifically intended to prohibit independent businesses from becoming 'associates' in a common plan which is bound to reduce their competitor's [sic] opportunity to buy or sell the things in which the groups compete. Victory of a member of such a combination over its business rivals achieved by such collective means, cannot consistently with the Sherman Act or with practical, every day knowledge, be attributed to *individual* 'enterprise and sagacity'; such hampering of business rivals can only be attributed to that which only makes it possible—the collective power of an unlawful combination. That the object of sale is the creation or product of a man's ingenuity does not alter this principle.[16]

---

[16] *Ibid* at 15.

According to Justice Black, each AP member 'surrendered himself completely to the control of the association' and the association passed rules which could not be considered 'normal and usual agreements in aid of trade and commerce.'[17]

Justice Roberts challenged this analysis in his strong dissent, urging that '[w]e must not confuse the intent of the members with the size of their organisation.' Justice Roberts stressed that AP was treated more harshly than its competitors just because it was a joint venture:

> The argument of the Government seems to assume that UP and INS, independent corporations, in spite of their size, are not monopolies or attempts to monopolise because they deal at arm's length with their patrons whereas there is something sinister about AP *because it deals on the same terms with its own members* . . . significant feature of the practices of the one is absent in those of the others.[18]

The difference is, of course, that Justice Black treated AP as a vast 'continuing conspiracy' of its members, while he saw its rivals—UP and INS—just as business corporations whose relationships with newspapers were purely vertical. On the other hand, the local licensing practices of UP and INS show quite clearly that local exclusivity was a regular and ordinary part of the news service relationships with newspapers. This is terribly important because it should bring into play the ancillary restraints doctrine of antitrust under which parties can justify an exclusivity rule.

The *Associated Press* plurality opinion clearly created a compulsory access rule of JVNs, going far beyond the precise conditions and limitations in *St. Louis Terminal*. First, its dangerously vague conception of 'conspiracy' reflects a very strong hostility to limited collaboration among competitors seeking to create something new. Second, it assumes away the importance of competition at the network level, so long as the primary market competitor is disadvantaged. Third, it is inconsistent with the whole thrust of modern intellectual property law, where governmentally created and protected property rights are viewed as an incentive to innovation and effort. The Court's remedy was, in effect, a compulsory copyright licence.[19]

---

[17] *Ibid* at 19.

[18] *Ibid* at 45 (emphasis added).

[19] The *Associated Press* decree turned out to be very bad for the continuation of the intense competition between AP and its two 'wire service news' competitors (i.e. 'network' market competition). Most newspapers joined the Associated Press, so that it became a utility that offered no product differentiation in local markets. The competing wire services declined, UP and INS merged (into UPI), and continued to

Overall, a vague rule of compulsory access to competitive JVNs flowing from the plurality opinion in *Associated Press* would tend to (1) encourage future antitrust litigation among the reluctant bedfellows; or (2) lead to the abandonment of a JVN's 'goodwill' or 'differentiation' rather than accept litigation risks and costs (as we have seen in bank JVNs); or (3) lead to reduced long-run actual and potential competition at the 'network' level (as we have seen in news wire services and credit cards); or (4) result in a tendency for differentiated network offerings to come from SFNs rather than JVNs (as we have also seen in news wire services).

The antitrust history of joint ventures was complicated further by post-*Associated Press* decisions involving non-network type joint ventures, in which the Supreme Court became even more willing to equate 'joint venture' with 'cartel' concepts with 'naked agreements' concepts, and thus to apply *per se* rules to the joint venture rules with little or no regard for the relative efficiencies of the former. [20]

Things have begun to change and joint ventures are now more often subjected to the rule of reason. The key modern landmark in the joint venture area is the *Broadcast Music* decision in 1979, in which the Supreme Court stated that 'easy labels do not always supply ready answers' and that a literal approach to *per se* rules can be 'overly simplistic and often over broad.'[21] The Court held that a joint venture representing the interests of a very large number of musical composers was entitled to license a large library of compositions by many different composers at a single package price without incurring the wrath of a *per se* prohibition against price fixing. The Court explained:

> [O]ur inquiry must focus on whether the effect and, here because it tends to show effect,. . . the purpose of the practice are to threaten the proper operation of our predominantly free-market economy—that is, whether the practice facially appears to be one that would always, or almost always, tend to restrict competition and decrease output,. . . or instead one designed to 'increase economic efficiency and render markets more, rather than less, competitive.'[22]

---

decline. Meanwhile, the traditional AP leaders (*New York Times, Los Angeles Times, Washington Post, Chicago Tribune*, etc.) created their own syndicated services that could be offered to local newspapers on an exclusive basis. See Baker, *supra* n , and the discussion of *Paddock Publications* v *Chicago Tribune Co.*, 103 F.3d 45 (7th Cir. 1996) *infra*.

[20] See, *United States* v *Sealy, Inc.*, 388 US 350 (1967) (pricing rules), and *United States* v *Topco Associates, Inc.*, 405 US 596 (1972) (territorial limitations on numbers).

[21] *Broadcast Music, Inc.* v *Columbia Broadcasting System, Inc.*, 441 US 1 (1979).

[22] *Ibid* at 19–20.

Six years later, in *Northwest Wholesale,* the Supreme Court held that the exclusion of a competitor from a wholesale purchasing co-operative which lacked market power should be subject to rule-of-reason analysis rather than being banned outright as a boycott under the *per se* doctrine.[23]

The net result of the Court's changed approach is that, today, a joint venture with a plausible efficiency reason for its existence can be reasonably sure that its particular membership and operating rules will be subject to fact-intensive review under the rule of reason or the 'essential facilities' doctrine—with the outcome turning on particular facts and the fact-finder's impression of them.[24] Regardless of outcome, the process is expensive for the JVN and the ongoing uncertainty is often debilitating.

VIII. Single Firm Networks Face More Certainty and Less Populism in Making Decisions on Exclusivity and Access

1. Refusals to Deal by Competitors

It is a cornerstone of the US antitrust system (under the so-called *Colgate* doctrine) that a competitor can refuse to deal for whatever reason it chooses and can threaten in advance to do so if the other party fails to do what it wants.[25] This is subject to the limited qualification (under Section 2) that a monopolist who competes in a dependent market may be compelled to deal with its competitors in that market.

What this means is that an SFN is only required to deal with its competitors in the 'primary' market if it is monopolist in the 'network' market. If the SFN does not compete in the 'primary' market, it is free to use its 'network' monopoly in arbitrary ways under the antitrust laws (in the absence of some other regulatory regime, e.g. that established by the Federal Communications Act, 47 USC. §101).

---

[23] See *Northwest Wholesale Stationers, Inc.* v *Pacific Stationery & Printing Co.*, 472 US 284 (1985).

[24] See *Board of Regents* v *NCAA*, 468 US 85 (1984) (joint venture found liable on exclusivity rule) and *SCFC* v *Visa USA, Inc.*, 36 F.3d 598 (10th Cir. 1994) *cert. denied* 515 US 1152 (JVN membership rule sustained after a contrary jury verdict).

[25] *United States* v *Colgate & Co.*, 250 US 300 (1919), discussed in n *supra*.

2. Leading Cases on Monopolists

There are relatively few Supreme Court decisions involving compulsory dealing by monopolists (and only two of them involved what might be regarded as 'network' markets). In addition, there are at least four critical Court of Appeals decisions that we should consider as part of a chronological review.

a) Eastman Kodak v Southern Photo Co., 273 US 359 (1927)
This landmark, decided eight years after *Colgate*, sets the duty of a monopolist to deal with its downstream competitors on reasonable terms. The plaintiff, a photographic stock house in Atlanta, purchased goods on the same terms as other Kodak dealers, but in 1910 Kodak unsuccessfully attempted to purchase the plaintiff's business. Kodak subsequently refused to sell its goods to the plaintiff at the normal dealers' discount—so the plaintiff claimed—in furtherance of the purpose to monopolise interstate trade in photographic supplies. In support of its allegations, the plaintiff had introduced evidence that Kodak had secured control of 75–80% of the market by acquisitions of competitors and the dismantling of facilities. The Supreme Court found that, even though there was no direct evidence that Kodak's refusal to sell to the plaintiff was in pursuance of the purpose to monopolise, the evidence disclosed circumstances that would support a jury finding that Kodak's refusal was pursuant to such a plan.

b) Otter Tail Power Co. v United States, 410 US 366 (1973)
This is the first clear Supreme Court decision under Section 2 in the 'network' market. The defendant was a dominant regional electric utility which generated power, and transmitted it over the only transmission system available (i.e. it was a monopolist in the 'network' market for transmission). The defendant sold power to retail customers in those areas where it had been granted franchises by the local government. Several local communities discontinued their Otter Tail franchises and took over their own electric retail distribution. Otter Tail refused to supply them power or to 'wheel' power to them from government agencies or other bulk power suppliers. This refusal to deal and wheel by a monopolist was held to violate Sherman Act §2, because it was done to eliminate potential retail competition.

*c) Official Airline Guides, Inc. v Federal Trade Commission, 630 F.2d 920
  (2nd Cir.) cert. denied, 450 US 917 (1981)*
The Commission (in a thoughtful opinion by then Commissioner Robert Pitofsky) had ordered the sole provider of published airline flight schedule

information to publish listings of connecting flights of commuter airlines, even though the respondent did not compete in the relevant markets. The Second Circuit upheld the Commission's factual findings that the failure to publish these listings was arbitrary and had an adverse effect on competition between the traditional main airlines (United, Delta, etc.) and the regional commuter air carriers. The court refused, however, to affirm the FTC's holding that arbitrary conduct by a monopolist, causing injury in a market in which the monopolist does not operate, was unlawful under Section 5 of the Federal Trade Commission Act, 15 USC. §45. 'We think that even a monopolist, as long as he has no purpose to restrain competition and does not act coercively, retains this [*Colgate*] right.'[26] The Second Circuit concluded that 'enforcement of the FTC's Order here would give the FTC too much power to substitute its own business judgement for that of the monopolist in any decision that arguably affects competition in another industry.'[27]

d) *MCI Communications Corp. v AT&T, 708 F.2d 1081 (7th Cir.), cert. denied, 464 US 891 (1983)*

This decision is the most frequently cited compulsory access standard in the network context. MCI had burst upon the scene as AT&T's major rival in long distance communications. This case asserted that AT&T had improperly refused MCI's access to the local monopoly network that AT&T controlled. The Seventh Circuit, relying on *Otter Tail*, held that MCI had proven 'that it was technically and economically feasible for AT&T to have provided the requested interconnections, and that AT&T's refusal to do so constituted an act of monopolisation.'[28] The court explained that '[s]uch a refusal may be unlawful because a monopolist's control of an essential facility (sometimes called a 'bottleneck') can extend monopoly power from one stage of production to another, and from one market into another. Thus, the antitrust laws have imposed on firms controlling an essential facility the obligation to make the facility available on non-discriminatory terms.'[29] The court's weighing of issues is clearly set out in this interesting passage:

---

[26] 630 F.2d at 927–28.

[27] To me, it seems reasonably clear that, had Respondent been a significant competitor in the air transportation markets, the FTC's Order would have been upheld. In the US , a monopolist seems to have a lot of room to refuse to serve, so long as its victim is not a competitor in some market.

[28] 708 F.2d at 1133.

[29] *Ibid.* at 1132.

Otter Tail provides an analogy to the instant problem. AT&T had complete control over the local distribution facilities that MCI required. The interconnections were essential to MCI to offer [its own competing long distance] service. The facilities in question met the criteria of 'essential facilities' and that MCI could not duplicate Bell's local facilities. Given present technologies, local telephone service is generally regarded as a natural monopoly and is regulated as such. It would not be economically feasible for MCI to duplicate Bell's local distribution facilities (involving millions of lines of cables and lines to individual homes and businesses), and regulatory authorisation could not be obtained for such an uneconomical duplication.'[30]

Since AT&T had no persuasive business or technical reasons for denial of access, the denial was held improper.

The *MCI* decision is celebrated because it articulated four elements necessary to establish this right of access: (1) control of the essential facility by a monopolist; (2) a competitor's inability practically or reasonably to duplicate the essential facility; (3) the denial of the use of the facility to a competitor; and (4) the feasibility of providing a facility.[31] It is the 'essential facilities' test that must frequently be referred to in relocation to single firm monopolists.[32]

e) Aspen Skiing Co. v Aspen Highlands Skiing Corp., 472 US 285 (1985)
The defendant operated three of the four ski areas in the famous resort in Aspen, Colorado; the plaintiff operated the fourth. The jury had found 'Aspen skiing' (rather than 'destination skiing') to be a relevant market and hence the defendant was dominant enough to be treated as a monopolist. For many seasons, going back to the time when there were three ski operators in Aspen, the parties had offered an 'all Aspen' ski ticket to allow the skiers to use the lifts at all four locations. Historically, the revenues from the 'all Aspen' ticket had been allocated on the basis of the usage; but the defendant began to force the plaintiff's share downward. Eventually, the defendant required the plaintiff to accept a fixed percentage of ticket revenues less than historical usage, and forced the sharing formula even lower the next year. After the parties ultimately proved unable to agree on a formula, the plaintiff attempted to market its own multi-area package, but was thwarted by the defendants' efforts to make such marketing 'extremely difficult.'[33] The defendant's decision to terminate the long-standing joint marketing arrangement, which the Court characterised as 'a decision by a monopolist to make an important *change* in the

---

[30] *Ibid.* at 1133.
[31] *Ibid.* at 1132–33.
[32] See ABA Antitrust Section, *Antitrust Developments*, (ABA 1997:276–277)
[33] 472 U.S., at 593–4.

character of the market',[34] coupled with the jury's apparent conclusion that there were no valid business reasons for this conduct, led the Court to find that the defendant's actions could properly be described as 'exclusionary, and hence illegal.

f) Alaska Airlines v United Airlines, 498 F.2d 536 (9th Cir. 1991)
Here, the 'network' market was 'computerised reservation systems' (CRS). In 1976, each of the defendant airlines (United and American) had established its own CRS after an industry joint venture CRS system had fallen apart for lack of funding. The plaintiffs, unintegrated airline competitors, objected to what they regarded as the high fees charged to them for listings on these two systems. They made 'essential facilities' and 'monopoly leveraging' claims that were rejected by the Ninth Circuit in sustaining summary judgments for the defendant. The court downplayed each CRS-operator's monopoly power. It emphasised that the CRS operators, which competed against each other and the plaintiffs in the air transportation market, each had less than 20% of the airline market and therefore had to get other airlines to list their flights on their own CRS. Thus, neither system was an 'essential facility.' The court explained:

> Although each defendant may have gained some leverage over its competitors through control of its CRS, each defendant's power fell far short of the power to *eliminate* competition seen in *Otter Tail* and *MCI*. At most, defendants gained a monetary profit at their rivals' expense. The exercise of this limited power is not actionable under Section 2.
>
> Our view of the essential facilities *doctrine* does not render the doctrine superfluous or otherwise inappropriately curtail its reach. When a firm's power to exclude rivals from a facility gives the firm the power to *eliminate* competition in a market downstream from the facility, and the firm excludes at least some if its competitors, the danger that the firm will monopolise the downstream market is clear. In this circumstance, a finding of monopolisation, or at least attempted monopolisation, is appropriate. . .'[35]

g) Eastman Kodak Co. v Image Technical Services, Inc., 504 US 541 (1992)
The defendant, Kodak, the manufacturer of large photocopying machines, had instituted a new policy of (a) refusing to provide spare parts and manuals to independent service organisations (ISOs) and (b) requiring that any purchaser obtain its servicing from Kodak, unless it were sufficiently large to have its own in-house servicing organisation. A reversal of the summary judgment for

---

[34] *Ibid*, at 604.
[35] *Ibid*. (emphasis in original).

Kodak was upheld on the grounds that there were disputed issues of fact regarding whether competition in the new-machine market would prevent Kodak from behaving monopolistically in after-markets for spares and repairs: 'Kodak's theory, although perhaps intuitively appealing, may not accurately explain the behaviour of the primary and derivative markets for complex durable goods: the existence of information and switching costs.' In other words, the patented Kodak equipment was assumed to give rise to separate markets in repair services and spare parts which Kodak could monopolise or attempt to monopolise. Dealing with the Section 2 claim, the majority stated that the conduct element of the offence was 'the use of monopoly power 'to foreclose competition, and to gain a competitive advantage, or to destroy a competitor.'' In dealing with Kodak's refusal to sell parts to ISOs, the Court commented in a footnote, 'it is true that as a general matter a firm can refuse to deal with its competitor. But such a right is not absolute; it exists only if there are legitimate competitive reasons for the refusal (*Aspen Skiing Co.* v *Aspen Highlands Skiing Corp.*). . .'[36]

h) Paddock Publications v Chicago Tribune Co. et al, 103 F.3d 42 (7th Cir. 1996) rehearing denied 103 F.3d 42, cert. denied 117 S.Ct. 2435 (1997)
This case, like *Associated Press,* involved a news service, but this time a single firm news service. The plaintiff, a publisher of local newspapers in Chicago, challenged the exclusivity agreements entered into by several 'supplemental news services' (e.g. *New York Times* syndicated service, King Features) with one or the other of the two leading Chicago papers (the *Tribune* and the *Sun Times*). The Court recognised what the *AP* court had not: 'Exclusivity is one valuable feature the service offers, for a paper with exclusive rights to a service or feature is both more attractive to readers and more distinctive from its rivals'. It went on to say, 'this is fundamentally an 'essential facilities' claim— but without any essential facility . . . [T]he existence of three competing facilities not only means that none is an 'essential facility' but also means that each of the three is entitled to enter an exclusive contract with a favoured user'.

3. Net Reckoning

A true network monopolist that competes with others in a dependent market will have to allow access on reasonable terms under the principles announced

---

[36] Query whether the Supreme Court would have said this had Kodak not *changed* its original policy of selling to ISOs. Note that in *Aspen,* too, the Defendant had changed its prior policy.

in *Otter Tail Power* and *MCI Communications*. On the other hand, an SFN that is strong but faces competition in the 'network' market appears free to refuse to grant access (as illustrated by *Alaska Airlines* and *Paddock Publications*). Here is where the differences with JVNs is most clear, because under *Associated Press* and its progeny such a JVN may still be compelled to grant access in such circumstances. The fact that *Paddock Publications* and *Associated Press* occurred in the same kind of copyrighted news market and yet came out with opposite answers underscores the point.

IX. A Brief Comparison: Network Exclusivity and Access Under Articles 81–82 [ex 85–86]

The European Union has developed an extensive and elaborate jurisprudence on 'essential facilities' and duty to supply doctrines.[37] Most of this has been based on the 'abuse of dominance' principles under Article 82 [ex 86] of the Consolidated Treaty.

It seems quite clear that the EU applies the same basic 'essential facilities' and exclusive dealing rules to joint ventures and single firms—using market power and 'essentiality' tests. This is quite a robust doctrine because European enforcers and courts have been willing to use narrower markets (which generate higher market shares) and lower market share tests in determining 'market dominance' under Article 82 [ex 86].

The clear majority of the Commission cases and European court decisions on essential facilities involve single firms. Because the Commission has seemed more sympathetic to the plight of those foreclosed and less reluctant to take on the 'regulatory' burden of determining 'reasonable' access than most American courts and antitrust enforcers have been, it has built up a substantially richer body of jurisprudence defining 'essential facilities' and 'reasonable access'.[38]

---

[37] See the especially illuminating and comprehensive review of the EU's efforts by John Temple Lang, James Venit and John Kallaugheat the 1994 Fordham Antitrust Conference, Temple Lang (1994); Venit and Kallaugher (1994).

[38] This includes providing for reasonable cost recovery by the dominant firm whose 'essential facilities' must be opened to access by a competitor. See ITT-Belgacom, *27th Competition Policy Report*, (ITT-Belgacom 1997) at 152, involving telephone directory information. Reasonable cost recovery is clearly important to avoid free-riding and the Commission and European Courts seem willing to tackle the issue. (US enforcers and courts tend to try to shift the price setting burden to a regulatory agency, as the Supreme Court did in *St. Louis Terminal* and *Otter Tail Power*.

Quite a number of the Commission's single firm 'essential facilities' cases involve 'network' environments. One type involved airline CRS systems controlled by a major carrier on relevant routes.[39] Another type involved control of ferry facilities and harbours to favour the leading ferry operator.[40] These seem to involve some situations where more than one firm in the same market could be deemed to 'essential,' or rested on lower market share thresholds than the US courts would require in determining 'monopoly' power under *Otter Tail* and *MCI*.

The Commission's joint venture network cases have focused hard on market dominance—either at network level or 'primary' market level—and seem not to set standards that go beyond what would have been applied to SFNs. Some cases have involved access to a JVN for which there was no apparent substitute.[41] Others have involved access to historic local monopolies of the JVN partners to assure that others can effectively compete against the JVN in the 'network' market (for global services). The important *Phoenix/Global One* case[42] involved a non-European carrier (Sprint) and led to a parallel order in the United States.[43] Other examples involved equal access rules directed at the historic monopoly telephone companies in France, Germany, Sweden, Holland and Switzerland, which were partners in new global JVNs.[44] In all of these cases, the Commission seemed to assume that the 'network' market for global business communications was very competitive.

Several of the EU's single firm essential facilities cases offer particularly interesting contrasts to the US experience.

1. United Brands Co. v Commission, Case 27/76, [1978] ECR 207

This case illustrates the point that the 'dominant firm,' the party with the essential facility, need not compete in the downstream (or 'primary') market. The Commission's order required the banana company to supply a distributor with

---

[39] See *Amadeus/Sabre, 21st Report on Competition Policy*, Amadeus/Sabre (1992) and *London European-Sabena*, OJ L 317/47 (1988) (Commission).

[40] See *Sea Containers v Stena Sealink*, 94/19/EEC, OJ L 15/88 (1994) (Commission), and *Port of Rødby*, 94/119/EEC, OJ L 55/52 (1994) (Commission).

[41] See *La Poste/Swift + GUF*, OJ C 335 (1997) (interbank payments network).

[42] Decision 94/547/EEC, OJ L 239, (1996)

[43] *US v Sprint Corp.*, 1996–1 Trade Cas. (CCH) ¶ 71,300 (D.D.C. 1996) (consent decree).

[44] *Atlas*, Case IV/35.337, OJ L 239 (1994) and *Unisource-Uniworld*, 97/780/EEC, L 318 (1997).

whom it did not compete. In discussing this case—which might just be regarded as vertical coercion to encourage downstream exclusivity—Mr. Temple Lang notes, 'What the Commission now calls essential facility cases were simply merged with what was regarded as the general class of cases in which dominant companies have a duty to supply, and it was not thought necessary even to distinguish between supply to competitors and customers not in competition with the dominant supplier.'[45]

2. Stena Sealink, [1992] 5 CMLR 255 (Commission)

This case involved allocation of harbour space and departure times for the UK-Ireland ferry service operating out of Holyhead harbour. The 'dominant' company controlled the harbour and the Commission entered an order regulating scheduled departure times because the Respondent had scheduled its ferries to interfere with the Complainant's operation.

3. Radio Telefis Eireann v EEC,[1995] 4 CMLR 718 ('Magill')

The European Court of Justice upheld 'essential facilities' decisions by both the Commission and the Court of First Instance requiring access to program listings from leading television networks that competed with others in providing their markets. The respondents were three broadcasters whose programs reached 'most households in Ireland and 30% to 40% of the households in Northern Ireland.' (Para. 6). Each published a program listing magazine and authorised newspapers to publish daily listing. They refused to let McGill have listing information so that it could publish a magazine covering all channels. In the Court's judgment, copyrighted program schedule information was treated as 'essential' because, without it, nobody could create a program magazine to compete with each network's own program guide. The Advocate General had recommended against this result.

Thus it would appear that *Official Airline Guides, Alaska Airlines*, and possibly *Paddock Publications* might well have had different outcomes had they been decided in Europe.

Yet, the gap between Europe and the United States on the SFN front appears to have been narrowed by the Court of Justice's acceptance of Advocate General Jacobs' opinion in *Oscar Brunner GmbH & Co.* v *Mediaprint*

---

[45] *Supra*, Fordham n at. 250.

Zeitungs,[46] where a local newspaper was seeking compulsory access to the newspaper delivery system of Austria's largest newspaper chain (which had about 47% of the country's circulation). The Advocate General had asserted that there are substitutes (although less comprehensive) and warned of the danger of excessive reliance on 'essential facilities' principles in potentially competitive situations. The key thing, said the Court, was not whether a small newspaper such as the plaintiff could establish its own delivery system—but whether another newspaper similar to the respondent could do so. Thus:

> For such access to be capable of being regarded as indispensable, it would be necessary at the very least to establish, as the Advocate General has pointed out at Point 68 of his Opinion, that it is not economically viable to create a second home-delivery scheme for the distribution of daily newspapers with a circulation comparable to that of the daily newspapers distributed by the existing scheme.'[47]

It was not clear to the Court that no other alternatives existed. Accordingly, it answered the question presented by the Austrian national court as follows:

The refusal by a press undertaking which holds a very large share of the daily newspaper market in a Member State and operates the only nation-wide newspaper home-delivery scheme in that Member State to allow the publisher of a rival newspaper, which by reason of its small circulation is unable, either alone or in co-operation with other publishers, to set up and operate its own home-delivery scheme in economically reasonable conditions, and to have access to that scheme for appropriate remuneration does not constitute the abuse of a dominant position within the meaning of Article 82 [ex 86] of the Consolidated Treaty.[48]

The *Magill* decision was distinguished on the ground that involved 'exceptional circumstances' in that it 'concerned a product . . . the supply of which was indispensable for carrying on the business in question' and the refusal 'was not justified by objective considerations'.[49]

Even after *Oscar Bronner*, the European approach still seems less likely to be wedded to a strong *Colgate*-like premise that any non-monopolist power is entitled to refuse to deal and, even a monopolist is entitled to refuse to deal with non-competitors. Rather, the core European idea may still be well captured in Mr. Temple Lang's opening statement (made before the Court's judgments in *McGill* and *Oscar Bronner*:

---

[46] C–7/97 [1998] ECR I–7791.
[47] *Ibid*, at Para. 46.
[48] Para. 50.
[49] Para. 40.

. . . if one competitor owns something for which access is essential to enable other competitors to do business, and which they cannot be expected to provide for themselves, European Community competition law obliges the owner of the essential facility to give equal access to its competitors because of the effect of a refusal of access on competition. This principle . . . that companies in dominant positions have a legal duty to provide access to genuinely essential facilities on a non-discriminatory basis is one of great and increasing importance. . .'[50]

The net effect would seem to be that:

a) an SFN is more likely to be forced under the 'essential facilities' theory to deal with competitors in Europe than in the US;
b) a JVN may be even more likely to be forced under a 'boycott' theory to deal with competitors in the US than in Europe; and
c) Europe seems more likely to achieve comparable enforcement parity between SFNs and JVNs on access questions than is true in the US.

Finally, I would note that the European Union has had a great deal of difficulty in trying to characterise joint ventures for merger analysis. It has tried to draw a line between 'co-operative' joint ventures subject to Article 81 [ex 85] and 'concentrative' joint ventures subject to the Merger Regulation. The task of drawing the line turned out to be difficult at best; consequently, it was abandoned and replaced with the concept of a 'full function' joint venture 'performing on a lasting basis all the functions of an autonomous business entity' in the 1998 Merger Regulation Amendments. This seems to me to be a conceptual step towards treating full function JVNs more like ordinary business enterprises and, as such, is a step forward.

X. Conclusion

The US seems bogged down in antitrust history at a time when clear thinking about networks and market power in 'network' markets is increasingly needed. In dealing with access to JVNs, our enforcers and courts have often given insufficient weight to competition at network level and the practical advantages to network users of having a more competitive 'network' market rather than a single 'open access' JVN monopoly utility. As *Paddock Publications* and *Alaska Airlines* illustrate, the courts have not generally applied the same principle to SFNs.

---

[50] *Supra*, Fordham n at 245.

The legal rules on JVN access were unnecessarily confused by the Supreme Court's *Associated Press* decision in 1945. Since then, an antitrust cloud has hung over joint efforts to create anything new and necessary in network markets. The historical body of thinking has rested on a somewhat obsolete view of antitrust law which placed more weight on competitive equality than on efficient competition. It has failed sufficiently to consider that the primary purpose of free markets is to provide incentives to pioneers to work hard and take risks, and thereby to maximise consumer choice.

These issues of discrimination against JVNs are apparently raised by the Justice Department's very recent complaint against Visa and MasterCard (a case in which I am involved).[51] The Department does focus on a 'network' market, apparently emphasising the product creating aspects more than the interchange aspects; and it does seem to reflect some special solicitude for Visa's and MasterCard's two main 'network' market competitors, American Express and Dean Morgan Stanley/Dean Witter, while downplaying the highly visible 'network' competition between Visa and MasterCard.

All this recent excitement, of course, still highlights, but does not answer, the question of whether it is wise competition policy for the United States to pursue anti-trust cases that echo *Associated Press* and which treat prominent and successful JVNs to more stringent access and exclusivity rules than successful SFNs are subject to.

Why is not something akin to the SFN standard the right one to apply to a permanent JVN that faces active competition in the 'network' market? Could we not take a page or two out of the Supreme Court's *Copperweld* decision and the European Union's amended Merger Regulation? Where a network is what the EU calls a 'full function' joint venture which has its own management, institutional infrastructure, interchange facilities, and perhaps even valuable intellectual property, should it not be treated as if it were an 'enterprise'' rather than a 'conspiracy'? As such its vertical or horizontal contracts with users or other networks would be subject to normal Sherman Act §1, rules; and its refusals to deal would be subject to the *Colgate, Otter Tail,* and *Aspen Skiing* rules under Sherman Act §2.

Whether the EU's 'essential facilities' rules are too stringent when applied to arguably competitive SFNs—or the US ones not stringent enough when applied to virtual monopolies—are different questions that I shall have to save for another day, or leave to others.[52]

---

[51] *United States* v *Visa USA, Inc. et al* (SDNY complaint filed October 7, 1998).

[52] Compare two very recent (and critical) articles: Treacy (1998) and, 'DOJ Gets No Credit For Visa Complaint,' *Legal Times of Washington*, November 2, 1998.

III

Eleanor M. Fox*

Alliances, Telecoms and the Problem of Access:
US and the World

I. Introduction

In this essay I address the US antitrust law regarding rights of access to the facility or technology of another enterprise. I note the genesis of the US doctrine of access to an essential facility (the *Terminal Railroad* case); the persistent uncertainty as to how far the law has moved beyond the narrow confines of that case, and the current flirtations with a much more robust access principle. I conclude by noting that the access question under US law is in flux; and the access question in world context is 'sleeping' in the GATS/Telecoms agreement. It will awaken; and the United States and its trading partners will be forced to confront the question: What does 'abuse of dominance through denial of market access' mean? And, 'is there already—or will there inevitably be—a common rule for the world?'

II. The Parent of the US Law on Access to an Essential Facility—*Terminal Railroad*

The problem of access to bottleneck facilities has been with us since the early days of the US antitrust law. In *United States v. Terminal Railroad Association*,[1] railroad companies bought and jointly operated all of the railroad terminal facilities in St. Louis, Missouri. The US Supreme Court held that they had the duty to admit to the railroad terminal association all railroad competitors that wished to join, 'upon a plane of equality in respect of benefits and burdens with the present proprietary companies'; and that they had the duty to grant non-discriminatory access to all railroads that wanted to use the facilities without joining the association. *Terminal Railroad* is the source of the essential facility doctrine in the United States. The doctrine, which arose in the context of collective action, has been extended to single firms (monopolists) under Section 2 of the Sherman Act.

---

* New York University School of Law.
[1] 224 US 383 (1912).

In the United States the essential facility doctrine is narrow. The US Supreme Court has not invoked the doctrine in modern times. It consciously avoided its use in *Aspen Ski*.[2] The right of property owners to refuse to deal is much stronger under US law than is any such right in the EU; and in the EU, at least at Commission level, the concept of 'essential facility' is much more robust than its US counterpart.

The *Terminal Railroad* case involved a quintessential essential facility— there was no alternative railroad access to St. Louis for hundreds of miles around the city, and geography prevented the construction of a competing access route. The railroads that ran the association had no good reason to deny their competitors access to the terminal facilities. Clearly there was a price that would have been profitable to an independent terminal facility owner and reasonable to a railroad user. The only purpose and effect of the exclusion and discrimination was to raise rivals' costs, or simply to exclude them.

As with many modern cases concerning network or bottleneck access, *Terminal Railroad* was a horizontal case (foreclosure of competitors in order to eliminate their competition) but involved the consortium's vertical integration into a business (terminal facilities) that was an input that the competitors needed to compete. This functional integration is what gave the railroads the power to exclude their competitors and raise their costs.

In *Terminal Railroad*, if we assume that break-up of the terminal facilities would not have been efficient and that spin-off of the terminal function to an independent third party was not an option, an order requiring competitor access was fair and probably efficient.[3] There was no prospect of the construction of competing terminal facilities.

The modern law of network access, including telecom, computer and media cases, is not so clear. It involves at least three additional dimensions:

In many cases, access is sought to intellectual property; but intellectual property involves statutorily granted rights to exclude in order to induce inventiveness.

Technology and markets are rapidly changing, raising questions of market power and its durability, and of either too much or too late antitrust intervention.

Complications are added by the global dimension, which includes the problem of negative externalities; positive externalities (and how to harness them); the costs of multiple applicable rules of law to the same transaction, and the various substantive and institutional challenges likely to arise from existing

---

[2] *Aspen Skiing Co.* v *Aspen Highlands Skiing Corp.*, 472 US 585 (1985).
[3] It would be efficient if access were granted at a competitive price and price-administration or surveillance were not required.

international agreements (Telecoms-WTO) and possible future ones. (Should there be overarching international principles of competition law? Do we already have them?)

III. The Law of the United States—The Legal Uncertainty of Access Rights Beyond *Terminal Railroad*

Mergers and alliances in information technology markets are increasingly raising questions of access; yet the relevant law of legal rights and remedies is in flux. This is true not only in the United States but in most other countries and jurisdictions, thus compounding the problem that such mergers and alliances are increasingly international and that the law of several jurisdictions, plus 'international law' under the GATS/Telecoms agreement, may apply at once.

In this section I focus on US law and the margin of uncertainty thereunder.

As noted, the law of the United States requires joint venturers to grant non-discriminatory access to essential facilities (narrowly conceived) under the circumstances of *Terminal Railroad*. Our inquiry here is, how much farther does the law go, and are any special principles applicable to communications or media network problems?

The US law in question is Section 1 of the Sherman Act. Section 1 prohibits combinations that unreasonably restrain trade. It flatly prohibits cartels and other naked restraints of trade, because naked restraints are designed simply to eliminate competition; they virtually never have pro-competitive or pro-efficiency effects. The approach to integrative collaborations—acquisitions, joint ventures and alliances—is entirely different, because integrative collaborations are (at least presumptively) designed to produce synergies.[4] Normally they are responses to the market and not attempts to control the market. The framework for analysis is: Does the alliance or other combination create or enhance market power? If the answer is affirmative: Are there pro-competitive or efficiency justifications such that consumers are better off with, rather than without, the alliance?[5] Efficiency justifications may include the need to protect

---

[4] See, *for example*, *Broadcast Music, Inc.* v *Columbia Broadcasting, Inc.*, 441 US 1 (1979); *Yamaha Motor Co.* v *FTC*, 657 F.2d 971 (8th Cir. 1981), *cert. denied sub nom. Brunswick Corp.* v *FTC*, 456 US 915 (1982). See Brodley (1982).

[5] See *SCFC ILC, Inc.* v *VISA USA*, Inc., 36 F.3d 958 (10th Cir. 1994), *cert. denied*, 515 US 1152 (1995); *National Bancard Corp.* v *VISA, USA.*, 779 F.2d 592 (11th Cir.), *cert. denied*, 479 US 923 (1986); *Yamaha Motor Co.* v *FTC*, *supra*. See *Rothery Storage & Van Co.* v *Atlas Lines, Inc.*, 792 F.2d 210 (D.C. Cir. 1986), *cert. denied*, 479 US 1033 (1987).

against free riders. If a power-increasing alliance is not justified by offsetting contributions to competition or efficiency, it is likely to be held illegal in essence. If it *is* justified, still, one asks: Does the alliance include ancillary anti-competitive aspects or restrictions that are either unnecessary to serve the market or are perceptibly[6] more restrictive than necessary to serve the market?[7] Unreasonably anti-competitive ancillary restrictions will be set aside.

The above analysis is traditional. A subsequent question is controversial. Does the law impose duties to deal, or duties to deal fairly, even though the circumstances fall below the thresholds of a *Terminal Railroad* essential facility? When, if at all, is a refusal to deal or refusal to deal fairly unreasonably exclusionary?[8] Does an alliance that gives a partner preferred access to a narrow market outlet have a duty to give outsiders access, or non-discriminatory access, to a facility or technology owned by it?

The US approach to this issue has changed over time. From approximately 1945 to 1980, US law was sympathetic to the view that antitrust should, among other things, prohibit firms with power from 'unreasonably excluding' competitors. The principle, which became part of tie-in law and other 'fencing out' violations, and indeed which had motivated the enactment of Section 3 of the Clayton Act in 1914, was based on fairness (fair rules of the game; fair opportunity to compete; freedom from coercion); not on efficiency;[9] but it was justified also by the hypothesis that giving powerless firms the right to contest markets on the merits conduces to efficiency.[10]

Beginning in the late 1970s, the US antitrust perspective became more nuanced. The Supreme Court began to qualify fairness principles. It examined the need of firms to prevent free riding, and it called attention to costs of imposing antitrust duties on firms that were simply trying to serve the market.[11]

In 1981 with the advent of the Reagan Administration, the US antitrust perspective changed dramatically. 'Unreasonably exclusionary conduct' was

---

[6] The law does not second-guess business judgments. 'Perceptibly,' as I have used it, implies that there is a rather clear available less anti-competitive alternative.

[7] See *VISA* cases, *supra* n 5; *see Yamaha Motor Co.* v *FTC, supra* n 5.

[8] See *Associated Press* v *United States*, 326 US 1 (1945). See *Aspen Skiing Co.* v *Aspen Highlands Skiing Corp.*, 472 US 585 (1985). See also, 1977 US Department of Justice Guidelines on International Operations, generally and Case C, 4 CCH Trade Reg. Rep. §13,110 [superseded by 1995 guidelines].

[9] See, for example, *Fortner Enterprises, Inc.* v *United States Steel Corp.*, 394 US 495 (1969).

[10] See Fox and Sullivan (1987); Fox (1981).

[11] Broadcast Music, Inc., *supra* n 4; *Continental T.V., Inc.* v *GTE Sylvania, Inc.*, 433 US 36 (1977).

virtually written out of the law as an antitrust restraint (by the agencies and a great deal of the case law), on grounds that firms, even monopoly firms, must be allowed to compete and compete hard; that they must be able to do so without pulling punches; that any rule recognising rights of allegedly foreclosed competitors will coddle inefficient competitors, handicap efficient firms, and harm competition, efficiency, and competitiveness.[12] Economic libertarianism found common ground with this conservative view of the requirements of efficiency. Some argued that, as part of our free enterprise system, people who owned property had a right to do what they chose with their property, and the law should not sanction its expropriation.[13]

By the late 1980s, some proclaimed that, in matters of US antitrust law, the Chicago School[14] had won. But this victory was overclaimed. While some Supreme Court opinions supported the view that efficiency is the sole guide to the law and that acts of private firms are presumed efficient,[15] these were split decisions. Other Supreme Court opinions pointed in the other direction.[16] In *Aspen Ski*, the Supreme Court approved a jury instruction that said:

> We are concerned with conduct that unnecessarily excludes or handicaps competitors. This is conduct that does not benefit consumers by making a better product or service available—or in other ways—and instead has the effect of impairing competition.[17]

In *Eastman Kodak v. Image Technical Services*,[18] the Supreme Court majority rejected Justice Scalia's argument that interbrand competition necessarily

---

[12] See Fox (1987) 50 *Law & Contemp. Prob.* 33. This argument was reminiscent of the dissenting opinions of Justice White in the earliest Supreme Court antitrust cases, arguing that, if the antitrust law forbade stock acquisitions of competitors, it would confiscate property in violation of the Constitution.

[13] *Ibid.*

[14] 'Chicago School,' as used here, refers to the position that antitrust law is merely a means to move us closer to allocative efficiency, and the assumption that private firm action is efficient.

[15] *Brooke Group Ltd.* v *Brown & Williamson Tobacco Corp.*, 509 US 209 (1993); *Business Electronics Corp.* v *Sharp Electronics Corp.*, 485 US 717 (1988).

[16] *Eastman Kodak Co.* v *Image Technical Services, Inc.*, 504 US 451 (1992); *Aspen Skiing Co.* v *Aspen Highlands Skiing Corp.*, 472 US 585 (1985); *Jefferson Parish Hospital District No. 2* v *Hyde*, 466 US 2 (1984).

[17] Aspen Skiing Co., *supra* n 15.

[18] *Supra* n 15. See Fox (1994) 62 *Antitrust L.J.* 3, arguing that Kodak's abuse of power in cutting off the independent service organisations, not consumer welfare, explains the decision. This essay rejects the thesis, argued by those who style themselves 'post-Chicago School,' that the law is solely 'efficiency law' but that the Supreme Court

prevents a seller from monopolising aftermarket service of its own machines.

In the Bush Administration the Department of Justice targeted for action practices abroad that foreclosed foreign markets and unreasonably excluded US exports.[19] Though harm to consumers in the closed foreign markets could probably be shown, protecting foreign consumers was not the reason for the initiative.

As we entered the second Clinton Administration, the two federal antitrust agencies began to take a harder line against acts by firms with market power having exclusionary, foreclosing, and preference-creating effects, especially but not only in high tech areas.

In a series of telecom and media alliances involving transatlantic service, the Federal Trade Commission and the Department of Justice bargained for consent decrees assuring that the American partner would not get preferred access over other American firms to valued foreign markets. Thus, in connection with the MCI/British Telecom alliance (now overtaken by the merger of Worldcom and MCI), the Antitrust Division feared that BT would have incentives to abuse its control of access to the UK market. The consent decree settling the case requires the alliance to disclose terms and conditions under which MCI and the alliance gain access to BT's network, and requires it not to discriminate against rival US carriers.[20]

In connection with the joint venture of France Telecom and Deutsche Telecom to acquire 20 percent of Sprint stock and to establish a Sprint/FT/DT joint venture called Phoenix, the Antitrust Division required terms parallel to those above plus: Sprint and the joint venture were prohibited from providing certain services until US competitors had the opportunity to provide similar services in France and Germany on non-discriminatory terms, and they were prohibited from obtaining more favourable terms of access by reason of their affiliations with the French and German monopolies.[21]

Time Warner's acquisition of Turner Broadcasting System, also involving TCI, which owned stock of Warner, combined cable operators with program suppliers. The FTC worried that rival programs would be discriminated

---

now understands better how to achieve efficiency. See also, *Image Technical Services, Inc.* v *Eastman Kodak Co.*, 125 F.3d 1195 (9th Cir. 1997), *cert. denied*, 118 S.Ct. 1560 (1998).

[19] See Justice Department Policy Statement, April 3, 1992, 5 CCH Trade Reg. Rep. §50,084.

[20] *United States* v *Concert plc and MCI Communications Corp.*, 1977–2 Trade Cas. 71,935 (D.D.C. 1997).

[21] *United States* v *Sprint Corp.*, 1996–1 Trade Cas. §71,300 (D.D.C. 1996).

against by TCI and Warner's cable operating systems and that rival cable operators would not have an equal chance to compete for the merging parties' programming. The FTC entered a consent decree prohibiting discrimination. FTC Chairman Robert Pitofsky said: 'the central issue [the merger] raises can be summarised in one word: access.'[22]

Two current, high profile cases involve the problem of access. The Federal Trade Commission brought proceedings against Intel Corporation alleging that Intel, the monopoly producer of microprocessors (the 'brain' of personal computers), used its power to coerce key customers (Compaq, Intergraph and Digital) to share their technological developments with Intel. Intel allegedly exerted coercive power by cutting off these customers from Intel's 'essential' technology after they sued Intel for infringing their own technology. The FTC alleged that the three customers have a right of non-discriminatory access to Intel's essential technology.[23]

In the closely watched *Microsoft* case, which at this writing is on trial, the Department of Justice and nineteen states allege (among other things) that Microsoft has monopolised the operating system market. One of the many alleged illegal acts is Microsoft's refusal to allow PC makers to customise the first screen users see in accordance with their understanding of consumer preferences. Netscape—maker of the Netscape browser—was developing a rival technology; by use of the Java language it threatened to 'commoditise' operating systems and dissolve Microsoft's power. The federal and state governments allege that Microsoft implemented strategies to destroy Netscape. The strategies include Microsoft's bundling its browser with its operating system, refusing to allow PC makers the right to customise the first screen by, e.g., including the Netscape icon on this scarce, 'essential' desk top real estate, promising service providers such as AOL a special place on the first screen if they refused to deal with Netscape, and threatening to cut off needed co-operation with Compaq, Apple and others if they dealt, or dealt favourably, with Netscape; or unless they (e.g. Intel) ceased efforts at developing competing technology. Among relief discussed is access to Microsoft's technology and to the first screen.

---

[22] See Warner/Turner Deal Requires Restructuring to Resolve FTC Concerns, 71 BNA Antitrust & Trade Reg. Rep. 255, September 16, 1996; Time Warner, Inc., 5 CCH Trade Reg. Rep. §24,104 at 23,911–12 FTC (1997). See generally, Fox and Fox (1999), chapter 11.

[23] In *re Intel Corp.*, complaint (summarised), 5 Trade Reg. Rep. paragraphs 24, 440 (1998); proposed consent decree filed, March 1999. In a private action, Intergraph at first obtained a preliminary injunction against Intel. 1998–1 Trade Cas. ¶ 72,126 (N.D. Ala. 1998); but the injunction was vacated by the appellate court whose opinion is inconsistent with the FTC action. 1992 Trade Cas. §92,691 (Fed. Cir. 1999).

A duty to give access can sometimes be efficient and progressive; but also it can be inefficient and can reduce incentives to invent. The empirical literature is inconclusive; we simply do not know what is 'optimal.' The new invocation of access by the US government in recent cases reveals the elasticity and inde-terminacy of the concepts of efficiency, technological progress, and protecting 'competition.' Perhaps, in the margin of efficiency-neutrality,[24] a right of com-petitors to fair, non-discriminatory access to a dominated market is a positive value that antitrust law can serve.

IV. The Global Element

The scene is set for a clash of jurisdictions. This is so even if, at the moment, the US law on access may be seen as converging with the EC law on abuse of dom-inance;[25] for each set of laws still moves on its own axis.

Near-explosive clashes of the past are windows on the future. In 1981 the United States withdrew its monopoly case against IBM because the Depart-ment of Justice thought that IBM had no market power and, even if it did, that it should have no duty to disclose its mainframe interfaces to its competitors who made peripheral equipment (disks, memories) plug-compatible with the IBM mainframe (PCMs). The Assistant Attorney General proclaimed that an order requiring IBM to grant its competitors rights of access to its proprietary information would create free riding, undermine IBM's incentives to invent, and undermine America's 'goose that lays the golden eggs.' Just as the United States withdrew its case against IBM, the European Commission's DG IV announced its position that IBM had a duty under EC law to disclose its new interfaces when it made product changes, so as not to squelch the PCMs' com-petition and unfairly deny them access to the users of IBM mainframes. As in the later case of *Boeing/McDonnell Douglas*, the battle that was brewing dis-solved when the respondent accepted conditions from the European Commission. But United States officials were angry; they believed that US pol-icy on technology, competition and competitiveness had been undermined; and

---

[24] This is the margin wherein efficiency benefits and costs may be more or less evenly balanced, or they may be so indeterminate that whoever has the burden to prove effi-ciency or its absence loses.

[25] Consider the government initiatives in *Intel*, *Microsoft* and *VISA*; the Supreme Court decision in *Kodak*; and the FTC decision in *Toys R Us*.

[26] See Fox (1986).

they had no place to go—no forum—for vetting the disagreement and testing their claims.[26]

How should we handle the problem of clashes with unavoidable spillovers? Do we need protocols for jurisdiction? For primary and secondary assertions of jurisdiction? Do we need rules prohibiting unreasonably extraterritorial relief? Do we need international rules for choice of law and limits to nationalistic policies? Do we need common international substantive rules? Are we bound to start developing a 'common law' of such rules in the context of particular disputes arising from alleged breaches of access obligations in the GATS/Telecoms Agreement? Do we already have an international law of non-discriminatory access under the Telecoms Agreement?

We may need international agreement on these questions.[27] The common stance of the antitrust bar in the United States is to the contrary, however; it seems to prefer the status quo to some level of internationalisation.

The United States might take note that the EU is far advanced in its thinking on harmonisation and co-ordination of legal rules on media sector market access in cases involving international spillovers. This is demonstrated in the Commission's 1997 Report on Competition Policy (1997), points 4 and 5, and in the Commission Notice of 31 March 1998 on the Application of the Competition Rules to Access Agreements in the Telecommunications Sector.[28] If the United States continues to regard the problems as national, or solvable by extraterritorial application of US law, and to regard international engagement as dangerous to sovereignty, the EU may, by default, write the rules for the world.

---

[27] I have proposed some possible frameworks for answers. See Fox (1997); (1996); (1998) and Fox and Ordover (1995).

[28] The Commission Notice says: 'this Notice will provide guidance to telecommunications companies and national regulatory and competition authorities on the Commission approach in three important areas. These are the access principles which flow from European competition law, the relationship between competition law and sector specific legislation and explanation of the application of competition law across the telecommunications and related sectors.' Mr. Ungerer explained the Competition Directive as follows: *the issue of access* will become a common denominator between the telecom and the media sectors. Access will be, to a large extent, the future name of the game. In legal terms, the cases concerning access will evolve in a complex interplay between Articles 81, 82, 86 [ex 85, 86, 90] and the EP and Council Directives based primarily on Article 95 [ex 100a], and their transposition into national law. In the telecom field, the main principles are now expressed in the Access Notice which reaches in its importance far beyond telecoms into the media field, and by ONP, the Open Network Provision Directives, based on Article 95 [ex 100a]. The access cases in the telecom/media field are likely to lead to major steps forward in the development of the legal doctrines concerning Article 82 [ex Article 86], as the liberalisation Directives have led to a substantial development of the doctrines concerning Article 86 [ex 90]'.

IV

Barry E. Hawk*

Co-operation in the Review of Telecommunications
Mergers and Joint Ventures

I. Introduction

It is a widely held belief in the telecommunications industry that the telecommunications market of the future will be characterised by a few large, international firms that provide a full range of multimedia services. This belief is fostered by the wave of mergers among cable companies, satellite providers, Internet access providers and telephone companies that have occurred as a result of changing regulation in the telecommunications industry, both in the United States and in Europe. In the last two years, we have witnessed a number of mergers and alliances that will change radically the shape of the telecommunications market.

The increasing number of cross-border mergers means that simultaneous merger reviews on both sides of the Atlantic will occur with greater frequency. In view of this development, competition authorities in the European Union and the United States, as well as other national competition authorities, will have to co-operate closely in order to ensure consistency and to avoid conflicts in antitrust enforcement.

Moreover, because of the complexity of the telecommunications industry—with respect to both technology and to regulation—and the inherently international nature of the services provided, effective co-ordination among different national competition authorities is of particular importance in this industry. Regulators need to evaluate alliances—and craft any remedies to competition problems—with an understanding of technological innovation, existing regulation and the network effects of telecommunications media. The difficulty of monitoring the behaviour of alliances and the implementation of remedies in light of these industry dynamics call for increased co-operation among national competition authorities.

First, competition authorities must understand the innovative and dynamic nature of the telecommunications industry. A principal reason for the global

* Skadden, Arps, Slate, Meagher & Flom LLP & Affiliates; Director, Fordham Corporate Law Institute. I would like to thank Stefanie Niebisch and Nikolaos Peristerakis for their invaluable assistance.

liberalisation of the sector has been dramatic technological progress, which has
allowed for the creation of new telecommunications products and considerable
cost reductions. As a result of this process, telecommunications is no longer
considered a natural monopoly. An immediate implication of this dynamic
process is the difficulty of defining product and geographic markets, as well as
assessing the competitive impact of a merger. The relevant markets are by no
means obvious: the technologies are constantly changing, as are the participants in alliances. Antitrust authorities need to identify the technological factors that are the key elements in the market structure.[1] To arrive at a common
market definition on both sides of the Atlantic, regulators will need to co-
operate in order to achieve a thorough understanding of the expected benefits
of a merger, as well as the potential for competitive harm.

   Second, the high degree of regulation of the industry calls for close co-
operation between regulators and competition authorities when evaluating
cross-border mergers and alliances. In many instances, an assessment of the
competitive effects of a transaction will depend on the degree of liberalisation
of the telecommunications market in question, as well as on the regulatory
implications of the transaction. At this early stage of liberalisation, oversight
of the industry by competition authorities alone is not deemed sufficient in
either the United States or the European Union. For this reason, additional
regulation relating particularly to network access has been imposed on dominant operators. In many instances, EU regulators have also required commitments of market access and further market liberalisation in order to give a
merger clearance.

   Significantly, the involvement of regulatory authorities in the telecommunications industry requires greater co-operation among international competition authorities because competition authorities in one country do not have as
good an understanding of what a regulatory authority in another country is
empowered to do. For example, when a European regulatory body is charged
with supervising compliance with a merger remedy, US antitrust authorities
will have to rely on their foreign antitrust counterparts to ensure that the regulators are carrying out the role envisioned by the consent agreement.

   One step toward defining the parameters of antitrust co-operation in the
telecommunications field was taken when the General Agreement on Trade in
Services (GATS) Telecommunications Agreement was adopted on 15
February 1997. Through this agreement, both the United States and the
European Union, as well as 65 other nations, have committed themselves to

---

[1] For more developments on the issue of innovation and EC antitrust law, see
Temple Lang (1997).

liberalising their national markets for basic telecommunications services and to abolishing any foreign ownership restrictions on telecommunications operators.[2] The United States and the European Union have gone one step further by providing, under their respective laws, for the liberalisation of all telecommunications services. The GATS Telecommunications Agreement, by setting forth minimal openness requirements, may help to establish a common approach toward competitive assessments in the telecommunications sector, thereby laying the foundation for closer co-operation among competition authorities.

II. The Importance of Conflicts

In spite of the desire to co-operate, to avoid duplication and to achieve consistent outcomes in a merger review, regulators do sometimes arrive at different conclusions about the competitive effects of a merger or alliance. One justification for differing conclusions may be that a transaction will have different effects on each market. At other times, differing national stances on a merger result from one agency's conditioning approval of the merger on achieving greater market access. The stance of the US Department of Justice (DOJ) toward the Sprint/France Telecom/Deutsche Telekom and BT/MCI alliances are examples of this link between competition policy and market access.

Minor differences in the results of merger reviews are unlikely to cause significant problems in the industry so long as remedies are as non-intrusive as possible and do not slow the development of new technologies. The dynamic nature of telecommunications (as well as the revolving membership in alliances) will allow telecommunications markets to be largely self-correcting so long as entry remains unimpeded.

III. Recent Enforcement Actions Involving International Mergers and Alliances

The following cases illustrate the extent of co-operation between US and EC competition authorities in the review of telecommunications mergers and alliances.

---

[2] Basic Telecommunications Services include all services that involve the end-to-end transmission of voice or data. Value added services are not covered by the agreement.

1. Joint Ventures and Strategic Alliances

a) BT/MCI (Concert)

In 1994 BT and MCI created a joint venture for the provision of corporate value added telecommunications services. In addition, BT acquired a 20 percent interest in MCI. In the United States the DOJ cleared formation of the joint venture subject to the parties' entering into a consent decree that prevented BT from using its market power in the UK to disadvantage MCI's competitors. The decree imposed certain information reporting requirements on BT and MCI as well as Chinese walls to prevent BT from sharing with MCI competitively sensitive information about MCI's competitors.

In the EC review of the venture, the Commission paid particular attention to the accessibility of the MCI and BT networks to potential competitors. The Commission found that the 1934 Communications Act ensured open and non-discriminatory third party access to MCI's networks and minimised the danger of cross-subsidisation from MCI to Concert. The Commission held that the UK regulatory framework provided similar safeguards. It did not impose any conditions for the clearance of this transaction, because it considered the regulatory framework sufficient for ensuring open and non-discriminatory access to the parties' networks.

b) Sprint/France Telecom/Deutsche Telekom (Global One)

In 1995, France Telecom, Deutsche Telekom and Sprint created a joint venture for the provision of value added corporate communications services. In addition, France Telecom and Deutsche Telekom were each to acquire a 10 percent interest in Sprint. In the United States the DOJ imposed a consent decree to approve the formation of the venture and the acquisition of stock in Sprint. As in the BT/MCI alliance a year earlier, the DOJ was concerned that the legal monopoly enjoyed by the European carriers in their home markets would permit them to discriminate against other US carriers in favour of Sprint. The consent decree prohibits Sprint and the joint venture from providing certain services until competitors have the opportunity to provide similar services in France and Germany. The decree also includes a Chinese wall that prevents FT and DT from sharing with Sprint competitively sensitive information about Sprint's competitors. During the merger review, the European Commission kept the DOJ informed of its concerns regarding the transaction by communicating non-confidential versions of warning letters addressed to France Telecom and Deutsche Telekom. Later in the procedure, the Commission also provided the DOJ with draft copies of the Article 19(3) notices with the consent of the parties.[3]

In its own analysis of the transaction, the Commission assessed the regulatory situation in the United States, France and Germany. The Commission concluded that the 1934 Telecommunications Act ensured that Sprint was subject to open access and non-discrimination requirements vis-à-vis potential competitors of the Global One venture in the market for corporate value added communications services. However, in the case of France and Germany the Commission obtained commitments from the respective governments to liberalise alternative infrastructure and voice telephony. In addition, the Commission imposed on France Telecom and Deutsche Telekom open access and non-discrimination requirements to avoid cross-subsidisation or discrimination in favour of Global One. Notably, the US consent decree contains two phases of remedies corresponding to the EC's liberalisation program. The first phase applies up until the time that France and Germany implement required liberalisation measures. The second phase, applied once areas are open to competition, merely imposes reporting, confidentiality and open licensing requirements.

2. Acquisition of a US firm by an EC Telecommunications Operator

BT/MCI (II)[4]

The DOJ approved BT's proposed acquisition of MCI in 1997 subject to modification of the 1994 consent decree. The modified decree required the combined company to increase the amount of information it reported to the DOJ so that the DOJ could adequately monitor instances of discrimination against other US carriers by BT. The modified decree also strengthened the Chinese walls that were designed to prevent BT from sharing competitively sensitive information about MCI's competitors. The EC imposed the further condition that BT divest overlapping cable capacity obtained through the merger, consistent with US concerns over BT's ability to impede new entry into the US-UK market by withholding use of its cable capacity from potential competitors. In its Competitive Impact Statement regarding the merger, the DOJ noted that

---

[3] Commission Report to the Council and the European Parliament on the application of the Agreement between the European Communities and the Government of the United States of America regarding the application of their competition laws, 10 April 1995–30 June 1996.

[4] *British Telecom/MCI II*, Case IV/M.856, OJ L 336/1 (1997).

more extensive remedial measures might have been required if the British government and its telecommunications regulatory authority, OFTEL, had not taken actions that reinforced the DOJ's non-discrimination objectives.

The frequent contacts between the DOJ, the EC,[5] and OFTEL that occurred during this proposed merger were necessary in order to adopt a consistent approach in defining the relevant product market, and to review the impact of the merger within the framework of the international accounting rate arrangements.[6] During its review, the Commission was very concerned with the risk of reinforcing the parties' dominant position in the market for international voice telephony services between the United Kingdom and the United States. This risk stemmed principally from a cable capacity shortage on the eastern end of the US-UK route. The capacity shortage, coupled with the fact that satellite capacity was not a perfect substitute for cable, increased the danger of a bottleneck for potential entrants. The Commission cleared the merger subject to the condition, among other things, of the divestiture of a certain amount[7] of cable capacity on the eastern end of the US-UK route for international voice telephony services, in order to allow established competitors to compete effectively with BT/MCI, and to ensure cable capacity availability to new entrants.

The Commission again took into account the significant degree of liberalisation of the US and UK telecommunications markets and the fact that the US regulatory framework allowed US carriers to agree to cost-based accounting rates with international carriers. In view of these facts, the Commission concluded that the US regulatory framework allowed potential competitors to provide international voice telephony services on an end-to-end basis. This analysis of the US regulatory environment led to close co-operation with the US authorities.

Moreover, OFTEL, the UK telecommunications regulator, was expected to give its assent to each sale of cable capacity, giving particular attention to the availability of capacity on a non-discriminatory cost basis. This case is a good illustration of the usefulness of having the co-operation of the local regulatory authority for the effective enforcement of remedies in the telecommunications sector.

---

[5] Commission Report to the Council and the European Parliament on the application of the EC–US Co-operation Agreement for the period between 1 January 1997 and 31 December 1998, available at http.\\europa.eu.int.

[6] Accounting rate is a negotiated rate between international carriers, premised on the idea that the carriers jointly provide international telephone services by handing off traffic to each other at the half-way point between two countries.

[7] The divestiture was limited to the overlapping capacity, that is, the incremental eastern end cable capacity acquired through the addition of MCI's capacity.

3. Acquisition of an EC Firm by a US Telecommunications Operator

Ameritech/Tele Danmark[8]
In 1997, the Commission cleared the acquisition of a controlling interest (34 percent of the share capital) by Ameritech in Tele Danmark. The Commission cleared the transaction by noting that in all possible relevant markets, the parties had a combined market share of less than 15 percent. Since the case did not involve the US telecommunications market, the Commission did not notify it to the US authorities.

4. Participation of US Telecommunications Operator in Consortium with EC Operator

a) ADSB/Belgacom[9]
In 1996 the Commission cleared the acquisition of 50 percent of the Belgian PTO (Belgacom) by a consortium comprised of Ameritech, Tele Danmark and Singapore Telecom. The three members of the consortium and the Belgian State, the holder of the remaining 50 percent, would jointly control Belgacom. The Commission cleared the acquisition and notified US authorities of the transaction.

b) GTS-Hermes Inc/HIT Rail BV[10]
GTS and a consortium of European railway operators created a jointly controlled venture for the provision of network infrastructure services throughout the EEA. In particular, the joint venture would use the railway network to provide high-bandwidth transit capacity between incumbent telecommunications operators. The Commission notified the operation to the US authorities. The Commission found that the joint venture would provide a completely new product, (i.e. carrier's carrier services), for which there was no competition yet at the time. In view of the anticipated future competition in the sector, the Commission cleared the transaction.

---

[8] *Ameritech/Tele Danmark*, Case No IV/M.1046, C 25/18 (1998).
[9] *ADSB/Belgacom*, Case No IV/M.689, C 194/4 (1996).
[10] *GTS-Hermes Inc/HIT Rail BV*, Case No IV/M.683, C 157/13 (1996).

5. Mergers or Strategic Alliances Between US Firms with Some Operations or Interests in the EC

a) Worldcom/MCI

The DOJ and EC initiated simultaneous investigations when this transaction was announced in October 1997. Although both companies are US-based, they are major carriers of Internet traffic and their merger will have effects on both sides of the Atlantic. The investigations were conducted separately, although there was a 'high degree' of co-operation, including information-sharing and joint meetings with the merger parties.[11] Also, the Commission formally requested 'pursuant to the 1991 US-EC Antitrust Co-operation Agreement, the Department's co-operation and assistance in evaluating and implementing the divestiture proposal, which had been submitted to both the Commission and the Department of Justice.'[12] Ultimately, the DOJ allowed the merger to proceed after requiring divestiture of MCI's Internet business. Without the divestiture, the merged company would have controlled a significant portion of the Internet backbone service in the United States, which service connects various high-capacity computer networks carrying Internet traffic. The EC, in addition to requiring MCI to sell its main Internet businesses, also required the parties not to recruit MCI's old corporate customers. After MCI initially agreed to sell its Internet backbone service to Cable and Wireless PLC, it was European regulators who pushed for further divestitures, resulting in MCI's agreement also to divest its retail Internet access services. Also, the FCC reportedly deferred to European regulators as to how much of the companies' Internet backbone services would have to be sold off in order to approve the deal.[13]

The Commission in its press release indicated that its investigation and negotiation of remedies were undertaken in parallel with the proceedings before the DOJ. The Commission explicitly stated that 'the process so far has been marked by a considerable level of co-operation between the two authorities, including exchanges of views on the analytical method to be used, co-ordination of information-gathering and joint meetings and negotiations with the parties'. The Commission found that the merger, due to the parties'

---

[11] DOJ Press Release, 'Justice Department Clears Worldcom/MCI Merger After MCI Agrees to Sell its Internet Business,' 15 July 1998.

[12] *Ibid.*

[13] Edmund L. Andrews, 'European Officials Move to Approve Worldcom-MCI Deal,' *The New York Times on the Web*, 20 June 1998.

network externalities,[14] would lead to a strengthening of the parties' position in the market for top level or universal connectivity.

The Commission cleared the merger subject to the divestiture of all of MCI's Internet interests, in order to ensure the entry of a new market player in the market for Internet access. The Commission indicated that the co-operation between the two authorities would continue until the undertakings are fully implemented and exchanged formal letters to this effect in accordance with the EC-US agreement regarding the application of competition laws.

b) Uniworld

Uniworld involved the creation of a joint venture between Unisource (jointly controlled by Telia, KPN and Swisscom), and AT&T. The published EC reference decision make to contact with the US authorities. The Commission however obtained direct undertakings from AT&T on several issues. AT&T undertook: (i) to advise the EC Commission of any complaint filed with the FCC regarding access to or interconnection with AT&T's international facilities, and to inform the Commission of the final decision in regard to a complaint; and (ii) to offer cost-based accounting rates, which will be no higher than the rates established between AT&T and any Unisource shareholder. The Commission cleared the joint venture subject to open access and non-discrimination undertakings on behalf of the Unisource shareholders (Telia, KPN and Swisscom), similar to those imposed in Phoenix/Global One.

6. Satellites

Until recently, the satellite sector was reserved to international consortia (international satellite organisations, or ISO's) formed by national governments and incumbent telecommunications operators, which were largely immunised from competition rules. However, most of these consortia, including Intelsat and Inmarsat, are in the process of being privatised. Faced with the introduction of a new global communications service (e.g. the satellite communications personal system (SCP-S)), the Commission has been more inclined to accept exclusivity clauses and other restrictions on competition because satellite ventures are usually substantial and risky investments. However, the Commission intends to prevent the ISO's from leveraging their power in markets where they

---

[14] The Commission defines network externalities as the phenomenon whereby the attraction of a network to its customers is a function of the number of other customers connected to the same network.

are dominant to gain an unfair advantage in new product markets or in gaining access to space segment capacity.

The satellite sector also has been the focus of several complex competition cases in Europe, such as NSD. These cases demonstrate the new role of satellites in the deployment of digital TV/multimedia, which has made satellites central in the new markets.[15]

Frequency allocation at a worldwide level will be central for the development of this sector. In that context the Regulatory Annex to the GATS Telecommunications Agreement specifies that the 'allocation and use of scarce resources, including frequencies, will be carried out in an objective, timely and non-discriminatory manner.'

a) Inmarsat[16]

In 1994 the International Maritime Satellite Organisation (INMARSAT), an international satellite organisation which provides mobile satellite services, created ICO, an affiliate for the provision of Satellite Personal Communications Systems (S-PCS). Its shareholders are national governments and certain incumbent telecommunications operators, such as Telefonica, Telecom Finland, OTE and PTT Netherlands. Although there is no indication of any special co-operation in this case, the Commission noted that in 1995 the FCC, contrary to the EC, had already granted frequencies to five SCPS.

b) Iridium[17]

Iridium is a joint venture that will provide global satellite personal communications services (S-PCS). It was created by Motorola, which holds a 20 percent stake, and other operators (including Sprint, Stet and Vebacom) that hold minority stakes (3–4 percent). There is no public indication of co-operation between US and EC authorities and the case is not among those that the EC notified to the US authorities during 1996. The Commission did note that the FCC granted the required licenses to Iridium in January 1995. In view of the high risks involved and the importance of the investments required for the provision of the service, the Commission concluded that the creation of the joint venture would not meet the criteria for the application of Article 81(1) [ex 85(1)].

---

[15] Herbert Ungerer. 'Market Restructuring, Alliances, Mergers.' speech in the 6th Satel Conseil Symposium. Communications Satellites and Market Realities. Paris, 8 September 1998.

[16] *Inmarsat*, Case IV/35.296, C 137/13 (1995).

[17] *Iridium*, 97/39/EC, L 16/87 (1997).

IV. Improving Co-operation

Existing co-operation agreements allow for effective co-operation between competition authorities, in particular between the EC and the United States. However, certain aspects of those agreements should be improved. First, the co-operation agreements that are currently in place between the EC and the US should be extended to other countries. Second, the existing EC-US co-operation agreements should be strengthened, particularly with respect to positive comity. Finally, a dispute settlement procedure and clearer rules on jurisdiction should be established.

1. Creation of a Stronger Framework for Co-operation at the International Level

Compared with the EC-US co-operation, co-operation between other competition authorities appears more limited. The EC of course has strong links with Member States and EEA competition authorities. Less strong links exist with Canada,[18] Australia and New Zealand. Co-operation also exists to some extent with the competition authorities of the ten countries with which the EC is associated. The United States, by contrast, has co-operation agreements in place with Canada, Germany and Israel, as well as a second-generation agreement with Australia that specifically permits the exchange of confidential information on a reciprocal basis.[19]

The EC has pushed strongly for the adoption of a multilateral framework of competition rules. The 'Wise Men Group' set up by Commissioner van Miert in 1994 proposed that co-operation between competition authorities should be strengthened by (i) development of the existing co-operation agreements, e.g. by sharing certain confidential information or by developing a

---

[18] On 4 June 1998 Canada and the EC announced the completion of the text of the EC–Canada co-operation agreement. The agreement, which is not expected to be signed before early 1999, is similar to the 1995 Canada–US co-operation agreement and calls for co-ordination of enforcement actions, information exchanges, and regular meetings of officials.

[19] The International Antitrust Enforcement Assistance Act confers upon the DOJ and FTC the authority to negotiate bilateral agreements with foreign antitrust authorities. The Act permits the agencies to exchange information collected through civil investigative demands or administrative subpoenas and through grand jury proceedings, but does not permit the agencies to share information obtained through the Hart-Scott-Rodino pre-merger notification system.

stronger positive comity principle, and (ii) developing a multilateral frame
work based on a minimum set of jointly agreed competition rules. It is note
worthy that the EC did not propose a minimum set of rules with respect t
mergers. Instead, reasoning that merger policy is still an instrument of compet
tion policy that comes very close to industrial policy, the Wise Men Group sug
gested merely a harmonisation of the merger review procedures and time limits.

The Commission proposed to the Council that it submit these recommen
dations to the WTO.[20] The 1996 Singapore Conference, in fact, gave a mandat
to a Working Group on trade and competition policy for the identification o
any areas that may merit further consideration under the WTO framework
The Working Group will have to examine which core principles are commor
in different countries, and how the effectiveness and coherence of nationa
competition policies could be enhanced. The working group will also deter
mine how to improve co-operation between competition authorities in th
WTO framework. The United States, for its part, is more reluctant to adopt
minimal common set of competition rules which would constitute a level play
ing field. The WTO General Council ultimately will decide whether it shoul
go further and adopt a plurilateral or multilateral instrument containing a min
imum set of competition rules. In the area of telecommunications, there i
already a minimal set of rules that is intended to establish a level playing fiel
among the WTO Members: the Regulatory Annex to the GATS Tele
communications Agreement contains competition principles and obligations
primarily concerning access to dominant operator networks.

2. Strengthening the Positive Comity Principle

The co-operation agreement currently in force between the EC and the Unitec
States contains a positive comity principle. One party can ask the other party
to initiate an investigation of practices occurring principally in the latter
party's territory, but the requested party retains full discretion as to whether it
will initiate any proceedings (Article V). The Agreement does provide that the
requesting party will normally defer or suspend its activities in favour of the
investigating party's proceedings. The requesting party may still initiate its
own proceedings, but the agreement contemplates such a case more as ar
exception than as the rule. The 1998 Agreement, however, does not cover

---

[20] *Towards an International Framework of Competition Rules*, 18 June 1996
COM(96)284.

merger investigations and it remains to be seen whether positive comity will play an important role with respect to review of mergers and acquisitions.

3. Creation of a Dispute Settlement Procedure

In view of the Boeing/McDonnell Douglas case, and the different outcomes in the EC and the United States, EC officials have proposed the establishment of an arbitration mechanism on a bilateral or even a multilateral (WTO) level.[21] The GATS Telecommunications Agreement now provides the necessary instruments intended to avoid such a deadlock in the telecommunications sector, primarily through the WTO Dispute Settlement procedures. Ultimately, a serious disagreement in the substantive approach to be followed could lead to an action before the WTO for violation of the other party's GATS Telecommunications commitments, including the violation of the minimum competition rules included in the GATS Telecommunications Reference Paper. US officials, however, have been more cautious about adopting such a dispute settlement procedure.

4. Clear Rules on Jurisdiction

The thresholds for a mandatory pre-merger filing in the EC are based on turnover, i.e. revenues from sales. However, in the telecommunications sector, it is particularly difficult to allocate turnover easily. It is difficult to determine, for instance, where the phone services are provided and whether they are provided to the subscribers, to the network operators or to the receivers. According to one EC official, DG IV is provisionally basing its calculations only on services that are provided to domestic subscribers, settlement inflows for international calls from other network operators and revenue from the direct provision of value-added services.[22] Clearer EC turnover calculation rules will avoid problems that may arise from controversial interpretations of what constitutes turnover in the telecommunications sector.

---

[21] Schaub (1998).
[22] Lowe (1994).

V. Differences Between the EC and the United States

In the United States, antitrust authorities have recognised that communica
tions industries 'are not the same as steel mills and grocery stores.'[23] Given the
rapid technological changes in this industry, the DOJ, for example, ha
expressed particular interest in the effect of telecommunications mergers or
potential competition. In the view of Joel Klein, head of the DOJ's Antitrust
Division, 'the ideal competitive environment should enable the development o
as many different conduits or points of entry as possible—be it cable, tele
phone, wireless, as well as other emerging technologies—in order to link people with all kinds of content–voice, video, and audio. . .'.[24] In addition to
scrutinising mergers, US antitrust authorities are also particularly watchful of
issues relating to network industries, exclusive dealing, control over essentia
facilities and other abuses of market power.[25]

US antitrust authorities have also lauded the high degree of co-operation
and consultation that occurs among US and foreign regulators during the
review of a merger or alliance that has cross-border effects.[26] This stance is consistent with the 1995 Antitrust Enforcement Guidelines for International
Operations, in which the DOJ and FTC make clear their commitment to vigorous enforcement of the US antitrust laws in the international arena while
recognising the importance of a strong co-operative relationship with foreign
competition authorities.[27] Robert Pitofsky, Chairman of the FTC, has noted
that positive comity agreements such as the recently-signed US-EC co-
operation agreement, though not applicable in a merger context, exemplify this
positive attitude toward international co-operation.[28]

Co-operation among competition authorities in telecommunications matters has also extended beyond the merger realm. In 1994 the DOJ began an
investigation into a requirement proposed by the European Telecom-

---

[23] Robert Pitofsky, 'Competition Policy in Communications Industries: New
Antitrust Approaches,' (manuscript), prepared remarks at the Glasser Legalworks
Seminar, at 2 (10 March 1997).

[24] *Ibid*, at 5–7.

[25] Joel I. Klein, 'Preparing for Competition in a Deregulated Telecommunications
Market', (manuscript) remarks at the Glasser Legalworks Seminar,' at 12 (11 March
1997).

[26] Robert Pitofsky, 'Merger and Competition Policy: The Way Ahead', (manuscript)
statement at the Annual Meeting of the American Bar Association, 4 Aug. 1998, at 3.

[27] US Department of Justice and Federal Trade Commission, Antitrust Enforcement
Guidelines for International Operations (6 April 1995).

[28] Robert Pitofsky, *supra*, n 26.

ιunications Standards Institute (ETSI) that firms wanting to sell technology ;ghts in Europe had to license their intellectual property on a worldwide basis. ′S competition authorities viewed this policy as a compromise of intellectual ιroperty rights and the DOJ began an investigation into whether the requireιent would raise antitrust concerns, including whether it would have a chilling ffect on innovation in the United States. When DG IV raised similar questions ιbout ETSI's proposals, the objectionable provisions were dropped from the ιolicy.[29]

′I. The Impact of National Regulatory Review on Co-operation

ίven after the liberalisation of the telecommunications sector on both sides of ιhe Atlantic, extensive regulation has been imposed on the industry in order to ιnsure that new entrants will have open and non-discriminatory access to the ιcumbents' networks and will be able to avoid bottlenecks. In view of the ιomplexity of the industry, it would be advisable to have more direct involveιent of the regulatory authorities in the co-operation process. As was apparιnt in many merger cases, the EC Commission's stance resulted in large part ιrom its assessment of the regulatory situation, not only in the EC, but also in ιhe United States.

   In that respect, it is noteworthy that after a recent internal reorganisation ιf DG IV, a specialised telecommunications unit of DG IV is responsible for ιelecommunications mergers and alliances. This reorganisation shows that the ∶ommission recognises the increasing complexity of the sector and the need to ιave telecommunications industry experts involved in merger review.

   In the United States, in addition to the DOJ and FTC, the Federal ∶ommunications Commission (FCC) has responsibility for reviewing the comιetitive effects of a merger. Under the 1996 Telecommunications Act, the FCC ∶s responsible for determining whether a merger is in the 'public interest', a test ιhat has been interpreted to require proof that a merger will enhance competiιion.[30] The 1996 Act repealed the FCC's authority to immunise mergers of teleιhone companies from the antitrust laws and amended section 7 of the Clayton ᇺct by revoking the FCC's ability to immunise a merger from section 7 by ιpproving the merger.

---

[29] DOJ press release, 'Opening Markets and Protecting Competition for America's Businesses and Consumers,' at 5 (7 April 1995).
[30] Klein, Comments Before the House, at 9. By contrast, the antitrust agencies ιttempt to determine whether a merger will *lessen* competition.

While the FCC has long had a role in evaluating the competitive impact a merger under the 'public interest' standard, the loss of its ability to immuni mergers and the consequent involvement of the antitrust agencies in reviewi mergers may have actually enhanced the FCC's role in antitrust enforcemer The difference in review standards between the FCC and antitrust agencies cr ates the potential that the FCC could withhold its approval of a merger th goes unchallenged by the antitrust authorities. Generally, however, t antitrust authorities work closely with the FCC during merger reviews in ord to ensure a consistent outcome. Even prior to the passage of the 19 Telecommunications Act, the antitrust agencies worked with the FCC resolve questions about competition. For example, as part of the DOJ's 19 settlement with BT and MCI, the DOJ referred to the FCC the 'issue whether regulatory action is appropriate to ensure that new entrants ha access to US backhaul facilities'.[31] Therefore, in spite of the DOJ's aggressi stance in assuming oversight of competition issues in the telecommunicatio industry, the FCC appears to have taken on an important supporting role reviewing mergers and alliances and in monitoring them after they have bee approved.

---

[31] DOJ press release, 'Justice Department Asks Court to Modify and Exten Previous British Telecom/MCI Settlement After Reviewing New Deal,' (7 July 1997).

V

Colin D. Long*

Competition Policy in Communications Network Markets:
Bottlenecks, Alliances, Regulation and Convergence

I. The Role of Regulation and Competition Law

The role of regulation in these matters is to try to secure that appropriate conditions exist for the attraction of investment, innovation and fair competition in the market. Therefore, in sectors such as telecommunications, until recently generally the preserve of utility-style state 'enterprise', liberalisation cannot immediately take on the mantle of so-called de-regulation but must first go through a transition period of re-regulation, to protect competition and consumers.

By contrast, the primary function of competition law is to deter anti-competitive activity and provide enforcement remedies, as well as private compensatory recourse, to bring such activity to an end. Inevitably, regulation and competition law overlap and to an extent regulatory bodies become quasi-competition authorities. Gradually, however, as the telecommunications services market(s) become more mature and stable, the need for industry-specific regulation to condition market behaviour should lessen and general competition law should be able to take its place.

Because regulators are typically creatures of statute and of a 'constitution' set for them by legislators, they face the risk of being trapped in their own time-warp, with technology and innovation in market practices continuously running ahead of their powers and adaptability. The solution for regulation, apart from the long-term strategy of abdication in favour of competition law, is to avoid the trap of regulating today's conduct and behavioural models, and at the same time to set general principles of behaviour supported by operational guidelines explaining the regulator's view and approach. The cry may then go up that general rules create uncertainty and paralyse investment, which is precisely why a mid-course must be found between the extremes of over-invasive,

---

* OLSWANG, London.
[1] Directive 97/33/EC of the European Parliament and of the Council on interconnection in telecommunications with regard to ensuring universal service and interoperability through the application of the principles of open network provision (ONP), OJ L199/32 (1997).

highly prescriptive, prohibition and a loose or over-indulgent approach to reg
ulatory management.

II. Regulatory 'Tunnel Vision'

There are numerous examples of regulatory thinking being captured by faddis
theories and concepts. Some have a justifiable consistency and longevity an
are a valuable addition to market control mechanisms. Others are more perni
cious and often take far longer to eradicate than the time it took to achiev
their introduction. In the meantime, permanent significant harm can b
inflicted on fledgling competitors. The access deficit contribution (ADC
regime which led a brief existence in UK regulation in the early nineties was
classic example of this.

More recently, interconnection pricing (to which ADCs were closel
related) has undergone a similar conditioning throughout the Member State
and has invariably produced a monopolist-type pricing structure bearing littl
relation to the services and activities performed. So far, based on the ONF
Interconnection Directive[1] and a few national variations, interconnection pricing is usage based and geared to minutes or seconds of traffic conveyed ove
interconnected networks. In form and structure this is in reality a top-down
approach based on the retail tariff model. There is really no good reason, in
fact, why retail pricing and wholesale interconnection pricing should be based
on the same structure—nor, in fact, are they constrained by Euro-regulation:
the Interconnection Directive expressly contemplates other possible charging
models, such as capacity-based.

There is, therefore, a risk that in giving in to the immediacy, the 'quick fix'
of regulatory solutions, we may sometimes lose the very flexibility and ability
to evolve which should be its greatest virtue.

III. Bottlenecks and Essential Facilities

There is currently much talk in regulatory and legal circles of bottlenecks and
their anti-competitive effects. There is, of course, no legal concept and certainly
no definition of a bottleneck: an alternative, sometimes substitute, theory is that
of 'essential facilities'—derived, in principle at least, from US anti-trust law.[2]

---

[2] The US essential facilities doctrine requires a company with monopoly power to
contract with a customer where five conditions are met: (i) an essential facility exists and

The essential facilities concept is not, however, represented by a new and separate legal norm; in the EU, it is but one example of the law enshrined in Article 82 [ex 86], the abuse of a dominant position. Within this context, the idea of an essential facilities 'doctrine' has been pursued in various Commission decisions,[3] in the Commission's Access Notice[4] and by different jurists, although it has not so far been fully reviewed, and certainly not specifically endorsed, by the European Court of Justice.[5]

The Access Notice, is a form of guidance as to the Commission's opinions and intentions with respect to the application of the competition rules to access (to telecommunication networks) and access agreements, such as for interconnection of networks and call termination.

In the Notice the Commission explains its view that a refusal to give access to telecommunication facilities may be prohibited under Article 82 [ex 86] 'if the refusal is made by a company which is dominant because of its control of facilities'. Where access to such facilities is essential in order for companies to compete on a related market, in the Notice the Commission continues:

> The key issue here is, therefore, what is essential. It will not be sufficient that the position of the Company requesting access would be more advantageous if access were granted—but refusal of access must lead to the proposed activities being made either impossible or seriously and unavoidably uneconomic.

This was the type of situation that recently came before the European Court of Justice for consideration, although the ECJ avoided direct reference

---

is controlled by a monopolist (a facility is essential where access to it is indispensable in order to compete on the market with the company controlling it); (ii) a competitor is unable practically or reasonably to duplicate the facility; (iii) use of the facility is denied to a competitor; (iv) it is feasible for the facility to be provided; (v) there is no legitimate business reason for refusing access to the facility.

[3] Notably, *B & I Line plc* v *Sealink Harbours LH and Sealink Stena LH* [1992] 5 CMLR 255 and *Sea Containers* v *Stena Sealink*, Commission Decision 94/19/EC, OJ L 15/8, (1994). In the latter case the Commission stated: 'The owner of an essential facility which uses its power in one market in order to protect or strengthen its position in another related market, in particular by refusing to grant access to a competitor, or by granting access on less favourable terms than those of its own services, and thus imposing a competitive disadvantage on its competitors, infringes Article 82 [ex 86]'.

[4] Notice on the Application of the Competition Rules to Access Agreements in the Telecommunications Sector: OJ C 265/02 (1998).

[5] However, see *European Night Services, Case T–374/94* [1998] II–3141.*Oscar Bronner GmbH & Co. KG* v *Mediaprint Zeitungs-under Zeitschriftenverlag GmbH & Co. KG and Others*, Case C–7/97, [1998] ECR I–7791.

to any essential facilities doctrine or concept. In *Oscar Bronner* v *Mediaprint Zeitungs*,[6] Bronner was seeking access for its daily newspapers to a home distribution system established by Mediaprint for Mediaprint's own newspapers and Mediaprint had refused. On an application from the Austrian national court for a preliminary ruling, the ECJ decided that Mediaprint was not committing an abuse of Article 82 [ex 86]. Bronner's publication was growing in sales and had alternative means of distribution open to it; to establish its own home distribution system was not totally impracticable and uneconomic in the longer term; thus, access to Mediaprint's distribution system was, in the context of Article 82 [ex 86], neither essential nor indispensable.

The Oscar Bronner Case is the latest in a line of cases applying Article 82 [ex 86] to a 'refusal to deal' situation. Indeed, it suggests that there is, in fact, no real need to rely exclusively on the essential facilities concept and that the Court is quite capable of assessing these cases under well-established Article 82 [ex 86] principles. It is also a useful and timely reminder (as the CFI had also given in European Night Services) that analysis of the impact of control of what may be an essential facility should take place in the context of determining the relevant market and the facility owner's position in it.

IV. Interconnection and Conditional Access

Closely related to the essential facilities concept are the rules introduced to cover interconnection (e.g. the ONP Interconnection Directive) and conditional access (e.g. the Advanced Television Standards Directive[7]).

In relation to Interconnection in the UK, whilst, so far, regulation has obliged the incumbent to connect its network in order to facilitate 'any to any' calls via the local and transit switching facilities of the incumbent, regulatory policy, in contrast to the US, has yet to embrace clearly and unreservedly the concept of mandating interconnection at any technically suitable point. In particular, allowing a competing operator to connect to the unbundled local loop facilities ('copper connections') of the incumbent and lease dedicated capacity over those facilities has been regarded hitherto as potentially undermining the UK sector policy of encouraging the building of new alternative network infrastructures. Even EU regulation has fought shy of going to this depth of manda-

---

6 *Ibid.*

7 Directive 95/47/EC of the European Parliament and of the Council on the use of standards for the transmission of television signals, OJ L 281/51 (1995).

ɔry access to an incumbent's facilities: the Interconnection Directive does not ҳtend to this type of (local loop) connection.[8]

Clearly, the economics of market entry would be substantially affected ₊epending on whether or not the entrant could acquire rights directly over the ᴀcilities connected to customers. Moreover refusal of an incumbent to make ₊s local loop facilities available is potentially challengeable under Article 82 [ex ₊6][9] even though neither national regulation (in the case of the UK) nor EU ƆNP legislation (though more for technical reasons) would appear to support ʜis proposition. This conflict between government sector policy and applica-ɒle competition rules is regrettable in that it can send a confused signal to the ᴍarket place as to the basis upon which market entry could or should be ₊llowed.

The European Commission's Green Paper on the regulatory implications ɒf convergence[10] unfortunately does little to clear up the confusion in the area ɒf unbundling, declaring it to be 'complex' and closely linked to the availabil-ty of viable alternative distribution channels, whilst admitting that this would ₊ot exclude 'appropriate safeguards being introduced under the Competition ⁊ules'.

In respect of conditional access agreements, the competition issue here is ɔest exemplified in relation to direct-to-home satellite communication of ₊ncrypted programming. Customers for such services will require a set-top-box ᴠhich will decode the broadcaster's signal. Customers may choose to have ₊nore than one set top-box but inertia and practicality are likely to lead to most ᴠishing only to have one. Any broadcaster or service provider wishing to ₊eliver a programme to such customers will, therefore, need to be able to access ₊he encryption technology embodied in the particular type of set-top box.

This situation can lead to the emergence of a dominant conditional access system operator with a powerful 'gatekeeper' role. Where this role is held by a ᴠertically integrated organisation which is also active in the retail market for ₊ay-television or other content, there may be incentives to use control of the ᴄonditional access system to keep competitors in the provision of programming ɒut of the retail market.

This potential importance of conditional access systems as gateways to pro-ᵍramming and other content was foreseen in the enactment of the Advanced

---

[8] See footnote (i) to Annex I, Commission Recommendation, OJ L 73/42 (1998).

[9] Commission Notice on the application of the competition rules to access agreements in the telecommunications sector, OJ C 265/02 (1998), at para. 127.

[10] *Green Paper on the Convergence of the Telecommunications, Media and Information Technology Sectors*, COM(97) 623.

TV Standards Directive. Pursuant to this Directive, operators of conditiona access services must offer such services to broadcasters on fair, reasonable an non-discriminatory terms. These terms are, of course, closely related to th Article 81/82 [ex 85/86] principles of non-discrimination.

This Directive is an example of a developing trend in EC legislative practice the setting of *ex ante* regulation inspired by Treaty competition law principles instead of and in contrast to the *ex post* application of Article 82 [ex 86] controls

V. Mergers and Alliances

Very often, it is the parties' control of essential facilities or of bottlenecks whicl are the key concern in merger investigations in this sector.

In the recent WorldCom/MCI merger control case, the Commission's view was that the combination of the Internet backbone networks of the two partie 'would create a network of such absolute and relative size that the combine entity could behave to an appreciable extent independently of its competitor and customers'. Indeed, the Commission event went so far as to suggest, con troversially, that the WorldCom/MCI combined network might constitute a essential facility to which all other Internet service providers would have n choice but to interconnect.

WorldCom/MCI is also a classic example of the 'network externalities principle: the Commission took the view that, given the way the Interne worked, there was a real risk that, by virtue of the parties' market position, cus tomers would be attracted to them simply because of their proliferation of con nections and network relationships.

The case suggests, however, as have other recent merger cases in this sector that the Merger Control Regulation is a somewhat 'rough and ready' contex in which to consider new markets and technologies, particularly given the stric time-limits imposed and the need to achieve resolution within relatively shor time-scales. Coupled with the fact that the Commission will not seek behav ioural remedies, decisions of the authorities under the Regulation are some times a subtle blend of law and pragmatism.

This pragmatism is not always confined to the parties, who may be keen t compromise in order to remove regulatory roadblocks; it may also come fron the regulators. Their proceedings under Article 81 [ex 85] and the Merge Control Regulation have sometimes been used as a lever to achieve regulatory change. This demonstrates that the Commission will not simply look at the parties' market positions but will also consider the regulatory environment and the effects that this will have on their freedom of action in the market.

VI. Relationship of Regulation and Competition Law in the Telecommunications Future

Issues relating to convergence are being widely canvassed at Community and national level.[11] Convergence is not a future prospect posing questions which can be pondered and resolved at some time in the distant future. It is already upon us and beginning to pose challenges for regulators. A number of areas where these challenges will be particularly pointed can be identified.

a) *Target of regulation*: in a converged world, there will be an infinite variety of services which previously could only be received over traditional media (e.g. broadcasting only for video, wireline only for voice) but which will now be offerable over every conceivable type of infrastructure, wireless or wireline, and will include the Internet. The medium and technology will thus become largely irrelevant to regulation which should focus, to the extent necessary, on the activity taking place (wireless frequency being the exception, in that it is a scarce resource which will, for some time, need to be administered and managed efficiently). In this regard, regulation must become increasingly technology-neutral and focus on the rights and obligations conferred and not the technology platform utilised.

b) *Markets*: as the markets converge so there will need to be a re-assessment of relevant markets in order that market power can be fairly and accurately determined; the impact of new technologies creates new services which, in turn, capture new communities of customers, thus attracting new service providers to meet their needs.

c) *Regulatory framework*: convergence of regulation is logically attractive because to do otherwise would risk inconsistencies of approach and discrimination between different operators and service providers employing different transmission media. In the European Commission's Green Paper on Convergence,[12] the question is posed as to whether existing regulatory approaches require adaptation to convergence and if so, whether their adaptation should: i) build on existing frameworks, ii) create a new framework for on-line and interactive services or iii) seek to create a comprehensive framework applying similar regulatory approaches to all sectors.

---

[11] See, in particular, the UK Department of Trade & Industry Green Paper on Regulating Communication: Approaching Convergence in the Information Age (HMSO).

[12] *Ibid.*

In fact, a preferred approach would seem to be to create a comprehensive framework which applies consistent and harmonised regulatory approaches whilst avoiding duplication and 'double jeopardy' for the players in the market. It does not seem indispensable to such a regulatory approach that there should have to be a single regulator, particularly as there is a powerful argument for the separation of regulation of content from the regulation of service delivery.

VI

Michael J. Reynolds*

Article 81 [ex 85] and the Merger Regulation:
Breaking the Network Access Bottleneck

I. Introduction

1. Alliances in the Telecommunications/Media Sector

Over the last few years, there has been a wave of alliances taking place in the telecommunications and media sector. In 1996, for example, more than 15% of the total value of worldwide mergers and acquisitions was generated by activity in the information and communications sector.[1] For the most part, they represent attempts by existing operators in these markets to respond to the rapid pace of evolution in this sector, with its twin characteristics of globalisation and convergence. The changes in the technologies available, the increasing scale of operations and the greater geographic coverage required to meet customers' demands, together with the fundamental changes in the regulatory framework, have all placed existing market operators under immense pressure to change and adapt in order to survive in their new environment, as well as creating enormous opportunities for new products and markets where potentially huge profits may be made. The significance of this 'information revolution' cannot be overstated. As one commentator puts it, 'These radical developments imply a transformation of the core of our economies comparable only to the industrial revolution which shaped the nineteenth century'.[2]

The Commission has been acutely conscious of the significance of these alliances, which have the potential to determine the future shape of the sector. One of the Commission's main objectives is to ensure that, with the full lifting of the remaining exclusive rights, former monopoly incumbents will not be able to entrench their dominant position or to extend it to emerging markets. Furthermore, with converging markets, companies may acquire control of essential segments which others need access in order to compete. 'The post-monopoly and future multimedia environment is likely to be characterised by

---

* Allen & Overy, Brussels.

[1] *Green Paper on the Convergence of the Telecommunications, Media and Information Technology sectors*, COM(97)623, page 12.

[2] Ungerer (1995: 467).

situations where firms singly or jointly control facilities—such as networks, conditional access systems or critical software interfaces—which may provide an essential route to customers'.[3]

Notwithstanding this risk, the Commission recognises that enterprises must be allowed to adjust to the dramatically changing market structures as these structures evolve out of demonopolisation and convergence. At the same time, the Commission aims to avoid foreclosure which would slow down market development if allowed to progress unchecked:

> On the whole we assume a positive attitude towards new vertical and horizontal partnerships and ventures as long as we can be convinced of the real synergies and benefits which should form the underlying logic for the moves. If on the other hand it looks more like a defensive strategy to sew up markets and shut out competition the competition rules must be used to block the agreement. In particular, we are watching out very closely for bottlenecks—preventing the creation of new ones and ensuring fair conditions of access where we have a *fait accompli*—and for any extensions of existing dominant positions.[4]

This paper considers the Commission's application of the Merger Regulation[5] and Article 81 [ex 85] EC in relation to horizontal and vertical alliances involving the control of a network access bottleneck, with reference, in particular, to some of the more significant examples of horizontal and/or vertical alliances that have taken place in the telecommunications/media sector over the last few years.

2. Definition of Network Access Bottleneck

At the outset, it is useful to establish a working definition of what constitutes a 'network access bottleneck'. According to the briefing paper for this workshop, the term refers to those facilities in evolving communications and information networks which represent 'essential gateways' between the provision and the

---

3 *Ibid*, page 468.

4 H. Ungerer, *Competition in the Information Society: Multimedia*, AGM, European MultiMedia Forum, 19.11.96, http://europa.eu.int/en/comm/dg04/speech/six/en/ sp96056.htm, page 5.

5 Council Regulation 4064/89 on the control of concentrations between undertakings OJ L257/14 (1990), as amended by Council Regulation 1310/97 amending Council Regulation 4064/89 on the control of concentrations between undertakings, L 180/1 (1992).

consumption of communications services. These include, for example, the local loop telecom infrastructure and conditional access systems. In the Commission's case law on this subject, this concept of a network access bottleneck appears to correspond broadly to the 'essential facilities' doctrine, referred to in both Commission decisions and sector specific telecommunications legislation.[6] The doctrine of essential facilities has been developed under Article 82 [ex 86], which prohibits the abuse of a dominant position. According to one commentator, the essence of the essential facilities doctrine is that:

> when a dominant company owns or controls a facility to which access is essential to enable its competitors to carry on business, it may not deny them access and it must grant access on a non-discriminatory basis in certain circumstances. In these circumstances, it must not use its powers as owner to give itself advantages as a competitor.[7]

The test is whether the essential facility is an insurmountable barrier to entry, i.e. whether the handicap resulting from denial of access is one that can be reasonably expected to make competitors' activities in the market in question either impossible or seriously uneconomical.

Examples of essential facilities identified by the Commission include leased line services, PSTN/ISDN services including access to such services and traffic over such services,[8] conditional access systems and navigation systems.[9] In BT/MCI II, the Commission identified a potential bottleneck on the eastern end of the transatlantic cables used to carry international direct dial and international private leased circuits (IPLC's) services between the United States and the United Kingdom, because BT's consent would be required for new competitors to enter this market.[10] In MSG Media service, the Commission was concerned at the parties' control of the provision of technical and administrative services to the pay-TV market.[11]

---

[6] 'Essential facility' is defined as 'a facility or infrastructure which is essential for reaching customers and/or enabling competitors to carry on their business and which cannot be replicated by any reasonable means', Commission notice on the application of the competition rules to access agreements, OJ C 265/02 (1998) paragraph 68. The WTO agreement on basic telecommunications services defines essential facilities as 'facilities of a public telecommunications transport network or service exclusively or predominantly provided by a single or limited number of suppliers and which cannot feasibly be economically or technically substituted in order to provide a service'.

[7] Temple Lang (1994), 486.

[8] *Atlas*, Case IV/35.337, OJ L239/23 (1996), paragraph 28.

[9] *Supra* n 1, at 29.

[10] Case No.IV/M.856, *British Telecom/MCI II* OJ L 336/1 (1997).

[11] Decision 94/922/EEC, *MSG Media Service* OJ L364/1 (1994).

In the past, in considering whether entry is either impossible or seriously uneconomical, the Commission has taken a 'short-termist' pragmatic, commercially realistic approach to what constitutes an essential facility, which concentrates more on achieving competition and new products in the short term. As noted by Temple Lang:

> The problem of choosing between short term and long term benefits sometimes presents itself acutely in those essential facilities cases in which it is theoretically possible for the plaintiff to develop its own alternative to the allegedly essential facility, but the plaintiff says it would take too long, be too unlikely, or cost too much to be a real and viable alternative. In the short term, competition in the downstream market in which the facility is needed, is promoted by requiring access to be given. In the long term, it may be that competition in the provision of facilities in question might be promoted by forcing the plaintiff to find some way of developing its own facility.[12]

There does, however, appear to be a certain reassessment of the essential facilities doctrine taking place. For example, Advocate General Jacobs in his recent opinion in the Bronner case notes that:

> First, it is apparent that the right to choose one's trading partners and freely to dispose of one's property are generally recognised principles in the laws of the Member States, in some cases with constitutional status. Incursions of these rights require careful justification. Secondly, the justification in terms of competition policy for interfering with a dominant undertaking's freedom to contract often requires a careful balancing of conflicting considerations. In the long term it is generally procompetitive and in the interests of consumers to allow a company to retain, for its own use, facilities which it has developed for the purpose of its business. For example, if access to a production, purchasing or distribution facility were allowed too easily there would be no incentive for a competitor to develop competing facilities. Thus, while competition was increased in the short term, it would be reduced in the long term. Moreover, the incentive for a dominant undertaking to invest in efficient facilities would be reduced if its competitors were, upon request, able to share the benefits.[13]

He concludes that an application of the essential facilities doctrine can be justified in terms of competition policy only in cases where the dominant undertaking has a genuine stranglehold on the related market, where duplica-

---

[12] Temple Lang (1996), Section III, page 1.
[13] Case C–7/97, *Oscar Bronner GmbH & Co. KG v Mediaprint Zeitungs-under Zeitschriftenverlag GmbH & Co. KG and Others*, [1998] ECR I–7791.

tion is impossible or extremely difficult for physical, geographical or legal reasons or highly undesirable for reasons of public policy. Cost may be an insuperable barrier but, if so, it must be such as to deter any prudent undertaking from entering the market.[14]

The main issue concerning bottlenecks which arises in the context of alliances is how the ownership of a bottleneck or essential facility, or the creation of a bottleneck, will influence the Commission's assessment of an alliance under the Merger Regulation or Article 81 [ex 85] and of the conditions and obligations which the Commission will require from the parties. Clearly, this will depend in part on the nature and structure of the alliance. The Commission's assessment of such alliances must also be seen in the context of the Commission's policy on the liberalisation of telecommunications and on the convergence of technology in the media, telecoms and broadcasting sectors.

3. Commission Policy on Telecommunications Liberalisation

The Commission perceives the telecommunications sector as vital to the emerging information society and to the economic well-being of the Community and its citizens as a whole. Set within the context of the Information Society Action plan and based on the concept of progressive evolution of competitive infrastructure,[15] the Community telecommunications regulatory package aims at market-opening based on the combined use of liberalisation measures to break down monopolies, harmonisation measures providing common rules and procedures in the markets opened to competition, the establishment of national regulatory authorities and the active use of competition rules to ensure fair competitive behaviour in the newly opened markets. The deadline for the full liberalisation of the telecommunications sector in most of the EU was the first of January, 1998. So, for example, the Directives on Open Network Provision (ONP) ensure that access is provided to users, service providers and other network operators on a transparent, non-discriminatory basis and at a fair and reasonable cost. The Directives on interconnection aim at ensuring that incumbent dominant telecommunications operators, who have no natural incentive

---

[14] One commentator has argued that the 'essential facilities' doctrine developed under Article 81 [ex 85] has a wider range of application than that developed under Article 82 [ex 86] and may be legitimately employed to restrict non-dominant companies' freedom to trade. However, this approach does not appear to have been followed in practice.

[15] H. Ungerer, 'Telecommunications Competition and Strategic Partnerships', (manuscript) speech at the 1996 European Communications Summit, page 1.

to interconnect, are required to do so. The sector specific and competition pro-visions of Community law are both important and mutually reinforcing for the proper functioning of the sector. Thus, in making an assessment under the competition rules, the Commission will seek to build, as far as is possible, on the principles established in the harmonisation legislation. It should also be borne in mind that a number of the competition law principles are also covered by specific rules in the ONP framework. The Commission has stated that proper application of these rules should often avoid the need for the applica-tion of the competition rules.[16]

The position of the Commission is less clear in relation to converging mar-kets. On December the third, 1997, the Commission adopted a Green Paper on convergence in the telecommunications, media and information technology sectors.[17] According to the Green Paper, digital technology is allowing 'a sub-stantially higher capacity of traditional and new services to converge towards the same transporting networks and to use integrated consumer devices for purposes such as telephony, television or personal computing'.

The Green Paper is intended to launch a Europe-wide debate on how this new generation of electronic media should be regulated in the next century. At present, the Commission is reviewing the current legal framework to ensure that it will still be relevant in the light of convergence. According to the Green Paper, as a general rule, issues of access to networks or to content are a matter for commercial agreement subject to the application of competition rules. Nevertheless, one issue which remains to be decided is whether the regulatory framework setting out the rules for open access currently applied to telecoms and digital television conditional access infrastructure should be extended to other sectors affected by convergence.

II. Alliances in the Telecommunications/Media Sector

'Horizontal' agreements are those made between firms that compete with each other at the same level of trade or industry. 'Vertical' agreements, on the other hand, are those between firms at different levels of trade or industry such as supplier and customer.[18] Most of the alliances in the telecommunications and media sector have involved a combination of vertical and horizontal elements.

---

[16] Commission Notice on the application of the competition rules to access agree-ments in the telecommunications sector, *supra*, n 16.

[17] *Supra*, n 1.

[18] Korah (1997: 170).

Nonetheless, they may be broadly separated into 'strategic' horizontal alliances involving competitors, such as BT/MCI[19] and Atlas[20] and 'convergence' alliances, characterised by an overlap between telecommunications and media services, where the vertical element predominates, such as MSG Media Services.[21]

A 'strategic alliance' is basically a wide arrangement between companies which may not reach the level of a full merger of all of their activities, but goes beyond a limited agreement to carry out some activities in common, as with a distribution agreement. They are mostly an attempt to respond to substantial and rapid changes to the market in which incumbent operators are active. Most of them include a possibility of evolution in accordance with further market changes. In other cases, they are attempts by companies not previously present on the telecoms market to respond to the new market opportunities created by these sudden changes. Of the two types, the former raise the most problems from a competition perspective. These alliances usually involve the setting up of a joint venture between the participating companies either as a holding company (Unisource) and/or to offer global value added and enhanced telecommunications services to very large users on a worldwide (e.g. Concert) or pan-European (Atlas) scale. 'Convergence alliances' are the more problematic subset of strategic alliances, primarily intended, as they are, to create vertical integration, for example by drawing together content provision and transmission systems. However, the key distinction in all of these cases is that made between the horizontal and the vertical aspects of a transaction as regards their perceived impact on competition.

As noted in the Commission's recent Follow-up Communication on vertical restraints, competition law generally regards vertical restraints as, on average, less harmful than horizontal competition restraints.[22] The main reason for treating a vertical restraint more leniently than a horizontal restraint lies in the fact that the latter may concern an agreement between competitors producing substitute goods/services while the former concerns an agreement between a supplier and a buyer of a particular product/service. In vertical situations, the product of the one is the input for the other, so that the exercise of market power to raise prices either up-stream or down-stream would normally hurt the demand for the product of the other (the 'self-policing character of vertical restraints'). However, this analysis falls down in a situation where one of the

---

[19] Case No. IV/34.857, OJ C93/3 (1994).
[20] *Atlas* Case No IV/35.337, OJ L 239/232.
[21] *Supra*, n 12.
[22] Follow-up Communication to the Green Paper on Vertical Restraints.

parties to vertical restraints/integration controls an essential facility, as it then dictates its competitors as well as its own costs in the downstream market. As a consequence, in a bottleneck situation, the Commission has been particularly concerned at the potential foreclosure effects inherent in vertical integration. Indeed as one commentator notes, 'Most policy disputes in telecommunications refer to vertical foreclosure'.[23] To carry out vertical foreclosure, a company must have market power in one market and the ability to use that market power to acquire an advantage in a vertically related market.[24]

1. Horizontal Alliances

Horizontal alliances may involve competitors, each of which has its own bottleneck or essential facilities, which are combining to enter into new product or geographic markets which may rely on the use of the existing bottleneck or essential facility (Atlas, Global One, Unisource). Ideally, the best way of dealing with that bottleneck would be to encourage competitors to bypass the bottleneck by creating alternatives. In its assessment under Article 81 [ex 85], therefore, the Commission considers whether the competitor could itself enter the relevant market and possibly 'break' an existing bottleneck.

   If it is accepted that the replication of a bottleneck or essential facility involves 'insurmountable' costs, then horizontal alliances are unproblematic from a competition point of view in relation to bottlenecks. The partners are, by definition, incapable of being potential competitors, as they are unable to replicate the other's bottleneck. As noted above, however, the Commission's willingness to treat a service or infrastructure as 'essential' could be viewed as 'short-termism'. Blocking horizontal alliances and forcing companies to enter both the upstream and downstream markets at once, with the added expense this would involve, would hinder the achievement of the goal of promoting new and innovative services over existing facilities, and thereby accelerating the emergence of the information society, which has been an underlying objective of the Commission since 1994.[25]

   For the most part, the Commission has chosen to categorise strategic, horizontal alliances as being pro-competitive and has concentrated more on restraining the potential for foreclosure through vertical integration. While, strictly speaking, partners in strategic alliances are often potential competitors

---

[23] Noll (1995).
[24] *Ibid* at 503.
[25] Hitchings (1998).

in the relevant market, the Commission's approach has been to conclude that for the short term, these partners are not realistically competitors and that to require them to enter the market individually would hinder the achievement of goals such as those mentioned above.

2. Vertical Mergers

As noted above, the Commission's main concern in relation to alliances in the telecommunications sector has been the vertical component. Vertical integration is seen as creating an incentive to use control of a network access bottleneck to foreclose and discriminate against competitors in the downstream market. There is an inherent conflict of interest for a vertically integrated undertaking which is active in both the upstream and downstream market. It has no interest in offering non-discriminatory access to its upstream facilities when this enables its competitors to compete with it more effectively in the downstream market. It is this that brings the risk of foreclosure of competitors, in particular as regards access by them to infrastructures, networks and/or services that can be viewed as bottlenecks and that are indispensable for the development of the competitors' activities. The problem is the extent of the foreclosure effect for other competitors in both the upstream and the downstream markets and the barriers to entry which would result if competitors had to enter the market on both levels at once. These cases require an assessment of the market power of both parties at both levels.

EC competition law has, in the past, viewed vertical restraints with suspicion, if not open hostility. By contrast, in the US, antitrust authorities have traditionally adhered to the Chicago School, which holds that most vertical mergers, viewed through the lens of neo-classical economics, are often pro-competitive (or neutral) as they enable the merged entity to realise significant efficiencies as a result of the vertical integration.[26] Nonetheless, even in the US, there appears to be a swing towards stricter enforcement, which, while relying on the Chicago School's economic analysis, looks at vertical mergers with closer scrutiny as regards aftermarket effects and barriers to entry. The key to the new view is to focus not on the effects of the merger on the immediate relevant market, where the merger will usually have pro-competitive or neutral

---

[26] This thinking is of course led by the Chicago School premise that, in a market economy, the aim of competition is to maximise economic efficiency (thus lowering costs to consumers) and that this can be better achieved by firms with vertically integrated systems.

effects, but rather on the effects it will have on competition in upstream, downstream or ancillary markets. By focusing on these markets, analysis of the vertical merger will reveal whether these neighbouring markets will suffer from foreclosure effects as a result of the vertical integration.

The Commission, in fact, has never shared the Chicago School's view that vertical mergers have benign or ambiguous effects. It has consistently been on the look-out for the possible negative effects of vertical integration between two merging parties: creating a barrier to entry for competitors and conferring an advantage to the parties which is such as to distort competition seriously. This divergence of approach between competition authorities is clearly illustrated by the recent *Boeing/McDonnell Douglas* case.[27]

An analysis of the cases examined by the Commission under the Merger Regulation reveals that vertical elements have been a matter of considerable concern. In a number of cases under the Merger Regulation,[28] the Commission has made clear that the vertical integration between the merging undertakings was an important factor in its decision to open a Phase II (more detailed) investigation.[29] More importantly, in three recent cases in the media sector,[30] the vertical foreclosure effects of a proposed concentration were the main factor in the Commission's decision to prohibit the transactions.[31] Under the Merger Regulation, where two merging parties operate in vertically adjacent markets, the Commission generally adopts a quantitative foreclosure analysis, focusing on the market shares of the merging firms at their different vertical levels as a means of assessing the risk of substantial foreclosure of non-integrated competitors. Aside from cases under the Merger Regulation, examination of the vertical aspects has played a significant role in its consideration of joint ventures and strategic alliances under Article 81 [ex 85], even though the focus here is usually on the extent to which parties may be expected to co-operate and co-ordinate their behaviour at the horizontal level.

---

[27] *Boeing/McDonnell Douglas,* 97/815/EEC, OJ L 336/16 (1997).

[28] Council Regulation No. 4064/89 on the control of concentrations between undertakings, OJ L 257/14 (1990).

[29] *Tetra Pak/Alfa Laval,* Decision 91/535/EEC, OJ L 290/35(1991); *Siemens/Italtel,* Decision 95/255/EEC, OJ L 161/27 (1995).

[30] *MSG/Media Service,*94/922/EEC, OJ L 364/1 (1994); *Nordic Satellite Distribution,* 96/177/EEC, OJ L 53/20 (1996); *RTL/Veronica/Endemol,* 96/346/EEC, OJ L 294/14 (1996).

[31] The only other case in which considerations of vertical foreclosure were an important factor in the decision to prohibit a merger was *Kesko/Tuko,* 94/409/EEC, OJ L 110/53 (1997) (Commission).

The Commission does seem to have accepted that the market foreclosing effect of an agreement is now a critical factor in assessing vertical agreements, as an essential tool in distinguishing between these vertical restraints that are benign in effect and those that must be considered carefully under relevant competition rules. However, some commentators have noted that the Commission's Green paper on vertical restraints does not propose the use of market foreclosure tests as a future option, relying instead on 'less sophisticated' market share tests.[32] Nonetheless, in a bottleneck situation, foreclosure analysis will surely continue to be the key element in assessing the competitive impact of vertical integration.

According to the Green Paper on Convergence, vertical merger activity in telecoms and media is seen as a significant indicator of a change in industry structures in response to the convergence phenomenon.[33] The risk of foreclosure effects with vertical mergers in the converging telecoms and media sectors, with the growing interdependency between upstream and downstream markets and the tendency towards bottlenecks is, of course, particularly acute. For example, in the case of mergers between content providers and carriers, if the content provider is dominant, a competing carrier might be unable to obtain enough valuable content in the appropriate language to offer a satisfactory selection of channels and programmes. On the other hand, if the carrier is dominant, a competing provider might be unable to find satisfactory alternative broadcasters.[34] If the carrier controls a high proportion of the set-top boxes or satellites in the relevant geographic markets, then, unless it can be required to give access to other content providers or broadcasters, it might be able to prevent competitors from getting access to all the households which have already bought a set-top box, or to the satellites which they need.

In cases involving integration between companies in sectors which are separate but converging, the extent of the foreclosure is extremely difficult to assess. While the problem is the same, the raising of barriers to entry because of the need to enter several markets at once, is, in such cases, 'a series of present and future markets may need to be looked at and the mutual dependence of many companies in the media sectors must be kept in mind'.[35]

---

[32] Pheasant and Weston (1997).
[33] *Supra*, n 1, at 13.
[34] Temple Lang, *Supra* n 6.
[35] Temple Lang, *Media, Multimedia and European Community Antitrust Law*, http://europa.eu.int/en/comm/dg04/speech/seven/en/sp97070.htm, 61.

III. Article 81 [ex 85] or the Merger Regulation?

In dealing with these alliances, and, in particular, the problems posed by the bottlenecks they create or strengthen, the Commission has several tools at its disposal. This paper focuses on the use that the Commission has made of Article 81 [ex 85] and the (recently amended) Merger Regulation in order to secure effective competition in a rapidly evolving environment. Both Article 81 [ex 85] and the Merger Regulation, enable the Commission to block or restructure alliances which would lead to the creation of anti-competitive market structures, whereas Article 82 [ex 86] is aimed at preventing the abuse of an already existing position of dominance.

Article 81 [ex 85] is designed to deal with agreements between undertakings which have as their object or effect the prevention, restriction or distortion of competition. An agreement which falls foul of the prohibition contained in Article 81(1) [ex 85(1)] may be exempted under Article 81(3) [ex 85(3)], if it can be established that the agreement promotes technical or economic progress while allowing consumers a fair share of the resulting benefit, as long as the agreement does not contain any restrictions which are not indispensable to the attainment of these objectives, and, crucially, does not afford the undertakings concerned the possibility of eliminating competition in respect of a substantial part of the products in question. According to Regulation 17 (the main Regulation implementing Articles 81 and 82 [ex 85 and 86]), 'a decision in application of Article 81(3) [ex 85(3)] of the Treaty shall be issued for a specified period and conditions and obligations may be attached thereto'.[36] Further, there is no time-limit imposed on the Commission for it to reach its decision.

The Merger Regulation contains a compulsory system of prior notification for substantial cross-border mergers and acquisitions, or 'concentrations' with a 'Community dimension',[37] as defined in Article 1. If a notified transaction is found to 'create or strengthen a dominant position as a result of which competition would be significantly impeded in the common market' or a substantial part of it, it is to be declared incompatible with the common market and prohibited. Companies risk fines and the invalidity of their transaction if they fail to notify. Investigation under the Merger Regulation is subject to strict time-limits, and the Commission has a maximum of five months within which to reach its decision. Significantly, the Commission does not have the power to

---

[36] Article 8, Council Regulation 17/62 OJ 204/62.

[37] In order to have a Community dimension, certain turnover thresholds must be met. New lower thresholds were introduced on 1st March, 1998, which will result in considerably more transactions being examined under the Merger Regulation.

exempt a merger for a limited period of time only; it must either clear the transaction in question permanently (with or without conditions) or prohibit it.

On March the first, 1998, a series of far-reaching changes to the Merger Regulation entered into force. Prior to these latest changes, the jurisdiction of the Merger Regulation over joint ventures was limited to concentrative joint ventures. This assumed the existence of a jointly controlled venture which did not afford the possibility of the parents co-ordinating their competitive behaviour. As a result, the Merger Regulation did not apply where two or more parents operated in the same product market as the joint venture or in an upstream, downstream or neighbouring market. In this instance, the joint venture was deemed co-operative, rather than concentrative, and was subject to Article 81 [ex 85] of the Consolidated Treaty.

Following the amendments, the potential co-ordination of the competitive conduct of the parties no longer prevents the application of the Merger Regulation, though subject to the important proviso that the issue of co-ordination will still be assessed according to the Article 81 [ex 85] criteria, even if, now, this will occur within the context and strict time-limits of a Merger Regulation inquiry. The investigation may be split, with the joint venture being examined by the Merger Task Force (MTF), while the Article 81 [ex 85] aspects are assessed by DG IV officials. The key issue now is whether the joint venture is a 'full-function' joint venture, i.e. if it fulfils, on a lasting basis, all the functions of an autonomous economic entity, in which case it falls to be examined under the Merger Regulation.

There are significant differences, both conceptual and procedural, in the Commission's approach to alliances under Article 81 [ex 85] and the Merger Regulation. The appropriate procedure has, in the past, largely depended on the structure of the alliance. It should, however, be borne in mind that the procedure selected can have a significant impact on the eventual result of an investigation, both in terms of the conditions imposed on the parties and, indeed, whether the proposed alliance is to be allowed to proceed.

Prior to the latest changes to the Merger Regulation, strategic horizontal alliances between Telecommunications Operators (TOs) going beyond the pure acquisition of shares were almost always examined under Article 81(1) [ex 85(1)] because, given their strong position in their respective domestic markets, their financial means and their technical skills, they could enter the new areas of the market on their own and had to be considered at least potential competitors. By entering together, they restrict independent R&D activities, production and the distribution of services, which are all restrictions that reduce current and future choice of alternative suppliers and services. Smaller joint ventures and new market entrants, however, were mostly determined to be of a concentrative nature

and examined under the Merger Regulation mainly due to the continued existence of separate national markets and the fact that the parents were still active
in different States or came from different sectors.

In the past, developments in the telecoms/media/information technology
sector have tested the consistency of the approach under European competition law to the analysis of alliances and joint ventures. As Ungerer notes, many
of these projects were inevitably constructed in such a way that it was not clear
whether they were rightly categorised as co-operative or concentrative joint
ventures, which in the past meant the difference between the application of the
Merger Regulation and Regulation 17. Choosing between the two, according
to Ungerer, involved:

> balancing the risk of co-ordination between parents and retaining the ongoing
> scrutiny of these risks, if necessary coupled with behavioural conditions, which only
> Regulation 17 offers, or giving priority to the concept of a joint venture as a new
> autonomous entity which should principally be considered in its own right as to
> market impact, as provided for under the Merger Regulation.[38]

Temple Lang argues that in most respects the Commission regards the differences between the cases dealt with under the Merger Regulation and cases
under Regulation 17 as merely procedural. He suggests that although on paper
the substantive tests appear different, in practice the Commission treats the test
under Article 81(3)(b) [ex 85(3)(b)] as a test of dominance, and tries to ensure
that the same or similar results are achieved under both Regulations.[39]

Nonetheless, as noted above, there are some significant differences. Merger
Regulation decisions are permanent, while individual exemptions under
Article 81(3) [ex 85(3)] are temporary. This leads, or could lead, to a different
result in a case where, by ensuring restrictive effects were only short term,
future potential competition could be secured. In other words, an authorisation under Article 81(3) [ex 85(3)] might be justified in some circumstances
where merger clearance would not. The Commission attaches great importance
to this ability to be able to subject transactions in a changing environment to
periodic review:

> Our current practice regarding exemptions in the media sector is very much influ-
> enced by its evolving nature. So, we are inclined to grant exemptions of a relatively

---

[38] Ungerer, *supra* n 2.
[39] *Supra* n 12, Section III, page 1.

short duration and strictly limited to the concrete range of services and/or business scope notified. . . . . [T]his practice reflects an intention to periodically re-assess market evolution and the effect of strategic alliances in the market.[40]

A behavioural undertaking is more readily accepted in cases under Article 81 [ex 85] than in merger cases. This issue has proven highly significant in relation to the Commission's approach to bottleneck issues in alliances investigated under the Merger Regulation. It has often been argued that the Commission may only accept structural undertakings.[41] This argument was based on the purpose of the Merger Regulation, which is to preserve competitive market structures, as well as on the wording of Article 8(2). While this limitation is somewhat disputed,[42] the fact remains that the Commission has, in the past, displayed a considerable reluctance to accept behavioural undertakings in several important telecommunications merger cases, relating to access to the relevant bottleneck, describing them as 'mere pledges of conduct which have no structural dimension and whose fulfilment cannot in any case be checked'.[43] This refusal resulted in the prohibition of the mergers in question.

It could be argued that this difference of approach is due to the fact that the Merger Regulation is more concerned with the impact of the newly created entity on the structure of the market, whereas Article 81 [ex 85] addresses the possible co-ordination of the competitive behaviour of the partners and the potentially anti-competitive effects of constraints.

Finally, the time-limits under the Merger Regulation are seen as a definite advantage and, combined with the permanent nature of clearance, they have led to a tendency for companies to structure the alliance to fall within the scope of the Merger Regulation. Nonetheless, the relatively short time-limits under the Merger Regulation may compel the Commission, in some especially significant or complicated cases, to prohibit a merger whereas under Article 81 [ex 85] the process of revision and negotiation could take many months, even years.

Following the latest changes to the Merger Regulation, which also include

---

[40] Miguel Angel Pena Castellot, speech to be found on the internet, 'The Application of the Competition Rules in the Telecommunications Sector: Strategic Alliances', http:\\europe.eu.int/eu/comm/dg04/speech/five/eu/sp95013.htm, page 5.

[41] Kerse and Cook (1996): '[I]n the first edition of this text we doubted whether undertakings as to future commercial behaviour were appropriate, or even legally valid or enforceable. These doubts are apparently shared by some members of the Advisory Committee and by the Commission itself'.

[42] Case 102/96, *Gencor* v *Commission*, currently under consideration by the Court of First Instance.

[43] Decision 94/922/EEC, *MSG Media Service*, OJ L364 (1994), paragraph 99.

new lower turnover thresholds, it can be expected that many more transactions in the telecommunications sector will be examined under the Merger Regulation, as the prospect of co-ordination of the parents' competitive behaviour is no longer a disqualifying factor. It will be possible for companies to structure their alliances in such a way as to ensure that the joint venture created to implement their alliance fulfils the criteria of a 'full function joint venture'. In the past, some commentators have identified a certain reluctance on the part of the Commission to characterise joint ventures for the provision of telecommunications services as being concentrative in nature and thereby subject to the more liberal and speedy review available for concentrations.[44] This possibility will no longer arise, although the Commission does have some room for manoeuvre, in relation to its characterisation of a joint venture as 'full function'. The risk is that the Commission may be tempted to expand the requirements for a 'full-function' joint venture in an attempt to bring transactions under Article 81 [ex 85], where they can be examined at leisure, in stark contrast to the fixed Merger Regulation time-table. Of course, the solution to this is the reform of the Article 81 [ex 85] procedure with the introduction of a more streamlined procedure and a timetable for the various stages in an investigation.

The changes should not, however, lead to any significant difference in the Commission's conceptual approach to bottlenecks and access issues. It will still be applying Article 81 [ex 85] to the conduct of the parent companies. As a result, it will still be able to impose behavioural restrictions such as non-discriminatory access on the parent companies. Furthermore, as Regulation 17 still applies, exemptions for the conduct of the parents under Article 81(3) [ex 85(3)] will continue to be for a fixed term only. Similarly, with regard to the joint venture itself, the Commission will still be applying the Merger Regulation criterion of dominance and concentrating on the impact of the joint venture on the structure of the relevant market. It will be interesting to see whether the Commission takes a more relaxed approach to the adoption of behavioural undertakings, in relation to the joint venture, given that the DG IV officials investigating the Article 81 [ex 85] aspects in tandem with the MTF's appraisal of the joint venture, will have considerable experience and presumably more confidence in the imposition and supervision of such under-takings.

Some support for this may also be gained from the change to the wording of Article 8(2) of the Merger Regulation. Previously, the Commission could attach conditions and obligations to the decision 'with a view to modifying the original concentration plan'; now, however, the obligations are those 'render-

---

[44] Long (1998: 292).

ing the concentration compatible with the common market'. Given that this phrase must also cover the obligations imposed under Article 81(3) [ex 85(3)], it must apply to behavioural as well as structural undertakings, although it remains to be seen whether the Commission interprets this as such.

The most significant difference is likely to result from the fact that the Commission's investigation of the co-ordination of the parents' behaviour under Article 81 [ex 85] will now have to be carried out in a maximum of five months. Given that in the *GlobalOne* and *Atlas* decisions, it took on average 18–20 months of investigations and discussions between the Commission and the parties for the transaction to be exempted, this restriction may cause significant practical difficulties. In some cases, Commission officials may feel that they have not had sufficient time to address the issues raised by the transaction in enough detail to feel sufficiently confident to allow it to proceed, with or without conditions. The Commission is very keen to ensure that the alliances that take place in these sectors do not result in foreclosure of markets before they have even had an opportunity to be opened up. It is therefore possible that the Commission might prefer to prohibit a joint venture rather than risk the consolidation or creation of bottlenecks in a situation where it was not completely satisfied that this risk had been properly assessed and dealt with.

One challenge for both the parties, and particularly interveners, is identifying which conduct should be examined under the two different tests set out in the new Merger Regulation. In other words, it may be difficult at times to identify when particular conduct creates or strengthens the joint venture's position, so that it is subject to the dominance test, or whether, in reality, it amounts to co-ordination of the parents' behaviour, for example, where the parent companies agree that the joint venture will be their exclusive distributor. This is significant, as it is often the cumulation of factors that leads to a finding of dominance, so the decision to categorise behaviour determines not only the criteria applied, but may also determine the perceived impact of the transaction as a whole. For interveners not privy to the details of the Commission's approach, it may be difficult to make submissions where they are unsure even of the test being applied. Of course, it may well be the case that the Commission will have a large degree of discretion as regards which test to apply and may even apply both tests to the behaviour in question. Interveners may decide to address competitive concerns in the alternative, under both the dominance and the restrictive practices tests.

A further issue which is not entirely clear is whether the amended Merger Regulation allows the Commission to take into account the 'creation or strengthening of a dominant position' of the parent companies. While the structure of the Merger Regulation does seem to suggest that the test in relation to the parent companies is the co-ordination of their competitive behaviour, the wording does leave some uncertainty on this issue, which may need to be clarified by the Commission in future investigations.

In the telecommunications sector, there have been four joint ventures which have been assessed under the amended Merger Regulation, all of which were cleared within the one month period. These included a joint venture for the provision of Internet services in Sweden, between Telia, Telenor Nextel and Schibsted Multimedia and a joint venture in Italy between Deutsche Telecom, France Telecom and the Italian electricity group ENEL.[45] Although press releases are available, the decisions have not yet been published. When published, it can be hoped that they will provide further clarification of the new procedure. In any event, it is clear from the press releases that the Commission is conducting a 'dual analysis' of the joint ventures, although the press releases do not provide any detail on how precisely the Commission broke down its analysis.

IV. Examples of Strategic Alliances Examined Under Article 81 [ex 85]

This section examines in more detail the Commission's approach in some of the more significant cases of strategic alliances examined in the last few years.

1. BT/MCI[46]

In July 1994, the Commission cleared the joint venture between BT and MCI, known as Concert, making it the first global strategic alliance in the telecommunications sector to have cleared all the regulatory procedures around the world. The new joint venture company was formed to address the emerging market for value added and enhanced services to large multinational corporations, extended enterprises and other intensive users of telecommunications services provided over international intelligence networks. The joint venture was originally notified to the Commission under the Merger Regulation in August 1993, but the Commission ruled that it was not a concentration and converted the notification to an Article 81 [ex 85] proceeding. The agreement fell under the scope of Article 81 [ex 85] because BT and MCI were, and for the

---

[45] IP/98/476, IP/98/557, IP/98/656, IP/98/755.
[46] *Supra,* n 19.

ɔreseeable future would continue to be, at least potential competitors in the ·verall market for telecommunications services and also in the enhanced and .alue added global telecommunications segment of the market which was to be ᵃddressed by Concert.

The Commission concluded, however, that Concert qualified for an individual exemption under Article 81(3) [ex 85(3)]. In particular, it would be able o offer a set of new services of a global nature to customers more quickly, heaply and of a more advanced nature than either BT or MCI would be capa- •le of providing alone under their existing technologies. Through Concert, ach parent would substantially reduce the costs and risks involved in offering ᵢew services on such a scale. The Commission examined whether the creation •f Concert would afford the parties the possibility of eliminating competition ɴ respect of the services to be offered by Concert. First, the Commission con- luded that there would be significant competition at the level of Concert from •ther alliances such as Unisource as well as possible future alliances of other ᶜOs. However, the Commission also examined in detail the extent to which ᵢccess to the MCI and BT networks by third parties was possible, as well as the ᵢssue of cross-subsidisation. It was satisfied, however, that the national regula- ory environment in the home markets of the parties (the US and the UK) ᵢnsured that both parties had to provide access to their networks to third par- ies on a non-discriminatory basis.

This case clearly demonstrates that the more competitive the home markets ɔf the parents are, the easier it is to obtain approval with less onerous condi- ions. As discussed above, one way of dealing with bottlenecks is to encourage he development of alternative infrastructures to bypass the bottleneck, which ᵢs one of the aims of the Commission policy on liberalisation. In a situation ᵥhere the Commission is satisfied with the progress towards liberalisation, ᵥith the 'gate-opening' process, and with the ability of national regulators to ɔrevent the abuse of existing bottlenecks through the strict imposition of non- ᵈiscriminatory access, it is far easier for a joint venture to obtain clearance.

In BT/MCI, the home markets of the parents were largely liberalised, and he Commission imposed only one condition: that the provision whereby MCI ᵥould be prevented from using certain IP rights if it sought to enter BT's core ᵐarket be limited to five years. This can be contrasted with the position in Atlas, (discussed below) where the home markets of the parties (France and ᵍermany) were far less liberalised. Under BT's Public Telecommunications ᴼperator Licence, BT cannot show undue preference or discrimination in the ɔrovision of certain services towards other persons, nor unfairly favour any ɔart of its own business against competitors. Further, the national regulator, ᴼFTEL, is empowered to act against any unfair cross subsidy by BT. These controls, together with the additional explanations provided by the parties led the Commission to conclude that it was not necessary, in its exemptio decision, to require the parties to give any non-discrimination undertakings.

As more markets become liberalised, it can be hoped that there will be trend towards decisions such as BT/MCI, where the Commission has sufficien confidence in the national regulatory framework to implement the sector spe cific telecoms legislation, with its in-built principles of essential facilities an non-discriminatory access, so that it does not burden companies with adminis tratively onerous decisions involving additional reporting requirements, an added uncertainty which risk disadvantaging a company in a fast moving envi ronment.

2. Atlas[47] and GlobalOne[48]

On July 17th 1996, the Commission granted an exemption pursuant to Articl 81(3) [ex 85(3)] for five years to Atlas, the joint venture between Franc Telecom (FT) and Deutsche Telekom (DT) and for 7 years to GlobalOne, a joint venture between FT, DT and Sprint. The joint ventures address the mar kets for the provision of non-reserved telecommunications services to corpo rate users both globally and regionally. In particular, they relate to the market for non-reserved corporate telecommunications services, the market for trav eller services and the market for carrier services.

The Atlas and the GlobalOne decisions are the most elaborate decision taken by the Commission in the field of strategic global alliances. They exem plify the two key elements of the Commission's approach, intended to ensur that these alliances do not allow the exploitation of network access bottleneck to prevent the development of effective competition in downstream markets The first is to use such notifications as levers to require Member States to brin about full liberalisation in their respective jurisdictions, thereby creating th environment for alternative infrastructures. Secondly the Commission impose detailed conditions designed to ensure the non-discriminatory access of thir parties, and to prevent any 'unfair' advantage to the parties' joint venture in th new market.

The Commission considered that the Atlas and GlobalOne joint venture would potentially lead to a substantial reduction of competition. DT and F1 had dominant positions in the two single largest Member States' telecommuni

---

[47] Case No. IV/35.337, OJ L239/23 (1996).
[48] Decision 94/547/EEC, OJ L239/57 (1996).

cations markets, reinforced by a legal infrastructure monopoly until liberalisation. Even after liberalisation, it was considered that FT and DT would, at least for a number of years, remain indispensable suppliers of building blocks for the relevant services in France and Germany. The cost of building infrastructure would impair competitors' ability to create a competitive network of similar scope and density to DT's and FT's in these countries. The link between commitments to liberalisation and clearance in these cases was strongly emphasised by Commissioner Van Miert:

> We are taking full advantage of the strong and effective link between implementation of government commitments to liberalisation and our conditions for allowing alliances involving dominant telecom operators . . . [N]otifications such as GlobalOne and Unisource, are a very effective lever to put pressure on the national governments concerned to make solid commitments as regards opening up the relevant market . . . [O]ne of the main conditions for us to give this joint venture the go ahead is that full implementation of the commitment to liberalise alternative infrastructure in both Germany and France is not only notified but actually effective—this means new licences granted and new players entering the market.[49]

For example, the exemption for the creation of the Atlas joint venture under Article 81(3) [ex 85(3)] was granted for five years and came into force when the first two alternative telecommunications infrastructure licences were granted.[50] The main underlying issue was the need to develop a viable infrastructure for real competition at customer access level.

The Atlas Decision imposes a very precise and detailed range of conditions aimed at ensuring third party access. It is *conditional* on DT and FT granting, to any third party that applies for interconnection of its telecommunication facility or system with DT or FT's networks, such interconnection on non-discriminatory terms vis-à-vis Atlas. The terms and conditions applied by DT and FT to Atlas have to be 'similar to the terms and conditions applied to other providers of similar services', for example in relation to price, quality of service, usage conditions, the timetable for installation of requested facilities, connection of apparatus or repair and maintenance services. Atlas is not to be granted terms and conditions or to be exempted from any usage restrictions which would enable it to offer services which competing providers are prevented from offering. DT and FT cannot discriminate in connection with a decision to modify technical interfaces for the access to reserved or essential facilities

---

[49] Commissioner Karel Van Miert, 'Preparing for 1998 and beyond', (manuscript), speech to the IIC Telecommunications Forum. 15 July 1996, page 3.

[50] Paragraph 76 of the Atlas decision, *supra*, n 47.

substantially, and competitors are to have access to technical information to which they can adapt, lest their quality of services be reduced.

Other conditions imposed included a prohibition on cross-subsidisation, and a prohibition on 'bundling' with an obligation to provide certain services under separate contracts. The obligations imposed on the Global One joint venture mirror those in the Atlas Decision. One of the most striking aspects of the Atlas and GlobalOne decisions is the fact that the Commission chose to impose conditions rather than obligations. The breach of any one condition can cause the GlobalOne exemption to fall automatically, whereas the breach of an obligation only leads to withdrawal of the exemption or part of it after a formal Commission procedure. This is a considerably more onerous burden than that imposed on BT/MCI or, indeed, Unisource/Uniworld. The risk with the imposition of such detailed conditions is that they can impair a company's ability to move and react quickly to changes in a rapidly evolving environment. The imposition of long and extremely detailed conditions and reporting requirements creates a heavy administrative burden, particularly for an entity which is just trying to get off the ground.

Further, even the best-intentioned regulations and decrees can lead to uncertainties in implementation and unexpected problems due to the rapidly evolving technology. This can lead to added expense and delay, which affects a companies' abilities to respond quickly to market demand. This is particularly significant in high technology industries, with their short product life cycles. For example, the commercial life of IP rights in the computer industry has been described as 'shorter than the growing season in Silicon Valley'.

Further, the Commission is putting itself into the role of regulator, thereby undermining the role of national regulators, when it does not really have the resources and structures to perform this function properly. It is to be hoped that with the full implementation of liberalisation throughout Europe, the Commission will have more confidence in the adequacy of sector specific regulation to deter anti-competitive conduct without the need for additional regulation of the type imposed in the Atlas and Global One decisions.

V. Vertical Alliances and the Merger Regulation

1. MSG Media Services[51]

MSG is representative of a new generation of cases which are directly linked to multimedia and the convergence phenomenon. In deciding to prohibit the

---

[51] *Supra*, n 11.

roposed joint venture, the Commission clearly demonstrated that while it avours restructuring to meet the needs of a rapidly evolving environment, it annot accept that markets may be closed before they start to develop. MSG Media Service involved a proposed joint venture involving Bertelsmann, a eading German media group, Kirch, the principal supplier of feature films and V programming in Germany and Deutsche Telekom, who own the cable etwork in Germany. The object of MSG was the technical, business and dministrative handling of pay-TV and other communication services. The Commission identified three relevant markets: (i) that for technical and administrative services for pay-TV and other TV services financed through subscription or payment by viewers in Germany, (ii) the market for pay-TV itself and iii) the market for cable television networks.

Firstly, the Commission noted that the most likely companies to enter the market for the supply of technical and administrative services for pay-TV are pay-TV suppliers themselves or cable network operators. With the setting up of MSG, there was, therefore, a concentration of those enterprises which would otherwise each have had to install an infrastructure for digital pay-TV and provide the corresponding services. Thus, the joint venture meant that the most likely potential competitors were being excluded in the development phase of the market. The Commission did not accept that the parents would not have been able to enter the market individually. It went on to conclude that:

> it appears scarcely conceivable that competing suppliers in Germany could enter the market for technical and administrative services for pay-TV once MSG had established itself on that market. The installation of an alternative infrastructure would require a large amount of investment that would be undertaken by other suppliers only if there was a chance of market penetration. However, such a chance would scarcely exist if MSG had already occupied the market. An alternative supply of services would have to impose itself against the combined competitive advantages and specific strengths of Telekom on the one hand and Bertelsmann/Kirch on the other. This appears hardly possible.

At the time of the decision, there was only one pay-TV channel in Germany, Premiere, which was owned by Bertelsmann, Kirch and Canal Plus. However, the Commission felt that it was to be expected that, as a consequence of the introduction of digital television over the next few years, the joint ventures downstream market would grow rapidly and new suppliers would enter the market. Following the transaction, all pay-TV suppliers who entered the pay-TV market in the future would be in a position of being forced to take supplies of services underlying pay-TV from an enterprise controlled by the leading pay-TV suppliers. They would, therefore, either have to accept MSG' conditions or stay out of the market, as is the case in the UK where a new prc gramme supplier is dependent on BskyB's infrastructure. Via MSG Bertelsmann and Kirch could significantly influence competition from futur pay-TV suppliers and, to a large extent, shape it as they wished whilst benefil ing from artificially high prices through their share in MSG's earnings.

By using the excuse of technical constraints that could only be verified wit' difficulty, MSG would have the possibility of supplying MSG's services in sucl a way that market access of programmes that ran counter to the interests o Bertelsmann and Kirch was, at least, delayed. The Commission concluded tha in view of the considerable competitive advantages that were involved fo Bertelsmann and Kirch in MSG and the possible adverse effects on future com petitors, it was to be expected that the proposed concentration would create ; durable dominant position for Bertelsmann and Kirch on the pay-TV marke in Germany.

The parties offered a number of undertakings in an attempt to meet th Commission's concerns but these were rejected for a number of reasons Firstly, the Commission felt that the undertakings were mostly behavioura rather than structural. MSG's undertakings not to discriminate merely com plied with the legal obligations incumbent on undertakings in a position o market dominance. In view of the various possibilities of hidden discriminatio and obtaining information that existed in practice, it would be difficult to prov that MSG was not behaving neutrally. Only the undertaking on the introduc tion of a common interface contained a structural aspect, but it was not enougl to prevent market dominance by MSG, and was subject to reservations whicl the Commission considered made it amount to a non-binding declaration o intent. The other undertakings were described as 'mere pledges of conduc which have no structural dimension and whose fulfilment cannot in any even be checked'. They were, therefore, inappropriate to solve the structura problem.

The parties argued that the rapid acceptance of digital TV would be pro moted by MSG, but the Commission felt that the hindering of effective com petition that would result from the proposed joint venture 'may even make th achievement of technical and economic progress questionable' and that poten tial suppliers of pay-TV may decide not to enter the market to the same extent The successful spread of digital TV would, in this situation, be hindered rathe than promoted.

Clearly, the assessment of the impact of the venture on the market as wel as the impact on future market evolution was vital to this decision. The Commission commented in its Annual Report on Competition Policy:

The affected markets are currently in a transitional phase, since the telecommunications markets were about to be liberalised and new technologies and services were continually being developed and some were about to be introduced. In this situation, the decision of the Commission took on a particular importance because future market structures were being defined. The Commission, therefore, acted to ensure that these future markets were not foreclosed.[52]

It is thought that the Commission would have allowed the joint venture to proceed if a common interface had been combined with a differently structured, more broadly-based company, as this would guard against the restriction of competition by a very small group of key players. Indeed, Commissioner Martin Bangemann is reported as saying that 'in principle, it is a very good idea and given a different ownership constellation, should have been encouraged'.

It is interesting to note that many of the Commission's objections to possible anti-competitive behaviour by MSG would have amounted to an infringement of Article 82 [ex 86] if adopted in practice. However, combined with the structural, long-term monopoly in the market for conditional access services, and the difficulty of policing discriminatory policies, it is evident that the Commission felt justified in blocking the creation of MSG.

2. Bertelsmann/Kirch/Deutsche Telekom[53]

Four years later the same parties notified two mergers, which together would have set the framework for the future development of digital pay-TV in Germany:

a) The acquisition of joint control by CLT-UFA and Kirch of the German pay-TV provider, Premiere, and of BetaDigital, which provides technical services for broadcasting digital pay-TV programmes. CLT-UFA is a joint venture between Bertelsmann AG and Audiofina SA. The aim of this merger was to develop Premiere into a joint digital pay-TV channel and marketing platform, using Kirch's current digital television activities, its d-box technology and technical services from BetaDigtal.

b) Acquisition of joint control by CLT-UFA, Kirch and Deutsche Telekom of BetaResearch, currently a Kirch subsidiary which holds exclusive licences

---

[52] 25th Competition Policy Report (1995), pp. 174–174: OJ L134/32, 5.06.96.
[53] *Bertelsmann/Kirch(Beta research)/Deutsche Telekom*, 99/154/EC, OJ L 53/31 (1999).

for Beta access technology in Germany, Austria and the German-speakin, areas of Switzerland. This merger was intended to give Deutsche Telekon access to the Beta technology.

Premiere joint venture: The Commission felt that through the mergei Premiere would achieve a dominant position on the market for pay-TV ii Germany and the German-speaking area, particularly since the assets of it only present competitor, the Kirch subsidiary DF-1, would be transferred to i following the merger. The pooling of their programme resources and Premiere's existing subscription base would prevent the development of an; additional broadcasting platform in the German pay-TV market. Premieri would be in a position to determine the terms under which other broadcaster could enter the market. Furthermore, in the market for technical services, fo: pay-TV, BetaDigital would attain a lasting dominant position in the satellit. sector in Germany.

BetaResearch merger: After the BetaResearch merger, Deutsche Telekon was to have provided the technical platform in the cable network for the pro vision and broadcasting of pay-TV programmes. The Commission concluded however, that the merger would result in Deutsche Telekom permanently becoming the only supplier of technical services for pay-TV in the cable net work. This would further strengthen Deutsche Telekom's still dominant posi tion on the market for cable network.

Under the terms of their agreement, CLT-UFA, Kirch and Deutsche Telekom had all committed themselves to using Beta access technology and the d-box decoder, which has a self-contained proprietary encryption system. After the merger, therefore, all current providers of digital pay-TV, and the future provider of technical services, Deutsche Telekom, would all be commit ted to this technology, and would jointly control the exclusive licensee, BetaResearch. The Commission felt that the development of an alternative decoder structure was not very likely, so that any other service providers would have to use the parties' Beta technology and would depend on obtaining a licence from BetaResearch. As a result, it could prevent market entry through its licensing policy. Further, CLT-UFA, Kirch and Deutsche Telekom, through BetaResearch, would control the future development of the decoder technology.

After last-minute negotiations failed to produce a settlement which would satisfy its competition concerns, the European Commission decided unani mously to prohibit the two mergers. Once again, as with the MSG Media Service merger four years previously, the Commission noted that it would have welcomed an agreement which met its competition concerns, but stressed the need for the digital TV market to be kept open and allowed to evolve on a competitive basis. It has been suggested that the first MSG decision marked a turnaround in the Commission's use of competition policy as an instrument to secure open competition in the media field. Previously, the Commission had relied on regulation as its principal tool and had been criticised for its failure to counter the market dominance of major media groups. Certainly, since this decision, the Commission has shown a new determination to assert itself in this field.

A possible problem with the MSG decision is that it may act as a deterrent to the formation of vertical alliances of this type in this sector, although, as one commentator has noted, perhaps the German market is perhaps exceptional in the level of concentration which exists at programme supply and cable operator level. As the Commission cannot, on the other hand, intervene to restrict the establishment of monopoly positions by single corporations, it may be that the development of single suppliers of services will be the pattern of development in the future. However, convergence is having a fundamental impact on the dynamics of the industry, as rapid technological changes bring businesses that were once distinct closer together. As a result, it is predicted that mergers and acquisitions amongst converging technologies, such as the recent acquisition by Ericsson, the Swedish telecoms operator, of the Internet business, Advanced Computer Communications, will set the pattern in the industry in future, and negative decisions by the Commission in highly particularised cases such as MSG are unlikely to reduce the general enthusiasm for such deals.[54]

3. Nordic Satellite

A similar case, which also led to a prohibition following a Phase II investigation, was Nordic Satellite Distribution[55]. The NSD joint venture was set up for the transmission of satellite television programming to cable television operators and home satellite reception dishes in the Nordic region. The joint venture's parents were all important companies in the transmission of television and media in the Nordic area. The three firms combined would control virtually all of the satellite capacity for the broadcasting of programmes into the Nordic region. The Commission considered that the operation would have an impact on the affected markets both horizontally and vertically, the markets being:

---

[54] *Financial Times*, 10th September, 1998.
[55] Decision 96/177/EEC, OJ L 53/20 (1996).

a) provision of satellite TV transporter capacity;
b) operation of cable TV networks;
c) distribution of satellite pay-TV and other encrypted TV channels direct to households.

However, it was the high degree of vertical integration achieved which seems to have caused most of the problem for the Commission. The down-stream market positions (cable TV operations and pay-TV) and those upstream (satellite transporters, provision of programmes) would have rein-forced each other. Through this vertically integrated operation, the parties would be put in the position of being able to foreclose the Nordic satellite TV market from competitors. The joint venture would have held a bottleneck monopoly controlling the Nordic market for satellite TV broadcasting:

> The vertical integration of NSD means that the positions of the parties in various markets reinforce each other. Particularly, it should be noted that the positions of the parties in the downstream markets (cable TV networks and distribution) rein-force the dominant position on transponders by deterring potential competitors from broadcasting from other transponders to the Nordic area.[56]

The parties had argued that NSD would achieve technical and economic progress through an improved distribution of satellite TV in the Nordic region. The Commission roundly rejected these arguments stating at paragraph 151:

> The Commission considers that an infrastructure as described by the parties could be highly efficient and beneficial to consumers. However, it must be an open infra-structure accessible to all interested parties. In particular, the Commission takes the view that the participation of such a strong broadcaster as Kinnevik in NSD means that there is a high risk that this will not be the case. Therefore, it is likely that the operation will lead to less variety in the offer to Nordic TV households in the future. Furthermore, in the opinion of the Commission, the vertically integrated nature of the proposed operation is not necessary in order to create such an integrated infra-structure.

As a result, the concentration was declared to be incompatible with the common market and prohibited.

---

[56] Decision 96/177/EEC, OJ L 53/20 (1996) at paragraph 69.

VI. Conclusions

The changes to the Merger Regulation should mean that the old balancing act between the Merger Regulation and Article 81 [ex 85] should no longer be such a problem. There will still, however, be issues of delineation as to what constitutes co-ordination of the parents' competitive behaviour warranting scrutiny under Article 81 [ex 85], and the classification of joint ventures as 'full-function'. Furthermore, it remains to be seen how the new time-limits affect the assessment and whether the Commission's approach to behavioural undertakings will change. It is to be hoped that the recent decisions in the telecommunications sector in relation to full-function joint ventures will provide some much-needed guidance in this area.

Nonetheless, these changes do not address the fundamental problem in EC competition law which arises from the vast differences in procedure under Article 81 [ex 85] and the Merger Regulation, which leads firms to restructure their proposals to meet regulators' requirements rather than to meet market needs. It is widely felt that the Article 81 [ex 85] procedure is in need of reform. Indeed, Commissioner Van Miert has indicated that the procedure needs to be streamlined.[57] In particular, a timetable needs to be imposed on the conduct of each stage of proceedings so that they are of an acceptable duration. According to Montag, based on a sample of decisions where fines of at least 3 million ECU were imposed, on average it takes the Commission three years and nine months to adopt a decision. Additionally, a considerable increase in staffing at DG IV is needed to allow the Commission to respond within shorter time-frames. Without reform of the Article 81 [ex 85] procedure, the incentive will continue to exist for the Commission to try to categorise a transaction as falling within Article 81 [ex 85] in order to benefit from the unrestricted timetable it offers.

In relation to vertical foreclosure, one element in the Commission's approach has been to require cost separation, in order to prevent cross-subsidisation and price discrimination. However, this approach should not be seen as a panacea for all ills. The most effective way of controlling the behaviour of the vertically integrated bottleneck operator is, of course, to divide the different services into structurally separate units and force the provider of the basic services to deal with the enhanced services unit on the same basis that it deals with independent service providers. However, the costs involved in structurally separating a company in terms of lost economies of scale and scope has meant that regulators such as OFTEL have not considered this as a realistic

---

[57] Montag (1996).

option. Nonetheless, it has been argued that the alternative of cost allocation, is not really reliable as, for example, both essential and enhanced services often share the same facilities, and are supported by the same personnel. Cost allocation can involve quite arbitrary decisions about how to divide what is really an indivisible whole. Given that the point of cost allocation is to ensure that each function covers its own costs in order to prevent cross-subsidisation, if it is not possible to establish a sound economic basis for apportioning the costs, the value of the process becomes questionable. As one commentator notes:

> Cost separation is fraught with problems that undermine its reliability. It is very much a second best solution when compared with structural separation.[58]

In the MSG case, the very difficulty of policing non-discrimination requirements seemed to be a key factor in the Commission's refusal to accept the parties' proposed undertakings. Proving the existence of degraded service or inaccurate and incomplete information about network capacities is very difficult. With technology evolving so rapidly, a series of even modest delays in compliance with non-discrimination requirements could still impose significant disadvantages on vertical competitors.

Indeed, Noll goes so far as to argue that the efficacy of behavioural rules to deal with vertical foreclosure is suspect, apart from cases where the activity is obvious and blatant. On 'close calls' or issues requiring detailed understanding of the technical and economic nature of an industry, the imposition of behavioural rules may lead to unevenness of regulatory treatment and uncertainty of application. Furthermore, there is a risk that more sophisticated and subtle forms of exclusionary practices may well go undetected while actions based on what subsequently prove to be valid technical and economic arguments, are prohibited.

The Commission finds itself in a difficult situation where uncertainty as to how precisely an industry will evolve, combined with the novelty and complexity of the workings of that industry, makes it unsure firstly, of the type of conduct which should be condemned, and secondly as to the efficacy of its traditional remedies in this new environment. In this context, it has shown an understandable caution in allowing transactions to proceed where their structure and scale could be such as to render regulatory controls to secure competition on the affected markets ineffective in years to come.

---

[58] Ryan (1997).

According to Ungerer, the MSG decision established the threshold at which point the concentration of power in the whole value chain becomes unacceptable. The Commission is keenly aware that with the present, evolving market structure and the rush by key market players to gain first-mover advantages and occupy the key growth positions, there is considerable potential for the creation of bottlenecks, using all the commercial muscle developed as former monopolists, which may prove unassailable in the future. As a result, its overriding concern is to prevent foreclosure of markets now, and it is not prepared to take the risk that bottlenecks may only in fact prove to be short term. 'The challenge is that we need to balance the positive synergies of integration and partnership against the risks of entry barriers and foreclosure of markets'.[59] There has been some variation in the past in the intensity of the regulation to which the Commission has subjected alliances, in the name of securing access to the bottlenecks. Uneven regulatory treatment can severely disadvantage a company vis-à-vis its competitors and, in particular, restrict its ability to react quickly to changing market conditions. Given the Commission's emphasis on the creation of a level playing field in the telecommunications and media sector, it is to be hoped that when it comes to review the various exemptions of strategic alliances, it will make a conscious effort to ensure even-handed regulatory burdens, or clearly set out the reasons for differences in treatment of one alliance compared with another. Hopefully the Commission will continue to develop its quantitative foreclosure analysis so that it can calibrate its decisions in situations where the level of foreclosure is diminishing. Furthermore, it is to be hoped that the Commission's efforts at securing access at this stage in the process of demonopolisation and convergence will allow competition to develop on future markets in a way that does not call for a similar intensity of intervention in the future.

In such a rapidly evolving industry, there is inevitably an element of crystal-ball-gazing by the Commission in its predictions as to how markets will evolve out of demonopolisation and convergence in the next few years. This does, however, call into question the legitimacy of the Commission's reliance on such predictions as the basis for its decisions, as it renders its application of both Article 81 [ex 85] and the Merger Regulation highly uncertain for companies in this industry and gives the Commission an unsettling breadth of discretion in deciding whether to allow a transaction to proceed.

For example, the Commission was clearly uneasy at what it saw as the huge potential market power of the Atlas and Global One alliances. However, several years later, it is clear that Global One still has a battle on its hands in a

---

[59] *Supra*, n 2.

niche market crowded with carriers jostling for a limited number of con-tracts.[60] Successfully bringing together vastly different corporate cultures and technical infrastructures has proven immensely challenging for alliances such as Unisource and Global One, and according to industry observers '[n]one of these alliances has really hit the big time yet'.[61] As a result, it is essential that the Commission recognise that, at best, it is engaged in an imprecise science, and that built into its decisions is the flexibility to respond to the changing environment in which the transactions it examines are taking place.

---

[60] *Wall Street Journal*, 19th December 1997.

[61] Keith Mallinson, of the 'Yankee Group Europe', quoted in the *Wall Street Journal* of 19th December 1997.

VII

Alexander Schaub*

Bottlenecks Access in Networked Sectors: Recent Practice
under Article 81 [ex 85] and the Merger Regulation

I. Introduction

The end of 1998 is an appropriate time to hold a competition workshop on
access issues. It is only now that the economic and legal context in a number of
key networked sectors of the economies of most Member States of the
European Union allows us to discuss these issues not only on theoretical
grounds, but also as they occur in practice.

The type of issue extensively dealt with under Panel One is that of the
behaviour of a dominant firm controlling a bottleneck, in general, terms, such
a dominant player is not expected to have any powerful incentive for granting
access to its network to would-be competitors. If it does grant access, it does so
on terms and conditions that would be unlikely to allow competitors to be any
real danger to its incumbent position. As has been previously described by my
colleague Herbert Ungerer, the Commission has a framework in place to try to
prevent such anti-competitive behaviour occurring, but if it does occur, it will
normally be addressed as an abuse of dominant position under Article 82 [ex
86].

This way of dealing with dominant firms and bottlenecks represents a policy choice in the European Union. Some of our main trading partners have
chosen different ways of coping with the problem. The break-up of AT&T and
the creation of the seven regional Bell operating companies in 1984, is an example of such an alternative approach. It is difficult to say which way is better, in
particular, when recent legislative changes in the US have largely eliminated
the distinction previously drawn between local and long distance operators.

Panel Two deals with the application of Article 81 [ex 85] and the Merger
Regulation in networked sectors, in particular, when issues regarding access to
bottlenecks arise. The European Commission has a rich and growing experience in dealing with these issues in different sectors.

Whereas, under Article 82 [ex 86], the structure of the market in which
abuses take place is given and largely static, under Article 81 [ex 85] and the
Merger Regulation, the structure of the market is constantly being modified

---

* Director-Commissioner General of Competition, European Commission.

or even created. So, our assessment has to be more dynamic and must make forecasts about what the structure of the market would look like if the transaction were allowed to proceed, often with the added complexity of structural remedies.

In some cases, the intention of the parties or, at least, the effect of the transaction, is the creation or reinforcement of a dominant position. This is a major concern for the Commission. Its goal under both Article 81 [ex 85] and the Merger Regulation, is to counter the creation or enforcement of a dominant position on the understanding that such a dominant position will be abused later. Thus, under Article 81(1)(3) [ex 85(1)(3)] assessment, we will typically conclude that an exemption in not possible because the condition which requires that competition is not eliminated in respect of a substantial part of the products in question is not fulfilled (Article 81(3)(b) [ex 85(3) (b)]). Under a merger control assessment, the Commission would show that the access issue is an example of restrictions of competition resulting from the dominant position having been created or reinforced and as such, the merger would be declared incompatible with the Common Market.

A possible exception to the above concern refers to exclusive rights of way notified as part of transactions between non-dominant players in the telecommunications field. Clearly, these do not create any dominant position. As I will show later, our approach towards these exclusivity conditions has been a negative one because they have the effect of removing the existing alternative infrastructures from the market, hence substantially raising the barriers for most would-be newcomers to the market.

In the course of the following discussion, I will present several typical issues which appear in the context of cases in networked sectors where dominant positions can be created or reinforced. I will try to point out the most recurrent ones in the context of several important recent cases dealt with or currently being dealt with by the Commission. These cases will also show the increasing relevance of international co-operation in the competition field.

II. The Typical Issues which Characterise Cases under Article 81 [ex 85] or the Merger Regulation in Networked Sectors.

Unlike Article 82 [ex 86], which deals with the unilateral behaviour of firms, Article 81 [ex 85] and the Merger Regulation deal with transactions concluded between two or more firms.

Most agreements are either innocuous under a competition analysis or are not important enough to create appreciable restrictions of competition. A few, however, are concluded by big players and have such wide reaching effects that they can significantly harm existing or future competition in a given market. It is logical that we pay special attention to these. Many such transactions occur in networked sectors, in particular, in those that have been recently opened to competition and where former State monopolists are emerging as powerful vertically integrated private firms.

1. Horizontal and Vertical Aspects

In standard competition policy practice a distinction is made between horizontal and vertical agreements. It has traditionally been considered that horizontal agreements, that is agreements between companies operating at the same level in the market, are more dangerous for competition than vertical agreements, that is those concluded between companies operating at different levels in the market, for example that of supplier and customer. In general, terms, in horizontal agreements the exercise of market power by one company will benefit its competitors, so that there may be a mutual incentive to induce each other to behave anti-competitively, whereas in vertical agreements, the product of one party is an input for the other. This means that the exercise of market power by either the up-stream or the down-stream company would normally hurt the other party, so that the companies involved have an incentive to prevent the exercise of market power by the other. As a result, competition policy is, in general, very strict as regards horizontal agreements and somewhat more flexible as regards vertical agreements. The competition policy of the European Union is not an exception to that approach, and although, as is publicly known, we are revising our policy towards vertical and horizontal agreements, that basic approach will remain valid within new, more flexible policies.

However, purely horizontal or vertical agreements are rarely seen in the context of networked sectors. Rather, our experience up to now is that we have to analyse complex deals that normally include both horizontal and vertical elements at the same time, because they involve horizontal co-operation by vertically integrated firms. For the sake of clarity, I will refer to these by using for convenience the term 'strategic alliances', which will include anything from loose non-full-function joint ventures between actual or potential competitors to fully fledged mergers. Such operations present several distinctive features that make their assessment particularly demanding.

2. Market Definition

First, it must be said that market definition is often very difficult. Many strategic alliances have as their object the development or launch of innovative products or services and/or entry into new geographic areas. Innovation is by definition dynamic: different technological approaches to the same problem can, however, co-exist. Their degree of development can be different. Some can even come to dead ends. In addition, data are often unreliable or simply do not exist. Defining markets on this basis is a complex task. We must not forget that what is meant by 'market' in a competition case is a rather static picture of the market structure. Taking a decision in a given case about what the substitutable services or technologies are has clear implications on the market position of the parties. For this reason, the Commission has to be very cautious.

The dynamic nature of innovation also means that market definition can be subject to change in cases where there are rapid technological developments. The advent of digitalisation, for instance, is rapidly blurring the borders between hitherto distinct markets. The *Bertelsmann-Kirch*[1] case is a good example of this.

Networked sectors also have particular features that must be taken into account when defining markets: the existence of network externalities in the form of large scope and scale economies benefits in particular, the largest network. In addition, some elements of networks can still be very close to natural monopolies (the local-loop, for instance). Such elements point to a naturally high level of barriers to entry and exit and to a small number of big players.

Secondly, the geographical scope of markets is also sometimes complicated. If we take the example of incumbent telecommunications operators in Europe, these have traditionally been very large national companies with very little direct experience abroad. However, in the case of strategic alliances, their business was often the provision of cross-border services to big customers having a widespread presence in the world. On this basis, the Commission has defined several layers for the geographic market: a national one and a cross-border (pan-European or worldwide) layer on top of the national layer. In other cases, for instance, those regarding Internet connectivity, we have conceded the existence of global markets.

---

[1] *Bertelsmann/Kirch (Beta Research)/Deutsche Telekom*, 99/154/EC, OJ L 53/31 (1999).

3. Defining Market Power

The definition of completely new or emerging product markets also implies that dominant positions on these markets, even by companies having significant market power in related fields, are difficult to prove. Broadly speaking, if a market does not yet exist, the current market share of any player is indeterminable.

The assessment of the market position of the parties (in particular, their market shares) is quite straightforward in some cases, but can be very complex in others. Sometimes, it has been necessary to approach the problem of market position by trying several methods at the same time. The consistency of results has then been sufficient to be able to draw a conclusion on the market position of parties. The *WorldCom-MCI*[2] case is a good example of this.

In addition, strategic alliances include a multitude of agreements and produce an impact on several markets at the same time; the competition assessment has to take all of them into account. Further, the alliances tend to be flexible and are built to evolve and/or grow in the future.

Even if the parties do not have a significant degree of market power in most or, at least, in the main markets affected by the transaction, they may very well be able to restrict appreciably competition between themselves on one or several markets. The *WorldCom-MCI*[3] case is again a good example of the above. Internet connectivity was a relatively minor part of the transaction.

4. Spillover Effects

Furthermore, given the presence of the companies involved in closely related markets, the assessment must take into account incentives for co-ordination of the parties in these related markets. This is what we usually refer to as spillover effects. For instance, a strategic alliance between infrastructure providers can very easily have a negative impact on independent providers of services, as the latter can either be foreclosed from that infrastructure or, at least, be put in a disadvantageous competitive position with regard to the service provider's subsidiary belonging to the strategic alliance. The same consequences can also be seen in agreements regarding the provision of interactive services, which have a negative effect on the access to decoders in the digital pay-tv market, or the

---

[2] *World Com/MCI*, 99/287/EC, OJ L116/1 (1999).
[3] *Ibid.*

accumulation of slots in congested airports that can make the entry of competing airlines on given routes more difficult. Generally speaking, the strategic alliance type of operation gives the parties the power to raise the costs of entry of competitors in other markets. By doing so, they erect or increase barriers to entry and preserve their own position in all markets. This is clearly an access problem.

5. Access Issues

A particular category of cases is where two bottlenecks are put together as a result of an alliance. The best example is provided by alliances among airlines. On hub-to-hub routes, provided that both ends are congested the double barrier so created will make barriers to entry even higher, thus reinforcing the position of the parties even further.

Thus, in general, terms, efficiency enhancing strategic alliances may also result in negative effects on competition in the market. The stronger the market power of the parties to the co-operation, the more this is likely. Our approach to this, particularly under Article 81 [ex 85], is to accept the strategic alliances provided that they are able to bring about significant efficiencies, while at the same time limiting the negative effects that also result from them. The most common way to do this is to impose remedies on the parties. In pure Article 82 [ex 86] cases, most remedies are of the behavioural type where, in other words, the firm undertakes to change its behaviour. In Article 81 [ex 85] and, in particular, in mergers, remedies are more structural, so, for example, we would see the establishment of interconnection points or the timely provision of leased lines, the disposal of slots and the reduction of frequencies or the divestment of an overlapping Internet business. The cases that follow include examples of remedies actually imposed on the parties.

The *WorldCom-MCI* and the airline alliance cases underline the need for co-operation between competition jurisdictions. On transatlantic alliances, each party is submitted to different jurisdictions, not only competition jurisdictions, but also aviation authorities. The same is true for other cases involving companies from within and outside the European Union, like *WorldCom* and *MCI* where the Department of Justice and the Federal Communications Commission of the US were also assessing the case. In the face of the increasing globalisation of our economies, without a measurable degree of co-ordination between competition and other jurisdictions both at bilateral and multilateral levels, the coherent assessment of cases would become increasingly difficult.

III. Overview of Recent Relevant Cases in Networked Sectors

As I indicated above, the Commission has gathered a rich experience in the last few years in dealing with these complex strategic alliances in networked sectors. I would like to outline here some of the most important ones that relate to access issues. By so doing, I will also explain the way we have been dealing in practice with the distinctive features that I outlined in the preceding section. Some of these cases are still pending, and for this reason I will not be in a position to enter into any great level of detail in respect of them.

I have left aside cases where the only or main concern was the application of Article 82 [ex 86] in the context of a bottleneck, because that was the subject matter of Panel One. I will only say here that there are many access cases under Article 82 [ex 86]. Their number and importance is growing and will presumably continue to do so in the near future, not only in the telecommunications field, but also in other sectors such as, for instance, access to airport premises and infrastructure.

It is also very important to show that access issues in networked sectors are not limited to telecommunications. Indeed, they arise in many other sectors. Thus, the cases that I have chosen come first from telecommunications, a pioneering sector as regards our assessment of access issues, then from air transport, a sector where the pace of announcement of new alliances is growing very fast. Both sectors have in common that full liberalisation has already been achieved. Finally, I have also chosen cases from the audio-visual field, which is a growing sector where liberalisation as such was not the most powerful engine behind the alliances, but where technological convergence is blurring the borders between markets that up to now were disparate.

I should mention why I have not included cases in other networked sectors (like energy or post). There are two basic reasons: first, liberalisation has not gone that far or is only now starting and second, access and bottleneck issues in these sectors will, generally speaking, not be very different from those that appear in the three sectors that I will be discussing.

1. Telecommunications

a) Alliances Between Incumbent Telecommunications Operators
The combination of full liberalisation of telecommunications achieved in most Member States by 1 January 1998 and the growing convergence of telecommunications and information technologies have put the traditionally quiet

European telecommunications sector on the move, basically from 1994 onwards. The gradual disappearance of traditional borders meant that new entrants or foreign telecommunications operators could start competing in markets traditionally reserved for incumbent monopolists. At the same time many customers started to ask operators to fulfil their increasingly global telecommunications needs. The reaction of many operators has been to go beyond their national borders in order to follow their customers—this was also intended to compensate for the expected decrease of market shares at home. The most common way for incumbents to cope with these challenges has been the conclusion of far-reaching flexible alliances with telecommunications operators in other countries.

I will briefly summarise two cases. First the *Unisource* case, which is an example of alliance between incumbent telecommunications operators resulting in positive effects but with a clear anticompetitive potential, which included very clear access issues. Second the WorldCom-MCI merger where the Commission acted to prevent a dominant position being created regarding Internet.

Unisource:[4] Unisource was a strategic alliance between the incumbent telecommunications operators of the Netherlands (PTT Telecom BV), Sweden (Telia) and Switzerland (Swiss Telecom). It intended to offer through its subsidiaries new advanced services, originally in carrier services, mobile telephony and calling cards, satellite services, and corporate telecommunications (data and voice). It operated both at pan-European and domestic levels of the telecommunications market.

The creation of Unisource was found to fall within the scope of Article 81(1) [ex 85(1)] because it restricted actual and potential competition between the parent companies, which were considered to be potential, if not actual, competitors in most of the markets where Unisource intended to be present.

The restriction of competition was made more serious at the domestic level of the geographic market because of the dominant position enjoyed by the parties in their respective home markets. The situation was nevertheless slightly different from the previous *Atlas* case (involving France Télécom and Deutsche Telekom),[5] in the first place because of the smaller size of the companies involved and secondly because the regulatory situation was better. Sweden had already fully liberalised telecommunications, the Netherlands was also quite advanced, and Switzerland had already declared its intention to liberalise its telecommunications sector fully by 1 January 1998. In addition, the

---

[4] Commission Decision 97/780/EEC, OJ L 318 (1997).

[5] *Atlas*, Case No. IV/35.337, OJ L 239/23 (1996).

three countries had granted or were about to grant licences for alternative infrastructure.

Despite the new services to be offered and the new pan-European markets to be addressed, an exemption was made possible only after the Commission had requested conditions and obligations from the parties to ensure that they were not in a position to eliminate competition within their respective national markets.

The conditions and obligations that were imposed were closely modelled on those imposed in the *Atlas* case. Major emphasis was put on the establishment and maintenance of interconnection to the parties' networks on non-discriminatory and cost-oriented terms especially as regards price, the availability of volume discounts and the quality of interconnection. As part of the condition on interconnection, the parties undertook to make interconnection available on a reasonable number of termination points and to meet all reasonable requests for interconnection. In addition, standard interconnection agreements would have to be published. Each party providing interconnection undertook also to define and attribute the costs of interconnection by using an analytical accounting system.

Finally, a specific condition was included regarding the continued access on a non-discriminatory basis to customer databases necessary for the provision of directory services at cost-oriented prices.

WorldCom-MCI:[6] The proposed merger between WorldCom and MCI notified on November 1997 and cleared with conditions on 8 July 1998 was the first big case concerning the Internet. The Internet was only a relatively minor part of the transaction.

Dominance in respect of access to the Internet was the fundamental concern of the Commission: allowing the merger to proceed as notified would have jeopardised the competitive structure that has characterised the Internet in its developing years. Between them, the two companies would have created a dominant top level network with universal connectivity which would have allowed them to control a substantial proportion of all traffic on the Internet.

Market definition was a complex task to undertake because the markets are emerging and data is difficult to obtain. At the end of the day, however, despite allegations to the contrary by the parties, our assessment allowed us to conclude that the relevant market was that of the provision of top level universal Internet connectivity on a worldwide basis. This merits some additional explanation.

---

[6] *Supra,* n 2.

The Internet market is characterised at its lowest level by a large number of relatively small national Internet Service Providers (ISPs) who deal with end-users. Although this is changing—indeed, analysts expect the market to become increasingly concentrated—for the foreseeable future, this is likely only to affect national markets and pan-European or global concentration of ISPs appears unlikely.

In order to provide universal connectivity, which is, after all, the essence of the Internet, each of these ISPs needs a link, direct or indirect, to each of the others. There are, therefore, two elements—the ability to provide international connectivity and the ability to provide access to the directly connected customers of a particular network—which distinguished a small number of networks (the so-called Top Level Networks or Backbone Networks) from all of the others. MCI and WorldCom were already without doubt among these few networks.

On the basis of this market definition, the Commission concluded that there was a real likelihood that the merged entity would create a dominant position. The parties, inevitably, disputed the reasoning behind this conclusion, although the interveners in the case agreed with it.

Another difficult area in this case was the methodology to be used in calculating market share. The parties proposed a revenue test that would have given them a market share of approximately 20% of all Internet revenues of ISPs. However, when dealing with a vertically integrated company, such a revenue test would inevitably under-represent the true position.

After examining a number of different possibilities, the Commission concluded that the safest means to measure market share was in terms of the traffic passing across the various networks. Extensive fact-finding was thus undertaken, leading to conclusions on market share that gave rise to concern. In any event, it has to be noted that the market share of the parties using the method chosen was consistent with that obtained using alternative methods being considered.

This market share figure, combined with a number of other important factors led the Commission to consider that the proposed merger would lead to the creation or strengthening of a dominant position on the Internet backbone market. These other factors included the general benefits that accrue to the largest single network in an industry where network externalities are important, and the opportunity that WorldCom-MCI would have had to degrade the connections between its network and third party networks, thereby encouraging end-users to migrate to its network.

In view of the above, a possible solution was discussed with the parties to divest the overlap resulting from the merger in the relevant market. At the end of the day, MCI offered to sell its entire Internet business to a third party. The Commission considered this disposal to be sufficient to remove any overlap and so to eliminate its concerns.

By removing any overlap between the two companies on the Internet market defined above, the Commission ensured that the Internet would continue to be competitive, and would not be dominated by any one player. The solution thus promotes innovation and investment in the Internet, rather than impeding it. The parties themselves admitted that of all the savings which would result from the merger, none would result from Internet related activities. In other words, there were no direct benefits to the Internet resulting from the merger as originally notified.

The outcome of the *WorldCom-MCI* case, moreover, shows that the Commission is well suited to the difficult task of market definition in a high technology sector, and also that the Commission is not afraid to intervene, even in highly public areas, when competition is threatened.

Co-operation with the Antitrust Division of the United States Department of Justice was continuous, smooth and fruitful for both competition bodies.

The WorldCom-MCI merger proposal was notified to both the European Commission and the Antitrust Division of the United States Department of Justice (DOJ). It was also notified to the Federal Communications Commission of the United States. The notifying parties granted appropriate waivers in order to enable the DOJ and the Commission to exchange information supplied by the parties to the two agencies. Many firms who responded to parallel enquiries from both the DOJ and the Commission were prepared to let the two agencies exchange information, or supplied the same submission to both.

In the course of the investigation and analysis of the merger proposal there was a considerable degree of co-operation between the two agencies, involving preliminary exchanges of views on the analytical framework, co-ordinated requests for information, the attendance of DOJ observers at the Oral Hearing, and joint meetings and negotiations with the notifying parties. In addition, the DOJ and DG IV conducted jointly the market testing of a first set of remedies. This included the presence of an official from DG IV's case team on the DOJ premises to take part in the DOJ market testing.

As regards the implementation of the undertakings offered, there has been an exchange of letters between myself, as the Director General of Competition, and the Assistant Attorney General in charge of the Antitrust Division, in accordance with Article IV of the bilateral agreement with the US. In this exchange of letters, we requested the DOJ's co-operation regarding the undertakings that were offered by the parties to both the Commission and the DOJ. The DOJ confirmed that it would take whatever steps were necessary and appropriate to evaluate the undertakings, and if it found them to be sufficient, would seek their effective implementation.

b) Cases in the Telecommunications Field: Rights of Way

Rights of way provide access to land wherever this is necessary for telecommunications purposes, e.g. by laying cables or building electricity towers on public or private ground. As full formal liberalisation has been achieved in most Member States, rights of way are becoming one of the most important obstacles to be overcome by new entrants wishing to get access to the market. The granting of a licence by a regulator is just the start of an often complex process of negotiations with owners of land whose permission is required to lay down a network. Thus, it is very important that new entrants get competitive access to these rights.

To this end, the EC liberalisation directives in the telecommunications sector contain an obligation to the Member States to provide within their national legislation for the granting of rights of way to companies. The main general principle is the one of non-discrimination, within which the Member States are left with a rather large discretion.

In addition, the granting or refusal of rights of way may lead to the artificial exclusion of certain companies from entering the telecommunications markets and has consequently to be assessed under the EC competition rules. Thus, rights of way for telecommunications purposes, as well as the closely related issue of the rights to use existing telecommunications infrastructure, have already been the object of various procedures carried out by the Commission in its application of the competition rules. Dominance was not a major issue in these cases.

(i) In merger cases, the Commission has taken the view that the mere access to capacities, in other words, the right to use telecommunications infrastructure, should generally be accepted. This is even true for exclusive rights of use, provided that the time period is not excessively long. These rights of use are thus usually considered as forming an integral part of the operation, which otherwise could not be carried out effectively among the parties. What matters, above all, is that third parties are not excluded from building their own telecommunications infrastructure.

(ii) On the other hand, the Commission generally considers exclusive rights of way as unacceptable, because they tend to prevent third parties from gaining access to the telecommunications infrastructure. Such rights, therefore, are not regarded as an integral part of the concentration and require a separate assessment under Article 81 [ex 85].[7]

---

[7] See, cases *DBKom*: M.827 + IV/36.226, C 168/5 (1997) and *Retevisión*: 97/181/EC, OJ L 76/19 (1997).

(iii) The Commission, under Article 81 [ex 85], generally follows an equivalent approach to the one adopted under the Merger Regulation as regards rights of use. The Commission, first of all, considers that such clauses generally fall within the scope of Article 81(1) [ex 85(1)]. However, exclusivity over a limited time period is held to be necessary in order to protect the legitimate interests of the parties. Usually, however, the granting of exclusive rights of way is found to be unacceptable.[8] Our position has been reinforced by the fact that in a similar case (*Cégétel*) the parties did not agree any exclusivity concerning the use of the French railways for the purpose of building a telecommunications network.

2. Cases in the Audio-Visual Field

The Commission has prohibited several mergers in recent years in the audio-visual field. Our overriding concern is that merging companies having dominant positions in related markets, by entering together in the audio-visual field, reinforce their pre-existing dominant position in their original markets and create a dominant position in the new markets resulting from technological convergence. In our opinion, if this were to be accepted, the mere emergence of these new markets would be jeopardised. It is evident that such a possibility is unacceptable to the Commission.

Coming back to bottlenecks and access issues, they are a major problem in these cases. In order to demonstrate this point, I have chosen two very recent cases.

The *Bertelsmann/Kirch /Deutsche Telekom* case concerned the introduction of digital pay-TV in Germany. In fact, the case concerned two closely related transactions (Bertelsmann/Kirch/Premiere and Deutsche Telekom/ Beta-Research) which were both examined under the merger regulation and prohibited on 27 May 1998.

The first transaction concerned the intended acquisition of joint control by CLT-UFA and Kirch of the German Pay TV-Provider, Premiere, and of BetaDigital which were solely controlled by Kirch. The aim of the intended merger was to develop Premiere into a joint digital Pay-TV channel and marketing platform incorporating Kirch's current digital television activities and on the basis of the d-box technology provided to Premiere by Kirch. The technical services required for the provision and broadcasting of digital Pay-TV programmes were to be supplied by BetaDigital.

---

[8] See *DBKom, ibid.*

The second proposed transaction consisted of the acquisition of joint control by CLT-UFA, Kirch and Deutsche Telekom of BetaResearch, a company until then solely controlled by Kirch. In the context of the intended operation, Deutsche Telekom would have built a technical platform for the digital distribution of pay-TV-programs over its cable TV network and supplied the technical services required for the provision and broadcasting of digital pay-TV programmes using Kirch's Beta access technology and its d-box decoder. The aim of the intended merger was to ensure Deutsche Telekom's access to the Beta-technology.

Both operations would have set the framework for digital pay-TV in Germany. Premiere would have achieved a monopoly position as a programme platform and as a marketing platform. BetaDigital would have achieved a dominant position for technical services for pay-TV for satellites and Deutsche Telekom for its cable network. At the same time, Deutsche Telekom would have strengthened its dominant position for cable networks.

The Bertelsmann/Kirch/Premiere merger would have had an effect, in particular, on the markets for pay-TV and technical services for Pay-TV in Germany. Currently Premiere and DF1 are the only providers of Pay-TV in Germany. Through the merger, Premiere would have achieved a dominant position on the market for pay-TV in Germany. The combination of the important programme resources of Kirch and CLT-UFA, and the subscription base of Premiere would have prevented the development of any additional broadcasting and marketing platform in the German Pay TV-market. After the merger, Premiere would have permanently become the only pay-TV broadcasting and marketing platform in Germany that would be in a position to determine the conditions under which other broadcasters could enter the pay-TV market. If we take the market for technical services for pay-TV, BetaDigital would have attained a lasting dominant position on this market for the satellite sector in Germany.

All current providers of digital pay-TV, as well as Deutsche Telekom as the provider of technical services in the cable sector, are committed to using the Beta-access technology and the d-box decoder, which incorporates a proprietary encryption system. BetaResearch could therefore, in fact, prevent, other service providers entering the market through its licensing policy. Furthermore, Bertelsmann, Kirch and Deutsche Telekom would have controlled the further development of the decoder technology.

An additional fact was that after the merger, Deutsche Telekom would have become permanently the only supplier of technical services for pay-TV in the cable network and would have strengthened its still dominant position on the market for cable network.

This case also provides an example of the fact that market definitions can be subject to change based on rapid technological development. While in the *MSG Media Service* decision in 1994,[9] the Commission found that the market for cable networks was distinct from the market for satellite DTH distribution, in two recent cases, the Commission has considered the possibility of the two transmission modes constituting one market.[10]

British Interactive Broadcasting (BiB): BiB is a joint venture created by BT, BSkyB, the Midland Bank and Matsushita Electric to provide digital interactive TV services, such as home shopping, downloading of games, and a limited collection of Internet sites, to consumers in the UK. In order to receive BiB services, consumers must have a digital interactive decoder. BiB will not be involved in traditional broadcast services such as those provided by its parent company BSkyB.

BiB is a good example of the complexity of market definition in new product joint ventures. BiB has an impact on 5 different markets: the markets for i) digital interactive TV services, ii) technical and administrative services for digital interactive TV services and retail pay TV, iii) retail pay TV, iv) the wholesale supply of films and sports channels for retail pay TV and v) local loop infrastructure.

Our assessment led us to formulate the following concerns to the parties:

(i)   First, BiB's control over the decoder could be used to impede the development of competition on the markets which are reliant on the box (i.e. those of retail pay TV and digital interactive TV services).

(ii) Secondly, a major aspect of Bib was the subsidy of the decoder. BiB intended to recover this subsidy from other users of the box (BSkyB, other broadcasters, and competing digital interactive TV services providers). Our concern in this respect was that the subsidy recovery mechanism could be used to impede the development of competition on the digital interactive TV services market, for example, by charging a substantial 'entry fee' before competitors are allowed to use the box.

(iii) Thirdly, BiB could help to strengthen BSkyB's dominant position in the retail pay TV market. BSkyB also has a quasi-monopolistic position in relation to the wholesale premium programming rights (sports and films) market.

(iv) Finally, we were concerned that BT's short to medium term incentive to innovate and invest in its existing telecommunications network, where it

---

[9] 94/922/EEC, OJ L 364/01 (1994).
[10] *Bertelsmann/Kirch/Premiere, supra,* n 1.

still has a dominant position, may be reduced and that BT could use its dominant position in the local loop to impede the supply of services competing with BiB.

Hence, our initial assessment was overall negative. And we thus informed the parties, who decided to make concessions to eliminate the Commission's concerns. As a result, the parties have accepted conditions on the legal separation of BiB's activities in respect of the subsidisation of the decoder, on the subsidy recovery mechanism and on fair, reasonable and non-discriminatory access to the decoder. At the same time, additional conditions have been included to eliminate the possibility of BSkyB strengthening its dominant position in wholesale and retail pay-tv services. Finally, BT has agreed to divest its existing cable-TV business in the UK.

On the basis of the above conditions, the Commission has just announced its intention to clear BiB.[11]

3. Access Issues in Alliances between Airlines

Following similar trends in other recently liberalised sectors, and in the face of an increasingly globalised market, airlines within and outside the European Union are forging big strategic alliances. The importance of this trend is such that it could very well happen that the sector is significantly concentrated in the hands of only a few global airline alliances in the very near future.

On 3 July 1996, the Commission started proceedings under Article 85 [ex 89] in order to examine whether the following four alliances between European and US airlines are compatible with the EC competition rules: British Airways (BA) and American Airlines (AA), Lufthansa (LH), SAS and United Airlines (UA), KLM and Northwest, and Sabena, Austrian Airlines, Swissair and Delta.

What follows is a summary of the two cases in which the Commission adopted its preliminary position on the 8 July 1998: British Airways/American Airlines and Lufthansa/SAS/United Airlines alliances. The Commission expects to adopt its preliminary position on the other two alliances before the end of the year.

The preliminary position of the Commission in both cases was, on the whole, favourable. However, it included substantial conditions regarding fre-

---

[11] See Article 19(3), Commission Notice, OJ C 322 (1998); Commission's execution decision of 15 September 1999, nyr.

1ency reductions, the reduction of slots and additional conditions relating to equent flyer programmes, computerised reservation system displays, rela- ins with travel agencies, and corporate customers and interlining.

Furthermore, in order to ensure that in both cases there would be sufficient impetition on the markets concerned, the UK authorities (in the BA/AA ise) and the German, Danish, Swedish and Norwegian authorities (in the H/SAS/UA case) were requested to permit all European Economic Area EA) carriers to enter air transport markets between the US and their respec- ve countries under conditions of tariff freedom.

British Airways/American Airlines Alliance: BA and AA wished to form a orldwide alliance that would require close co-operation covering practically ie full range of their activities. The Commission considered that, without the roposed conditions, the implementation of the agreement would amount to n abuse of the parties' dominant position on hub-to-hub routes. The ommission also considered that the BA/AA agreement restricted competition intrary to Article 81 [ex 85] of the Consolidated Treaty. The key competition incerns were the reinforcement of BA/AA's dominant position on three hub- i-hub routes and the significant barriers to entry that would be created by the lliance.

The proposed specific conditions were the following:

) Reduction in frequencies: On three hub-to-hub routes (London-Dallas, London-Miami, and London-Chicago) BA/AA would be obliged to reduce their combined number of weekly frequencies, if so requested by a com- petitor during a period of six months following authorisation of the alliance.

i) Slots and airport facilities other than on hub-to-hub routes: When a rival airline wishes to launch a new service or to expand an existing service and cannot obtain the necessary slots in accordance with the procedure laid down in the EC slot regulations, the alliance would be obliged to make available the necessary slots in London.

The maximum total number of slots to be released under these two reme- lies amounts to 267; they are to be released without compensation. In addition, vherever necessary, the alliance should also give up airport facilities necessary or the effective use of the slots to be given up.

Lufthansa/SAS/United Airlines Alliance: The Commission considered that he LH/SAS/UA alliance restricted competition contrary to Article 81 [ex 85] if the Consolidated Treaty. The proposed conditions, which are equivalent to hose to be imposed on BA/AA, were the following:

(i) Reduction in frequencies: On two hub-to-hub routes (Frankfur Washington and Frankfurt-Chicago) LH/SAS/UA would be obliged t reduce their combined number of weekly frequencies, if requested to do s by a competitor during a period of six months following the authorisatio of the alliance.

(ii) Slots and airport facilities other than on hub-to-hub routes: When a riv. airline wishes to launch a new service or to expand an existing service an cannot obtain the necessary slots in accordance with the procedure lai down in the EC slot regulations, the alliance would be obliged to make th necessary slots available in Frankfurt and Copenhagen.

The maximum total numbers of slots to be released under these two rem dies amounts to 108. Again, no compensation is available for release and whe ever necessary, the alliance should also give up the airport facilities necessar for the effective use of the slots released.

IV. Lessons for the Future

The above cases show that the approach of the Commission across sectors ha been that strategic alliances between very large firms are, on the whole, nece sary. In order for firms to benefit fully from liberalisation, carry out the nece sary R&D activities, launch new services of a better quality and wide geographical coverage and reduce costs, the alliances should not endanger th efficiencies which derive from giving participants the opportunity to consoli date or create dominant positions. The Commission has requested remedie where necessary to correct this situation.

We can see that in telecommunications, the main concern of th Commission was the domestic situation of the parties to a strategic allianc with an international scope. In the audio-visual field, the Commission has pro hibited mergers where dominant positions could put the new markets create by convergence in danger. As far as airline alliances are concerned, the cumu lation of slots controlled by alliance partners, which control most slots in othe important airports in the US, together with other elements, like the combina tion of frequent flyer programs, code-sharing, and so on, would impede th development of competition in that liberalised market.

In the cases I have discussed, the Commission had key concerns regardin access to bottlenecks.

In *telecommunications*, the crucial importance of the existing infrastructur for the entry into the market of competitors in this phase, in which the effect of liberalisation are starting to be felt, led the Commission to require access to incumbent networks as a condition precedent to any exemption. This concern also justifies the negative position of the Commission towards exclusive rights of way and exclusive rights of use of a very long duration in cases where dominance was not an issue. Finally, the possibility that access to networks by small providers in the context of the Internet would be degraded in the future was the basis for the firm approach of the Commission in the *WorldCom-MCI* case.

In the *audio-visual* field, the two following specific areas could potentially result in significant access or bottleneck concerns: decoders and content.

Providers of pay-tv services are normally also providers of technical services. When they entered the market, the necessary technical services did not exist. It was, therefore, logical that they developed them themselves. In theory, a new entrant into the pay-tv market could develop its own decoder and technical services. In practice, however, the scale of investment required and the understandable reluctance of consumers to buy or rent more than one decoder means that the new entrants' most realistic option is to provide a pay-tv service using existing decoders. New entrants need, then, to get access to the decoder and, in particular, to the proprietary elements that it includes, namely the conditional access system, which constitutes the actual entry door, the electronic programme guide, a device which helps the viewer through the multiplicity of chains made possible by digitalisation and compression techniques and the application programming interface, software which allows the decoder to be programmed. The Commission considers it essential to keep access open and available on a non-discriminatory basis, otherwise competition will not develop.

The success of a pay-TV channel is directly linked to the availability of attractive content, in other words, movies and sports. At the moment, exclusive arrangements in respect (mainly) of sport events and premium films are a controversial topic in many Member States in the context of the launching of digital TV. On the one hand, lack of access to such contents is a substantial barrier to entry to the market. On the other hand, however, exclusive arrangements, in particular where they have been obtained through a prior competitive process, can be accepted, at least, for an initial period. This is the position we have taken up to now; and so, in a recent case concerning broadcasting rights of Spanish first division football, we have accepted an exclusive arrangement for pay-per-view for three seasons. After that period, the rights will be again be put out for tender in the market.

It must be mentioned that it is not out of the question that the cumulation of exclusive rights in respect of attractive contents could result in the creation or reinforcement of a dominant position, however, this will need to be assessed on a case-by-case basis.

Finally, our main concern regarding access in the air transport sector was that members of alliances with a very substantial presence on transatlantic routes usually control large numbers of slots at highly congested airports. This is due to historic or other reasons, but in respect of most European big carriers, they were former flag carriers that are now using main airports in the Member States as hubs. Lack of slots would impede competition to develop.

I think it is clear that all these access concerns were similar across all sectors. They tend to make entry by other competitors more difficult or impossible. Indeed, similar concerns are expected to arise in the energy and postal sectors. Logically, our assessment of and answers to these concerns have to be consistent across all the sectors.

V. The Future Need for International Co-operation

In the light of the cases described, I have already given you hints of the growing importance of co-operation between the Commission and other jurisdictions, either sectoral regulatory agencies or competition authorities. As I indicated above, in the face of the increasing globalisation of our economies, without a measurable degree of co-ordination between competition and other jurisdictions both at the bilateral and multilateral levels, the coherent assessment of cases will become increasingly difficult.

I will explain the policy of the Commission regarding co-operation first, with sector-specific regulators and second, with other competition jurisdictions.

VI. Co-operation with Regulatory Agencies

Many of the issues dealt with regarding access will fall, at least to some extent, within the field of competence of newly created National Regulatory Agencies (NRA) within the Member States, or with sector-specific regulators in third countries.

Regarding the first, the Commission as a practical matter recognises that certain issues will be covered by regulation regardless of Commission intervention in a competition case. Where the regulation can be shown to be based on the same principles as would apply under the competition rules, then the Commission can appropriately leave certain matters to the regulatory authorities. However, I want to make it clear that the competition rules continue to apply even where there is overlapping sector specific regulation.

What is more, a number of cases, which could be brought to the Commission under the competition rules, could also be brought under the sector specific regime established under Community law and applied by NRAs. The Commission's Notice on Access Agreements,[12] to which ample reference was made in Panel One, indicates that where an issue falls within the jurisdiction of a NRA, it should first be taken to the NRA. Only if the NRA fails to protect effectively rights arising under Community competition law, would the Commission then intervene.

I should also add that there is always a general caveat that applies when the Commission is deciding whether to deal with a case or whether to leave it to a national authority. If the matter is of sufficient interest to the Community as a whole—for example—if the matter is likely to crop up in a number of different Member States—then, in the interests of efficiency, it may be more appropriate for the Commission to deal with the case immediately.

Regarding co-operation with other sector-specific regulators in third countries, we have recent experiences of cases that were notified to the competition authorities of both the US and the European Commission, but also to sector-specific regulators in the US, like the FCC (WorldCom-MCI) or the FAA (the transatlantic alliances). The policy of the Commission in this respect is developing. It is clear, however, that our natural counterparts are the competition authorities which are looking at a given transaction from a perspective broadly equivalent to ours.

2. Co-operation with Other Competition Authorities

In the future, co-operation with other competition authorities either in a multilateral context or on a bilateral basis will have an ever-increasing importance. As markets become global, the competition policies of different countries come into more direct contact, so that there is more potential for overlap and possible conflict between competition authorities in concrete cases inside and outside the European Union.

As a consequence of this, the international laws to cope with anti-trust violations need to evolve. For the EU, we have pursued two strategies. In the first place, we have encouraged discussions on multilateral approaches in fora such as the OECD and the WTO and we intend to continue to do so in the future. We think that, at present and for the foreseeable future, these fora are the

---

[12] Commission Notice on the application of the competition rules to access agreements in the telecommunications sector, OJ C 265/02 (1998).

appropriate places to discuss and co-operate on general competition issues on an international basis. In addition, a clear borderline must be maintained between trade issues and competition issues. Any attempt to blur the borderline between them has to be avoided.

Secondly, we have developed close bilateral relations with our major trading partners. We have a long tradition of co-operation with the competition authorities of the Member States and a fast developing practice in co-operating with other competition authorities, in particular, with those of the US.[13]

As far as Member States are concerned, in 1997 the Commission adopted a Notice on co-operation between national competition authorities and the Commission in handling cases falling within the scope of Articles 81 and 82 [ex 85 and 86] of the Consolidated Treaty,[14] which sets guidelines on case allocation between the Commission and the national competition authorities.

We are working together more and more with the antitrust authorities of the US. This co-operation is proving to be increasingly frank and useful for both sides, although we should not expect to be able to come to equivalent conclusions in all cases because the European and the US anti-trust authorities do not apply the same rules. This was the case with the Boeing/McDonnell Douglas merger of last year where different conclusions were reached in the end. However, the very recent WorldCom-MCI merger tells a different story of both excellent co-operation and shared conclusions, which I hope, will be a model for the future.

VI. Conclusion

Access issues and bottlenecks are a crucial issue for companies trying to enter newly liberalised markets. The clash with very big vertically integrated companies has been unavoidable and will continue to be of critical importance for the coming years. We, as a competition authority, are aware of the importance for newcomers to overcome bottlenecks and to have fair access to the existing infrastructures built over the years by incumbents under the protection of monopolies and closed markets. In this presentation, I have tried to look at these issues from the point of view of Article 81 [ex 85] and the Merger Regulation. Our basic concern is the creation or reinforcement of dominant

---

[13] Directive 95/47/EC of the European Parliament and of the Council on the use of standards for the transmission of television signals, OJ L 281/51 (1995).

[14] OJ C 313/3 (1997).

positions. Access issues have arisen in several sectors in this context. We can mention particular cases in emerging or recently liberalised markets where strong players could endanger the development of these markets to their full potential. In most cases, access issues increase barriers to entry into the relevant markets by competitors. The Commission has been dealing with access issues in a consistent way across all sectors. Remedies (including prohibition decisions) have been imposed where necessary to eliminate artificial barriers to entry erected in the context of those strategic alliances.

The basic overall aim of the Commission is for competition to develop and be maintained in these markets in accordance with what the evolving structure of the market can support. The Commission is not necessarily looking for perfect competition in the economic sense if the features of the industry exclude it. In the context of networked sectors, therefore, the Commission is aware that the establishment of large networks requires big investments in fixed capital that need to be made before a new network starts to generate revenue. Such costs can be irrecoverable (or sunk in the language of economics) if the investor wants to exit the market. So, we can accept that entry (and exit) barriers can be naturally high. In addition, very big scope and scale economies can exist. Indeed, for some elements of networks natural monopoly conditions can still exist. All these elements are indications that in networked sectors the structure of the market can be such that perhaps only a few players can coexist and that these players will be big and strong. However, we think that no additional obstacles should be put in place as a result of strategic actions by those already in the market.

The aim of the Commission is not to destroy or harm big or even dominant firms. Contrary to what has happened in some countries in the past, this is not the policy we are pursuing. To give just one example, when we request interconnection, we do not ask for free interconnection, but only for fair, cost-oriented, non-discriminatory interconnection. Our role is simply to apply our competition rules on a neutral basis and in this context, it is clear that bigger firms will have more potential to harm competition than smaller ones.

VIII

Klaus-Dieter Scheurle*

Major Tasks and Fields of Activity of the German Regulatory Authority for Telecommunications and Posts

I. Introduction

The privatisation and liberalisation of the German telecoms market have been successful. The telecoms market was fully liberalised, on time, on the first of January 1998; the initial period of liberal market interchange has been highly positive, and has exceeded all our expectations.

To date, some 170 licences have been granted for fixed voice telephony and transmission paths. Close to 180 further licences are being processed. Additionally, in the area not subject to licence, there are currently some 1,000 telecommunications service providers operating in the market. These figures show that companies are very confident about market liberalisation. They rate their profit opportunities within the newly deregulated markets very highly. Thus, a bare six months after the launch of a fully competitive market, competition is now, happily, already intense.

The licensees are a heterogeneous group, comprising, for instance, local network operators, regional providers, companies offering their services in one or more Länder (states), and various providers with a nationwide presence. About 70 cities and municipalities have already established their own telecommunications company; a further 50 are about to do the same.

II. Market Volume and Economic Importance of Telecommunications

In 1998, the German telecoms market achieved revenues in excess of DM100 billion. Communications services accounted for sales of 83.5 billion, while communications equipment accounted for sales of DM17.8 billion.

In Germany, a daily average of about 489 million call minutes accrue in the fixed network, of which approximately 10 million were handled, in March 1998, by competitors of Deutsche Telekom. Only six months after the opening up of the market this share had—according to estimates by Deutsche Telekom AG (DT) and its rivals—increased to roughly three percent.

---

* President of the Regulatory Authority for Telecommunications and Posts.

The volume of the postal market is estimated at DM 40 billion. In Europe, market growth in the field of telecommunications is currently eight percent. The growth rate of telephone services, which make up the major part of telecommunications services, has even reached 10 percent in Germany. At world level, European lines account for 36 percent of the main existing telephone lines and Europe receives 30 percent of the revenues from telecommunications services. In Western Europe, the German telecommunications services market is the most important national market, its share being 25 percent.

Employment prospects are similarly good. Despite the fact that general unemployment is currently high, many of the information technology companies are often unable to fill their vacancies. In 1997 and 1998, 102,000 new jobs were created within Germany's information industry, while the industry expects a further 91,000 posts to be created in 1999/2000.

The lower cost of modern communications—driven by competition and the availability of better or even totally new communications services—will also enhance competitiveness in other branches of industry, for example, in the postal and information sectors, through the introduction of teleworking or through the centralisation of distribution and customer support functions in so-called 'call centres'. Therefore, the dynamic development of this industrial sector is central to Germany's desire to be 'a place to do business', and, thus, to the development and the future of the German economy as a whole.

III. Prospects for the Development of the German Telecommunications Market

Optimistic forecasters expect Deutsche Telekom's competitors to achieve a share of 14 percent of the fixed voice telephony market by the year 2000. By 2005, their revenues may have doubled again. Experience from telecommunications markets that were liberalised some time ago indicates that monopolists suffer a greater market share loss the more the communications distance increases. Thus, it is to be expected that alternative carriers will, first and foremost, increase their market share in the field of long-distance and international calls. It has to be borne in mind, however, that the regulatory framework for competition in Germany is extremely favourable, so that, in the longer run, intense competition will not just be witnessed in the long-distance market.

Incumbent operators forecast that Deutsche Telekom will see a considerable growth in sales and, above all, will enjoy an enormous potential for a sustainable increase in its profitability. Judging by UK and US experience, it can be expected that DT will also be able to defend its dominant position with regard to market share for a considerable period to come.

IV. Regulation for the Benefit of Competition

With liberalisation, competition and thus regulatory 'normality' have become possible within the telecommunications market. If, however, markets were simply to be left to themselves, the incumbent companies would have the whip hand: new entrants could easily be kept out of the market, not only through discriminatory pricing, but also through a refusal to provide interconnection with the existing telecommunications networks. Moreover, new competitors are particularly dependent, in the initial phase of competition, on the shared use of existing infrastructures, particularly the local telecommunications networks.

The Regulatory Authority's role, laid down in the Telecommunications Act and in the Postal Act, is not an end in itself: without licensing, *ex-ante* regulation of interconnection prices, state-guaranteed network access at reasonable prices, *ex-post* control of end user charges, state dispute settlement, state frequency and number management, or, in short, the activities of the Regulatory Authority, there would be no workable competition within the telecommunications market.

The tasks to be fulfilled by the Regulatory Authority are laid down in the Telecommunications Act and the Postal Act. The aims behind its activity can be subsumed under four major headings.

(1) In view of the incumbent's dominant position, it need be ensured that all players can compete on reasonable terms.

(2) It need be ensured that any co-operation, among competing providers is focused solely on technical standards and specifications and does not lead to discrimination.

(3) The economic and technical framework needs to be adapted to the current state of the art. Moreover, it has to be shaped so as to foster technical progress.

(4) As part of the infrastructure guarantee, an appropriate and adequate provision of telecommunications and postal services is to be ensured throughout the country.

Thus, the goal is not one of impairing entrepreneurial freedom. On the contrary, what is at stake is the fostering of competition in the telecommunications sector and the encouragement of technological and organisational progress. The creation of equal opportunity and workable competition is, at the same time, also the decisive tool for achieving other public policy aims. Users' best interests are safeguarded by competition; technical progress can be made a reality, while, in the long run, the provision of basic services at favourable prices can also be guaranteed.

V. The Powers of the Regulatory Authority

In order to achieve these aims, the Regulatory Authority has not only been equipped with effective procedures and instruments, including, for instance, information and investigative rights, but has also been given the power to enforce various sanctions.

The Regulatory Authority may request information from the companies engaged in telecommunications, and inspect and audit their business records. To this end, the Regulatory Authority has the right to be given access to business premises during normal business and working hours. It can make searches by virtue of an order from a local court and may seize business records. Records that are not delivered voluntarily can be seized. Violations of such administrative orders are subject to fines of up to DM one million.

VI. Decision-Making Procedures Within the Regulatory Authority

The transparency and independence of decisions are, first and foremost, guaranteed by the procedures of the Ruling Chambers. The Ruling Chambers are conciliation boards whose decisions are taken in a manner similar to judicial proceedings. They are composed of a Chairperson and two assessors. For decisions which concern licensing, the allocation of scarce frequencies and the imposition of a universal service obligation, the President's Chamber (Ruling Chamber 1) has jurisdiction and is composed of the President of the Authority, acting as Chairperson, and the two Vice-Presidents, acting as assessors. Ruling Chamber 2 is responsible for rate regulation in the field of voice telephony for the public, as well as for transmission. Ruling Chamber 3 deals with the special control of anti-competitive practices and *ex-post* rate regulation in the field of telecommunications. Ruling Chamber 4 is concerned with special network access, including interconnection. In addition, there is a Ruling Chamber dealing with the postal service.

Proceedings are public and the companies that are directly concerned may take part. Additionally, persons, associations of persons or representatives of business affected by the proceedings, may also be summoned to attend. Since proceedings are based on the judicial system and as procedural principles are respected, objective decisions, which are readily comprehensible to all parties, are guaranteed.

The work of the Ruling Chambers is supplemented and supported by three administrative departments, one of which deals with postal matters and, therefore, is not relevant in this context. Department One (telecommunications regulation) is responsible for basic economic and legal issues, for licences and frequency management. Department Three (technical telecommunications regulation) addresses technical issues such as, for example, frequency assignment, licences, standardisation, testing and measurements. In addition, where necessary, it supports Department One in many other specific fields, such as numbering, security in telecommunications and data protection.

The independence of the Regulatory Authority is also guaranteed by the ruling whereby Regulatory Authority decisions cannot be quashed by the supervisory authority (i.e. the Federal Ministry of Economics) in the event of legal action. Any action against a decision of the Regulatory Authority must be brought directly before the administrative courts.

While the Regulatory Authority is responsible for the implementation of laws and regulations, Department Seven, which deals with telecommunications and postal issues within the Federal Ministry of Economics, works out proposals for new laws and regulations, or for the amendment of existing regulatory provisions. Moreover, it represents German interests in international bodies and in the EU. The Regulatory Authority for Telecommunications and Posts co-operates closely with the Cartel Office in matters such as market delimitation and definition of a market-dominant position. However, in view of the complexity of the issues involved, these two bodies may differ in their approach to a single case. Should it not be possible to reconcile such differing views, even after an exchange of opinions has taken place, the opinion of the body given competence for the decision under the law shall prevail.

VII. Areas of Activity of the Regulatory Authority

Four major areas of activity can be identified: market access and licensing, universal service, rate regulation and network access and interconnection. The tasks and competences of the Regulatory Authority are explained for each of these four areas below. The activities of the Authority in each area of competence are further illustrated by examples of cases dealt with in 1998.

1. Market Access and Licensing

In general, anyone who so wishes is allowed to offer services in the telecommunications market. A licence is nonetheless required for the provision of mobile services, for satellite services, for the operation of other transmission and for voice telephony for the public, paths provided through self-operated networks. By contrast, no licence is necessary for the provision of, for example, data services or multimedia services on leased lines. In the areas subject to licence, anyone with proven specialised knowledge, reliability and efficiency in their intended field will be granted a licence. In addition, however, potential providers must also ensure that their activities will not prejudice public safety or order. Auctions or competitive bidding are only held by the Regulatory Authority in relation to frequencies whose supply is limited.

In mobile communications, decisions must be made on the distribution of the remaining frequencies in the 1800 MHz band. The two D1 and D2 network operators have already made applications for frequency assignment. Under the Telecommunications Act, any decision on the distribution and usage of the remaining frequencies must be based on an assessment of the implications for the relevant mobile radio market and, thus, for the network operators active there: that is to say, D1, D2, E1 and E2.

Within the context of the 1997 E2 licence, the E1 and E2 operators were given a considerably larger chunk of the frequency spectrum than the D1 and D2 operators (22.5 MHz/12.5 MHz) because of the prevailing competitive situation in the cellular mobile radio market. This decision was based on extensive studies of the competitive and technical aspects of the market. Additional studies are now being undertaken, in order to determine whether and, if so, to what extent, competitive conditions have since changed.

The Regulatory Authority's decision on the final distribution of the frequencies will need to pay due regard to the justified interests of all parties concerned—especially with a view to their future possibilities for development. The decision must ensure equal opportunity and workable competition.

Special attention needs also to be given to the new technologies such as UMTS (Universal Mobile Telecommunications System), wireless local loop, global mobile satellite service networks and broadband ISDN. Standardisation in these areas is to be based on the principles of openness, transparency interoperability and safety, while individual providers should not be subject to discrimination. Meanwhile, agreement has been reached within ETSI on the standardisation of the air interface. From the regulatory point of view, this agreement is to be welcomed since it should foster the speedy introduction of innovative and efficient technologies into the market. Following the first frequency assignments—limited to one year—to companies operating local UMTS experimental networks in 1997, further assignments can be expected each year. We must map out the path for the introduction, throughout Europe, of commercial UMTS operation by the year 2002.

In relation to this innovative technology, and technology for wireless multimedia applications in particular, we hope to repeat the success with the GSM standard. If we can do so, the public will be able to see how swift, forward-looking regulatory initiatives can encourage and promote innovation and create new competitive markets.

Frequency assignments to Digital Audio Broadcasting (DAB) are also on the agenda. In August 1997 a decision was made on the frequency distribution procedure. This was preceded by a comprehensive public comment procedure on the list of specifications and by discussions with the federal states on the time schedule and the regional coverage zones. The first DAB licences were issued in late October 1998.

Furthermore, digitisation will also affect licence applications. Digitisation allows a substantially greater number of channels in the existing bands, so that arrangements must be made to enable balanced and non-discriminatory access for the programme providers.

2. Universal Service

With regard to universal service, the Regulatory Authority must ensure the provision of a minimum set of telecommunications services. Every citizen, irrespective of place of residence or place of work, must have affordable access to this minimum set of services, for which a particular quality content has been defined. This set of services includes ISDN voice telephony, directory information and regular publication of directories, provision of public telephones with an emergency call facility, and the provision of leased lines.

We assume that these services will, in any case, be offered on competitive markets anyway. Therefore, the Regulatory Authority will only intervene where gaps in supply are identified. In such cases, the Regulatory Authority will either oblige the dominant company to offer the service, or will solicit bids for the universal service in question. Either the dominant company or the lowest bidder will be obliged to provide the services. Losses experienced by the service provider will be compensated for by a levy on all licenses with a market share of at least four percent.

Currently, given the competitive market's satisfactory coverage, no company is obliged to provide universal services. Only DT must notify the Regulatory Authority one year in advance of any changes in its universal service offers.

In this context, the municipalities, demand for fees for public telephones must be addressed. Agreement must be reached between the telecommunications companies and the municipalities on the distribution of public call boxes and on reasonable rates to be charged for the operation of boxes, irrespective of the frequency of use. In order to establish a workable system of co-financing for less frequented call boxes, charges in profitable locations should also be moderate. This is the only guarantee that the network of public telephones will not be reduced, which is surely in the best interests of the municipalities.

Standard agreements to this effect have been entered into by DT and the central associations of municipalities. These will form the basis for contracts concluded between DT and the local authorities, governing the operation of public telephones on public ground or communal premises.

3. Rate Regulation

With regard to rate regulation, the Regulatory Authority must approve the rates proposed by dominant operators for transmission paths and voice telephony before they can take effect. The purpose of this regime is to prevent customers from being put at a disadvantage by a company holding a dominant position in the market. Such disadvantage would occur if the company requested prohibitive prices in an area of low competition. Moreover, a company with a dominant position should not be allowed to disadvantage its competitors. An impairment of competition would exist were the dominant company in a position to drive competitors out of the market through predatory pricing.

Normal practice, at least for the time being, is that the rates are approved on the basis of the costs of the efficient provision of each individual service. This determines that the rates for each service must be approved individually. Currently, price cap regulations, which relate to the basketing of several services and which set regulatory targets for the average increase or decrease in the rates for these services, only apply to specific end user rates.

The practice of individual rate approval determines that the companies concerned must submit extensive cost statements. The statements show the individual costs of a given service, and the common costs which are determined according to fixed standards. These costs must be broken down into payroll costs, hardware costs, depreciations and cost of capital. Capacity utilisation must also be accounted.

Moreover, service specifications, general terms and conditions, the revenues generated, the quantities sold and contribution margins must be indicated, and their financial impact on customers and suppliers analysed. The submitted accounts must cover the past five years and must also include forecast figures for the coming four years.

The Regulatory Authority may reject rate proposals if full documentation is not provided. Where the documentation is correct, the Authority must examine the figures given with a view to establishing whether, and to what extent, the rates proposed are based on the costs of efficient service provision. The costs of efficient service provision are derived from the long-run incremental costs of providing the service, plus an appropriate amount for volume-neutral common costs, inclusive of an appropriate return on capital employed, to the extent that these costs are required to provide the service.

For purposes of comparison, the Regulatory Authority must review the prices and costs applicable in comparable competitive markets. Stated costs exceeding the costs of efficient service provision will only be taken into account if they derive from a legal requirement or if other, proper, justification is given for them.

With regard to telephone charges end users must pay for the fixed network, it was decided in 1997 that DT must reduce these rates by an average of at least 4.3 percent (price cap). This decision was taken prior to the passing of the Telecommunications Act, but is binding for the Regulatory Authority. The target figure of a 4.3 percent cut was derived from an assumed increase in productivity of about 6 percent less an inflation rate of 1.7 percent. In March 1998, the Regulatory Authority found that Deutsche Telekom had comfortably achieved the target set. Its proposed rate cuts were approved accordingly.

Much more decisive, from the customers' point of view, will be the increasing reach of competition, which will, in the future, put pressure on telephony prices. This is not a shortcoming in the law, on the contrary, it is entirely in line with the philosophy of market liberalisation. So, the question is one of whether DT would be well advised to limit its price cuts to just slightly more than the required minimum amounts. This, however, is not a question to be decided by the Regulatory Authority, but by market forces.

Internet telephony is not subject to voice telephony regulation. The underlying reason for this is that packet-based transmission of data cannot guarantee real-time transmission of speech as is the case with regard to voice telephony. It is doubtful whether the current cost structure, lower than the traditional telecommunications cost structure, can be maintained in the medium and long term. In the long run, compared with traditional voice telephony, however, internet telephony offers better possibilities to integrate different communications services, in the form of video-conferences, mailboxes, pagers, facsimile and e-mail, and allows for the integration of telephone services with the services provided on the World Wide Web. In the future, the current price advantage will be overtaken by a qualitative advantage.

The rates that DT charges for preselection and number portability (numbers can be retained after a change of network), and their extensive coverage in the press in 1998, caused a great deal of confusion among customers. The responsible Ruling Chamber of the Regulatory Authority immediately wrote a letter to DT ordering the company not to levy any charges for preselection and number portability, as long as these rates were not approved. Nevertheless DT was obliged to render the services. After DT had withdrawn a first rate proposal, the Ruling Chamber partially approved the second rate proposal from DT on 15th June 1998. Since there were doubts about DT's efficiency in supplying these services, the approval was based on extensive surveys of comparable rates charged in the US, Canada, Australia and New Zealand. Furthermore, a rate reduction from DM27 to DM10 was to be achieved during the years 1998–2000. The Ruling Chamber had already decided in April 1997 that number portability should continue to be free of charge.

Telecommunications services other than voice telephony, for instance the transmission of sound and video broadcast programming in cable networks, are also subject to rates regulation.

On account of the numerous complaints received about the 1997 15 percent increase in the broadband cable prices charged by DT, the Regulatory Authority, *ex officio*, ordered formal abuse proceedings which, however, did not give rise to any objection to the price increases seen by the end of 1997. However, it became evident that DT was inefficient in this area. The Ruling Chamber responsible established that the costs it had approved had to be reduced by 7 percent before the end of 1998. DT was thus ordered to reduce its price increase by at least 64 percent.

With regard to other price issues, there have been numerous complaints about abusive practices on the part of DT. For example, DT has been obliged to grant its competitors access to its in-house cabling systems. Furthermore, DT has also been subject to investigation in relation to charges levied for the feeding of programmes into the broadband cable network.

4. Network Access and Interconnection

To ensure that new entrants enjoy opportunities equal to those of the incumbents, the law provides that dominant operators may be obliged to grant access to their network. Moreover, they must grant access—on a non-discriminatory basis—to all the essential facilities they offer on the marketplace and use themselves internally. Competitors must have access to the facilities under the same conditions as the dominant providers. The 'bundling' of service offers to competitors is also restricted.

Workable competition in the telecommunications market is only possible if all subscribers can reach one another over a public telecommunications network. Hence, the providers, regardless of their market power, are obliged to negotiate with other operators on network interconnection. Only when such private negotiations fail will the Regulatory Authority order interconnection. This ruling will include decisions on disputed issues such as volume of service and charges due.

In this regard, DT was required, in 1997, to set an average interconnection rate of 2.7 Pfennigs a minute. Together with the decision to provide new competitors with the right of unbundled access to the local loop of DT, this decision prepared, in a timely, clear and reliable fashion, the ground for competition. The rates which DT charges its competitors for access to its local loop are assessed on the basis of the cost records submitted. A first proposal, filed by DT, was rejected by the responsible Ruling Chamber on 9 March 1998 because it judged the cost documents submitted to be incomplete and non-verifiable. Instead, the Chamber set a provisional price of DM 20.65 for access to the bare copper wire, not inclusive of any switching facility.

With this temporary order, Germany met an important requirement for competition in the local network. Thus, a very high degree of market opening has been achieved, even judged by global standards.

In addition, the Regulatory Authority, assisted by the Scientific Institute for Communication Services (*Wissenschaftliches Institut für Kommunikationsdienste*) is drawing up a general model in the field of interconnection to cost the local network. The model's assumptions and calculation methods have been discussed with all the operators concerned. The model is currently being extended to include the long-distance network to provide a benchmark for the costs of certain essential services.

International experience shows that the application of strict but fair cost benchmarks may result in a further marked reduction in the level of interconnection charges and increased planning safety for the telecommunications companies.

VIII. Assessment of the Current Competitive Situation

After a 125-year monopoly, it would be unrealistic to believe that the transition to competition would be perfectly smooth. All concerned, and that includes Deutsche Telekom, made enormous efforts to make competition possible as from January 1998. The German regulator has intervened rapidly, effectively and in an entirely consistent manner to ensure that the market is not made unattractive to new providers on account of high switching fees; though of course, new services allowing every German consumer to opt, completely free of charge, for another provider to handle his call simply by dialling the appropriate carrier preselection code, means that competition is now established without any switching fees at all.

Thus overall, the initial phase of liberalisation can be assessed entirely favourably. Admittedly, not all the offers expected are actually available in the marketplace. Set against that, however, is the fact that customers are being wooed intensely in the long-distance market. The consistent regulation of interconnection prices was the main contributory factor in this development. Smaller providers, who began with only a few resources of their own, were, surprisingly, very soon successful in the basic business of fixed voice telephony. Many of them have used this success as a basis for further developing their network. This means that, to date, regulation has successfully lessened the danger of a market dominated by just a few major providers, charging very high rates.

Price competition will continue to be a decisive driving force for the development of infrastructure, for innovations and for the implementation of technical progress. However, quality and the availability of innovative services are also used as arguments to attract customers. The mobile picturephone is just one outstanding example of this.

IX. Liberalisation of Telecommunications: Advantages for the Customers

Since January 1998, every telephone customer in Germany has been able to opt for another provider, completely free of charge, to handle his call, simply by dialling the appropriate carrier preselection code. There are about 50 different companies offering telephone calls. This fierce competition in the area of long-distance traffic has already paid dividends for the German customer. In some areas, prices have gone down by more than 60 percent, and this downward trend is continuing.

Contrary to expectations prior to the introduction of competition, the price reductions are by no means for the benefit of business customers alone. The call-by-call option has transformed a large number of residential and small business customers into a market target group, whose changed telephony habits now underpin the success of the new competitors.

Consumers have also seen their rights improve. From January 1998 they have been able to demand itemised bills free of charge and bills from a subscriber network operator which specify the services rendered by other providers. In case of complaints against the telephone bill it is no longer the customer, but the operator who has to furnish proof of the service in question. Telephone lines can only be blocked if the arrears payable amount to DM 150. In all cases of dispute with the telecommunications service provider the customer may turn to the Regulatory Authority for conciliation.

Finally, as expected, medium-size and large business customers have been provided with a whole variety of customised offerings tailored to their individual communications needs, offerings which will result in considerable cost savings and service improvements. In many cases such cost savings have opened up completely new business areas, for instance in the field of tele-learning. All groups of customers, however, are now provided with innovative products and services at a rate far quicker than that seen prior to liberalisation.

X. Liberalisation of Telecommunications: Advantages for Companies within the Industry

In a monopoly situation where there is artificial protection from the influences of the world market, where there are no incentives for innovation, no need to increase efficiency and no pressure on market prices, telecommunications would simply become a sector supported by state subsidies, with no prospects for the future.

Liberalisation, however, has given rise to a completely new economic sector in Germany: the telecommunications sector. Today's young, and remarkably successful companies, could not have developed without liberalisation. Even if some of the new businesses do not survive on the market, it can be expected that all the new competitors will add a proportionally higher share to the growth of the overall market and that many of the investments that they are making will be profitable.

The incumbent company, DT, will benefit considerably from the expansion in market volume. Competition will force it to make its operational processes more efficient, and will enable it to step up its innovative activities, financed by private capital. This will increase its ability to benefit from a globalised market and the information society.

XI. Liberalisation of Telecommunications: Advantages for Germany as a Place to do Business

The lower cost of communications, driven by competition, and the availability of qualitatively better, or even totally new communications services will also enhance competitiveness and employment prospects in other industrial sectors. Teleworking, for instance, will be introduced, or medium and larger-sized companies will concentrate their distribution and after-sales services in what are known as 'call centres'. In call centres alone, the number of new jobs expected by the year 2000 will amount to roughly 140,000. Thus, the impact of the dynamic development of the telecoms industry goes far beyond the bounds of the sector. For Germany's industrial base as a whole, telecoms is vital.

XII. Concluding Remarks

Liberalisation in Germany has been a huge success to which all concerned, including DT, have contributed enormously. Fierce price competition is the driving force behind new technologies, for example, in the field of least-cost-routers. In the long run, however, price will not be the only competitive parameter. Quality, customer service and innovative services will play an increasingly important role.

The Regulatory Authority for Telecommunications and Posts ensures easy access to the German market and equal opportunities for competition through independent regulation. It intervenes quickly and efficiently to stop anti-competitive practices. It thus creates sound and predictable investment conditions. Its regime aims to promote competition in the telecoms sector and to encourage technical and organisational progress.

This is of advantage to all—to customers, to DT, to the new competitors, to the workforce—and will enhance the future prospects of the German economy generally. The WTO estimates that a quarter of all future economic activity in the industrial countries will take place by electronic means. Germany is preparing for these global challenges, and the excellent outlook for the communications and information technology markets is one of the reasons why Germany's overall economic situation has markedly improved.

IX

*Mario Siragusa**

Access and Discrimination in the Creation and Consolidation of
Networks Under Community and Italian Law

I. Introduction

The communication, information technology, and media industries are currently undergoing a process of intense and dramatic restructuring in response to deregulation and technological development. Companies are trying to establish themselves in international markets and to reap the rewards of changing commercial and technical conditions. One of the principal ways in which companies expand is to establish stronger horizontal and vertical links, by entering 'strategic alliances'.

Whilst the Commission generally favours this restructuring process, which it considers necessary to allow companies to benefit fully from liberalisation, carry out research and development activities, and launch new products and services, it tries to ensure that liberalisation is not affected by restructuring initiatives that might prevent new companies from entering previously monopolistic markets, or by any other abuse or strengthening of dominant positions.[1] Competition authorities are particularly sensitive to the behaviour of companies inheriting advantages from special or exclusive rights previously enjoyed and fear that such companies may retain assets or control access to networks and infrastructure on which new competitors must rely to enter the market. The Commission clearly wishes to prevent holders of 'bottleneck' positions

---

* Cleary, Gottlieb, Steen & Hamilton.

[1] The Commission has stated that: 'Competition policy as it relates to the information society is, therefore, a balance between, on the one hand, a liberal attitude towards restructuring and, on the other, the need to keep a watchful eye on how such restructuring is carried out, or even to impose a ban in some cases. There is also a link between the degree of actual liberalisation of the relevant markets, which evolves over time, and the conditions which may be attached to restructuring operations. In particular, the acceptability of alliances, which are often pro-competitive outside domestic markets must be assessed in the light of the extent to which those markets have been liberalised' (European Commission 26th Report on Competition Policy, para. 66). On this issue, as it relates to the media sector, see also *ibid*, para. 81).

from foreclosing on markets,[2] and imposes special duties on companies holding privileged positions.[3]

Commission policy in the telecommunications, information technology and media sectors is our starting point in discussing the treatment of agreements dealing with the creation and consolidation of networks, under competition law where control of a network may enable its owners to affect the development of the market and this paper discusses the rules under which third parties are granted access to networks. We begin by defining the term 'network' and then identify the principle competitive concerns raised by networks. We go on to examine specific issues relating to network agreements: agreements relating to contractual networks; agreements on the creation of structural networks; and agreements for the consolidation of networks.

II. Networks Defined and Principal Competitive Concerns

A network is a set of nodes connected by a set of links,[4] a prime example being the telephone network, where the nodes are the switches and the links are standards, protocols, copper, and fibre. Other structures that can be described as networks include airline routing systems, airline computerised reservation systems, and ATM, credit card and cross-border transfer systems, linked by contracts and standards. Similarly, suppliers or distributors linked to a particular company may be described as a 'network of suppliers' or 'network of distributors'. The term network encompasses a variety of structures that arise in

---

[2] 'Dominant players cannot claim technological progress for extending their dominance. That would stifle innovation and not encourage it. So we will not allow gatekeepers to block entry into markets. This is true in the case of joint control of cable networks and telecoms infrastructure, of digital set top boxes and of Internet Web browsers.' (Van Miert, Commissioner for Competition, Speech to BEUC, Brussels, November 21, 1997.)

[3] 'Particularly where an industry emerges from a long period of strict regulation, it is likely that certain firms will inherit some of the advantages which arise out of special or exclusive rights granted previously . . . In the interest of creating genuine opportunities for competition, it may be necessary to impose particular duties on companies holding such a central position. In several industries, open and non-discriminatory access to networks or other key facilities provided by dominant companies appears to be a necessary condition for effective competition.' (European Commission 21st Report on Competition Policy, para. 16).

[4] See R. Schmalensee, 'On Antitrust Issues Related to Networks before the Federal Trade Commission', Testimony of 1 Dec 1995.

different situations,[5] but in each situation, when the networks involve agreements between competitors, two sets of antitrust concerns arise.

First, issues relating to co-operation between competitors must be resolved by applying traditional rules on the evaluation of the advantages and disadvantages of encouraging partial integration through joint ventures, or complete integration through mergers. Since network agreements often arise in advanced and innovative sectors, the level and nature of the innovation is often significant in their assessment.

Second, network agreements raise the issue of access to the networks concerned. A network can consist of a physical infrastructure, software, or assets to which competitors must have access in order to offer their products or services. The network owners are effectively 'gatekeepers' able to prevent third parties from reaching the market by denying them access to the network or granting access on disadvantageous conditions. A network can also be a system that connects competitors for the provision of services to end-users, or involves the exchange of data. Participation in such a system can be decisive for the ability of third parties to compete effectively, especially where there are a large number of participants. Finally, a network can consist of outlets for the distribution of products to consumers. In such a case, the imposition of exclusive purchasing obligations may obstruct competitor access to the market.

In assessing network agreements, competition authorities take into account both the exclusion of third parties and the inclusion of specific undertakings, as exclusion from certain networks may exclude companies from the market altogether or limit their ability to compete, while the inclusion of certain undertakings can reduce competition from other networks. In particular, the participation of a company holding a competitive advantage may enable parties to network agreements to restrict competition. Imposing a duty to allow third parties to participate in agreements, networks, or systems raises the question of the extent and cost of such participation, and requires a kind of 'economic regulation' that competition authorities cannot always perform. It also introduces uncertainty for the joint undertakings that create a network or system, thereby possibly reducing incentives to innovate.

---

[5] The literature on networks describes the characteristics of networks as the presence of network externalities, that is, factors that 'cause the value of network to increase more than proportionally as its size increases.' See Schmalensee, *supra n* 4, who adds: '. . . when network externalities are present, the total value of one network is greater than the total value of two competing networks, and there is an element of increasing returns that tends in principle, all else equal, to drive the system toward monopoly.')

Under Italian law, when dominance or joint dominance is involved, issues of access and the imposition of exclusive purchasing obligations are Article 82 [ex 86] Consolidated Treaty or Article 3 of Italian Law No. 287/90. The issue of access is frequently analysed as a refusal to deal, or under the 'essential facilities' doctrine. Finally, for structural operations, the combination or consolidation of two or more networks may be examined under merger control rules as the creation or reinforcement of a dominant position. Imposing a non-discrimination obligation on network holders, or prohibiting exclusive purchasing obligations for distributors, is consistent with the well-established principle that dominant undertakings have a special responsibility not to allow their conduct to impair competition in the common market.

The Commission and the Italian Antitrust Authority (IAA) have also assessed network agreements under Article 81 [ex 85] EC and Article 2 of the Italian Law. In general, these provisions are applied where operators have held significant positions in the affected markets, irrespective of the characteristics of the facility concerned. Consequently, in some cases, agreements have been annulled or the parties obliged not to discriminate against competitors, without consideration of dominance. The requirements for the imposition of such obligations, in the light of recent developments in the case law of competition authorities and the Court of First Instance, and the extent to which control of a network gives rise to a special responsibility for the undertakings party to it are discussed below. Finally, we will examine whether the distinction between Article 81 [ex 85] and 82 [ex 86] issues is blurred.

III. Agreements Relating to Contractual Networks

Contractual networks are typically created by companies for the distribution of their products or services. Two categories of agreements may be envisaged. The first includes agreements for the creation of a network in the strict sense, i.e. agreements between a supplier and a number of distributors, or distribution networks. In these cases, competitors may be denied access to distributors and prevented from operating on the markets in which the distributors are active. The second category covers situations where a joint venture is established to distribute products, or an association of undertakings is entrusted with such a task. In these cases, the distribution network may be constituted by only one undertaking. Foreclosure can take place not only at the level of competing undertakings, but also at the level of other distributors, especially where the product to be distributed is not generic or interchangeable and is essential to compete. In the first category of cases, the Commission generally clears the agreement or orders the removal of restrictive clauses.[6] By contrast, in the second category, the Commission may require the parties to allow competitors to participate in the network.

1. Contractual Distribution Networks

The first category of network agreements raises the issue of the foreclosure of competitors by the undertakings establishing the network. This is particularly true when the agreement contains an exclusive purchasing obligation on distributors. Generally, the competition authorities are concerned about those agreements that might restrict competition for access to retailers between the supplier and its competitors, and make access to the market difficult or even impossible for competitors. The applicability[7] of Article 81 [ex 85] EC or Article 2 of the Italian Law depends, respectively, on whether an agreement, either alone or in conjunction with other agreements between the same or different companies, may have an appreciable effect on trade between Member States and on competition,[8] or significantly restrict competition in the Italian

---

[6] The Court of First Instance (CFI) has stated, with respect to distribution agreements containing exclusive purchasing obligations, that the Commission may order termination of the agreements or withdraw the block exemption, although it cannot prohibit undertakings from concluding new agreements of the same kind in the future. See Cases T–24/92 R e T–28/92 R, *Lagnese-Iglo GmbH e Scholler Lebensmittel GmbH & Co. KG* v *Commission*, [1992] ECR 1713.

[7] As a general rule, the Commission adopts a favourable position towards agreements providing for exclusive purchasing obligations, recognising that such agreements have an important business function because they guarantee sales to one party and continuous supply to the other (European Commission VII Report on Competition Policy, para. 9). Agreements may also be covered by Commission Regulation (EEC) No. 1983/84, on the application of Article 81(3) [ex 85(3)] of the Treaty to categories of exclusive purchasing agreements, OJ L 163/5 (1983), ('Regulation No. 1983/84'). The IAA also considers that issues raised by exclusive distribution networks do not make for a simple application of competition rules (see Italian Antitrust Authority Decision of December 23, 1996, Bollettino dell'Autorità Garante della Concorrenza e del Mercato No. 52/1996, p. 5).

[8] As to the visible impact of an agreement on competition, the Notice on agreements of minor importance which do not fall within the meaning of Article 81(1) [ex 85(1)] of the Treaty establishing the European Community (Commission Notice, OJ C 372/13 (1997)) provides that agreements do not fall under Article 81(1) [ex 85(1)] Consolidated Treaty if the aggregate market shares of the parties on any of the relevant markets do not exceed 5 percent in the case of horizontal agreements, and 10 percent for vertical agreements, unless the agreements are serious infringements of competition law and

market. In this assessment, one must take into account the legal and economic context and the existence of similar agreements that might have a cumulative effect on competition.[9]

The test is whether or not there is a real possibility of competitor access, that is, whether it is particularly difficult for competitors to enter the market or increase their market shares, for example, by buying existing outlets or opening new outlets.[10] In conducting this assessment, the decisive elements are the number of outlets tied to the supplier compared with the number not tied; the duration of the commitments; and the quantity of products to which the commitments relate and proportion of products sold by independent distributors.[11] In addition to establishing a real possibility of entry, one must consider the legal rules on company acquisitions and opening of outlets, and to the minimum number of outlets necessary for the viable operation of a distribution system.[12] Finally, we must identify the contribution of the individual agreement to the cumulative foreclosure of the market, by examining the market position of the parties and the duration of the agreements.[13]

An agreement may be exempted where certain conditions are fulfilled. First, the agreement must allow the parties to plan their production, distribu-

---

competition is restricted by parallel networks of similar agreements. In Commission Decision 93/406/EEC, OJ L 183/19 (1993) (*Mars/Langnese-Iglo GmbH*), the Commission found that agreements covering approximately 15 percent of sales outlets and sales volume on the relevant market appreciably restrict competition.

[9] See, for example, Case C–234/89, *Stergios Delimitis* v *Henninger Brau AG*, [1991] ECR 935 (*Delimitis*). The IAA applies the same reasoning as the Commission (see Italian Antitrust Authority Decision of December 23, 1996, *supra* n 7; Italian Antitrust Authority Decision of May 28, 1997, Bollettino dell'Autorità Garante della Concorrenza e del Mercato, No. 22/1997, p. 25).

[10] In its decision 78/172/EEC, OJ L 53/20 (1977) (*Spices*), the Commission found that an agreement between a supplier of spices and certain major distributors which prevented distributors from selling other suppliers' brands of spices was incompatible with competition law. The decision does not refer to an 'essential facility' but clearly assumes that access to a facility (in this case, three major supermarkets) may be essential for competitors. The Commission found that the main brands of spices for domestic consumption are marketed in wide ranges that can only be adequately launched and sold in large self-service stores. The effect of the agreements at issue was to prevent competitors from gaining access to a sizeable proportion of distribution outlets, and therefore restricting opportunities to canvass for sales or to launch products.

[11] See *Delimitis, supra* n 9, para.19.

[12] *Delimitis, supra* n 9, para. 21. Account must also be taken of all other conditions under which competitive forces operate on the relevant market, as listed in *Delimitis, supra* n 9, para. 22.

[13] *Delimitis, supra* n 9, paras. 25–26.

tion, and sales more precisely and over a longer period of time, limiting the risk of market fluctuation, and to lower the costs of production, storage and marketing. It is not sufficient that an agreement is advantageous for one party. Rather, the agreement must offer appreciable advantages to the public to compensate for any competitive disadvantages.[14] Second, the agreement must allow consumers a fair share of benefits. Third, the agreement must not make it more difficult for third parties to be active on the market and must not erect barriers to entry.[15]

a) Mobile Telephone Services in Italy

The IAA dealt with the issue of foreclosure of a number of market outlets by the major player in the market in *Costituzione Rete Dealer GSM*.[16] It found that the creation of an extensive exclusive distribution network by Telecom Italia Mobile (TIM), the dominant provider of mobile telephone services in Italy, limited its competitors' access to the Italian markets for the management and sale of mobile telephone services.[17] TIM's network comprised a number of dealers that generally sold mobile telephones and collected subscriptions for the mobile telephone services to be provided by TIM. Dealers undertook to sell subscriptions to TIM's services exclusively.

---

[14] *Mars/Langnese-Iglo GmbH, supra* n 8, para. 118, where the Commission found that an agreement that reinforced the strong position of the parties could not be exempted.

[15] European Commission VII Report on Competition Policy, *supra* n 7, p. 15.

[16] Italian Antitrust Authority Decision of May 2, 1996, Bollettino dell'Autorità Garante della Concorrenza e del Mercato No. 18/96, p. 9. The Commission faced a similar issue in a merger case, *TNT/Canada Post*, Case No. IV/M.102, 1991 OJ C 322/9 (1991), where it found that a joint venture involving TNT and five national post administrations could not, as regards its international express delivery system, provide exclusive access to outlets of the postal administration, since '[t]his would have provided the [joint venture] with a segment of customers, which would only be available to other private operators through establishing a separate network and which would have given the joint venture a significant advantage over its private operator competitors' (paras. 46–47). Based on this analysis, the parties reduced the scope of their exclusive access, and limited it to a period of two years. On the issue of the pre-emption of certain qualified sales outlets, see also *Spices, supra* n 10.

[17] The IAA dealt with the compatibility with Article 3 of the Competition Law of the creation of a distribution network by incumbent telecommunication operators in *SIP-Società Italiana per l'esercizio delle telecomunicazioni*, (Italian Antitrust Authority Decision of March 24, 1993, Bollettino dell'Autorità Garante della Concorrenza e del Mercato No. 6/1993, p. 23). There, the IAA held that SIP's exclusive franchising network for the sale of cellular telephones was incompatible with competition law because it raised barriers to entry and hindered the development of competition.

The IAA found that this system tied dealers to TIM, and limited their freedom to choose a supplier. The system was reinforced by the provision of a fidelity bonus for dealers generating a minimum number of subscriptions on TIM's behalf, by minimum stock requirements, and by a non-competition clause.

In addition, the IAA found that TIM had tied those retailers most qualified to sell subscriptions and had the highest distribution capacity. The IAA noted that the sale of GSM subscriptions was closely linked to the sale of mobile telephones. Despite the significant number of potential sales outlets (30,000), only 9,700 sold mobile telephones, 78 percent of the sales being attributed to 1,940 outlets (high-segment dealers). TIM's network was composed of 1,875 outlets, most of which were high-segment dealers, and within the network 77 percent of subscriptions were collected by only 451 dealers. Given that TIM's market share exceeded 80 percent, the IAA estimated that 25 percent of TIM's dealers accounted for 70 percent of the subscription market.

As a result of the exclusivity obligation, TIM's competitors in the provision of mobile services were at a serious competitive disadvantage. They were foreclosed from the high-segment dealers, and could only operate through outlets that were not specialised and/or had limited distribution capacity. Even though TIM's competitors had access to a large number of outlets, most of them were staffed by people with little experience in the sale of mobile telephones and required training. Thus, the effect of the exclusive distribution system was to raise TIM's competitors' distribution costs significantly, which were estimated at 35 percent of total costs. The IAA found that exclusivity was not justified by the dealer's obligation to provide after-sales services. There was no risk that, if able to market competing services, dealers would provide inaccurate information to consumers in order to promote the service most profitable for the dealer.

b) Amex and Dean Witter/American Express
Another interesting example of market foreclosure analogous to that produced by exclusive dealing arrangements and involving an important market player and its dealers is *Amex and Dean Witter/American Express*.[18] Visa proposed adopting a rule prohibiting member banks from issuing Discover Cards, American Express cards, or any other card deemed competitive, but not including MasterCard, Diners Club and JCB cards. Visa operates a network system, in that member banks issue cards and acquire outlets within the frame-

---

[18] See European Commission, 26th Report on Competition Policy, *supra n* 1, pp. 140–41.

work of Visa's association rules.[19] The Commission found that the proposed rule would have restricted competition between card payment systems and between banks offering international cards, since it would have impeded card systems other than Visa from licensing the vast majority of EC banks, and prevented the introduction of new systems and the expansion of existing ones. A substantial majority of the major European banks were Visa members. Thus, if the rule were adopted, it was unlikely that any bank would have used a competing card and risked exclusion from Visa's system, and would have stood to lose substantial sums if they renounced membership. Moreover, the system would have restricted competition between banks by limiting the range of products they could sell to customers.[20]

2. Pooling Exclusive Rights and Distribution Joint Ventures

This category typically includes horizontal agreements between competitors involving the pooling of patents and exclusive rights, or the creation of exclusive distribution structures. Exclusivity is not, generally, *per se*, incompatible with competition rules, and can be justified because it safeguards the value of, for instance, the copyrighted product and is essential for its exploitation. However, in specific circumstances, agreements relating to exclusive television rights, sporting events, and feature films, all of which are essential components of television programming,[21] may be illegal because of the extent and duration of the rights. An exemption from the usual competition rules is only possible if

---

[19] By contrast, Amex is a 'closed loop' or proprietary system. It controls the issue of cards, the acquisition of merchants and the processing of merchant receipts. Similarly, Discover operates a proprietary system.

[20] Commissioner Van Miert issued a warning that Visa's proposal could not be accepted, after which Visa decided to drop the proposal. The complaints were withdrawn and the case closed without the Commission taking a formal decision.

[21] In *Federazione Motociclistica Italiana/Telepiù* (Italian Antitrust Authority opinion of February 8, 1996, Bollettino dell'Autorità Garante della Concorrenza e del Mercato No. 7/1996, p. 65), the IAA confirmed that the test of compatibility with Italian antitrust law for exclusive television programme licensing is whether transmission of the programmes which are the object of the license represents 'a factor of particular relevance for the composition of a television programming schedule which could guarantee an adequate audience in the provision of television services'. The exclusive right to broadcast the World Motorcycle Championships granted to Telepiù by the World Motorcycle Federation was not a crucial factor for entry to the television market (the share was approximately 4.7 percent of the total audience of Telepiù) and, although the exclusivity lasted five years, it did not restrict competition.

suitable access facilities are available to third parties. In *ARD*,[22] for example, the Commission objected to agreements between an association of German broadcasting organisations and a subsidiary of three American film companies under which the association obtained the exclusive right to transmit a number of films.[23] The Commission found that the agreements limited ARD's freedom of action because it could not grant sub-licences in Germany and competitor access to the films. The agreements restricted competition because of the unusually high number of particularly interesting films involved and the extensive duration of the exclusive agreements (15–16 years). The Commission only granted an exemption when the parties granted third parties access to the films.[24]

UIP

The Commission also exempted an agreement between Paramount, Universal, and MGM, which created UIP, a joint venture that distributed feature films produced by parent companies.[25] The latter pooled distribution activities in the Community and granted UIP exclusive distribution rights for their films. The Commission considered that this exclusivity prevented third-party distributors from marketing the films of three large, but not dominant, companies, which accounted for almost 20 percent of Community box-office receipts. The Commission objected that the exclusivity granted to the joint venture limited competition between the parents and reduced the likelihood of the parents entrusting the distribution of their films to other distributors. Following the Commission's objections, the exclusivity provision was modified to only allow UIP a right of first refusal over the parents' films. The parent companies first

---

[22] Commission Decision 89/563/EEC, OJ L 284/36 (1989).

[23] The decision does not contain a detailed assessment of the market position of ARD. It is worth noting that the acquired movies amounted to 4.5 percent of the total stock available worldwide.

[24] The parties agreed to license films to other television stations during so-called 'windows'. In such periods, exclusivity was lifted and members of the association could not use the films. The length of the windows varied from two to eight years. ARD agreed to release the television products which its members had not themselves selected. The Commission considered that the remaining exclusivity was necessary to allow a fair share of return for the relevant investment costs, such as licence fees and dubbing costs. Similarly, in *EBU* (Commission Decision 93/403/EEC, OJ L 179/23 (1993)), the Commission exempted a system for the joint purchasing of broadcasting rights for international sports events operated by the European Broadcasting Union, Eurovision following agreement by the parties to grant non-member channels access to the sports programmes purchased by Eurovision.

[25] Commission Decision 89/467/EEC, OJ L 226/25 (1989).

had to offer each film to IUP for distribution in the Community. If UIP refused, the parent company could require UIP to distribute the film or distribute it through alternative channels. In addition, the parents undertook to make the joint venture available for the distribution of third-party films in their commercial judgement.

IV. Agreements to Create Structural Networks

'Structural networks' consist of physically linked facilities, such as telecommunication or railways infrastructure, or electronic payment systems. Structural networks create more concrete links between participants than contractual networks. Parties can agree to create a network, and in some cases enter into a joint venture to operate it. These agreements usually involve structural changes and are designed to enable the parties to implement projects involving high risks and requiring considerable investments.

1. *Iridium*

Structural network agreements generally involve projects that the parties may not undertake unilaterally. If the parties are not competitors, the agreements do not fall under Article 81(1) [ex 85(1)] of the Consolidated Treaty or Article 2. For example in *Iridium*,[26] the Commission cleared the creation of Iridium, a company led by Motorola and sixteen strategic investors, including STET and other telecommunications service providers, and equipment manufacturers. Iridium was to be the first operational provider of global satellite personal communications services, using a constellation of sixty-six low-earth orbit satellites. The Commission concluded that the creation of Iridium fell outside Article 81 [ex 85]. None of the investors could reasonably be expected to take on the very high level of investment, and technical and commercial risk associated with the system. In addition, no investor held all the licences necessary to operate the system.[27] The Commission considered that the creation of Iridium introduced a viable competitor in a completely new telecommunication field.

---

[26] Commission Decision 97/39/EC, OJ L 16/87 (1997).

[27] In particular, the Commission considered that: (i) the implementation of the network programme involved a considerable risk; (ii) no investor could reasonably be expected to make the necessary financial investment to set up and operate a world-wide S-PCS system; (iii) no investor was in a position to assume the substantial financial risk of technical failure inherent in space operations, and the risk of commercial failure

The Commission did not find that Iridium held a dominant position (
would have been able to enjoy any competitive advantage. However, give
STET's strong position in the provision of satellite services in Italy, th
Commission requested an additional safeguard to ensure that the creation (
Iridium would not affect the ability of others to gain access to STET's Italia
telecommunications infrastructure, apart from the facilities specifically deve
oped for the Iridium system. Interestingly, the parties were asked to 'confirn
that this would be the case, despite the fact that the Commission did not find
violation of law. The parties also had to 'confirm' that STET would not di;
criminate with respect to facilities other than those developed for Iridiun
These 'commitments' not only appear to be aimed at ensuring the ability (
third parties to provide services competing with Iridium's, but also at guarar
teeing the use of telecommunications networks and facilities for any purpose

2. *GEN*

In *GEN*,[28] the Commission approved the Global European Network agree
ment between France Télécom (FT), Deutsche Telekom (DT), British Telecor
(BT) and Telefonica for the provision of high quality digital links betwee
Member States and the creation of a fibre optic telecommunication network
Under the agreement, each operator agreed to dedicate a certain amount o
optical fibre capacity to GEN and to install on its network at least one node (o
network access system), and associated data packet re-transmission links con
forming to the X.25 standard. The Commission recognised that the networl
would improve the speed of circuit provision, network availability, and th
quality and reliability of services. However, since the parties were dominan
operators, the Commission required amendments to ensure that 'eacl
signatory will offer in its public tariff access to GEN capacity on a non
discriminatory basis to third parties.[29]

---

inherent in the fact that the system was new and would be expected to encounter toug
competition; (iv) given the global reach of the system, no investor in Iridium holds th
necessary authorisations and licences to provide international services on a world-wid
basis through satellite; and (v) the array of technologies required for a S-PCS systen
was outside the individual capabilities of the parties.

[28] Case IV/34.820 (GEN), OJ C 55/3 (1994). The Commission did not adopt a forma
decision.

[29] The Commission warned the parties that the negative clearance of the agreemen
does not mean that the parties could abuse '*strong if not dominant positions*' in the mar
ket for leased lines.

From the discussions on *Iridium* and *GEN*, it appears that when major telecommunications operators holds a dominant position in the national markets for telecom services, the Commission requires certain commitments to prevent possible abuse of such a position. However, when major public telecommunications operators are not involved, the Commission seems ready to clear agreements without imposing conditions, even though the parties may have a significant market share in a new market.

3. *Hermes*

In *Hermes*,[30] the Commission cleared a joint venture between telecommunications operators, ten national railway companies, and a company providing business and operational telecommunications services to the British Railway Board. The joint venture combined the telecommunications expertise and infrastructure of the parties to introduce a pan-European telecommunications network centred around the cross-border transport of traffic, primarily along railway tracks. The network would be used by public telecoms operators, carrier consortia, cellular telephone companies, and other authorised telecommunication operators. Hermes would supply cross-border basic transport capacity to carriers who would, subsequently, supply end-users in competition with traditional PTO systems.[31]

4. *Eurotunnel*

If agreements lead to the co-ordination of competitive behaviour, the competition authorities also assess the impact on third parties. In some cases, the Commission and the IAA follow an essential facility approach and focus on the nature of the 'resources' at issue. In *Eurotunnel*,[32] for example, the Commission

---

[30] Case No. IV/M.683, OJ C 14/6 (1996).

[31] As the first entrant in the new market for the provision of pan-European transport networks, the joint venture would have high market share, possibly even 100 percent. However, the Commission found that: (i) Hermes' market power would be limited by a number of potential competitors (i.e. PTOs, telecommunications operators, international alliances, and owners of infrastructures such as national energy and water undertakings); (ii) customers were knowledgeable companies that could limit the joint venture's market power; and (iii) the main barrier to entry, national regulation, would diminish in the future.

[32] Commission Decision 94/894/EC, OJ L 354/66 (1994).

found that an agreement between Eurotunnel, British Rail (BR) and Société Nationale des Chemins de Fer Français (SNCF) reserved all the hourly paths available for international trains made available by Eurotunnel to BR and SNCF.[33] The Commission found that the agreements limited competition between the parties[34] and caused significant foreclosure because the Channel Tunnel was an 'essential facility' for railway undertakings wishing to provide services between the UK and continental Europe. The reservation of all of the hourly paths available for international trains by BR and SNCF is not essential for the provision of their transport services. Indeed, the contract provides that BR and SNCF may be requested to surrender part of their entitlement to the use of the fixed link and that their agreement cannot be unreasonably withheld. The Commission found, however, that the Channel Tunnel project was unique and that its operation involved high risks and investments. It therefore exempted the agreements but required a limitation of the capacity reserved to BR and SNCF.[35]

Where joint ventures create a facility necessary for parties to compete, the Commission and the IAA are concerned to ensure that third parties are able to use the facility under non-discriminatory conditions. Competition authorities apply a rule that regulates membership of the joint venture and the conditions

---

[33] The Commission identified two relevant markets: the market for the provision of hourly paths for rail transport in the tunnel, including the tunnel and its access areas; and the market for international transport of passengers and freight between the UK and continental Europe. It also found that in the market for the provision of hourly paths, the contract provides that the applicants were at all times entitled to 50 percent of the capacity of tunnel. Since under the terms of the contract, half of the tunnel was reserved for shuttle services and the other half for international passengers and freight trains, BR and SNCF are entitled to 100 percent of the hourly paths available for the latter category of transport. Upon appeal of the parties, the Court of First Instance (CFI) annulled the decision because it found that the Commission misinterpreted the contract and no provision in the agreement between the parties reserves, expressly or implicitly, half of the tunnel capacity for shuttle services (Joined Cases T–79/95 and T/80/95, *SNCF and British Railways v Commission*, [1996] ECR II–1491).

[34] In particular, the Commission found that the parties agreed that Eurotunnel concentrated on the operation of shuttles and BR and SNCF in the provision of international trains.

[35] The Commission required that for a period of twelve years the reserved capacity for BR/SNCF be limited to 75 percent of the hourly capacity reserved for international transport. After a twelve-year period the level of capacity allotted to BR and SNCF could be revised. BR and SNCF could use more than 75 percent of the capacity if the other railway undertakings do not use the remaining 25 percent, and, conversely, the latter could use more than 25 percent of the capacity if BR and SNCF do not use the 75 percent which is reserved to them.

of third-party use of the joint venture services. Case law is unclear as to whether, and under which conditions, authorities will require parties to open up membership of joint ventures to third parties.

5. *DISMA*

In *Disma*,[36] the company managing Malpensa airport collaborated with a number of oil companies operating in the airport to create a joint venture for the installation and operation of equipment for storing jet fuel and transferring it to supply points within the airport.[37] The equipment would have been the only means of refuelling aircraft at the airport. The Commission considered that the system was advantageous in terms of Community environmental legislation and that consumers also benefited. However, it objected to clauses in the joint venture agreement preventing non-Disma companies from gaining access on non-discriminatory terms to the joint venture's services, including a limitation on the transfer of shares in Disma to third parties, and the imposition of higher charges to non-members. The Commission issued a comfort letter once the parties agreed to adopt a uniform tariff with actual charges on a sliding scale according to the quantities of jet fuel supplied,[38] and agreed that non-members should have easy access to Disma's capital once Malpensa's refuelling facility is operational.[39]

6. *AgipPetroli/Kuwait Petroleum Italia/Esso Italiana-PAR*

The IAA applied similar reasoning in cases involving jet fuel storage and refuelling joint ventures. In *AgipPetroli/Kuwait Petroleum Italia/Esso*

---

[36] European Commission 23rd Report on Competition Policy, paras. 80, 223–24.

[37] The agreement envisaged the creation on the site of the airport, of a new fixed aircraft-refuelling installation essentially comprising a fuel and lubricant depot directly linked, via underground pipelines, to supply points.

[38] The principle of a sliding scale was justified by the existence of fixed costs associated with the services supplied to each customer.

[39] In *Gas Interconnnector*, the Commission cleared an agreement between leading European gas companies for the construction and operation of an underwater gas interconnection that would have been the first connection between the UK and continental gas markets (European Commission 25th Report on Competition Policy, para. 82). The Commission took into account the ability of third parties to acquire access to transport capacity on freely negotiated terms, in light of the fact that the project created the possibility of competition between isolated markets.

Italiana-PAR,[40] the IAA cleared an agreement between oil companies for the creation of a co-operative joint venture for the construction and operation of a jet fuel storage and provision system at Naples Airport. The IAA found that the agreement had no anti-competitive effects, as the parties would continue to act autonomously in the downstream market for the sale of jet fuel to air carriers. In addition, third parties were allowed to acquire a stake in the joint venture and the parties could be compelled to transfer their stake. Finally, third parties could benefit from the joint venture's services at non-discriminatory prices. The prices they were charged were different from those charged to the parties. However, the difference was due to the fact that third-party prices were fixed so as to cover the cost of the parties' investment.[41]

Finally, in assessing the compatibility with competition rules of electronic payment systems, the Commission has referred to the 'essential' nature of the systems, in order to impose substantive and procedural requirements on the operators running them.

---

[40] Italian Antitrust Authority Decision of November 21, 1996, Bollettino dell'Autorità Garante della Concorrenza e del Mercato No. 47/1996, p. 6.

[41] Similar conclusions were reached by the IAA in: (i) *Agip/PAR* (Italian Antitrust Authority decision of March 12, 1998, Bollettino dell'Autorità Garante della Concorrenza e del Mercato No. 11/1998, p. 11, concerning an agreement on the basis of which the parties entrust the joint venture of the activities in the airport of Palermo); (ii) *RAM-Rifornimenti Aeroporti Milanesi* (Italian Antitrust Authority Decision of July 20, 1995, Bollettino dell'Autorità Garante della Concorrenza e del Mercato No. 29/1995, p. 15); (iii) *Agippetroli/Esso Italiana/Kuwait Petroleum Italia* (Italian Antitrust Authority Decision of May 20, 1998, Bollettino dell'Autorità Garante della Concorrenza e del Mercato No. 21/1998, p. 6, concerning an agreement for the creation of a joint venture for the provision of oil product storage and loading in Linate Airport and the oil product loading at Fiumicino and Malpensa Airports. The IAA accepted the pricing system for third parties and noted that its implementation was easier than the *Agip/PAR*'s system; (iv) in *Agippetroli/Esso Italiana* (Italian Antitrust Authority Decision of June 4, 1998, Bollettino dell'Autorità Garante della Concorrenza e del Mercato No. 23/1998, p. 13), concerning the creation of a joint venture for the provision of oil product handling and storage services. In this case the third parties' price for the joint venture services was determined on the basis of the same criteria used to determined the price paid by the parties; and (v) *Colisa-Continental/Sigemi* (Italian Antitrust Authority Decision of July 21, 1998, Bollettino dell'Autorità Garante della Concorrenza e del Mercato No. 29–30/1998, p. 16), concerning the creation of a joint venture for the provision of oil product handling and storage services. The IAA cleared the transaction despite the fact that the parties did not undertake to allow third parties to acquire a stake in the joint venture.

[42] Commission Notice, OJ C 251/3 (1995).

7. Cross-Border Credit Transfers

According to the Notice on the application of EC competition rules to cross-border credit transfers,[42] a system constituting,

> [a]n essential facility . . . must be open for further membership (as distinct from ownership) provided that candidates meet appropriate membership criteria. . . . An essential facility is a facility or infrastructure without access to which competitors cannot provide services to their customers. A cross-border credit transfer system will be an essential facility when participation in it is necessary for banks to compete in the relevant market. In other words, lack of access to the systems amounts to a significant barrier to entry. . . . This would be the case if a new competitor could not feasibly gain access to another system or create its own system in order to compete in the relevant market.[43]

No reference is made to the position in the markets of banks that set up or participate in the system, or, more specifically, to their position of dominance. Based on the preparatory draft, it could be argued that quantitative criteria may be relevant in defining an essential facility.[44] It is not clear, however, how significant the lack of access must be to qualify the system as an essential facility, or what constitutes the relevant market in which competition must be ensured.[45] It could be argued that essential systems are those occupying such a

---

[43] *Ibid*, para. 25.

[44] In the draft Notice circulated prior to completion of the current text (OJ C/322/7 (1994), the Commission states (para. 6): 'As a general rule, a system which constitutes an 'essential facility' should be opened for further membership (provided that candidate meet appropriate criteria) and must not prevent individual members from taking part in other systems. Factors indicating that a system might be an essential facility include a high market share or a significant number of participants.' In Annex C to the Commission Working Document (SEC (92) 621), *Easier Cross-Border Payments: Breaking down the barriers*, it is stated that (para. 1a): 'As a general rule, co-operation agreements which embrace the majority of credit institutions of one country or are likely to process a significant part of payment traffic between different countries either totally or in a given market segment . . . may be considered to provide an 'essential facility' and, therefore, should be opened for further membership provided that candidates meet appropriate criteria.' The 1994 draft Notice also states that (para. 6): 'A system which does not have a significant position in the overall market may be important for particular types of banks and could also constitute an essential facility for the type of bank in question.'

[45] 'The economic realities of multilateral interbank agreements for performing payments . . . can never be deemed to be essential—in the sense of being critical to a third party's competitive viability. Banks can always use correspondent banking, which,

prominent place in the market that 'outsiders would have to invest in an alternative facility at a cost which might be prohibitive or at least disproportionate in light of the expected performance of that new facility.'[46]

An essential facility holder must apply membership criteria that are objectively justified.[47] In addition, those who run the system must provide written justification for any refusal of membership, and allow for the refusal to be subject to an independent process review.[48] The Commission distinguishes membership from ownership of the system, and allows parties to envisage different forms of membership, such that participation is direct or indirect depending on the level of responsibility undertaken by the banks.[49]

The issue of identifying different levels of membership was faced in the *SWIFT* case.[50] The Commission suspended its investigation of the Society for Worldwide Interbank Telecommunications (SWIFT)[51] when SWIFT undertook to allow access to its network to all entities with access to EU third-party fund transfer systems, and no longer to offer its network and services to banks only. In view of the imminent arrival of the Euro, SWIFT created a totally new category of participants, called Non-Shareholding Financial Institution (NSFI), to be granted full access to the SWIFT network, products and services.

---

though less convenient, is always an alternative to multilateral arrangements on netting or settlement.

[46] Gyselen (1996), argues that the yardstick is not so much whether the facility is dominant, either alone or collectively, but whether there is room to create another.

[47] Membership criteria should be written down, accessible and non-discriminatory. Criteria may relate to the financial standing of members, their technical and management capacities, and compliance with creditworthiness levels. They may not make membership conditional upon acceptance of other unrelated services, and an essential facility system should permit membership by banks with only a small number of transactions. Payment of an entry fee may be required, but must not exceed a fair share of the real cost of past investments in the system.

[48] *Ibid*, para. 28.

[49] For details of access rules, see paras. 26–29 of the Notice, *supra n* 27.

[50] Publication of an undertaking, OJ C 335/3 (1997).

[51] SWIFT is a co-operative society owned by some 2000 banks throughout the world. It owns a telecommunications network and provides an electronic message transfer system to its users, which use the SWIFT network for various types of interbank messages, including national and cross-border payment messages. Only banks and 'entities in the same type of business' have full access to the totality of the network, products and services of SWIFT. The Commission issued a statement of objections against SWIFT upon receipt of a complaint by the French Post Office, which had unsuccessfully applied to become a member of SWIFT. Following the opening of proceedings by the Commission, SWIFT offered the Commission an undertaking which led the Commission to suspend its investigation.

NSFI included all institutions satisfying criteria laid down by the European Monetary Institute, the forerunner of the European Central Bank, for access to European payment systems.[52] The SWIFT undertaking is a good example of the type of undertaking that may satisfy the Commission, while not forcing the company to grant full access to all potentially interested applicants, or to share ownership in the network with all users. To this extent, the undertaking might be considered as an example of the recognition of the need to comply with the principle of proportionality.

V. The Consolidation of Networks

The agreements discussed below are not necessarily related to the creation of networks, but involve undertakings that own and/or manage networks. The agreements involve either the combination of different networks, or co-operation/integration between competitors, one or more of which control a network.

In network combination cases, the Commission is concerned about the strengthening of the position of undertakings and possible foreclosure effects, due to the integration of essential infrastructure or to 'network externalities'.

Agreements between airline companies involve the integration of networks, in terms of slots, computer reservation systems, and frequent flyer programmes.[53] In *Lufthansa/SAS*,[54] the Commission found that Lufthansa and Scandinavian Airlines would have increased their market power by pooling their resources, networks, and frequent-flyer programmes. The Commission also noted that they controlled a substantial proportion of slots at the main German and Scandinavian airports. The Commission applied Article 81(3) [ex 85(3)] to the transaction but conditioned its decision on the provision of undertakings including the giving up of slots and the granting of access to frequent

---

[52] The requirements to quality as an NSFI are: (i) the entity must be authorised to hold accounts for customers; (ii) its direct participation in one or more EU fund transfer systems processing third-party payments must have the approval of the central bank; and (iii) its public nature must ensure little risk of failure, or its financial service activities must be supervised by a recognised competent authority. Pending the creation of the NSFI category, SWIFT will offer any institution applying for full access and meeting the EMI criteria a co-operation agreement that grants full access to the whole range of SWIFT network, products and services.

[53] See Case No. IV/M.616, *Swiss Air/Sabena*, OJ C 200/10 (1995).

[54] Commission Decision 96/180/EC, OJ L 54/28 (1996).

flyer programmes. In *LH/SAS/UA* and *British Airways/American Airlines*,[55] the Commission held that the alliances restricted competition because they created barriers to entry. The Commission therefore proposed several conditions, including the reduction of frequencies, where requested by a competitor, and the obligation to make slots available free of charge to competitors wishing to launch a service.

1. *BT/MCI II*

In *BT/MCI II*,[56] concerning the merger of MCI and BT, the Commission found that the relevant markets were those for the provision of audio-conferencing and international voice services in the UK. BT held a dominant position in both markets, underpinned by its control of the local loop, a position that was likely to remain in place in the future given the investments and lead time required for the development of local networks. The transaction would have reinforced BT's dominant position in both relevant markets, particularly in the market for the provision of international voice services, where BT carried over 70 percent of traffic. The Commission found that, given the current shortage of existing international transmission capacity between the UK and the US, together with the parties' significant entitlement on existing transatlantic submarine cables, it could only clear the transaction subsequent to the parties' commitments to: (i) make available to new operators in the UK without delay and at reasonable prices all their current and prospective overlapping capacity on the UK/US route resulting from the merger on the transatlantic cable; (ii) sell BT's capacity leased to operators on the UK/US route at their request and on reasonable terms and conditions; (iii) sell to other US carriers, at their request and without delay, the Eastern end matched half circuit owned by BT to enable them to provide international voice telephony services on the UK/US route on an end-to-end basis, and to arrange for the divestiture of MCI's audio-conferencing business.

---

[55] Commission Notice concerning the alliance between Lufthansa, SAS, and United Airline, OJ C 239/04 (1998); Commission Notice concerning the alliance between British Airways and American Airline OJ C 239/05 (1998). The proposals of the Commission impose on the parties the obligations to give up frequencies, airport facilities and slots without compensation, and to grant competitors the possibility of interlining and sharing frequent flyer programmes. However, the extent of these obligations is limited to allow competitors to enter the relevant markets.

[56] Case No. IV/M.856, OJ L 336/1 (1997).

. *MCI and WorldCom Inc.*

'ollowing *BT/MCI II*, the merger between MCI and WorldCom Inc., which ould have led to the consolidation of the internet backbone of the parties, was uthorised upon the divestiture of MCI's internet business activities. The Commission found that, as originally notified, the transaction would have led ɔ the consolidation of the networks of the global market leader, WorldCom, nd one of its main competitors, MCI. The parties would have had approxi- nately 50 percent of the market for 'top level' internet connectivity which was onsidered to be the relevant market. The Commission found that network xternalities (i.e. where the attraction of a network to its customers is a func- ion of the number of customers connected to the same network) would have nabled the merged entity to act independently of competitors.[57]

√I. Co-operation and Integration Between Competitors Controlling Networks

ɔome cases do not involve the creation of a network or the combination of dif- erent networks, but rather situations where the undertakings concerned con- rol networks or facilities that might confer competitive advantages. Where one ɔf the parties owns a network and other parties may gain privileged access to his network, this generally induces competition authorities to impose non-dis- crimination obligations on the parties, even without a finding that the under- akings hold an individual or joint dominant position.[58] However, in case of ɔonvergence agreements and joint ventures, this obligation is sometimes not ɔnough to remove competitive concerns, and transactions may be prohibited despite undertakings not to discriminate. Three categories of cases are dis- ɔussed below, namely agreements and joint ventures involving a competitive

---

[57] IP/98/639.

[58] With regard to the means by which third party access is guaranteed, the Commission has recently distinguished a 'condition' from an 'obligation' and stated that: 'The essential difference between a condition and an obligation under Regulation No 17 is that a failure to comply with a condition means any exemption is inapplicable without further action by the Commission, whereas a breach of an obligation can lead to a formal Commission decision withdrawing the exemption. National authorities (including both regulatory authorities and national courts) can therefore themselves determine whether the conditions have been fulfilled. A national authority could no longer permit continued operations under its regulatory regime if the conditions were not fulfilled.' (see case IV.36.539, 1998 OJ C 322/6 (1998)).

advantage in a related market, strategic alliances, and convergence network agreements.

1. Agreements and Joint Ventures Involving a Competitive Advantage in a Related Market

The Commission and the IAA may impose on one or more of the parent companies of a joint venture or the parties to an agreement which control a network, an obligation not to discriminate against third parties, even where there is no finding of dominance in the relevant market.

In joint ventures, the Commission may impose on the parents an obligation not to discriminate in favour of their joint venture if they have a large market share and even if they do not control an 'essential facility' in the strict sense. The Commission is concerned that the joint venture may hinder competitors, especially where the parents supply their products and services exclusively to the joint venture or where they discriminate against competitors in providing such goods and services. In *DHL International*,[59] on the acquisition by Lufthansa, Japan Airlines, and a Japanese trading company of the express delivery service company DHL,[60] the Commission decided not to oppose the agreement when the parties undertook not to discriminate against DHL's competitors in the provision of services and facilities.

Similarly, the Commission issued a comfort letter in respect of an agreement for the provision of a joint product by Amadeus and Sabre, two computer reservation systems owned by leading airlines,[61] after the parties gave detailed undertakings to open the Amadeus parents' home markets to increased competition from other computer reservation systems.[62]

---

[59] European Commission, 21st Report on Competition Policy, paras. 88–89.

[60] The Commission has announced that it will authorise the acquisition by Deutsche Post AG of joint control of DHL when Deutsche Post AG undertook not to subsidise DHL from its reserved activities and to publish separate accounts for its reserved and non-reserved activities, and not to discriminate against parcel delivery rivals wishing to use the German Post Office network (*Deutsche Post/DHL* Case No. IV/M.1168, OJ C 154/6 (1998).

[61] European Commission 21st Report on Competition Policy, *supra n* 43, paras. 93–95

[62] In particular, carriers owning shares in Amadeus or Sabre must not discriminate against other CRSs when distributing their products. Amadeus and Sabre must not impede non-associated carriers from distributing their products through other CRSs and must treat equally all carriers, shareholders or not, whose products they display. To ensure that all CRSs operating in Europe were subject to the same rules the Commission adopted a group exemption.

a) *EPI/Postel*

The IAA cleared a distribution agreement between the Italian post office, Ente Poste Italiane (EPI), and Postel S.p.A. (Postel), a joint venture between EPI and Finmeccanica, active in the provision of 'hybrid' e-mail services that permit customers to send e-mail messages to a service provider who transmits the messages to branch offices for printing and delivery.[63] Under the notified agreement, EPI undertook to provide hand delivery services of Postel's e-mail messages on a non-exclusive basis, charging an amount covering direct costs and general fees, plus a profit margin. During the proceedings before the IAA, EPI agreed to: (i) provide non-discriminatory access to its distribution network to all other hybrid e-mail service providers; (ii) organise separate accounting for delivery services provided to such undertakings and arrange for verification of the costs of these services by qualified external auditors; and (iii) not to impose exclusivity clauses.

b) *Infonet*

The Commission has adopted a similar policy in the telecommunications sector. In *Infonet*,[64] for example, the Commission declared that certain agreements for the provision of global value added services between several public and private telecoms operators would not be covered by an Article 81(3) [ex 85(3)] Consolidated Treaty exemption unless the participants agreed not to discriminate against third parties. Infonet used an international packet-switch network constructed with lease lines from the participant telecom operators (TOs) or other TOs. The Commission found that there was a risk of cross-subsidisation and discrimination by the TOs against other suppliers of telecommunication services, but was satisfied when the parties undertook that: (i) Community TOs would supply third parties with services on similar terms and conditions to those applied to Infonet; (ii) Infonet would not be granted terms and conditions for reserved services that would allow it to offer services that other suppliers were prevented from offering; (iii) Community TOs would not discriminate between Infonet or its distributors and competing suppliers in relation to the release of any decision to make substantial changes to technical interfaces providing the means of access to reserved services or in the release of other technical information relating to the operation of the public telecommunications network; and (iv) Community TOs would

---

[63] Italian Antitrust Authority Decision of 30/3/1997, Bollettino dell'Autorità Garante della Concorrenza e del Mercato No. 18/1997, p. 29.

[64] Commission Notice, OJ C 7/3 (1992).

not discriminate against Infonet's competitors in relation to the provision of commercial information.[65]

c) Eirpage

Similarly, in *Eirpage*,[66] the Commission requested Irish Telecom (IT) to ensure that companies interested in competing with a joint venture between IT and Motorola in the wide-area interconnected paging sector be treated on the same footing as the joint venture. The joint venture was created to establish and operate a nation-wide paging service in Ireland connected to IT's telecommunications infrastructure. The joint venture would be the only operator in the market until new licences were granted. The Commission found that the agreement was anti-competitive, but decided to exempt it, since it would allow the rapid introduction of a paging service in Ireland, offering features not previously available. The Commission required a number of changes to the agreement and, in particular, that IT: (i) make the facilities necessary for operating such a service available to persons satisfying relevant licensing and financial requirements, on the same conditions as applied to its joint venture; (ii) inform the Commission of any request and the outcome of the request; and (iii) make the full text of the undertaking available to interested parties.[67]

Finally, in certain cases,[68] the Commission imposes the obligation not to

---

[65] In order to monitor compliance with these undertakings the Commission imposed the following obligations: (i) each Community TO agreed to keep records of any application by Infonet or its distributors for reserved services (indicating the services and the supply conditions) for three years following the application; (ii) Infonet agreed to supply an annual report indicating applications to Community TOs; (iii) Infonet agreed to indicate any transaction of 2 million ECU in value between Infonet, a Community TO, and any other facilities provided by a Community TO to Infonet; and (iv) Infonet agreed to provide details of any agreement entered into between Infonet and a Community TO and relating directly to the notified agreements.

[66] Commission Decision 91/562/EEC (*Eirpage*).

[67] Eirpage paid IT an annual fee to amortise the investment in the paging infrastructure and full commercial rates for all IT's facilities such as the use of leased lines. The parties also gave assurances that Eirpage would not unfairly favour sales of Motorola equipment. For other cases of agreements involving telecommunication operators in which the Commission requested undertakings not to discriminate, see *MDNS*, a case concerning an agreement between telecoms administration and private parties to create a joint venture for the provision of managed data network services (IP/89/948 of December 14, 1989), and *FNA*, concerning a joint venture between leading telecommunications organisations for the provision of telecommunications services in the financial services sector (IP/93/988 of November 15, 1993).

[68] See Commission Decision 94/594/EC, OJ L 224/28 (1994) (*ACI*); Commission Decision 94/663/EC, OJ L 259/20 (1994) (*Night Service*).

iscriminate on the basis of the existence of a 'special relationship' between the
ɔint venture and its parents. By imposing the obligation not to discriminate,
ḥe Commission tries to ensure that the conditions under Article 81(3) [ex
᠈5(3)] are met. As will be seen below, the CFI appears to adopt a more restric-
ḷve approach as to the imposition of the obligation not to discriminate and to
ịpply an 'essential facility' type test.[69]

ɪ) Night Services

n *Night Services*,[70] the Commission considered certain agreements for the for-
ṃation of a joint venture (European Night Services Ltd, ENS) between British
Ṛail (BR),[71] Deutsche Ban (DB), Société Nationale des Chemins de Fer
·rançais (SNFC) and Nederlandse Spoorwegen (NS), either directly or
ḥrough their subsidiaries. ENS's business consists of providing and operating
ɔvernight passenger rail services between points in the UK and the Continent
ḥrough the Channel Tunnel. ENS also concluded operating agreements with
ẹts parents and with Société Nationale des Chemins de Fer Belges, in which
ẹach undertook to provide ENS with services including traction over its net-
ẉork, cleaning services on board-servicing equipment and passenger handling
ȿervices. The Commission found that these agreements had restrictive effects in
ḥe markets for the transport of business travellers and in the market for leisure

---

[69] It appears that the Commission adopted an 'essential facility-type' approach in
Télécom Development, where it announced its intention of approving a joint venture,
Télécom Development (TD), between SNCF and a telecommunications operator
(Commission Notice pursuant to Article 19(3) of Council Regulation No 17, OJ C 293/4
(1998)). TD was created to develop and run a long-distance telecommunications network in France using the surplus capacity on the SNCF optical fibre network and optical fibre capacity made available by Cégétel or its subsidiaries. SNCF granted TD a
non-exclusive right to occupy public railway land for a period of thirty years and a priority right of access to SNCF's land, guaranteed by a penalty clause applicable for a
period of three and a half years. However, the Commission objected to the priority right
granted to the joint venture, and demanded for a revision of the initial agreements in
such a way as to limit the priority right and a clarification of its implementing modalities. In order to obtain Commission approval, the parties spelt out the conditions under
which the penalties would be applicable and explicitly undertook that such a right
would not apply in the event other companies seeking access to railway-owned land if
the installation of cables on the rail network was the *sole way* to create a telecommunications network. The Commission was concerned that railways lines are one of the
infrastructures that allow for the rapid deployment of a national telecommunications
network (Agence Europe 24/9/1998).
[70] See *supra* n 67.
[71] Subsequently, BR's interest was transferred to European Passenger Services Ltd
(now Eurostar (UK) Ltd) (EPS).

travellers in the four routes served by ENS.[72] In fact, the agreements had the effect of partitioning the markets. In addition, given that ENS's parents continued to hold a dominant position in the supply of rail services in their Member States of origin, the formation of ENS might impede access to the market by competing transport operators. In particular, the existence of a 'special relationship between the parent companies and ENS might place other operators at a disadvantage in competition for necessary rail services'.[73]

However, the Commission held that the formation of ENS is likely to enhance economic progress and to benefit users directly. In addition, the restrictions were indispensable since the services were new and their provision involved a substantial degree of financial risk. The Commission granted the parties an eight-year exemption, subject to the condition that the restriction '*remain within which is indispensable*'. To this end, it imposed on the railway undertakings party to ENS an obligation to supply to any international grouping of undertakings or any transport operators wishing to operate night services through the Channel Tunnel, the same essential rail services that they have agreed to supply to ENS on the same economic and financial terms as they grant ENS.[74]

The CFI annulled the decision because the Commission had made a wrong assessment of the restrictive effects of the agreements.[75] In particular, the CFI

---

[72] The routes were: London/Amsterdam; London-Frankfurt/Dortmund; Paris-Glasgow/Swansea and Brussels-Glasgow/Plymouth. It is worth noting that the Commission did not make any reference to the position of the parties in the relevant markets and the visible impact of the restriction brought about by the agreements at issue.

[73] *Night Services, supra n* 67, para. 46. The Commission also considered that BR and SNCF control a significant proportion of the available paths for the international trains in the Eurochannel pursuant to an agreement with Eurotunnel. The Commission found that the restrictions of competitions were enhanced by the fact that ENS forms part of a network of joint ventures between the parent undertakings.

[74] *Night Services, supra n* 67, paras. 80–84. The Commission specified that the parties must not be obliged to supply the services if the new entrant is able to supply them itself or if the railways do not have the necessary traction available. In any event, the railway companies are not obliged to provide paths to groupings of railway undertakings which are entitled to request a path from the infrastructure managers under Directive 91/440/EEC.

[75] Joined Cases T–374/94, T–375/94, T–384/94 and T–388/94, *European Night Services and others* v *Commission*, [1998] II–3141. The CFI annulled the decision on several grounds. In particular, it found that it did not contain a sufficient statement of reasons to enable the Court to make a ruling on the shares of the parties in the relevant markets and, therefore, to assess whether the agreements had an appreciable effect on trade between Member States. In addition, the CFI found that the Commission's

rejected the Commission findings on anti-competitive behaviour vis-à-vis third parties, considering that the Commission failed to demonstrate that the rail services were essential for ENS's competitors,[76] and even issued its own guidelines for the imposition of a non-discrimination obligation under Article 81(3) [ex 85(3)].[77]

> [w]ith regard to an agreement . . . in the present case, setting up a joint venture which falls within Article 81(1) [ex 85(1)] of the Treaty, the Court considers that neither the parent undertakings nor the joint venture thus set up may be regarded as being in possession of infrastructure, products or services which are 'necessary' or 'essential' for entry to the relevant market unless such infrastructure products or services are not 'interchangeable' and unless, by reason of their special characteristics—in particular the prohibitive costs of and/or time reasonably required for reproducing them—there are no viable alternatives available to potential competitors of the joint venture which are thereby excluded from the markets.[78]

---

finding that the ENS agreements restricted competition among the parents and between the parent and the joint venture was vitiated by inadequate reasoning and error of assessment.

[76] The provision of paths to international groupings such as ENS was already ensured by Directive 91/440/EEC and, in any event, transport operators not ensured access played no role in the market for rail passenger services. With respect to locomotives, the CFI found that given the market shares of the parties, it could not accept that a possible refusal to deal by the parties could have the effect of excluding competitors from the market. Furthermore, the decision contained no evidence that the parties could not obtain locomotives from other manufacturers or rent them from other undertakings. On the contrary, the parties stated that locomotives could be freely bought on the market and ENS parents were free to provide locomotives to third parties. The CFI held that the fact that only notifying undertakings actually possess the locomotives and had been the first to acquire them did not mean that they alone were able to do so. Similarly, the CFI found the Commission assessment as to crews was vitiated by an absence or insufficiency of reasoning.

[77] In particular, the CFI cited *RTE and ITP* v *Commission and Tiercé Ladbroke* v *Commission (ibid*, para. 208).

[78] *Ibid*, paras. 207–209. However, the Commission appears to adopt a different approach in its response to the parties' arguments. It states that 'Although in theory undertakings other than ENS's parent undertakings may have special locomotives and crews and although such locomotives may in theory be purchased or rented by any transport operator . . . in reality only ENS's parent undertakings actually have them. It is thus a real and practical impossibility for transport operators to find an alternative. Consequently, it is undeniable that the railway undertakings concerned occupy a dominant position on the essential services market, which according to the case law (see judgements in *Commercial Solvents, CBME, RTE and BBC,*. . .) justifies the condition imposed' (*ibid*, para. 197). According to the Commission, such a condition 'reflects a

2. Strategic Alliances

Strategic alliances are broad ranging arrangements between companies that fall short of a full merger but that go beyond limited agreement on joint activities.[79] In the telecommunications sector, strategic alliances generally concern the provision of global enhanced telecommunications services. They are beneficial in terms of economic progress and the introduction of new services. According to the Commission, the markets affected by these alliances are generally global, cross-border, or regional, given cost and price differences,[80] and the global position of the parties is usually not significant. The Commission focuses its attention on the impact of the transaction at local level, taking particular account of the fact that participants may control the national network infrastructures necessary for competitors to enter the market at both national and international levels. In order to avoid discrimination against competitors in favour of the joint venture, the Commission tends to require strict compliance with the obligations imposed, and will take immediate steps in the event of breach. National courts may also participate in enforcement procedures. The Commission recognises, however, that the principle of proportionality requires that far-reaching legal and commercial consequences do not result from an occasional individual failure to comply with the strict terms of an undertaking, particularly where the effect on the market of the failure to comply is negligible.[81]

The Commission expressed its concerns in the first case involving a strategic alliance, *BT/MCI*,[82] and stated that third-party access to MCI and BT networks was central to its assessment. The Commission did not take any further steps because existing US and UK legislation prevented cross-subsidisation and/or discrimination.[83]

---

concern distinct from the 'essential facilities' doctrine, seeking in this case to ensure that the conditions for exemption required by Article 81(3) [ex 85(3)] . . . are satisfied (*ibid*, para. 203).

[79] Pena Castellot, M., 'Strategic Alliances in the Telecommunications sector and the Competition Rules of the European Union', conference paper, 1995 ERA Conference 'Taking EC Telecommunications Law into the Future'.

[80] See, for example, Commission Decision 96/546/EC, OJ L 239/23 (1996) (*Atlas*).

[81] *Ibid*, para. 77.

[82] Commission Decision 94/579/EC, OJ L 223/36 (1994).

[83] *Ibid*, para. 57.

Atlas-Global One

By way of contrast, in *Atlas* and *Global One*, where no national protective legislation was in force, the Commission imposed several conditions on the parties. In *Atlas*, the Commission was particularly concerned with the effects of the formation of Atlas in the French and German markets for data transmission via terrestrial networks, since DT and FT held market shares in excess of 70 percent in Germany and France respectively, and enjoyed a monopoly over the supply of infrastructure. In addition, the proposed joint venture provided for the elimination of a competitor in Germany, namely FT's local subsidiary. The Commission found that no adequate competitive alternatives to Atlas currently existed in Germany and France,[84] with respect to the provision of data communications services to customers which demand casual, low-speed, low-volume applications provided through the packet-switched data network.[85] These services require wide-coverage networks, which would have not been available to competitors for some time.[86]

Consequently, the Commission held that the formation of Atlas would strengthen the parties' dominant position in their national markets and prevent entry in these markets.[87] The transaction would also have an impact at the

---

[84] The Commission held that there were not effective competitive alternatives despite: (i) the existence of operational expandable alternative infrastructure to provide the service, such as the ISDN 'D' channel, which was widely used in Germany and France to provide nation-wide X.25 data services; (ii) the outstanding economic importance of the French and German telecommunications markets to telecommunications operators; and (iii) the existence of a number of strong competing alliances. In this respect, the Commission also noticed that the mere presence of competing Europe-wide operators had little impact on the markets (para. 62).

[85] According to the Commission, these customers comprise one of the two market segments for packet-switched data communications services.

[86] The Commission stated that 'Generally, competitive alternatives must be effectively available to have an appreciable impact on market conditions' (*ibid*, para. 70). It concluded that there were not effective competitive alternatives in the French and German markets due to two considerations. First, all alternative infrastructures available in France and Germany amounted to only a third of DT's and FT's infrastructure, respectively. Second, the market was characterised by low margins. Therefore, investments in an alternative infrastructure could reduce the gap with the incumbent operators only when such an infrastructure could carry any telecommunications service and, thus, provide a better return on such investments. This would only have been possible subsequent to the full liberalisation of telecommunications markets.

[87] 'The elimination of competition between the parents is substantial as the Atlas joint venture was created by two internationally active TOs and covers the joint development and provision of services throughout the EU. DT and FT's respective dominant positions in the [. . .] Member State Telecommunications markets is reinforced by a legal

international level, because for both economic and geographic reasons, service provision into and across Germany and France, the two largest telecommunication markets in Europe, is key to competition in the markets for Europe-wide non-reserved telecommunication services.[88]

In order to meet the Commission's concerns the French and German governments undertook to liberalise alternative infrastructures, thereby reducing competitors' dependence on the parties. The Commission conditioned its decision on the granting of the first two licences in France and Germany. These licenses were granted in December 1996. Furthermore, the parties postponed the transfer of their domestic data transmission networks to the joint venture pending full liberalisation of the infrastructure in France and Germany. FT also undertook to sell its German corporate telecommunications services subsidiary, Info AG.

Finally, the parties were obliged to agree not to discriminate against competitors of Atlas who required access to their network infrastructures. In particular, clearance of the transaction was conditioned upon several behavioural constraints relating to: interconnection to the public packet-switched data networks on terms economically equivalent to those available to Atlas in France and Germany;[89] non-discriminatory interconnection to the PSTN and the ISDN in France and Germany;[90] and non-discriminatory interconnection to DT's and FT's other networks and facilities.[91]

---

infrastructure monopoly until such markets are fully and effectively liberalised . . . and will continue to rely on a dominant position for terrestrial transmission capacity for years thereafter. Current prices for infrastructure access—leased lines tariffs and interconnection, rates—together with DT and FT's strengthened joint market position impair competitors' ability to create a competitive network of similar scope and density to DT and FT's in these countries.' (*Atlas, supra n* 55, para. 40).

[88] *Ibid,* para. 62.

[89] FT and DT must also publish standard terms and conditions for the X.25 interface standards and not disclose to Atlas sensitive confidential information (Article 4(c)).

[90] In particular, the parties must not: (i) grant Atlas terms and conditions dissimilar to those applied to competing service providers with regard to leased lines services, PSTN/ISDN services, including access to such networks and traffic over such networks. This obligation also concerns services and facilities which will remain 'essential' after the liberalisation of the telecommunications markets in France and Germany; (ii) grant Atlas terms and conditions dissimilar to those applied to any competing third party operating a telecommunications facility that apply for interconnection with DT's or FT's networks; and (iv) discriminate between Atlas and other service providers in connection with the modification of technical interfaces for the access to services or essential facilities, the disclosure of technical information on the PSTN/ISDN, and the disclosure of any commercial information which could grant a substantial competitive advantage and is not available elsewhere (Article 4(b)).

[91] 'Such terms shall enable the telecommunications operator to provide

Besides undertakings to ensure that the conditions and scope of services available and the disclosure of technical and commercial information, were equivalent to those available to Atlas, the Commission imposed obligations on he parties to monitor compliance, in particular regarding maintenance and supply of detailed accounting information and Commission inspection of ecords, together with a reporting and auditing obligations.

In *Global One*,[92] which involved a joint venture between Atlas and Sprint, he Commission imposed similar obligations to prevent the parties from discriminating in favour of the joint venture and Sprint,[93] together with obligations not to discriminate against correspondent operators.[94]

The Commission adopted the same approach in *Unisource*,[95] an alliance between PTT Telecom of the Netherlands, Telia and the Swiss PTT, and *Uniworld*,[96] the alliance between Unisource and ATT.

3. Network Convergence Agreements

This category comprises forms of integration characterised by the presence of operators active in converging markets and who control telecoms infrastructure,

---

telecommunications services or [. . .] facilities without limitation in any respect within the reasonable capabilities of the telecommunications operator concerned' (Article 4(d)).

[92] Commission Decision 96/547/EC, OJ L 239/57 (1996).

[93] *Ibid*, Article 2(a) and (b).

[94] *Ibid*, Article 2(c).

[95] Commission Decision 97/780/EC, OJ L 318/1 (1997). The Commission found that the parties had a dominant position in the market for the provision of leased lines and national services and tried to ensure competitors' access to the networks and the publication of standards of interconnection agreements and terms and tariffs of leased lines, and to avoid the misuse of confidential information. The Commission contacted the national governments, but did not condition approval of the operation upon their actions. In Sweden, the markets were already liberalised, while the Dutch government confirmed its intention to meet the deadline for the liberalisation of alternative infrastructures and the introduction of full competition. Switzerland is not a Member State, but the Swiss government nonetheless agreed to liberalise the market by January 1998.

[96] Commission Decision 97/781/EC, OJ L 318/24 (1997). The Commission made its finding regardless of whether Uniworld was active in domestic markets. However, it still considered the impact of the links between Uniworld, Unisource, and their shareholders who held a dominant position, and imposed obligations not to discriminate. AT&T undertook certain obligations and, in particular, agreed to abide by the relevant legislation to grant access to competitors for its US infrastructure, and to advise the Commission of any complaints filed with the FCC regarding access and the final decisions taken.

and hold a substantial amount of transmission capacity or conditional acces
technology. In these cases, irrespective of whether such facilities are considere
'essential', they are apt to confer on the parties a competitive advantage in nev
and developing markets. Moreover, the combination of the parties' activities ca
strengthen their position in their original markets.

The Commission has clearly stated that dominant positions formerly hel
by national operators as a result of Member State legislation should not b
replaced by dominant positions for private parties produced by commercia
agreements.[97] As a general rule, the Commission does not prohibit integratior
in converging markets, especially in the media sector, when there is no risk o
foreclosure because parties do not have a strong market position, or because a
number of competitors are able to counteract their market power.[98] By contrast, where the parties enjoy a significant competitive advantage which woulc
enable them to control the development of the market, the Commission may
well prohibit the transaction, even if the transaction might contribute to technical and economic progress.[99]

At the time of writing, four transactions[100] involving the creation of joint
ventures for the provision of services in new or developing markets betweer

---

[97] *Nordic Satellite Distribution*, Commission Decision 96/177/EC, OJ L 53/2(
(1996).

[98] *CLT/Disney/Super RTL*, Case No. IV/M.566, OJ C 144/23 (1995); *Kirch,
Richemont, Multichoice Telepiù*, Case No. IV/M.584, OJ C 129/6 (1995); *Kirch,
Richemont/Telepiù*, Case No. IV/M.410, OJ C 225/3 (1994); *Bertelsmann-CLT*, Case
No. IV/M.779, OJ C 364/3 (1996); *Cable I Television de Catalunya/STET International,
GET-Gruppo Electrico de Comunications, Endesa and Intercatalunya Cable*, Case No.
IV/M.1148, OJ C 101/31 (1998); *Matsushita/MCA*, Case No. IV/M.037, OJ C 12/15
(1991); *Bell Cablemedia/Cable & Wireless/Videotron*, Case No. IV/M.853, OJ C 24/22
(1997); *ATT/NCR*, Case No. IV/M.050, OJ C 16/20 (1991).

[99] In its decision 94/922/EC, OJ L 364/1 (1994) (*MSG*), the Commission stated (paras.
100–101) that '[t]he reference to this criterion under Article 2(1)(b) . . . is subject to the
reservation that no obstacle is formed to competition. . . . The hindering of competition
does in fact make even the achievement of technical and economic progress questionable.'

[100] In 1996, the Commission considered a joint venture between the Spanish telecommunications company and Sogecable, a subsidiary of Canal+, the leading French pay
TV company, whose aim was to provide cable television and audio-visual services in
Spain. The Commission considered that the joint venture would have reduced competition in several markets for telephone, pay-TV and cable services. In particular, the joint
venture would have led to foreclosure in the markets for services to operators of cable
audio-visual and television services, and delayed the effects of liberalisation of the
market for voice telephony in Spain. Since the joint venture was abandoned, the
Commission did not take a formal decision (*Telefonica/Sogecable*, European
Commission 26th Report on Competition Policy, *supra* n 1, paras 150–51).

leading telecommunications and media operators have been prohibited. In each case, the transactions would have led to the strengthening of the parties' position on the markets where they were active and/or the creation of long-lasting dominant positions in new, developing, or recently deregulated markets. The transactions generally involve, *inter alia*, the creation of joint ventures that would have acquired a bottleneck facility. In other cases, the parent company held a bottleneck facility to which the joint venture would have had preferential access, compared to its competitors.

a) MSG Media Service

In *MSG Media Service*,[101] the Commission prohibited an agreement between Bertelsmann, Kirch, and DT,[102] on the grounds that the operation would have restrictive effects in the German markets for administrative and technical services for suppliers of pay-TV and other financed communications services, pay-TV, and cable television networks.

MSG would be active in the market for administrative and technical services. This market did not exist in Germany but was expected to develop rapidly following the introduction of digital television. MSG would have acquired a long-term monopoly, and been able to restrict or prevent access to competitors, given DT's strength in the cable networks field and the exceptional film and programming resources of Kirch and Bertelsmann.[103] Competitors would not be likely to enter the market.[104]

---

[101] See *supra* n 69.

[102] Bertelsmann is the leading German media group with interests in book and music publishing, sound recording, and commercial television. Kirch is the principal German supplier of feature films and television programming. DT is the public telecommunications operator that own the German cable network.

[103] In particular, the Commission found that 'Thanks to the business potential of Bertelsmann/Kirch in the pay-TV area, MSG will [. . .] probably benefit from economies of scale (subscriber base, number of programmes handled) that would make competition from other service providers much more difficult. On the other hand, Telekom's participation in the joint venture allows MGS to provide pay-TV suppliers with the necessary user contracts for Telekom's broad-band cable network, even if these contracts are legally made between Telekom and the users. MGS can therefore [. . .] offer programme suppliers a comprehensive service covering all the technical prerequisites for pay-TV' (*ibid*, para. 70).

[104] The Commission stated that, 'although a monopoly in a future market [. . .] should not be regarded necessarily as a dominant position within the meaning of Article 2(3) of the Merger Regulation, the assumption that non-market dominance exists presupposes [. . .] that the future market in question remains open to future competition and that the monopoly is consequently only temporary' (*ibid*, para. 55).

In the pay-TV market, Bertelsmann and Kirch would have had sufficient resources to obtain a strong position and, through MSG, would have been able to control and influence access by their competitors to consumers and hence hold a dominant position. Any new pay-TV provider would have been obliged to buy services from MSG. Through MSG, Bertelsmann and Kirch could delay the launch of competitors' programmes, acquire valuable information about them, and influence the location of competitors' programmes on the screen modulator of the decoder and in the smart card. In addition, the Commission found that MSG could limit free access to decoders and require that viewers not use the decoders of other pay-TV or service providers.

Finally, DT would have an advantage in the cable market due to the possibility of access to the wide range of Bertelsmann and Kirch programming.

The notifying parties proposed to undertake that MSG would not discriminate against competitors, or transfer information to its parents, and that DT would open up its cable network.[105] These proposals were considered inadequate, since they were conditional or were only declarations of intent, and did not resolve the underlying structural problem.

b) Nordic Satellite Distribution

Similarly, in *Nordic Satellite Distribution,*[106] the Commission blocked a joint venture (NSD) between the national Norwegian and Danish telecommunication operators, Norsk Telekom (NT), Teledenmark (TD) and Industriforvaltings AB Kinnevik (Kinnevik), a television and media conglomerate.[107] NSD intended to transmit satellite TV programmes to cable operators and households receiving satellite TV on their own satellite dish. The Commission found that the joint venture would have created or strengthened dominant positions

---

[105] The parties proposed, *inter alia,* that: (i) MSG use a decoder base that operates on a common interface; (ii) MSG agree not to disclose any information to its parents on programme or subscriber data of other pay-TV suppliers; (iii) MSG choose a non-discriminatory electronic programme guide style; (iv) MSG adopt a transparent and non-discriminatory pricing policy; and (v) DT agree to open up its network to further digital transmission of programmes.

[106] *Nordic Satellite Distribution, supra* n 67.

[107] NT was the largest cable TV operator in Norway, with about 30 percent of the connections controlling the satellite capacity on the 1 West satellite position (one of the two Nordic positions), and an important pay-TV distributor in Norway. TD was the largest cable operator in Denmark, with about 50 percent of the connections, and enjoyed a privileged position in relation to its cable TV operations until January 1, 1998. TD and Kinnevik controlled most of the satellite capacity on the 5 East satellite position (the other Nordic position). Kinnevik was the most important provider of Nordic satellite TV programmes, and the largest pay-TV distributor in the Nordic countries.

in three relevant markets. In particular, NSD would have had a dominant position in the market for the provision of satellite TV transponder capacity to the Nordic region, enabling it to foreclose other satellite operators from leasing transponders to broadcasters, given its links with Kinnevik as an important distributor of satellite TV channels direct-to-home households, and through links to the parents as cable TV operators. Furthermore, TD's dominant position on the Danish market for operation of cable TV networks would have been strengthened. Finally, NSD would have obtained a dominant position in the markets for the distribution of satellite pay-TV and other encrypted channels to direct-to-home households.[108]

The Commission considered the parties' proposals—relating to the waiver of rights over certain transponders, making additional transponders available to third parties, and the arm's length relationship between the parents and the joint venture—insufficient to eliminate competitive concerns. They were '*too limited in scope, mostly behavioural and would be very difficult to enforce.*'[109]

c) RTL/Veronica/Endemol

In *RTL/Veronica/Endemol*,[110] the Commission blocked a joint venture between a Dutch-language commercial broadcasting corporation, a public broadcasting association in the Netherlands, and Endemol, the biggest independent programme producer. The joint venture would have affected three markets, including TV broadcasting, TV advertising, and the market for independently produced Dutch-language programmes. In TV advertising, the joint venture would have obtained a dominant position. In the market for TV programmes, Endemol's dominant position would have been strengthened

---

[108] In commenting on the decision, the Commission stated that: 'The vertically integrated nature of the operation means that the downstream market positions (cable TV operation and pay-TV) reinforce the upstream market positions (satellite transponders and provisions of programmes) and vice versa. . . . The affected markets are currently in a transitional phase since the telecommunication markets were about to be liberalised and new technologies and services were continually being developed and some were about to be introduced. In this context the decision of the Commission took on a particular importance, because future market structures were being defined. The Commission therefore acted to ensure that those markets were not foreclosed. However, the Commission recognised that joint ventures and particular transnational joint ventures can be instrumental in developing the media and telecommunications sectors to their full potential. Furthermore it is the Commission policy to take new developments into account' (European Commission 25th Report on Competition Policy, p. 174).

[109] *Nordic Satellite Distribution, supra* n 67, para. 159.

[110] Commission Decision 96/346/EC, OJ L 134/32 (1996).

because the joint venture would have guaranteed a significant sales outlet for Endemol's programmes, since Endemol would have obtained a structural link with the leading broadcaster in the Netherlands, providing it with preferential access to the largest customers in the Dutch TV production market. At the same time, the joint venture would have had preferential access to Endemol's wide range of programmes.[111] Following Endemol's withdrawal from the joint venture and the receipt of certain undertakings by the parties, the Commission authorised the transaction.[112]

d) CLT-UFA—Kirch/Premiere

In this case, the Commission prohibited the proposed acquisition of joint control by CLT-UFA and Kirch of Premiere and Kirch's subsidiary Beta Digital, to avoid foreclosure in the German pay-TV and technical services for pay-TV

---

[111] Similar issues arose in *Screensport/EBU* (Commission Decision 91/130/EEC, OJ L 63/32 (1991)), in which the Commission found the creation of Eurosport, a transnational satellite sports channel, contrary to EC competition rules. Eurosport was established as a joint venture satellite television sports channel by the Eurosport Consortium, Sky Television, and News International. Almost all EBU members participate in the Eurovision system, an institutionalised system of TV programmes, including sports programmes, for which the Eurovision members jointly purchase rights. The agreements extended to Eurosport the benefits of the Eurovision system. The Commission found that the benefits of the introduction of a new transnational channel were outweighed by the limitation of market entry opportunities.

[112] The Commission noted that: 'The withdrawal of Endemol from HMG had removed the structural link between the largest Dutch producer and the leading commercial TV broadcaster in the Netherlands, a link which resulted in the strengthening of Endemol's dominant position.' (European Commission, 26th Report on Competition Policy, *supra* n 1, p. 185). The Commission dealt with the issue of preferential access to contents in *Numericable/Exante/Canal+* (IP/98/1062). The case involved an operation whereby BankAmerica Investment Corporation (BankAmerica) and Capital Communications CDPQ Inc. (CDPQ) was to acquire joint control of Numericable Holding (NCH) together with Canal+. NCH operates cable television networks in France. The Commission conditioned its clearance upon Canal+ and Sogecable, a Spanish company jointly controlled by Canal+, undertaking to negotiate with Spanish cable operators regarding theme or other television programming over which they held distribution rights and to distribute such programming in a fair and non-discriminatory manner consistent with Community and national competition rules. Such undertaking would remove the risk of Sogecable, which holds a strong market position in the pay-TV market and is a very important distributor of content, granting a preferential treatment to Cableuropa, a joint venture between BankAmerica and CPDQ and a licensed operator of cable pay-TV and telecommunications services via fourteen franchises in Spain.

markets.[113] As a result of the transaction, the parties would have transferred to all their digital pay-TV business assets to Premiere would have been the sole operator in the market. The Commission found that the combination of the programme resources of Kirch and CLT-UFA and the subscription base of Premiere would have prevented the development of any additional broadcasting and marketing platforms in the market. At the same time, Beta Digital would have obtained a dominant position in the market for technical services for satellite pay-TV in Germany, given that all digital pay-TV providers were committed to use its access technology. The development of an alternative technology was also considered unlikely.

The Commission also prohibited the acquisition of joint control by CLT-UFA (Bertlesmann), Kirch and DT of BetaResearch, a subsidiary of Kirch that held exclusive unlimited licenses for the Beta access technology on the basis of the d-box decoder. DT would have built a technical platform for the digital distribution of pay-TV programmes over its cable TV network on the basis of this technology. As a result of the transaction, competition in the German markets for technical services for pay-TV and cable networks would have been restricted and DT would have become the only provider of technical services for pay-TV in the cable network, strengthening its already dominant position in the cable network market, to the disadvantage of private operators. According to the Commission, private cable operators wishing to offer technical services for pay-TV in their own networks would use Beta's technology. DT would have controlled the company, and could have prevented the entry of other service providers into the market through its licensing policy.[114]

The Commission displayed the same concerns about market foreclosure in objecting to the launch of a digital platform by Canal+, Rai, Telecom Italia, Mediaset, and Cecchi Gori, by the acquisition of interests in the capital of Canal+'s subsidiary, Telepiù Srl.[115]

The IAA has examined cases in which Telecom Italia (TI), the incumbent Italian operator, acquired two companies active in converging markets.

---

[113] IP/98/477 of May 27, 1998.

[114] To avoid reaching a negative decision, the Commission proposed that: (i) DT broadcast programmes of possible rivals; (ii) Premiere offer some of its rights to sports events and part of its film stocks; and (iii) reasonable prices for sporting rights and for Premiere films be set, with an arbitration procedure in the event of disagreement (Agence Europe 28/5/98).

[115] The IAA also stated its position on the potentially anti-competitive effects of such an initiative in challenging the provision on which the right to create the platform was based, Article 52(19) of Law No. 249/97 (see Italian Antitrust Authority Opinion of July 10, 1997, Bollettino dell'Autorità Garante della Concorrenza e del Mercato No.

e) Telecom Italia/Video On Line

In the first case, *Telecom Italia/Video On Line* (VOL),[116] the IAA cleared TI's acquisition of the main Italian internet access provider. The IAA expressed concern at TI's monopoly of the telephone infrastructure and its presence in the market for telecommunications services. In the provision of access to internet services, TI would have had advantages over its competitors, such as significantly lower costs for the use of its own transmission capacity and the ability to provide a more widespread network. Without starting formal proceedings, the IAA authorised the transaction after TI had agreed to several conditions, including communication to the undertaking active in the provision of on-line services of all relevant information concerning infrastructure development and tariff changes; the conclusion of interconnection agreements and agreements for the creation of joint-point internet access; and the creation of a separate business unit with separate accounting activities within the relevant product market.

f) Telecom Italia/Intesa

In the second case, *Telecom Italia/Intesa*,[117] the IAA prohibited TI's acquisition of Intesa, a joint venture between IBM and Fiat.[118] The IAA focused on the impact of the transaction on the relevant national markets. In particular, it considered that, in the market for leased lines, TI still enjoyed a *de facto* monopoly, and that the acquisition of Intesa would prevent potential competitors from supplying one of the main users of leased lines. In the market for standardised data transmission services, the IAA found that TI's dominant

---

26/1997, p. 62). It affirmed that the acquisition would inevitably create a 'unity of objectives in the global management of the controlled company'. The agreement, according to the IAA, would not only cover technological aspects, but would inevitably have horizontal effects on organisational and commercial strategies, such as common management of clients and common planning. Accordingly, the acquisition of a controlling interest in the only pay-TV operator by the most important domestic competitors on generalist and thematic television markets and the public telecommunications operator would have led to serious distortions of competition by establishing a barrier to entry to the Italian pay-TV market.

[116] Italian Antitrust Authority Decision of June 19, 1996, Bollettino dell'Autorità Garante della Concorrenza e del Mercato No. 25/1996, p. 66.

[117] Italian Antitrust Authority Decision of November 13, 1997, Bollettino dell'Autorità Garante della Concorrenza e del Mercato No. 46/1997, p. 19.

[118] The agreements between IBM and STET were notified to the Commission on April 10, 1997. The notification was withdrawn after the acquisition of Intesa was blocked.

position would be permanently reinforced, thanks to the competitive advantages it enjoyed. First, TI operated the public switch data transmission network (Itapac), which could be used to gain access to clients and distribute competitors' services, on an exclusive basis. Furthermore, on completion of the operation, TI might integrate its offering with Intesa's customised data transmission services and value-added services to offer a full range of products. Broadening TI's offer would generate a barrier to entry for new competitors, since none of them would be able to offer a comparable range of services, particularly in the standardised data transmission services area. Finally, in the market for customised data transmission services, the IAA considered that a substantial market share, together with a monopoly in the provision of leased lines, and a dominant position in the provision of standardised data transmission services, indicated the existence of a dominant position.[119]

VII. Conclusion

We can conclude that the Commission and the IAA employ different approaches in imposing the obligation to grant non-discriminatory access to third parties, making it impossible to identify uniform criteria in cases where control of a network generates a special responsibility. Moreover, in most cases regarding structural network agreements, the Commission tends apply a different test from that applied under Article 82 [ex 86], particularly in essential facility cases.

The *legal basis for the obligation not to discriminate* is found in Article 81(3) [ex 85(3)] Consolidated Treaty, Article 4 of the Italian Law, and Community and Italian merger control rules. The crucial requirement under Article 81(3) [ex 85(3)] is the fourth test, which provides that exempted agreements must not allow the parties to eliminate competition with respect to a substantial part of the products and services concerned. In theory, application of Article 81 [ex 85(3)] can only follow a finding of infringement of Article 81(1) [ex 85(1)]. However, in *Iridium*, the parties had to 'confirm' that access would be given to third parties, even though the Commission found that the agreement did not fall under Article 81(1) [ex 85(1)]. The obligation to grant non-discriminatory access

---

[119] The IAA considered TI's competitive advantages as a monopolist in the market for leased lines and standardised data transmission services. The cost of leased lines for competitors was much higher than the internal cost for TI, and TI had access to information on the commercial policy of competitors that used Itapac to provide customised services.

is aimed at ensuring that the elimination of competition is not significant, and, in particular, that a number of competitors are present in the market.

Legal analysis under Article 81 [ex 85] does not require finding of a dominant position. The market position of the parties to an agreement is relevant only as one of the elements for evaluating the applicability of the restriction, and, in case of contractual networks, the extent of the contribution of the agreement to the restriction of competition. However, in some cases, the fact that the parties to the agreements are major or dominant operators in neighbouring or connected markets appears particularly important in the Commission's assessment.

The test establishing foreclosure varies. In case of contractual network agreements, such as *Costituzione Rete Dealer GSM*, the authorities focused on the impact of the agreements in the market and, in particular, on the extent to which they foreclose it. The Authorities found that foreclosure consisted in raising rival's costs, and condemned the parties even though foreclosure was not absolute or there was a number of outlets available (*Costituzione Rete Dealer GSM Dealer*). In cases of pooling of rights or distribution joint ventures, the analysis is focused on the content and extent of the exclusivity. However, in *UIP* the Commission considered that the parties held almost 25 percent of the market.

In cases of structural networks, the authorities took into account a variety of circumstances to impose the obligation not to discriminate. In some cases, they focused on the nature of the network (indispensability) and applied an 'essential facility' approach. In other cases, the Commission's approach has been to impose the obligation not to discriminate on operators who create, own or operate an important facility, access to which is necessary to ensure that third parties are able to compete without serious handicap. This is true, in particular, in joint venture cases where the Commission and the IAA are concerned that parents active in upstream markets may discriminate in favour of their joint venture. In general, the Commission and the IAA did not establish that the network created or owned by some of the parties was an essential facility or that the services/products that the parent companies could provide were essential. Moreover, the Commission and the IAA do not assess the extent of the competitor's handicap. In particular, they do not assess whether the lack of access entails elimination or substantial reduction of competition to the detriment of the consumer in both the short and long-term. In addition, they focus on the market power in the upstream market and do not ascertain whether the parties have a significant position in the downstream market.

Instead, they appear to base their decision on the fact that the parent companies are incumbent operators or hold significant market shares in related markets. In *Night Services*, for example, the Commission considered the special relationship between the parent companies and the joint venture and found that as a result of such a relationship, the joint venture's competitors could be placed at a competitive disadvantage.

Finally, in cases of convergence agreements and consolidation of networks, the Commission applies the traditional 'dominance approach' under the merger control rules. However, it should be noticed that dominance is also established by taking into account the position of the parties in upstream and downstream markets. The prevention of the creation of a long-lasting dominant position, is considered particularly important in developing markets. A 'hybrid' test of dominance was applied in *Atlas*, where the Commission dealt with the strengthening of the dominant position of the parties in the national markets under Article 81(3) [ex 85(3)].

To enforce policy, authorities adopt a number of different *measures* are used to enforce policy. Requiring termination of agreements, especially in the case of contractual networks; prohibiting proposed transactions in the case of mergers; and imposing on one or more of the parties an obligation not to discriminate against third parties. Obligations can even be imposed on foreign companies in relation to access to their infrastructures outside the EU, but the obligation not to discriminate is less likely to be imposed if existing legislation prevents those who run the network from discriminating against competitors.

The types of obligations imposed under Article 81(3) [ex 85(3)] Consolidated Treaty vary. In contractual networks based on the pooling of rights, competition authorities generally require sub-licensing. In structural networks, competitors may be allowed access to a network to be able to provide their services. In particular, they may be allowed to use the network services and/or to interconnect their own networks. In some circumstances, they may even become members of a system, for example a payment system, for which there can be different levels of membership. Where a network is run by a joint venture, it is not clear whether the competition authorities will require compulsory admission of shareholders to the joint venture. From the case law, it appears that the Commission takes into account whether third parties can become shareholders of the joint venture, but focus on the simple opportunity for access to the network. The IAA is more careful in ensuring that third parties can have access to the shareholding of the joint venture. In certain circumstances, the Commission required the parties to transfer their assets in favour of their competitors.

The duty not to discriminate may be accompanied by other obligations, including a prohibition on the misuse of confidential information, and accounting and reporting obligations. The latter may often seek to ensure the possibility of monitoring compliance by the parties.

The extent of the duty to grant access, and the parties to whom it should be granted, is not always clear from case law. In most instances the agreements and implementing measures are not published. As a general rule, however, it appears that under the principle of proportionality, access to infrastructure should only be granted within the reasonable capabilities of the network owner. In addition, access should be imposed only to the extent necessary to allow third parties to compete. Third parties should not be placed in a better position than the owners of the network.

It is unclear who may claim access. Competition authorities seek to allow access for competitors, but have not defined the category of persons. The requirements necessary for third parties to be able to claim access are never defined and, in some cases, the authorities seem to impose a very broad 'public service obligation' on the network owner.

As discussed earlier, the Commission will not accept agreements not to discriminate in mergers that create a dominant position. The Commission does not consider that such mergers can be made lawful by the parties agreeing not to abuse their dominant position. The Commission instead requires structural remedies, but is willing to accept amendments to the originally notified agreements. In this respect, it is significant that the Commission authorised the transaction between RTL and Veronica after Endemol's exit from the agreement. It is arguable that, if the transactions which have so far been prohibited were notified under Article 81 [ex 85] EC, the Commission would have had the opportunity to consider behavioural aspects more carefully and accepted agreements not to discriminate against competitors. By contrast, the IAA in *VOL* and *PI/SDA* cleared the acquisition of Video On Line by TI on the basis of an undertaking not to discriminate.

In most cases involving infrastructures which might grant a competitive advantage to the parties to a network agreement, the Commission appears to set aside the analysis of the nature of the facility and/or bases its findings on other grounds. This approach can be criticised because it does not include an in-depth assessment of the situations and, in particular, of the implications of the imposition of the obligation to share facilities granting a competitive advantage in the long term.

As a result of this policy, discrimination and the exclusion of competitors are assessed differently, depending on whether the exclusion or discrimination is made by a single firm or by a joint venture. The first type of case is usually dealt with under the essential facility doctrine, whereby an undertaking controlling a facility or infrastructure without access to which competitors cannot provide services to their customers, may not refuse access to such a facility to a competitor or grant it access on less favourable terms than those for its services. The imposition of such a duty is to prevent the undertaking controlling the facility from imposing a competitive disadvantage on its competitors. However, imposition of such a duty is exceptional and requires a rigorous analysis of the conditions for the application of Article 82 [ex 86], in particular, as to the definition of the relevant market and the existence of a dominant position. In particular, the essential facility test is based on the assessment of the following requirement: whether the undertaking controlling the facility occupies a dominant position in the provision of the essential facility and itself uses the facility; the facility at issue is essential, i.e. access to such a facility is indispensable for competitors to be able to compete. The non-duplicability of the facility must be an objective one and concern all competitors, and the Commission, in deciding whether a facility is essential, seeks to estimate the extent of the competitors' handicap and whether it is temporary or permanent; there is no objective justification for the refusal of access or for the discrimination.

The reason why the Commission follows a different approach in assessing network agreements could be related to the fact that generally, in cases of agreements falling under Article 81 [ex 85], competition is restricted by co-ordination of the parties behaviour. Thus, the need to ensure that other competitors are present and able to compete in the market is stronger, and the requirements not to discriminate are more relaxed. Another reason for the Commission's attitude is that in most cases of network agreements, the Commission intends to keep newly liberalised markets open to competitors, even if competitors are already protected by Community or national legislative measures. In *Atlas*, for example, the Commission found that there were alternative network infrastructures available to competitors, but it held that these did not constitute adequate competitive alternatives to provide services to some customers and that competitors did not have a real possibility of entry, at least until the full liberalisation of the telecommunications markets was accomplished.

In the *Night Services* judgment, the CFI appears to have 'imported' an essential facility test into Article 81(1) [ex 85(1)]. The judgment indicates that foreclosure of third parties relates to the fact that the parties to the agreement are in possession of infrastructure, products or services which are necessary or essential for entry to the relevant market. The indispensability is assessed by ascertaining whether the products and services are interchangeable and whether there are viable alternatives for competitors which do not impose prohibitive costs on the new entrant in terms of expense or time. Consequently, the obligation not to discriminate can be imposed only upon such a finding.

It is desirable that the Commission adopts such an approach in the future. The essential facility approach would be more consistent with certain established principles in Community and national law: the right to choose trading partners and freely to dispose of property. In addition, a uniform approach would allow the shortcomings which derive from the policy currently followed by the Commission to be overcome.

A group of competitors party to a network agreement are subject to the duty to share the network without being able to claim any objective business justification. They could argue that the agreement is indispensable and improves distribution and fosters technological progress. This might not prevent the Commission from imposing access to the facility on the basis that the agreement restricts competition significantly. The parties may not, for example, be able to claim that third parties are unable to meet certain standards to interconnect or use their network. They could, moreover, be compelled to grant access even if the facility can be duplicated or their joint venture does not have a dominant position in the downstream market.

From the public policy perspective there are three main concerns. First, a broader application of the obligation not to discriminate undermines the development of competitive ventures. Third parties have an incentive to claim access to these ventures in order to free ride on the successful venture, rather than undertaking risks on their own. Consequently, market operators do not have incentives to create joint ventures. This could impede market development in sectors such as communications where ventures are necessary to explore the new possibilities that this sector offers. In some networked industries co-operation is essential to carry out operations as in the case of payment systems and airlines interlining arrangements, or to benefit from economies of scale. Second, joint ventures may be deterred from competing and gaining a higher market share, due to fear of more severe scrutiny and being compelled to share their facility. Third, joint ventures have an incentive to operate at a sub-optimal level for fear that an efficiently sized venture would lead to compulsory access.

Even if the Commission follows such an approach, and focuses its analysis on the nature of the infrastructure, there will always be differences in the application of Article 81(1) [ex 85(1)] and 82 [ex 86]. Article 81 [ex 85] does not require the finding of a dominant position and the assessment of the relevant market is less detailed. In addition, as with the merger control rules, Article 81 [ex 85] can be applied irrespective of the finding of actual exclusion and/or discrimination. It is an instrument of preventive control which can be used to scrutinise agreements which have not yet produced effects. Generally, Article 81 [ex 85] proceedings start upon voluntary notification by the parties which seek the clearance of their agreements prior to implementation. During proceedings the Commission may prevent discrimination by informing the parties and requiring them to amend the agreements. In *Iridium*, for example, the Commission did not find a violation, but the decision does contain a reference to the fact that STET would have not discriminated against competitors. Furthermore, when the Commission finds that an agreement falls under Article 81(1) [ex 85(1)], it can persuade the parties to undertake certain obligations to obtain an exemption under Article 81(1) [ex 85(3)].

PANEL THREE

INSTITUTIONS AND COMPETENCE

1

PANEL DISCUSSION

GENERAL RAPPORTEUR:

Ulrich Immenga
Professor, Dr., University of Göttingen, Göttingen, Germany

PARTICIPANTS:

Guiliano Amato
Professor, Minister for Finance, Rome, Italy

J.C. Arnbak
Professor, Chairman OPTA, the Netherlands

Donald I. Baker
Baker & Millar PLLC, Washington, United States

Tod Barnes
Policy Advisor, OFTEL, United Kingdom

Mr Boettcher
Regulierungsbehörde für Telekommunikation und Post, Bonn, Germany

Stuart Brotman
Professor of Law, Harvard Law School, United States

Henry Ergas
Professor, University of Auckland, Australia

Ian S. Forrester
QC, Professor White and Case, Brussels, Belgium

Eleanor Fox
Professor, School of Law, New York University, New York, United States

Herbert Hovenkamp
Professor, University of Iowa, Iowa, United States

Frédéric Jenny
Professor, Vice-President, Conseil de la concurrence, Paris, France

Günter Knieps
Professor, Dr., Institut für Verkehrswissenschaften und Regionalpolitik, Freiburg, Germany

Bruno Lasserre
Secretariat d'Etat à l'Industrie, Paris, France

Colin Long
Partner, Olswang, London, United Kingdom

Santiago Martinez Lage
Martinez Lage & Associates, Madrid, Spain

Vincenzo Monaci
Autorità per la Garanzia nelle Comunicazioni, Rome, Italy

James F. Rill
Collier, Shannon, Rill & Scott, Washington, United States

Daniel L. Rubinfeld
Professor of Law and Economics, University of California, United States

Michael Salsbury
MCI Communications Corp, Washington, United States

Alexander Schaub
Dr., Director General, DG IV, Brussels, Belgium

Joachim Scherer
Professor, Dr., University of Frankfurt, Partner, Baker & Mckenzie, Frankfurt a,M., Germany

Mario Siragusa
Professor, Avv., Cleary, Gottlieb, Steen & Hamilton, Brussels, Belgium

Guiseppe Tesauro
President, Autorità Garante della Concorrenza e del Mercato, Rome, Italy

Herbert Ungerer
Dr., Head of Unit, DG, Brussels, Belgium

Robert Verrue
Director General, DG XIII, Brussels, Belgium

Dieter Wolf
President of the Bundeskartellamt, Berlin, Germany

Dimitri Ypsilanti
Directorate for Science, Technology and Industry, OECD, Paris, France

Panel Three

▶ AMATO—In this panel, we will discuss which institutions, at national, European, and multi-national levels, might be the source of authority and rules for international transactions. This is becoming quite a crucial issue. Of course, as the former head of an antitrust authority, my personal belief is that the ideal world would be one in which sector-specific regulators are not necessary, and antitrust authorities are responsible for the entire range of issues.

However, there is, at the very least, a transitional period in which sector-specific regulators are required. What are they supposed to do? Do they take care of the same goals, interests, and conflicts as antitrust authorities? My personal view is that there is some confusion about their role, at least in our country.

People generally think that all of these authorities promote competition, fairness or the equal treatment of consumers and users. Personally, I do not think this is the case. I think that competition is one thing and fairness is another. Likewise, taking care of the market is one thing, but taking care of consumer claims is something else. Perhaps this needs to be clarified.

The second enormous issue that we must face, at least in Europe, concerns the length of time for which we can foresee that telecommunications, an increasingly integrated market at the European level, can be handled by national level sector-specific regulators. Can it work? Do we need something at European level? At the moment, the Commission limits itself to its directives and leaves Member States to pursue other issues. Eventually, however, the size of the regulated companies might require something at a higher level. This is an open question.

Another open question is the global market and the increasing difficulty that we have in handling disputes among different regions of the world. Mergers, for example, can have effects in different continents.

Consequently, in the few hours that we have left, let us see whether we can go through these three issues: the identification of goals for sector-specific regulators, the issue of control at European level, and the need for international coordination. Our colleague, Immenga, will open, followed by the regulators and then by open discussion. Therefore, Professor Immenga, the floor is yours.

▶ IMMENGA—Regarding today's business, the least one can say is that there is a great deal of confusion about institutions. One very brief observation: institutional questions are often neglected. This is particularly true, I must admit, in academic circles.

Nevertheless, I think it is quite evident that even the most sophisticated law has no real value without strict application and enforcement. As we will discuss today, this is not only a problem of the institutions and their competences, but also a question of the strength and independence of the institutions.

The focus of this panel is on the different bodies of law that are applied to the sectors of the economy with which we are concerned: network markets. The papers submitted contain some very illustrative examples, concerning not only telecommunications, but also other specific sectors, such as broadcasting and energy. I am sure we will touch upon these sectors in the context of convergence.

In these network markets, we are confronted with both sector-specific regulatory laws and general antitrust laws. Such parallel legislation requires an institutional framework. In Europe, the general approach to this issue is to create sector-specific regulatory authorities alongside existing antitrust authorities. The existence of these parallel institutions is partly a result of EU directives, and is not necessarily to be found all around the world.

Apart from creating parallel antitrust and sector-specific institutions, the possibilities for regulation include abolishing (or never creating) sector-specific regulations and trusting the national antitrust authority to apply the general competition law to all sectors. As we have already mentioned, this is the case in New Zealand. We have another pattern in Australia, and I hope Mr. Fels will talk about that during the discussion. The Australian approach entrusts the antitrust authority with the task of applying sector-specific regulations (with the help of special provisions provided in the law).

Before turning to the two-agency system used in Europe, it is worth noting that these institutional questions have been intensively discussed in both France and Germany. Mr. Wolf's paper demonstrates that there was much discussion on whether the Federal Cartel Office in Germany should apply, in addition to competition law, sector specific regulations. Regulatory proposals included the creation of a separate department within the Federal Cartel Office, charged with preparing and participating in telecommunications decisions. Finally, however, Germany followed the general European pattern and created a separate agency.

Among the papers, however, there seems to be a consensus that pure competition law cannot adequately respond to the specific issues arising in newly deregulated markets. I will outline some questions which, in my opinion, should be discussed here. These are questions that emerged from reading the papers and from following yesterday's discussion.

First, some normative questions. In effect, regulation tackles three different subject matters. The first comprises technical requirements, for instance, numbering, licensing and distribution of frequencies. The second involves economic regulation: universal services, interconnection, market access, and tariffs. The third includes competition issues: domination, definition of markets, abuse control, merger control, alliances, and vertical and horizontal agreements. The question is: to whom should we attribute each of these regulatory objectives?

As far as the sector-specific regulatory agencies are concerned, the issue of competence may be further broken down into two questions. The first is the question of what the vision of the future landscape of the market should be. Another question asks whether the regulators should focus exclusively on telecommunications, or whether they should also regulate broadcasting. There seems to be a debate on this issue in the United Kingdom. Moreover, in Germany, the regime is not limited to telecommunications, but also covers the postal service. This problem is a part of the general issue of convergence and technical developments.

With regard to the antitrust authorities, the question is whether we should introduce specific rules requiring the transparency of telecommunications oligopolies. Another core issue is the question of interaction between the two forms of authority. Do the decisions of the sector-specific regulatory authorities have supremacy over general competition rules? This seems to be the case in the United States, where the Federal Communications Commission (FCC) has precedence over the Department of Justice (DOJ). An alternative system, which is probably at work in Germany, creates a kind of subsidiarity between the two agencies.

Furthermore, it is important to discuss examples of interrelation and coordination between the two types of agency. For example, the question of mutual information is particularly important in the French papers. Is it necessary to have an area of concerted action in specific issues? We do have this in Germany, for example, in the case of the definition of domination.

A further question concerns the notion of transitional regulation that surfaced yesterday. There seems to be a broad consensus that the rules should sunset at some time in the future; but the real question is that of who decides that they should have no further application. The papers revealed some interesting points, and I will leave the panellists to propose their answers to this question.

After discussing the division of competences between the institutions, we should move on to the issue of institutional independence. There are problems concerning who will nominate officers, what their qualifications will be, and what the period of their tenure will be.

A further problem is that of judicial review. Does it exist, and to what extent? How is it provided for? There are some problems in Germany, in particular, but I understand there has been a much better solution in France.

Finally, I will touch upon the problems of the internationalisation and the potential objectives of international institutions. I think we primarily must view these developments in the light of technological convergence; though, of course, globalisation also plays a role in creating difficulties.

The first institution that comes into play is the EU. One of the papers asks: may regulatory principles differ? The Commission may have competence based on Article 86(3) [ex 90(3)]. We might consider, for instance, the implementation of universal service obligations, the framework for numbering policies, the guidelines for interconnection agreements, or the harmonisation of requirements for mobile licences. These might be some examples to touch upon. However, we have to ensure that we will not regulate too much at one level.

Finally, I would like to turn, in the context of globalisation, to the WTO. To date, we are examining regulation and national regulatory authorities within the framework of the EU Treaty. However, if it becomes necessary to enlarge the authority to examine technological problems and development across borders, it might be possible to enlarge the existing WTO agreement on telecommunications. This might be one path to follow.

Regarding antitrust in the context of the WTO, one question is unavoidable. Should we have a multilateral agreement for an international antitrust system? In Mr. Rill's paper, there is a reference to the international competition policy advisory committee that was created in 1997. The first hearings have taken place. Therefore, it will be very interesting to listen to the opinion of the United States, while we also have the opportunity to hear the views of the Chair of the WTO working group, Mr. Jenny. I hope he might touch upon this problem as well.

▶ LASSERE—Professor Immenga's introduction makes my job much easier this morning. I would like to focus my presentation on the interrelation between regulation at national and European levels. Thus, I will not discuss the issue of competition authority versus sector-specific regulators, nor will I focus upon national regulation versus European regulation. Instead, I will consider general competition authority and sector-specific regulation at both national and European levels. This task is easier for me because I was once the French telecommunications regulator and I am now a member of the French competition authority, although much less experienced than Mr. Jenny.

The first item on my agenda involves sector-specific regulation and competition authorities. I would like to make three short remarks. The first one is that emulation is good. Just as it is better for a consumer to choose than to be forced to accept services from a monopoly, it is also better to have a choice of institutions. The fact that the institutions do not have the exclusive right to deal with a particular matter can stimulate them into better performance, because each institution wants to provide the best services. Consequently, there is a race among them to be the quickest and the most able to provide the best service.

Second, I think it is possible to define these interrelations articulately. There are two modes of doing so. The first is to set up bridges, which lead each institution to inform the other of any pertinent issues and to benefit from the added value provided by the other. The second, and we do this in France, is to appoint the same court of appeal for the two institutions. This helps to unify the jurisprudence.

Of course, each institution has its own strengths and weaknesses. The strengths of the sector-specific regulatory authority are its proximity to the industry, its less judicial nature, its degree of informality and its ability to take action *ex ante*. The strength of the general competition authority is its very important power to unify general competition rules, regardless of the industry concerned.

The third remark I would like to make is that this interaction among institutions is not stable. It changes depending on the regulatory and market-building phase. Personally, I see three successive stages in the opening of a market. The first stage is the regulation of entry, which aims to define the legal and technical conditions under which new entrants can operate. One requires lawyers and engineers to undertake these legal and technical tasks. Moreover, in this stage, which involves licensing conditions, interconnection, and access to scarce resources, such as numbering and frequencies, the sector-specific regulators must be involved because they must create the new rules of the game. In fact, they must guide this transition from monopoly to competition. Of course, the general competition authority has to provide intellectual support to develop general concepts, such as definition of the relevant market and definition of predatory prices.

The second stage is a stage of dominance. The market is *de jure* open to new entrants, but the ex-monopolist enjoys a very strong position. In this stage, regulation becomes less and less legal and technical, and more influenced by economic and financial concerns. It is largely based upon accounting. In this stage, we must find the best way to control end-user prices, interconnection fees, and the allocation of costs. These tasks demand a very strong degree of collaboration between the sector-specific regulator and the antitrust authority. In fact, they must work with the same concepts. The only difference is that the sector-specific regulator will try to prevent damage to the competitive situation, while the antitrust authority will try to repair the damage created.

The third stage is the regulation of competition after the industry is fully liberalised. In this stage, the sector-specific regulation can be phased out, and more and more faith can be placed in the general authority of the competition authority.

Personally, I do not believe that we can ever completely phase out the sector-specific regulator. This is only a dream. As every national experience, particularly in the US, shows, one may think hypothetically about the disappearance of the sector-specific regulator, but this will never happen. There are strong reasons for the maintenance of sector-specific regulation in order, first, to safeguard the universal service requirement and, second, to ensure the fair allocation of scarce resources. In fact, it is a very long voyage before one arrives at a 'normal' competitive situation.

Consequently, each country has had a debate about the need to create a sector-specific regulator. Generally, through a political compromise, governments have created sector-specific authorities, but have maintained that they will be transitory in character. In practice, however, I think we have created an eternal regulator.

However, I do think that everyone can accommodate this situation. I do not think any country is ready to allow the telecommunications sector to operate without this strange animal, the telecommunications sector-specific regulator.

This point may also be applied to European level. Personally, I am very much in favour of creating European sector-specific regulators. This comes from my personal experience, which includes one general feeling and one factual observation. The feeling is, of course, that sector-specific regulators in each Member State are part of the same club. We see each other. We exchange documents.

Moreover, when I see my British or Belgian colleagues, we exchange the information which is provided to us by our own national operators. My supervisor was surprised when I was reading the report given by France Telecom's UK office to the British regulator, and the report given by French Telecom's Belgian office to the Belgian regulator. They proved to be exactly the same form of report, which I had received from France Telecom's own competitors operating in France. Of course, I was very happy, but also rather frustrated with the manner in which the telecommunications operators are able to divide their brain into two parts: one as an incumbent and the other as a challenger. The two parts, however, never meet. Given this experience, I would be very pleased if someone at European level could tackle these schizophrenic individuals, and reconcile them as parts of a complete whole.

The second reason why I am inclined to push for European regulation stems from a factual observation. Everybody knows about the Leo constellation (Low earth orbit satellite constellation). Some American firms, like Iridium or Teledesic, had a problem gaining world-wide credibility. What did they do? They went to the FCC and applied for an American licence. With this document in hand, they were recognised in the United States and they could claim to provide world-wide service. They had a sort of world-wide ticket provided by a continental regulator.

Skybridge is another Leo constellation, which was invented in Europe, mainly by Alcatel (with some American and Japanese partners). They were in a similar position. That is, they wanted to provide a world-wide service. Normally, they would go to the French or German regulator to be licensed in these nations. They did not do that. Instead, they also went to the FCC, so that they, too, could have a continental ticket, which furnished them with the credibility that they needed to access the world-wide market. I found that rather shocking. If we had a Euro-regulator with the ability to give a similar ticket, it would have been better respected and would have provided a good deal of influence.

Therefore, I do not understand the taboo about a Euro-regulator. I do not understand the resistance from the Member States, the shyness of the Commission, and the antipathy from national regulators. I think of the fact that we have been able to build a single currency, we are familiar with subsidiarity, and we can use the same arguments for a Euro-regulator.

In conclusion, I think the problem is not so much the answer but the question. I think the question is incorrectly worded. If we say, would we deprive national regulators of some of their competences were we to establish a Euro-regulator, we will fail. If, instead, we ask whether we can work together to bring an added value to the Euro-regulator, we would succeed. I sometimes think of a joke about smoking and praying:

A Dominican wants to smoke during high offices. He is very candid, and asks his superior if he may smoke. The answer, obviously, is no. The Jesuit, however, understands that changing the question will change the answer, and, more subtly, he asks : may I pray while I am smoking? The answer is, maybe.

The same is true for the Euro-regulator. The answer will depend on how the question is posed.

▶ VERRUE—I will make three memorandum-type remarks to begin my presentation, and then I will look at telecommunications regulatory policy within the EU from three different perspectives. First, I will examine where we stand and what we have achieved. Second, I will examine how EU policy is being challenged by the reality of markets and technology. Third, I will make a few observations regarding whether or not we should think about a European regulatory competence or a European regulatory authority.

In this sector, as in many others, the EU institutions should ensure that the Community economy is, as much as possible, an open and level playing field. This is why we have constructed a fairly complicated set of (decentralised) rules for the telecommunications sector. We also, however, try to keep differences in the application of these rules to a minimum. This problem will probably resurface in the next few years because differences in the transposition of the rules are beginning to appear.

Second, we are in a sector in which technology is changing at a very rapid rate: in fact, to such a degree that it is extremely difficult to define this market sector. The problem of trying to define stable reference points will exist for quite a long time, and I will later say a few words about convergence.

The third of these introductory remarks is that we must make one point very clear when we discuss the creation of a new Euro-regulatory authority or a new Euro-regulatory function. What tends to be forgotten or ignored when we talk about a new institution or function, is that we are dealing with something that can not happen for three to five years, because that is how long things take at EU level. Therefore, we must, with some foresight, look at the question of what the technological and market situation will be in the future. Of course, perfect technological forecasting is impossible, but we must try to take future developments into account in discussing new institutions.

Enough of the introduction: now, what have we done so far? We managed to de-regulate the EU telecommunications services market by the first of January 1998. Momentarily setting aside the countries with a deferment—certain of them have yet to come to the independent conclusion that deferment was counterproductive, while the others are relatively small markets—we can consequently say that this deregulation policy was on schedule. Deregulation took around 10 years from the first Green Paper, or about 4 years from the most extensive policy commitment made by Member States.

As will be shown in a report to be published in a few days by DG IV and my own department at the Commission, transposition of these rules has, on the whole, been encouraging. Sometimes, it is even satisfactory. Moreover, several positive economic results are emerging from this policy. For example, the number of new market players is fairly high, so entry is not completely closed. Services are obviously diversifying, and many indicators point to the conclusion that the quality of service is also substantially improving. Meanwhile, I do not see genuine universal service problems in the EU; so, the fears about threats to universal service have not been confirmed.

We can, therefore, be content with what we have done and say that we have done a serious piece of work. However, things are, fortunately and unfortunately, moving extremely quickly from the point of view of technology. Consequently, every time we try to identify phenomena that would reflect the effectiveness of competition, we encounter the difficulty of defining markets and finding proper price indicators. This presents problems simply because technological changes are moving far quicker than bureaucratic or legal work could ever hope to.

For example, there is a disproportionate relationship between the cost of voice telephony over the internet and the cost of voice telephony by other methods. Depending on which tariff you examine, you have the impression that you are doing very well or very poorly in ensuring reasonable prices. Similarly, if you look at the balance between mobile and fixed voice telephony, you conclude that they are now in competition. However, when you examine the statistics more closely, you also discover that they are in competition in some markets but not in others. In other words, the rapid pace of technological advance is blurring our perception of the market.

One thing of which I am certain is that if you examine the European situation from an international perspective, we still have a long way to go towards lower tariffs. This is true not only because lowering prices is a value in itself, but also because the increase in consumption of new services is highly correlated to the tariff level. We still have a good deal of work to do in this area.

Furthermore, life is much more complicated now than it was in the late 80's and early 90's when the EU governments opted for the de-regulation of telecommunications services. Frankly, I am amazed by our collective inability to predict the key forces driving structural changes in markets. The internet, for example, was vastly underestimated, even in the research community. Yet, today, the primary factor that is substantially changing the balance in telecommunications markets is the availability of internet services.

The second, correlated phenomenon, which was mentioned by Professor Immenga, concerns the combined effect of the digitalisation and the development of much more powerful components for information treatment and storage. Together, these factors increase network capacity exponentially, making it possible to transmit an immense volume of information. Further, digitalisation eliminates the distinction between bits of information, whether voice, data, image, etc., or any combination thereof. This challenges the distinction that has heretofore existed between the telecommunications and audio-visual sectors.

Certain countries, Italy in particular, grasped this development early on, but the reaction has sometimes been very strange. Various countries have anticipated the institutional consequences, others have anticipated the legal consequences, and very few countries have anticipated both. I must say that, at EU level, we have not yet anticipated any of them, but we must work with 15 countries, which sometimes renders life even more complicated. At any rate, if we look out of the front, rather than the rear window, convergence is the major phenomenon that we are predicting.

My final point concerns the institutional dimension. I could be very brief and simply agree with Bruno Lassere, but I would like to be a bit more provocative and say that I do not agree. We often forget the fact that there are already quite a few regulatory functions fulfilled at European level in the field of telecommunications services. Sometimes, they are to be found in the hands of the Commission. Sometimes, they are to be found in the joint hands of the Commission and the national regulators. And sometimes, they are in the hands of the Commission, even though they are not exercised through clearly visible instruments.

Furthermore, if you ask what people expect from a Euro-regulatory authority or function, a large number of the responses concern things that already exist. We discovered this fact when we asked network operators and service providers what they desired of a Euro-regulator. A number of the tasks were already carried out at European level, but they were not perceived to be co-ordinated and centralised within a particular authority or institution.

Second, we have to be quite frank. Even if we can only talk about a Euro-regulatory authority in three years' time, the technology and the nature of the market structure are such that if we were to have a Euro-regulatory authority tomorrow morning, we would immediately be struck with very thorny subsidiarity problems. In my view, it is impossible for Brussels to deal with all of the regulatory issues that we must tackle in order to ensure that this de-regulatory policy would function.

Thus, the only scheme we could imagine is some variation on the structure prevailing in the United States, which is a network with a central organisation. However, as we can see in America, the relationship between the FCC and the state regulatory agencies is sometimes very Freudian. I am trying to be as diplomatic as possible, but they have not provided operators with a regulatory environment characterised by a great deal of clarity. Moreover, operators have learned to exploit these agencies in some very clever ways.

▶ Tesauro—I would like to speak about the Italian experience regarding the relationship between the sector-specific telecommunications regulator and the general antitrust authority, but I must qualify my remarks, since, at the moment, we have had very little experience. As you know, although our telecommunications regulatory authority was not born yesterday, it has only been in service for a year. Thus, although we cannot draw upon a wealth of experience in this field, we can speak about the initial situation in which we have found ourselves.

First, I must note that the Italian antitrust authority had quite a good relationship with the former regulator, who was the Minister of Communications. We now have a different situation, and our interests may diverge from those of the telecommunications authority. We have, as an antitrust authority, just a single public interest: the protection of competition. Our objective is the normal goal of a competition authority; we must analyse competition problems and promote the adequate functioning of the market.

The interests of the regulatory commission are quite different. In their own way, they also promote competition, but they simultaneously balance other interests. For example, their mission includes the ensuring of adequate quality standards and widespread, homogeneous services throughout the national territory, without prejudice to the profitability of such activities. Meanwhile, they are entrusted with establishing an objective, transparent, and non-discriminatory tariff system and protecting customers and consumers.

Therefore, it is possible that we will have differing views from those of the regulatory authority. Fortunately, we have not yet had any experiences in which the regulatory interests have conflicted with the promotion of competition. Nevertheless, given the fact that the complex goals of the regulatory institution could conflict with our single goal of competition, it is possible that we will face such conflicts in the future.

I will now turn to the way in which our laws promote co-operation between the two agencies. Presently, the law is that we give non-binding advice to the regulatory authority on competition issues. Likewise, the regulatory agency provides us with advice concerning sector-specific problems. Similar systems apply, for example, with regard to the insurance regulatory authority and the central bank in the banking sector. That is, in both of these sectors, we give some advice and so do the sector-specific regulators. There is, however, an important difference between our relationship with the central bank and our relationship with the telecommunications agency. In the case of the central bank, we tend the same garden. That is, Italian law gives the central bank some competition functions. With regard to the telecommunications regulatory agency, in theory, we tend different gardens. That is, we have the responsibility for competition issues and they have the responsibility for universal service, quality standards, and so forth. It is possible that this division of powers will lessen conflict with the telecommunications agency in the future, but we will have to wait and see to be sure.

Generally speaking, the Italian regulatory system comprises a competition authority and many sector-specific regulatory authorities. The competition authority has the final say on competition matters, while the sector-specific regulators deal with issues peculiar to their sector. I think this is a good system, because uniformity in the application of national and European competition rules is crucial. From this perspective, it is preferable to have a single competition authority applying its rules to all sectors.

Thus, I do not think it would be helpful to give the sector-specific regulators authority over some or all of the competition function, at least in Italy. I feel that the situation is more or less the same in all of the European countries.

In my view, another important point is the role of the European regulator. The European Commission has many regulatory functions. These functions may not be formalised, but the Commission is present in the regulation of telecommunications and other public utilities. Do these regulatory functions also include the co-ordination of the work of national regulatory authorities? I think the co-ordination function is inherent in the Treaty. We have common principles, and common rules that derive from these principles. Consequently, there already is a European regulator. It is the Commission.

The Commission's profile in telecommunications may have been low until the late 80's and early 90's. Nevertheless, it now clearly operates as a regulator, and there is room for it to co-ordinate national policies more actively.

Regarding developments outside the EU, such as globalisation and the internationalisation of regulation, I believe it is very interesting to look at the United States and to look toward the WTO. However, we must first solve our own problems in Europe. We need to co-ordinate and achieve the same level of liberalisation of our national telecommunications systems and our other public utility systems.

▶ WOLF—I would not like to expand very much on what has already been said about the advantages or disadvantages of integrating the different authorities. Mr. Immenga mentioned this issue, and I suppose it will be a topic for further discussion.

Nevertheless, I would like to focus on the consequences of technological convergence for the authorities concerned. What are the implications of this convergence, for instance, for the competition authorities?

We have already acknowledged that telephone calls, songs over the radio, images on television, and internet chatting are all, or very soon will all be, reduced to digital impulses. Meanwhile, fusion of terminal equipment, such as telephones, televisions and computers, is becoming apparent. This fusion is easier for the consumer to see. Meanwhile, the problem we used to have with scarce frequencies and transmission stations will soon become history.

Unfortunately, in my view, convergence is in no way matched by a convergence of regulatory systems, for example, through the streamlining and reduction of regulatory density. Regulatory systems do not yet reflect the fact that the allocation of scarce frequencies is rapidly becoming an obsolete task.

Let us take the example of Germany, where, in some areas, over-regulation has emerged. I believe such over-regulation could become one of the most serious threats to economic development. Moreover, it seems to me that over-regulation is not only a German problem, even if it is particularly pronounced in Germany because of overlapping competences arising from our federal system.

Broadly speaking, in Germany, the tasks are allocated as follows. As far as monitoring competition is concerned, general competition law exists alongside sector-specific control, which is carried out by the newly created regulatory authority for telecommunications and post. It goes without saying that the competences of the European Commission are not affected by this. Specifically, pursuant to the Telecommunications Act, the regulatory authority is responsible for granting licences and for price and abuse control. Meanwhile, pursuant to the Act Against Restraints on Competition (AARC), the Bundeskartellamt is responsible for monitoring cartels and for merger control. Abuse control under the AARC is subordinated to abuse control under the Telecommunications Act.

Under the Telecommunications Act, the two authorities must co-operate with each other. This is easier said than done. For example, to ensure that competition under the Telecommunications Act is as consistent as possible with the general competition law, issues of market definition and determinations of dominance are to be analysed jointly. In practice, in the first few months of our co-operation, this has not always been easy, but there is now evidence that things are running more smoothly.

However, this is not all. Market access and the control of concentration in radio and television is subject not only to the general competition regime, but also to special media law regulation, which is exercised by separate agencies. Internet services are subject to special, but far from uniform, rules. That is, depending on whether the services are aimed at individuals or at the general public, they are subject to different provisions. They can also be categorised as broadcasting services, in which case they are subject to broadcasting regulation.

You will perhaps suspect that I am deliberately exaggerating the problem in order to confuse you with this network of regulations. I assure you, however, that the matter is genuinely so complicated. I regret, in fact, that I have simplified it for you.

I want to underline that it is dangerous to over-regulate this sector, which should be a main driving force for growth. In my opinion, the only exit from this quagmire of special and sector-specific regulations is a radical change of policy. We must pursue what I would call a model of 'lean' regulation.

I would imagine the following as elements of such a lean regulation. Sector-specific authorities and their expertise should be brought under a single roof: that of the competition authority. This general competition authority should be responsible for monitoring competition in all sectors. It might, however, require sharper teeth for this purpose. In sectors that were once monopolies, such as telecommunications and energy, a legislative framework is required. This legislation should be geared to the active promotion of competition. It must include clear rules on the joint use of essential facilities, as well as the power to immediately enforce decisions by the competition authority. For example, in our general competition law, we introduced a clause, which denotes the refusal of access to essential facilities, an abuse of a dominant position.

This national authority should be responsible for all matters that are mainly national in scope. When necessary, it should apply EU competition rules in a decentralised manner. The Commission, by contrast, should examine cross-border issues. This would avoid the duplication of control measures. I will not go into more detail in this respect because I do not think this is the proper setting to do so. However, I believe it is important for competition authorities to have the power to monitor competition in a lean regulatory model.

Sector-specific agencies are not really, in my view, a necessity if one integrates their expertise into the competition authority. The Australian example is a very interesting one in this respect.

Technological convergence in telecommunications is well underway, and capacity problems are becoming less and less important. The German regulatory framework has not yet been adapted to this convergence. I think the same is true in other countries. In contrast, we are proceeding on the wrong path by creating or maintaining the artificial separation of these sectors through the work of sector-specific authorities and rules.

The right answer to this regulatory labyrinth can, therefore, only be lean regulation. That is, to ensure legal certainty and efficiency, we should focus on the enforcement of competition law and try to bring sector-specific regulation under the same roof. If politically desired—I add this only to be complete—one could set up an authority to monitor cultural aspects in the context of information technology. However, there is really no need for multiple institutions.

▶ JENNY—Listening to this debate, it is obvious that the field of competition oversight and regulation has itself been subject to competition. The incumbent antitrust authorities are losing market share to the newcomers, the sector-specific regulators. Fortunately, in many countries, they tend to keep a monopoly over the enforcement of competition law, although this is not always true (in the UK, for example). Therefore, the sector-specific regulators tend to keep to certain narrow niches. There are some exceptions to this. For example, in the Australian case, 'Tsar' Fels has defeated an army of regulators and driven them out of the market. In New Zealand, by contrast, they were never admitted into the first place.

I have begun this way because I believe that when we ask why this is happening, we highlight a factor that has not yet come out in our debate. It is linked to our discussion at last year's seminar and it has to do with the goals of competition law. This, in turn, is the fact that competition authorities tend to see themselves as applying economic theory and developing competition for efficiency reasons. In the field of the sectors that have newly been opened to competition, in particular, telecommunications, there are three disadvantages to economic theory.

The first disadvantage is that economic theory does not tell us very much about how to create competition. It tells us how to preserve competition, but not how to create it. Second, I do not think that the strong point of economic analysis is the trade-off between short-term competition and dynamic efficiencies, particularly in sectors where the technology is unstable. If we examine the economic point of view, it assumes that technology is fairly stable, that market definition is fairly clear and is independent of practices, etc.. Finally, economic analysis does not tell us very much about bottlenecks, particularly when they are integrated into firms who also operate on the downstream market. We heard yesterday from Henry Ergas that the best theoretical models are basically useless for decision-making because they are so complex.

I would add a fourth issue, which I think has not yet been generally recognised. Deregulation, like opening networks to competition, is not only about efficiency. Yesterday, Bruno Lassere mentioned the fact that there are other objectives. Fairness is certainly one of them. Promoting entry, promoting investment and ensuring universal service are examples of others. So, there are social-economic and political goals at issue. Therefore, I do not think that it would be correct to analyse regulatory activity only from the standpoint of competition and efficiency, because regulation in these sectors has much broader goals.

This may not come as a surprise because I think the conclusion we reached at last year's seminar was that competition policy itself had broader goals than mere economic efficiency. Consequently, it should not be shocking that this is also true of regulation. But, because antitrust authorities have narrowed themselves to a discourse of promoting competition for the purpose of efficiency, they have disqualified themselves, to some extent, from participating in the regulatory exercise. On top of this, the instruments that the competition authorities have traditionally controlled are not particularly well adapted to the problems of the regulated sectors.

Interestingly, I think this is one reason why, in different countries, there are very diverse ways to solve the problem of the interface between regulation and competition. Moreover, even within each country, the solutions are quite different, depending on the sector concerned. I explore this issue more fully in my paper. However, I wish to point out that you see very different answers between railways, electricity and telecommunications, because you have a different political set-up for each sector. That is, regulation is, to a large extent, the result of the political forces that are concerned with the sector.

I will not go into the various details, but a division of labour between regulators and competition authorities seems to be the dominant model. There are risks of overlap, gaps, or contradictions, because of the vertical integration of the dominant operator. This means that the decisions made at the level of the regulators—entry, prices, and so forth—must be co-ordinated with the competition authorities, usually examining the service markets. This leads to various models, as Mr. Lassere mentioned.

If one believes that regulation is not only about competition and efficiency, but also about other values, including fairness and a level playing field, then the international question comes into play. This is particularly true in telecommunications, which is the sector that is most likely to be globalised rapidly. If you start from different bases, with different regulatory constraints, you immediately face the problem of creating a level playing field at international level. How can you have fair competition among firms who face different regulatory environments at home?

Consequently, if we momentarily limit the problem to the EU, I do believe that the nature of the problem dictates some degree of European level regulation. This is necessary because we do not have a level playing field among the regulatory environments of the Member States, and having a level playing field is what international competition is all about.

I now turn very rapidly to the globalisation problem beyond the borders of the EU and the United States. We all know that there is an ongoing discussion about whether competition, in its broad sense, should become part of the WTO commitments. This discussion is taking place for the very reason I mentioned earlier: to have something approaching a level playing field. This discussion is also taking place, however, because other private practices, or behind the border regulations, can either defeat trade liberalisation or prevent trade liberalisation from providing its expected benefits.

From that point of view, there are various solutions being considered. Some solutions have been generally excluded. For example, I would say that an international competition code is excluded because the level of development of countries is so different that no agreement could be found. Pure extraterritorial enforcement of one country's competition law is also excluded because it leads to legal chaos. The intermediate, or conceivable solutions, involve cooperation or some kind of multi-national role within the WTO.

Could we use the principles of the WTO—non-discrimination, transparency, most favoured nation and due process—as a basis for an international competition regime, or do we have to add something to them? Telecommunications is quite interesting in this regard, because it is practically the only sector in which we already have a multinational level. In the annex to the WTO agreement, there has been an integration of the considerations of competition and regulation. That is, each signatory must ensure that its monopoly, or the firm to which it has granted an exclusive right, does not abuse its dominant position in a way that prevents market access.

The interesting question is: why was it possible to reach such an agreement in the context of telecommunications, when there is so much resistance to this type of provision in the general context of competition? Presumably, this was agreed because telecommunications is the sector where the problem was most obvious. That is, we are progressing rapidly from a situation of protected, purely national markets toward open international markets. This process is accompanied by rapid technological advances. Consequently, there was an appreciation of the need to develop rules.

If this discussion continues at international level, one important question will be whether one should continue to make sector-specific adaptations to the general rules. That is, should there be one provision for each sector, or instead, should there be a general competition regime worded somewhat along the lines of the Telecommunications Annex? In the latter case, I imagine that a general regime would not be limited to rules against the abuse of dominant positions.

▶ BROTMAN—I am going to use my time to discuss a case study based on personal experience in the United States. Hopefully, these cases will provide some insight into the contemporary debate. In particular, I hope these cases will illustrate the ways in which the different agencies' shared competences can be marshalled in competition policy. Moreover, my discussion may clarify the way in which marketplace reality can be wedded with the economic theory that Mr. Jenny discussed.

During the Carter Administration, I was one of the founders of a United States agency known as the National Telecommunications and Information Administration (NTIA). In the late 1970's, the Federal Court of Appeals in Washington struck down the rules that governed the cable pay television industry. As a result, the FCC was largely barred from regulatory involvement in the area. Consequently, the NTIA was able to work upon a relatively clean slate.

After these rules were struck down, the cable industry began to organise and take advantage of the pay cable opportunity, since there was tremendous pent-up demand to view unedited, uninterrupted movies. As a result, three major companies organised vertically. Time Inc., which was the second largest cable operator in the nation, organised a pay cable service around Home Box Office (HBO). The largest cable operator in the country, Teleprompt, joined the seventh largest, Viacom, and formed the second leading pay-TV service, known as Showtime. Meanwhile, Time-Warner Cable, the third largest operator, organised something called The Movie Channel. Consequently, we had three different firms, each of which was organised around this vertically integrated model.

Very quickly, HBO achieved about a 60% market share, and the movie studios, who were licensing films to the pay cable operators, became very concerned. Frankly, these studios had not paid much attention to licensing for pay cable. They had missed the mark in terms of understanding the shape the market was taking, and had, therefore, granted licences at a very minimal price. Thus, when they began to see HBO aggregating such a large market share, they knocked on the door of the DOJ and of the NTIA and began negotiations which continued for the better part of a year. The movie studios argued that there were potential monopoly and monopsony problems associated with an entity as large as HBO.

This development took place against the background of bipartisan government sentiment in favour of separating content provision from the cable conduit. This policy strain began in 1974, when the Republicans suggested the possible divestiture of the cable industry. The Democrats raised a similar proposal in 1976. Given the popularity of such proposals, the DOJ and NTIA considered dividing the content and conduit portions of the cable industry to avoid potential monopoly and monopsony powers.

This theory seemed to strike a chord with both agencies: the NTIA and the DOJ. The DOJ initiated a massive civil investigation of the pay cable industry. This was one of the largest civil investigations carried out during the Carter

Administration. The NTIA did not only examine HBO, however, we also analysed structural issues that might have an impact on the entire development of pay cable. In fact, we decided to commission long-term research in the area. Probably the most important thing we did was immediately to inform the DOJ of this project. Hence, we developed a very informal but co-operative arrangement in which the DOJ shared its economic theories with us and we shared our perceptions of the marketplace reality with them.

Equally important, we asked the DOJ to avoid filing suit until we had completed our research, which took roughly a year. They agreed. Obviously, the DOJ had to withstand considerable pressure from the movie studios, who asked virtually every day when the complaint would be filed against Time Inc.. Our research was interesting because, with the help of enormous databases and resources, we ultimately discovered that the marketplace reality was much different from the economic theory focused on market share and vertically integrated structure.

In fact, the key aspect involved urban cable franchising. In the late 1970's, most of the United States, particularly the larger cities, had not been franchised. As a result, there was a counterweight, since the cable franchise authorities could essentially demand that any cable operator would offer all of the services. Thus, we projected that, over a two-year period, the pronounced bottleneck would wither away. This was the essential conclusion of the study. We brought that information to the DOJ—obviously, they had been informed throughout the progress of the research. At the end of the day, the DOJ decided to fold its civil investigation, and did not file suit against HBO or Time Inc..

Fortunately, our projections were precisely on target. Within two years, virtually the entire market in the pay television area had opened up. Coming back to Mike Salsbury's rule of three, I am happy to say that there are currently three vibrant competitors. Moreover, they are the same competitors who existed 20 years ago. Therefore, vertical integration was not necessarily the evil that economic theory might suggest. Certainly, the notion of a large market share, in and of itself, was not the barrier that would ultimately be harmful to the cable industry.

I would like to drop in a quick footnote before I close. The movie studios were not very pleased with this result. They decided to create their own pay cable operation, called Premier, which they organised shortly after our study was concluded and after the DOJ dropped the suit. The DOJ had, by that time, become so well educated in this area that they understood the marketplace reality of having the movie studios organise their own network. The critical feature of this network was that the movie studios created a nine-month window in which they would have the exclusive right to show new films. The DOJ moved very aggressively, and there was an injunction against this practice. The operation was shut down before it started. Thus, there was a direct consequence in terms of competition policy. Specifically, the DOJ almost completely changed its point of view. It learned that the movie studios would not necessarily be the victims in the process but could potentially be the aggressors. Hence, I think this case history has a happy ending.

The larger point on which I would like to close is the metaphor of two prisms. We have the prism of television policy and the prism of telecommunications policy. I think that we often use these prisms as monocles. I would suggest that, in our case, and probably also in other cases, we can use these prisms as spectacles. We can put these two prisms together and improve our overall vision.

▶ FORRESTER—Till now, we have largely focused upon technological factors, within telecommunications, as they impact upon competitors. However, I would urge you not to forget that the sector also serves its customers. More specifically, the telecommunications sector is distinctive, not only because of particular market factors, but also because it is tremendously important to those who use it.

Europe has traditionally imposed fierce barriers upon access, which have also impacted upon those attempting to use the voice telephony network. I think the United States offers us a model of what can be done with a more user-friendly telecommunications infrastructure. I very much hope that, in the next decade, the regulators who govern European telecommunications will succeed in releasing the creative power that we can now see in operation in California.

My next comment is that the technology is developing at an astonishing rate. In 1993, the European Commission commissioned a study concerning what would happen over the next few years in the electronics and telecommunications sectors. This study contained no mention of the internet—not a word about it. Yet, last year, internet commerce was 12 billion Euro, this year it will be 35 billion Euro and in a few years' time it will be hundreds of thousands of billions of Euros. We have seen what unregulated success can do, in the form of the success of the internet and in the form of the success of GSM technology.

It seems to me that the only certainty is that we are underestimating the pace and depth of change. We are moving from a world of scarcity to a world of abundance, which is marked by a wide choice of technological solutions. Consequently, we do not need more regulation for the protection of the competitive process. We need more regulation for the protection of the citizen.

Yet, if we look at what has happened over the last ten years, we can observe a somewhat troublesome pattern. First of all, we have privatisation. The telecommunications operators say, '[W]e want to be free.' The price of privatisation is liberalisation. We call liberalisation de-regulation, and now we are in the process of re-regulating. So what do regulators do? I have nothing against regulators; indeed, I am married to one, and many regulators are entirely congenial. Regulators always want to do the right thing, but, sadly, they sometimes do the wrong thing.

For example, General Fuller in the British War Office in the 1930's was faced with budget cuts. He looked at the available technologies and resources, and he made a wise decision: he increased the purchase of fodder for horses by 60% and cut the purchase of petrol for tanks by 90%. That is what regulators, doing their best, do.

Regulators generally opt for specific, detailed rules that constrain behaviour and channel activities to what is known and safe. Regulators are criticised for the mistakes that others see, but they are almost never criticised for the successes that are invisible.

To move on and give examples: fibre optic cables and satellite transmission will soon be competing with traditional telecommunications technology. So, why should we severely handicap the incumbent operators well into the first half of the next decade? I think it is much better to look for a softer approach, for a milder, more flexible type of regulation, because regulators will surely be wrong in their predictions about the future.

Those were remarks about the 'whether' and the 'what' of regulation. Turning now to the 'whos', the national regulatory authorities are the ones who are making the hard, daily decisions that either empower or wound telecommunications operators. Like the gentleman in the Molière play who did not realise that he had been speaking prose all of his life, the telecommunications regulators are practising competition law without knowing it.

The national regulatory authorities are doing one thing very well. They are making decisions. The weakness of DG IV has been that, in the past, it has confused rule-making with decision-making. They are two different things. The national regulatory authorities, by contrast, are very successfully making regulatory decisions; that is splendid. However, they are operating on a national basis, whereas we need a European vision. Further, of course, national regulatory authorities must deal with trans-national issues, but they are addressing them largely along national lines.

Second, they are pursuing, what seem to me to be, micro-managerial goals rather than pursuing a broader vision of where we want to be. Now, the European Commission has produced a stunning selection of regulations and directives over the past 10 years, which the national regulatory authorities are actually implementing, although they may not know it. There are wide differences between how this is done among countries. I can understand such variety, but I fail to understand why there is so little active co-ordination. We should pursue common solutions to common problems with a view towards a European perspective.

This is not a new problem in EU policy. There are dozens of management committees, presided over by the Commission as scribe, note-taker and initiator, which are attended by national delegates. I think that there could be something that does not cost too much, that is not too institutionally burdensome, but that will work when we need it: for the next two to three years. That is, I think that DG XIII, DG IV or someone else inside the European Commission, could establish a task force to bring together, on a regular basis, national telecommunications regulators and national competition authorities involved in telecommunications. This group could systematically review developments in the field with a view to achieving local enforcement of Community principles. Such a system works in the field of customs valuation. It works for many subjects. And it could work—I will probably be told that it does work—but it could work better in the field of EU regulation of telecommunications.

This means that I define myself as an optimist. I think I am a minimalist optimist. That is, I believe that if we stand out of the way, it will be possible for national telecommunications regulatory authorities to disappear, or greatly diminish in the course of the next decade. Therefore, I suggest that Mr. Ungerer, who yesterday offered us his vision of the past, should build a 'poison pill' into the regulations that are being elaborated by DG XIII. To phrase this more cheerfully, perhaps we could call it an exit clause, a retirement fund or a sunset arrangement. The point is that we should not do this any longer than is necessary.

Regulators here present, I am very sorry, but as long as you are regulating, you get a taste for it. Unless you insert a clause into the regulations saying, '[T]his will end 31 December 2000,' you are likely to keep regulating indefinitely. Therefore, I encourage the regulators to think about putting a dissolution clause into European Community super-regulation for telecommunications.

▶ Amato—That might be a good idea. Mr. Ungerer suggested, 'from now until eternity'. You are suggesting, '2–3' years. A compromise might be something analogous to the history of bread regulations, which were initiated in the thirteenth century, and disappeared in the nineteenth. It only took six centuries.

▶ Martinez—There are two particular ways for the European Commission to promote competition in this market. The first is under the traditional, although only recently discovered, system of Article 86(3) [ex 90(3). As lawyers we should encourage the use of these provisions. However, such use is subject to the threshold requirement that the companies involved enjoy an 'exclusive' or 'special' right. This factor will not always be satisfied in the future.

The second manner in which the Commission can promote competition, is through proceedings under Article 226 [ex 169]; an option that has been reinforced by the ECJ's 1988 Judgment in the Italian CNSD case. The case concerned legislation that required custom agents to enter into fee agreements. The Commission challenged this legislation before the Court of Justice. This, I think, is the first time that the Court has held that the Italian government has failed to satisfy the general co-operation requirement in Article 10(2) [ex 5(2)], by depriving the competition rules (Articles 81 and 82 [ex 85 and 86]) of their *effet utile.*

I think that, in the future, this could be a very useful tool with which the Commission might attack any infringement of the liberalised regime through anti-competitive legislation and measures, even when they are taken by national regulatory authorities. As you see, Mr. Schaub, we, Spanish lawyers, have a very favourable view of Commission intervention in this field.

▶ RILL—Speaking of lawyers, I think the institutional issues of dealing with the telecommunications market in the United States are particularly dicey. I would like to talk about them briefly with respect to mergers and market access. Thereafter, I would like to touch upon the international sharing of jurisdiction with respect to telecommunications arrangements.

Let me say at the outset that the area of telecommunications is only one example of shared competition authority in the United States. Indeed, it is an area that probably works better than some other instances in which competition authority is invested in non-antitrust agencies. For example, the surface transportation board is responsible for approving railroad mergers. We saw what a wonderful job they did in approving the now very sluggish Union Pacific and Southern Pacific merger, over the objection of the United States DOJ. Just in passing, the Surface Transportation Board (The Surf Board) observed than it was concerned with greater issues than the 'trivial' question of competition policy.

Let us now turn to telecommunications and talk about mergers, first, from the purely domestic standpoint. The DOJ and the FCC share authority to review mergers with respect to wire line companies and the internet. Both agencies have authority to enforce Section 7 of the Clayton Act. The FCC also has authority over licence transfers. This has not always worked well.

For example, in the Bell Atlantic-Nynex merger, the DOJ adopted an analytical approach based upon traditional theory about potential competition. After a very thorough review, it concluded that Bell Atlantic was not one of the more likely entrants into the Nynex area. Consequently, applying traditional potential competition theory, the DOJ elected not to challenge the merger.

Thereafter, the FCC applied its public interest standard, which is, theoretically-speaking, a broader inquiry than Section 7 of the Clayton Act (which asks only whether the merger is likely to lessen competition substantially). Applying the broader standard, however, the FCC imposed various requirements that were, generally-speaking, competition related. They called for monitoring of performance, monitoring of uniform support systems, prices based on forward-looking economic costs, shared transport facilities and payment plans for non-recurring charges. One must, particularly with respect to pricing, view these requirements as being motivated by a concern about competition entering into the market.

Interestingly, Commissioner Ness implicitly criticised the DOJ. He said that the FCC does not look at the current significance of the merging partners, but, rather, their expected significance as the act is implemented. This suggested that the DOJ takes a snapshot, while the FCC takes a much more forward-looking view. I would politely suggest that this is not at all true. The notion that the DOJ does not take a forward looking view is, of course, erroneous.

This kind of dual authority can lead to uncomfortable situations. For example, when presented with rumours of the AT&T-Southwestern Bell acquisition, Reed Hunt, who was then Chairperson of the FCC, gratuitously opined that such a transaction would be 'unthinkable'. I, for one, cannot imagine the DOJ delivering advisory opinions on rumoured mergers with such abandon.

Moreover, the duplication of authority has even been criticised within the FCC. For example, in a concurring statement in the FCC's approval of the Worldcom-MCI merger, Commissioner Michael Powell suggested that the FCC should stay out of competition analysis. In his view, the FCC should let the DOJ review the competition aspects of the transaction and should restrict itself to a review of the other, non-competition, public interest factors, such as, safety and universal service. To be more specific, Commissioner Powell said: '[B]ased on my acknowledgement of the analytical overlap, and my deep respect for the diligence and considerable expertise of the Department [of Justice], I am hopeful that the Commission will, in the future, be able to minimise duplication of the effort in the area of competitive analysis and thereby use our regulatory resources much more efficiently'.

A similar statement was made by Commissioner Roth, who suggested that competition issues are best left to the DOJ and other issues are best left to the FCC. I also think that this is the right solution. One could even go so far as to say that there is no need for an FCC; but, politically, this is an impossible recommendation. Nonetheless, there is simply no reason for the FCC to duplicate the effort of the DOJ. There is no reason why the DOJ should not be empowered to make binding determinations with respect to the vitality of competition. The FCC could then perform its task of examining other public interest factors.

Let me turn to access for a moment. Section 271 of the Telecommunications Act of 1996, governs the ability of the Bell Operating Companies (BOCs) to enter the long-distance market. The FCC applies a 14 point test, which is set out in the legislation, and gives substantial weight to the opinions of the DOJ. (The DOJ is required to analyse the 14 points, and also to review other points which it may see fit to analyse.) Strangely, it seems that the DOJ has never gone beyond the 14 points. In contrast, the FCC has, on occasion, done so, but has then co-ordinated very closely with the DOJ, so that the analytical path does, in fact, appear to be parallel. If this is the case, why should there be two agencies undertaking the same review?

Again, Commissioner Michael Powell has suggested that better co-ordination might produce less overlap in work. Further, he suggested that the DOJ might appropriately consider competition factors, including the pro-competitive factor of the BOCs entering into the long-distance market, which itself is not a model of competitive vitality. If the 14 points are to be covered, perhaps they should be reviewed by the FCC, while the DOJ undertakes the more traditional competition analysis, including possible pro-competitive effects.

In this case, I think the legislative framework is more at fault than either of the two agencies. We may not wish to know the political processes which lead to such compromises; compromises which Bismarck might have called 'treaties'. Nevertheless, we must acknowledge that such compromises have established hurdles that make it difficult for the BOCs to enter the long distance market. Such entry may be even more difficult than Congress intended.

Let me turn to international aspects. We now have 60–70 countries who have systems, which call for some form of pre-notification or a merger review. In the telecommunications area, this is particularly significant, and, of course, the WTO includes a telecommunications agreement that has a competitive factor within it. The Worldcom-MCI merger was, in my view, a paradigm of excellent co-operation between the DOJ and DG IV's Merger Task Force. As was discussed yesterday, I think that this type of bilateral arrangement is the model for improving multinational merger review, not only in telecommunications but also in other, broader, areas. Moreover, I think that bilateral agreements, such as the 1991 agreement between the United States and the

European Commission, could serve as a blueprint to remove the friction and co-ordinate international merger regulation.

This issue is currently being considered by the DOJ advisory committee on international competition policy, to which Dieter Wolf and others have made major contributions. We hope that, in about a year, this committee will issue a report concerning the removal of friction and initiation of better co-ordination in international merger reviews, including those within the telecommunications sector.

▶ YPSILANTI—I am neither a sector-specific regulator nor a competition regulator. Nevertheless, I have been fascinated with the discussion and think that one of the conclusions which we can safely reach is that both sector-specific and competition regulators agree that, in the long run, they wish to treat telecommunications in the same way as any other sector.

Therefore, we have a common goal. What is clearly missing, however, is how we arrive at that goal. Certainly, I have yet to hear a clear message from the competition regulators on how we are to proceed; nor, have I seen the form of supervisory toolbox that would move us into a competitive environment. Structural solutions have been mentioned, but, in Europe, for example, I have not seen any competition authority attempt to implement them. In my opinion, one step that would assist in the process is the divestiture of cable television from incumbents; but there has been little or no movement in this direction.

Today, we have heard that sector-specific regulators make mistakes; but I think the competition regulators also make mistakes. For example, if we return to yesterday's discussion on mergers, we can see that the various merger approvals were, arguably, mistaken in the context of bringing competition to the US telecommunications market.

Clearly, this does not mean that the sector-specific regulators are doing a great job. I also think there are problems on this front. One of the key problems which was mentioned earlier is the lack of any clear forbearance, streamlining, sunset clause or any other such policy. However, you cannot be mechanical about these issues; I am not sure that we can easily set specific time limits or specific market share requirements. Nonetheless, we do need a review of the regulation, and even of the regulator; and we do need to roll back regulatory tendencies. This is important, and a few countries have, in my opinion, good procedures to review the whole regulatory framework.

Another problem with regards to sector-specific regulation, is that there is a movement towards increasing complexity within regulation. Regulations are becoming much more detailed; while the more detailed they are, the more embedded they become in the system and the harder it is to rescind them. New entrants and incumbents acclimatise themselves to these regulations, and this makes it difficult to withdraw them.

The issue of complexity is linked to the a process of convergence, which further complicates the regulatory process, as broadcasting network regulations become intertwined with telecommunications regulations. However, while in telecommunications we have moved toward pro-competitive regulation, broadcasting is still characterised by a regulatory philosophy of relative market closure, at least in most countries.

Convergence will complicate the whole regulatory framework. It will require us to tackle broadband issues and the allocation of costs within the broadband network. In my view, this will be much more complicated than dealing with a public switched network or dealing with voice telecommunications alone. Given convergence, the model I would like to see is similar to OFTEL, where you have a single regulatory framework dealing with networks irrespective of their use. However, I do recognise that there are complexities involved.

Other institutional solutions have also been mentioned. The first one is streamlining, *i.e.*, trying to develop clearer criteria for streamlining. The second is moving certain issues away from the sector-specific regulator and giving them to the competition authority. For example, I believe that interconnection falls under the jurisdiction of the Danish competition authority. A number of such issues exist, which, over time, can be transferred from the sector-specific regulator to the competition authority.

The third solution involves the creation of an authority like the ACCC, as has been done in Australia. That is, the creation of a bureau within the competition authority that deals with sector-specific regulation. This, however, poses dangers in that it is difficult to justify the creation of a telecommunications bureau, in the absence of an electricity, railway or transportation bureau. Where a roller-coaster effect takes hold, there is a danger that the competition authority will no longer look at the economy as a whole, but will dissolve into a bundle of sector-specific bureaux whose actions may distort overall competition.

Moving to international issues, the WTO has been mentioned. As you all know, all OECD countries have signed up to the 'reference paper' and have attached it to their schedules. The reference paper is, in a sense, an implicit listing of regulatory safeguards, and, to a certain degree at least, an implicit understanding that members will proceed towards sector-specific regulation. The danger for the future is that, as arbitration and case law flesh out some of the safeguards mentioned in the reference paper, certain sector-specific regulations may be institutionalised. Institutionalisation may also result from forthcoming multilateral discussions within the context of the WTO; the year 2000 should see a further round of negotiations.

I would like now to move very quickly to multi-level governance issues. One of the points that we have not yet discussed is the fact that conflict is not limited to disagreements between sector-specific and competition authorities, but may also extend to encompass other bodies involved. For example, Ministers of Finance have, in a number of cases, taken steps to prevent pro-competitive measures from being put in place. Again, we come back to cable TV networks, where, in the process of privatisation, the divestiture of cable TV has been halted by Finance Ministers.

For example, in Greece, the regulator is trying to bring forward market opening to the year 2000. The Greek Finance Ministry is opposed to accelerated market opening, since they believe a sale of government shares in the monopoly will maximise the funds realised through privatisation. This, in turn, could have a positive impact on Greek efforts to join EMU.

At the multi-government level, the European Union faces various problems. Thus, while Member States have agreed on the principles of liberalisation, uneven implementation is leading to a significant divergence among the national markets. Divergence is augmented by the different rates at which competition is building up in the different markets. One suggested solution is the creation of a European regulator. I have my doubts as to whether this is the best route to take, unless it is in the form of a federal or collegiate system that allows decentralised national implementation of common rules.

One last point, again on the multi-governance level, is the issue of municipalities. I do not think anyone has touched upon this, but municipalities are 'getting in the way' of pro-competitive policies. In certain countries, municipalities are in a position of providing or not providing the rights of way. In other countries, they are involved in the cable TV consortia. National governments are reluctant to confront municipalities and are, by contrast, attempting to identify solutions that push them out of the field. Of course, this is primarily a political problem, but, in certain countries, these political problems have lead to corollary difficulties with regard to access to rights of way controlled by municipalities.

▶ AMATO—That was the last report and the floor is now open for questions. I expect that the main questions that we will discuss will concern convergent technologies and the issue of too many authorities.

Another point that we have not touched upon, however, is whether we necessarily have to invent a regulator simply because we have regulation? In other words, could some regulations be viewed as private systems of ordering, and be managed by existing institutions?

▶ LONG—With some hesitation, as I am surrounded by so many professors and regulators, I recall a story about a Greek professor who went to Oxford to deliver a speech. He delivered the speech entirely in ancient Greek, and the others listened in stony silence. Nobody understood a word. So that when I say *custodius custodiae*, I hope that our Italian colleagues at least will understand me.

One rather thorny question which we have yet to tackle is: who will regulate the regulators? I have been involved in the issue of judicial review in my country. It is one of the most difficult places to seek review when you feel you have been unfairly treated by a regulator.

While we do have access to some supervision processes available, they nonetheless boil down to a case of one regulator attempting to overrule another. Sometimes this is a good thing; sometimes it is not. We must, in any case, address these 'turf wars'. In the past, DG IV has, for example, quite usefully intervened to bring existing telecommunications agencies into line, as regards their over-regulatory tendencies.

However, if we are going to move closer to having a regional or global regulator, I hope we will bear one thing in mind. An eighteenth century jurist said to us: '[B]e ye ever so high, the law is above you'. Well, if we are going to create supranational regulators, how in this world will we ever find someone who can be their judge?

▶ BOETTCHER—I personally feel somewhat pressurised: in the very near future, I must take a 'poison pill'. On that basis, I do not think it makes much sense to defend the present position; instead we must take a proactive stance.

I would like to pick up on a question posed by Mr. Lassere. He asked whether there should be a European regulator in certain fields, and he pointed to this need, especially in the field of satellite communications. I would argue that we need to go even further. If we look at this special segment of the telecommunications sector, we have to keep the following in mind. In order for a company to operate a satellite in the geo-stationary orbit, it must apply for a satellite position at the International Telecommunications Union (ITU). This procedure can only be initiated by governments and is only a technical notification. The notification process aims to co-ordinate the frequencies used by the satellite in order to avoid interference.

However, the ITU does not examine the economic impact of the positioning of a new satellite with regard to competition law. This is true even though orbital slots are scarce and even though satellite capacity forms a market with typical bottleneck characteristics. Today, the ITU does not review satellite cartels, nor does it review mergers and possible abuses of satellite capacities.

Of course, we cannot blame the ITU: it is not mandated to apply competition law. In fact, nobody is mandated to do so in this field, at least not on a global basis. We have certain decisions made at European Commission level, and we have national decisions in this area, but we do not have decisions with global application.

According to the European Commission, the revenues generated in the geostationary satellite sector will reach 200 billion dollars over the next ten years. It is, thus, a rather large market, and if we look at the satellite systems with mobile characteristics, a further 400 billion dollars will be generated over the next 10 years. So, we have a huge market, but no one is taking an overall view of the competition issues involved.

I think that the need for competition law enforcement in this sector is quite compelling. Therefore, we might justifiably ask why there is no entity controlling abuses in this field? Should a European entity do so? I do not think so. It should be a global entity—UN or UN-like—with global, rather than European, competence. This type of institution may, of course, also be responsible for other economic questions. Mr. Wolf has already pointed this out several times, and I think he is quite right in this regard.

I am also convinced that it is possible to find the appropriate regime to guarantee competition in this sector. It is not necessary to create new competition rules. Rather, we could apply internationally accepted common rules on competition, especially those concerning merger and abuse control. Personally, I am very much in favour of a global entity, and I would favour further discussion of this issue, not just at the European level, but on an international basis.

▶ ARNBAK—When I took office in July 1997, I had to swallow the 'poison pill' immediately. In Holland, in 2002, there will be a review of whether the regulatory agency should continue to exist.

I want to touch upon judicial review. In the Netherlands, there has been an effort to streamline judicial review, so that the competition authority and the regulatory authority will be subject to the same judicial review. Thus, where our views diverge, they will be reviewed by the same court, which is, in my view, extremely important.

I also wanted to note that, in contrast to what Mr. Jenny from the French competition authority suggested—*i.e.*, that competition authorities are always older and more dignified—that this is not the case in Holland. As those of you who are familiar with Dutch competition law know, European transactions contain what is known as the 'Dutch clause.' This clause refers to the fact that, until very recently (January 1998 after the creation of the regulatory authority for telecommunications), the competition authority was inactive. Prior to January, competition issues were resolved by the Minister of Economic Affairs. Today, even under the new regime, this Minister can overrule decisions of the Antitrust Authority. Therefore, the 'Dutch clause' provides that politically delicate matters are referred to DG IV.

I would also like to discuss the recent development discussed yesterday: the fact that DG IV can refer questions to the national regulatory authorities. This could be due to resource reasons. For two reasons, we, in the Netherlands, are in the process of developing a similar protocol between the national sector-specific regulatory authority and the national competition authority. First of all, if we are both empowered to deal with a particular issue, then *lex specialis* will take precedence. Thus, the national competition authority will refer the issue to the national regulatory authority, so that we can deal with it first under telecommunications law. After that, once we have set out a draft decision on the matter, the competition authority will review it to see if there is any conflict with competition law.

▶ AMATO—Is it informal?

▶ ARNBAK—I am referring to a protocol that we are currently trying to establish. Earlier, the government tried to set up a legal arrangement in which the Minister would have the final word. However, we found this to be flawed because it was contrary to our regulations. Moreover, because the Minister is a shareholder in the incumbent firm, it was contrary to the idea of an impartial regulation, as stipulated in the WTO agreement.

The protocol we have proposed would not only be used in the event of overlapping powers, but also for situations in which we use the same legal terms for different purposes. For example, this protocol would be used for defining terms like 'reasonable return on investment' and for the developing of market definitions. In the latter case, we have agreed to create a public list of such terms and to consult each other when new cases arise. In most cases, this would mean that the regulatory authority would consult the competition authority. In this way, we believe that the poison pill may not have to dissolve unpleasantly in the regulator's stomach. We see this as a way of sharing work, especially because the competition authority, as young as it is, is completely overloaded with mergers and concentration approval requests. Consequently, the national regulatory authority will be the front line soldier in telecommunications matters. Where fundamental competition issues arise, of course, we will refer to the competition authority.

▶ BAKER—It seems to me that there are some fundamental questions that we should be asking ourselves. First of all, do we want the competition authority to be an administrator or a law enforcer? These are both reasonable alternatives, but they lead you down different paths.

Secondly, do we want it to be independent or a part of the executive establishment? This is a subject of considerable debate. I would like to point out that although the DOJ is technically a part of the United States executive establishment, it has probably acted more independently that the regulatory agencies. This can be explained by a variety of factors, including the fact that the sector-specific authorities were sometimes captured by industry or held back by caution.

Third, there are nice issues about judicial review. For example, in the United States, if you want to appeal a decision of the FCC, you have to sue both the FCC and the United States. The DOJ represents the United States as respondent, which gave me (in the DOJ) substantial leverage in dealing with the FCC because we could threaten to intervene against them in the Court of Appeals. Obviously, the judicial review issue is also important in Europe, where the Court of First Instance has become a big thing.

The next issue is the possibility of the antitrust agency bringing cases against transactions that were approved by the sector-specific regulator. We have a leading case involving the FCC, *United States v RCA*, in which the FCC had approved a merger and the DOJ overturned it. We have had a large number of such cases in the banking area. In these cases, the banking agencies may intervene on behalf of the merger they have approved during an antitrust case brought by the DOJ.

The next kind of case is the antitrust case challenging the structure of an industry that the regulatory agency has either approved or coddled. *United States v AT&T* is an interesting example of that scenario. In this case, the DOJ more or less overturned the industry as it then existed. An unsuccessful effort was made to overturn the agency regulating the stock exchange. We ended up in the Supreme Court with the DOJ on one side and the Securities and Exchange Commission (SEC) on the other. The SEC won. Fortunately, we were able to turn the tables on them through legislative action in Congress.

The next possibility is the antitrust agency participating as a formal party in a case before the regulatory agency. A case de-regulating terminal equipment was a landmark, where the DOJ did just that. It was one of the first cases I worked on.

Finally, you have got Jim Rill's idea—I am not quite sure how it works—of the antitrust agency binding the regulatory agency on a competition question. The question that then comes to my mind is: how do you get judicial review of that? If the regulatory agency says they rejected the merger because the DOJ told them to do so, do we then review the DOJ or the regulatory agency?

As a footnote, I will mention the one area in which the DOJ has become a regulatory agency. This is in approving failing newspaper mergers. In this context, the DOJ has failed in its functions, just as miserably as the classic sector-specific agency. It has approved every newspaper case it has faced. There has then been judicial review of the Attorney Generals' decisions in these areas.

My final thought is that, in the United States, the independence of the antitrust agency is such that we have been able to place professionals at the head of antitrust. People like Bill Baxter, Jim Rill and Donald Turner had independent reputations and could simply go home if they were unpopular with the political parts of our government. If we make the antitrust agency a general administrator of all that effects competition, I am not so sure that the political authorities are going to be willing to have independent professionals running the operation. They might well prefer people who are more like political operators. Anyway, it is not an easy question and it is a great subject for a morning like this.

► ERGAS—I wanted to intervene briefly about the specific lessons that might be drawn from the New Zealand experience in terms of the balance between industry-specific and general competition regulation. The typical commentary about the New Zealand experience is that it demonstrates the need for some type of sector-specific regulation. The popular view is that the courts (who make decisions under general competition policy) have failed as regulators of telecommunications policy in New Zealand. The observation made in this respect is that it has taken some time for the courts to determine the very substantial matters before them.

Is this really a good indicator that New Zealand's system of light regulation has failed? In my view, for a small country like New Zealand, it is extremely important to set the signals which guide large-scale investment correctly. The fact that the courts have struggled for some time with these issues, does not necessarily indicate failure, in particular, if we have ultimately achieved a good outcome. Moreover, I believe that when you examine what has happened in the New Zealand market, the impression you derive is that the outcomes achieved are good ones.

In addition to these indications that the courts may not have failed, as some would suggest, it is, in my view, important to ask whether other countries actually offer superior alternatives to the system of light-handed regulation that has operated in New Zealand. Looking around this room, it is my impression that New Zealand is not the only country witnessing lengthy litigation in the context of telecommunications and competition matters. We have a monopoly in some areas, but litigation is not one of them.

Rather, when I examine countries with sector-specific regulation, I see that they not only have sector-specific regulation, but also have litigation associated with this regulation. This is certainly true in Australia and the United States, and probably true in many other countries. Consequently, in some senses, they achieve the worst of all possible worlds. Not only do they bear the kinds of costs that are undoubtedly borne in New Zealand, but they also get the distortions, rent-seeking, strategic gaming and all the other consequences associated with sector-specific regulatory regimes.

What has New Zealand attained from not having sector-specific regulation? I think the first thing that we have achieved, is a market of immense commercial freedom. We do not have the kinds of detailed, prescriptive rules that Mr. Forrester pointed to as a sign of, and in some sense an understandable consequence of, sector-specific regulation. The absence of such detailed rules has made it much easier for New Zealand to adapt to changing circumstances and, in particular, to changing technologies. If I may provide one very specific example: I noticed that almost all other countries are still grappling with establishing immense 'forward-looking cost models' of the networks of the 1950's, *i.e.*, PSTN networks. That is, they are struggling to define interconnection prices for narrowband networks. In New Zealand, by contrast, the debate has moved on from that, and we are involved in designing an interconnection system for broadband networks. Indeed, we are quite advanced in developing interconnection agreements for broadband networks. As far as I know, we are the only country that has done so. Therefore, I hope there will be great potential to export this model to the rest of the world.

Furthermore, this commercial freedom has provided fantastic adaptability and flexibility, which translates into good outcomes for consumers. In addition, it means that, rightly or wrongly, New Zealand has not been brought into the problem of managing the eventual transition from sector-specific to general competition regulation. You will correct me if I am wrong, but it is my perception that, similar to the Marxist idea of the withering away of the state, the euthanasia of the regulator is viewed with, at best, mixed feelings by the potential euthanasees. Consequently, although market dominance (a bit like love) comes and goes, regulation (like a diamond) can be forever. Precisely because of this enormous persistence, it appears as though regulation may prove to be the rent-seekers' best friend.

Ultimately, there is a trade-off and a choice. There are costs associated with the absence of sector-specific regulation. However, the way that has been perceived in New Zealand is that the trade-off is between mechanisms such as the courts applying general competition policy, and conventional sector-specific regulators. The courts have limited institutional capabilities, but, at the same time, have a very low vulnerability to rent-seeking, capture and gaming by special interests. The sector-specific regulators, by contrast, are much more capable—they have armies, they can mobilise, they are Weberian bureaucracies. However, they obtain this greater institutional capability at a relatively high price in terms of their vulnerability to manipulation by special interests.

It may be that New Zealand has leaned very heavily, perhaps too heavily, toward one end of the spectrum. But surely, there is an even more compelling case for the proposition that there are many countries who have leaned far too heavily towards the other end.

▶ GOSLING—Perhaps this will bring the discussion down to a rather practical, but I think quite important level, which is about offices, buildings and personnel. This has not really been discussed yet.

There seems to be a consensus that we need to develop better the relationship between the competition authorities and national regulatory authorities, at least as concerns pro-competitive economic policy. There is less consensus on how that solution looks from the point of view of institutional architecture of the solid and not the abstract kind.

This might be very simplistic and I might be challenged on this, but it seems to me that there have been three models based upon the metaphor of the architecture of houses and bridges. The first one is that you have two houses: the regulatory house and the competition house, with the solution to more efficient interaction depending on better bridges, better co-operation between them. I had the feeling that this was the Italian point of view and maybe that of the Commission.

The second model is bringing the two houses under the same roof, literally bringing the offices and the people into one agency. Very simply, it seems that has happened in Australia, where the telecommunications people were brought into the ACCC. Perhaps, to a certain extent, it has gone the other way in the UK, where OFTEL is bringing a large number of competition people into the regulatory agency.

The third model is the structure in which you have only one house, that is, the competition house. Perhaps the German solution is that you just demolish the second house. The New Zealand solution is that it should never be built.

▶ Fox—I would like to continue talking about architecture. I want to think about this problem as a multi-level chess game. In so many countries we have regulation and competition, yet the issues span across the world. Consequently, I am going to refer to two points. One relates to the point that Mr. Martinez made earlier regarding impermissible State action that buys access. I want to dwell on this as a very important point for the world. Mr. Jenny mentioned that there is discussion at the level of the WTO working group on some multi-lateral rules. They might involve transparency, non-discrimination and due process.

I propose that we should also add something for the world that looks like Article 86 [ex 90] or something like the *'effet utile'* doctrine within the EU Treaty. This is necessary because there is no disciplining of excessive state-led anti-competitive regulation at the global level. The *Fuji-Kodak* case has just shown us that the WTO, as it stands, is insufficient to deal with such issues, unless people first have a reasonable expectation of entering a market, which is then defeated. Consequently, I think a market access addition would be very important. Your particular cases are very good examples of situations in which the incumbent is protected by the state, which you could call a regulator (here it was legislation) and the outsider cannot enter. This outsider may or may not be on the other side of the world.

Secondly, for some years, we have seen cross border clashes between regulatory and competition systems. One case that comes to mind is the *Freddy Laker* case, from some time ago. Of course, this case involved airline regulation, but a similar situation could arise in telecommunications. The allegation was that the major airlines entered into a predatory pricing conspiracy to push Freddy Laker out of the market. Laker was a very good upstart in the market who was causing a vast reduction in prices. At least one American airline was allegedly involved, while British Airways, British Caledonian and perhaps Sabena were also alleged conspirators. There were different regulatory systems on the opposite sides of the ocean. There was some agreement and regulatory approval of tariffs on either side of the ocean. On the British side, the claim was that they had been immunised by the regulator. On the United States side, they probably did get immunisation from the regulator. Freddy Laker, or more accurately his trustee in bankruptcy, brought suit. The case was ultimately settled.

This is exactly the type of problem that will arise again. Whose regulation trumps? Whose competition law trumps? How do we develop a common rule for thinking about sanctions and immunities? This kind of problem should be discussed and resolved by people who are thinking about some kind of common system. It should be thought of, in Europe for example, from the point of view of the Community citizen. That is, all interests should be taken into account in making such decisions, and some framework should be agreed upon that could be inserted into the multilateral structure that I believe will ultimately evolve.

Thus, I think that we must think globally because our problems are worldwide. I also think that if people come together to talk about such a problem, it is possible to reach a point of consensus. Under this consensus, competition policy will take the upper hand following liberalisation, unless regulators can demonstrate a non-parochial, specific, national public interest.

Knieps—From my point of view, the idea of competition among institutions is a fallacy because competition policy and sector-specific regulation should be seen as complementary, not as substitutes for each other. Their instruments are applied in different ways. I think what we have learned is that there is a large potential for fading out of sector-specific regulation, once market failure is overcome. The opening of markets is increasing. Network markets are becoming much more complex.

Taking this a step further, there is a large amount of literature which analyses the asymmetric information problems that the regulator has with respect to the firms. The role of the market is increasing, but this does not mean that the role of government intervention has to increase with it, since a wide range of solutions can be found in the market.

Going back to the essential facilities doctrine or the bottleneck problem, I believe that minimizing regulation of bottlenecks might lead to the conferral of this task upon the competition authority. In Germany, for example, the essential facilities doctrine is included in the sixth amendment of the competition law, so that the remaining tasks will be entrusted to the competition agency. Thus, the inefficiency in the application of institutional powers may disappear. Ultimately, we should have the market in mind as the objective of competition policy. Deregulation, and not rent seeking among different regulators, should be the end result.

Hovenkamp—I want to say that I fully agree with what Mr. Baker and Mr. Gill said about internal inconsistencies and chaos in federal oversight in the United States. However, I think they both understate the level of chaos in one particular respect, and that is, the expansive nature of private enforcement in the United States. If a merger is within Section 7 of the Clayton Act, it is generally reachable in actions by private parties. This is also true of actions under the Sherman Act. Furthermore, the fact that the FTC or DOJ has (conditionally or definitively) approved a practice or a merger does not preclude private parties from subsequently challenging it. The Supreme Court also made it clear, in 1990, that such a challenge may include a request for structural relief. Related to this is the problem of whether agencies are captured by the industries they oversee, while private plaintiffs unabashedly serve their own private interests when they bring suits challenging mergers. Finally, I see significant potential for legislative modifications eliminating some of the jurisdictional contests that Mr. Baker discussed. However, I do not see much potential, in the United States, for eliminating private enforcement in this area.

Incidentally, there has been one preliminary injunction this year in a case brought by a private party against a newspaper. There was another private party challenge to a merger of two public utilities, which the third circuit Court of Appeals ultimately rejected on merits, but not on grounds of standing. Perhaps the best example in the communications industry is the Rupert Murdoch/Fox News challenge to the Time-Warner/Ted Turner acquisition. In this case, Time-Warner acquired Turner interests, including CNN, and then threatened to eliminate Fox News on cable systems controlled by Time-Warner Cable. That was subject to two different private challenges in two different federal districts in New York. Fox was ultimately able to negotiate a much more aggressive conditional remedy than the FTC.

▶ AMATO—Has anyone ever suggested the elimination of private litigation of antitrust cases?

▶ HOVENKAMP—Thousands of times. It is certainly not on the political horizon as far as I can see, but the study of the infirmities of private litigation has become almost a cottage industry in antitrust scholarship.

▶ RUBINFELD—And it's going that way in the world. Are there not other places that are now thinking about private remedies to make up for inadequate government resources?

▶ AMATO—Exactly, we could be thinking about introducing the horrible treble damages all over the world.

▶ EHLERMANN—But remember in the 1996 seminar, it was advocated that we increase private suits in Europe.

▶ BARNES—I am now going to adopt a more optimistic point of view than the one I adopted yesterday, in the sense that I think it is possible to invent the future. Therefore, it is possible to invent institutional arrangements that are better than those we currently have.

I also think, however, that the perfect should not be the enemy of the good. What I would like to do in the next few minutes is to outline some of the experiences that OFTEL has had over the past two years in dealing with overlapping and concurrent jurisdiction. Hopefully, this will provide some information about problems that might be avoided in building future institutions to deal with this issue.

I would like to make one other point. In inventing institutional structures, I think it is extremely important to keep independent variables separate. Therefore, the issue of who regulates the regulators, whether you use a litigation system or some other system of judicial review, is, to some extent, an issue independent from the question of institutional structures. There are certain problems along independent variable lines. It is important for policy makers to avoid confusing the problems which the individual solutions focus upon.

Let me now look at the institutional structures in terms of overlapping powers. In the UK, we have had concurrent powers, under the competition rules, for the sector-specific regulators and the general regulator, the Office of Fair Trading (OFT). This will be maintained in the future, when the UK moves to a much better set of general competition rules. In particular, we will move to a direct prohibition system along the lines of Articles 81 and 82 [85 and 86], in which there will be concurrent powers between the regulator and the OFT. However, in any particular instance, only one institution can exercise these powers. There is no dispute resolution procedure.

Nevertheless, to date, perhaps slightly counter-intuitively, in cases where something could reasonably been done by both, the two bodies have tended to say 'you do it', rather than 'let me do it.' This may be an indication of the extent of their resources. However, I also think that it also indicates that, as some hope, regulators are aware of the need to minimise regulation. At least some institutional bodies realise that they should be shrinking their field of intervention, rather than expanding it. In summary, I think the lesson is that, if you have concurrent powers, you should ensure that only one institution will exercise the power at any particular time.

I underline this conclusion because there is another bit of the forest that OFTEL regulates, where we have overlapping jurisdiction with the Independent Television Commission (ITC). In this sector, there is no rule about only one institution exercising power. Indeed, the same issue is looked at by two regulatory organisations using slightly different rules. Ensuring co-ordination and achieving sensible outcomes under these circumstances, is extremely difficult. It can be done, and, to some extent, we have been reasonably successful in the UK, but this is a structure that makes it much more difficult to have efficient regulation and co-operation. Thus, the worst outcome is,

I believe, two people looking at the same thing using different rules. Probably the best system, if you must have concurrent jurisdiction, is to have the same rules applied by one or the other of the institutions, in which only one of them decides any particular issue.

In the UK, we also have a system to ensure that the two sectoral and general regulatory institutions do not go in different directions. The appellate body, called the Competition Commission, is the same irrespective of whether OFTEL or the OFT has made the initial decision. So, to keep the two organisations on track, the same appellate body will be used. I think that, at least in one little area, without dealing with the international issues, this furnishes us with the following operational rule: avoid, at all costs, a system where two or more institutions have overlapping jurisdiction and use different rules.

▶ FELS—The Australian debate on this topic took place when certain things were easier to do than others. Australia is a relatively small and homogeneous country, which made certain things easier. We started out with the debate mainly in the energy and transport areas, because telecommunications is national. It is not a state issue. As the process of deregulation of public utilities got underway, we faced the possibility that, in each state in Australia, there would be a separate water regulator, gas regulator, electric regulator, etc.. It was thought that, at the very least, in our small country, we should have one regulator taking care of all of these functions.

After deciding that we needed some kind of general regulator for all of these utilities, the next question was whether it should be at the state or national level. A number of these markets are national in dimension. Indeed, regulation itself is one of the reasons why some state markets had not become national. We therefore thought that we probably needed a general national regulator.

The next issue that then came up was whether we would set up a major national regulatory institution and what its relationship with the competition agency would be. On the whole, the prevailing view was that it was better, on balance, for the competition regulator to oversee this job. We believed a sector-specific regulator was not likely to have pro-competition values, but was more likely to give precedence to other values. Therefore, it was better for the necessary national regulation to be driven by the cultural approach of a competition body, rather than having a separate culture.

Going back to the question of the states, however, I should mention what has actually happened in the energy sector. Where there is some kind of national issue, such as a pipeline or a grid that crosses state boundaries, this issue is handled by the national regulator. This includes pricing questions and so on. Where you have, instead, state markets in the distribution of electric or gas (in which there are a number of political issues and cross-subsidies), decisions remain in the hands of state regulators and state legislation. There are some national control overrides and it is likely that, over time, these functions will drift to the national regulator. In the meantime, however, we are in no hurry to take over these functions.

As far as the question of independence is concerned, there has not really been any change in the independence of the Commission. Further, it has been argued that it is better to have a big, overarching commission, because we are happy to fight any interest group whatsoever. In contrast, there is some doubt about whether sector-specific regulators are fully able to fight the interest groups in the sectors under their supervision.

A couple of other arguments came up. The essential argument, which carried the day, was that a competition culture should drive necessary regulatory activity. However, it was also recognised that, in an era of convergence, it was better to have the general competition regulator operating across sectors. You even have some convergence, after all, between the energy and the telecommunications sectors. We also had consistency, some economies of scale in the work to be done by the competition authority, one-stop-shopping for business, and the possibility for enhanced co-ordination of the application of various instruments, all of which we thought could be best achieved in a unified agency. Against this, we recognise that our approach does put a large number of eggs in one basket. It does take quite a few risks in this regard.

The technical regulation has been kept separate in the communications area. We have set up something a bit like the FCC without its competition and economic regulatory functions. It is called the Australian Communications Authority. Although, at this stage, it has not been merged with the broadcasting agency, this might happen in the future, giving us the 'slimmed down' FCC model.

Further, in a very general way, when technical issues come up that raise major competition issues, then the ACCC has oversight of them.

On the staffing and knowledge issue, we took a few people from the ACCC, but we mainly brought new people in. It is true that we have a separate branch that deals with telecommunications, which makes up nearly 10% of the staff of our organisation. Nevertheless, this group is very much controlled by the Commission and by senior staff and others. They are eager to impart the competition culture and approach to these matters. So, that is basically the system that has emerged in Australia.

There are also some important pieces of legislation, which override everything. For example, there are laws regarding cross-subsidies. I will leave it at that.

► MONACI—Naturally, since I am truly a newcomer here, I cannot yet offer very much background on the debate that has followed the creation of our telecommunications authority. I would like to express, however, that it has been very useful for me to gain the insights offered here on the debate in other countries, not just in Europe, but across the world.

I was also very happy to learn that, although we were only recently born, we may soon approach our death. At any rate, we do exist, and as you may already be aware, our law on telecommunications assumes that convergence will be the real driving force for the market, today and in the future. Perhaps this will allow us to jump over many hurdles and be in the front-line of development.

The one comment that I want to make on this debate is the following. In the absence of a regulatory authority in our country, I wonder who would have taken decisions on issues like new frequencies and interconnection tariffs. We have already decided upon both of these issues. In the latter case, we have moved into a stage of collaboration with DG IV and our own competition authority. In this sector, there is a sense of urgency with regard to the need to prevent monopoly growth, not only in the telecommunications sector but also in the broadcasting sector. In the latter sector, we have a unique situation, with a variety of broadcasters and a substantial degree of dominance on the part of two operators.

► SALSBURY—I would, again, like to bring to the table the perspective of a victim of regulation and competition authorities. I believe that it really is necessary to have both types of authority. You could have neither, as the New Zealand experience shows, but then you do not have meaningful competition there either. Thus, I think competition authorities and sector-specific regulators each serve useful purposes.

The competition authority should have primacy in the areas of mergers and industry structure. The competition authority also serves as a useful backstop for situations in which regulation fails to allow competition to develop, as happened in the United States. But the competition authority alone is not sufficient, because it involves itself in structural issues and tends to shun behavioural issues, as we heard yesterday.

Meanwhile, the sector-specific regulator primarily concerns itself with behavioural issues. It is not possible to have the competition authority work out the terms and conditions of interconnection, which is the primary issue here, because the parties cannot accomplish this by themselves and antitrust law does not do a very good job on pricing issues. But you must recognise that there is a need for a sector-specific regulator because there is a very uneven bargaining position between the incumbent and the new entrants when it comes to interconnection issues. It is necessary, and I think that sector-specific regulators do serve a useful purpose, particularly when the merger authorities make errors.

Because the competition authorities feel themselves constrained to structural solutions, they tend to overlook behavioural conditions that should be included in a merger. They tend to look at things in black and white when, in fact, there is a rich variety of greys in the universe of our industry. So, when the DOJ made what was widely perceived to be a mistake in the Bell Atlantic-Nynex transaction, the FCC was able to step in and impose some behavioural conditions. Unfortunately these conditions have not yet been enforced, but they made sense at the time. For that reason, both agencies have an important role, and I would prefer that they be in separate houses so that each can serve as a check upon the other.

We have difficulties when there are overlapping competition authorities and sector regulators at different governmental levels (state and federal). We do not have problems where they overlap each other on a subject matter basis, but we do have problems where they overlap each other on a geographical jurisdictional basis. So I would urge you to consider a European level sector-specific regulator because, frankly, the product you are regulating is not a national product. Our communications cross national boundaries. Our biggest customers are in all of your jurisdictions. The technology is advancing at such a rate that it is very difficult for any one national regulatory authority to keep place with these developments. Thus, I urge you to consider one European authority, at least for the terms and conditions of interconnection.

In the United States, we find that multi-level policy with overlapping jurisdictions on behavioural issues is a problem. What you end up with is forum shopping by the industry participants. We certainly participate in that as much as anyone else. We will go to states if we think they will be more favourable to us; we will go to the FCC if we think that it will be more favourable.

So, you do need to have authorities on each side—competition and sector-specific regulation. That is very helpful. But if you do not have a European level regulator, you run into several risks. The first is that it is much easier to have regulatory capture at the national level. The second is that you will not promote uniformity of result. For example, because the terms and conditions of interconnection are decided at two levels in the United States, we have seen a perverse outcome. A call within a state costs more than a call across the country because the cost of access is by far the overwhelming cost function in the telephone call. So, a call from New York City to Los Angeles costs a fraction of the cost of a call from New York City to upstate New York. That is why you really need uniformity and one sector-specific regulator.

▶ SCHAUB—I think Mr. Amato deliberately called upon Bruno Lassere to open our discussion in order to provoke debate. Our discussion this morning has illustrated that there is a very confused and confusing situation in this area, and that there are really quite a number of people working in the same garden. It takes some courage to consider this a permanent mode of operation. How do we, as a European competition authority, consider this situation and the prospects for the future?

I would distinguish between the short term and the medium and long term perspectives. In the short term, we are not behaving as Bruno Lassere has proposed. That is, entering into competition issues to fight for market share with the other competition authorities and sector-specific regulators. On the contrary, I am very much in favour of subsidiarity. I have indicated to all of our colleagues in the national regulatory authorities that we would be perfectly happy if they solve the maximum number of disputes. The more they resolve the better, as long as the result is satisfactory and acceptable from the point of view of European competition rules. Of course, if they do decide in a way contrary to European competition rules, we have and we will intervene in a determined way.

How do we limit the number of cases in which there is a conflict between the national decision and European competition rules? I think we must maximise co-operation between the two levels. Our co-operation with national competition authorities is increasingly close, and our co-operation with the US competition authorities has also improved. We do perceive a very strong desire on the part of the FCC in Washington to co-operate closely with us. Some of the national regulatory authorities, such as the Dutch and the Germans, are also very interested in co-operating closely with us, in order to avoid misunderstandings and divergence. Some of the national regulatory authorities find it difficult, however, to invite DG IV or DG XIII people to their meetings. We can easily live with that, but I am not sure it is the best way to avoid conflict.

Now, in the medium term, when the dust from the initial battles has settled, I believe that we have to undertake a serious streamlining of the situation. I would not say that this should necessarily lead to the disappearance of the regulators. That is, using Louisa Gosling's architecture terminology, I am not sure that a scenario in which most of the houses would be destroyed is the best way of solving the problem. But I am sure that we need a regulatory network at European and international level. The various elements in this network must be able to co-operate satisfactorily and limit themselves to tasks that can reasonably be accomplished at their various levels.

In the development of such a future networking system, I am not sure that we can proceed in a mechanical way, applying the New Zealand or the Australian model. Rather, I believe that we are working, at least in Europe, in a very sensitive environment with deep historic, regional, and cultural differences. Therefore, in the elaboration of this future networking system, we have to take this specific environment into account. The result may be a kind of trial and error process where we progressively reach a solution that offers more satisfactory results to our clients—the companies and the European citizens. But whatever we do, we must respect the somewhat difficult environment in which we are working.

▶ RUBINFELD—As Jim Rill outlined in his paper, my understanding is that the differences between the opinions expressed by the FCC and the DOJ in the *Nynex* case mentioned by Mr. Salsbury are primarily due to the difference in the standards applied by the two agencies in examining mergers. Moreover, let me point out something else that you might find interesting. From an economist's perspective, I have been surprised to find that not only are there substantial economies of scale, but there are also substantial economies of scope in looking at competition issues.

For example, I supervise 10–15 economists who work in the areas of telephony, radio, TV and internet access. That staff is much larger than the comparable staff at the FCC. This capacity is one reason why the FCC is quite happy to collaborate with us. In fact, one of their key people is someone I loaned them for the year because they were so short-staffed. The only reason we do not have more co-operation is that we are legally limited as to the extent to which we can provide information about our merger review process.

▶ SCHERER—Thank you. I would like to make two preliminary remarks, followed by two substantive points. The preliminary remarks are of a 'motherhood and apple pie' nature. I think that regulation should be light-handed and that over-regulation is bad. Secondly, I think that sector-specific regulation should be phased out over time.

Now the two substantive points. First, I think we urgently need to establish a European regulatory body. Mr. Schaub has probably said that, albeit in more couched terms. He said that, in the medium term, we need some serious streamlining. I read that as saying we need a European regulatory body. I do not think that it should be in the medium term, however. It should be very soon, because the market needs it.

The second point is that this regulatory body needs to be in charge, not only of the supra-national aspects of telecommunications regulation, but also of the supra-national aspects of media/communications regulation. In other words, it needs to reflect the regulatory needs of convergence. We are a long way away from that, but we need to think seriously about it.

I would like to give a couple of reasons for these two proposals. We already have numerous European regulatory bodies in place, in addition to DG IV. Mr. Verrue hinted at them in his presentation. We also have numerous regulation procedures in place, but they are in need of serious streamlining. At the European level, we have ONP committees, we have a somewhat cartel-like meeting of the national regulatory authorities, we have frequency regulatory bodies and we have mediation bodies.

Looking at the picture from a new entrant's point of view, however, I do not think that this regulatory chaos, which is probably second only to the system in the United States, works very well. For example, it is very difficult to attempt to license one of these LEO systems in Europe. We tried to do it in 20 different jurisdictions. We took it to frequency management. It is a very long and very tiresome process. Try to get access to sea cables at different landing points within the European Union. There is no co-ordination whatsoever. Try to get a service provider licensed. There is no such thing as a one-stop-shop. You go to each of the different national regulatory authorities, and I do not think we can afford the delays involved in that.

The Commission has attempted to use a few crutches to help industry with that. These crutches are known as communications, access notices and warning letters. Sometimes they are just plain arm-twisting of the national regulatory authorities. But I do not think that will help us in the medium and long term.

The second point concerns regulatory needs with regard to convergence. Some say that the Internet has developed so well because it is a totally unregulated market. This simply is not true. The internet has very serious regulatory issues that need to be tackled. I do not need to quote child pornography, data protection issues, encryption issues. These can no longer be tackled at the national level. They probably cannot be tackled at the supranational level either, but that would, at least, be a starting point. Thus, my plea would be to establish a European regulatory authority and to establish it very quickly. You can dissolve it once the market has evolved, but for the time being, I think the challenge is to establish it.

► SIRAGUSA—Yes. We all agree, but the reality is that the sector-specific national regulatory authorities are alive and kicking. Therefore, I am afraid we have to contend with them at least for the next few years. This means that the Commission has an extremely important role to play. The Commission should not swallow a 'poison pill'. Without the Commission, we would revert back to a situation even worse than national regulation.

Let us not forget that without Articles 82 and 86 [ex 86 and 90], there would be no liberalisation in many of the European countries. Thus, the role of the Commission as the guardian of the situation should continue.

Therefore, I am happy that we have Dr. Verrue and Dr. Schaub here, so that we can suggest two or three practical things that they should do as soon as possible. Some of the national authorities are approaching their role with the principle that nothing can be done without prior authorisation. I already detect such a trend in the very first decrees of the Italian national regulatory authority. In my view, such a requirement of prior authorisation is contrary to the spirit of the Commission's work in this area. Therefore, I think the Commission should give some guidelines regarding the proper role of the national regulatory authorities regarding whether or not a system of prior authorisation is the best way to enhance competition.

The second thing that the Commission could do regards the technological development mentioned earlier. I think we have to look very closely at market definition. We are in a very dangerous situation. We are faced with decisions, some of them Commission Decisions, which establish very narrow market definitions. Remember that they defined TACS and GSM as two separate markets. Now national regulatory authorities are going to apply such a definition. Consequently, I think the Commission should quickly develop new market definitions in line with the technological development. This is necessary because the national regulatory authorities are going to be heavily influenced by the position that the Commission has taken. If the Commission does not correct the situation as soon as possible, we are in deep trouble.

▶ UNGERER—I want to make three points. One point I would add to Mr. Ergas' remark is that it is success that counts. If you look at the situation we face now, you must admit we have made progress. On this issue, as Mr. Verrue has also mentioned, I would recommend that those of you who still have doubts read the implementation report. It is available on the Commission's website and it would make good reading, particularly for those of you who doubt that we have made progress.

Secondly, I wanted to point out that we have not really had an internet discussion here. We have only discussed phone networks. What the internet really means is a regulatory concept that proposes far-reaching privatisation of regulation. Now, that is a different concept, which we have not discussed. In my view, the real issue is to what degree Europe accepts this type of private regulation. Do we really wish to fold the internet into the current regulatory system? If we were to do so, the internet would look very different in Europe, with huge implications. This is a fundamental point for me.

Point three returns us to the European regulatory concept. I think we should also look at the positive effect of competition between regulators in Europe. Do not forget that we have interconnect rates that are based on best practice. You do not have best practice when there is only one regulator. You must simply be correct from the start. My personal conviction is that if we had created a European regulator in 1990, we would not have achieved the degree of liberalisation and competition that we have today.

I wish to make a final, personal, point. It was mentioned that I was deeply involved in the 1987 Green Paper. In fact, I was responsible for that paper and the subsequent liberalisation. There is one lesson to be learned from our experience. We had one basic concept in mind which summarised the whole liberalisation process: less regulation is better than none.

That philosophy dictated that we never define what a value added service was. Instead, we simply identified which voice services had to be protected in the initial stage. This philosophy was fundamental throughout the whole process. It is quite correct that we did not foresee all of the benefits of this liberalisation at this outset. For example, the real benefits came not from liberalisation itself, but from the substantial improvement of the incumbents' competence and services in anticipation of the arrival of competition. We also did not foresee mobile, but the base for mobile development was set by our philosophy. We did not foresee internet, but the liberalisation of value added services was the very base that allowed the development of Internet Service Providers (ISPs) in Europe. These facts indicate that it is important that the basic underlying philosophy is correct.

I like the idea about sunset provisions; but do not believe we have 10 years' time. I think that it must come much quicker.

▶ WATERS—Perhaps I might finish with a non-European perspective because I think that it is not possible to regulate through competition law alone. I think the answer lies in unbundling the retail and wholesale issues. At the wholesale level, you need sector-specific regulation. That may continue, but that must be flavoured with competition law. At the retail level, you need competition law flavoured with sector-specific issues.

At the wholesale level, as Professor Fox noted yesterday, the bottleneck concept is, in its legal and economic terminology, far too narrow to comprehend and support an interconnection regime. So many things that are made available under interconnection agreements are not bottlenecks in the true economic sense: interconnection of databases, provision and carrying of information, for example. Thus, if you rely only on competition law and the essential facility concept, your interconnection regime will be too narrow.

However, it is also important to recognise that there is an emerging wholesale market in the provision of services. If you do not have a competition expert at the interconnection level, you will swallow, and may crush, wholesale competition. Therefore, you must constantly ask yourself whether this regulated interconnection service is now competitive, in which case it should be moved out of the basket of regulated access. That is sector-specific regulation with the flavour of competition law.

At the retail level, the problems with using competition law are not theoretical. They are very practical. The task of market definition is extremely complex. For example, in my jurisdiction, which has a common law administrative law system, the incumbent can take pre-emptive legal action. The incumbent can discipline the regulator by applying for judicial review of each step in the process, including market definition, market power, and abuse. By that stage of this constant judicial review process, the regulator can barely stagger over the finish line. Worse, the courts can actually enjoin the regulator's decision. Of course, if the incumbent does that, it is the end of the matter. Therefore, I think that if you rely on competition law at the retail level, you need to alter it to deal with these practical legal problems.

Finally, I think that Australia provides a good model for moving economic regulation into the realm of competition regulation. We must keep in mind, however, that the only thing Australia has done is to move the boundaries over which the regulators fight. As Alan Fels said, the technical issues remain with another regulator.

However, it is a mistake to think that technical issues are not competition issues. Number portability is a very clear example. It is dealt with in Australia by the technical regulator. The competition regulator can send some directions, but basically it has failed to do so. This system is not working well. The decision about whether to adopt an intelligent network solution is not an engineering question. Rather, it is a pricing question and a competition question. So, unfortunately, if you go along the road to giving competence for these issues to the competition regulator, you have to import an entire truckload of instruments, including technical regulation.

On a concluding note, as an external advisor to Cable & Wireless, I should say that my views are just my own, idiosyncratic views.

▶ AMATO—Thank you. We have gone a bit over time, but I could not strangle such a lively discussion. Before passing the floor to Professor Immenga for his final remarks, let me say a word on this risky dilemma that we are creating between Member State authorities in Europe and regulation at the European level. In the final analysis, the merger of this architecture must be very carefully managed for two simple reasons. One, Europe has subsidiarity; a profoundly rooted principle throughout Europe. Second, the Commission must not be overloaded.

Therefore, the model of the network is ultimately the only practical one. I do not understand why we have been so successful in creating a system of central banks, yet, whenever we analyse other areas, we forget that model. It is a good model. Even though Member State central banks may resent it more than it would be polite for them to admit.

We now turn to Mr. Immenga for the final comments.

▶ IMMENGA—We really could not have expected a richer discussion, both yesterday and today. I cannot attempt to summarise all that we have covered. I will simply close with three remarks about the consensus that I see emerging from our discussion.

The first remark goes back to the architecture and Ms. Gosling's houses. I get the feeling that the house of the antitrust division should be the more prestigious and spacious one. That is what I understand. As Mr. Wolf has recounted, there is a very rigid approach in Germany. In fact, it comes very close, not to the destroying of the sector-specific house, but to the Australian model of the absorption the two houses under one roof. There are other suggestions put forward, such as the codification of competition rules, be they the sector-specific rules or the general competition rules. We talked about the joint decision-making that might be employed, or the bridges that might be used to enhance co-operation between agencies.

As I understand, there is a total consensus on the transitory character of regulatory rules, and that the EU should decide upon their passing. It was quite interesting to hear that there is already a sunset provision in the Dutch regime.

Examining the potential for regulation at the European level, there is strong support for European level regulation, albeit, under the proviso of the maintenance of subsidiarity through network agency forms. European regulation is preferred to ensure the enforcement of Community principles, the maintenance of a level playing field, industry access to world-wide credibility and a single licensing authority for satellite operations going beyond Europe. These are very strong arguments, although one has to see how this might work in practice, particularly given the subsidiarity rule.

My final point concerns convergence. Convergence is a reality in this field. The technological developments have been described in a very convincing manner. Emerging markets, abundance of facilities and new services, suggest that we will have fewer hardware problems. I think the general understanding of this panel is that all of this should not lead to more regulation, but instead to an regulation that does not restrict the emergence of new products and serices.

AMATO—Thank you. Claus Ehlermann, who deserves our gratitude for the organisation of this workshop, will provide the final words.

EHLERMANN—After what we consider to be a very successful meeting, I am grateful to all of you, and my mind is now churning. My special thanks goes to Louisa Gosling for her physical and intellectual input regarding the development of themes. If we carry this work to publication, it is thanks to her and Laraine Laudati.

PANEL THREE

INSTITUTIONS AND COMPETENCE

2

WORKING PAPERS

I

*Ulrich Immenga**

Statement of the Rapporteur on Panel Three

I.

The discussion of panel three warrants three preliminary observations. Firstly, although there is an intensive discussion concerning the development of rules and regulations, institutional questions have often been neglected and the institutions responsible for the application of these rules and regulations have not generally been the core of the debate. This is particularly true in academic circles. Secondly, it must be stressed, that the best, the most modern, and the most sophisticated legislation will not attain its objectives, and will be of little substantive value, if the tools for a strict application and enforcement of the law are lacking. The danger of a tiger without teeth really does exist. Thirdly, law enforcement does not depend solely on the potential and professional competence of law enforcers. The independence of the institution plays a crucial role. This is, in particular, a question of the composition and legal status of commissioners. Laws which are designed to ensure workable competition on deregulated markets must be protected against politics or pressures from the industries concerned.

II.

This panel focusses on the different bodies of law which are applied to specific sectors of the economy which may be described as network markets. Regulatory laws and antitrust laws determine the structure of these markets. This parallel legislation requires a framework for institutions, their competences, and their co-ordination. The general approach, at least in Europe, following a process of deregulation, is the creation of national regulatory agencies (NRA) to replace or complement (the traditional) antitrust authorities (AA). This development is partly due to directives of the European Community. This is the case in the field of telecommunications which accounts for the greater part of the analyses presented in this panel, although some also make observations about the media and other sectors.

* Professor of Law and, Director, Institute of International Economic Law, University of Göttingen, Germany.

The European pattern, however, is clearly not universal. In New Zealand, for example, there is no specific agency in the telecommunications sector nor any specific legislation. The development of market forces in telecommunications is left solely to the antitrust laws. It appears that a sufficiently competitive market structure has indeed emerged in the wake of deregulation.

The Australian legislator entrusted the evolving telecommunication markets exclusively to the existing antitrust authority. As is explained in the discussions of the panel, there were several reasons for this decision. With regard to existing deregulations in different fields there was a general understanding of a predominance of the culture of antitrust. This policy had been enforced by a completely independent commission. The responsibility of a general competition regulator should produce economies of scope and allow for a coordination of instruments. Furthermore, the advantages of a 'one-stop shop' have been taken into consideration. In practice, a new branch of the existing antitrust commission had been instituted to resolve the technical problems emerging in the telecommunications sector and to introduce the indispensable expertise.

In Germany, not unlike the situation in Australia, there was a comprehensive and serious debate on whether the Federal Cartel Office should be the sole institution to apply—besides the general competition laws—those specific regulations deemed necessary for the regulation of particular issues in the telecommunications sector or whether a special department should be added to the Federal Cartel Office to prepare and participate in any decisions affecting the sector of telecommunications. On the academic level, the prevailing view supported this policy which might have helped avert several conflicts which had emerged and which will be discussed later. In the last instance, however, Germany joined the general European pattern.

III.

There appears to be a consensus, however, that pure competition law is not able to respond to the specific issues of newly deregulated markets. This consensus arises from the analyses presented and the general discussion. Several arguments supporting this view emerged. First of all, one must bear in mind that, contrary to the objectives of general competition laws, competition does not exist in newly deregulated sectors but has to be created, in particular, by the introduction of access rules. In this context the imposition of prices for interconnection would appear to be unavoidable. Rules of transparency in matters of accounting and financial reports have to be introduced as well as instruments of preventive control. Competition laws are generally considered to play an important role, both now and in the future, in the development of market structures in the telecommunications sector. A number of cases discussed in the papers (e.g. France, Spain, Italy) confirm this assumption. They deal in particular with dominant positions of former state monopolies and issues related to the doctrine of 'essential facilities'. Furthermore, it has been pointed out that competition law will have to play a crucial and more important role in the context of converging economic sectors such as telecommunications, audio-visual (broadcasting) and information technology (the Internet). A cable directive of the EC partly addresses these problems.

In particular, the Spanish paper presents an interesting suggestion regarding future developments in the telecom markets. It starts from the assumption that the most successful upcoming competitors, including the former monopolists, will create oligopolistic market patterns. Therefore, specific obligations should relate to transparency (separate accounting, publication of prices, and so forth), and to information requirements with regard to rebates, service quality, etc. This is described as 'light-handed regulation', or regulation which might make regulations disappear gradually.

In sum, there is little doubt that competition law will always constitute an indispensable element in evolving network markets.

IV.

The main focus, therefore, is on the debate concerning the lines between regulation and competition law, the status and competences of agencies, and their interaction. The arguments turn on the pre-eminence of NRAs, the subsidiarity of AAs, requirements of mutual information and interaction, and on the obligation of joint decisions in specific issues. A German example in this context is the determination of relevant markets and their domination.

The nature of specific issues and obligations should determine the relevant lines of demarcation. A more systematic approach appears in discussions in Germany and in the French paper by Jenny. Accordingly, we can make a necessary distinction between technical regulation, economic regulation, and antitrust enforcement. Obviously, the NRAs are responsible for technical regulation: for instance, the distribution of frequencies (licensing), the safety of equipment, or numbering. Two important questions, however, have to be answered. What are the subjects and institutional requirements of economic regulations? And to what extent should the application of competition law be entrusted to AAs on their own, or to the AAs and the NRAs together?

As far as technical issues are concerned the role of NRAs is not debated in a controversial sense. Economic regulations are, for example, universal service obligations, market access provisions, and rules on interconnection, their mechanism and prices. The general view presented by the papers attributes these competences to the newly created NRAs. There are, however, no distinct lines of demarcation. Who, for instance, controls prices to end users? In Germany it is the NRA, whereas in France it is the competence of the AA. In general, this is a field which requires a great deal more exploration and which raises serious questions for each (national/domestic) legislation.

The first issue is how to handle overlapping competences. Market access regulations as a part of the above mentioned category of economic regulation may also concern the antitrust authorities which control the abuse of dominant positions by the application of general competition laws. On the EC level, the respective instruments are provided under Article 82 [ex 86] of the Treaty. The emerging importance of the essential facilities doctrine must be stressed in this context. This rule, originally developed in the United States, has been applied in the EC in recent years and has even been implemented into German law. In addition to the issue of market access, the antitrust law is also competent to focus on the price payable, for instance, for interconnection. Furthermore, some legislation, as in Germany, includes competition rules in the regulatory scheme. Other legislation applies different standards to antitrust issues in specific sectors. In the United States, for example, merger control authorises the Federal Communications Commission to evaluate mergers under a public interest standard beyond antitrust considerations which are determining the control of mergers by the Department of Justice.

The solutions which are presented to resolve potential conflicts are quite different and not really clear in the various bodies of (national) legislation. Different kinds of co-operation and agency interaction are applied. The papers presented by France, for example, describe the bridges between both authorities in the form of (mutual/reciprocal) information requirements. The NRA may seek non-binding advice from the AA on any competition matter. The NRA must refer to the AA in cases of potential abuse of a dominant position or anti-competitive practices. In Italy, similarly, mutual information and consultation is required. The AA must apply to the NRA for a prior non-binding advice on decisions concerning agreements, the abuse of dominant positions, or mergers which involve enterprises operating in the communication industry. The NRA must apply to the AA for prior advice in order, for example, to identify significant market power of a firm, or to decide on the conditions of interconnection with, and access to, a network.

This system of mutual information and collaboration before a decision may be taken by one agency which includes material aspects of the other sector, also appears to shape the Spanish and German approach. In Germany, even a joined decision is required between the agencies to decide on competition issues such as the definition of relevant markets.

In general, priority is accorded to the regulatory rules if they are adequately specified. This is obviously not the case, if the regulatory provisions rely on a broad 'public interest standard' as in the case of the provisions of the US Federal Communications Act, as compared to the general antitrust rules. On the other hand, the AAs retain their powers within their traditional areas of competence. The allocation of competences, however, generally requires a mutual respect for elements and experiences of the other agency's objectives. The general debate has indeed confirmed this comprehensive view.

V.

Some of the papers advocate a transitional character of regulatory provisions, a kind of 'sunset rules'. This idea is based on the—perhaps optimistic—expectation that the markets concerned will gradually become more competitive so that regulations will not ultimately be necessary and may simply fade away. A convincing example presented in the Spanish paper are markets for voice telephony. Based on particularly fixed networks, regulation is needed during a longer period of time than in the field of mobile telephony where parallel networks already have been developed. There is a clear consensus that the power to decide on the end of the transitory period should not lie with the NRAs as the latter tend to identify themselves with the industry being supervised. It has been argued that this power might be placed with the European Commission (DG IV). In the Netherlands, the need for regulatory provisions is reconsidered every four years. Germany entrusts the independent Monopolies Commission with the evaluation of the activity report of the NRA with regard to the level of workable competition attained in the telecommunication markets. In particular, the Monopolies Commission is asked to evaluate whether specific regulatory provisions are still necessary.

VI.

In the context of interrelationship between the respective authorities the judicial review of their decisions may generate conflicts. Germany instituted different appeals mechanisms for the two agencies: administrative courts for the NRA and the general civil courts for decisions of the Federal Cartel Office. This two-way judicial review is by no means justified and may lead to serious conflicts. France, altogether more enlightened and prudent, decided to bring the appeals of both agencies to the same judicial body, the *Cour d'Appel* in Paris. This solution provides consistency, particularly in areas of potential conflict.

The question of the institutional independence of the agencies has not really been discussed intensively and is, indeed, a predominantly political matter. To what extent does the nomination of Commissioners reflect governmental intentions? In this context it is important to know whether the parliament or the government is in the more influential position. The United Kingdom is an example of where head of an NRA, in this case OFTEL, is appointed for five years by a parliamentary process. In Spain, the members of the NRA are selected by the government on the recommendation of the Ministry of Public Works. This procedure provides a broad margin of discretion to the government, and the NRA has been accused of a certain degree of politicisation. In Germany, there had been a public discussion with regard to the first appointment of the head of the NRA. The focus was on the background of the candidates and whether this should be of a more regulatory or a more competitive nature. This debate underlines the importance of individuals who must in fact perform their duties with a high degree of responsibility. A thorough examination of the legal status and nomination process of the members of the NRAs and AAs should provide more information in this field.

The potential objectives of international institutions were discussed, particularly in the light of the convergence of telecommunication and media and the globalisation of the economy. With regard to the European Union, the discussion revealed broad support for the competences of the Commission. One of the most convincing arguments was that a system whereby national licences on frequencies would be bound together to create a 'continental ticket', would generate world-wide credibility for the European system. Furthermore, there was a strong opinion in favour of the harmonisation of regulatory principles, based on the firms' need for a 'level playing field', and for a uniformity of rules and regulations so as to avoid 'forum shopping' within the industry. The Community principles should be locally enforced. These were the principle answers to the broad question as to whether regulatory principles might, or actually do, differ within the European Community. The broad support was cautioned by a remark which underlined the limits of EC competences in the light of the subsidiarity principle. The papers refer in particular to a harmonisation of numbering policies, guidelines for interconnection agreements, and the allocation of mobile cellular licences. Furthermore, universal services obligations should be implemented on the basis of common rules.

On the international level, furthermore, the WTO is emerging as a policy forum for telecommunications in addition to the International Telecommunication Union, which has traditionally been a key player in terms of standardisation. The first achievement on this level is the WTO Agreement. The competences of the WTO were invoked particularly in relation to two challenging issues. One is the increasing globalisation of the industry and the parallel convergence of telecommunications and media. The second issue is for the involvement of the WTO on the basis of the policy underlying Article 86 [ex 90] of the Consolidated Treaty. This is a, to date, unique instrument to attack those restraints on competition that are caused by Nation States. State-led anti-competitive tendencies, camouflaged as national public interest, may well be due to a desire to defend incumbent authorities.

Convergence is evidently supported by the process of digitalisation which needs less hardware to perform an increasing number of functions. In this way, convergence will lead to merging markets and an abandoning of facilities and new services. This process will constitute an institutional challenge—to what extent should existing regulatory authorities extend their present competences? In this context it is interesting to note that Italy has already brought broadcasting, together with telecommunications, under the auspices of a single authority. The paper in question, by the Director General of DG XIII, reports a substantial support for the separation of transport functions and content rules, thus moving towards a common set of rules for networks. On the other hand, a clear majority are in favour of building on current regulatory structures rather than introducing an integrated regulatory framework for all services. The discussion linked to this context supported in general a cautious approach with 'lean regulation' being the relevant catch phrase. This position was principally based on the argument that the process of convergence which leads to multimedia networks and services should not be restricted. Emerging new products should be able to make their way.

II

Stuart N. Brotman*

Developing a New Institutional Framework to Reconcile Communications and Competition Policy Concern

Introduction

iewing market developments through the separate lenses of communications olicy and competition policy often creates different perceptions and out-omes.[1] Since the late 1970s, US communications policy-makers, especially nose within the Executive Branch who are not delegated with regulatory ɛsponsibilities, have been pursuing long-term strategies to support the dual olicy goals of competition and deregulation. In contrast, antitrust law nforcers, such as those in the US Department of Justice (DOJ), view compe-ltion policy more on a case-by-case basis, their remedies are crafted to reflect he facts at hand, and often developed to impose structural rather than behav-ɔural solutions to anti-competitive problems.

Fortunately, there have been exceptions to this general principle, perhaps ɩone more striking or successful as the joint efforts of the National ʾelecommunications and Information Administration (NTIA) of the US Department of Commerce and the Antitrust Division of the US Department of ustice in considering the development of pay cable television during its nfancy.

In 1979–1980, while serving as Special Assistant to the Director of the NTIA, I experienced first-hand how these agencies developed a durable—ɪlbeit *ad hoc*—process to share information and perspectives regarding the levelopment of the pay cable industry. This industry, then dominated by a sin-ɟle distributor, Home Box Office (HBO), became the focus of a Justice Department civil investigation at the beginning of 1979, after a group of film ʂtudios and their trade association, the Motion Picture Association of America, mounted a concerted lobbying effort in Washington, DC.

---

* Research Fellow, Harvard Law School.
[1] Both approaches work well in their own domains, but the different focal points—ɔne concentrating on the forest, the other on the trees—can create conflicting agendas. Lacking formal mechanisms for institutional co-operation, agencies within the US Executive Branch usually support their own activities rather than actively seek to coor-dinate them.

The core of their argument related to the alleged bottleneck power that pa cable distributors generally, and HBO in particular, had with respect to keep ing film licence fees low. Under this analysis, the alleged bottleneck also create anti-competitive effects because pay cable distributors were vertically inte grated with large cable multiple system operators (MSOs). These MSOs, b virtue of their vertical linkage to pay cable distribution and coupled with the grant of exclusive municipal franchises to operate, created an environment tha foreclosed competition by a non-affiliated pay cable network.

When the outline of this case was brought to the Antitrust Division, attracted immediate attention. To antitrust enforcers, it merited further factua analysis to determine the patterns of practice at hand. If such patterns were i place, the Justice Department believed it had a strong monopolisation cas against HBO and its parent company, Time, based on anti-competitive vertica integration under the Sherman Act.

During this period, NTIA met with film studio lobbyists and viewed th alleged bottlenecks as serious, too. Its prism, however, was not confined to tra ditional antitrust analysis. Rather, as an agency responsible for developin, long-range communications policy, NTIA was more focused on crafting national plan for cable development for the 1980s and beyond. To the greates extent possible, NTIA sought to foster policies that would enable marketplac forces rather than government regulation to prevail.

This philosophy differed sharply from the traditional American model o regulated monopolies developed during the New Deal and embodied in th Communications Act of 1934, as amended. The new model, as compared to th old, sought to create an environment that supported competition by nev entrants rather than maintain the status quo of monopoly (e.g. AT&T) or oli gopoly (e.g. the broadcast television networks) industry operations that wer kept in check by pervasive government regulation.

NTIA did not want to develop policies without a well-formed factual back ground detailing past practices and future trends, nor did it want to create a collision course with other Executive Branch agencies such as the Department of Justice. After all, if the DOJ imposed a structural remedy for pay cable (tha is, a forced divestiture of HBO by Time) through a consent decree, or if a court ruling fashioned such a remedy, NTIA's policies would need to reflect that remedy. NTIA preferred developing policies in this area with a less-constrained set of options.

The Justice Department, which had a great deal of antitrust experience in evaluating mature industries with relatively minor technology aspects, realised early on in its HBO/Time civil investigation that this case posed special prob lems. Foremost among these problems were the relative infancy of the pay cable market, the rapid technological changes that the cable television industry was experiencing, and the scope of relevant market definition. Lacking both the specialised expertise and a research budget and staff to undertake a sustained analysis of pay cable developments, the Justice Department looked with considerable interest at NTIA's policy activities. Like NTIA, the Antitrust Division of the DOJ was sensitive to potential conflicts within the Executive Branch that might arise if it proceeded down one road (i.e. an antitrust prosecution or consent decree), while NTIA was making recommendations that either contradicted DOJ or suggested that the Justice Department was basing its case on an incomplete or inaccurate record.

The heads of both agencies, Henry Geller of NTIA and John Shenefield of the Antitrust Division, agreed to have their agencies work in a parallel yet complementary fashion. This consisted of NTIA staying in close contact with the DOJ when NTIA was developing a Request for Proposal (RFP) to retain a contract research firm to assist in data and information analysis. NTIA also promised to keep DOJ lawyers in the loop as this pay cable study commenced, including making available databases and other information that would be compiled internally and externally. For its part, the DOJ agreed to make available to NTIA, for confidential review, a complete set of background memoranda prepared for the HBO/Time, civil investigation as well as updates regarding the interviews and depositions generated throughout the civil investigative process.

Each agency would continue with its work and neither would have the ability to interfere with the other's internal processes. The emphasis was on good faith, ongoing coordination so that both sides, irrespective of the policy direction pursued, would have confidence that their analyses would be based on the best available context for decision-making, encompassing both macro and micro concerns. This case study represents a heretofore untold success story. The details concerning how US pay cable policy reached a unified vision follows.

II. Pay Cable Policy Development

In September 1979, following a six-month RFP publication and review process, NTIA awarded contract #NT-79-SAC-00027 to Technology and Economics, Inc. (T+E), a contract research firm with headquarters in Cambridge, Massachusetts and a branch office in Washington, DC. This study was performed for the NTIA by T+E to provide NTIA with background information, data and a description of events and trends in the fields of cable television and pay cable.

While NTIA specified that the study was to cover both the cable television and pay cable fields, it also stated that the purpose of gathering data was to provide NTIA with background information to assist the agency in policy formulation in the pay cable field, and that the emphasis of the study therefore would be on pay cable.

In the project's statement of work the NTIA indicated that its interest in reviewing questions relating to the pay cable industry stemmed from the new thrust of federal regulatory policy in the communications field that emphasises deregulation. 'Federal regulations regarding cable television programming—both signal carriage and pay services—have been, or are in the process of being eliminated,' the agency said:

> Accordingly, the cable industry will be freer to operate in the marketplace than it has been. The elimination of a federal regulatory scheme here is partially dependent, however, on full and fair competition among cable operators and those supplying programming services.

NTIA thus sought to obtain a comprehensive picture of the marketplace, and a projection of its future, so that it could assess 'whether or not new federal efforts are needed to insure competition.'

Underlying the NTIA's emphasis on pay cable services was the agency's belief that revenues from this source would provide the most important impetus for the building of cable systems in urban centres and major metropolitan areas. For this reason, a full understanding of the pay programming industry was essential for NTIA's policy-making as cable was set to emerge as a major US communications medium in the 1980s.

In the late 1960s and early 1970s, when urban planners, social scientists and futurists became aware of the potential of cable television for expanding viewing options and delivering other communications services, they propagated a wave of enthusiasm for the 'wired nation' and a 'television of abundance' whose coming they regarded as imminent and whose impact they regarded as substantial.

When the 'wired nation' and its alleged benefits failed to materialise swiftly, a reaction set in. Extravagant forecasts of the functions that cable would perform became known as 'blue sky' and the notion of cable's importance as the new communications medium was dismissed as 'the cable fable.'

Neither side in the controversy clearly foresaw the development that would create an economic base for building high-capacity cable systems in urban and metropolitan environments. These developments were set in motion in 1972 when a small company, Home Box Office (HBO), signed up several cable systems in Pennsylvania to carry a pay TV service. For this service, the cable subscriber paid a regular monthly fee in addition to the monthly charge for the cable service, and the cable operator shared a substantial portion of the revenues generated.

Pay cable, thus introduced, grew slowly and had little impact until HBO decided to begin disseminating its programming by satellite in 1975, and the Federal Communications Commission (FCC) approved use of relatively inexpensive small antennae to receive satellite transmissions in 1976. This placed satellite reception of pay cable programming within reach of virtually every cable system.

The overwhelmingly favourable response of cable subscribers to pay programming, coupled by a federal court decision that lifted prior regulatory restraints on pay cable programme offerings, caused the pay cable industry to 'take off' in 1977. At the same time, the potential of the satellite earth-station technology for the relatively inexpensive national dissemination of many kinds of programming, supported by a variety of economic arrangements, became clear. Programming services proliferated to a point at which, by 1979, the full capacity of RCA's Satcom I, the satellite used for cable programming, was insufficient to meet the demand. In effect, a new television system had been born.

This expansion of US television, so earnestly sought for so long by many parties concerned with oligopoly control of over-the-air TV, and so often urged as the proper destiny of cable, came without extensive government or civic intervention when both technology and demonstrated consumer demand provided an economic underpinning.

The coming of pay cable and of networking by satellite produced several consequences. One of these was to make the building of cable systems in urban and metropolitan areas, where the marginal economics of old-style cable service had retarded or prevented system construction, suddenly appear attractive to investors and to large communications companies. This produced a 'gold rush' for urban cable franchises beginning in 1979.

In conducting the study for NTIA, T+E carefully noted how often planners and policy-makers, carried away by the movement and excitement in the fields of satellite transmission, programming expansion and cable growth, failed to relate their views to the status of the cable industry 'as it exists in the US today' (that is, at the end of the 1970s). There was, in fact, a wide gulf separating tomorrow's dreams from today's cable plant, and this fact had an important bearing on policy formulation, including decisions at the DOJ regarding whether to pursue an antitrust suit against HBO and Time, Inc.

In many respects, cable television in 1979 could be regarded, not as one industry, but as three. They can be described as follows:

- *Community Antenna Television:* This group consisted of systems that delivered no more than twelve channels of material to their subscribers. In most such systems, a majority of channels was devoted to the retransmission of local and distant over-the-air signals. There often was competition for use of the few remaining channels, which could be devoted to pay TV or other non-broadcast satellite transmitted programming, and locally-originated material. Figures for 1978, the latest available at the time of preparation of T+E's report, showed that 70% of all US cable systems fell into this category.

- *Cable Television:* Systems in this category delivered more than twelve, and up to thirty-five, channels. A sub-group consisted of systems with twenty channel capacity and interactive capability, built in accordance with the FCC's 1972 cable rules. For most policy purposes, however, these systems could be viewed as a whole. In general, cable television systems transmitted a number of non-broadcast satellite-transmitted and locally-originated services in addition to local and distant signals. In 1978, 12% of US cable systems had 13–20 channel capacity, and 14% had channel capacity in excess of 20 channels. Combined, this total represented about a quarter of all cable systems in the country.

- *Broadband Communications Systems:* These systems, which deliver over thirty-five channels, with full interactive capabilities and feature a wide range of non-broadcast programming, were the type being proposed in urban franchising competitions. At the time of T+E's study, none existed.

Other important types of divisions, not fully correlated with the above groupings, related to the number of subscribers served and location of systems in rural, urban and metropolitan areas. For example, in 1978, the number of communities with cable systems serving less than 5,000 subscribers was 3,794; the number of communities with cable systems serving more than 5,000 subscribers was 3,675. Roughly half of all cable systems, therefore, served a subscriber base far smaller in size than the urban population groupings to which the attention of policy-makers and others increasingly was being drawn.

To summarise, the United States at the time of the NTIA study and the DOJ pay cable civil investigation had no experience with broadband communications. Rather, it had, at best, only moderate experience with cable television systems as defined above. The only form of cable with which there had been considerable experience was twelve-channel community antenna television, whose resemblance to the projected broadband communications systems that were to be built in urban centres in the 1980s was weak.

The fundamental differences among the three categories of systems with respect to existing or potential subscriber bases; pressures from consumers; and economic incentives inevitably would differentiate them in their development and the types of services offered. In addition, consumers had yet to indicate definitively their choices and preferences in the area of programming—namely, how much they would pay for what services over time.

Additional problems were posed by the pace of change in the cable, pay cable, satellite and related software industries. These industries had been growing and changing so rapidly that any compilation of data and information suffered from near-instant obsolescence. In fact, since certain material in the NTIA report itself was compiled by other sources at some date significantly prior to the time when it became part of the report's text, T+E's researchers often had the sensation of the astronomer who looks back in time when looking out into space. New events were transpiring so quickly as to make even the best and most recent compilations seem like period pieces.

Thus, almost from the time of publication, the report, its background and data volumes were not serviceable as a fully current source of information. They did, however, provide significant value as a portrait of the pay cable industry at a certain point in time, with historical information taking the story back to its beginnings. They were also useful as a seedbed of information from which policy questions could be framed in ways that would far outlive the currency of the specific data.

This portrait showed that for many years, the cable industry enjoyed steady growth, despite both restrictive FCC regulatory policies and the 1974–1976 recession. In 1979, there were about 4,100 cable systems in the US, serving some 16 million homes, which represented about 20% of all homes with television. About 26.4 million homes were passed by existing cable installations, which meant that about 55% of all homes where cable was available took the service.

At the beginning of the 1980s, this portrait depicted cable as standing poised at the threshold of important growth and change. During the first half of that new decade, cable franchises would be granted in many major cities and metropolitan areas. Cable systems would be built in these locations with greater channel capacity and would offer a greater mix of services than had characterised the previous generation of systems. At the same time, many existing systems would be rebuilt, enlarging their channel capacity and enabling their subscribers to receive a larger selection of broadcast and non-broadcast material. By the middle of the decade, cable was projected to reach some 30% of all US TV homes, at which time its impact on the entire existing system of television broadcasting, television advertising and programme distribution was expected to become substantial.

The prime moving force behind this new era of cable television would be the advent of satellite-transmitted pay programming. If the expansion of the cable industry could be described in economic terms as fully satisfactory, the expansion of the pay cable industry could be described as meteoric. In 1975, when the transmission of pay programming to cable systems by satellite began, the total number of pay subscribers was 265,000. By 1977, when small TVROs—television receive-only earth stations—were coming into general use by cable systems for the reception of pay services, the number of pay cable subscribers had risen to 1,174,000. In each of the two succeeding years it more than doubled, reaching 4,353,00 by mid-1979. Moreover, by mid-1979, 36% of all cable systems were carrying pay programming, and 40% of all cable subscribers who had a pay service available to them took it. Both these figures, moreover, were projected to continue on an upward curve in the early 1980s.

By mid-1979, HBO and its affiliate, Telemation Program Services, together controlled 65% of the US pay cable market, with 3 million subscribers and 1,200 cable system affiliates. As of 30 June 1980, the standing of three major pay cable suppliers was as follows: HBO (4,705,000 subscribers); Showtime (1,150,000 subscribers); and The Movie Channel (401,000 subscribers).

HBO had also entered the programming field and operated a syndication division that developed original programming for cable. By 1979, it had produced over 100 shows and had another 50 in development with a budget of $13 million US. HBO's parent firm, Time Inc., also owned American TV and Communications (ATC), the nation's second largest cable MSO, which had 905,000 subscribers in 1979, 364,000 of whom were subscribers to a pay service.

Showtime, the second largest supplier, was jointly owned by Viacom, a communications conglomerate, and Teleprompter, the nation's largest MSO, with 1,180,000 subscribers in 1979, of whom 341,600 subscribed to a pay service. Launched in 1976, Showtime began to disseminate its programming via the Satcom I satellite in March 1978. Like HBO, Showtime increasingly became involved in original movie and programme production, with a 7–8 million dollar budget in 1979.

The Movie Channel, the third largest pay cable network, was operated by Warner-Amex Cable Communications, a company jointly owned by Warner Communications (a diversified communications firm with interests in publishing, motion pictures, TV programming and music recording) and the American Express Company. Warner-Amex was the nation's fourth largest cable MSO, with 630,000 subscribers in 1979, of whom 113,000 were pay subscribers. Originally called the Star Channel, the service initially was intended only for Warner-Amex cable systems, but in 1979 it was renamed, expanded to a 24-hour-a-day service offering movies only and made available to all cable systems.

Ownership concentration in the cable industry was not heavy, however, and ad not been increasing. In 1978, for example, the eight largest MSOs accounted >r 35.6% of all cable subscribers, down from 39% in 1975. Each of the three major pay suppliers was affiliated with one of the nation's top cable MSOs.

As the pay cable industry grew, distinctions between and among producer, supplier and exhibitor had become blurred through vertical integration of comanies and by the increasing tendency of major pay suppliers to engage in film nd programme production and all forms of software distribution. Meanwhile, he software procurement scene continued to be dominated by the failure of major film suppliers to be reconciled with the payment arrangements for pay V rights that HBO had succeeded in forcing on film producers, and from which other suppliers had chosen to benefit rather than seeking to undercut.

For their best films, movie studios hoped to earn fifty to sixty cents per subcriber or more for pay TV rights, but instead, they found themselves accepting orty cents per subscriber from major pay distributors, who controlled the only meaningful access to the pay market. Moderately successful films were obtained at twenty to forty cents per subscriber, and relatively unimportant films were purchased by the distributor at a flat fee regardless of subscriber count.

In 1978, a cable system in Thibodaux, Louisiana owned by Wometco— which did not have an ownership affiliation with any pay cable service— became the first system to offer HBO and Showtime to its customers. Many subscribers took both, and the pattern was repeated as other systems experimented with tiering in 1979. It became clear beyond doubt that the consumer appetite for pay cable was not satiated with a single pay programming service.

As late as July 1979, however, no system owned by Time Inc.'s ATC carried Showtime as a second tier, and no system owned by Teleprompter carried HBO as a second tier. But in the ensuing months, the resistance of vertically integrated systems to carrying the pay service of competitors substantially dissolved. By June 1980, Showtime was available as a second tier in some ninety HBO markets, including some ATC systems, and the trend toward tiering was continuing to gather momentum. One reason for the change in corporate approach was the demonstrated fact of increased profitability. Another was the increased tempo of franchising activity in urban metropolitan centres, in which each bidder, regardless of vertical linkage sought to remain competitive; this meant that each was forced by the marketplace to offer a number of channels of pay service.

III. Discovering the Critical Unknown Factor

As work on the NTIA study progressed, NTIA and T+E increasingly became

aware of the impact of current activity in the field of cable franchising on th
shape and form of pay cable services, and on the evolution of cable televisio
generally. Consequently, NTIA authorised a supplement to T+E's contract t
study the current cable franchising scene and simultaneously briefed the DO
so that the Antitrust Division could recognise that a critical aspect of its civ
investigation might be subject to new information. The Justice Departmen
appreciated being made aware of this, and requested another briefing after
more complete analysis was submitted by T+E.

For most of the 1970s, the urban franchising scene proceeded along line
that were largely determined by three factors: the general history of the indus
try; certain requirements of the FCC's 1972 cable rules; and the rise and fall o
the expectations that were generated by the initial enthusiasm for the 'wire
nation' and the 'television of abundance.' During the last two years of th
decade—the years when NTIA and the DOJ were pursuing their analyses—
events transformed this scene beyond recognition.

Cable television was originally developed to provide better reception o
over-the-air TV signals and a wider selection of such signals than could b
received in various areas with inferior TV reception. The transmission capability of some of the early equipment did not exceed five channels, but by the early
1950s, twelve-channel equipment had been introduced, and by 1970 it still wa
the staple of the industry. Until 1970, cable systems were used almost exclusively for such retransmission.

An additional type of transmission that had become the subject of experi-
mentation by 1970 was the origination of local programming directly over an
otherwise unused channel of the cable system. Time and weather channels were
also introduced, with the camera fixed on a clock and/or weather information.

The FCC asserted regulatory jurisdiction over cable in the 1960s. From that
time until the mid-1970s, this power was used principally to protect the over-the-
air broadcasting industry from what was regarded as the competitive threat of
cable. The FCC's most ambitious rule-making effort in the field resulted in its
1972 cable rules that established immensely complicated limitations on the number and type of broadcasting signals that cable systems could retransmit.

By 1975, franchising activity followed a predictable pattern. The basic service offered by cable—its only meaningful source of revenue—continued to be
the retransmission of broadcast signals. The value that a given area or community might have had for the purpose of building a cable system was determined by the number of persons in that community who might want such a
service compared with the cost of building the system to provide it. Well-established formulas and substantial experience gave the industry the tools which to
predict the relevant costs and returns with great accuracy.

Under the FCC's new rules, new systems in communities of any significant size were required to have twenty-channel capability, although in many instances only twelve were activated. Most systems made provisions for a channel of local programming, although this offering was based on its community relations value rather than on its ability to generate revenue. In certain medium-sized cities, a 35-channel capacity was installed. Such systems, however, constituted a small minority of new systems being built.

According to the calculations of the cable industry, there were many places in the country where the building of cable systems would not have been profitable. These included the nation's largest cities, where construction costs would be high and where the availability of a good assortment of over-the-air signals reduced the saleability of cable's only revenue-producing service.

That service—pay cable programming—had struck a gush of unmet public demand which astonished even the most optimistic of its commercial backers. It could be sold anywhere, regardless of the relative availability of over-the-air TV fare, which formerly dictated the economics of cable when cable was solely a retransmission service. Suddenly, with pay cable as the driving force, the wiring of major cities and urban centres became attractive. In 1979, the 'gold rush' for the remaining ungranted big-city and metropolitan cable franchises began in earnest.

The limited number of franchises still available became so valuable to the competing companies that they began offering systems and services in hopes of outstripping competitors and receiving the coveted awards. The meaning of the term 'state-of-the-art' shifted from month to month, with untested equipment and services routinely being offered in franchise bids. The cities, for their part, were aware of the value of the franchises and used their bargaining position to secure the most they could from the bidders.

Franchise demands and promises thus began a swift upward spiral. The externality of urban franchise competition represented a critical unknown factor that neither NTIA nor the DOJ foresaw when they began their work on separate policy tracks. It was destined to change the ability of pay cable networks to maintain market share by virtue of having a bottleneck vertical linkage with a cable MSO.

By the end of 1980, cable franchises under construction, when completed, were to add 27 million homes to the 27.3 million passed by cable at the end of 1979. By the end of 1981, only 17 million of the 75 million homes in the top 100 markets were projected to be without installed or franchised cable systems. Lucrative franchises in suburban areas, when put out for a bid, usually attracted ten or more bidders, while bids for major cities often attracted five or six. In both situations, the externality of intense franchise competition would erode any bottleneck between jointly-owned pay cable distributors and MSOs.

IV. The Aftermath

After this analysis was shared with the DOJ staff, the Antitrust Division independently concluded that regardless of the seriousness of the anti-competitive effects it had documented in its civil investigation, if it proceeded with a formal complaint, the erosion of the pay cable bottleneck through new urban franchising would seriously undermine its case. Like NTIA, it remained sensitive to any potential future bottlenecks that might occur regardless of franchising.

As a result, the DOJ turned its attention to a new pay cable distributor—Premiere—organised by four major film studios (Columbia, Paramount, Twentieth Century Fox and Universal) in 1980. Premiere was the move industry's self-help remedy to combat HBO, since neither NTIA nor the DOJ had moved as aggressively as the studios had wished. Premiere was designed to create a nine-month distribution window, so that films by the equity partners would be made available exclusively to Premiere for nine months before they would be made available to competing pay cable networks such as HBO and Showtime.

Given the popularity of pay cable movies, the import of Premiere was that it would, in effect, eliminate real competition in the pay cable market by ensuring that only the network that was vertically-linked at the production end would offer unedited, uninterrupted movies when consumers desired them the most—soon after they had left cinemas and not nearly a year after they had been aired on another pay cable network.

Thus, with some irony, the bottleneck in pay cable that was ultimately pursued by the DOJ was one created by the companies that had first brought the allegations to both NTIA and the Justice Department. Moving swiftly and with an enhanced understanding of pay cable market dynamics by virtue of NTIA's briefings and the T+E study, the Antitrust Division successfully sought a federal court injunction against Premiere launching its operations.

With Premiere out of the picture, the other pay cable distributors continued to compete, as NTIA had projected, ultimately negotiating higher licence fees with the film studios to gain exclusive access to certain films or to entire libraries of a single studio (e.g. Showtime negotiated an exclusive deal with Paramount in the early 1980s).

V. Conclusion

And so this case study comes to an end, indeed to a happy end for both the communications policy and competition policy agencies involved. It would have been highly unlikely, and probably impossible, for such a positive outcome to have emerged had both NTIA and DOJ followed protocol and ignored what the other agency was discovering independently. Foresight and patience prevailed. By following the moving target of pay cable development rather than making decisions based on an analysis of a series of freeze-frames, both NTIA and the DOJ could factor in what was likely to develop in the future, including taking into account external forces such as the dynamics of urban cable franchising. In this case, the powerful prisms of communications policy and competition policy melded together. Two monocles were converted into a pair of spectacles, which in turn created a better policy vision.

There are doubtless other examples of inter-agency cooperation that have followed, both in the United States and elsewhere. Hopefully, this case study will inspire other participants to detail their own experiences after a sufficient passage of time. Individually and collectively, such experiences can inspire renewed *ad hoc* efforts. They may also inspire the development of ongoing inter-agency and transnational institutional arrangements that allow communications and competition policy agencies to collaborate and, in doing so, to strengthen the foundations of their separate but highly-related missions.

III

*Ian S. Forrester**

Achieving and Safeguarding Conditions for Fair and
Efficient Competition

I. Introduction

This is a very difficult but fascinating assignment. Difficult, because we are asked
to comment on how to regulate a field in a consistent way, yet European experience tells us that inconsistencies and very different styles of judicial and regulatory tradition can each succeed. Difficult, because the field is evolving rapidly and
it seems certain the answers will vary from situation to situation, depending on
the sector: if we try to lay down universally valid guidelines we may be wrong or
platitudinous; the technological trends are not so difficult to predict, but market
developments in response to them are very unforeseeable; difficult because
telecommunications deregulation involves the construction of a deliberately
unlevel playing field which will rig competition against one category of operator,
yet the goals being pursued by this effort are by no means agreed (pro-European?
pro-efficiency? pro-innovation? pro-employment? totally disinterested? pro-
competition? pro-competitors?). Fascinating, because the field is enormously
important for all kinds of reasons; and because where telecommunications deregulation leads other important sectors will follow, since information technology,
multi-media, broadcasting and conventional telecommunications are converging
(to such an extent that one of the common handicaps imposed on telecommunications operators is restraints on their entering other sectors).

We accept that European competition law holds dominant companies
to a higher level of pro-competitive conduct than non-dominant companies,
by the application of Article 82 [ex 86] of the Consolidated Treaty.[1] Yet

* Q.C., White & Case, formerly Forrester Norall & Sutton, Brussels; Visiting
Professor in European Law, Glasgow University. The author gratefully acknowledges
the very generous assistance and advice offered by his colleagues, in particular, David
Eisenberg, Sandra Keegan, Krzysztof Kuik, Rolf Olofsson, Mark Powell, and a number of helpful persons who have answered technical, policy and legal questions. Mark
Powell authored a Forrester Norall & Sutton study for the EC Commission, entitled
'Efficient Co-operation with the National Telecommunications Authority'.
[1] A classic formulation of this notion is to be found in the Michelin judgment: 'A
finding that an undertaking has a dominant position is not in itself a recrimination but
simply means that, irrespective of the reasons for which it has such a position, the
undertaking concerned has a special responsibility not to allow its conduct to impair

telecommunications deregulation goes much further, both as to the threshold ('significant market power' is much lower than 'dominant position') and as to remedy (duty to refrain from abuse is much easier to tolerate than a duty affirmatively to render a service to the opposition).[2]

I summarise my contentions. First of all, when considering how to apply competition rules in the telecommunications sector, consider not only the interests of companies which want to compete there, but also the interests of customers who are operating in a continent which is generally risk-hostile, certainly when compared with the United States. Second, the evolution of the technology is making possible, technically and commercially, a wide range of options in terms of modes of delivering service. Third, regulations almost always evolve more slowly than the marketplace requires; regulators and the businesses they regulate consistently underestimate the pace of change; and regulators generally favour what is familiar. Fourth, the mass of national and Community legislation was conceived for a period of limited resources and modes of service; as new options evolve, we should need less legislation. Fifth, it seems that the handicapping of incumbent operators on a daily basis by telecommunications regulators is done conscientiously and skilfully, but with an insufficient vision of broad competition principles, as opposed to micro-managerial issues of costs and details. Sixth, that there should be an effort to avoid falling back into re-regulation after de-regulation, and that the European Commission has a key role to play in this regard.

II. Introductory Doubts

The task we are set is to state whether the application of competition rules, or the promulgation of sector-specific technical regulations, will be the better means of achieving a successful network in the marketplace. And should the enforcement and supervisory task be assigned to competition watchdogs or telecommunications watchdogs, European or national?

I shall be submitting that we need to identify the best candidates to perform the task of enforcing the rules on telecommunications for a period of time, after which the playing field will be made level again; and separately consider who are the best candidates to continue to supervise the marketplace thereafter. I

genuine undistorted competition on the common market.' (Case C–322/81 *Michelin* v *Commission*, ECR [1983] 3461 at para. 10).

[2] Herbert Ungerer of DG IV, speaking on Telecoms Pricing Policies and their effect on the European Internet, EUROISPA Conference, June 4 1998, refers to the need for 'sharper tools' in the telecoms sector.

shall argue that the most effective regulators today are the national telecommunications authorities, and their resources appear capable of doing both the immediate job and the medium-term job. However, while I accept their good faith and their dynamism, I question whether they are currently following principles which are oriented on regulating the market or which are oriented at creating a competitive market. I fear they are doing the former, not the latter. However, before considering who should be entrusted with the task, it is useful to consider how necessary that task is.

In a well-functioning hypothetical transparent economy, clear principles of fair behaviour are probably the best underpinning of healthy competition. It may be that sector-specific rules will be appropriate to govern railways, the health industry and privatised coal mines. However, in the telecommunications sector I have no confidence at all that today's sector-specific rules will even be relevant tomorrow. Such regulations apply to the exploitation of existing technology, not emerging technologies. We have no idea what technologies will be extant in 2010 or 2005, so lengthy rule-making in 1998 about how telecommunications operators must co-operate in the future with new entrants is very likely to be a waste of time, save insofar as it is intended to handicap the incumbent operator this year or next year from competing too aggressively with new entrants.[3] Worse, micro-managing how a marketplace operates may well eliminate potentially attractive goods or services.

The major drawback of regulation is that it does not foster innovation in most cases. The Internet shows what largely unregulated innovation can deliver:

> The International Data Corporation (IDC) projects that global Internet commerce spending—which includes everything from retail sales to business-to-business transactions—will reach $32.4 billion this year, up from $12.4 billion in 1997. Indeed, the

---

[3] Standardisation and technical harmonisation are unobjectionable exceptions to my remarks about the pointlessness of rule-making in the long term. One consequence of the rapid technological change and the near disappearance of traditional economic frontiers between countries may be a change in the approach to the setting of standards. This is true within companies and within countries. Whereas in the past, companies developed proprietary standards and enforced them to keep away competitors, many standards are now elaborated through consensus between companies. Technical standards are no longer set to favour national champions (of course, interconnection standards have needed, for decades, to be neutral and non-national in orientation, because otherwise services across a frontier would not function). CEN, CENELEC, ETSI seem to function well, albeit with occasional disputes about copyright and patents, which protect all or part of a standard which is a candidate for being generalised as the standard.

research firm is projecting explosive growth for the next few years. By 2002, says IDC, annual e-commerce spending will total $425 billion.[4] (The Commerce Department offers a more conservative estimate of $325 billion).

The huge commercial potential of the Internet offers incentives not only to those who are developing Internet-related goods and services, but also to quite traditional shops. A cigar shop called Greybeard's has had great success, maybe because of the quasi-pornographic nature of its merchandise, which politically correct persons will wish to buy furtively:

> While Greybeard's already serviced a modest number of summer customers year-round via mail order, its long-distance business has doubled to about 8 percent of the store's $700,000 in annual revenue since launching its Web site in January, says George Kalvinsky. Moreover, the Web site has generated more walk-in traffic for the store this season by people who [. . .] never knew about the store until they saw it on the Web.

> The Kalvinsky's Web site illustrates how mom-and-pop shops are boasting the appearance of big business on the Web and transcending borders to reach far-flung customers. A depth of selection of merchandise, detailed product information written with flair and professional, high-quality graphics can all work together to make even the most humble enterprise look like a big-time operation.[5]

I presume that in Europe we would have more multi-media and Information Society services if there were fewer rules on how service providers could function. Can we draw conclusions from the different success stories of the GSM and of earth satellite receivers as to the 'modalities' of innovation? Would GSM technology have been a bigger success, sooner, if there had been fewer telephone regulations? (For that matter, why did the telephone monopolists get their hands first on GSM technology?) Could the inventors find no better outlets than the entrenched interests who might not have welcomed the advent of the new rival technology? Very likely, fewer regulations might have helped things move even faster, but the GSM is such a success story in Europe that it would be unfair to carp (the US example is telling: conflicting standards and frequencies often make GSM services local and not national).

The competition law challenge is distinctive. It is presumed that in each Member State there is a dominant incumbent, with a high market share, a

---

    [4] (*http://www.herring.com/mag/issue58/internet.html*), *Internet Commerce and Infrastructure: Gaining Momentum.*

    [5] (*http://www.cnn.com/TECH/computing/9808/26/mompop.idg*), *Mom-and-pop businesses go boom on the Web.*

hugely expensive infrastructure and the consequent capacity to exclude new entrants. The ONP (Open Network Provision) legislation which has been the driving force of Commission liberalisation efforts in the 1990s contemplates something more than mere respect for the traditional competition rules. 'Mere competition' will not be enough to achieve competitive conditions; therefore the playing field needs to be made unlevel to disadvantage the dominant operator and favour the successful arrival of new entrants. It is presumed that 'super-competition' or 'competition plus' will be necessary for some period. It is hoped that the incumbent will survive the advantaged arrival of new entrants without suffering fatal damage.

Deciding the dozens of individual controversies is generally handled at national level but may also require the intervention of DG IV. My impression is that most of these individual conflicts are arbitrated by telecommunications regulators rather than by competition specialists, and it seems to involve a lot of rough-and-ready decision-making which generally disfavours the incumbent. The press releases of national telecommunications operators read in a triumphalist, scalp-counting manner. OFTEL announces that it has determined that it has regulated Cable & Wireless international tariffs, or found that BT is free to set tariffs on calls from Ulster to Eire or that someone else has significant market power in mobile telephony. Worse, I have heard a number of examples (in an admittedly anecdotal and unscientific survey) of decision-making by national regulatory authorities which are worryingly unsound. The authorities seem to take tough, well-intentioned positions upon their understanding of purely national criteria, without considering what competition lawyers would regard as the relevant marketplace. The addressees of these decisions will often regard them as perverse or eccentric, or as part of a generalised campaign against the established order. I shall say that there seems to be a lot of rough justice in the decision-making about particular controversies in national telecommunications.

I find myself surprised to have sympathy for the formerly dominant incumbents, who are now being exposed not just to normal competition but to measures which sharply constrain their ability to react by making competing counter-offers. I question whether national regulators are making these decisions well and consistently, and with a clear vision of the long-term and mid-term objectives.

Competition policy is the main pillar underpinning the whole legislative programme. Will conditions of competition be better achieved by entrusting the supervision of sector-specific rules to competition agencies or to telecommunications regulators? How can we ensure that these agencies do not impose a deadening weight upon a market which must be free to evolve rapidly? The rules intended to disfavour the incumbent must have an in-built obsolescence:

how can we ensure that they actually disappear when they are no longer needed? Are we satisfied that concentrating on establishing good conditions for competition in the telecommunications sector as such is a meaningful exercise, given that alternative methods for delivering the key services of telecommunications operators are developing rapidly?

I shall be saying that we need to consider whether the regime we adopt needs a social component and an industrial policy component;[6] that we need to consider who are the intended beneficiaries of the exercise; and that we need more closely to consider the needs of the ordinary consumer because thus far I believe too much attention has concentrated on the process of competition between rival suppliers, without customer satisfaction as such being sufficiently taken into account.[7]

All this is in the nature of a health warning: any marketplace will usually move more rapidly than regulators' pens; the telecommunications market is evolving very fast indeed. Footnotes are being added to this paper to remedy statements made in September. Competition principles can be timeless and open-ended, but applying them can have unforeseen consequences.[8] I am therefore very unconfident of my ability to make recommendations with any confidence. Let us begin by recording a few points where we can be confident.

III. Monopolies, Public Service and the Need for Good Telecommunications Services in Europe

There are a number of activities/functions which in our youth looked like natural monopolies. Post; gas; electricity; telephone; rail travel; maybe health.

---

[6] Access to the US market: while ATT, GTE, US West and Ameritech each have big stakes in European telecoms operators, the reverse is not the case; and foreign companies cannot take a controlling interest in a US telecoms operator. US-based alliances are much bigger than Europe-based alliances. Should we bear this in mind when regulating?

[7] One subject about which we have not been asked to comment is taxation. An industry's success, and its attractiveness to new entrants, will reflect how it is taxed. Rate-setting is nominally (and in reality, to be fair) a different exercise, but its effect may be close to taxation. In the *Echo de la Bourse* (28 October 1998) the Belgian electricity giant Electrabel complains that its freedom of commercial manoeuvre is seriously compromised in dealing with competing bids to its customers from other Member States by the imposition on it of a 'one time' but thrice repeated special tax, which does not apply to a foreign electrical utility supplying a Belgian customer.

[8] Sometimes, those who claim that the application of classical competition rules for a given sector without making due adjustment for the specificities of the sector are proven not to have been wrong. I respectfully submit that those who claimed the application to the training and employment of professional footballers of Community rules without taking account of the game's special features would have grave consequences, have been shown to be correct.

Certainly there were obviously wretchedly bad monopolists: I will offer the French telephone system, where telephone lines were so scarce that landlords would specifically mention the presence of a telephone when advertising apartments for rent,[9] and Sabena as examples of the worst of the bad old days. Does being a monopolist guarantee bad service, exploitation of the customer, languishing technology? No, I think not, though the evidence is uneven. I submit that the Bell Telephone System (before the dismantling of ATT's ownership of twenty-three operating companies twenty years ago) may be the best example of the enlightened despot monopolist. Any European who is old enough to remember May 1968 and who spent time in the United States remembers the shock of discovering a country where telephones could be installed within a week, often less, where bills were itemised and where dealing with the telephone system bureaucracy was pleasant; indeed, the relationship then between the American citizen and Ma Bell was like the relationship between Brits and the BBC.

Can we see an explanation of why it was so bad in one democracy and so good in another? America has made a success of public service businesses for a long time. Benjamin Franklin ran a private post office, profitably, some sixty years before the advent in 1840 of prepaid postage stamps in the United Kingdom, the brainchild of Sir Rowland Hill. Local calls were subsidised by the relatively high price of long-distance calls. In many cities, local calls were free. Whether demand was stable or expanding, there was a fanatical preoccupation among the engineering staff with delivering consistent, rapid and uninterrupted service. Yet competition was absent from the American telephone system, at least in terms of customer choice; one probable explanation of the excellence of the service is the presence of extremely strict regulatory standards. The very high general level of performance was closely monitored by both the service provider and public authorities. These performance standards emerged from a consensus between the Bell system and its regulators: number of days within which a new subscriber must be connected in an area already served by telephone lines; number of seconds' delay before a dial tone in normal circumstances, number of unsuccessful calls; and the telephone company, in order to

---

[9] Though Belgium was not perfect either. When I first lived in Belgium, it was too painful and unpredictable for those who lived in real time to rely on the repair service of the Régie des Télégraphes et des Téléphones. So, in my building the concièrge, and one of his friends ran a user-friendly telephone service. They arrived on time they wanted to give satisfaction, and their rates were modest. Their equipment was probably procured from the RTT: as in the Soviet Union, private initiatives palliated the rigidities of the institutional system. Hostility and resentment to the incumbent operators, who are the heirs of such a system, is surely not a trivial element in the motivation of the deregulatory movement.

qualify for more income in the form of higher rates, had to prove it was doing its job in trying to meet these standards. Another factor, difficult to quantify, but surely relevant, is popular will and consumer sentiment. People in a democracy or in a totalitarian regime will usually accept what they expect.

There may be circumstances where market forces are unavailable or incapable of effecting a change in the behaviour of the incumbent service provider. As users lack market power, public intervention is the only way of producing the wholesome benefit of market forces. There are bad monopolies in the US: the railway system used to be, and in many places still is, squalid, slow, poorly maintained, slovenly. There were alternatives and people used them. Federal subsidies to motorway construction in the US show how government intervention can also distort competition.

I fear that in the excitement about how to fine-tune competition between competitors, the interests of the user may get forgotten. It is not obvious to me that many offerors is necessarily a guarantee of customer satisfaction. It may mean merely customer confusion or irritation: Californian customers may discover that their telecommunications supplier has changed hands only when they get a bill from the new incumbent. So let us consider whether consumer satisfaction can be achieved only by competition. The American experience shows plainly that the answer is no. There were good regulators on both sides of the Atlantic; I find it difficult to believe that the key difference is that the American regulated monopoly was owned by shareholders whereas the European ones were owned by ministries. Maybe it is the case that we can achieve what consumers want from a service provider in either of two ways. One is by regulation which sets targets and rewards for meeting these targets. The other is by competition. In each case, the incumbent service provider receives guidance from the marketplace, either a real marketplace or a theoretical one. Competition is an easier means of achieving a good result than elaborate regulations unless these are extraordinarily well-drafted, by setting the right standards for the right parameters, and are strictly respected. In the days of telephone monopolies in Europe, I presume that the rules were not strictly respected.

We are moving from an era of scarcity of resources, where in many cases a single monopolist was the natural service provider, to an era of abundance. There are several alternative modes by which telephone services can be provided, they are expanding very rapidly, the infrastructure to carry the messages is expanding exponentially, and customers know they have choices. Yet the field is still very closely regulated, with the incumbents in particular being handicapped in a finely calculated manner. That may have been necessary to aid the transition from protected monopoly to competition, but I submit that it will not remain necessary for very much longer.

Who should benefit? One reason to promote competition is to encourage the results associated with the benefits of competition, such as efficient allocation of resources. Another reason is to protect against predators. I can offer a particular reason why. Less technically, I feel that it must be obvious that regulating the telecommunications sector well in Europe is especially important. Many successful businesses find it easier to thrive in North America than in Europe. European governments and officials have made the launch of new enterprises too difficult. The risk and the cost of corporate failure is far too high. The 'barriers to exit' for a small or medium-size enterprise in Belgium, and in other European countries, are unacceptably high. An enterprise in Nebraska or in New York may fail, without acute economic risk, whereas the risks of failure for an enterprise in Belgium, its owners, the employers, are so high that they constitute a real brake on innovation and risk-taking.[10] It is very important that we should achieve an environment in which there is a possibility of launching new services and products, the launching of attractive alternatives resulting from technological innovation. Because the barriers to success and the barriers to exit are so very severe, it is especially important that Europe must have an effective telephone system, producing answers with which individual enterprises can cope. The commercial potential of the Internet is enormous, as are the businesses associated with delivering telecommunications and computer-related goods and services. I am certain that the emergence of Silicon Valley in California is due to the excellence of the local telephone infrastructure. Many companies in California have only two or three employees, the head of technology being aged fifteen, and the business manager being the grandfather aged fifty-five. University students using campus computers develop websites which bring them revenue directly or indirectly. Most Americans do not have to pay telephone charges for access to the Internet if the call is local (it is included in the local flat fee paid for all local calls). I think this is crucial for people to take advantage of the Internet as a medium for commerce. Will regulation add to costs? As an example of the new technology helping those who use the Internet, consider XML, the new 'Internet Extensible

---

[10] In 1981, I set up an SME (small-to-medium-sized enterprise) in Brussels with Chris Norall. Launching it was stressful, notably because of the need to overcome bureaucratic and infrastructural problems. A law practice needs a telephone. Getting ours required the investment of banknotes to encourage R.T.T. interlocutors to do their best to do their job. I remain sceptical about interventionist programmes to encourage employment: no business manager can doubt that government regulation and fiscal policy are the biggest factors in determining whether employment increases or shrinks.

Markup Language'. This is a step towards the idea that a user should be able to make a pin-point search for a product:

> A primary goal of XML is to label with tags information throughout a document to make it easier to find and retrieve. Anyone who has come up with hundreds of thousands of mostly irrelevant results on a search engine query can understand the value of such a technology to the Web.[11]

So it will allow for more targeted searching. But:

> XML faces a number of hurdles before the average Web surfer can use it to hone his or her searches. One such hurdle is lack of browser support. Browser market leader Netscape Communications does not yet make a browser that supports XML. And while Microsoft's Internet Explorer 4.0 browser supports XML, that browser was built before the first version of XML received a final recommendation from the World Wide Web Consortium.[12]

It is, I submit, of huge importance to Europe's industrial future that we make it not too difficult for such enterprises to get launched.

IV. The Marketplace is Unpredictable

There are many reasons to fear that whatever we do to shape the healthy development of the market will be wrong. Recent industrial history offers plenty of examples of skilled and experienced companies which made the wrong choice: electro-mechanical typewriters were swept away by electronic typewriters. The fax machine could have been made in Europe, Japan or North America, but it was the Japanese (who routinely used hand-written messages and could readily see the potential) who made the photocopier and the fax machine their own. We can also see examples of the completely unexpected success of new products. Peter Drucker, the management guru, quotes a Japanese 'leading electronics executive' as saying in 1952 that 'Japan would not have television for many, many years; the Japanese simply do not have the money to buy television sets'. Yet by 1955, the penetration of television sets in Japanese households was almost as high as in the US. Consumers have a capacity for enthusiastic adoption of telecommunications which consistently confounds the expectations of even the manufacturers of telecommunications equipment. Six

---

[11] *Mark-up language wins praise* (http://www.news.com/News/Item/0,4,24215,00. html).

[12] *Ibid.*

years ago, a few private cars had mobile telephone equipment housed in a box the size of a normal briefcase. Two years ago, GSM services were becoming more and more widely recognised. Today, significant numbers of children have GSM telephones the size of a packet of long cigarettes; and in Bangladesh, demand is rising rapidly, ownership frequently being communal, as a response to the inadequacies or absence of conventional telephone services.

Today, the number of Internet subscribers doubles every hundred days. Telephone companies can offer burglar alarm services; webcasting is the reception of radio channels via the Internet. Legislation is drafted over the Internet. A Website operated by an independent California lawyer, Carol Kunze, the '2B Guide', is an example of a completely Internet-based information source on the adaptation of the Uniform Commercial Code to shrink-wrap licensing by the development of a new set of principles (Rule 2B). It allows people the opportunity to follow the law as it is being written, to get updates on developments by e-mail, and to submit comments which are sent on to the Rapporteur who is writing the law. Comments are sent to all members of the 2B drafting committee, as well as all the participants who come to the meeting, and an e-mail list of over 650 lawyers and other interested persons. In fact, anyone can submit comments through Ms. Kunze's site: they will be sent on and reviewed by the committee. This really is an unparalleled opportunity to participate in the legal drafting process. The European Commission could, had it chosen, have submitted comments. Internet access is all that is needed.[13]

Internet use in Europe is currently growing at three times the rate of the US. If this rate of growth continues, European use of the Internet will reach that of the US in 2002. The iMac (Apple's new computer) has no disk-drive: this is a major technology change. It means that the user cannot upload from, or download to, a disk. Thus iMac users wanting to add software or send files somewhere will be heavily dependent on the Internet. The development of new technology for the internet is a major economic activity. Then again, Oracle is starting a programme to lease software and computer space to business over the Internet. This means that small businesses can outsource some of their work, do not have to buy and then service a lot of software, and can store their files offsite.[14] A portion of this paper has been dictated at 140 words per minute

---

[13] 'The 2B Guide—A Guide to the Proposed Law on Software Transactions: Draft UCC Article 2B—Licences' (<http://www.2BGuide.com). See also, 'The ETA Forum—A Public Forum on the Proposed Uniform Electronic Transactions Act' '<http://www.webcom.com/legaled/ETAForum/>).

[14] 'Company will Lease Programme Space to Small Businesses over the Internet' '(http://cnnfn.com/smbusiness/wires/9808/26/oracle_wg/).

and converted into text via an astonishingly accurate voice-driven word pr
cessing programme called Naturally Speaking.

Seven years ago, there was talk of an information superhighway, dim
understood by those who talked about trans-European networks. Studies wri
ten in 1992 for the European Commission on the technological future did ne
identify the Internet as a field where something interesting was likely t
happen.

My point is that providers of goods and services constantly try to predic
market trends, and constantly get it wrong. It is consumer choice in a compe
itive marketplace which offers a reality check and ultimately decides the con
mercial fate of a given good or service. If one company's 'Call Waiting' servic
causes confusion and dissatisfaction, new offerors should be able to supply
better one. At the moment, we are trying to achieve the right for new entran
to offer a competing service without being confronted with great difficultie
while also imposing super-competition burdens via the imposition of specifi
largely regulatory, obligations on the incumbents. I have doubts about the sec
ond part of that effort: assuming that it is right for today's conditions, I a
sure it will be damaging if it is retained too long.

V. Do No Harm

There is a high probability that regulators will not get it right, a certainty the
will not be right all the time, and a probability they will sometimes be com
pletely wrong. It takes months or years to draft a new regulation, yet the life c
an electronic product may be measured in months. A perceptive article b
Steven Wallman, a former Commissioner of the Securities and Exchang
Commission, the world's premier market regulator, notes the tendencies of a
well-intentioned bureaucracy to make the familiar compulsory and to slov
down the arrival of the novel.

> Any regulator runs the risk of building on what had been a good foundation but
> due to shifting fault lines, is now quite unstable. A detailed, incremental regulator
> perspective continues to add weight to an increasingly shaky structure; when mak
> ing small changes, one is apt not to look at the fundamentals. In particular, detailed
> incremental regulation fails when the underlying economics or competitive context
> or the technology itself, moves other than in slow incremental steps.[15]

---

[15] Wallman (1998: 348).

It is particularly interesting to observe that a securities regulator is faced with choices about whether or not to protect the marketplace by enforcing a prior approval regulatory regime.

This means seeking to eliminate where possible advance approvals for innovative products or services, and providing fewer detailed command-and-control regulatory requirements.

Mr. Wallman notes, sometimes acknowledging his own failures, sometimes taking modest credit for successes, the difficulty of enacting quite limited reforms:

In a world marked by accelerating change and competition from other industries, forcing all new products and services to obtain advance regulatory approval [. . .] is unwise. Investors are denied the benefits of speedy innovation. Worse, investors may be denied all the benefits of some innovations as delays and costs to obtain regulatory approval present true barriers to entry or raise the hurdle rates for products, thereby precluding them from coming to market at all.[16]

As one might expect, those presently on top frequently have an incentive to resist change, or at least that change for which they may not have an advantage. Those presently on top also have the loudest voices and serve then to reinforce a preference for the regulatory status quo.[17]

Those participants who are most nimble at navigating the current system are able to profit most from it. Conversely, changes to the system provide proportionately greater opportunities for those who are not faring the best under the current structure.[18]

[. . .] regulators seek precision and detail in their requirements, so they can be easily inspected and enforced.[19]

The flip side of regulation designed to ensure appropriate enforcement, and an enforcement orientation generally, is the demand for certainty that is to be expected from those who are regulated [. . . .]. The result is a desire for specific and detailed guidance—not the kind of pronouncements that reflect fundamental concepts and allow the market to develop on its own.[20]

He ruefully describes the difficulties he encountered in persuading his officials, who were doubtless conscientious, experienced and skilled in the field

---

[16] *Ibid*, at 348.
[17] *Ibid*, at 347.
[18] *Ibid*.
[19] *Ibid*.
[20] *Ibid*.

they were regulating, to move from denominating share prices in vulgar fractions (like $19⅝) to decimals. Fierce resistance, great difficulties, great dangers:

> Frequently, criticism is levelled at regulators concrete failure to protect someone who is hurt, rather than for precluding something new or experimental that might— although no one is sure—have led to a better world. Consequently, regulators opt for specific and detailed rules that constrain behaviour and channel activities to what is known and safe. One is criticised for the mistakes others see, not for the mistakes barring something new the critics never know about; and no one keeps statistics on the number of good ideas that were never allowed to happen.[21]

I expect that any telecommunications expert will have no difficulty in listing several products which never saw the light of day because a regulator did not approve them in time.

Vice President Gore has said that the first precept for government is to do no harm. This is an elegant formulation, but a perceptive Scot had already identified the problem 220 years ago. Adam Smith said:

> Every individual necessarily labours to render the annual revenue of the society as great as he can. He generally, indeed, neither intends to promote the public interest, nor knows how much he is promoting it. By preferring the support of domestic to that of foreign industry, he intends only his own security; and by directing that industry in such a manner as its produce may be of the greatest value, he intends only his own gain, and he is in this, as in many other cases, led by an invisible hand to promote an end which was no part of his intention. Nor is it always the worse for the society that it was no part of it. By pursuing his own interest he frequently promotes that of the society more effectively than when he really intends to promote it.[22]

I note an echo of this in an opinion of Justice Brennan,[23] who rejected the argument of a city that its power-generating activities, being in the public interest, were entitled to a kind of immunity from the antitrust laws. He was unpersuaded by the argument:

> [The City's] argument that their goal is not private but public service is only partly correct. Every business enterprise, public or private, operates its business in furtherance of its own goals [. . .] the economic choices made by public corporations in the conduct of their business affairs, designed as they are to assure maximum benefits for the community constituency, are not inherently more likely to comport with the broader interests of national economic well-being than are those of private corporations acting in furtherance of the organization and its shareholders.

---

[21] *Ibid*, at 346.
[22] Adam Smith, *The Wealth of Nations*, Book IV, Chapter 2.
[23] *City of Lafayette* v. *Louisiana Power & Light Co.,* 435 US 389, at 403 (1978).

In any event, Adam Smith concluded that 'kings and ministers [. . .] are themselves always, and without any exception, the greatest spendthrifts in the society.' We cannot expect the state or the civil service or self-regulatory bodies to be any better than anyone else at identifying what will be the consequences of regulatory initiatives. The conclusions of the well-informed and well-intentioned can be completely wrong. Consider the reactions of the British government and bureaucracy[24] to bovine spongiform encephalopathy eight years ago. Officials conscientiously asked the right questions, consulted, and decided to adopt a disastrously wrong course of action. Sense of perspective can be wildly distorted even for experts. When it was proposed that fixed brokerage commissions for stock exchange transactions should be abolished, the President of the New York Stock Exchange said:[25]

> One does not remove the keystone to an industry which is responsible for billions of dollars of public money, which operates the largest securities market in the world, and which facilitates the raising of the bulk of new capital for this country without presenting irrefutable evidence. We are dealing with a delicate mechanism. This is not an area where one experiments, tries a new system, and returns to the old if the results are unsatisfactory. Destruction of the minimum commission rate would produce irreversible consequences. An erroneous decision will have far-reaching effects.[26]

We can see with the benefit of hindsight that Mr. Haack was over-excited. The American securities markets remain vigorous. The world has not come to an end, despite the end of fixed commissions. Yet Mr. Haack was perfectly sincere, and one may assume, given his position, that many experts shared his views. I fear that those who are in charge of applying telecommunications rules may, like him, be misguided at important moments.

This is only one more example of my proposition: there is no certainty that either regulators or the industry's leaders will accurately identify future trends, threats or opportunities or even accurately assess current needs.

VI. Technology in Evolution

This weakness is especially forgivable when one considers the pace of technological innovations, particularly in the field of telecommunications. AltiGen Communications, Inc. in Fremont, California headlines its advertising 'The

---

25 The European Commission hardly covered itself in glory either.
25 Wallman, *supra*, n 15, at 350.
26 Seligman (1995), quoting comments of NYSE President Haack during SEC hearings on fixed commissions, at 409–10.

BEST Telephone System for your business may *not* be a 'Phone System' at all' AltiGen is offering a system combining personal computing, fax, e-mail, voice mail, and conventional voice communication. That sounds to me rather like a telephone system, but maybe I am technically uninitiated.

What is certain is that new products and new technologies are constantly emerging. For example, in the field of traditional telephony, there are four methods of getting access to the local loop:[27]

1) interconnection to the network of the incumbent operator, who either laid or owns the tons of underground copper wiring to houses and businesses;
2) laying a new alternative cable, either alone or in a consortium (for example with others in a fibre optic consortium);
3) using an existing alternative network (railway lines, cable television networks, gas pipelines);
4) using a new local loop, based on wire-less technology (e.g. Ionica (UK) operates a wire-less system using a small aerial fixed in the home, which then relays the call to a conventional telephone; the company can sign up new customers more cheaply than its competitors and when a customer cancels the service, Ionica simply retrieves the aerial from the customer's house and sets it up in another one; like many new entrants, the company aims to compete on innovative service as well as on price; it routinely offers customers three telephone numbers as well as allocated billing, useful for splitting a residential phone bill between social and work calls.[28] Wire-less local loops are being developed in the Central and Eastern European countries (in Hungary, more than 200,000 customers have signed up).

It is not just the young Turks who are offering new technologies. Incumbent operators are defending their positions. BT has introduced a device called the Onephone which offers a dual-mode handset that uses digital cordless technology at home but GSM beyond it, to provide mobility without wholly transferring the fixed capacity to the mobile network. *The Economist* suggested that 'The Future Looks Unwired'. Over the next four years, cellular data speeds will increase rapidly. An ISDN-like capability will be available in 1999, and when third generation mobile services based on UMTS technology are launched in 2002, wire-less systems will be capable of transmission rates forty times higher than today's fastest fixed-line dial-up modems. The speed of a new personal computer in 1996 was maybe 100 megahertz; in 2000, it is

---

[27] The physical link which leads to subscribers' homes.

[28] As noted below, the originality of Ionica's approach did not save it from competitive pressures.

pected to be 1 gigahertz. Transmission speeds will go up, say the experts, ten mes in five years. As the speed, quality and range of performance increase, the mount of bandwidth or spectrum required will be reduced by data compress- g techniques, but the demand will increase enormously. The supplying of nventional telephone connections will become a mass-market commodity oduct, presumably cheap. The growth of the Internet means that there is ore data transmission across the Atlantic than voice transmission. Prices for xed and mobile calls are quite different today. However, as the prices of obile calls decrease and mobile operators begin to offer fixed telecommuni- ations services (see Mobistar's Offering Circular), the borderline will disap- ear. Come the next enlargement of the European Union, there will be more obile subscribers in Europe than orthodox telephone connections.

I have mentioned only a few intriguing technological possibilities. Some ill fail, some will succeed; all need to be given the chance of success. Whether e follow the *ex-post* or *ex-ante* model, deregulation is intended to achieve atisfactory conditions for users, suppliers and service providers by releasing arket forces to maximise economic benefit. And the benefit is not just for the ser/consumer, but also for all marketplace operators, even though the former onopolists will not be grateful for the experience. This brings me to the ext comment, which relates to why we are discussing competition and regula- ion.

Competition implies winners and losers; failure is a necessary element. Alan Cane of the *Financial Times*, a perceptive observer, noted (18 October 1998) hat telecommunications operators' licences now permit them to go bankrupt, n unprecedented phenomenon. Ionica, which I mentioned above as offering a ovel wire-less local loop, has only enough money to trade until January, and other young Turks are vulnerable.[29] Even the incumbent operator has no blank cheque: incumbents can fail, like other companies. The field is getting crowded. At least one-and-a-half billion Euros per year will be spent on new fibre optic capacity over the next few years. Germany alone will have issued nearly three hundred operating licences in the next year. If demand for Internet access con- tinues to double every 105 days, then maybe there will not be a glut of capac- ity. But it looks likely that there will be a lot of failures, and I presume that they will include one or more national incumbents. It is probable that huge economies of scale will be necessary to survive. It is likely that we will see con- solidations, mergers and acquisitions. It is not impossible that we will move

---

[29] Indeed, by the date of this conference in November 1998, Ionica had gone into receivership. A sympathetic letter from Professor Gordon Edge to the *Financial Times* (5 November 1998) spoke of the challenges confronting such companies.

from a world of fifteen national incumbents and a small number of terriers ya
ping at their heels, through a period of turbulence, innovation, failures a
consolidation, to a world of four or five continental-scale incumbents, most
them based in the United States.

Is anyone considering the social dimension of the competitive scenari
before us? The typical incumbent is today the heir of a once-hated dinosau
Dinosaurs employed civil servants, not employees. When Belgacom was priva
tised, it had 27,000 employees, of whom four hundred were university grad
ates; today, it has 20,000 employees, of whom 1,800 are graduates. The civ
servants had security of tenure, since performance reviews could in effect nev
be so bad as to justify termination, and they were entitled to a pensio
Typically, that pension was not funded, so the newly-privatised company ha
to fund past obligations and future obligations out of present incom
According to Belgacom's published data, it will take twelve more years befor
it has purged itself completely of the need to fund its predecessor's pensio
obligations, at a cost of about 400 million Euros per year. (It is not only i
Belgium that pension obligations have heavy consequences: I believe tha
France Telecom made one up-front payment to the French government to hel
the latter meet its Maastricht criteria.) I presume that there are ten or mor
telecommunications operators whose situation is characterised by high marke
share of a market which is declining in profitability; suffering from high labou
costs and inflexibility, a public service mandate, numerous competitors toda
and even more with new techniques in the future; and arousing very little sym
pathy from regulators, customers or even their former shareholders, the gov
ernment for which privatisation came as a relief.

Hugeness does not and should not confer immunity from the competition
rules. Competitive pressures have to touch every operator, not just the lean an
mean; but the challenge of adopting to a new environment is especially sever
for companies like Deutsche Telekom. Prohibiting them from offering security
alarm services or from offering cable television services is evidently a severe
handicap. The answer of the regulators today to these concerns would probably be that such constraints are mere pinpricks, and that the squeals of outrage
from Mr. Sommer of Deutsche Telekom in October 1998 about the unfairness
of the regulatory constraints placed upon it are to be disregarded as predictable. For the short term, there seems to be no alternative, but I submit the
short term should not last very long.

VII. Convergence and Regulation

The providers of different categories of service will shortly be able to offer the same service to customers. Thus, cable television distributors can, via satellite, offer access to Internet services; telephone companies can offer video on demand; Internet service providers can offer broadcasting and voice telephony services. Personal computers are entertainment centres, Internet terminals and data-processing tools. Consumers will have a choice between different modalities of delivery, provided that regulations do not stifle that choice; the technological obstacles are already disappearing. The objective of the regulators who have to supervise competition should be to foster innovation, to foster competition and to foster consumer choice.

There will remain a place for regulatory concerns which are not discharged by competition alone or by abundance of choice: consumer protection would be one, universal service would be another. We may not sufficiently realise how far the competition and sectoral rules governing the telecommunications, information technology and broadcasting fields need to be reappraised in light of the new technological environment. Rules developed in the context of scarcity (limitations on the number of available broadcast channels, number of local telephone providers, other natural monopolies) have to be re-examined in the context of technological abundance to see if the objective of the rule requires its continued application. For example, rules on 'European content' in the field of 'Télévision sans Frontières' were adopted for a world of scarcity of content providers. The huge abundance of content now available should justify leaving the determination of content to consumer choice while allowing the rules to stand undisturbed for traditional public service broadcasters whose influence is such that the social goals of ensuring plurality in the media and respect for cultural diversity continue to apply. It is otherwise for broadcasters who enter into individual transactions where the consumer exercises a specific choice, such as video on demand: it seems difficult to see why rules on European content should apply if the consumer selects a video without leaving his home but do not apply if he goes to the cinema or the video shop. Yet I have been told that one or two telecommunications operators have been informed that they could provide video on demand services only if they respected European content rules.[30] The relevance of this episode is as an illustration of the tendency of regulators to impose regulations.

---

[30] In the days of scarcity of channels, rules on content could seem reasonable, but it is difficult to say they remain necessary in the new environment. How to create enough content in Europe, whether or not rules exist compelling its use, is a big challenge beyond the scope of this paper.

Licensing is a classic reaction to limited resources. Eliminating *ex ante* approval procedures may well be the best way of enhancing competition. I am sure that regulating individual services on a case by case basis is undesirable in terms of enhancing competition and innovation; the Japanese financial services sector shows the danger of not being bold enough in this respect.

That said, there remain real problems which need regulating: the protection of privacy, which has traditionally been very closely and effectively policed in the telecommunications sector, is scarcely regulated on the Internet; repression of criminal activity conducted over the Internet (who has jurisdiction? which law applies? what rules of evidence? what procedure governs the *instruction*? regardless of who has theoretical jurisdiction, is someone competent going to investigate?); and protection of consumers against fraud or their own carelessness or gullibility (can we assume that the technologically alert Internet user will be less prone to acting unwisely than the customer who buys a bottle of expensive wine or a miracle cleanser or a domestic gadget in the supermarket? The rights of the latter are elaborately protected, yet the interests of the former are virtually unprotected. The rules of the non-electronic marketplace do not apply, or at least are in real-life likely not to be respected in the on-line marketplace). These are real difficulties which were adequately regulated in the world of conventional telecommunications, and which are not adequately regulated in the Internet world.

Any operator will need to be regulated in some respects, even if there are no limits on market entry for regulatory reasons otherwise: GSM operators should be able to offer a service without any limitation or quota, but the safety of their equipment and the frequencies they will use cannot be left to market forces. 'Competition simply does not and cannot further the interests that lie behind most social welfare legislation' said Chief Justice Rehnquist in *Community Communications Co. v. City of Boulder.*[31]

Some economic functions may need a legal monopoly: the postal service for letters might appear to be one such. But other methods of delivery on-line may render traditional postal services obsolete, for example letter-to-letter delivery via the Internet on personal computers. But not all services for post offices need be subject to monopoly, such as worldwide package deliveries. The Commission has already tabled a proposal to introduce liberalisation in the same way as has been done in telecommunications (that is either step-by-step or piecemeal) until deregulation leaves the bedrock universal service of a standard format letter weighing less than 200 grammes. Other services, argues the Commission, should be available to those who want to offer them.

---

[31] *Community Communications Co. v City of Boulder*, 455 US 40, at 60 (1982).

Once upon a time, it seemed to be that local telephone calls and cable television distribution were natural monopolies, as it seemed wasteful to contemplate two parallel wiring infrastructures to connect into people's homes. Yet in Belgium, which has a very comprehensive cable television network, the cable distributors enjoy a monopoly which is not especially enlightened. They are 'intercommunales', which means they are owned by local public authorities—which foreign (or other linguistic minority) broadcaster they allow on their network is the subject of intense current litigation, as is the amount of copyright royalties they should pay to foreign and Belgian broadcasters. The consumer who does not like the cultural or linguistic or aesthetic choice made by the 'intercommunale' which supplies the viewer's cable has no choice. And if the consumer elects to abandon cable distribution for a satellite dish, the local commune will charge a tax on that dish equal to the subscription for one year of the cable: the public authority taxes you the same amount as you would have paid if you had been satisfied with cable service.

VIII. The Range of European Experience

The questions put to us ask whether the challenge of telecommunications regulation (and I would suggest that in large part what we really mean is re-regulation) is best handled by competition people or regulatory people, by Euro officials or enlightened technicians, by *ex ante* or by *ex post* regulations. There is a great range of regulatory and enforcement styles in Western Europe. I am doubtful if there is any universally desirable attribution of responsibility as between prior regulations (*ex ante*, laid down by the telecommunications regulator), and general rules of fair play (*ex post*, enforced by competition authorities).

A system may work adequately, even well, despite ideological or jurisdictional inconsistencies or peculiarities. If we were rewriting European competition law today, we would frame Regulation 17 differently. The Commission's jurisdictional reach has been beyond its administrative grasp, and it has at times found it hard to choose between rule-making and decision-making. But European competition policy has been a great success in a remarkably short time. The big divergences between how European countries regulate their affairs should be regarded as strengths rather than automatically deemed defects. The pursuit of common goals according to locally appropriate methods is presumably what subsidiarity means. So diversity as such is not to be criticised.

There are extraordinary variations in the vigour and efficiency with which regulatory and antitrust issues are pursued in Europe. Compare Belgium, the northernmost Latin country, and the United Kingdom. Belgium has little tra dition of either encouraging competition with public enterprises or enforcin competition law domestically. The competition agency is miserably undei resourced. There are a number of EC cases where Belgian protectionism wa challenged at European level. And the Belgian Ministry for Telecommunica tions is also a shareholder of Belgacom. (The general WTO principle is tha national regulatory telecommunications authorities should be independent c the operator and of the ministry: of course, it is helpful to have the expertise c the staff, but there is a potential for damage to the competitive process). Ye despite the traditions of the country, there is a rapid evolution of market driven change. Belgacom is jumping thirty years forward in terms of regulator and competitive environment. Consumers are getting a choice, there is a ding doing battle between two (soon to be three) GSM mobile service providers (tw is too few, but still), and Belgacom is getting ready to be a predator in othe countries. The UK story is very different: a strong tradition of independent civi service, a period of great social and economic turbulence between twenty and fif teen years ago, and strong agencies (though, remarkably, competition authori ties with a very limited remit). In both countries there is healthy change. But if were guided by history, I would say that change in Belgium will have a sounde future if the Belgian supervisors of change are braced by European standards.

If we want to have an example of an un-reconstructed national authority we may look at the recent past in Spain and the Commission's decision witl respect to GSM radiotelephony services there.[32] Telefónica de España is one o the world's largest telecommunications operators, with 70,000 employees anc multiple stock exchange listings. The Spanish government was by far its larges shareholder, appointing eighteen out of the twenty-five board members. It wai therefore held to exert 'decisive influence' over the company. The decisior records the prolonged battle between the Commission and Telefónica to ensure parity of treatment with respect to the award of licences to operate a GSM net work, leading ultimately to a formal decision condemning the government': behaviour on the basis of Article 82 [ex 86] read in conjunction with Articlε 86(1) [ex 90(1)] of the Consolidated Treaty. The Commission noted that the European Conference of Postal and Telecommunications Administrations had recommended that competition between GSM operators be encouraged and that regulatory barriers to such competition be abolished. It also noted that several Member States had granted three licences. It then recorded the various curious features of the Spanish licensing regime. The award of the second oper- ator's licence was made to a company, Airtel Móvil, which offered 85 billion

---

[32] *GSM radiotelephony services in Spain*, 94/181/EEC, OJ L 76/19 (1997).

pesetas for its licence, four billion pesetas less than the highest bid. Telefónica had made no such payment when receiving its licence. The Commission intervened, calling for equality of treatment. The Spanish government refused to redress the balance, by collecting 85 billion pesetas from Telefónica, and instead proposed to reduce interconnection tariffs to both operators over the next fifteen years. This was rejected, and there ensued several weeks of sharp correspondence between the Commission and the Spanish authorities, without any material concession being offered.

In a robust decision, the Commission had little difficulty in finding that Telefónica had a dominant position on the market for cellular digital mobile radiotelephony services in Spain. Telefónica had many advantages, including an existing distribution network, long experience of the Spanish market, economies of scale in terms of infrastructure, and a 'head start' of several months over its rival. The discrepancy of 85 billion pesetas in favour of Telefónica involved an extension or strengthening of its dominant position. It could use the money not spent at the time of obtaining the licence to make special offers to subscribers or otherwise reinforce its market position. The Spanish government's proposal to reduce interconnection tariffs in favour of all licencees was unacceptable: only an asymmetric tariff reduction in favour of Airtel Móvil would have been effective. The improbable argument that the payment of 85 billion pesetas had been 'voluntary' was rejected. The Commission sharply criticised the reluctance of the Spanish authorities to supply information about the real financial implications of its suggested remedies, noting tartly that the 'most obvious step would be to reimburse [the] sum paid by Airtel Móvil'.

The decision states that revoking the licence to Airtel Móvil would not remedy the breach, because it would leave Telefónica in a monopoly position, rendering ultimate competition even more difficult. The Commission found,

> [t]he competitive disadvantage in the form of the initial payment imposed on the second operator alone for its concession to operate a GSM network in Spain constitutes an infringement of Article 86(1) [ex 90(1) of the Treaty read in conjunction with Article 91 [ex Article 96].[33]

The Commission thus decided that Spain should remedy matters either by:

> (i) Reimbursing the initial payment imposed on Airtel Móvil, or (ii) adopting, after receiving the agreement of the Commission, corrective measures equivalent in economic terms to the obligation imposed upon the second GSM operator.[34]

---

[33] *GSM radiotelephony services in Spain*, 94/181/EEC, OJ L 76/19 (1997) at paragraph 31.
[34] *Ibid*, Article 1.

It would be tempting to be sharply critical of the Spanish authorities as pro tectionist, nationalist and narrow-minded. Maybe, but maybe not. The officia were presumably offering a defensible interpretation of specific legislative text an interpretation which was favoured by their government and the incumben against a hostile Commission. These officials are doubtless still in their jobs, st doing their best to implement the relevant texts. Do they share the same vision the OFTEL officials? I doubt it. Could they come closer in vision? I am sure the could, given leadership and facilitation by the Commission.

The acceptance of the need for change in Finland came much more easil Liberalisation happened there early in 1994, as the Finnish authorities imple mented the directive on carrier pre-selection for long distance calls. Local ope ators have a local loop monopoly: this involves a huge infrastructur investment, especially in Finland. There is intense competition for intern tional calls. So the caller chooses a prefix and thereby chooses which long distance operator to use. If the user dials 00, the revenues are distributed pr rata among all the operators. (Alternatively, the customer may have done deal with, say, Global One, whereby all its international calls will call up th services of Global One, in which case 00 will get Global One).

In Switzerland, the old PTT was partially privatised under the name c Swisscom, the state retaining 51% of the shares; its regulation is supervised b OFCOM, whose determinations can be litigated before the Federal Commissio for Communication (ComCom). The state remains closely involved in the settin of parameters relevant to the obligations of the universal service provider. I would seem that the Swiss implementation of telecommunications liberalisatio will trust less to market forces than the régime in other countries.

I have tried in a rather anecdotal way to get an impression of the pattern o regulation and enforcement in the Member States. I submit that regulator authorities are usually staffed by technicians, engineers and others familia with the technology almost to the exclusion of the consequences of th technology in the market. So they may measure arcana-like line seizure rate rather than the number of seconds to obtain a dial tone and the number o unsuccessful calls. Regulators commonly have a preoccupation with costin which does not encourage them to take a non-cost approach to particula problems. In past years, they devoted much skill to eliminating fat from the costs claimed by the incumbent operator. It is not so obvious to me that they are well adapted to fine-tuning their area of operations, so that there is an ini tial slope which favours new entrants without obliterating existing operators.

Their task is made more difficult by the fact that every operator desires to use whatever advantages it possesses not just to offer better products but also to squeeze out a little monopoly benefit. For example, the supplier of television conditional access services (by cable or by satellite) may wish to market television decoder boxes which allow the subscriber to receive television signals. The loser in the set-top-box example would be the consumer who can use the decoder for only one broadcast system. In an ideal world for consumers, content providers would compete in terms of quality and programming, and not by excluding other content providers. The controversy has related to how far the supplier could go in developing a box to suit his own portfolio of programmes while not suiting competing television programmes (either completely excluding them or somewhat discouraging the subscriber from receiving them by making it difficult to have a multi-channel guide). So there is an understandable reluctance on the part of regulators to believe that any provider of goods or services is behaving in a neutral manner. While regulators may find it fairly easy to identify the direction they wish to persuade companies to take in such circumstances, it is much more difficult to determine completely fair access conditions.

The fair price of allowing interconnection between the terrestrial telephone network of the incumbent and the new offeror is always very debatable. There appears to be a lot of rough justice in arbitrating these questions: it is natural that one side or the other side will feel disadvantaged by the outcome. At the moment, the incumbents seem to be taking more punishment than the new entrants. That said, competition in the GSM sector seems to be a success for the moment. The technicalities of interconnection appear to be functioning well; there is some customer lock-in due to the fact that numbers are not portable.

The consistently and persistently knotty problem in national telecommunications regulation is determining the terms of competition for long-distance calls and the enjoyment of the incumbent's inherited infrastructure supporting the local loop: a massive asset of great value. When the foreign operator competes on new markets, it must rely on the infrastructure of a local competitor. An operator with significant market power must offer cost-oriented non-discriminatory tariffs. If the local operator behaves badly, problems could in theory be presented as a question of rate-fixing (probably a matter for the competition people), or as a matter of technical regulation (probably a matter for the relevant telecommunications regulator).

In actual practice, it seems (and this is based on a very anecdotal survey) that most competitive disputes at national level are settled by the national competition authorities. The size of the teams available would confirm this. In Ireland, the ODTR has fifty people, whereas the Competition Authority has twenty-two in total, of whom 'one or two' have some telecommunications experience. In the UK, OFTEL has 160 people, great *esprit de corps*, confidence in its righteousness, and the OFT deals only with mergers in the telecommunications field, so has no involvement at all (so far as I understand it, based on the (beautifully) hand-written paper *Procedural Safeguards: an Alternativ Approach* by Jeremy Lever QC, delivered at the 1998 Fordham Conference). I the Netherlands, the OPTA has seventy people and the NMA has fifty people of whom 'five to six' are said to have telecommunications experience. I Germany, the regulator has some 3,000 people, while the Bundeskartellamt ha about 240. This seems to confirm that it is the telecommunications regulator who are doing the handicapping of the runners in the competitive race. It als confirms that the regulators of telephony for a country are always much mor numerous than the regulators of competition for the economy of the sam country. This may mean that we have invested too cautiously in competitio regulation, or that we are spending too much on telecommunications regula tion. Maybe it would be possible to draw conclusions about the utility of th latter by examinig the market share, or diminution of market share, of th incumbent, or the number of competing suppliers. On this basis, I suspect tha the return on investment might seem disappointing.

IX. The European Commission and its Role

The rules being applied at national level to telecommunications operators ar hugely influenced by EC legislation. Directives based on Article 86 [ex Articl 90] (and a few based on Articles 95 and 49 [ex 100a and 59]) required Membei States to allow new licensees to offer telecommunications services under the supervision of independent regulators who should ensure interconnection on non-discriminatory and economically justifiable terms. The original 1990 directive has been joined by subsequent ones on Satellites, Cable & Mobile ser-vices. The revolution in deregulation would certainly not have arrived so far in every Member State had it not been for EC legislation.

The Community regime contemplates the establishment of a playing field which is unlevel, by what I have called competition-plus conditions (EC Directive 96/19 deals with competition in particular). So the operator who has significant market power (often over 25 percent of the market) has to play uphill against smaller and numerous opponents. The incumbent must make its infrastructural assets available to the new entrant. This is most severely true in the case of basic voice telephony services, which are fast becoming a basic com-modity service, and less so in respect of more advanced services. The European deregulation train left the platform with the adoption of Directive 96/19 and, despite the cries of alarm from its passengers, reached the destination of full liberalisation of voice telephone and the supply of infrastructure advantages on January 1, 1998. The ferment due to Community and national deregulation forces continues, with the elaboration of a directive limiting the consequences of joint control of cable and terrestrial networks.

Almost nothing is sacred. Emergency call numbers have been harmonised (999 in the UK, so we were told, could be dialled in darkness or smoke; I once confused 'cent' in Belgium with 'sang' at a road accident: 112 is the European-wide number). 00 is the international access code, replacing 011, 19 and other pre-fixes. Number portability is supposed to allow consumers to switch telephone companies without changing numbers. What has astonished me is how many of these very perceptible local changes are attributable to European initiatives.

Some of these issues are covered by soft general principles. The hardest and toughest deal with interconnection rates, the price of allowing connection with the incumbent's local loop. Correspondingly, the attractiveness of universal service rules is sharply constrained by very tight definitions. In other words, a Member State cannot bury favours for its incumbent in the unlevel playing field by attributing over-generous compensation for the provider of universal public service. I hope that universal service obligations will not be regarded as the commercial dregs of the market; unprofitable, uninteresting, and to be left to the providers offering yesterday's technology.

Implementing these principles is, obviously, the task of the Member States, nearly always the National Regulatory Authorities. I believe that the experience, training and psyche of the Authorities' officials lead them to be excellent at solving concrete, precise problems, especially those involving costing. They will also apply their abilities to settling other precisely defined controversies, like the terms on which an incumbent must deal with the publisher of a rival telephone directory. Like the character in the Molière play who discovered that he had been speaking prose all his life without even knowing it, the National Regulatory Authorities are practising competition law while deciding individual regulatory controversies. This is a strength and a weakness. On the one hand, they are familiar with the market and very ready to decide. On the other hand, I believe they are approaching their roles without a consistent view of the pro-competitive environment which must be the overall goal. They seem to exchange ideas and solutions too infrequently. We may compare European experience in the field of classical competition law, where up until recently one could note disparities of approach and the lack of cross-fertilisation between competition agencies facing common tasks.

My concern is that by faithfully trying to apply at local level to local controversies very detailed cost-driven solutions to fundamental or minor issues of competition, the National Regulatory Authorities are imposing—under Commission compulsion—their own rigidities and inflexibilities on a national basis. They are working diligently, but—unless we remedy matters—they are working towards goals defined by micro-managerial criteria.

The current telecommunications regime should lapse in a given sector once there is sufficient competition in that sector. This is easy to say, but the entity best placed to appreciate whether this has happened is the National Regulatory Authority, which is free to discontinue the application of competition-plus in that circumstance. Can we set a date at Community level? Built-in sunset clauses are arbitrary. So it is preferable to lay down conditions to help decide when the legislation will no longer apply. I submit that forcing the deregulating of telecommunications should be a high priority by, say, the year 2000.

The current enforcement results are, I submit, too inflexible and insufficiently driven in daily practice by Community-wide principles which are intended to deliver fair but vigorous competition on a Community-wide basis. This is partly a problem of who regulates; but it is also a consequence of how the regulations are drafted at Community level in the first place. The enforcement structures are not in themselves bad, but the enforcers need to recognise the weaknesses of the current system and build on them for a more efficient and effective regime. So we moved from monopoly to privatisation and liberalisation to de-regulation; and now we risk embarking on re-regulation.

Even if good sense did not tell us that markets cannot be regulated for ever, the sheer speed of change will make the regulations irrelevant. Fibre-optic cables and satellite transmission will soon be competing vigorously with traditional telephony. Why bother to handicap the incumbent once that happens? There is no time to adjust EC legislation to each scenario. Therefore it is better to be guided by broad notions of competition, supplemented by sector-specific requirements appropriate to competition in the telecommunications industry, such as rules on essential facilities, bottleneck monopolies and so on; these concepts cannot be applied in a vacuum; they need an understanding of the industry (where the National Regulatory Authorities are very well qualified) and of broader competitive goals (where these Authorities are less well qualified).

More generally as to whether competition people or telecommunications people should ply the labouring oar, I have a number of general thoughts. First, the European experience is very vast, rich, varied. We have huge differences in how laws are made, interpreted, litigated and applied in specific cases. There is no single best way. An incoherent and patchwork quilt approach to the enforcement of Articles 81 and 82 [ex 85 and 86] has not prevented the evolution of a rich competition law. We would not draft Regulation 17/62 that way again if we were starting from zero. But the combination of political will and talented people has yielded something very successful. One of the lessons we should generalise is that co-operation between the EC and national agencies is absolutely vital. On the other hand, the level of government readiness to make hard choices varies greatly. We cannot yet trust the Member States. Worse, in

some Member States there is not much local competition law (I am thinking of Belgium and Austria).

In the short-term phase of super-competition, I can see no realistic alternative to the National Regulatory Authorities as front-line decision-makers. DG IV cannot do it. DG XIII cannot do it. The weaknesses in the current regime are, in my view, of attitude and approach rather than lack of will or lack of skill. We need rapid decision-making with readily-available appellate procedures, rather than perfectly-reasoned decisions that take six months to produce. I propose that we should continue to give the National Regulatory Authorities the benefit of the doubt, while improving mechanisms to encourage co-operation between them. To address the weaknesses of disparity, rigidity and absence of a Community vision, I would propose the creation of a Task Force within the Commission. I suggest the appointment of a set of officials in DG IV or DG XIII to give advice rapidly on the practical competition issues in concrete cases (as quickly as the Merger Task Force), and on corrective, rapidly available measures. These officials should not have the remit of perfection. They should address the issues brought to them, offer the insights of Europe-wide experience, and encourage a decision which is consistent with EC goals.

Do we need a European Telecommunications Authority, as the European Parliament proposes? Certainly not if the goal is to have a telecommunications DG IV: back to the old debate about a European Cartel Agency; but in the case of telecommunications we need an agency which will function today, next year and a year or two longer. Thereafter it will become a supervisor, not an innovator. No doubt a European Telecommunications Institute would do valuable work in setting frequencies and standards, but I doubt if it would have the prestige of DG IV, or its ability to disagree with governments successfully, or the capacity of DG XIII in terms of production of new legislation. Let us set up new bodies only if we are sure they will work well within the time needed. The role of the Commission as secretary, minute-taker, initiator and theorist is a good model in all cases.

The European Parliament has recommended the creation of a European Telecommunications Agency. The subject has been addressed in a variety of fora. It seems clear to me that it could not possibly be put in place in the short term to play a useful role during the phase of super-competition. Could it play a useful role thereafter? Certainly, some tasks which the Commission does or could engage in could properly fall within the remit of a European Telecommunications Agency. Obviously, to the extent that National Regulatory Authorities lack cross-border jurisdiction or vision, the Commission's role is essential. Likewise, it is the Commission which had the political prestige to switch on the engine of deregulatory reform, and (even if we may doubt that an independent agency could have taken that initiative so successfully) the adaptation of that legislative programme could be tackled by a European Telecommunications Agency. The danger is that a new agency takes time to become operational, and will not naturally stand up to Member State pressure. Therefore the tasks best entrusted to it, at least at the beginning, are matters such as frequency licensing, numbering and relations with international standards bodies. Conceivably, the protection of privacy, the protection of children, fraud and consumer protection could better be addressed by such a body than by the Commission, where I have the feeling such issues may sometimes seem neglected. These are important tasks, politically sensitive, but ultimately capable of being solved by reason and logic, in co-operation with other agencies around the world where necessary. They should *not* be regarded as competition issues: one of the vices of the past is the abuse of regulatory principles to achieve anti-competitive objectives.

I question whether it would be wise to launch the European Telecommunications Agency in the very near future. The National Regulatory Authorities are new creations, or at least newly independent ones, in several Member States. It will take time for them to evolve from 'national regulators' to regulators applying locally principles which are agreed at Community level, in partnership with each other and the Commission. During this phase of development, it seems desirable to concentrate the process of consultation rather than diluting it. Indeed, advantages can perhaps be derived from identifying the occasions where an issue is presented as a regulatory matter when it is really a restriction of competition masquerading as a regulatory matter. If there is a scandal in some country about Internet fraud, we may expect a politician will (understandably) demand tough measures which may either distort competition or be Internet-hostile. I have at this stage more confidence in the Commission's ability to resist political pressure for undesirable measures than in the ability of the National Regulatory Authorities to do so.

In the longer run, I would continue to oppose the allocation of competition responsibilities to a European Telecommunications Agency, for the same reasons as I have opposed the creation of a European Cartel Agency. I accept that a European Telecommunications Agency could play a valuable role in international negotiations about international competition questions, ideally alongside the Commission; and it may be that the Commission's role in supervising normal competition will diminish. But let us focus most attention on surviving the next two years and equipping ourselves with minimalist regulations for the next ten, rather than drawing up organigrammes.

IV

Frédéric Jenny*

Safeguarding Conditions for Fair and Efficient Competition
in Complex Markets: Institutional Issues

I. French Competition Law and Access to Essential Facilities

The problem of access to essential facilities is not specific to the telecommunication sector or even to network industries. For example, in France, in 1996 in a case involving the organisation by a hospital in southern France of an emergency medical service to fly victims of road accidents to the hospital, one of the constraints was that the helicopter used for this service be stationed in the vicinity of the hospital so that doctors could be flown as quickly as possible to the sites of the accidents. However, the only helicopter station in the vicinity of the hospital was run by a company which already ran a helicopter service. After a competitive bidding process, the hospital chose another operator of helicopter services. The company already operated at the station then attempted through various means (including abusively high pricing of access to its facility) to prevent the helicopter company which had won the bid from gaining access to the station and to fulfil its contractual obligations with the hospital in the hope that the contract of its competitor would be cancelled. The Conseil de la concurrence ruled that this behaviour was a violation of the French competition law (Art. 8 of the law which prohibits practices of abuse of dominance) and the operator of the station was fined and given an injunction to price its services for the use of the station at a reasonable level compared to its costs and on a non discriminatory basis (compared to the price it was charging for the stationing and servicing of other helicopters).

An earlier case of a somewhat similar nature involved the discriminatory pricing conditions under which a cable operator which had a dominant position (and also belonged to a group vertically integrated in the production of programmes) undertook to carry programmes produced by independent producers on its cable network. It was found by the Conseil de la concurrence to be offering independent producers only a third of the price that it paid for programmes produced within its group. This behaviour was considered to be an abuse of its dominant position. However the Conseil's decision was overturned by the Court of Appeals on the basis of the fact that it was not

---

* Professor of Economics ESSEC; Vice President, Conseil de la concurrence, France.

sufficiently established that the independent producers' programmes had the same appeal as the programmes produced within the group.

Thus, competition law, and in particular provisions prohibiting the abuse of dominant position, can be used to ensure access to an essential facility even if one has to recognise that to adjudicate this type of cases the competition authority will undoubtedly face some difficulties in assessing the costs incurred by the operator of the essential facility and the maximum access price which could be charged.

II. Competition Law and Regulation in the Telecommunications Sector in France

At present the main regulation in France dealing with access to network industries concerns the telecommunication sector,[1] although a new law is being discussed in the context of the gradual opening to competition of the electricity sector.

The basic model followed in France in the telecommunication sector is that of a mandate-driven division of labour between the telecommunication regulatory authority (ART) and the competition authority. The problems raised by access to the network (whether technical conditions or access prices) and the granting of licences are handled by the regulatory authority whereas the competition authority has jurisdiction over the pricing of services to end users in the area which is open to competition.

Different reasons were offered to justify such a division of labour between both institutions. First, it was considered that in the initial phase of the opening up of the telecommunication sector to competition, competition law provisions on abuses of dominant position and competition law procedures were insufficient to ensure a speedy resolution of conflicts which would inevitably arise between France Telecom and its new competitors in view of the fact that these competitors would be dependent on France Telecom to gain access to the local network (at least in an initial phase). From that perspective the New Zealand experience (or the US experience of the late 1980s) were generally presented in a negative light and offered as proof that more efficient procedures than quasi-judicial procedures were required.

Second, it was considered that the opening up of the telecommunication sector to competition necessitated a certain dose of regulation (including establishment of a numbering plan, granting of licences for the use of scarce fre-

---

[1] Loi no 96–659 de réglementation des telecommunications.

quencies, definition of public service obligations and the establishment of a financing mechanism to cover their cost, rebalancing of the tariffs of the former public monopoly, establishment of accounting principles which the operator of the network would have to follow so as to eliminate possible cross subsidisation between its monopolistic markets and its activities in markets open to competition) requiring that a specific regulatory agency be established. This was considered to be all the more necessary because France Telecom is to remain for the foreseeable future a public firm with universal service obligations. There was some discussion of the fact that eventually, under the influence of technological convergence and the development of competition, the fixed point local network would lose its essential facility nature and that some of the regulations necessary in the initial phase of the development of the industry would be eliminated (thus allowing a greater role for competition law enforcement). However no explicit mechanism was established in the law to ensure the gradual phasing out of obsolete regulations.

As regards the problem of interconnection, operators of networks open to the public and having a significant influence on a telecommunication market, must publish an interconnection offer and must grant interconnection rights to service operators and to other network operators in an objective, transparent and non discriminatory way. The interconnection tariffs must be cost oriented and reflect the effective cost of using the network. Network operators having a market share of more than 25 percent of a relevant telecommunication market are presumed to have a significant influence and must thus publish a tariff of interconnection. The interconnection tariffs must be approved by the Regulator.

The regulatory authority is entrusted with the power to make a decision in case of a conflict between the operator of a network and a service provider over the interconnection price or technical conditions or in case of a refusal by the network operator to grant interconnection rights. It can issue temporary injunctions during its investigation of the matter. Its decisions can be appealed to the Paris Court of Appeal.

The Telecommunication Regulator can impose sanctions such as revoking the licence of a network operator or a service provider who does not meet its licence conditions or impose administrative pecuniary sanctions.[2] The regulatory authority can also act as a conciliator for disputes unrelated to interconnection problems between network operators and service providers if one of the parties to the dispute requires such conciliation. Finally, the

---

[2] Within the limits of 3 percent of the total sales of the offender or of 1,000,000 FFr. if the offender is not an enterprise.

Telecommunication Regulator gives a non-binding opinion to the Minister fc Telecommunications who must approve the prices charged to end-use cu tomers by the network operator for universal service obligations or for service which were not previously open to competition.

It is worth noting though that several provisions of the telecommunica tion law are designed to establish bridges between the telecommunicatio authority and the competition authority. First, before establishing the list o network operators who must offer interconnection services because they hav a significant position on a telecommunication market, the Telecommuni cations Regulator must seek the opinion of the Conseil de la concurrence The opinion of the Conseil, however, is non-binding. This provision arose ou of a concern over the fact that the division of responsibilities between th Telecommunications Regulator and the Conseil de la concurrence would leac each of these institutions to offer inconsistent definitions of relevant tele communication markets. Secondly, when it acts as a conciliator th Telecommunications Regulator must inform the Conseil de la concurrence. I a referral to the Conseil has been made on the same matter (for example or the basis of the fact that the network operator is abusing its dominant posi tion through excessive or unjustified demands on the service provider), the Conseil may (but is not required) to stay its investigation until the results of the conciliation. If, on the other hand, the conciliation fails and if the matter is relevant to competition law, the Telecommunications Regulator must make a referral to the Conseil. Third, the Regulator must refer any potential abuse of dominant position or anti-competitive practice which it may come across to the Conseil. If the matter is urgent, the Regulator may require that the Conseil make its decision within thirty days. Fourth, the Regulator may seek the non-binding advice of the Conseil on any competition matter. Finally the competition law enforced by the Conseil fully applies to the pro vision of telecommunication services to end-use customers and its decisions can be appealed before the same body as the decisions of the Telecommunica tions Regulator, i.e. the Paris Court of Appeal. Furthermore, before making any decision on a competition matter regarding the telecommunication sector, the Conseil de la concurrence must seek the non-binding advice of the Telecommunication Regulator.

This system delineates the responsibilities of each body: the Minister for Telecommunications is responsible for setting tariffs for universal services and services offered by the operator of the network when there is no competition; the Telecommunications Regulator is responsible for interconnection tariffs and technical conditions between the operator of the network and the service providers; and the competition authority are responsible for the relationship between service providers and end-use customers for markets open to competition. Consistency between the approaches of the regulatory decisions and of the competition law enforcement body is ensured both through consultations between the regulatory agencies and the competition authority and because the decisions of both bodies can be appealed before the Paris Court of Appeal.

The relationship between the Conseil de la concurrence and the Autorité de regulation des télecommunications has so far been one of mutual respect and co-operation. The Telecommunication Regulator has sought the advice of the Conseil in cases in which it was not required to do so (for example regarding the specific conditions which should be included in the licence of France Telecom to ensure the development of fair competition between the network operator and the service providers for services open to competition). Similarly, in a case concerning the awarding of a contract by the Ministry for Education for the provision of access to the internet to all public high schools (a new service for which France Telecom was for the first time bidding competitively with private service operators), the Conseil supported the view of the Regulator that the offer made by France Telecom prevented competition.

In this instance, the France Telecom tariff for the provision of the Internet services to high schools had been approved by the Minister for Telecommunications because this was a new service for which previously there was no competition and France Telecom had been awarded the contract by the Ministry for Education. In approving the tariff for access to the internet proposed by France Telecom, the minister had disregarded the non-binding opinion of the Telecommunication Regulator who had considered that the rates offered by France Telecom for internet access to high schools (which were lower than the interconnection rate for the interconnection of the Internet service providers to the local loop) were predatory given the unavailability of technical alternatives at the time of the bidding process. The losing competitors then made a referral to the Conseil de la concurrence arguing that the squeeze they were facing constituted an abuse of the dominant position of France Telecom prohibited by Art. 8 of the 1986 ordinance on the freedom of competition. The Conseil shared the opinion of the Regulator, particularly in view of the fact that if cable operators could conceivably offer internet services without having to interconnect with the local loop network, this possibility existed only to the extent that cable networks were upgraded and that France Telecom, which is technically responsible for the cable networks, had delayed the upgrading of such networks. Thus, the Conseil gave a temporary injunction to France Telecom to revoke its offer to the Ministry for Education and/or its interconnection rate for providers of the Internet service to high schools.

Subsequently the Telecommunications Regulator mediated the conflict between France Telecom and its competitors.

In only one case was there a disagreement between the Conseil de la concurrence and the Telecommunications Regulator. As mentioned, the Regulator establishes an annual list of network operators who must publish an interconnection offer to their network, because they have a significant position on a telecommunication market after having sought the opinion of the Conseil de la concurrence. The question arose as to whether a private mobile telephone operator had a sufficient market share on a relevant telecommunication market to be considered to have such a position and whether he should be subjected to the obligation of offering interconnection to its network. Whereas the Conseil de la concurrence in its non-binding opinion was of the view that this was indeed the case, the Telecommunication Regulator disagreed and did not include this operator in the list.

II. Regulation of the Audio-visual Sector and Competition law

The audio-visual sector is also regulated in France,[3] and the regulatory body (Conseil Supérieur de l'Audiovisuel, CSA) has the following functions:

- to give opinions to the government on a variety of matters including the conditions of the licensing of operators of radio or television services, the public service obligations of public television stations, the technical specifications applicable to cable and hertzian television services operators;
- to appoint the board members of publicly owned television companies;
- to allocate frequencies for hertzian television and radio services and to grant licences to broadcasters;
- to control television and radio broadcasters and sanction them or revoke their licences if they do not meet the conditions of these licences.

The law imposes various constraints on the ownership of hertzian television and radio broadcasters designed to guarantee a 'pluralism' of opinions. No individual or undertaking can own, either directly or indirectly, over 49 percent of a licensed television broadcaster. No individual or undertaking owning more than 15 percent of a television broadcaster can own more than 15 percent of another licensed broadcaster, and so forth. Finally, the law imposes constraints on the programming of licensed television broadcasters, including quotas of French-made films and programmes.

---

[3] Loi no 86–1067 du 30 September 1986 relative à la liberté de communication.

Whereas the competition law provisions concerning abuses of dominant position and anti-competitive cartels apply to the audio-visual sector (the enforcement of these provisions being entrusted to the Conseil de la concurrence), merger control does not apply to the audio-visual sector. Indeed, it was felt that the above mentioned constraints on ownership of radio and television broadcasters (enforced by the CSA) were sufficient.

This has led to a great degree of confusion. It is clear that the purpose of the constraints on ownership written into the telecommunication law (designed to ensure pluralism of ownership) differ from those of competition law provisions on merger control (designed to maintain competitive market structures). Furthermore, merger control applies to mergers between broadcasters to the extent that such mergers have an effect on a market other than the audio-visual market (such as, for example, the advertising market).

There are only a few bridges between the Audio-visual Regulator and the Conseil de la concurrence written into the competition law or the audio-visual law. The CSA must refer any evidence it comes across of a potential anti-competitive cartel or abuse of dominant position to the Conseil. So far the CSA has never referred any such evidence to the Conseil. The Conseil must seek the prior (non-binding) opinion of the CSA whenever it examines a case of potentially anti-competitive practices in the audio-visual sector.

III. The Electricity Sector

Intense discussions have started in France on the opening up of the electricity sector to competition and on the sort of regulatory regime to establish for this sector. Some of the problems raised are similar to the problems raised by the deregulation of the telecommunications sector. The electricity grid is an essential facility to which independent producers will have to be interconnected to supply electricity to large industrial users. Edf, will remain a public firm with universal service obligations, and a system of licences will allow private producers to compete on (at least part of) the market with Edf.

However, it is argued that there are differences between the two sectors and that the regulatory framework for electricity should not be same as that for telecommunications. In the first place, the technology in the electricity sector is more stable than in the telecommunication sector which means that the electricity grid is likely to remain an essential facility for much longer than telecommunications networks. Secondly, the scope of deregulation in the electricity sector in France will be much more limited as only a small portion of the market will be open to competition (and the incumbent will retain its legal monopoly on the provision of electricity to most customers) in the next few years. Thirdly, the (modest) opening to competition will take place in the context of governmental planning of the production of electricity (both with respect to what production capacities should be and to what types of installations should be allowed). Fourth, in order to avoid failure, there is a constant need to instantaneously adjust demand and supply and the government plans to entrust this function not to an independent 'technical' regulator but to an 'independent' division of Edf. And finally, the electricity sector in France is characterised by an excess supply due to the over-ambitious past programme of investment in nuclear power plants pursued by Edf and there are serious questions as to the present and future competitiveness of nuclear power compared to other sources of energy.

As a result, there has been much stronger resistance to the deregulation of the electricity sector in France than to the deregulation of telecommunications. It has been argued that the type of solution adopted for the telecommunications sector is either inappropriate or impossible in the case of electricity. It is, in particular, argued that the Ministry for Energy, or a division of such a ministry, should in any case retain the bulk of the regulatory powers to ensure consistency between deregulation and planning.

Although it is too early to say what the regulatory framework for electricity will be, it seems that the role assigned to the Regulator will be more limited than in the telecommunication sector. The role of competition law enforcement is, at this point unclear.

IV. Conclusion

In assessing the situation in France there is no substantive reason to believe that problems arising from access to essential facilities or networks could not be adjudicated under competition law provisions dealing with abuses of dominant position. There is, however, a real concern that competition law procedures are too slow and too cumbersome to guarantee a rapid solution to conflicts. Thus sector-specific regulators tend to be given powers to arbitrate conflicts or to make rapid decisions on interconnection problems.

Furthermore in most cases establishing a competitive environment for the industry is only one of the goals pursued. Promoting fairness (in the case of telecommunications), guaranteeing pluralism (in the case of the audio-visual sector), ensuring security and national independence (in the case of the electricity sector) are important policy goals justifying the existence of a specific regulatory body.

The division of jurisdiction between the regulator and the competition authority varies across regulated sectors reflecting varying levels of commitment to the goal of promoting competition. The mandate-driven division of labour between the competition authority and the sector-specific regulatory body can be drawn in such a way as to reduce potential conflicts (although it can also create gaps as we saw in discussing the audio-visual regulatory framework). In such a model, the competition authority (rather than the regulator) is responsible for enforcing the provisions of the competition law applicable to the regulated sector. Even a carefully drawn division of labour between the two authorities can lead to some overlap in jurisdiction between the two bodies (for example, in France, the arbitration of conflicts by the Telecommunications Regulator does not preclude the applicability of competition law) and the risk that both bodies will possibly interpret in different ways the same concepts (such as relevant markets). The Paris Court of Appeal which is the appellate body both for the decisions of the telecommunication regulator and for the decisions of the Conseil de la concurrence will, however, provide consistency.

IV

Frédéric Jenny

Chairman's Note on the Mini Round-Table on the Relationship
Between Regulators and Competition Authorities Held at the
OECD–CLP Committee, June 1998

I. Introduction

There seem to be specific regulatory regimes in many sectors of the OECD
countries, although, of course not all of the countries necessarily have specific
regulators in the same industries. Besides the obvious case of sectors such as
telecommunications, electricity, or railways for which we find specific regulatory regimes (and often industry specific regulators) in natural gas, radio and
television broadcast, civil aviation, cable television, ocean shipping, pharma-
ceuticals, petrochemicals, radioactive minerals, alcoholic beverages, insurance,
banking, coach transportation and trucking, water distribution and so forth.

A quick look at the contributions indicates that there is no unique model of
relationship between specific regulators and competition authorities either
across countries or (sometimes) within a country, even if there is a model which
seems to have the favour of a majority of contributors, that is, the mandate-
driven division of labour model.

Whereas in countries which have deregulated their economy earlier, the
relationship between specific regulators and competition authorities was established following a pragmatic case by case approach, in countries which are now
in the process of deregulating their economies and/or upgrading their competition law, there seems to be an attempt to think about the relationship between
specific regulators and competition authorities in a more systematic way.

Finally, in some contributions the same words do not always seem to have
the same meaning. In particular, I would draw your attention to the distinction
which is sometimes made between technical regulation, economic regulation
and competition law enforcement. What we mean by economic regulation
needs to be more precisely defined and I hope that the oral contributions will
shed light on this (as well as give us a precise understanding on who is responsible for economic regulation)

Before we examine specific cases, I would like to start with three contributions
which explore in the most systematic way the relationship between competition

law and sector-specific regulation and offer views as to the principles which should govern the relationship between competition authorities and regulators.

II. Principles

In Norway, an expert report discussed the extent to which responsibility for competition policy should be delegated to subordinate authorities and how competition and regulatory enforcement tasks should be allocated between the competition authority and the sector-specific authorities in the context of an administrative system where both the regulatory agencies and the competition authorities retain close links with the technical ministries and the Ministry for Economic Affairs.

In Denmark, a government appointed committee in 1997 suggested three reasons for leaving competition issues exclusively to the Competition Authority. It also found three reasons for having sector-specific regulators (i.e. regulation on quality, safety and the environment, ensuring public service at fair prices and access to infrastructure facilities) and recommended giving the Competition Authority a supporting role in each.

In the Netherlands primacy is given to competition law. In the context of the Project on the Supervision of Privatised Utilities begun in 1996, extensive discussions took place on the differences between sector-specific regulation and competition law, on the principle of restraint in the introduction of sector-specific regimes and on the relationship between sector-specific regulators and the Competition Authority. What is of particular interest in the case of the Netherlands is that in two out of three options explored for sectoral super-vision, the Competition Authority would in fact regulate both the competition and the economic regulator.

III. Diversity of Models

Irrespective of what we think should be the ideal model, there is a diversity of regimes across countries (and sometimes within one country across sectors).

In the case of New Zealand there is no specific regulator but the principle of light-handed regulation applies. For such a model to work, however, it seems that the government must be have the power to intervene to ensure speedy resolution of some disputes.

Australia follows a different model. Its competition authority, the ACCC has some regulatory power. In particular, it seems that it plays a role in access regimes. Thus, the solution in Australia appears to differ from the regime in

New Zealand, which relies entirely on competition law to solve deregulation issues. The questions raised in this context are: why was it felt necessary to establish specific access provisions (rather than use the general provisions against abuse of dominant position)?; why was the enforcement of this regulatory regime entrusted to the ACCC rather than to specific regulators?; and how does the behaviour of the ACCC in enforcing these rules differ from that of a specific regulator?

As we all know, the division of labour between the German Cartel Office and the Telecommunication Regulator has been the subject of intense debate in Germany. The provisions of the Telecommunication Act take precedence over the Cartel Act, and some of the responsibility for competition enforcement was transferred to the Telecom Regulator even though the Federal Cartel Office remains competent to supervise the activities of dominant suppliers of telecommunication services in relation to customers who are not competitors. The questions raised are: why was it felt that the provisions of the Telecommunications Act should take precedence over those of the Cartel Act?; how effective is the provision which requires the Bka and the Telecommunications Regulator be given an opportunity to hear each others views?; in which instances does the Bka give a binding opinion to the Regulator?; and, why is the opinion of the Bka binding in those cases and not in others?

The United Kingdom is unique in that it is a country in which specific regulators can apply competition law concurrently with the Director General for Fair Trading (except for merger control) and in which the Competition Bill, before parliament, will retain this principle. Thus, the existing and planned concurrence between authorities appears to be more widespread (and systematic) than in Norway, Spain and the United States. What are the reasons which militate for this model, and what are the conditions under which such a model can avoid conflicts and distortions?

Finally, at the general level the US contribution is of particular interest since it seems that several models of relationship between regulators and competition authorities are used concurrently.

IV. Overlaps and Co-operation between Regulatory Agencies and Competition Authorities in countries which have adopted the Model of a Mandate-driven Division of Labour

Most of the other countries seem to fall in the general model of mandate-driven division of labour. The organisation of co-operation between competition authorities and sector-specific regulators in countries which follow the model of mandate-driven division of labour between these two authorities may lead to two kinds of problems. In the first instance, both authorities may use the same concepts but interpret them differently. And secondly, there may be a partial overlap of responsibility, making it unclear which law should apply to specific practices (and who should enforce these laws).

However before we explore what specific problems are encountered in this model or the relationship between regulatory and competition agencies at the enforcement level, the situation in Canada underlines the fact that competition authorities can (and should) play an important role in the formulation of specific regulatory regimes through their advocacy function. Beyond this general point the Canadian contribution discusses at some length the concept of 'forbearance' and the role of the Bureau in this respect.

Along the same lines, the Mexican contribution emphasises the importance of competition advocacy in the design and implementation of sector-specific regulatory mechanisms. But it also states that a number of sector-specific laws and regulations explicitly provide a role for the Competition Commission (something which appears to be lacking in Canada). Yet, it seems that in the case of Mexico, even in sectors where there is a specific role for the Competition Authority, there are difficulties due to the fact that the same practices may fall simultaneously within the purview of competition law and sector-specific regulators.

In Italy the competition authority strictly interprets the regulatory exemption for anti-competitive practices and co-operation between regulatory and competition authorities has been institutionalised by the provision of non-binding opinions delivered by regulatory authorities to the competition authority and *vice versa*. Furthermore, the Autoritá also offers its views on desirable regulatory regimes to parliament. As regards publishing and broadcasting, the specific regulator had competition law enforcement functions but lost them due to a change in the law whereby these functions were transferred to the Autoritá.

The case of Finland underscores the potential difficulties associated with overlapping responsibilities of sector-specific regulators and the competition authority particularly in the telecommunications sector. It suggests, however, that the OFC and the regulatory authorities have in practice (and in a rather informal way) agreed on how overlapping situations should be addressed without however publishing any concordats. An interesting question is whether the solution found so far can be generalised to other sectors which are about to be deregulated, such as the railways.

In Japan, as in some of the other countries, the JFTC has sole responsibility for enforcing the Antimonopoly Act and economic and technical regulations are implemented exclusively by regulatory agencies. But regulatory laws and the AMA clearly have different objectives and requirements and even though procedures have not been established to resolve problems that arise between competition agencies and regulatory agencies, the usual 'administrative co-ordination' has been effected in an attempt to achieve appropriate resolutions to these problems. It seems that in some areas at least technical regulators reformed their regulation following representations by the JFTC. An interesting question is whether the JFTC takes the initiative to review these regulations, whether such reviews are systematic, whether they apply to individual decisions by regulators and whether regulators have to take into account the remarks of JFTC.

In Sweden, the Telecom Act of January 1997 gave the National Post and Telecom Agency (PTS) extensive power as a sectoral regulator. PTS has been given a co-ordinating and unifying function in relation to the Competition Authority and the Consumer Protection Agency. It also seems that there are cases in which the competition authority made decisions both in the area of interconnection and in the area of pricing of services by the dominant operator to its own end-customers.

In Hungary, another country which follows the mandate-driven division of labour model, the Competition Authority may only intervene in practices which are not regulated by the regulatory authorities although, at least in some sectors such as gas, electricity and television broadcasting, in the area of merger regulation the competition authority and the regulatory agency have to come to a unanimous positive decision for the merger to proceed.

Lastly the EU can intervene in various ways in the national regulatory process either through decisions based on Article 226 [ex 199] or Article 86(3) [ex 90(3)] or through directives. Furthermore, Articles 81 and 82 [ex 85 and 86] are applicable to firms in regulated sectors even if their practice has been authorised, approved or tolerated by a national regulatory agency if the regulation itself violates Article 86(1) [ex 90(1)] of the Treaty. National courts can directly apply Article 86(1) [ex 90(1)]. Thus, it seems that national competition authorities may have wider powers to intervene in the regulatory process on the basis of European law than on the basis of their own domestic competition law.

But one should note a comment made about the Netherlands Report, which states that 'often directives that regulate liberalised markets stipulate that Member States establish national regulatory agencies (e.g. telecom, postal service, electricity, etc.). Such a solution is indeed not stimulating as to situations where national competition authorities are empowered to enforce sectoral regulations. In this respect, EU directives that prescribe national regulatory authorities may well contribute to the problem of proliferation and supra-national remedial actions could be necessary'. So the question is whether in the EU, the action of the Community is in fact adding confusion on the issue of the applicability of competition law to regulated sectors.

V

*Bruno Lasserre**

Competition or Regulatory Authority? European or National Level?

. Introduction

The opening up of telecommunications in France—where the Conseil de la concurrence operates as a strong, recognised authority for the horizontal monitoring of competition—illustrates the duality of institutions responsible for regulating both the industry and competition alike.

II. Why Two Authorities? The Debates Preceding the 1996 Reform of French Telecommunications

The debate began in 1993/4 and became properly structured in late 1995, at the time of the public consultation organised by the Directorate General for Posts and Telecommunications with an eye to drafting the law on telecommunications regulation. In 1993/4, when competition in France was limited to mobiles and business services—with the exception of fixed public telephones—France Télécom's behaviour in the competitive sector had given rise to complaints from professional organisations and new market entrants alike. The criticism related less to the principle of its presence within the market than to the dysfunctionality associated with certain types of commercial conduct, and did not lead to legal action, but to repeated appeals on the part of the regulator—the DGPT. The Conseil de la concurrence (Competition Board) was rarely called on.

Following public consultation with all interested parties, the regulator published a series of recommendations taking account of the viewpoints expressed. These related to the status of the regulator—then an integral part of the state. The introduction of an appeals body to complement the regulator was also discussed.

The desires then expressed by competitive operators were simple: the regulator should be able to intervene rapidly, should be in posession of a full range

* Secretariat d'Etat à l'Industrie. I would like to thank Ms. Martine Georges, advocate with Moquet-Borde et associés of Paris, for the work she has done, particularly in clarifying the tables.

of penalties and should be able to take preventative measures. When operator recognised that the Competition Board and the courts had an entire range of instruments at their disposal—injunctions, temporary orders, financial penalties, and published judgments—they signalled that they would withdraw from judicial proceedings since this was too lengthy a procedure and was tantamount to 'going on the warpath'.

At the time, appeals to the regulator seemed natural for three reasons. First there is a continuity between regulatory activity proper and the treatment of problems that may subsequently arise. The *a priori* monitoring of tariffs and the correct allocation of costs run hand in hand with *a posteriori* verification of absence of cross-subsidisation. It is difficult to separate the regulation of the content of licences from the implementation of regulatory stipulations when it comes, for example, to settling access to the public network. Secondly, the regulator is able to mobilise expert capacities and can also promote use of informal mediation procedures. And finally, the regulator has the power to propose and amend rules that may tend to create distortions of competition.

Such, then, were the findings on which the then consensus was based. The regulator sought to respond to the demands made by publishing a series of recommendations addressed to France Télécom, and brought together in the form of a 'good conduct code'. This, however, never got beyond the draft stage because of the hefty opposition from France Télécom and the serious reservations of the Competition Board, which rightly felt that this initiative was encroaching on its prerogatives.

In 1995, during the drafting of the telecommunications law that was to liberalise the whole sector as from 1 January 1998, the debate fired up again. It was split between two opposing 'schools'. The first brought together private operators and, defended by the DGPT, advocated a specific regulator for the telecommunications sector with extensive powers and a high degree of independence. The second, France Télécom supported by the competition directorate in the Economics Ministry, instead advocated 'normalisation' of the sector such that the ordinary competition law would act as 'regulator' of a liberalised telecommunications market. The idea of a 'public utilities section' (telecoms, electricity, transport) within the competition board was again raised.

When consulted, the Competition Board reconciled the two positions by supporting the idea of an independent regulator while suggesting the creation of 'bridges' between the two institutions to prevent the 'fractionalisation' of general competition law.

III. The Links Between the Two Authorities: Practical Solutions

The telecommunications regulation law of 26 July 1996 radically changed the institutional landscape by creating a regulatory authority for telecommunications (ART), as the successor to the DGPT, to regulate the now fully liberalised sector. By contrast with other European countries, France rejected any degree of ministerial influence upon the regulator and opted for a fully independent authority subject to *a posteriori* judicial control.

Its five members are appointed for a period of six years, and may not be dismissed during that period or reappointed after it. ART decisions which arbitrate between operators can only be challenged before a judge in the Paris Appeals Court. The Conseil d'Etat is responsible for other cases. But despite this independence, the new authority's powers are not unlimited and are shared, on the one hand, with government, and on the other, must be compatible with those of the competition authorities who retain full powers in the telecommunications sector. The situation is summarised in the following table.

Table 1

Principles	Consequences
(1) No specific competition law for telecommunications and no exclusive competence for the ART	Linkage of the institutions
(2) Respect for telecommunications; regulations do not pre-empt respect for competition rules laid down in either European or national law	Cumulation of rules

A linkage between the ART and the Competition Board was established by the setting up of institutional 'bridges' compelling both bodies to consult each other and inviting them to benefit from the 'value added' of the other, as well as through unified judicial review. The institutional bridges can be summarised in the following table.

Table 2: Powers of the ART and one-off actions by the Competition Board

ART	Competition Board
(1) General Duties Obligation to bring before the Competition Board abuses of dominant positions or practices in restraint of free competition in the telecommunications sector	(2) General Duties Obligation to notify the ART of any case in the telecommunications sector and to secure its opinion on cases before it
(2) Specific Powers Licences: consideration of public telephony requests; authorisation of independent network	(2) Specific interventions at ART or government request Opinion on the 'Competition Clause' in the list of charges; opinion on accounting separation
Interconnection: setting of technical and financial terms; list of major operators on the market; approval of catalogue; decisions on disputes (injunctions possible); amendments of agreements	Opinion on the list of 'major' operators; opinion on changes to agreements
Universal Service: assessment of costs of universal service and contributions payable by operators	Possibility of giving an opinion at ART or government request
Rates: opinions on charges for universal services and services with no market competitors	

Allocation of scarce resources (frequencies and numbers)

Technical regulation (Standards and agreements)

Conciliation (articles L.36–9) to promote friendly settlement of disputes not having to do with interconnection

Notification of Competition Board by ART (Board may decline to intervene at this stage); invocation of Competition Board by ART should conciliation fail

(3) Penalties

(3) Penalties

Delay: total or partial suspension of authorisation; financial penalties

Conservational measures; injunction to cease anti-competitive behaviour; fines

As regards the judicial review of disputes on interlinking networks or the supply of telecommunication services, the law prevents operators from choosing to submit an appeal either to the ART or to the Competition Board, by giving the Paris Appeals Court, which is the 'appeals judge' for the Competition Board, final competence to handle all appeals. This solution, which has the merit of unifying the cases, has been accepted by the Conseil Constitutionnel on the grounds that it favours the good administration of justice. In all other cases—rejection of licences, approval of rates, allotment of frequencies or numbers—ART decisions must be challenged before an administrative court, in this case the Conseil d'Etat, which must also verify whether the administrative authority has complied with competition law.

IV. The Strengths and Weaknesses of Each Institution

We may summarise the strengths and weaknesses of each of the two bodies—the ART and the Competition Board—as follows. The main strength of the ART is its capacity to mobilise its economic and technical resources to deal with the often complex questions relating to the functioning of the telecommunications sector. The publicity which its opinions and decisions receive also constitutes a trump card, giving the authority a form of 'magisterial influence'. Finally, the ART's ability to forestall potential restraints of competition make it an effective recourse.

The youth of the ART is nonetheless a weakness, since authority is often acquired with time. The fact that the ART shares its powers with the government in a great number of cases, is also a handicap: this is the case for approval of France Télécom's rates, where by contrast with Britain's OFTEL the French ART only has the power to give opinions which the government need not follow. Finally, the ambiguity of the regulatory function also weighs upon the institution: it is an intermediary function, almost 'in suspension' between the definition of policy, something which is always up to government and parliament, and business administration, which is a matter for the actors within the market. The regulator must maintain the balance desired by the legislator—a balance which is often in movement—without encroaching on the role of normal market forces. He is expected to reduce uncertainties precisely when the weight of technical and economic development is amplifying them: a difficult job where legitimacy can only be attained over time through a capacity to guarantee the predictability of the basic rules.

The Competition Board, has one incomparable strength, deriving from its comprehensive power, since the ordinary competition law it is mandated to apply transcends sectoral barriers or specificities. Its unchallenged authority, born of now well-established experience, gives it more clout than the sectoral regulator, and often makes it the call of 'last resort'.

There are several reasons for its relative weakness. Its remoteness from the sector, which, though sometimes an advantage, does not allow it to acquire technical expertise. Its *modus operandi*, which resembles that of a court, may mean longish delays, even though the Competition Board has been able to show (as, for instance, when it came to freezing a rate charged by France Télécom for access to the Internet in schools) that it can take rapid measures when the stakes are high. Finally, its task is simply that of repairing *a posteriori* damage caused to the competitive functioning of the market rather than the *a priori* prevention of anti-competitive conduct.

V. Conclusion

In assessing the present position, one must acknowledge that there is a relatively satisfactory sharing of roles. The bridges have worked well in so far as they enable each institution to benefit from the 'value added' generated by the other. In relation to both France Télécom's rate offers or the concept of the relevant market when defining the list of 'major operators' for the publication of an interlinkage catalogue, the Competition Board has provided 'horizontal' expertise, based on the experience of years of case law. Conversely, in assessing complaints arising out of anti-competitive behaviour by France Télécom or its subsidiaries, the ART's opinion has supported the Competition Board's approach.

Similarly, the Competition Board has compensated for weaknesses in the legislation in certain cases. This was the case for the supervision of rates, where as we have seen the ART only has the power to issue an opinion. In the case of schools' access to the internet, the Competition Board was able to take measures to freeze the government's decision to approve rates which the ART had regarded to be 'predatory'.

This does not mean the position is stable or definitive. The situation is essentially one of transition from monopoly to competition, and is thus marked by the laying down of new ground rules. I believe that regulation will change in accordance with the state of the market in three stages. First, the *regulation of market entry,* involving the definition of the legal and technical conditions applying to new competitive actors (licences, access to scarce resources, conditions of access to public networks, financing of universal services). This stage requires the strongest involvement on the part of the industry regulator, given that before laying down new ground rules he must also guide the transition from monopoly to competition. Second, the *regulation of dominance,* corresponding to a liberalised market still largely dominated by the former monopoly: here the need is to define the—economic and accounting—conditions necessary in order to guarantee a level playing-field, or equality of competitive conditions for those present in the market. The relevant instruments are rate control (consumer charges or interconnection rates), stipulated accounting or legal separation and consideration of correct cost allocation. This stage calls for close collaboration between the competition and regulatory authority, since the same concepts are being used (anti-competitive practices, abuses of dominant positions), the only difference being that the regulator seeks to forestall anti-competitive conduct, whilst the competition authority makes corrections subsequently. And thirdly, the *regulation of competition,* corresponding to a market situation not just liberalised but 'normalised', taking account of the re-balancing of market segments and the progressive disappearance of structural barriers to competition. In this third stage, which places trust in the application of market forces whilst reserving the power to apply penalties for anti-competitive action, the industry regulator takes second place to the competition authority, since its added value declines.

The question of principle—'which will survive?'—undoubtedly calls for an affirmative answer as regards the competition authority. But the real question is 'for how long?', given that developments may be so slow as to seem eternal. Which countries can seriously claim that their telecommunications markets have entered the third stage? And who can predict, particularly when observing what is happening in the United States, that the regulator's days are numbered since, with the passage of time he may become such an essential figure in the landscape as to confirm the poet's words: 'one man fell, and all was depopulated. . .'?

VI

*Santiago Martínez Lage and Helmut Brokelmann**

The Respective Roles of Sector-Specific Regulation and Competition Law
and the Institutional Implications

I. Introduction

The liberalisation of telecommunications markets throughout the European
Community has generated a vast amount of sector-specific regulation at a
national and Community level and led to the creation of national regulatory
authorities (NRAs) whose powers are liable to conflict with those of the
traditional antitrust authorities. This paper analyses the role of sector-specific
regulation and pure competition law in the new environment and the relation
between the new regulatory authorities and the antitrust authorities with particular emphasis on the Spanish telecommunications market.

II. The Respective Roles of Competition Law and Sector-Specific
Regulation

Although there are regulatory obligations that apply to any company operating in the telecommunications sector, the main task of sector-specific regulation is to create competitive conditions through asymmetric regulation to
remove existing imbalances generated by entrenched legal monopolies. There
are two basic differences between asymmetric regulation and the general application of competition law. First, under existing rules on Open Network
Provision (ONP) operators enjoying 'significant market power' are subject to
additional burdens even if they are not 'dominant' within the meaning of
Article 82 [ex 86] of the EC Treaty. That is, an operator with a market share of
around 25% alongside other competitors with lower market shares is subject to
supplementary obligations without necessarily being able to behave independently of its competitors, which would be the relevant criterion for 'special
responsibility' under the competition rules.[1] Indeed, the definition of 'significant market power' in the ONP Directives refers to the 'organisation's
ability to influence market conditions' rather than to its ability to 'behave

---

* Martinez Lage & Asociados.
[1] See, 322/81, *Michelin,* [1983] ECR 3461, para. 57.

independently of its competitors, customers and ultimately of its consumers'.[2] Secondly, Article 82 [ex 86] does not empower the Commission to carry out an *ex ante* control of potentially anti-competitive conduct, whereas the ONP rules allow for preventive control by the regulatory authorities so that operators with significant market power are subject to these regulatory obligations without even having abused their—potentially—dominant position.

In principle, sector-specific regulation allows regulators to address a broader range of issues and to impose more specific and far-reaching obligations than pure competition law. For example, under Article 82 [ex 86] of the EC Treaty, or the equivalent provisions of national competition law, a competition authority has the power to declare that prices charged by an operator are excessive, discriminatory or predatory, to order the termination of the abusive conduct, and to impose fines. It lacks, however, the power to impose a determined price on a dominant operator as provided for in the Interconnection Directive, which gives NRAs the power to require charges to be adjusted and to request changes in the interconnection after.[3] The same can be said with respect to obligations concerning transparency and non-discrimination,[4] and to those relating to access to, and interconnection between, networks and services,[5] all of which go beyond what is required under Article 82 [ex 86].[6]

An example of the different scope of obligations imposed on the basis of the competition rules and regulatory requirements is provided for in the Commission's Access Notice,[7] which states that, in contrast to Article 7 of the Interconnection Directive, Article 82 [ex 86], which prohibits dominant undertakings from 'applying dissimilar conditions to equivalent transactions', cannot

---

[2] See 27/76, *United Brands*, [1978] ECR 207, para. 65.

[3] See Articles 7–8 of Directive 97/33/EC on interconnection in telecommunications with regard to ensuring universal service and interoperability through the application of ONP principle, OJ L 199/32 (1997).

[4] See Articles 6–7 of Directive 97/33/EC on Interconnection; Article 16(7) Directive 98/10/EEC, on the application of ONP to voice telephony, OJ L 101/24 (1998).

[5] See Article 4a of Directive 90/388/EEC, as amended by Directive 96/19/EC on the implementation of full competition, OJ L74/13 (1996); Articles 3–4 of Directive 97/33/EC on interconnection; Articles 13 and 16 of Directive 98/10/EC on the application of open networl provision to voice telephony, OJ L 101/24 (1998); on access to other facilities see Article 15.

[6] As regards the quality of services, Article 12 of Directive 98/10/EC even allows Member States to set performance targets in individual licences granted to operators with significant market power and to keep up-to-date information concerning their performance.

[7] Notice on the application of the competition rules to access agreements in the telecommunications sector, OJ C 265/2 (1998).

normally require a dominant company to treat different categories of customers differently and that, 'Community competition rules are not sufficient to remedy all of the various problems in the telecommunications sector'.[8]

Hence, problems relating to issues such as interconnection, numbering, universal service, transparency or pricing are regulated in more detail in the respective Community Directives, particularly the ONP Directives, and the national laws implementing them. It is unlikely that the application of general competition law would serve a purpose of its own as competition rules do not normally extend as far as the obligations imposed by sectoral rules. One should, however, bear in mind that, as the Access Notice states, the Commission will build on the ONP Directives in applying the competition rules and that certain competition law principles are covered by specific ONP rules. The Access Notice seems to imply that there is no need to apply Articles 81 and 82 [ex 85 and 86] where the ONP framework is properly implemented by the NRAs (paragraph 58). This confirms that the space left for pure competition law in the first stage of regulating the recently liberalised telecommunications sector by sector-specific regulation is relatively narrow. Nonetheless, the Commission considers compliance with national or European sector-specific regulation does not obviate the need to comply with the Treaty's competition rules, making enterprises subject to a double compliance standard.

1. The Space left by Sector-Specific Regulation

In spite of the pre-eminence of regulations over the application of pure competition law, the latter still plays an important role within the framework of ONP rules. This is illustrated by an investigation of mobile phone charges across the EU initiated by the Commission under Article 82 EC [ex 86]. The investigation was launched against mobile telephone operators of several Member States (all of them former public monopolies) for charging excessive and discriminatory prices on calls between fixed and mobile phones. Of the fourteen inquiries originally initiated by DG IV, one (British Telecom) was suspended because the issue was already subject to an inquiry by the MMC and another four were referred to the respective national regulatory authorities. These four cases related to excessive and discriminatory interconnection fees charged to mobile phone operators which could be better addressed with the tools provided for in the Interconnection Directive and the national rules implementing it.[9] The remaining nine cases concerned excessive prices charged

---

[8] See paragraphs 14–15 and 123–4.

[9] See IP/98/707, of 27.07.98. According to the Commission, the four operators (Telefónica, Deutsche Telekom, KPN, and Telecom Italia) charged mobile operators

to consumers for mobile call termination (as opposed to origination of mobile-to-mobile calls) and fixed-to-mobile calls (in order to offset reductions in mobile termination rates). Here the Commission did not indicate why it opted for pursuing these cases under Article 82 [ex 86] rather than applying the ONP Directives, be it itself pursuant to Article 226 [ex 169], or asking the relevant NRAs to carry out the instruction. The reason for this choice may be a desire to set a tough precedent in a case directly affecting the consumer which displays sufficient 'Community interest', and which can be dealt with under Article 82 [ex 86].

The interplay between NRAs and the Commission is also evident in the case of Deutsche Telekom (DT) accused of charging excessive fees for the provision of carrier pre-selection and number portability. The Commission initiated proceedings because DT's proposed fees could have set a negative example, or even an incentive for abuse, for operators in other Member States contemplating the introduction of similar services. Nevertheless, the proceedings were terminated and the case referred to the national authorities following the German Regulatory Authority's rejection of DT's fees. Other instances where the Commission has initiated proceedings under Article 82 [ex 86] suggest that the threat of an unfavourable decision by the Commission may stimulate an early settlement in exchange for terminating the infringement procedure.

Despite the residual role of pure competition law in the immediate wake of liberalisation, there are situations where the application of competition rules is still relevant, particularly in those areas not covered by sector-specific regulation which can only be dealt with under antitrust law. The main field of application for general competition law is to *fill loopholes left by sector-specific regulation,* and this role will arguably become increasingly relevant over time as existing regulations become outdated and the application of pure competition law is faster and more flexible than legal process leading to the amendment of the ONP rules. For example, the review of the Cable Directive[10] deals with some of the problems generated by convergence, but many convergence-related issues in telecommunications, audio-visual, and information technology, are not covered by sector-specific regulation. Pure competition law plays

---

more than fixed operators for call termination of mobile-to-fixed calls. The Commission stayed its proceedings for 6 months in favour of action by the respective NRAs (cf. para. 30 of the Access Notice).

[10] Commission Communication on the review under competition rules of the joint provision of telecommunications and cable TV networks by a single operator and the abolition of restrictions on the provision of cable TV capacity over telecommunications, OJ C71/4 (1998).

a crucial role in this converging environment given that sector-specific regulation cannot anticipate new developments and movements by market players nor react with the necessary swiftness. In situations of this kind the Merger Regulation will not always be the best instrument because the acquisition of companies in adjacent, but different, markets will not always create or reinforce an incumbent's dominant position. Therefore, Article 82 [ex 86] plays an important role where incumbent telecommunications operators move into neighbouring markets, thus foreclosing opportunities for their rivals.[11]

Article 86 [ex 90], read in conjunction with Article 82 [ex 86], may also play a role where undertakings hold exclusive or special rights in a non-telecommunications field,[12] or if the state or NRA interferes with, or authorises, a specific operation. In 1997 the Spanish digital satellite television operator Canal Satélite Digital filed complaints with the Commission against measures adopted by the Spanish government and the NRA designed to hamper its penetration of the emerging satellite television market until its rival, Telefónica was ready to offer its own satellite television service seven months later (infra, p. 648).

Another area where the competition rules play an important role despite the existence of ONP legislation is *access to facilities*, in particular, access to the network facilities of dominant telecommunications operators (TOs). The Access Notice stipulates that the role of the competition rules is to guarantee the development of prospective access markets, and to prevent incumbent TOs from using their control over access to stifle the development of service markets. Although there are areas where the two sets of rules overlap, the Access Notice states that if the rules are properly applied this should often avert the need to apply the competition rules.

Sector-specific access regulation imposes obligations to negotiate interconnection and access from the start, whilst Article 82 [ex 86] only provides for an *ex post* control of abusive conduct, in this case a refusal to grant access to an essential facility on fair and non-discriminatory terms. The Access Notice identifies three situations where the refusal to grant access by a dominant operator

---

[11] See, for example, the complaint filed by Canal Satélite Digital against Telefónica's (the former public telecommunications operator in Spain) acquisition of Antena 3TV (a commercial free access TV network) in 1997. The complaint was filed pursuant to Articles 82 and 85 [ex 86 and 89] as this vertical concentration neither had a 'Community dimension' (Article 1(2) Reg. 4064/89) nor was it notified to or investigated by the national antitrust authorities (notification of concentrations was by then still voluntary in Spain). The case is mentioned in the Commission's Green Paper on Convergence, COM(97) 623 final, of 3.12.1997.

[12] For example, in the broadcasting or cable sector.

is liable to infringe Article 82 [ex 86]. While the first (discrimination), and thir (withdrawal of supply), situation are fully in line with the Commission's prac tice and the case law of both Community Courts, the application of Article 8 [ex 86] in the second case is questionable and has not yet been endorsed by th Courts' case law.

In this second case, the Notice provides for the obligation to grant access t a downstream operator where the network provider has not allowed access t another enterprise in order to provide the service in question, and is not itse present in the downstream service market. The Commission ostensibly relie on its own practice and ECJ case law to justify the application of the essentia facilities doctrine. In our opinion, however, this situation is not covered by EC case law or by Commission practice in other sectors. The main feature in th precedents cited in the Access Notice is that the dominant undertaking refus ing to grant access was either itself present or about to enter the downstrean market where the enterprise seeking access wanted to operate. This anti-com petitive element was even present in most withdrawal cases where the dominan undertaking willing to enter a downstream market ceased to supply an estab lished customer.[13] The need for a 'horizontal element' is even more important if the refusal is directed against a new customer of the dominant undertaking.[14] As case law stands, Article 82 [ex 86] is only applicable if the new customer is simultaneously an actual or potential downstream competitor of the dominant undertaking.[15] Thus, in the *Magill* case,[16] in addition to the fact that the TV stations were preventing the appearance of a new product for which there was a potential consumer demand, the TV stations sought to eliminate a potential competitor in the downstream market of TV listings where they were them selves present.[17] The ECJ's judgment in *BP/Commission*[18] shows that refusal to

---

[13] Case 6 and 7/73, *Commercial Solvents*, [1974] ECR 223; Case 311/84, Télémarketing, [1985] ECR 3270; Decision 88/518/EEC, *British Sugar*, OJ L 284/41; Decision 87/500/EEC, *BBI/Boosey&Hawkes*, OJ L 286/36.

[14] That is, where the element of dependence is lacking.

[15] While the ECJ confirmed in the *Volvo/Veng* (238/87, [1988] ECR 6211) and *CICRA/Renault* (53/87, [1988] ECR 6039) judgments that Article 82 [ex 86] could also apply to a refusal to supply a new customer, albeit in exceptional circumstances, it was not until the *Magill* case that the Commission (and both Community Courts) applied Article 82 [ex 86] to the refusal to supply a new customer (89/205/EEC, OJ L 78/43 (1989); on appeal case T–69/89, *RTE/Commission,* [1991] ECR II–485; and C–242/91P, *RTE and ITP/Commission,* [1995] ECR I–743).

[16] *Ibid.*

[17] The same applied in the port cases (*B & I Line plc* v *Sealink Harbours LH and Sealink Stena LH* [1992] 5 CMLR 255; *Sea Containers/Stena Sealink,* 94/255/EEC, OJ L 15/8 (1994); and Dec. 94/119/EC *Port of Rodby,* 94/19/EEC, OJ L 55/52 (1994), in

supply a new customer in a purely vertical relationship is not contrary to Article 82 [ex 86], and the Court of First Instance (CFI) has confirmed the need for a 'horizontal' element for applying Article 82 [ex 86] to a refusal to supply a new customer in the *Ladbroke/Commission* judgment. The Court held that, 'in the absence of direct or indirect exploitation by the *sociétés de courses* of their intellectual property rights on the Belgian market, their refusal to supply cannot be regarded as involving any restriction of competition on the Belgian market.'[19]

This brief analysis of case law shows that the Access Notice is breaking new ground in the interpretation of Article 82 [ex 86] as regards access to essential facilities.[20] The obligation to grant access in purely 'vertical' relationships goes beyond the obligations which Article 82 [ex 86] requires from dominant undertakings because of their special responsibility. From a policy perspective, it is reasonable to expect the former state monopolist, whose network has been largely built with public funds, to be under an obligation to grant access so as to facilitate the emergence of new products or services, even where the incumbent has no interest in the downstream market. Nonetheless, in order to avoid the future application of far-reaching requirements to other sectors or telecom operators that have not enjoyed long-standing legal monopolies, such obligations should instead be imposed by sector-specific regulation than via the general application of the essential facilities doctrine in the context of Article 82 [ex 86]. It is also important that such far-reaching regulatory requirements are not applied by the antitrust authorities, but by the NRAs so as to avoid the risk of these obligations 'feeding' themselves into other sectors, diluting the scope and content of the competition rules.

---

which the port operators were themselves present in the downstream market for provision of ferry services which they sought to monopolise. Similarly, in the airline cases (*Aer Lingus/British Midland*, 92/213/EEC, OJ L 96/34 (1992); and *London European/Sabena*, 88/589/EEC, OJ L 317/47 (1988) the refusal in the dominated upstream market aimed at excluding competing airlines from specific routes. For a more detailed analysis see Brokelmann (1997).

[18] Case 77/77, [1978] ECR 1513 (appeal against Commission Decision 77/327/EEC, OJ L 117/1 (1977)).

[19] See Case T–504/93, ECR [1997] II–923, paras. 129–30.

[20] To our knowledge, the only precedent in which the Commission has successfully applied Article 82 [ex 86] to a refusal to give access to in a purely vertical relationship is the *ICG/CCI Morlaix* case; *see* XXV Report on Competition Policy (1995), points 40 and 43 and IP/95/492, of 16.5.1995.

644 *Working Paper VI*

2. The Transitional Character of Sector-Specific Regulation

Compared with the duties of companies under the competition rules, asymmetric sector-specific regulatory requirements are generally more far-reaching and burdensome. It is therefore essential that the existing regulatory regime has a transitional character and does not impose burdensome obligations on operators once workable competition is in place. Obligations which go beyond what is strictly necessary to achieve competitive market structures in the various telecommunications markets may prove counterproductive and even act as a disincentive to investments, thus stifling innovation. Where more or less competitive market structures exist, it is arguably better to rely on market forces and the general application of competition law than to continue enforcing the stricter and less flexible regulatory framework. The role played by competition law should therefore increase as competitive market structures are implemented, and that of specific regulation should gradually become obsolete. The exception to this principle concerns key transparency and information requirements that should be maintained as long as markets are oligopolistic (albeit competitive).

An example of the need to limit the application of the ONP framework are the obligations imposed by current regulation (Community and national) on operators with 'significant market power', that is, with a market share of 25% or even less.[21] It is clear that once markets have been successfully liberalised, and effective or workable competition exists, the imposition of specific (asymmetric) regulatory obligations on non-dominant operators is no longer justifiable and questionable whether, for example, it is lawful to impose interconnection and access obligations on new entrants (*vis-à-vis* other newcomers) with a 25% market share competing against the incumbent operator and still investing heavily in its own network. This suggests that the imposition of strict regulatory obligations may be counterproductive in some situations and should progressively give way to the sole application of the more flexible competition rules. A distinction should at least be made between dominant positions held as a consequence of long-standing legal monopolies and those achieved by the efforts of the enterprise concerned.

This kind of limitation is provided in respect of specific regulatory obligations. Thus, Article 10(4) of Directive 92/44/EEC[22] provides that the NRA

---

[21] See Article 4(2) and (3) of Directive 97/33 on Interconnection; Article 2 of Directive 97/51 (amending Articles 1 and 2 of Directive 92/44, on the application of ONP to leased lines); and Article 2(2)(i) of Directive 98/10.

[22] Directive 92/44 on the application of open network provision to leased lines, OJ L 165/27 (1992), as amended by Directive 97/51/EC, OJ L 295/23 (1997).

'may decide not to apply the requirements of paragraph 1 in a specific geographical area where it is satisfied that there is effective competition in the relevant leased-lines market'. The Reference Framework for the Application of ONP Conditions annexed to Directive 90/387/EEC contains a similar provision, 'Where an organisation no longer has significant market power in the relevant market, the requirement for cost orientation may be set aside by the competent national regulatory authority'.[23]

One can argue that the opportunity to lift obligations imposed by sector-specific regulation should be a general principle governing the entire ONP framework which applies to all asymmetric requirements. This process should be gradual and decided specifically for each product and territorial market. By way of illustration, where it is difficult to build up networks (particularly fixed networks for voice telephony) sector-specific regulation is needed for a longer period than in markets where parallel networks, and consequently a competitive market situation, already exist (as in the mobile telephony sector where the incumbent also has to build up an own network).

Moreover, it is important that the decision to suspend regulatory obligations is taken by an independent body and not the respective NRA. Experience in other countries indicates that sector regulators have a natural tendency to perpetuate themselves and even expand their fields of activity. The institution best suited for this task is the Commission's Joint Team (DG IV and DG XIII), which could supervise the transition to competitive markets led by the NRAs lifting regulatory obligations in markets where workable competition already exists. DG IV instead of the NRAs should thus decide in each market when sector-specific requirements should be, first, relaxed and, subsequently, abandoned altogether to give way to the general application of competition law. A first step towards such a supervisory role of the Commission can be found in Article 25(2) of Directive 98/10/EC (voice telephony) and Article 18(2) of Directive 97/33/EC (interconnection), which establishes that 'the Commission may request national regulatory authorities to provide their reasons for classifying an organisation as having or not having significant market power'. In this context it should also be recalled that Article 12 of Reg. 17/62 already gives the Commission the power to carry out general inquiries into whole economic sectors.

Whilst the task of establishing competitive market structures through asymmetric regulation should be of a transitional nature, there are certain regulatory obligations which should have a more durable, if not permanent, character in the

---

[23] Para. 3 of the Annex (as amended by Annex I of Directive 97/51/EC), which sets out harmonised tariff principles).

telecommunications sector. We are not referring to those regulatory provisions which impose asymmetric duties on operators with significant market power—which should be strictly limited—but to the regulatory obligations related to transparency and information.

In the wake of full liberalisation, telecommunications markets will tend to be dominated by the incumbent operator, and subsequently be of an oligopolistic nature for a considerable period of time. Economic (interdependence) theory indicates that enterprises in concentrated markets will behave in parallel in order to maximise their joint profits without, however, necessarily colluding but as a result of each firm's natural response to market conditions. Experience in the application of European competition law in concentrated markets shows that it is difficult for antitrust authorities to establish a violation of either Article 81 [ex 85] or 82 [ex 86] of the Treaty or even to control such markets via the Merger Regulation. Thus, in its *Wood Pulp II* judgment,[24] the ECJ held that parallel behaviour could not be regarded as proof of concertation unless it was the sole plausible explanation for such conduct. As the operation of market forces could in that case be regarded as a more plausible explanation for parallelism in prices the Court held that a concerted practice could not be inferred from parallel behaviour and quashed the Commission's decision. As regards Article 82 [ex 86], the CFI, whilst confirming that it was possible to apply this provision where two or more undertakings together held a collective dominant position, annulled the Commission's *Italian Flat Glass* decision for lack of evidence of the 'economic links' necessary to prove such collective dominance.[25] Similarly, the ECJ recently quashed the Commission's merger decision in *Kali und Salz*.[26] Although the Court confirmed that collective dominant positions are within the scope of the Merger Regulation, it nevertheless annulled the decision on the facts because the Commission had not sufficiently established that the concentration would have led to the creation of a collective dominant position on the part of Kali+Salz/MdK and SCPA.[27]

The difficulties encountered by the Commission in controlling oligopolistic

---

[24] Joined cases C–89, 104, 114–17, 125–29/85, *Ahlström and others/Commission*, [1993] ECR I–1307.

[25] Decision 89/93/EEC, OJ L 33/44 (1989); on appeal Joined Cases T–68, 77 and 78/89, *Società Italiana Vetro/Commission*, [1992] ECR II–1403, paras. 358–68.

[26] Case IV/M.308, *Kali und Salz/MdK/Treuhand*, OJ L186/38 (1994). On appeal joined cases C–68/94 and C–30/95, *French Republic v Commission*, Judgment of 31.03.1998, nyr.

[27] Eventually, the Commission acknowledged that the concentration would not lead to the creation of a dominant duopoly and authorised the concentration; see *Kali und Salz/MdK/Treuhand*, see the decision of 9.7.1998

market structures highlight the need to maintain regulatory obligations in the telecommunications sector even beyond the legal and *de facto* de-monopolisation of markets through asymmetric regulation. During the transition period towards fully competitive market structures in the period immediately following liberalisation, telecommunications markets will tend to be of an oligopolistic nature for a long time. The specific experience in Spain, where duopolies have been created in the mobile and voice telephony markets during the transition to full liberalisation, shows that initially only a few players will operate in these markets and access for new entrants will remain difficult. It is important, however, that the long-term regulatory obligations are not asymmetric as this could constrain innovation and optimal market development. These obligations should therefore only relate to transparency and information requirements and be more in line with what is known as 'light-handed regulation'.[28] For the rest, the strict enforcement of pure competition law, supported by the information available due to the above-mentioned requirements, will ensure that effective competition is not distorted. As the Access Notice points out, 'Commission recommendations concerning accounting requirements and transparency will help to ensure the effective application of Article 82 [ex 86]'.

3. The Application of EC Competition Law in the Context of Over-Regulation

Another key field of application of Treaty competition rules concerns the control of measures adopted by the Member States in the implementation of ONP Directives and their enforcement by the NRAs. Pursuant to the INNO/ATAB doctrine,[29] Member States, and in particular NRAs acting within the ONP framework, are under an obligation to respect the effectiveness (effet utile) of the competition rules. In this respect the Access Notice states that, 'under Community law, national authorities, including regulatory authorities and competition authorities, have a duty not to approve any practice or agreement contrary to Community competition law'.[30] Apart from the possibility of

---

[28] See, Knorr (1998).

[29] Case 13/77, *GB-Inno-BM/ATAB*, [1977] ECR 2115, para. 33.

[30] Para. 13; *see* also para. 19: 'The NRAs must ensure that actions taken by them are consistent with Community competition law. This duty requires them to refrain from action that would undermine the effective protection of Community law rights under the competition rules. Therefore, they may not approve arrangements which are contrary to the competition rules. If the national authorities act so as to undermine those rights, the Member State may itself be liable for damages to those harmed by this

initiating proceedings under Article 226 [ex 169] against Member States for failure to implement an ONP Directive (Article 249(3) [ex 189(3)]), there are two ways for the Commission to take action against state measures which specifically deprive the competition rules of their effectiveness.

First, the Commission can proceed under Article 226 [ex 169] against the respective Member State for contravening Article 10(2) [ex 5(2)] read in conjunction with Articles 3(g) [ex 3(g)], 81 and 82 [ex 85 and 86]. The first case where the Commission had recourse to the Article 226 [ex 169] procedure in order to challenge the compatibility of national legislation with the 'effet utile' of the competition rules is in *CNSD*, where the ECJ upheld the Commission's action brought against Italy.[31] Second, where an NRA adopts a measure that is contrary to the competition rules, e.g. by favouring a public undertaking or those having a special or exclusive right, the Commission can adopt a decision under Article 86(3) [ex 90(3)] against that Member State for infringement of Article 86(1) [ex 90(1)] read in conjunction with Articles 81 or 82 [ex 85 and 86].[32] Thus, the 'effet utile' doctrine plays an important role where Member States 'over-regulate' specific markets through the adoption of legislative or administrative measures which hinder the effectiveness of Articles 81 and 82 [ex 85 and 86].

An example where the Commission has had recourse to Articles 86 and 82 [ex 90 and 86] in such circumstances are the Italian and Spanish GSM cases.[33] Prior to the full liberalisation of the market, the Telecommunications Ministries of both countries (then still the national regulatory authorities) required an initial payment to obtain a licence to operate from the second operators of mobile telephony services (Airtel Móvil in Spain and Omnitel in Italy). As they did not charge licence fees to the incumbents, Telefónica and Telecom Italia, these measures clearly distorted competition between the public TOs

action.', and para. 61: '[i]f an NRA were to require terms which were contrary to the competition rules [. . .], the Member State itself would be in breach of Article 3(g) [ex 3(g)] and Article 10 [ex 5] of the Treaty and therefore subject to challenge by the Commission under Article 226 [ex 169]. Additionally, if an undertaking having special or exclusive rights within the meaning of Article 86 [ex 90] of a state-owned undertaking, were required or authorised by a national regulator to engage in behaviour constituting an abuse of its dominant position, the Member State would also be in breach of Article 86(1) [ex 90(1)] and the Commission could adopt a decision requiring termination of the infringement'.

[31] Case C–35/96, *Commission* v *Italy,* [1998] I–3851.

[32] See the *Ahmed Saeed* judgment, Case 66/86, [1989] ECR 838. For a detailed analysis, Temple Lang (1997).

[33] Decisions 97/181/EC, *GSM Spain*, OJ L 76/19 (1997), and 95/498/EC, *GSM Italy*, OJ L 280/49 (1995).

and new entrants. The Commission eventually adopted a decision under Article 86(3) [ex 90(3)] against Spain and Italy for having infringed Article 86(1) [ex 90(1)] read in conjunction with Article 82 [ex 86], by adopting a measure to strengthen the incumbents' dominant position in the voice and analogue mobile telephony markets and favouring its extension into the neighbouring (but separate) market of mobile GSM telephony services.[34] The decisions obliged both countries either to reimburse the fees paid by the private operators or to compensate them by adopting equivalent corrective measures.

Another example is the *Spanish Canal Satélite Digital* (CSD) case reported on in the Commission's Development of the Market for Digital TV in the EU (Com 1999 540). Following the launch of Spain's first digital satellite television platform, CSD, in January 1997 the Spanish government enacted emergency legislation to implement Directive 95/47/EC into Spanish law. This legislation regulated standards for transmission of television signals, in particular, the technical specifications for conditional access systems used in decoders for digital television. The Act provided for a national type-approval procedure for decoders incorporating a conditional access system, which was precisely what Directive 95/47, in making reference to the voluntary code of conduct developed by the DVB (Digital Video Broadcasting), wanted to avoid. This requirement created a significant degree of uncertainty in the market in respect of the legality of CSD's operations, which increased when the grant of type-approval was refused by the Spanish NRA in May 1997. Furthermore, the (amended) final version of the Act[35] also obliged operators of conditional access systems to use the 'multicrypt' encryption system if those operators using the 'simulcrypt' system did not have an access agreement with other operators within two months of the entry into force of the new legislation in May 1997. However, CSD, whose decoders used the simulcrypt system, was by then the only digital TV broadcaster operating in Spain. The rival platform led by Telefónica (Vía Digital), which was to be launched in September, had announced that it would employ the multicrypt system, even though this system was not yet available on the market. In enacting this legislation the government was trying to impose the multicrypt system on the first operator in the market, effectively forcing it to replace all simulcrypt decoders already installed in thousands of homes, thus offsetting the competitive advantage gained over the rival platform for having been launched seven months earlier.

Following its enactment, CSD filed two complaints with the European Commission. The first, filed under Article 226 [ex 169], alleged that the Act

---

[34] Alternatively, the Commission argued that the initial payment would limit the development of the emerging GSM market contrary to Article 82(b) [ex 86(b)] EC.

[35] RD Law 1997, of 31 January 1997 was replaced by Act 17/1997, of 6 May 1997.

infringed Articles 28 and 49 [ex 30 and 59] for creating obstacles to the free movement of decoders, and the second complaint, brought under Articles 86 and 82 [ex 90 and 86] of the Treaty, alleged that the measures had been adopted to offset its competitive advantage over Vía Digital, the second platform led by Telefónica, the former state monopolist. CSD alleged that the state measures favoured Telefónica, a firm with exclusive and special rights in neighbouring markets. The measures—both of a legislative (the Act itself) and administrative (refusal by the NRA to grant type-approval to CSD's decoders) nature—were thus contrary to the principle of equality of opportunities developed by the ECJ in its case law on Articles 86 and 82 [ex 90 and 86],[36] and therefore infringed these two provisions. When the Commission was about to apply to the ECJ for interim measures to suspend the application of several provisions of the Digital TV Act for contravening Articles 28 and 49 [ex 30 and 59], the Spanish government agreed to amend the provisions.[37] The case was eventually settled although CSD is claiming damages, under the *Brasserie du Pêcheur/Factortame III* doctrine,[38] against the Spanish state.

Even though the Commission decided to pursue the case under Article 226 [ex 169],[39] it shows that excessive regulation by Member States which distorts competition or favours incumbents can be dealt with using the tools provided for by Community competition law. As can be seen in the Court's *Ahmed Saeed* judgment, the same is true in respect of measures adopted by NRAs which must equally be consistent with the Treaty's competition rules.

III. Institutional Issues

1. The Spanish Antitrust Authorities: Powers and Procedures

In Spain, competition law is the competence of the Competition Office (*Servicio de Defensa de la Competencia*, SDC), which is part of the Ministry of

---

[36] Case C–202/88, *France/Commission*, [1991] ECR I–1259, para. 51; Case C–18/88, *RTT/GB-Inno*, [1991] ECR I–5941, para. 25.

[37] RD Law 16/1997, of 16 September 1997.

[38] Joined cases C–46 and 48/93, [1996] ECR I–1029.

[39] Article 226 [ex 169] action brought against the Kingdom of Spain led to the adoption of a Reasoned Opinion but was settled following the amendment of the Digital TV Act in September 1997. In its reasoned Opinion, the Commission set out that both the legislative measures requiring Canal Satélite Digital to submit its decoders to a type-approval procedure as well as the denial of said type-approval by the TMC (May 1997) were, among other things, contrary to Articles 28 and 49 [ex 30 and 59] Consolidated Treaty.

the Economy, and the Competition Tribunal (*Tribunal de Defensa de la Competencia*, TDC), which is an administrative body formally dependent on the Ministry of the Economy, although functionally fully independent.[40] To guarantee this functional independence, the Competition Act limits government discretion in the selection of the president and members of the TDC, which may only be selected from lawyers, economists and other qualified professionals. Their five-year mandate is renewable, and cannot be revoked for reasons other than those specified in the Competition Act.

As regards procedure, the SDC investigates proceedings and makes pro posals to the TDC which then adopts a final decision in the case of infringement proceedings and applications for individual exemptions and delivers non-binding opinions to government in the case of concentations. The TDC is also designated to apply Articles 81 and 82 [ex 85 and 86] on a national level,[41] although here too the SDC carries out investigations and co-operates with European Commission in antitrust proceedings.

As regards concentrations, since the amendments introduced into the Spanish Competition Act by RD Law 6/1999,[42] the notification of concentrations is no longer voluntary. Concentrations must be notified to the SDC within one month of closing if either the participant undertakings have an overall turnover in Spain exceeding Ptas. 40 billion and at least two of them individually have a turnover exceeding Ptas. 10 billion or if the market share acquired or increased as a consequence of the concentration is equivalent to or represents more than 25% of the Spanish market.

The acts of the SDC may be challenged before the TDC in specific circumstances, whereas the TDC's final resolutions may be appealed against before the administrative jurisdiction. The competent administrative court to review the decisions of the TDC is the *Audiencia Nacional,* a court with special nation-wide competences in specific areas of law. The judgments of the *Audiencia Nacional* may be appealed against before the Spanish Supreme Court.[43]

---

[40] Article 20, Spanish Competition Act.

[41] Pursuant to RD 295/1998 of 27 February 1998.

[42] Act 16/1989 on the Defence of Competition, as amended by RD Law 6/1999, of 16 April, BOE of 17.4.1999.

[43] Article 58(2) of the Act on General Jurisdiction.

2. TDC Practice in the Application of the Competition Rules to Access Problems

The importance attached by the TDC to the liberalisation of the telecommunications sector became clear in a report submitted to the government in 1993 which recommended not to delay the liberalisation of the telecommunications sector[44] and to introduce competition in the mobile telephony market by issuing a second GSM licence before January 1995; to pass a Cable Television Act in order to introduce competition in the cable market through the creation of local duopolies for the provision of television and telecommunications services, and to liberalise the satellite sector. All these proposals were accomplished, although full liberalisation was delayed until December 1998. The TDC's report also recommended the supervision of prices and charges in the telecommunications sector during a transitional period, thus laying the foundations of a sector-specific regulatory authority.[45]

As early as 1993 the TDC had the opportunity of applying Article 6 of the Spanish Competition Act together with Article 82 [ex 86] EC to the refusal of the then state monopolist, Telefónica, to grant a potential downstream competitor (3C Communications) access to its network.[46] In order to provide value-added credit card pay-phone services on several Spanish airports 3C depended on the provision of leased lines by the public telecommunications operator. Telefónica, however, was preparing to launch its own service and refused, thus delaying the provision of leased lines arguing that 3C intended to offer a monopolised service and lacked the necessary type-approvals for its telephone terminals.

In its final resolution, the TDC imposed heavy fines on Telefónica for having abused the dominant position it enjoyed as a consequence of its legal monopoly over the public telecommunications network. Interestingly, the TDC based its reasoning on the obligation provided for in Directives

---

[44] The Community Directives, however, provided for additional implementation periods for Spain of up to five years.

[45] Together with the obligations to create independent regulators imposed in the respective Community Directives.

[46] Resolution A 46/93, of 3.6.1993, in which the TDC ordered the SDC to further investigate the case; Res. MC 6/94, of 8.4.1994, in which the TDC adopted interim measures against Telefónica; and Res. 350/94, of 1.2.1995, in which the TDC adopted its final decision fining Telefónica for having abused its dominant position. In another resolution of the same year the TDC fined Telefónica for abuse of its dominant position by tying the rental of terminal equipment to the subsequent sale of the apparatuses (Case 328/93, *Habana Films*, resolution of 1.10.1993).

90/388/EEC and 88/301/EEC to ensure that an independent body, different from the public telecommunications operator, carries out the regulatory activities. Having confirmed that the service offered by 3C clearly constituted a 'value added service' open to competition pursuant to Directive 90/388/EEC, the TDC went on to declare that, in any case, it was the job of the competent regulatory authority, and not Telefónica, to determine whether the service in question had been opened up to competition and whether 3C was in possession of the necessary type-approvals for its terminals. The TDC concluded that Telefónica, in refusing and delaying the concession of telephone lines to 3C, had taken on the role of the regulator, thus abusing its dominant position. In a similar case decided in 1997,[47] the TDC held that Telefónica's refusal to grant Esprit access to its network did not constitute an abuse of its dominant position. Esprit had requested Telefónica to provide a leased line between its offices in Madrid and London invoking Directives 90/388/EEC and 92/44/EC. In this case the TDC considered that there was no abusive conduct on the part of Telefónica as the competent telecommunications regulatory authority had previously informed Telefónica that Esprit did not have the necessary administrative licence to provide the value-added services in question.

The fact that the fine imposed on Telefónica in the 3C case was one of the highest ever imposed on an enterprise for infringing the competition rules stresses that the TDC considered the refusal by the then state monopolist to be of particular gravity. Nevertheless, it should also be said that due to the peculiarities of the Spanish antitrust procedure the rights of the complainant were not effectively protected in so far as 3C had filed its complaint in May 1992, but the TDC did not grant interim relief until April 1994. This case therefore also shows the need to create a specific regulator for the rapidly developing telecommunications sector that has the means of providing relief within a reasonable period of time.

3. The Spanish NRA

In recent years, Spain has witnessed a proliferation of regulatory agencies. As regards the supervision of competition, apart from SDC and TDC, which are the competition authorities responsible for applying competition law in general, the Spanish legislator has created several sectoral regulatory authorities whose task it is to supervise specific markets. Besides the existing regulatory agencies in the electricity, energy and tobacco sectors, in 1996 the Spanish legislator created the *Comisión del Mercado de las Telecomunicaciones*

---

[47] Res. 382/96, *Telefónica*, of 18.7.1997.

(Telecommunications Market Commission, hereinafter TMC), the regulatory authority competent for the telecommunications market. The TMC became operative in February 1997, although it could not exercise certain tasks, such as the those related to tariff-setting or interconnection charges, until December 1998 when the Spanish telecoms market was fully liberalised.[48] Until then, the Ministry of Public Works remained competent to decide these issues, although following the non-binding consultation of the TMC.

The TMC was created by Royal Decree (RD) Law 6/1996 to safeguard the principles of free competition, transparency and equal treatment in the telecommunications market. Its principal task is to supervise and facilitate the transition to full competition and to guarantee public service obligations. The legal framework governing the TMC is rather confusing and contains no less than seven pieces of legislation.[49] The TMC enjoys autonomy in exercising its functions,[50] but this is not absolute due to its organic dependence on the Ministry of Public Works.[51] This is why regulatory activity in the telecommunications sector is, in principle, in the purview of the Ministry of Public Works, the role of the TMC being limited to implementing these regulations. Nonetheless, the TMC has the power to adopt 'circulars' of a clearly regulatory, i.e. normative, character.

In contrast to regulatory authorities in other Member States the TMC is governed by a board, whose membership guarantees representation of all main political parties, selected from among telecommunications experts by government upon proposal of the Ministry of Public Works—a criterion which gives the government ample room for discretion. The fact that in Spain, parliament is merely informed about the candidates in this selection process, whereas in other European countries, such as France and Germany, parliament is active in the selection process appears to ensure a lower degree of independence of the appointed members. The members of the TMC have a six-year mandate, renewable for a further six years. They cannot be removed for reasons other than those explicitly specified in Article 35 of RD 1994/1996. In this context it

---

[48] Order of 31.01.1997. Pursuant to the Fourth Transitional Provision of the General Telecommunications Act, the Government is still empowered to authorise the tariffs charged by dominant operators for fixed telephony services. This transitional competence is attributed to the *Comisión Delegada del Gobierno para Asuntos Económicos.*

[49] The new General Telecommunications Act of April 1998, however, empowers government to elaborate a consolidated version of various laws that regulate the telecommunications sector.

[50] Article 3, RD 1994/1996 (the implementing regulation which governs the TMC).

[51] This formal dependence, which does not imply a hierarchical relationship, is necessary to comply with Article 97 of the Spanish Constitution, which attributes regulatory power exclusively to government.

should be noted that the TMC has been accused of a certain degree of politicisation. Indeed, its members have been designated by the main Spanish political parties following political horse-trading. One example of this politicisation could be seen in the refusal to grant Canal Satélite Digital type-approval for its decoders. The members of the TMC, appointed on the proposal of the governing political party, voted against granting such type-approval, while the members designated by other parties voted in favour. Although the procedure to select its members is similar to that of the TMC, there is no such politicisation of the members of the Spanish antitrust authority, the TDC.

Apart from its arbitration and advisory functions, the TMC has several means of intervention at its disposal. The main instruments of intervention in the market are 'resolutions',[52] directed at specific operators in order to protect free competition; and 'circulars',[53] of a general, quasi-normative nature. The TMC also has the power—as does the TDC upon proposal of the SDC—to adopt interim measures,[54] although both authorities may request a security if a complainant has applied for interim relief. The TMC also has the power to request information in pursuance of its tasks.[55]

In matters of judicial review, the Audencia Nacional enjoys exclusive jurisdiction to review both the resolutions of the TDC and those of the TMC.[56] A further appeal may be made before the Supreme Court.

Although the Notice on Access Agreements allows for direct actions before a judge as an alternative remedy for an infringement of Article 81 [ex 85] or 82 [ex 86], in Spain the likelihood of obtaining judicial review by bringing an action before the ordinary jurisdiction (e.g. against a competitor or incumbent operator for refusal to grant network access) is remote due to the CAMPSA doctrine of the Spanish Supreme Court.[57] According to the Spanish Supreme Court's case law, national and EC competition rules may only be applied by ordinary tribunals.[58] If, on the contrary, a party's principal claim before an

---

[52] Article 1.Two (c), Act 12/97.

[53] Also denominated 'instructions', Articles 1.Two (2)(f) Act 12/97 and 20 RD 1994/1996.

[54] Article 31 RD 1994/1996.

[55] Article 30 RD 1994/1996.

[56] Prior to the new Act on Administrative Jurisdiction (Act 29/1998), appeals against the TMC first went to the High Court of Justice of Madrid. The appeal of Canal Statélite Digital against the TMC's refusal to approve its decoders was the first case under the new procedure.

[57] Case 211/1991, judgment of 30.12.1993.

[58] This case law does not affect the administrative tribunals' competence to judicially review the resolutions adopted by the TDC. See, for example, Cases 127/73, *BRT/SABAM*, [1974] ECR 51; and C–234/89, *Delimitis*, [1991] ECR I–935.

ordinary court is based either on Articles 81 or 82 [ex 85 and 86], or under the corresponding provisions of national competition law the civil court does not have jurisdiction to hear the action brought before it. According to the Supreme Court, in these cases application of the competition rules is reserved to the administrative authorities in charge of enforcing these provisions.[59] Although it could be argued that this doctrine is contrary to the ECJ's case law on the (horizontal) direct effect of the competition rules,[60] as things stand no ordinary judge would be prepared to hear an action based on a claim of incompatibility with the competition rules.

Although there are no precedents in this matter, the Supreme Court's reasoning could equally well apply to the provisions of the General Telecommunications Act and other legislation regulating the telecommunications sector as these provisions are also enforced by a specialised regulatory authority, the TMC. On the other hand, the Telecommunications Act does not contain provisions that could be regarded as equivalent to Articles 81(2) and 82 [ex 85(2) and 86].[61] It appears to be more difficult for private parties to invoke specific regulatory provisions in the course of ordinary civil proceedings. Nonetheless, we can imagine cases where an operator charged with, for example, demanding excessive interconnection tariffs, claims the amounts paid in excess from another operator alleging that the prices charged contravene specific provisions of the Telecommunications Act or decisions adopted by the TMC pursuant to the Act. It remains to be seen how the courts will address these issues.

Under the 1997 Act,[62] the jurisdiction of the TMC was initially limited to the telecommunications market as such, but this was subsequently extended to other sectors closely related to telecoms,[63] including the markets for audiovisual, telematic and interactive services. The TMC also has extensive competences in the market of digital satellite television, in matters such as granting authorisations for the provision of digital satellite television services, the type-approval of digital conditional access systems, or the approval of the standard contracts used by broadcasters of digital conditional access television. Indeed,

---

[59] That is, the Commission pursuant to Article 9(3) Regulation 17/62 (OJ 13, 21.2.1962, p.204) and the TDC pursuant to the Spanish Competition Act.

[60] See, for example, *BRT/SABAM* and *Delimitis*, supra, n 58.

[61] Articles 1(2) and 6 of the Spanish Competition Act.

[62] Act 12/1997, of 24 April, on the Liberalisation of Telecommunications, which replaced RD Law 6/1996.

[63] Despite the adoption of the General Telecommunications Act (Act 11/1998), those provisions of Act 12/1997 related to the TMC remain in force.

it was in this market that the TMChad its first prominent case, which even led to an intervention of the European Commission.[64]

In safeguarding effective competition in the market, the TMC has the following competences:[65]

- the arbitration of conflicts between network operators and service providers;
- issuing general authorisations and individual licences in cases where a tender is not required;
- the management of scarce resources;
- the binding resolution of conflicts in the context of interconnection and network access;
- the monitoring of universal service obligations;
- the supervision of tariff proposals of services offered on an exclusive basis or by a dominant operator;
- setting maximum interconnection charges;
- advising government in the formulation of legislative measures and tendering procedures;
- to require the technical inspection of services and equipment and the reporting of any offences by the Ministry in cases where the TMC is not competent to prosecute;
- the registration of network operators and service providers.

The TMC also has the task of protecting free competition in the markets under its jurisdiction. In this respect, the different pieces of legislation applying to the TMC have caused some confusion as to the scope of these competences and particularly the relationship between the TMC and the Spanish antitrust authorities (SDC and TDC). Under the 1996 Law, the TMC was competent to 'adopt the necessary measures to safeguard free competition in the market, in particular with respect to the plurality of services offered, access to telecommunications networks by operators and interconnection of networks.'[66] This broad attribution of powers, however, had to be read in conjunction with paragraph (e) of the provision, which provided that, where necessary, the TMC 'instigate the intervention of the antitrust authorities'. In principle, this provision could be interpreted as preserving the pre-eminence of the antitrust

---

[64] On the *Canal Satélite Digital* case, see *supra*.
[65] Article 1.Two (2), Act 12/97.
[66] Article 1.Two (2)(d), RD Law 6/1996.

authorities *vis-à-vis* the TMC in the supervision of anti-competitive practices in the telecommunications sector.

Subsequently, the 1997 Act significantly modified the TMC's competences to safeguard effective competition in the telecommunications and related markets,[67] in particular by enabling the TMC to adopt measures 'with respect to the plurality of services offered, access by operators to telecommunications networks, interconnection of networks and open network provision; the service providers' policy on prices and marketing, and in general with respect to activities which could constitute anti-competitive practices'.[68] To this end, the TMC is empowered to adopt 'circulars' that are directed at the entities operating in the sector and are binding upon them once they have been published in the Spanish Official Journal. Non-fulfilment of circulars is regarded as a serious infringement subject to administrative sanctions pursuant to the General Telecommunications Act.[69] Circulars[70] adopted by the TMC are of a normative nature[71]. The 1997 Act not only maintains the TMC's competence to adopt measures necessary to safeguard competition, but adds another explicit competence with respect to the control of concentrations and other agreements which gives the TMC the competence to 'exercise control over concentrations of enterprises, capital shareholdings, and agreements between enterprises operating'[72] in the markets within its jurisdiction. This provision, however, has arguably been abrogated with the entry into force of the new General Telecommunications Act which provides that the TMC must merely be consulted in concentration proceedings which enter the third stage (i.e. only if the government is requested to authorise a concentration that neither the SDC nor the TDC have previously authorised). Nonetheless, the TMC has already attempted to reassert its competence to control concentrations in the telecommunications sector *vis-à-vis* both the European Commission and the Spanish authorities.

---

[67] It should be noted that in spite of the recent adoption of the General Telecommunications Act 11/1998, those provisions of Act 12/1997 which refer to the TMC have not been abrogated and thus remain in force.

[68] Act, 12/1997, Article 1. Two(2), para. f.

[69] Article 82 of Act 11/1998: either a percentage of the operator's turnover or five times the benefit obtained as a consequence of the infringement.

[70] Circular 1/1997, on the use of short numbers, of 13.11.1997; and Circular 1/1998, on publicity campaigns by dominant operators, of 31.7.1998.

[71] See Article 20 of the TMC's Regulation (adopted by RD 1994/1996, of 6 September) and Article 26 of Order of 9.4.97.

[72] Para. (g) of Article 1.Two (2) Act 12/1997.

4. Overlaps and Areas of Conflict between the TMC and the Antitrust Authorities

Turning to the rules which explicitly govern the relationship between the TMC and the Spanish antitrust authorities with competence to enforce both national and EC competition law, the 1997 Act[73] provides for the intervention of the antitrust authorities upon the request of the TNC.[74] Under the 1997 Act, the institution with competence to carry out the investigation (SDC), must consult the TMC before adopting a proposal to the TDC in all those cases referred to it by the TMC. If the SDC wishes to deviate from the report delivered by the TMC in the course of this consultation, it can only do so by providing a specific justification for adopting a different position. Nonetheless, this provision appears to confirm that the TMC's competence to adopt measures necessary to safeguard free competition leaves the exclusive competence of the antitrust authorities to apply the competition rules untouched. Furthermore, RD 1994/1996 contains a provision which regulates the relationship between the TMC and the antitrust authorities more precisely than the 1997 Act, in so far as the TMC may request the initiation of infringement proceedings from the antitrust authorities whenever it detects the existence of anti-competitive practices. Similarly, as regards concentrations in the telecommunications sector, the TMC may inform the SDC of such operations if the thresholds provided for in the Competition Act are met. RD 1994/1996 also provides that the TMC must be consulted in proceedings initiated by the antitrust authorities if they are related to the telecommunications market. It is not clear whether this also refers to other related markets over which the 1997 Act confers jurisdiction upon the TMC as the Decree only refers to the 'telecommunications market'.

The recently adopted General Telecommunications Act has clarified the relationship between both institutions. Apart from the duty to consult the TMC in the context of authorisations of concentrations, the only reference to the relationship between the TMC and the antitrust authorities is contained in the Seventh Additional Provision, which regulates the 'co-ordination between the TMC and the TDC' and stipulates that 'the TMC will perform its tasks in full respect of the competences which Act 16/1989, of 17 July, on the Defence of Competition, confers upon the antitrust authorities. When the TMC detects signs of restrictive practices prohibited by the Act on the Defence of Competition, it brings them to the attention of the SDC together with all

---

[73] Article 1.Two (2)(m) Act 12/1997.

[74] Mirroring the previous rule under para. (e) of Article 1.Two (2) of RD Law 6/1996.

available factual elements and, if appropriate, a non-binding opinion express-ing its own assessment of said practices.' However, the same provision con-cludes that 'this must be understood as being without prejudice to the tasks which the 1997 Act on the Liberalisation of Telecommunications attributes to the TMC', thus leaving the door open for jurisdictional conflicts between the institutions.

In the course of the legislative process which led to the adoption of the Telecommunications Act in April 1998, the Spanish legislator was tempted to confer additional competences upon the TMC to enforce general competition law in the telecommunications sector. Several parties proposed an amendment to the government bill so as to give the TMC exclusive competence to apply competition law, that is, the competition rules of the Spanish Competition Act, in the sectors under its jurisdiction.[75] They argued that being as independent and autonomous as the TDC, the TMC had the advantage of being more spe-cialised in the field of telecommunications. In the last instance, however, par-liament opted for a clear separation of the tasks of the TMC and the Spanish antitrust authorities, even though the law leaves room for conflicting interpre-tations.

This decision is to be welcomed for several reasons. First, it limits the dan-ger of a 'regulatory capture' of the telecommunications regulator, whose rep-resentatives are closely linked and thus influenced by the actors in the sector. Additionally, regulatory authorities have a tendency to balance and satisfy the interests of the (few) actors operating in the sector under their control, without focusing their enforcement activity on the needs of consumers. In other words, sector-specific regulatory agencies are in danger of acting as a mere arbiter between the operators under their jurisdiction instead of acting as a guardian of effective market competition. Lastly, it is debatable whether it is more diffi-cult for competition lawyers to become familiar with the peculiarities of another sector (telecoms), or for specialists in the sector to gain an in-depth knowledge of competition law. Therefore, it is arguably preferable for the enforcement of competition law to remain in the hands of the traditional antitrust authority.

In spite of this apparently clear delimitation of competences between the Spanish NRA and the antitrust authorities, there is ample room for potential jurisdictional conflict because the TMC appears to have adopted a rather generous interpretation of its tasks and competences. For example, in a case

---

[75] The proposal read as follows: '[I]n conformity with the Competition Act, the TMC shall be the only organ with competences as regards the defence of free competition in the markets for telecommunications, audio-visual, telematic, and interactive services'.

brought before the TMC by Cableuropa and other associated cable operators against the simultaneous presence of two companies (GET, belonging to the ENDESA Group, and STET International, belonging to the Telecom Italia Group) in Retevisión (the second Spanish voice telephony operator) and several cable operators.[76] Cableuropa alleged that this simultaneous presence in a telecommunications operator and various cable operators infringed national and Community competition law as well as several sector-specific regulatory requirements. Consequently, Cableuropa requested the TMC to prohibit the simultaneous participation of the two companies in operators of both markets and also demanded the adoption of interim measures. The TMC initiated proceedings[77] but interrupted them when the enterprises involved notified two concentrations under Regulation (EEC) 4064/89 to the Commission.[78] Following the Commission's authorisation of these operations the TMC resumed its proceedings, but eventually dismissed the complaint.

Nevertheless, the TMC's reasoning as regards the possible infringement of the competition rules implied that it in principle regarded itself as competent to adopt measures necessary to prohibit anti-competitive conducts in the markets under its jurisdiction. The only reason for denying its jurisdiction in this specific case was the fact that the Commission had already cleared the conduct complained of in the above-mentioned merger decisions. The TMC held that in qualifying the notified operations as a 'concentration' the Commission had ruled out the option of co-ordination between the parent companies (among others ENDESA and STET), which were not considered to be market competitors. For this reason the TMC considered that it was not competent to find an infringement of the competition rules, a finding that is underlined by the fact that it made express reference to the Merger Regulation.[79] This decision indicates that the TMC considered itself competent to adopt a resolution in a case of infringement of the competition rules.[80] According to press reports, the CMT is also investigating the simultaneous presence of ENDESA and Unión Fenosa in the capital of Airtel Móvil and Retevisión Móvil on the grounds that this concurrent participation in two direct competitors could distort competition in the mobile telephony market.

---

[76] *ME* 8/97, Resolution of 9.7.1998.
[77] Pursuant to Article 1.Two (2)(c) and (f) of Act 12/1997 and RD 1994/1996.
[78] *Cableuropa/Spainco/CTC*, IV/M.1022 (CTC) and IV/M.1091, OJ C 97/8 (1998).
[79] Article 21(1) and (2).
[80] It is not entirely clear whether the TMC would have applied the provisions of the Spanish Competition Act or the broad and rather vague enabling provisions of Act 12/1997.

These cases show that the TMC's resolutions are liable to create a sector-specific body of law which may partly overlap with the enterprises' duties under the general competition rules. As long as this occurs on the basis of sector-specific regulation and not on the basis of the competition rules, there is little risk of conflicting results or parallel procedures. From a substantive perspective, neither the TMC's 'circulars' nor its 'resolutions' can be adopted on the basis of the competition rules because the national antitrust authorities remain the institutions with exclusive competence to apply the provisions of the Spanish Competition Act as regards their administrative enforcement.[81] The same is true with respect to Articles 81 and 82 [ex 85 and 86] as RD 295/1998 expressly confers the exclusive competence for the administrative enforcement of Community competition rules on these two institutions. Nonetheless, the competence to adopt binding 'circulars' and the power to adopt 'resolutions' in order to protect free competition may conflict with the tasks of the antitrust authorities to prosecute infringements of the competition rules.[82] The task of the regulatory authority must therefore be confined to applying sector-specific regulation, and should not include the application of the competition rules as such. Were both the regulatory agency and the antitrust authorities competent to apply pure competition law, there would be a clear danger of creating a sector-specific body of competition law.[83] The application of the same rules by different bodies will lead to divergent interpretations of these rules which would in turn lead to legal uncertainty: it would only be a question of time until the sector-specific interpretation of competition law 'spilled over' into other industrial sectors. In principle, this reasoning should also apply conversely: the duties imposed on operators having 'significant market power' should be applied by an authority other than the antitrust authorities in order to maintain the distinction between the duties deriving from this notion under sector-specific regulation and the duties of dominant enterprises under the competition rules.

The—potential—jurisdictional overlaps of the TMC's activities with those of the antitrust authorities do not end here as the Cableuropa case discussed above also led to a conflict with the European Commission. In *CTC*, the TMC sent a lengthy letter to the Commission setting out its competences in the field of control of concentrations in the Spanish telecommunications market. As a consequence of these powers, the TMC argued, the Commission was under a duty to consult the TMC on concentrations in the telecommunications sector

---

[81] See the fourth recital and Article 25 of Act 16/1989.

[82] See *Cableuropa* discussed above.

[83] See Martínez Lage (1997a) and (1997b).

notified to it under Regulation (EEC) 4064/89.[84] Although the TMC had previously requested the Commission[85] for information on the existence of a procedure under Regulation 4064/89, the Commission carried out its usual consultation procedure with the 'competent authority of the Member State', i.e. the SDC. The Commission was arguably right in doing so as RD 295/1998 provides that the SDC is the competent authority for the purposes of the Article 19(2) consultation procedure.

5. The Need for an EU Regulator?

The most obvious advantage of creating a European telecommunications regulatory authority is the higher degree of independence from governmental and political interference and the influence exercised by companies operating in the respective national markets (regulatory capture) enjoyed by a supranational institution compared to national regulators. Given that national regulators have now been established in all Member States, the "duplication' of this existing regulatory and supervisory framework through the creation of another regulatory authority on an EU level would appear ill-advised as it would simply increase bureaucracy in a dynamic and fast changing market. In this respect the regulators' task may be adequately carried out by the Member States according to the principle of subsidiarity.

Nevertheless, the Commission should have a supervisory role *vis-à-vis* the activities of NRAs particularly to ensure the independence of their decisions. As guardian of the Treaties, the Commission has the task of ensuring that national legislation in matters of telecommunications implements existing Community Directives correctly. In this respect, the Commission should not hesitate to initiate actions pursuant to Article 226 [ex 169] against Member States failing to meet their obligations under Article 249(3) [ex 189(3)]. The same is true as regards administrative or normative measures of an NRA inconsistent with Member States' obligations under Community law. As the ECJ made clear in the *Ahmed Saeed* judgment, measures adopted by NRAs must be compatible with the 'effet utile' of the Treaty's competition rules.[86]

---

84 Pursuant to Article 19(2) of the Regulation.

85 In the context of the complaint filed by Cableuropa against GET and STET.

86 The Commission has the power to intervene either under Article 226 [ex 169] for infringement of Articles 10(2) [ex 5(2)] and 81/82 [ex 85/86], or to proceed under Article 86(3) [ex 90(3)] against the respective Member State for contravening Article 86(1) [ex 90(1)] read in conjunction with Articles 81 or 82 [ex 85 and 86]. See above II.3.

In addition to this supervisory role the Commission should have the power to decide when a given market can be released from strict regulation as NRAs could be in a conflict of interest when having to decide that the sector-specific regulation which they enforce should no longer apply because there is already workable competition in the respective market. Experience in other countries confirms the tendency of sector-specific regulators to expand their competences. In order to ensure the strictly transitional character of sector-specific regulation it is vital that the Commission adopt a supervisory role over the activities of the NRAs. To this end, the Commission's Joint Team should be given the task of gradually releasing individual markets from regulation when workable competition is established in a specific product (and geographic) market.

IV. Conclusion

One of the distinctive features of sector-specific regulation is its transitional character. In order not to hamper future market developments or act as a disincentive to investments in the telecommunications sector, the application of sectoral rules should be strictly limited to ensure that former monopolies are effectively broken up and more or less competitive market structures are established. Once achieved, asymmetric requirements should be derogated and make way for the general application of competition rules, coupled with some additional information and transparency obligations applicable to all operators due to the oligopolistic nature of these markets during the transition to full competition. This gradual phasing out of sector-specific rules, both from a substantive and an institutional perspective, giving way to the exclusive application of general competition law is crucial for a successful transition to fully competitive market structures as well as for the further development of these markets.

The transitional character of sector-specific regulation to some extent determines the institutional issues arising in the telecommunications sector. These transitional rules impose more far-reaching and burdensome obligations than the general competition rules and should not be applied by the antitrust authorities so as to maintain a clear distinction between the two sets of rules. This avoids a situation where related but different concepts inherent in the sectoral rules—particularly the notion of 'significant market power' as opposed to that of 'dominant' undertakings—gradually become part of the interpretation of general competition law. If the antitrust authorities were to apply sector-specific rules, these concepts would soon 'spill over' into other industrial sectors, thus diluting the scope of the competition rules. At the same time, the regulatory authorities' task must also be confined to applying sector-specific regulation, and must exclude the application of the competition rules as such. Otherwise, if both the regulatory agencies and the antitrust authorities were competent to apply the general competition rules, there would be a danger of creating a sector-specific body of competition law through the distinct or even contradictory interpretation of the same material rules by different institutions.

Finally, although there is no need to create a specific EU regulator alongside the existing national authorities, the Commission's role should not be limited to supervising the implementation of ONP Directives by the Member States, but should instead be to generally control the activities of Member States, and particularly of their national regulatory authorities, in this field, especially as regards the compatibility of their legislative or administrative measures with the 'effet utile' of the competition rules. Apart from initiating proceedings against a Member State, the ECJ's judgment in *CNSD* confirms that the Commission may also challenge measures that run counter to the 'effet utile' of the competition rules pursuant to Article 226 [ex 169]. In addition to these tools, the Commission should also be given powers to determine when a particular market should be released from the application of sector-specific regulation, giving way to the exclusive application of general competition law. National regulatory authorities have a natural tendency to perpetuate themselves, thus delaying the arrival of a truly deregulated sector, whereas the application of the general competition rules guarantees competition and innovation. It is thus the Commission, as an independent supranational institution, which is best placed to carry out this sensitive task.

VII

James F. Rill, Mary Jean Fell, Richard C. Park,
*Sarah E. Bauers**

Institutional Responsibilities Affecting Competition in the Telecommunications Industry

I. Introduction

In both the US and internationally, various industries exist where responsibility for the assessment and regulation of transactions and practices is vested concurrently with antitrust and specialised governmental agencies. In the US, agencies that maintain some degree of responsibility for antitrust enforcement exhibit mixed influence and differing roles to that end. For example, control of international airline alliances rests with the Department of Transportation (DOT), while the Surface Transportation Board (STB) serves as the ultimate authority for approving railroad mergers. The results reached by these specialised agencies have not always been satisfactory from the perspective of the antitrust enforcement agencies. In recent years, the US Department of Justice Antitrust Division (DOJ) has expressed its strong disagreement with DOT's immunisation from the antitrust laws of the market overlaps arising from the Delta Airlines/Sabena/Swissair/Austrian Airlines alliance, and with the STB's approval of the Union Pacific/Southern Pacific railroad merger.[1]

Since passage of the Telecommunications Act of 1996,[2] the concurrent jurisdiction of DOJ and the Federal Communications Commission (FCC) over telecommunications transactions has become another area where the actions of the specialised regulatory agency are not always consonant with those of the antitrust enforcement agency. Moreover, because of the astounding developments in technology and the nature of telecommunications itself, telecommunications companies increasingly operate at national and global levels, thereby

* Collier, Shannon, Rill & Scott, PLLC.

[1] See, 'Joint Application of Delta Airlines, Inc., Swissair, Sabena S.A., Sabena Belgian World Airlines, and Austrian Airlines for Approval of and Antitrust Immunity for Alliance Agreements', Department of Transportation Order 96–6–33 (14 June 1996); Remarks by Anne K. Bingaman, the then Assistant Attorney General, Antitrust Division, US Department of Justice, 'Statement on the Surface Transportation Board's Approval of the Union Pacific and Southern Pacific Merger' (3 July 1996).

[2] Telecommunications Act of 1996, Pub. L. No. 104–104, 110 Stat. 56 (1996) (codified at 47 USC §§151 et. seq.).

implicating not only review by US agencies but also by international agencies. Thus, competition policy and enforcement in this rapidly evolving industry presents interesting regulatory challenges, both domestically and internationally. This analysis examines aspects of the overlapping review processes and how the enforcement objectives of DOJ and the policy objectives of the FCC affect the telecommunications industry. It discusses how the differing roles and objectives of various agencies may lead to diverging assessments of the same transaction. It identifies the ramifications and costs of dual agency review and explores the likelihood and benefits of increased inter-agency co-ordination. This paper will also identify telecommunications competition issues at the international level, examine the degree and nature of co-operation and co-ordination between US and European competition authorities, and discuss whether the recent co-operative international efforts provide a framework for future multijurisdictional co-operation.

II. The Concurrent Jurisdiction of the DOJ and the FCC in the Domestic Telecommunications Arena

1. Telecommunications Merger Review in the Domestic Arena

Mergers and acquisitions in the telecommunications industry are subject to review by both the FCC and DOJ. Although both agencies have concurrent jurisdiction to review telecommunications mergers and often undertake similar competitive analyses, the underlying principles guiding each agency's review process differ in some significant aspects. The FCC applies a broad 'public interest' standard, which includes an assessment of the pro-competitive benefits of the merger, while DOJ focuses on whether possible anti-competitive effects of the transaction might violate the antitrust laws.

The FCC's jurisdiction to review telecommunications mergers is derived from two statutory sources: the Communications Act of 1934,[3] which gives the FCC the authority to review mergers between telecommunications common carriers under a 'public interest' standard;[4] and the Clayton Act,[5] which grants

---

[3] Communications Act of 1934, Pub. L. No. 73–416, 48 Stat. 1064 (codified as amended in scattered sections of 47 USC).

[4] See, for example, 47 USC §§214, 310(d) (requiring FCC determination that the transfer of control of a company holding radio licences will serve the 'public interest, convenience and necessity').

[5] 15 U.S. C. §§21(a), 18 (1994).

the FCC the authority to bar acquisitions of 'common carriers engaged in wire or radio communications where the effect of such acquisition may be substantially to lessen competition, or tend to create a monopoly'. The Clayton Act also grants the DOJ the statutory authority to review mergers, and prohibits the acquisition of stock or assets by any 'person' where 'the effect of such acquisition may be substantially to lessen competition, or tend to create a monopoly'.

Although the FCC also may challenge a proposed transaction under Section 7, because of the broader powers conferred to it by the Communications Act, the FCC rarely, if ever, uses its statutory authority under the Clayton Act as a basis for proceeding.[6] The fact that the FCC does not generally challenge mergers under its Clayton Act authority may be attributable to the Commission's belief that 'the proper role of competitive forces in an industry must [. . .] be based not exclusively on the letter of the antitrust laws,' but on the 'special circumstances of the industry'.[7] This statement illustrates that the FCC operates under a different ideological premise than DOJ. The FCC elaborated on this difference in *Federal Communications Commission* v *American Satellite Corporation,*[8] where it argued that 'the Sherman and Clayton Acts assume that the public interest is served by competition, in and of itself. Under the statutory fabric of regulation and of the Communications Act, however, we are required to decide where the public interest lies, and competition is but one element of a determination of the public interest.' Thus, the FCC's public interest inquiry differs from DOJ's antitrust analysis insofar as the Commission's 'examination of a proposed merger under the public interest standard includes consideration of the competition policies underlying the [antitrust laws] but the public interest standard necessarily subsumes and extends beyond the traditional parameters of review under the antitrust laws.'[9]

The fundamental difference between the agencies is that the DOJ approaches merger review from an enforcement perspective while FCC approaches merger review from a policy perspective. With respect to the telecommunications industry, the FCC can be characterised as a regulatory agency responsible, among other things, for setting and implementing the policy objectives of the 1996 Act. By contrast, DOJ is strictly an enforcement agency responsible for, *inter alia*, ensuring that mergers and acquisitions do not

---

[6] See Weiss and Stem (1998: 198).

[7] *United States* v *Federal Communications Commission*, 652 F.2d 72, 88 (D.C. Cir. 1980).

[8] 652 F.2d 72 (D.C. Cir. 1980).

[9] Weiss, *supra* note 6, at 198.

violate the antitrust laws. In essence, while DOJ's merger analysis must ensure that a proposed merger is *not harmful* to competition, the FCC is required to conclude that a proposed merger will *enhance* competition and benefit consumers.[10] Therefore, although both agencies necessarily examine competition issues, they do not share the same underlying functional paradigm that competition ultimately dictates the outcome of merger review.[11]

In her testimony before the House Judiciary Committee in June 1998, FCC Commissioner, Susan Ness, articulated how these differences influence the scope and process of each agency's merger review:

> [T]he Justice Department carries the burden of proof, should it decide to challenge a proposed merger; at the FCC, the burden of persuasion is on the proponent of the merger. The Justice Department functions more like a litigant, for a decision to challenge a merger is often brought to a district court for resolution; the FCC functions more like a judge deciding a contested proceeding. The Justice Department's processes involve greater use of investigatory tools than do those of the Commission, which is feasible largely because of confidentiality protections that the Commission cannot provide; the FCC's proceedings are generally open and based upon a highly public record.[12]

Because the FCC applies a broad 'public interest' standard construed to 'secure for the public the broad aims of the Communications Act', while DOJ's review is focused on whether the proposed merger violates antitrust laws, it is not surprising that the two agencies could reach different results regarding the same merger, as they did in Bell Atlantic/NYNEX.[13] The likelihood of a similar occurrence in the future is enhanced further if one considers the numerous differences between the two agencies' merger review processes outlined by Commissioner Ness in her testimony before the House Committee on the Judiciary.

---

[10] See, Memorandum Opinion and Order in the Application of NYNEX Corp. and Bell Atlantic Corp. for Consent to Transfer Control of NYNEX Corp. and Its Subsidiaries, No. NSD–L–96–10, at §37 (14 August 1997).

[11] The FCC, however, adopted the 1992 Horizontal Merger Guidelines as part of its assessment of telecommunications mergers.

[12] Susan Ness, Commissioner, Federal Communications Commission, Address Before the Committee on the Judiciary, US House of Representatives, 'Mergers and Consolidation in the Telecommunications Industry' at 5 (24 June 1998).

[13] See, for example, 'Antitrust Division Statement Regarding Bell Atlantic/NYNEX Merger', US Department of Justice Press Release (24 April 1997); 'FCC Approves Bell Atlantic/NYNEX Merger Subject to Market-Opening Conditions', Federal Communications Commission Press Release (14 August 1997).

2. Different Standards of Review and Policy Objectives Affect Agency Competition Analysis

The Bell Atlantic/NYNEX transaction is the most recent and most significant telecommunications transaction in which the FCC and DOJ merger review processes reached different results. The transaction involved the merger of two of the largest providers of local telephone service in contiguous regions of the Eastern United States. Moreover, some argued that the merger could eliminate the possibility of either or both companies entering and competing in the service territories of the other.[14] Despite contentions by some that the merger was anti-competitive, DOJ did not oppose the merger. The FCC, however, imposed several conditions before allowing the merger to close.

The fact that the FCC and DOJ came to different conclusions as to the competitive impact of the Bell Atlantic/NYNEX merger does not necessarily indicate that one agency is more qualified to review mergers than the other, but highlights the different nature and scope of the respective agency's merger review processes. Specifically, DOJ is not required to consider whether a proposed merger's effect on an industry's future market structure is consistent with a particular policy objective or congressional mandate unrelated to antitrust concerns,[15] while the FCC's public interest inquiry seems to focus precisely on such factors:[16]

---

[14] Weiss and Stem (1998: 202).

[15] See, for example, US Dept. of Justice & Federal Trade Comm'n, Horizontal Merger Guidelines (1992), reprinted in 4 Trade Reg. Rep. (CCH) 13, §194. The 1992 Guidelines 'describe the analytical process that the [DOJ] will employ in determining whether to challenge a horizontal merger, [that is] the process of assessing market concentration, potential adverse competitive effects, entry, efficiency and failure [. . .] to answer the ultimate inquiry in merger analysis: whether the merger is likely to create or enhance market power or to facilitate its exercise'.

[16] The difference in review standards is best illustrated by an examination of some of the actual conditions which the FCC imposed upon the merging parties. As described by Commissioner Ness, these conditions include: '(1) performance monitoring reports, negotiated performance standards, and enforcement mechanisms; (2) carrier-to-carrier testing of uniform operations support systems, which enable resale and unbundled network elements; (3) prices (other than for resale) based on forward-looking economic costs; (4) shared transport facilities on a minutes-of-use basis; and (5) easy payment plans for non-recurring charges, so that even relatively thinly capitalised new entrants can establish a toehold in the marketplace'. Ness, *supra* note 12, at 4. These conditions, which are directed more at ensuring competition as it applies to the Telecommunications Act rather than competition in a pure antitrust perspective, clearly indicate the policy driven framework under which the FCC operates.

The ultimate goal of the [FCC's] competitive analysis of a merger is to determin
how the merger will affect the development of competition as the transition to
deregulated environment envisioned by the Telecommunications Act evolves. Thus
[the Commissioners do] not look at the current significance of merging partie
today, but rather their expected significance as the Act is implemented. This is espe
cially important in the telecommunications markets.[17]

In the same way, DOJ is not required to consider how the proposed merge
affects network reliability, the ability to perform benchmarking analyses, o
other 'public interest factors', but instead focuses on whether a proposed
merger is likely to create market power or enhance a firm's ability to exercise
market power.[18] Thus, the 'public interest factors, specifically mentioned by
Commissioner Ness when discussing the Bell Atlantic/NYNEX merger are no
necessarily relevant in a strict antitrust analysis.[19] In most basic terms, DOJ':
inquiry is focused on how a proposed merger affects current and future competition in well defined geographic and product markets. Thus, to suggest that
the FCC's decision to impose conditions on the Bell Atlantic/NYNEX merger
implies that DOJ was recalcitrant in its antitrust duty ignores the fundamental
differences in the agencies' merger review processes and competition objectives.[20]

Given the distinct roles of these two agencies, the fact that they reached
seemingly different results in Bell Atlantic/NYNEX is not surprising.
Nonetheless, unless a concerted effort is made to more clearly define the review
process and increase inter-agency co-ordination, the costs and criticisms associated with the dual agency review and outcomes such as Bell Atlantic/NYNEX
will never fully be resolved. One particular problem arising from an ill-defined
and overlapping review process is the potential for inter-agency pre-emption.
For example, when posed with the hypothetical merger of AT&T and a
Regional Bell Operating Company (RBOC), then FCC Chairman Reed Hundt
responded that '[u]nder conventional and serviceable antitrust analysis, a

---

[17] Ness, *supra* n 12, at 3.

[18] 15 USC §18; *United States* v *E.I. du Pont de Nemours & Co.*, 353 US 586, 589, 77
S. Ct. 872, 875, 1 L. Ed. 2d. 1057 (1957) (Section 7 is 'designed to arrest in its incipiency
[. . .] the substantial lessening of competition [. . . .]'.

[19] Ness, *supra* n 12 at 4.

[20] The 1992 Guidelines stipulate that while the DOJ will challenge 'competitively
harmful mergers, the Agency seeks to avoid unnecessary interference with the larger
universe of mergers that are either competitively beneficial or neutral'. As an enforcement agency, the DOJ has no authority to impose conditions on a merger that, after it's
investigation, it finds 'competitively beneficial or neutral'.

merger between [AT&T] and the Bell incumbent is unthinkable'.[21] On the face of it, this statement suggests that his conclusion is based more upon pure antitrust analysis rather than a public interest inquiry as to the effect of the hypothetical merger on the goals of the Telecommunications Act. This 'conventional and serviceable antitrust analysis' falls squarely within the purview of the DOJ. Thus, even well intentioned advocating of policy statements or the declaration of a possible response to a merger scenario by one agency may signal to the market problems with a proposed transaction that are based upon another agency's merger review process and statutory charge. This situation may not only confuse the market but could also operate to deny the silent agency the opportunity to review the merger applying its own standards and with its own regulatory/enforcement objectives in mind.

III. Telecommunications Market Access in the US and the Review Standards Employed by the FCC and DOJ

1. DOJ and FCC Roles in the Evaluation of Section 271 Applications

Prior to enactment of the 1996 Act, RBOCs were prohibited from offering inter-exchange services by the Modified Final Judgement (MFJ).[22] This prohibition was grounded in the belief that the RBOCs would use their monopoly control of local telephone service to obtain an unfair advantage in the inter-exchange market.[23] With the enactment of the 1996 Act, Congress established a new statutory framework which allows RBOCs to offer out-of-franchise inter-exchange services immediately, but conditions authority to provide in-franchise inter-exchange services upon the opening of the RBOC's local market to competition.[24]

This statutory framework emphasises one of the important goals of the 1996 Act—the opening of local telephone markets to competition.[25] In order

---

[21] © FCC 'Chairman Reed Hundt calls combination of AT&T and RBOC 'Unthinkable',' Federal Communications Commission Press Release (19 June 1997).

[22] The MFJ is the settlement of the Department of Justice's antitrust suit against AT&T. See *United States* v *American Telephone and Telegraph Co.*, 552 F. Supp. 131 (D.D.C. 1982), *aff'd sub nom.*, *Maryland* v *United States*, 460 US 1001 (1983).

[23] *United States* v *American Telephone and Telegraph Co.*, 552 F. Supp. at 165.

[24] 47 USC §271 (Supp. 1998).

[25] H.R. Rep. No. 104–204, at 48 (1996), *reprinted in* 1996 U.S.C.C.A.N. 10, 11. The House Report indicates that 'the bill promotes competition in the market for local telephone service by requiring local telephone companies [. . .] to offer competitors access to parts of their networks'.

to achieve this goal, the 1996 Act established a structure whereby RBOCs ha
an incentive to comply with the fourteen-point competitive checklist designe
to encourage the opening of local service areas to competitors, and there
gain authority to provide inter-exchange services in their franchise areas.
This structure commonly is referred to as the 'carrot and stick approach'—t
carrot for the RBOC is the ability to offer in-franchise long-distance servic
while the stick refers to the condition that the RBOC demonstrate that its loc
market is open to competition before being permitted to offer such services.

In order to gain approval to offer in-franchise inter-exchange services,
RBOC either must provide interconnection and access to at least one compe
ing facilities-based local exchange carrier (LEC) pursuant to an agreemen
approved under Section 252 of the 1996 Act (Track A),[27] or alternatively, if
RBOC has not received requests for interconnection and access, that RBO
may still demonstrate that it generally is offering 'interconnection and access t
prospective competing LECs under a statement of terms and condition
approved under Section 252(f)' (Track B).[28] In either case, the interconnectio
and access being provided, or being made available by the RBOC, must satisf
the requirements of a fourteen-point competitive checklist, and approval of th
application must be in the public interest.[29]

According to the statutory scheme established by Congress, the FCC ha
ultimate approval authority over Section 271 applications. As part of th
approval process, however, it must consult with DOJ and give DOJ's evalua
tion 'substantial weight,' although the FCC is not bound by DOJ's assess
ment.[30] Likewise, DOJ is not bound to an evaluation of the fourteen-poin
competitive checklist. Instead, the Act provides that DOJ may use any stan

---

[26] With the enactment of the 1996 Act, RBOCs were permitted to offer interLAT/
interexchange services that originate out of their franchise areas as well as incidenta
interLATA services which include audio and video services, alarm monitoring services
Internet services over dedicated facilities for elementary and secondary schools, an
commercial mobile services. 47 USC §§271(b)(2), (b)(3), and (g).

[27] 47 USC §271(c)(1)(A). Section 252 describes the procedures for negotiation an
arbitration of agreements for interconnection, services, and unbundled elements. 4
USC §252.

[28] 47 USC §271(c)(1)(B). Section 252(f) describes the statement of generally applica
ble terms that a RBOC may file with a state commission indicating that it is in compli
ance with the 1996 Act's requirements to provide competing carriers with
interconnection, services, and unbundled elements. 47 USC §252(f).

[29] 47 USC §§271(d)(3)(A), (C).

[30] 47 USC §271(d)(2)(A). DOJ was granted this statutory authority as a result of its
historical role in telecommunications competition policy. The FCC also must consult
with the appropriate state commission. 47 USC §271(d)(2)(B).

dard that it determines is appropriate.[31] Ideally, this interactive scheme between the two agencies takes advantage of the unique expertise of each agency and their historical roles in monitoring competition and policy issues in telecommunications and does not merely result in multiple agency review of the same factors.

Within ninety days of a RBOC's filing an application under Section 271, the FCC must issue a written statement either approving or denying the application and must give appropriate consideration to DOJ's evaluation which is made in the same ninety-day period. Before approving an application, the FCC must find that the RBOC has met the requirements of either Track A (entering into interconnection and access agreements with competing LECs), or Track B (offering to provide interconnection and access), and has complied with the fourteen-point competitive checklist. The FCC also must find that the RBOC has met the separate subsidiary requirements of Section 272, and that approval of the application is in the public interest. The FCC may not limit or extend the terms of the fourteen-point competitive check list, which are as follows:

- interconnection in accordance with Section 251(c)(2) and 252(d)(1);
- non-discriminatory access to unbundled network elements pursuant to Sections 251(c)(3) and 252(d)(1);
- non-discriminatory access at just and reasonable rates to poles, ducts, conduits, and rights-of-way pursuant to Section 224;
- unbundling of local loops;
- unbundling of local transport;
- unbundling of local switching;
- non-discriminatory access to 911 services, directory assistance and operator services;
- white page directory listings;
- non-discriminatory access to telephone numbering;
- non-discriminatory access to signalling systems and databases;
- interim number portability through remote call forwarding, direct inward dialing trunks, or comparable arrangements;
- non-discriminatory access to information or services to allow the LEC to implement local dialing parity pursuant to Section 251(b)(3);
- reciprocal compensation in accordance with Section 252(d)(2); and

---

[31] 47 USC §§271(d)(2)(A). The House Conference Report indicates that DOJ may analyse a Section 271 application under any legal standard, including 'the Clayton Act, Sherman Act, other antitrust laws, section VIII(c) of the MFJ, Robinson-Patman Act or any other standard'. House Conf. Rep. No. 104–458, at 144 (1996), *reprinted in* 1996 U.S.C.C.A.N. at 124, 157.

* resale availability in accordance with Sections 251(c)(4) and 252(d)(3).

While the FCC and DOJ have different roles in the Section 271 approval process and although ultimate approval authority is vested with the former, neither agency to date has determined that a Section 271 application should be approved. Indeed, each agency has developed a strikingly similar approach in their role in the evaluation process.

2. Evaluating Section 271 Applications in the Real World

Despite the statutory authority to use any standard it deems appropriate, in practice DOJ has focused strongly on both the fourteen-point competitive checklist and competitive conditions in local service markets. In developing its standard under the 1996 Act, DOJ sought 'to establish a concrete standard so that applicants would know in advance' how DOJ would evaluate an application.[32] In determining what its basic standard for evaluating Section 271 applications should be, DOJ solicited extensive comments from industry officials and participants and determined that 'before a RBOC should be allowed to enter long-distance, it must be able to demonstrate that its market is truly open [which] is different from saying its market is fully competitive'. To reach its goal of determining whether a market is open to competition, DOJ considers the fourteen-point competitive checklist and the public interest inquiry as equally important:

> [T]here can be no doubt as to the critical importance of the checklist [. . .] The equally critical importance of the public interest requirement is unmistakable. Its importance is not only reflected in the express terms of the statute itself, where the requirement is given co-equal billing with the checklist and the other requirements that the Bells must establish that they satisfy. It is also indicated time after time in the legislative history.[33]

In addition to assessing compliance with the fourteen-point competitive

---

[32] Joel I. Klein, Assistant Attorney General, US Department of Justice: 'Preparing for Competition in a Deregulated Telecommunications Market' (manuscript), address at the Glasser Legalworks Seminar on Competitive Policy in Communications Industries (11 March 1997).

[33] David Turetsky, Deputy Assistant Attorney General, Antitrust Division, US Department of Justice, 'Bell Operating Company InterLATA Entry Under Section 271 of the Telecommunications Act of 1996: some thoughts' (manuscript), address before the Communications Committee NARUC Summer Meeting, (22 July 1996).

checklist, DOJ's public interest inquiry under Section 271 focuses on competition issues 'as informed by the principles of antitrust' and considers competitive conditions 'in all the affected markets' in each of its Section 271 evaluations. Thus in practice, the approaches of both the FCC and DOJ to evaluating Section 271 applications are strikingly similar.

For example, in its first Section 271 evaluation—the SBC Oklahoma Application—the DOJ found that SBC had failed to meet the public interest standard because its local market in that state was not 'fully and irreversibly open to competition'.[34] In making this determination, the DOJ considered several factors including: whether each path of entry by a competing LEC is available in the state; the 'nature and extent of actual local competition'; the existence and adequacy of the RBOC's performance standards; in those instances where actual competition has not flourished, why it has not; and whether 'the complex systems needed to support the provisioning and maintenance of resale services and unbundled elements are sufficiently functional and operable [. . . .]'.

In addition to the public interest analysis of the competitive environment in SBC's Oklahoma region, DOJ also assessed whether SBC had met the requirements of Track A or B and the fourteen-point competitive checklist. DOJ recommended denial of SBC's application because SBC did not 'satisfy either of the two entry tracks set forth in Section 271(c)(1)(A) or (B), [failed] to comply with the statutory competitive checklist, and because approval of the application would not be consistent with the public interest in competition'. The FCC also declared that SBC failed to satisfy the requirements of Section 271, but rested its denial on its finding that SBC had not met the requirements of either Section 271(c)(1)(A) or (B), and thus, did not make any findings regarding the fourteen-point competitive checklist or public interest.

In its Memorandum and Order in the Ameritech Michigan Application, the FCC articulated the relevant factors that are considered as part of its public-interest assessment under Section 271. Finding that the FCC has 'broad discretion in undertaking [. . .] public interest analyses', and that 'Congress granted the [FCC] broad discretion under the public interest requirement in Section 271 to consider factors relevant to the achievement of the goals and objectives of the 1996 Act', the FCC determined that its public interest

---

34 'Evaluation of the United States Department of Justice, In the Matter of Application of SBC Communications, Inc. et al. Pursuant to Section 271 of the Telecommunications Act of 1996 to Provide In-region, InterLATA Services in the State of Oklahoma', before the Federal Communications Commission, CC Docket No. 97–121, 36–37 (16 May 1997) ('DOJ Evaluation of S.B.C. Oklahoma Application').

concerns under Section 271 are broader than determining whether RBOC 'entry would enhance competition in the long-distance market.'[35] The FCC concluded that its public interest assessment would focus on 'whether all pro-competitive entry strategies are available to new entrants' including 'an assessment of the effect of BOC entry on competition in the long-distance market.' Significantly, the FCC determined that compliance with the fourteen-point competitive checklist alone is insufficient as it 'will not necessarily assure that all barriers to entry to local telecommunications markets have been eliminated, or that a BOC will continue to co-operate with new entrants after receiving in-region, interLATA authority.' Instead, the FCC identified several factors that would be probative of whether a RBOC's local service area is open to competition—several of which were similar to those identified by DOJ in its SBC Oklahoma Evaluation. These factors include:

- whether all entry strategies contemplated by the 1996 Act are available in the state, evidenced by 'new entrants actually offering competitive local telecommunications services to different classes of customers [. . .] through a variety of arrangements [. . .] in different geographic regions [. . .] at different scales of operations';
- an assessment of the actual nature and extent of local competition and whether a lack of entry is due to the RBOC's 'failure to co-operate in opening its network to competitors, the existence of barriers to entry, the business decisions of potential entrants, or some other reason;'
- whether agreements with one competing LEC are available at the same rates and terms of other LECs;
- whether the RBOC has agreed to performance monitoring to gauge compliance with existing interconnection obligations and provide information to establish a benchmark against which to measure performance over time; and
- whether the RBOC agrees to optional payment plans for non-recurring charges, whether there are other legal or regulatory barriers to entry, and whether the RBOC has engaged in discriminatory or anti-competitive conduct.

In Ameritech's Application to provide in-region interLATA services in

---

[35] 'Memorandum and Order in the Matter of Application of SBC Communications, Inc. et al. Pursuant to Section 271 of the Telecommunications Act of 1996 to Provide In-Region InterLATA Services in the State of Oklahoma', before the Federal Communications Commission, CC Docket No. 97–121, and 66 (25 June 1997).

Michigan, the FCC found that while Ameritech did meet the requirements for Track A filing, it did not meet all the requirements of the fourteen-point competitive checklist, and thus denied the application. DOJ also recommended that Ameritech's application be denied because Ameritech failed to comply fully with the fourteen-point competitive checklist, and because its local markets were not fully open to competition.[36] In the subsequent Section 271 evaluations and orders, both agencies have acted in parallel and relied on virtually the same criteria in their assessments.

IV. International Telecommunications and Concurrent Jurisdiction Issues

As globalisation increases, overlapping jurisdictional issues no longer solely pertain to bifurcated domestic authority but instead implicate multinational merger review issues, especially as the effects of anti-competitive conduct occurring in one jurisdiction often can negatively impact the commerce of another jurisdiction.

1. Mergers and Concurrent Jurisdiction in the International Arena

Statutory Authority for Concurrent International Jurisdiction
Mergers involving two companies located within one jurisdiction can trigger pre-merger filing requirements and review processes in other jurisdictions. With over seventy jurisdictions having enacted some form of legislation governing anti-competitive conduct, instances of overlapping jurisdiction are becoming increasingly prevalent. Moreover, the proliferation of merger laws has significantly increased the number of jurisdictions in which a proposed merger may be reportable. With today's interdependent economies as a backdrop, an increasing number of mergers affect multiple national economies and, hence, trigger competitive reviews in more than one jurisdiction. According to recent remarks by US Federal Trade Commission Bureau Director, Bill Baer, currently half of all mergers analysed by the US antitrust enforcement agencies

---

[36] 'Evaluation of the United States Department of Justice, In the Matter of Application of Ameritech Michigan Pursuant to Section 271 of the Telecommunications Act of 1996 to Provide In-region, InterLATA Services in Michigan', before the Federal Communications Commission, CC Docket No. 97–137, 34 (25 June 1997).

involve some level of interaction with the competition authorities of a foreign jurisdiction.[37] In addition, as mergers in the telecommunications industry are often subject to overlapping domestic jurisdictional issues, the potential for multiple-agency oversight and the emergence of non-competition based principles affecting the outcome is increased.

The US also maintains a long-standing policy approach to asserting jurisdiction in antitrust matters regardless of where the anti-competitive conduct occurs, if US consumers are adversely affected by the conduct.[38] In fact, the US government recently expanded its jurisdictional reach to include conduct that not only affects US consumers but also US exporters.[39] If conduct has a 'direct, substantial, and reasonably foreseeable' effect on US commerce,[40] US law permits the assertion of jurisdiction over the conduct and the offending parties. While the broad reach of US antitrust law has attracted some scepticism on the international front, other jurisdictions are moving closer to acceptance of the 'effects test' approach, including the European Union (EU). This policy of unilateral enforcement holds the potential to generate political friction between jurisdictions based on the perceived infringement of domestic sovereignty.

2. Effects of Concurrent Jurisdiction in the International Merger Review Process

As the potential grows for competition agencies in more than one jurisdiction to be concurrently investigating and analysing a merger, myriad conflicts and new obstacles have been imposed on antitrust authorities and businesses on the global scale.

In brief, most problems arise because a single international merger frequently falls within the jurisdictional and substantive scope of more than one country's law (including, for this purpose, the merger control system of the EU). From the point of view of regulatory authorities, this overlap can have several undesirable consequences, due to factors such as disagreements over the proper scope of jurisdiction, frustration in efforts to collect information

---

[37] William J. Baer, Director, Bureau of Competition, Federal Trade Commission, 'Report From the Bureau of Competition', (manuscript), address before the ABA Antitrust Section, 15 (2 April 1998).

[38] For an overview of US and EU jurisdictional reach, see Hawk (1996).

[39] US Department of Justice Press Release (3 April 1992). See, also, Joint Antitrust Enforcement Guidelines for International Operations, §3.122 (April 1995).

[40] Foreign Trade Antitrust Improvements Act of 1982 (FTAIA), 15 USC §6a (1988); *International Guidelines* at §3.12.

located within another country, different opinions about the proper remedy, and, perhaps most importantly, policy differences about the appropriate regulatory response. From the point of view of the business community, the consequences can be equally undesirable: the multiplicity of jurisdictions leads to greater uncertainty over the legality of an arrangement, simply because more than one approval is formally or practically necessary; it may lead to conflicting resolutions, where one authority approves and another seeks to block the same deal, often forcing the company to respond to the most restrictive regime; and finally, it leads to increased transaction costs as the parties must defend the transaction before several reviewing authorities.[41]

One of the most significant consequences of cross-border mergers is the potential for incompatible enforcement decisions; that is, when reviewing jurisdictions reach disparate decisions regarding the competitive analysis and viability of a proposed merger. In some instances, those divergent conclusions are not mutually exclusive and the merger can proceed while satisfying both jurisdictions.[42] In other instances, the differing conclusions cannot be adequately resolved and the most restrictive outcome will generally prevail.[43] The review of a merger by two (or more) jurisdictions also creates potential for political friction between the governments of both jurisdictions. The level of co-ordination or co-operation between the competition authorities in different jurisdictions, therefore, has become a paramount concern. The telecommunications industry provides several recent examples of the actual implementation of multi-jurisdictional merger review between the US and the EU. These cases also exhibit varying degrees of co-ordination between the enforcement officials of each respective jurisdiction. While no international telecommunications merger to date has resulted in divergent outcomes by different jurisdictions that would lead to conflict over the viability of the merger, there are several scenarios which may, arguably, illustrate the evolution of multi-jurisdictional merger review and give us some clues as to its future.

---

[41] Prof. Richard Whish and Prof. Diane Wood, *Merger Cases in the Real World: A Study of Merger Control Procedures* 11, prepared for the OECD Competition Law and Policy Committee (1994).

[42] See, for example, 'Commission Clears WorldCom and MCI Merger Subject to Conditions', European Commission Press Release (8 July 1998); 'Justice Department Clears WorldCom/MCI Merger After MCI Agrees to Sell Its Internet Business', US Department of Justice Press Release (15 July 1998).

[43] See, for example, 'FTC Allows Merger of the Boeing Company and McDonnell Douglas Corporation', US Federal Trade Commission Press Release (1 July 1997); 'The Commission Clears the Merger Between Boeing and McDonnell Douglas Under Conditions and Obligations', European Commission Press Release (30 July 1997).

Most recently, the co-ordination and co-operation that occurred during the review of the MCI/WorldCom merger has been highlighted as an example, not only for the telecommunications industry, but for multi-jurisdictional merger review in general. When MCI and WorldCom announced their plans to merge, concerns arose regarding the combined company's control over the Internet backbone.[44] Although both companies are US-based, the Internet's global presence prompted a merger review not only domestically, but also in the EU. Because parallel investigations would occur in both jurisdictions, the parties agreed to waive any confidentiality restrictions imposed on documents submitted to each competition agency. Without the restraints imposed by the confidentiality provisions statutorily imposed on company documents submitted to the US government in the course of a merger review, in this instance DOJ and the EU were allowed to communicate more directly regarding the competitive analysis. In so doing, the parties were afforded the benefit of reduced transaction costs, while the enforcement agencies were permitted greater latitude in their co-operative enforcement efforts. The agencies conferred with each other regarding potential competitive concerns of the proposed transaction, and importantly, discussed appropriate remedies designed to alleviate those concerns. In the end, the EU announced a settlement arrangement with the parties that included the divestiture of MCI's Internet business while permitting the remainder of the transaction to proceed as planned. The settlement satisfied DOJ's concerns with the Internet backbone issues although DOJ continued to investigate those aspects of the transaction that implicated US markets and consumers, for example, the US long-distance telephone market. Following its investigation, DOJ decided to forego additional remedies pending the completion of the Internet backbone divestiture arrangement required by the EU. Assistant Attorney General, Joel Klein, commented that the US 'enjoyed a close and constructive relationship with the EU in pursuing [each agency's] separate responsibilities throughout the investigation. [The US] looks forward to this kind of co-operation continuing beyond this matter into the future.'

While the governments on both sides of the Atlantic praised the level of co-operation and co-ordination that occurred during the merger review process, at least some in the US voiced concern that the US might have been forced to play a secondary role in the investigation due to timing issues.[45] Although co-ordination was taking place, the US and EU operate under separate laws and

---

[44] See, 'Justice Department Clears WorldCom/MCI Merger After MCI Agrees to Sell Its Internet Business', US Department of Justice Press Release (15 July 1998).

[45] Transcript from US Senate Judiciary Committee Hearing on Effects of Corporate Mergers and Consolidations (16 June 1998).

regulations guiding their respective merger review processes. In the EU, the European Commission is bound by stringent time requirements for the completion of a merger investigation,[46] whereas DOJ is afforded somewhat greater leniency in its investigatory time frame which can be further relaxed due to concurrent FCC jurisdiction.[47] In order to comply with the EU timing regulations, the European Commission's final decision pertaining to the merger was determined in advance of the decision reached by DOJ. While US government officials stated unequivocally that, regardless of timing constraints, the US retained complete control over its investigation and possible remedies, some have questioned whether the timing discrepancies placed the US at a disadvantage during the merger review process.[48]

Using a less formal approach to co-operation and comity, the US entered into a 1994 consent decree with British Telecommunications (BT) and MCI pertaining to an acquisition and attempt to form a joint venture by the two companies. As part of the transaction, BT (based solely in the UK) would acquire 20% equity stake in MCI which would provide BT with access to internal MCI information and board representation.[49] Additionally, a joint venture would be formed by MCI and BT and incorporated in the UK and would provide international enhanced telecommunications services to multinational businesses. The transactions would result in a 'vertical affiliation between the dominant telecommunications carrier in the UK and the second largest long-distance provider in the United States.'[50] DOJ reviewed the transaction and asserted jurisdiction because the transaction allegedly had the potential to disadvantage US competitors and consumers, specifically in the provision of telecommunications services between the US and the UK. The transaction as structured included a provision that restricted the ability of each company to compete in the other company's core market.

The then Assistant Attorney General, Anne Bingaman, extolled the efforts by both the US and the UK to alleviate the potential for anti-competitive harm

---

[46] EU Merger Control Regulation, 4064/89/EEC, OJ L257/14 (1990), Article 10 (21.12.1989).

[47] There are strict time frames laid out for merger review by the DOJ and FTC in the Hart-Scott-Rodino Act. Hart-Scott-Rodino Antitrust Improvement Act of 1976, Pub. L. No. 94–435, tit. II §201, 90 Stat. 1380. (codified as amended at 15 USC §18a (1994)). The FCC, however is not bound by these timing restrictions.

[48] See, Remarks of Senator DeWine, Transcript from Senate Judiciary Committee Hearing on Effects of Corporate Mergers and Consolidations (16 June 1998).

[49] *United States* v *MCI Comm. Corp.*, 59 Fed. Reg. 33009 (2 June 1994) (competitive impact statement).

[50] *Ibid*, at 33016.

associated with the transactions, while not infringing on sensitive jurisdictional matters between the two countries.[51] While the UK's Office of Telecommunications (OFTEL) and other regulatory agencies oversee competition and telecommunications-related issues within the UK, the US asserted its jurisdiction because those agencies have no responsibility to ensure competitive conditions for US consumers. According to documents filed with the consent order:

> [the US] considered issues of international comity in shaping the proposed Final Judgment. Consistent with its long-standing enforcement policy, the United States sought in the substantive provisions of the Final Judgment to avoid situations that could give rise to international conflicts between sovereign governments and their agencies. The substantive requirements imposed on MCI and NewCo have been tailored so as to avoid direct United States involvement in BT's operation of its telecommunications network in the United Kingdom on an ongoing basis, minimising the potential for conflict with United Kingdom authorities.[52]

Despite the pronouncements of the US regarding co-operation and comity issues, in private conversations, some in the UK viewed the settlement with MCI and BT as US 'unilateralism'.

3. International Market Access

In 1997, the World Trade Organisation (WTO) reached an agreement (WTO Telecom Agreement) among its member countries regarding basic telecommunications services. The Agreement requires member countries to open up their domestic telecommunications markets to foreign competitors to varying extents. In addition to facilitating the entry of competition into domestic markets, the WTO Telecom Agreement contains safeguards designed to protect against anti-competitive conduct based upon the provisions set forth in the 1996 Act.[53] The WTO Telecom Agreement represents one of the WTO's first

---

[51] Anne K. Bingaman, Assistant Attorney General, US Department of Justice, 'Antitrust Policy For The 21st Century', (manuscript), address Before the ABA Antitrust Section, (17 November 1994).

[52] *United States* v *MCI Comm. Corp.*, 59 Fed. Reg. at 33023.

[53] The Agreement states: '[A]ppropriate measures shall be maintained for the purpose of preventing suppliers who, alone or together, are major suppliers from engaging in or continuing anti-competitive practices'. In this context, anti-competitive conduct includes anti-competitive cross-subsidisation, the unfair use of competitor's

forays into competition-related issues. The commitments made by the member countries are enforceable through the WTO's dispute resolution mechanism. While only a portion of the overall WTO Telecom Agreement relates to competition issues, it represents a new step in multilateral convergence efforts. Currently, the WTO Telecom Agreement extends some level of market access to almost 99% of total basic telecommunications service revenues in WTO Telecom countries.[54] US Trade Representative, Charlene Barshefsky, applauded the completion of the WTO Telecom Agreement and noted that US firms 'will gain not only the opportunity to compete but they will also benefit for the first time from fair rules and effective enforcement.' While it is not yet apparent whether the WTO Telecom Agreement will be successful in dealing with international market access issues, it represents a unique and slightly divergent method for the establishment of international competition. Traditionally, DOJ uses bilateral arrangements to enhance co-operation and co-ordination to combat anti-competitive conduct on an international scale. The WTO Telecom Agreement represents a policy choice by the US government to pursue a multilateral approach, as the WTO Telecom Agreement clearly limits the ability to enter into separate bilateral telecommunications arrangements with non-WTO countries.[55] Continued study and analysis should be pursued to further determine the effectiveness of the WTO's jurisdiction in promoting a competitive international telecommunications environment. If US interests, however, are not appropriately addressed at the WTO level, the US will be forced to review other mechanisms to achieve the benefits of market access for US consumers and businesses.

V. Conclusion

Is the single agency authority the answer for US telecommunications policy in the context of mergers? The costs associated with overlapping jurisdiction for merger review by the FCC and DOJ are much lamented and recognised by merging parties, legal pundits, and the agencies alike. Undue delays resulting from multiple layers of review, increased transaction costs, duplication of

---

information, and the of denial of essential facilities or commercially relevant information. See *Reference Paper from the Negotiating Group on Basic Telecommunications* (24 April 1996).

[54] Statement of US Trade Representative Charlene Barshefsky on Basic Telecom Negotiations (15 February 1997).

[55] See, Atwood *et al.* (1997: 901).

effort by the reviewing agencies, and uncertain precedential guidance are all justifiable criticisms of dual agency review. However, the system is not ultimately unworkable. The very fact that DOJ and the FCC have different underlying statutory charges in reviewing a merger suggests that both agencies are necessary in order to fulfill their own individual responsibilities in the merger review process: compliance with the antitrust laws, and the implementation of the policy goals of the 1996 Act. Neither obligation is more nor less important than the other.

The practical difficulties with the concurrent jurisdiction, however, have been recognised even at the FCC. Commissioner Michael Powell recently stated that:

> [T]he Commission should focus its public interest merger analysis on factors relating to its unique expertise. In my view, there is potential in the future for the Commission to devise ways—formal or informal—to take into consideration how the Department deals with a particular merger in our own merger analysis. I believe this potential exists even where the Commission performs an independent analysis or the method and scope of our analysis differ from that employed by the Department. As our reliance on the Department's· horizontal merger guidelines demonstrates, there may at times be significant overlap between the analytical frameworks employed by the Commission and the Department. To suggest otherwise would strain credulity. Based on my acknowledgement of this analytical overlap, and my deep respect for the diligence and considerable expertise of the Department, I am hopeful that the Commission will, in the future, be able to minimise duplications of effort in the area of competitive analysis and thereby use our regulatory resources most efficiently.[56]

Commissioner Harold Furchtgott-Roth also was concerned about the 'cumbersome review process' in the WorldCom/MCI matter and stated that:

> Our staff has invested substantial talent and resources in the review of this merger, as is evident by the accompanying Order. But our staff is hard working and has many demands placed on their time. Another agency of the federal government, one with specific statutory authority to review mergers and with substantially more staff that specialises in nothing other than merger analysis, has already examined this merger in all market contexts in great detail and has found it acceptable. The heroic efforts of our staff notwithstanding, we have little to add or to subtract from the

---

[56] Separate Statement of FCC Commissioner, Michael Powell, Regarding the Application of WorldCom, Inc. and MCI Telecommunications Corp., CC Docket No. 97–211, at 4 (14 September 1998).

market analyses or the judgement of this other federal agency but a more detailed public record.[57]

One potential resolution would be to vest competition analysis solely with DOJ. Its recognised antitrust expertise and its greater access to information and investigatory authority under the Hart-Scott-Rodino Act may make the DOJ better positioned to review the competitive effects of mergers in the telecommunications industry.[58] Similarly, implementation of the policy goals of the 1996 Act could be left to the FCC. The practical application of such a resolution would require significant agency co-operation. For example, what if DOJ determines that a transaction does not violate the antitrust laws but the FCC denies or imposes conditions on the same transaction as was the case in Bell Atlantic/NYNEX? Even more challenging, what if DOJ wants to block a merger but the FCC determines that the anti-competitive effects are mitigated by public interest considerations?

Consistent with Commissioner Powell's call for utilising the unique expertise of each reviewing agency, in our view it would be desirable for the FCC to defer altogether to DOJ's analysis as to whether a given merger is anti-competitive. There is no principled reason for the FCC to duplicate the work of the DOJ in this regard or to second-guess its conclusions. The FCC could independently focus on any social-policy based public interest standard, accepting DOJ's analysis as to competitive effects. Such a scenario, of course, begs the overarching question as to whether competition-based analysis pursuant to the antitrust laws is sufficient to protect the public interest.

A less far-reaching resolution could be for both agencies to continue to recognise and appreciate the unique objectives that each brings to the merger review process, but to work towards greater sharing of information and resources. DOJ's procedures for reviewing mergers pursuant to the Hart-Scott-Rodino Act provide merging parties with a predictable review process and provide the government with information necessary to evaluate these complicated mergers fully. The FCC's public interest inquiry can only benefit from increased co-ordination with DOJ and the sharing of information gained through the Hart-Scott-Rodino process. The lessons learned from recent telecommunications mergers in the international arena relating to increased co-operation and information sharing are lessons that the domestic agencies can learn from as well.

---

[57] Separate Statement of FCC Commissioner, Harold Furchgott-Roth, Regarding the Application of WorldCom Inc. and MCI Telecommunications Corp., CC Docket No. 97–211, at 1 (14 September 1998).

[58] Weiss and Stem (1998: 207).

How then should redundancies between the agencies be resolved in the Section 271 application process? With the two agencies responsible for market access in domestic telecommunications acting in concert and relying on fundamentally the same standards for assessing compliance with Section 271, one might conclude that this system is functioning appropriately. Such a conclusion, however, would ignore the tremendous criticism the Section 271 process has received from the industry and even from the FCC Commissioners. As Commissioner Powell stated in his White Paper:

> Our present time-restrictive, paper-intensive, adjudicative approach to evaluating section 271 applications, has left our talented and dedicated staff powerless either to give detailed guidance on all aspects of section 271's 'competitive checklist' or to co-ordinate as fully with the applicants, the Justice Department and State Commissions as I believe is necessary to achieve our collective end: the promotion of competition in local and interexchange markets.[59]

There is a need for more predictability in the Section 271 application process, and for increased collaboration among state commissions, DOJ and FCC. Commissioner Powell has suggested that the new approach include more deference for each agency's unique area of expertise in an effort to conserve agency resources and streamline the overall Section 271 process.

The fundamental question may be whether the Section 271 approach itself constitutes sound policy. Arguably, industry-specific entry hurdles (such as those created by the Section 271 application process) are themselves anti-competitive, even given the history of the telecommunications sector. The congressionally mandated process reflects not only this history but the horse-trading that sought to accommodate the divergent interests of all industry segments. The end result is reminiscent of Bismarck's remark on treaties: 'If you like laws and sausages, you should never watch either one being made.'

Of more immediate relevance to the EUI programme, does the sequential responsibility of the FCC and DOJ contribute to the correct outcome? Would a better outcome be achieved if traditional antitrust principles were applied exclusively by DOJ, while the FCC, in turn, were to give conclusive deference to DOJ's assessment in its separate public interest review? While both the FCC

---

[59] *Wake Up Call:* FCC *Commissioner Michael Powell Calls for New Collaborative Approach to Section 271 Applications,* http://www.FCCgov/commissioners/powell/271essay.html. While the FCC has provided guidance on several items of the fourteen-point competitive checklist, it has provided little or no guidance on a handful of items in the context of its 271 Orders. See, for example, 47 USC §271(c)(2)(B)(viii) (white pages directory listings); 47 USC §271(c)(2)(B)(xii) (local dialing parity); 47 USC §271(c)(2)(B)(xiii) (reciprocal compensation).

and the individual state commissions are statutorily required to reach determinative conclusions on the fourteen-point competitive checklist, the Act designates that DOJ may use 'any standard' in its analysis of Section 271 applications. Thus, it may be appropriate for DOJ to utilise its expertise in the antitrust arena and analyse the competitive factors of the application rather than focus on the policy issues outlined in the fourteen-point competitive checklist. Such an outcome would eliminate unnecessary duplication of efforts by the reviewing agencies and maximise the benefits flowing from DOJ's unique understanding of competitive markets.

While there may well be valid arguments to support a single-agency approach to domestic competition enforcement in the telecommunications industry, the current international environment does not support the utilisation of a multinational mechanism for merger control enforcement in telecommunications or any other industry. As each jurisdiction's merger laws are so divergent in scope and nature, the potential for worldwide convergence on a substantive level at this time does not appear to be a feasible option. In addition, most jurisdictions maintain strict statutory time limitations for their merger review processes that would, in effect, prohibit the use of any mediation mechanism to resolve conflicts over jurisdictional merger issues.

There has been debate, both in the US and internationally, regarding whether or not an organisation, such as the WTO, should function as a worldwide dispute resolution body for antitrust enforcement. While the WTO may appear to be a suitable forum for such action due to its broad membership base, there is the fear that the vast discrepancy in substantive competition and particularly merger laws among member countries would create a system based on the 'lowest-common-denominator' approach to enforcement.[60] In addition, the WTO does not yet have the necessary experience in dealing with intricate antitrust matters. While the WTO is not suitable for providing a dispute resolution mechanism, it does offer a useful and appropriate forum for continued education on the benefits of enacting and enforcing competition policy.

Instead of efforts toward full substantive convergence or a dispute resolution mechanism, discussion should focus on increased efforts toward co-operation and co-ordination, including the prospect of more co-ordination on the procedural aspects of the merger process.[61] As evidenced by the multi-jurisdictional merger reviews discussed above, co-operation plays a vital role in the efficient

---

[60] See, Commentary by Joel Klein, 'No Monopoly On Antitrust', *Financial Times*, 13 February, 1998, at 20.

[61] Efforts are currently being made to study certain aspects of procedural harmonisation of the multi-jurisdictional merger review process. The OECD recently issued a

cross-border review process for both enforcement officials and business.[62] While the benefits derived from the use of co-operation in the international competition arena to date have been noticeable, more initiatives need to be pursued to improve such co-operation.

While efforts toward co-operation in the antitrust arena in general have placed significant importance on the ability to share information, US law prohibits the exchange of information obtained through the Hart-Scott-Rodino process without prior authorisation from the involved parties. Furthermore, the International Antitrust Enforcement Assistance Act (IAEAA) specifically excluded cross-border sharing of documents submitted in accordance with the Hart-Scott-Rodino process.[63] Without the ability to share documents and information, enforcement authorities are severely limited as to the types of discussions that can occur between jurisdictions. This limitation becomes particularly relevant when discussions regarding remedies arise. If parties choose not to waive their confidentiality rights, the agencies are often prevented from discussing the rationale behind potential remedy options. Such a scenario could pose difficulties if separate agencies reach conflicting remedy options and discussion regarding competitive effects is not possible. Continued discussion may be warranted as to whether further initiatives (besides the voluntary waiver method) are necessary to promote the US agencies' ability to share

---

draft recommendation on common pre-merger filing forms and timetables. Such convergence on a procedural level holds the potential to reduce transaction costs and to facilitate enhanced coordination between reviewing agencies. According to the business community, these procedural discrepancies and the subsequent uncertainties appear to cause significant concern. Progress in this area of harmonisation should be pursued and encouraged.

[62] While co-operation has worked well thus far in telecommunications mergers, it should be noted that the potential for conflict despite co-operation remains a possibility. The telecommunications industry is not immune from the conflicts that hold the potential to confront any industry or business. Substantive conflicts on outcome will always be a possibility because dual jurisdiction involves the application of different laws and standards to a single transaction. Thus far, one of the most controversial instances of dual jurisdictional conflict occurred during the US and EU's review of the Boeing-McDonnell Douglas transaction. Based on each jurisdiction's respective laws, different outcomes were reached. While, in the end, the merger proceeded in such a way as to accommodate both sides, the case may foreshadow events to come.

[63] To increase the ability of the US to co-operate with foreign competition enforcement authorities, the IAEAA was passed in 1994 and authorises the US to enter into agreements with foreign authorities under which investigative information to help in the prosecution of anti-competitive conduct is reciprocally exchanged. The law provides for exclusive safeguards to ensure that confidential information provided to a foreign jurisdiction is subject to adequate conditions of confidentiality.

information during the course of a merger investigation with their foreign counterparts conducting a parallel investigation. In addition, the increasing globalisation of transactions militates in favour of consolidating authority for competition review solely within antitrust agencies in the US. At the very least, it impels greater deference to the antitrust agency and avoidance of duplicate investigations.

As an indication of its magnitude, the future direction of international competition enforcement is being addressed by a committee established by the DOJ in 1997.[64] The International Competition Policy Advisory Committee (ICPAC) was given a mandate by Attorney General, Janet Reno, and Assistant Attorney General, Joel Klein, to study and evaluate the current and future status of international competition policy enforcement and report back to DOJ with its findings. The Advisory Committee's report will be the basis for the development of future US policy in this area. Under consideration by the Advisory Committee are three distinct yet intertwined subject areas, including multi-jurisdictional merger review, the interface between trade and competition, and co-operative enforcement of cartel activities. Part of the overarching analysis by the Committee will also encompass the ramifications of concurrent jurisdiction over competition-related issues.

---

[64] The Committee, co-chaired by James F. Rill and Paula Stern, is comprised of leading representatives from the worlds of business, law and academia. 'Reno, Klein Unveil First-Ever Committee to Attack Anti-competitive Cartels', US Dept. of Justice Press Release (24 November 1997).

VIII

Giuseppe Tesauro*

Relations Between Relations Regulatory and Competition
Authorities in the Communications Industry: the
Italian Experience

I. Introduction

In Italy, the Antitrust Authority (Autorità garante della concorrenza e del mercato) is responsible for enforcing the Competition Act (Law No. 287 of 10
October 1990) in all sectors, whereas regulatory bodies perform specific sectoral regulatory functions. The only exception is represented by the banking
sector, where the sectoral supervisory authority, the Bank of Italy, is responsible for enforcing competition rules with respect to agreements, abuses of dominant position and mergers which involve banks. On such matters the Antitrust
Authority has to provide the Bank of Italy with a non-binding advice.[1]

As far as regulation is concerned, the wide and far-reaching process of liberalisation, often fostered by EU interventions, which took place in many public utility industries in recent years, was accompanied by a thorough reform of
the institutional setting. In communications, similarly to what happened in
1995 in the gas and electricity industries, regulatory tasks previously carried
out by the Ministry have been recently transferred to a sectoral independent
regulatory agency. More specifically, Law No. 249 of 31 July 1997 has established the Communications and Broadcasting Regulatory Authority, called the
'Autorità per le garanzie nelle comunicazioni'. The new agency has, among
others, the following duties: to identify universal service obligations and the
conditions for the allocation of their costs; to define a set of objective and transparent criteria for network interconnection and access; to issue general authorisations and individual licences; to adopt guidelines regarding the quality of
services.

For telecommunications, Law No. 249/97 simply confirms the pre-existing
functional division of tasks, giving the communications agency regulatory
functions only while the Antitrust Authority remains competent to apply competition rules. For publishing and broadcasting, the law modifies the previous
institutional structure. In particular, the law gives the Antitrust Authority the

---

* Presidente, Autorità Garante della Concorrenza e del Mercato.
[1] Law No. 287/90, section 20, pars. 2–3.

power, previously assigned to the former Publishing and Broadcasting Authority, to enforce competition law in these sectors. This was an important step in the direction to create a unique antitrust authority, while maintaining regulatory functions within specialised institutions.

Since its establishment in 1990, the Competition Authority has repeatedly intervened in the communications sector, both as an antitrust enforcer and as a competition advocate. These interventions may be fully appreciated only if considered in the wider context of the progressive liberalisation of the sector, to which they have contributed in a substantial way. On the other hand the transformation of the Italian sectoral regulatory setting is very recent, so that it is particularly difficult to draw definite conclusions on the advantages and disadvantages of the current institutional framework.

II. Access to Infrastructure Networks and Antitrust Enforcement: the Italian Experience in Telecommunications

In Italy the general competition law applies to all undertakings, irrespective of their private or public nature. Competition rules, however, do not apply to undertakings which, by law, are entrusted with the operation of services of general economic interest or operate on the market in a monopoly situation, in so far as this is indispensable to perform the specific tasks assigned to them.[2] The Antitrust Authority has given a strict interpretation of this provision, stating that competition rules do not apply only when a specific conduct represents the less restrictive way to achieve the institutional goals entrusted by the law to an undertaking. Therefore, the restrictions of competition have to be strictly necessary and proportionate to the correct fulfilment of the tasks assigned to the undertaking by law.

Given this legal background, the Antitrust Authority has been able, since the very beginning of its activity, to deal with network access issues in the telecommunications sector, identifying abusive behaviour on the part of the former legal telecommunications monopolist with respect to its downstream competitors in liberalised markets. The following cases seem particularly relevant: 3C Communications, Telsystem-Telecom and Albacom-Telecom Italia.

---

[2] Law No. 287/90, section 8, par. 2, similar to Article 90, par. 2 of the EC Treaty.

1. Communications

In 1992, Sip (now Telecom Italia), the national telecommunications company, holding the exclusive right to operate the Italian telephone service, abused its dominant position by refusing to grant to 3C Communications the use of telephone lines and hence preventing this company from providing services consisting in the possibility of using credit cards to gain access to the telephone line and as a means of paying for telephone calls.

2. Telsystem-Telecom

In 1994, Telecom Italia abused its dominant position on the market for services for closed user-groups by refusing to lease telecommunications lines to Telsystem, a company created to provide telecommunications services among a closed group of users. Despite repeated requests, Telecom refused to lease the lines to Telsystem, justifying this refusal on the grounds that the Telsystem service was within the exclusive domain of the public carrier. Considering that EC Directive 90/388 restricted the scope of the telecommunications monopoly to the provision to the public of voice telephony and therefore liberalised the activity Telsystem was planning to enter into, the Authority ruled that Telecom was abusing its dominant position by not supplying Telsystem with the links it required. Unfortunately, even though the decision of the Authority was very timely, the seriousness of the abusive behaviour of Telecom Italia was so strong that Telsystem, a very small new entrant, had to exit from the market and file for bankruptcy.

3. Albacom-Telecom Italia

In 1997 the Authority ascertained that Telecom had abused its dominant position in the provision of dedicated circuits (or leased lines). One abuse consisted of the fact that Telecom Italia did not differentiate the tariff of intermediate speed transmission circuits according to capacity demanded by its competitors, strongly increasing the cost of entry for competitors demanding medium capacity circuits. Telecom also abused its dominant position by supplying high capacity lines only to its own final customers without publicising this option, *de facto* preventing competitors from gaining access to this service. Finally, Telecom had used a cheaper system of transmission, alternative to dedicated lines, without informing competitors of this possibility. In view of the seriousness of all these violations, the Authority ordered Telecom to pay a fine (950 million lire) equivalent to 1 percent of the relevant annual turnover.

The Antitrust Authority has intervened in the telecommunications sector in a few other instances, not directly related to network access conditions, with the aim of allowing entry into already liberalised markets. The following cases have been particularly relevant: Ducati-SIP, Cellular telephone system GSM and Telecom Italia-GSM dealers.

4. Ducati-Sip

In 1992, the Authority ascertained an abuse of dominant position by SIP in the mobile telephone retailing market. Mobile phones were bought by SIP from producers and then resold to clients with SIP trademark through its own distribution network. The abuse consisted in the inclusion in the distribution contract of exclusive clauses: distributors were obliged to buy their products from SIP and could not sell products other that the ones with the SIP trademark.

5. Cellular telephone system GSM

In 1992, SIP abused its dominant position on the new GSM market, where it was operating on an exclusive basis for 'experimental' reasons, pre-empting a soon to be liberalised market. Considering Sip monopoly on vocal telephony and on mobile services with TACS technology, the Authority ruled that acquiring GSM customers before any other competitor entered the market gave the company considerable competitive advantages, hampering the future development of competition.

6. Telecom Italia-GSM Dealers

In May 1996, the Authority ruled that exclusive rights and other loyalty clauses in the distribution contract between Telecom Italia Mobile (TIM) and its network of dealers for subscriptions to the GSM service were in violation of the Competition Act. In the course of the investigations, the Authority found that TIM held a dominant position on the GSM mobile telephone market in addition to its statutory monopoly over the adjacent and even broader market for TACS analogue mobile services. It therefore ruled that by organising an exclusive distribution system, and granting a TACS exclusivity only to those dealers

hat also had obtained a GSM exclusivity, Telecom abused its dominant posi-
ion by increasing access costs to competing service providers.

II. Advocacy Powers

These antitrust interventions were accompanied by an intense competition
advocacy activity by the Authority, aiming at fostering a fast and effective liberalisation process in the telecommunication sector. There is, in fact, a significant link between the activity of the Antitrust Authority in the enforcement of
competition rules and its advocacy activity. The investigations of alleged
abuses of dominant position or anti-competitive practices provide an opportunity to carry out a thorough examination of the regulatory context, making it
possible to identify obstacles to competition originating from unjustified rules
and regulations. At the same time, the effectiveness of the Authority's advocacy interventions is considerably enhanced when one or more investigations
are being carried out previously or simultaneously on conducts restricting
competition, giving more urgency to the requested regulatory or legislative
changes.

Since 1990, the Antitrust Authority has exercised its advocacy powers in a
wide range of economic sectors where regulations unduly prevented or
restricted entry on the markets, or otherwise distorted competition. Half of the
reports issued by the Authority refer to legislation concerning transport,
telecommunications and energy. With special reference to telecommunications, regulations governing value-added services and mobile telephony have
been changed as a result of a number of advocacy reports.

Although it is not easy to assess accurately the impact of the Authority's
advocacy activity in relation to the complex system of laws and regulations
which distort competition, a recent paper shows that the Authority has generally been more effective when its advice referred to a bill under discussion.[3] In
fact, in about one third of the cases, the Authority's positions have been
broadly taken up by Parliament and/or by the competent authorities, which in
some cases have repealed rules and regulations imposing unjustified restrictions on competition or, more frequently, have amended certain anti-competitive provisions of draft legislation. As far as the relations between the Antitrust
Authority and the competent regulatory body are concerned (generally the
Ministry, since the sectoral regulatory authorities have only recently being
established), the experience developed so far shows that the intervention of the

---

[3] Parcu (1996).

Antitrust Authority is more likely to be effective when it involves issues that have already been dealt with, in some degree, by the EU, in the form of direc tives, resolutions, infringement procedures or judgments by the Court o Justice.[4] On the other hand, where the Antitrust Authority has addressed issue of purely domestic relevance, its recommendations have often been ignored.

IV. Co-operation between Antitrust and Communications Regulatory Authorities

As in other sectors, the co-operation between the Antitrust Authority and the Communications Regulatory Authority, apart from general informal consul tations, has been institutionalised by the provision of prior non-binding advice delivered by the regulatory authority to the competition authority, and vice versa. More specifically, the Antitrust Authority is required to ask for a prior not binding advice to the Communications Regulatory Authority on decisions concerning agreements, abuses of dominant position or mergers which involve undertakings operating in the communication industry. This provision is sim ilar, to that in the insurance sector, whereby the Antitrust Authority is required to ask for a prior not binding advice from the insurance regulatory agency (ISVAP) on decisions concerning agreements, abuses of dominant position or mergers which involve undertakings operating in the insurance sector.

Similarly, the Communications Regulatory Authority is required to ask for a prior not binding advice from the Antitrust Authority, on a number of issues: the identification of undertakings active in the telecommunications sector with significant market power; the conditions of interconnection and of access to the network; the decisions concerning accounting separation.[5] The Antitrust Authority is therefore required to contribute to the decisional process of the Communications Authority by providing its specific technical expertise con cerning the evaluation of market power. As for the decisions concerning the conditions of interconnection to the network and those regarding accounting separation, the Antitrust Authority advice relates to an evaluation of the impact of the proposed solution to the development of competition.

---

[4] Parcu (1996) shows that in 73 percent of cases where the Authority suggestions were accepted, the Authority intervention was supported by a EU intervention.

[5] Presidential Decree No. 318/97, section 1, letter *am*; section 4, par. 9; section 4, par. 17; section 9, par. 2.

V. Some Concluding Comments

The Communications Authority has only recently been established and it is really too early to draw any conclusion concerning the day to day co-operation and co-ordination with the Antitrust Authority. Only some general remarks can be made:

1. Different Goals and Duties of the Two Institutions

With respect to the aim of protecting competition in public utilities, the activity of the Antitrust Authority mainly relates to the prevention of abusive behaviour by dominant firms aiming at impeding the development of competition on liberalised markets. The regulatory authorities recently established in communications, gas and electricity pursue different sets of objectives. According Law No. 481/95, they have been established with the aim of 'promoting competition and efficiency in the provision of public utility services, as well as adequate quality standards without prejudice to the profitability of such activities, while ensuring their widespread and homogeneous availability throughout the national territory, establishing an objective, transparent and non-discriminatory tariff system, protecting the interests of customers and consumers interests, taking into account the EC relevant law as well as the general policy guidelines set by the government'.

Therefore, while the Antitrust Authority pursues a single public interest, the protection of competition, the sectoral regulatory authorities have to draw a balance between different interests, within the limits defined by law. In this respect, what matters most from the point of view of the correct functioning of institutions is that the legal framework (independence of the Authorities, jurisdictional control on their activities etc.) is adequate to prevent improper external interference in the fulfilment of their institutional goals.

2. Functional Division of Tasks

The described developments of the institutional framework confirm the general trend towards a division of tasks between competition and regulatory authorities based on functional criteria rather than on specific sectoral expertise. This trend deserves a positive evaluation. Also due to the removal of some regulatory line of business restrictions, it is becoming increasingly difficult to design an effective and stable system in which a subset of markets or undertakings is not under the jurisdiction of the economy-wide competition authority, but of sector-specific competition law enforcer. In particular, product market bound aries are not stable over time, but change as a result of changes in technologic and in demand. However, the most important advantage of the genera approach of assigning regulatory tasks to sectoral regulatory agencies an tasks of competition law enforcement to the Antitrust Authority is that it gua antees a consistent interpretation and enforcement of the antitrust rules. In fac in the enforcement of general competition rules in different sectors, th Antitrust Authority applies similar principles, while the specific economi characteristics of each market may be taken into account; on the other han regulatory authorities, when they are assigned also the task to apply the com petition law in their sector, are not able to build up enough experience, leadin to possible contradictions in the interpretation of the antitrust law.

3. Regulatory Tasks

It has been argued that when competition is well established in a particular sec tor, there is no need for sectoral regulation (and for a sectoral regulatory author ity), since it is the functioning of the market itself that guarantees competitive prices and the widespread availability of goods and services of the desired quali ties. In this scenario, which implies a full working of competitive forces, abusive conduct by dominant firms could simply be regulated by general antitrust rule: and no regulatory authority would be needed. Furthermore if a sector is rapidly becoming competitive, the establishment of a separate regulatory body could even be disadvantageous, delaying the move towards full market liberalisation.

As far as the communications sector is concerned, however, this scenario is far from being attained and some form of regulatory expertise is definitely nec-essary. Of course, the approach followed in Italy of assigning regulatory tasks to sectoral regulatory authorities is just one of the possible solutions. Among the alternatives, one may mention:

(1) abolishing regulation, leaving the antitrust authority the power to apply general competition law to all sectors (e.g. New Zealand);
(2) assigning to the antitrust authority of the task of applying specific sectoral regulation (e.g. Australia);
(3) assigning regulatory tasks to a single regulator (no country to my knowl-edge has followed this route);
(4) assigning regulatory tasks to a number of regulators (United Kingdom, Italy, France, Spain etc.).

Every solution has its advantages and disadvantages. Abolishing economic regulation altogether has the disadvantage that, in the transition towards a fully competitive market, some specific 'regulatory' problems arise (financing universal service obligations, regulating tariffs etc.) that cannot be easily solved through the application of general competition rules. On the other hand the Australian approach of assigning the regulatory tasks to the antitrust authority has the advantage that interventions might be more inspired by competition principles. Moreover, such an approach would make the transition of a specific sector from regulation to deregulation easier. However the simultaneous application of regulation and competition law by the same body, according to the different philosophies involved, might reduce the transparency of the decision making process.

The choice of establishing one or more sectoral regulators is also not without problems. The solution of creating one single regulator has the advantage that similar problems (access, tariffs, universal service) are treated in the same way. On the other hand, due to the complexity and the novelty of the matters involved, a single regulatory body would eliminate all kind of beneficial 'competition' among regulators. In this regard, the Italian solution to create specialised regulators with a broad sectoral mandate seems quite appropriate.

IX

Robert Verrue*

Challenges Facing the European Telecommunications Regulatory Framework

I. Introduction

Since January 1998, telecommunications services have been fully liberalised in the vast majority of European Union countries. The results, which have been anticipated in some cases, are already visible. There have been significant decreases in tariffs—especially in the long-distance and international markets, many new actors in the sector with a total number of almost 300 operators authorised to provide national voice telephony services in the fifteen EU countries as against 100 at the end of 1997, a marked improvement in the quality and diversification of services, and a rapid increase in the overall consumption of communication services.

At the same time, investors are putting considerable capital into new communication infrastructures and services throughout Europe, and incumbent operators are expanding their activities beyond their domestic markets. Both trends pave the way for further competition in the coming years. The result of these developments is the genuine onset of competition, with benefits for both citizens and the business sector alike.

Against this background, this paper will show how the current regulatory framework, put in place only recently, is already being challenged by market and technology developments, and the impact of such challenges on the evolution of this new regulatory framework and its main institutional elements. The paper starts with a brief examination of the rationale of the liberalisation process, its key-elements, and will assess—as far as is possible at this stage—its current state of transposition, both in regulatory and in market terms. In the second part, we describe the emerging new technologies, notably the phenomenon of convergence in services and networks, and outline some of the implications for the current regulatory framework for telecommunications and media. The third part of the paper examines the 1999 Telecommunications Review, describes the current debate on convergence, the prospects for a European Regulatory Authority, and outlines the main features of a future regulatory framework for communications services.

---

* Director General, Directorate General Information Society of the European Commission.

II. The Evolution of the European Regulatory Framework for Telecoms Services

1. The Progressive Liberalisation of Telecoms Services

The formulation of the new European regulatory framework for telecommunications and the liberalisation of telecoms service in Europe has been a decade-long process starting with the publication of the Green Paper in 1987.[1] At this time, the EU telecom market was fragmented along national lines, with each national market being controlled by national monopolies and no separation between regulatory and operational functions.

Several factors called for the introduction of competition into telecommunications market. The new commercial telecom services, such as databanks, email, and call centres, were looking for non-discriminatory and cost-efficient access to networks. The progressive digitalisation of telecommunications networks favoured the competitive provision of these new services and generated significant reductions in transmission costs. Monopolies, which mainly delivered telephones and telex services, were no longer in a position to provide the benefits of all new technological developments to all sectors of the economy. The international environment was also evolving as a result of the AT&T break-up in the US and the shift to a duopoly market in the UK with the full privatisation of British Telecom (BT) in 1984. These two countries were followed by Canada, New Zealand, and Australia. Soon all those countries which had developed an alternative telecom regulatory model began to exert increasing pressure to open up markets.

There was striking evidence that the innovatory potential offered by digital technologies, and the consequent significant cost reductions to end users, could only be fully realised in a competitive environment. But in spite of the clear economic rationality of opening up markets, the full liberalisation of European telecommunications markets in 1998 was the result of a long and complex process of negotiation in which the replacement of the existing monopoly structures with a harmonised and competitive framework proved to be politically very demanding.

The European Commission promoted political consensus through the publication of Green Papers launching large public consultations and discussions with all relevant market players (i.e. national administrations, telecom opera-

---

[1] *Green Paper on the Development of the Common Market for Telecommunications Services and Equipment* COM(87) 290, 30.6.87.

tors, users groups, trade unions). This was followed by Resolutions from the Council, notably defining fixed deadlines to provide for predictability, transparency, and confidence in the process amongst investors and potential competitors.

Following the first of these Green Papers in 1987, the Commission assumed a pro-active role, using Article 86 [ex 90] of the Consolidated Treaty to introduce competition in a progressive manner to the various markets.[2]

* The Terminal Equipment Directive of May 1988,[3] as amended by Council Directive 1993 on satellite terminals.[4]
* Services Directive of June 1990,[5] as amended by the Satellite Directive of October 1994,[6] Cable Directive of October 1995,[7] Mobile Directive of January 1996,[8] and the Full Competition Directive of March 1996.[9]

Both voice telephony and infrastructure provision, were liberalised on 1 January 1998. Whilst the political agreement for voice telephony dates back to

---

[2] The use of the Article 86 [ex 90] by the Commission in the telecommunication sector has been confirmed by the rulings of the European Court of Justice in the British Telecom Case which allowed the completion of the 1998 telecommunications liberalisation process. Case 41/83, *Italy* v *Commission*, [1985] ECR 873, where the Italian government challenged a Commission decision under the competition rules taken against BT This case confirmed the full application of Treaty competition rules to the telecommunications sector. Case 202/88 *France* v. *Commission*, [1991] ECR I–1259, this upheld the Commission's Article 86 [ex 90] Directive on competition in the markets for telecommunications terminal equipment in all essential points. Joined Cases 271/90, 281/90 and *Spain, Belgium* and *Italy* v. *Commission*, [1992] ECR I-5833, upheld the Commission's Article 86 [ex 90] Directive on competition in the markets for telecommunications services in all essential points.

[3] Council Directive 98/301/EC on competition in the markets in telecommunications equipment, OJ L 131/73 (1998).

[4] Council Directive of 29 October 1993 supplementing Directive 91/263/EEC in respect of satellite earth station equipment, 93/97/EEC, OJ L 290/01 (1993).

[5] *Supra*, n 3.

[6] Directive 94/46/EEC, amending Directive 88/301/EEC and Directive 90/388/EEC in particular with regard to satellite communications, OJ L 268/15 (1994).

[7] Directive 95/51/EC amending Directive 09/388/EEC with regard to the abolition of the restrictions on the use of cable television networks for the provision of already liberalised telecommunications service, OJ L 256/49 (1995).

[8] Directive 96/2/EC amending Directive 90/388/EEC with regard to mobile and personal communications, OJ L 20/59 (1996).

[9] Directive 96/19/EC amending Directive 90/388/EEC with regard to the implementation of full competition in telecommunications markets, OJ L 74/13 (1996).

a Council Resolution in 1993, there was no consensus at that time for the liberalisation of infrastructure. A final breakthrough on infrastructure liberalisation was not made until the Telecom Council in December 1994. The publication of the Bangemann Group Report on 'Europe and the Global Information Society'[10] gave a powerful impetus to reach this objective. In making a strong plea for a break with the past, ending monopolies and making rapid progress towards a fully liberalised environment, the report was highly influential in changing the telecoms landscape in Europe.

2. The 1998 Framework

The 1998 regulatory framework for telecommunications is based on a set of Article 95 [ex 100a] Directives and Decisions from the Council and the European Parliament and on Article 86 [ex 90] Directives from the Commission. The following key elements are to be stressed. Ensuring interconnection of networks in order to allow interoperability of services, drawing on the basic principles of proportionality (limiting the regulatory burden to what is indispensable), transparency, and non-discrimination found in the Open Network Provision (ONP) rules.[11] Harmonising the public voice telephony services in the EU and defining the services available to all users in the context of Universal Service.[12] Defining a common framework for authorisation and licensing based on the Licensing Directive,[13] and the Full Competition Directive. It establishes the form that licences may take, the timetable and other procedures for granting licences, the fees that can be requested and the

---

[10] *Europe and the Global Information Society*, Recommendations to the European Council, 26.5.1994.

[11] Directive 97/33/EC of the European Parliament and of the Council of 30 June 1997 on interconnection in telecommunications with regard to ensuring universal service and interoperability through the application of the principles of open network provision (ONP), OJ L199/32 (1997).

[12] The original Directive on the application of ONP to voice telephony services was adopted by the European Parliament and Council in December 1995, Directive 95/62/EC of the European Parliament and Council on the application of open network provision to voice telephony services, OJ L 321/6 (1995). A new Directive on Voice Telephony was adopted on 26 February 1998, Directive 98/10/EC on the application of open network provision to voice telephony, OJ L 101/24 (1998), and has replaced the 1995 Directive

[13] Directive 97/13/EC of the European Parliament and of the Council on a common framework for general authorisations and individual licences in the field of telecommunications services, OJ L117/15 (1997).

conditions which may be attached. Establishing independent National Regulatory Authorities (NRAs) in all Member States in order to implement the European regulatory framework in an objective manner.

3. The Transposition of the Regulatory Framework

In order to ensure that the broad policy objectives described above are achieved, the Commission has been monitoring the implementation of the Directives and Decisions which make up the regulatory framework for telecommunications. As of November 1998, the situation can be reported as the following. The NRAs have begun operations in all Member States. There is, however, some concern as to the sufficiency of the competences and resources available to them, the degree of separation from the body controlling the incumbent, and the clarity of the division of powers with the competent Ministry. Secondly, the national frameworks for licensing in place appear to be functioning well, with a large numbers of new players authorised to enter the market. The procedures applied in practice conform broadly to the requirements of the framework. Concerns relate in particular to onerous licence conditions, lack of transparency with regard to conditions and procedures, the level of fees and the length of time required in certain cases to issue licences. Third, a significant number of interconnection agreements are in place. There are concerns as to the excessive length of negotiations, the scarcity of agreements in the fixed market, the inadequacy of reference interconnection offers and the lack of transparency relating to cost accounting systems. There is evidence that interconnection charges are beginning to converge on best practice charges, thereby contributing to efficient service competition. Fourth, schemes for financing universal service have been set up in only a limited number of Member States. There are concerns relating to the amount of the contribution from market players in most of those countries. Fifthly, while operators do not appear to be squeezed due to lack of availability of numbers, the incumbents in a small minority of Member States appear to exercise an undue influence on their allocation. Carrier selection is operating at least partially in most Member States, while number portability has been introduced ahead of schedule in some of them. Finally, all Member States have issued at least two GSM and one DCS 1800 licence. Concerns relate to the period required in some Member States for the phasing out of analogue systems.

In summary, the national regulatory frameworks are broadly in line with the EU regulatory framework. There appear to be no areas in which significant failures have occurred at EU level, although corrective action is required on a number of points in various countries. For this reason, quite a number of infringement procedures and competition investigations have been initiated.

4. Market Developments and Competition Issues

The European telecom services market will produce total revenues of around 148 billion ECU in 1998, a 9% increase over 1997. Mobile communications account for almost 20% of it, amounting to 28 billion ECU, which represents a 22% increase over the year 1997. Overall, the telecommunications sector is now widely regarded as one of the most important contributors to economic growth within the European Union.

There have already been benefits to business users and consumers. The most visible has been a significant increase in the number of providers across the range of telecommunications services.[14] Although it is still too early to detect a decrease in the market share of incumbents in fixed telecom services for most Member States, the market for mobile services clearly shows that the market power of the leading operators can be successfully challenged.

In general, tariffs for telecom services have started to fall. This concerns in particular business, long-distance, and international tariffs. By way of comparison, Member States with a longer experience of liberalisation enjoy significantly lower tariffs. However, in view of the need to rebalance tariffs in line with costs, some of the reductions are partly offset by increases in the cost of local calls, together with rental charges. Leased line prices have shown significant falls, with considerable differences between Member States. Another matter for concern is the persistently higher level of tariffs for cross-border leased lines.

The emerging competitive environment has also generated an increasing number of industrial alliances as market players position themselves to enter the market. In 1997, the value of merger and acquisitions announced in the telecommunication services industry in Europe totalled ECU 28.2 billion, a 45% increase over 1996.

---

[14] There are now 218 operators in the Union with authorisation to provide national public voice telephony, excluding a large number which are authorised on the basis of general legal provisions. As far as international voice services are concerned, 284 operators are authorised, while a total of around 73 national mobile licences have been granted. The network services market has also been thrown wide open: 647 operators are now authorised to offer local network services, while 189 can offer network services at national level and 253 at international level.

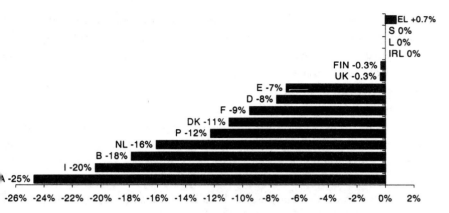

Fig. 1. *Annual variation of Nation Leased Line Basket Changed (Source: Implementation of regulatory package III, Com (98) 594)*

With this new framework, competition policy is increasingly being applied in antitrust and merger cases. Already some major telecom competition cases came up in recent years (e.g. BT-MCI, Unisource and AT&T-Unisourc, Global One; and more recently WorldCom-MCI). On the basis of Article 81 [ex 85] of the Consolidated Treaty (anti-competitive agreements), Article 82 [ex 86] of the Consolidated Treaty (abuse of dominant positions, including issues of unfair pricing and refusing access and interconnection), and the Merger Regulation, the Commission examined the planned mergers or alliances. Some of the cases were only acceptable from a competition point of view with sufficient remedies (e.g. MCI WorldCom had to divest substantial Internet assets to obtain Commission clearance).

Increasingly competition cases involve telecom companies and companies from neighbouring sectors, indicating the emergence of convergence. Two crucial cases concerned planned mergers in Germany in the digital TV market.[15] The growing number of competition cases is not so much a sign of increasingly collusive behaviour or distortion of competition, so much as an indication of the dynamism of the telecom market where actors are trying to position themselves through horizontal and vertical joint ventures and alliances.

III. New Regulatory Issues as a Result of Convergence

Whilst the competitive framework for the provision of telecommunication services has been put in place and competition has started to work, we are

---

[15] See, for example, the 1994 decision to block Media Service Group (MSG), a digital TV venture of Bertelsmann, Kirch and Deutsche Telekom *MSG/Media Services*, 89/205/EEC, OJ L 364/1 (1994).

observing—not least as a result of liberalisation—the rapid emergence of ne⁺ technologies and services. The key feature of this development is the digitalisa tion of virtually all networks and services leading to 'convergence' in the sens that networks can carry several different services or, on the other hand, a pa⁴ ticular service can be offered through various networks.

In order to be concrete and categorical in the analysis, even at the risk c leaving aside some specific features of convergence for the moment, thre major trends can be identified. First, Internet-based services will eventuall⁴ encompass text and image based services (e.g. email, file-transfer, etc.), 'tradi tional' telecom services (e.g. voice telephony and faxes), and audio-visual ser vices (e.g. video-on-demand). Second, mobile (and satellite) communication will converge with fixed communications. And finally, digital television plat form will also be used for interactive multimedia services.

1. The Internet as a Driver for Convergence

The Internet is the most significant and most unanticipated market develop ment in the telecom services sector of the last ten years, yet none of the majo⁴ studies commissioned as part of the '1992 Telecom Review' identified th⁴ Internet as a significant market phenomenon. Its strong and continuing growth presents a number of challenges to NRAs as market players move rapidly into this new business.

The Internet has become an important driver of demand for faster access New entrants now require much easier access, i.e. unbundling, to the local loop. Their objective is to introduce xDSL[16] technologies which multiply by 100 the capacity of a twisted copper pair traditionally used in the local loop. At present, only five Member States allow local loop unbundling, under specific conditions.

The demand for rapid access is also a major driver of backbone invest- ments, potentially stimulating the wide-scale deployment of ATM switching. Over time, the percentage of data traffic on networks is likely to substantially overtake the volume of voice traffic. In the medium term (3–5 years), this⁴ points to a shift away from circuit-switched services to packet-switched net- works which may increase competition in infrastructure services.

The Internet has the potential to become the competitive platform for many traditional services, be they public voice telephony or broadcasting. The main reason is that the use of the Internet Protocol (IP) allows the integration of dif-

---

[16] DSL refers to different variations of the digital subscriber line technology (DSL).

ferent services on the same network, which is much cheaper than running several networks in parallel (for example, voice telephony and cable-TV networks) and brings clear marketing advantages (i.e. package of services, one-stop-shopping, etc.). In response to the strategies of new entrants (e.g. the American IP long-distance operator, Qwest, which took over the pan-European Internet access provider Eunet in March 1998), many European telecom operators are now offering Internet-based voice telephony services, in competition with their own voice telephony business: Telecom Finland, Deutsche Telekom, Telecom Italia already provide examples of such strategic changes. Similarly, an increasing number of telecom operators are also investing in digital TV platforms (e.g. Telefonica, France Télécom, Telecom Italia, and BT).

Beyond traditional services, the Internet is also becoming an important platform for electronic commerce. According to the OECD,[17] on-line business done at world-wide level is estimated worth close to 22 billion ECU in 1997. Speculative forecasts from management consultancy and market research firms estimate that this figure could increase up to 270 billion ECU by 2001–2002 and 800 billion ECU by 2003–2005.

The Expansion of the Internet in the EU, although growing at a current annual rate of 53%, against 17% for the US, is very much correlated to the

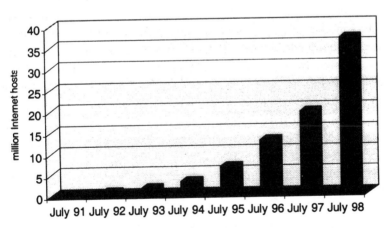

Fig. 2. *World-wide expansion of the internet (Source: Network Wizards, www.ww.com)*

Internet host: a computer connected to the Internet with an IP number address and a domain name(s).

---

[17] Report on the social and economic impact of electronic commerce presented to the OECD. Ministerial Conference on electronic commerce, Ottawa, 7–9/10/98.

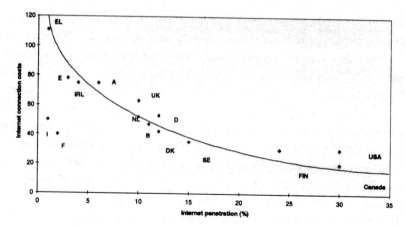

Fig. 3. *Internet connections: The Relationship to Costs*
Source: Commission calculations from OECD and NUA Ltd

Internet charges—levied at the local rate, which are still on average more than twice as high in the EU than in the US.

2. The Convergence of Mobile (and Satellite) Communications with Fixed Communications

The continued growth of mobile communications in Europe, with a current total of 74 million cellular subscribers in the fifteen countries (+65% over the last twelve months) has been a huge business and policy success in the European Union. Forecasts shows that there should be almost 160 million subscribers in the EU by 2002. The mobile communication sector in Europe is making major contributions to job creation and growth of the economy.

The success of GSM as a global standard is mainly due to a sound technology based on open standards and a clear industrial strategy. More specifically, the signing of a Memorandum of Understanding in 1987 by thirteen European incumbent telecommunications operators,[18] the role of the newly created ETSI[19] in matters of standardisation, and the formulation of a co-ordinated

---

[18] France, Germany, Italy, Sweden, Norway, Denmark, Finland, Spain, the Netherlands, Belgium, Portugal, Ireland and the UK.

[19] In 1989, the responsibility for specification development passed from the GSM Permanent Nucleus to the newly created European Telecommunications Standards Institute (ETSI), which accorded equal status to administrators, operators and manufacturers, which in itself had a considerable impact on the speed of development. This allowed for the co-operative environment and improved resources that enabled the majority of Phase 1 of the GSM 900 specifications to be published in 1990.

European policy for the reservation of common frequencies,[20] supported by the introduction of competition in key Member States and later through an Article 86 [ex 90] Directive,[21] all contributed to this success.

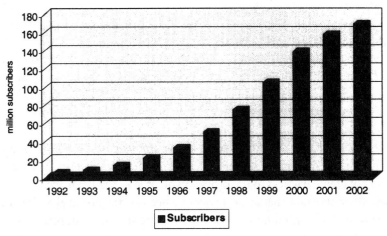

Fig. 4. *Mobile subscribers in the EU: 1999–2002 (Source EC/DG INFSO, 1998)*

The emerging third-generation mobile system, namely the universal mobile systems (UMTS), will accelerate the penetration of mobile communications for business and residential use. Building on the success of GSM, the Commission has proposed to the European Parliament and the Council in February 1998 an UMTS Decision designed to harmonise the allocation of frequencies, conditions and procedures for the award of UMTS licenses in Europe by 1 January 2000.

Mobile communications is becoming a substitute for fixed telephony, notably as wireless local loop can offer a cost-efficient alternative to existing copper wire, and will in the future offer broadband access. The fixed-mobile network convergence should allow users to access a consistent set of services from any fixed or mobile terminals via any compatible access point. In this new network environment, roaming agreements will have to be extended to different kind of networks, i.e. PSTN, cable-TV, mobile networks, and so forth.

---

[20] The harmonisation of frequency attribution in Europe was initiated by Council Directive Directive 87/372/EEC of the Council on the frequency bands to be reserved for the co-ordinated introduction of public pan-European cellular digital land-based mobile communications in the European Community, OJ L 196/85 (1987).

[21] Directive 96/2/EC amending Directive 90/388/EEC with regard to mobile and personal communications, OJ L 20/59 (1996).

As a consequence, it will become increasingly difficult in the future to justify different treatment of fixed and mobile communications. This does not mean the application of current ONP rules to mobile, but may mean the application of 'modified' rules to both of them.

In addition to mobile communications based on cellular technology, personal satellite communications services will be offering increased global mobility. This concerns both narrowband services (e.g. ICO, Iridium, Globalstar), and ('Internet in the sky') broadband services (e.g. the most advanced projects being Europe-led Skybridge and US-led Teledesic). Geostationary platforms (Astra, Eutelsat) are also moving into these new services. These satellite-based systems interworking with existing fixed or mobile networks will offer global coverage, particularly in remote or developing regions.

From a regulatory point of view, a key challenge is to co-ordinate the licensing of such systems, so that the operating conditions and frequency bands used do not create barriers to the provision of, at least, pan-European services. It is equally important that such services be licensed to start at the same time. To ensure such co-ordination a Satellite PCS decision was adopted in March 1997 by the Council and European Parliament to help usher in commercial satellite services by 1 January 2001.[22]

3. Using Digital TV as a Platform for Interactive Multimedia Services

The important technological progress made in the field of digitalisation of content in parallel with the increasing bandwidth of networks allow the distribution of many more channels over the same infrastructure (cable television, satellite transponders, terrestrial spectrum) by using digital compression rather than existing analogue transmission.

As a result, new digital television services are appearing on the market which consist mainly in digital bouquets and thematic channels, near video on demand (NVOD) and pay-per view. In spite of starting-up difficulties in most Member States digital TV will eventually be unstoppable. On the user side, digital TV distribution requires either a set-top box along with an analogue TV receiver or a fully integrated digital TV set. From a technical point of view, a set-top box is nothing more than a computer system with the main purpose of decoding digital into analogue signals and equipped with a conditional access

---

[22] The Commission is also working in close collaboration with the satellite industry to identify barriers to the use and provision of satellite services as part of its Satellite Action Plan of Spring 1997.

system, an electronic programme guide and application programme interface allowing the supply of interactive services. Unidirectional TV networks (terrestrial, satellite, cable) are already evolving towards a bi-directional network with asymmetrical (combining a broadcasting and an interaction channel over another technology such as telephony or GSM) and symmetrical traffic (full interactivity of the broadcasting channel, to be expected with the cable network, e.g. video-telephony requires symmetry). This means a new technical platform for interactive services is emerging, thus reinforcing the trend towards convergence.

IV. Institutional Issues in a Regulatory Framework for Communications Services

1. The 1999 Telecom Review

As required by the 95 [ex 100a] Directives constituting the telecommunications regulatory framework, the Commission will undertake a review of the new EU telecom regulatory framework for telecommunications in the course of 1999. The reason for this relatively rapid review is that although not all effects of competition may be fully visible by 1999, an early review will give regulators the opportunity to adjust the framework more or less in time with market and technology developments.

Much of the 1998 framework is designed to introduce competitive mechanisms into a market characterised by strong 'incumbent' positions, particularly over the local loop. This is particularly the case for requirements to interconnect, to introduce cost-accounting mechanisms, or to offer cost-oriented tariffs. A timely assessment of the extent to which the objectives are being achieved through the chosen approach will allow (policy-makers) to avoid undesirable developments by adjusting the rules accordingly.

The need to adapt rules stems from the changing environment. The telecoms market is particularly affected by the rapidly changing parameters as regards the development of digital technologies, increasingly global competition, and the emergence of convergence. Irrespective of the precise outcome of the telecom review, there are three key issues that will need to be addressed in the future: the regulatory consequences of convergence; the prospect of creating a European Regulatory Authority; and the evolution of specific-sector regulation in a framework for communications services.

2. The Regulatory Consequences of Convergence

The convergence issue has been the subject of a broad public consultation exer cise based on the publication, in 1997, of the Green Paper on the convergenc of the telecom, media and information technology sectors, and the implication: for regulation. In July 1998, the Commission adopted a Working Documen summarising the results of the five-month consultation. In short:

- a broad agreement on technological convergence, but differing views as to the speed and scope of its impact on markets and services;
- a general recognition of the continuing need for certain sector-specific rules, for example, to secure public-interest objectives with regard to the audio-visual sector;
- a broad agreement that self-regulation will play an increasingly important role in the on-line world; most respondents wish to retain a sector-specific approach to audio-visual content;
- substantial support for separating transport functions and content rules, thus moving towards a common set of rules for networks.

Reflecting these orientations, a clear majority of respondents are in favour of building on current regulatory structures rather than introducing an integrated regulatory framework for all services. Some, however, suggested that the latter be applied to networks and transmission.

Without attempting to predict the final results of the consultation and the policy conclusions that will be published by the Commission, common rules for networks will raise the question of access to cable television networks and to technical platforms, notably conditional access systems, electronic programme guides, and the application programme interface of set-top boxes. Convergence may also affect the availability and re-allocation of frequencies, currently used up by analogue terrestrial television broadcasting, once fully digitalised. Indeed, several Member States have already decided, or are in the process of deciding, a complete analogue switch-off for terrestrial broadcasting at a certain date within the next ten years. Such a process may well call for a harmonised European policy both as regards the switch-off date and the re-allocation of former analogue frequencies.

---

[23] See also, 'Issues Associated with the Creation of a European Regulatory Authority for Telecommunications', NERA and Denton Hall for the European Commission, March 1997.

3. A European Regulatory Authority for Telecoms Services?

The issue of the potential need for a telecom regulator at the European level, once so much in the spotlight, has become less imperative, as Member States and market players focus on putting the existing framework into place. The European Parliament has remained the most vocal advocate of a European authority and the Commission is under an obligation to examine the potential added-value of a regulatory function at a European level as part of the 1999 Review. This issue will cover several inter-related aspects.[23] First, the Commission already carries out a certain number of functions which correspond to those of a European telecom regulator, for example, guidelines for interconnection agreements, monitoring of tariff structure. Second, there are identified areas of concern related to the allocation of resources for pan-European operation (e.g. licences, numbers and radio-frequency), and cross-border dispute resolution mechanisms in several Directives which were felt to be too weak and nationally focused. Another aspect to take into consideration is subsidiarity and which functions could be better carried out at the European rather than the national level. Once the functions are agreed, the form of such a body is easier to define. And finally, it will be appropriate to review the role and achievements of CEPT (ECTRA and ERC), particularly in areas such as licencing, numbering and frequency harmonisation.

Further reflections and analyses will be necessary to better assess the scope and the possible functions of any European Regulatory Authority. To this end, another study will be completed during the first half of next year to assess the level of support for a European Regulatory Authority and to identify possible tasks in the light of the work already carried on by bodies, such as ECTRA, ETO or ERO. The need for a European authority will also depend on the experience made with the current network of National Regulatory Authorities (NRAs).

The NRA's appear to have made a satisfactory start in most Member States and play a key role in implementing the 1998 framework. In this respect, regular meetings between the NRA's and the Commission services have been of considerable help in the progressive building of the European Regulator's network. One way of moving towards a European authority would be to build on a network of NRA's, not always substituting certain functions, but offering a complementary alternative service.[24]

---

[24] Similar to the establishment of a 'European Agency for the Evaluation of Medicinal Products', EMEA, now based in London (cf. http://www.eudra.org).

4. The Evolution of the Specific Telecommunications Framework

The objective of the 1998 framework is to create a competitive telecoms market throughout the European Union. It can be assumed that the more this objective is achieved, that is, the more telecoms markets become mature, the less detailed sector-specific rules will be needed. There is little doubt that competition policy will play an increasingly important role in telecoms markets and in markets with converging services. The conclusion is sometimes drawn that sector-specific regulation must be gradually replaced by the application of competition law. Indeed, the application of competition rules can correct anti-competitive developments or interpret initially unforeseen challenges according to the spirit of the framework (e.g. Internet Telephony Notice). However, competition policy will not entirely replace regulation for at least three reasons. First, many issues relevant to market actors, such as licence procedures, frequency allocation and numbering, are not related to the abuse of dominant market positions or mergers. We cannot therefore assume that all undesirable developments can be ironed out by competition decisions. Second, policy-makers are concerned not only with the introduction of efficiency and competition in the market place but also with public-interest issues such as the provision of universal services, data protection, public safety, and consumer protection. Although some of these 'public-interest issues' can indeed be resolved through competition, politicians will still demand appropriate safe-guards. Finally, market forces alone, or the application of competition rules on a case-by-case basis, cannot always remove bottlenecks, particularly in cases of local access, which are unlikely to disappear within the next decade. *Ex ante* asymmetric regulation, that is, regulation that imposes strict obligations on the incumbent operator, offers more predictability to new entrants than the prospect of *ex post* competition decisions. As a consequence, the issue is not one of sector-specific regulation versus competition rules, but of how the existing regulatory framework should evolve. This evolution will be accompanied by competition cases and nurtured by the experience they bring with them.

Any reform of the regulatory framework must take into account the results of the Convergence Green Paper and the Telecom Review, complemented by related policy measures, such as those dealing with frequencies or electronic commerce. The relaxation of current rules will depend on the pace of convergence and the emergence of new services, and on the speed with which incumbents loose their dominant positions—that is, the degree of effective infrastructure and service competition. Irrespective of its precise structure, the evolving framework will probably develop along the following lines:

- by undertaking a comprehensive adaptation exercise to simplify provisions and lower the level of technical details;
- by establishing principles and guidelines that progressively replace detailed regulation but should be immediately applicable;
- by introducing more elements of flexibility in areas where detailed regulation is still required, that is, through self-regulation;
- by building on market mechanisms rather than introducing corrective measures or reserving monopoly areas in order to safeguard public interest;
- and finally, by taking into account global developments, through international negotiations on the basis of a regulatory framework and intensified co-operation in preparing and implementing legislation.

V. Conclusion

The 1998 telecommunications framework has begun to deliver the first tangible results in the shape of lower tariffs and more consumer choice. Incumbent operators are increasingly feeling the impact of competition and are starting to voice their concern that the regulatory balance has swung against them. This means that we have reached a critical period in the development of the telecommunications sector. Regulators must continue to apply the rules of the 1998 framework and do everything in their power to maintain a competitive environment. New services, with their huge potential for economic growth and job creation, can only develop properly if there is a significant drop in prices for telecommunications services. The objective must be to exploit this potential through a consistent policy designed to introduce competition in a sector so crucial for the entire economy. The regulatory framework must evolve if it is to take convergence, technological developments, and globalisation properly into account, and it is the 1999 Telecoms Regulatory Review which will launch this process of adaptation.

X

Peter Waters, David Stewart and Andrew Simpson*

Regulation of Telecommunications Liberalisation: The
Australian Experience

I. Introduction

Australia has recently undergone a public debate on the nature and scope of
regulation which is appropriate after the initial rounds of telecommunications
liberalisation. Despite seven years of vigorous competition and intensive industry-specific regulation, Telstra remains Australia's largest telecommunications
carrier. It is extensively vertically integrated, owning and operating comprehensive network facilities including the vitally important customer access network (CAN) or 'local loop', and offers a full range of wholesale and retail
services. Yet, the alternative infrastructure deployed by Telstra's competitors
means that Australia now has three national mobile networks and another two
or three new regional mobile networks currently being deployed, two national
fibre networks connecting most major cities, another two to three new fibre and
microwave networks currently being deployed between the main East Coast
cities, and two broadband local networks passing 40% or more of the country's
homes. There is also vigorous competition between the infrastructure-based
carriers in supplying wholesale services to the new wave of resellers and value-
added service providers which have entered the market since the last round of
liberalisation in 1997.

The introduction of competition demands that special attention be given to
the development of industry structures which allow fair competition between
the established operator and new market entrants. In particular, the reliance of
new entrants on infrastructure and services provided by the incumbent makes
them particularly vulnerable to anti-competitive conduct by the latter. This is
the reason for regulating telecommunications differently to other similar
industries (e.g. goods transport, aviation). The dilemma facing policy-makers
is whether these special features will be 'competed out', or at least decline, to a
level which can be dealt with using the more lighthanded, *ex post* regulation of
general antitrust law.

This analysis examines the progress of telecommunications liberalisation in
Australia and focuses on the strengths and weaknesses of the shifting balance

---

* Gilbert and Tobin Lawyers, Sydney.

between generic or 'antitrust' regulation, on the one hand, and industry-specific rules on the other. Key features of telecommunications industry structure, competitive (or anti-competitive) conduct, and the pattern of industry transition may well prove common to both Australia and Europe and allow policymakers to draw significant lessons from Australian experience in determining an appropriate balance regulation as the European telecommunications industry moves beyond the initial stages of liberalisation.

II. Progressive Industry Liberalisation

In Australia, facilities-based competition was introduced in a limited form in 1991, when Optus Communications (now Cable & Wireless Optus) was issued a license to provide fixed-line and mobile telephony services, and Vodafone was issued with a mobile licence. With the Telecommunications Act 1997, Australia moved from a structured duopoly fixed-line networks (and a 'triopoly' in the operation of mobile networks) to a regulatory system was characterised by:

— open entry to all network operators,
— no licensing requirements for the provision of services but only for the operation of network facilities,
— network operators specifically obliged to permit interconnection between telecommunications networks offering similar services,
— and the allocation of regulatory responsibilities impacting on competition to the general competition regulator, the Australian Competition and Consumer Commission (ACCC), and the technical regulation to the Australian Communications Authority (ACA).

In numerical terms, market entry into Australian telecommunications has been dramatic. In contrast to the period 1991–1997 when there being three licensed operators, as of January 1999 over twenty carrier licences have been issued. Each licence grants a broad right to own network infrastructure used to provide services to the public. There are no specific licensing categories for the provision of services by particular technologies (e.g. mobile or fixed-line services), there are very few qualifying requirements to hold a carrier licence, and the licence fee is only $10,000.

There are no licensing requirements for the provision of services by a person who does not own network infrastructure. In practice, this means that the provision of all 'carriage services' or 'content services' (roughly equivalent to the distinction made law between 'basic' and 'enhanced' telecommunications services) to the public takes place without substantial regulatory involvement.

For example, resellers of carriage services, such as long-distance resellers, ISPs or companies which integrate telephony services from different operators to provide a 'seamless' corporate solutions service, do not need to be licensed.

III. Industry-specific Regulation and General Competition Law Administered by a Single Agency

Between 1991 and 1997 a telecommunications-specific regulator, the Australian Telecommunications Authority (AUSTEL), had primary responsibility for regulation of the telecommunications industry, covering both significant competitive safeguards and technical regulation. Although general competition law under the Trade Practices Act 1974 (Cth) (TPA) applied to the telecommunications industry, aggrieved parties relied almost exclusively on the industry-specific competitive safeguards contained in the Telecommunications Act 1991. These industry-specific competitive safeguards, unlike general competition law, applied *ex ante* regulatory rules prescribing pricing and other competitive behaviour of Telstra on the basis of its dominance and without the need to demonstrate that this type behaviour actually lessened competition. For example, Telstra was required to file publicly available tariffs with AUSTEL, was not permitted to discount off-tariff and its tariffs could be disallowed if too narrowly targeted at particular market sectors.

Following Australia's 1997 review of the general carrier duopoly, regulatory responsibilities were reallocated. A new industry-specific regulator, the Australian Communications Authority (ACA) took over responsibility for the technical regulation of telecommunications and spectrum management. However, most of AUSTEL's key regulatory powers were transferred to the Trade Practices Commission, now renamed the Australian Competition and Consumer Commission (ACCC).

Hence, in competition matters, telecommunications industry participants are subject to both general and industry-specific laws, both administered by the same regulator, the ACCC. Moreover, while technical and spectrum issues are the sole competence of the ACA, the latter is required to consult with the ACCC and must comply with its directions when making any decision which may have an impact on competition. For example, the ACA may implement number portability requirements in the National Numbering Plan, for which it has responsibility, only if the ACCC has determined that portability is required for particular services having regard to specified competition and consumer objectives.

The ACCC's capability to handle competition issues in the telecommunications sector was enhanced at the time of the 1997 reallocation of regulatory responsibilities. AUSTEL staff who had worked in the area of carrier competition were transferred to the ACCC. The latter remains a general competition regulatory agency, but one with specialist knowledge and specific responsibility in respect of competition in telecommunications. There have certainly been teething problems as the ACCC has struggled with unfamiliar issues but it appears that the combination of general and industry-specific responsibilities within a single agency is a strength of the current regime.

IV. The Regulation of Competitive Conduct in Australia

1. Why is General Competition Law Inadequate?

Australian trade practices law resembles EU competition law in its principles and methods (e.g. market definition and assessment of dominance or competitive effect), and in the kinds of conduct held to infringe the law. Part IV of the TPA prohibits anti-competitive conduct such as: contracts, arrangements or understanding which have an anti-competitive effect or purpose, price-fixing; secondary boycotts; abuse of market power for certain prohibited purposes; exclusive dealing with an anti-competitive effect or anti-competitive purpose; resale price maintenance; mergers and acquisitions which have an anti-competitive effect.

There is provision for the authorisation by the ACCC of conduct, which would otherwise be prohibited under Part IV in cases where the public benefits of that conduct outweigh the anti-competitive effects.

A more recent innovation is Part IIIA which sets out a statutory National Access Regime, which is comparable, albeit not exactly equivalent, to the 'essential facilities' doctrine of United States antitrust law. The National Competition Council is an administrative body which can recommend, after a public inquiry, that certain services should be subject to the statutory access regime if they are of national significance, are required for competition in an upstream or downstream market, and cannot be practically or economically duplicated by competitors. If the ACC's recommendation is accepted by the Government and the facilities are declared by the Federal Treasurer, the ACCC has the power to arbitrate access disputes or to accept binding access undertakings from the owner of the facilities, which operate as a binding 'access tariff'.

It is no accident that former monopoly carriers are the main advocates of relying on general competition law to regulate telecommunications, particu-

arly after an initial period in which they have been subject to heavy industry-
pecific regulation. However, experience suggests that general competition law,
even when modified to include specific essential facilities rules, is inadequate
when it comes to safeguarding the development of competition in the telecommunications industry.

First, general prohibitions may not catch forms of conduct which may have
a significant anti-competitive impact on entrants. The usual tests for predatory
pricing applied under general competition law are inappropriate in the
telecommunications setting. The high ratio of fixed to variable costs in the
telecommunications industry inhibits entrants from leaving the market during
below-cost pricing by a rival, as some analyses assume.[1] The revenue 'recoupment' test[2] fails to take account of the strategic benefits to a telecommunications industry predator of establishing a reputation for 'toughness' and
deterring innovation and investment by its rivals.

Strict costs-based tests[3] are difficult to apply in the telecommunications
industry because of constant change in cost levels and information asymmetries between the incumbent and entrant carriers, and between the carriers and
the regulator. Similarly, 'essential facilities' tests for access under general competition law may not help entrants requiring access to individual exchange
buildings or radio-communications sites, billing systems, network planning
information, and operator and directory services. Access to such facilities and
services determines entrants' ability to compete with the incumbent, but
arguably duplication by each incumbent would be technically and economically feasible.[4] Mandating access to the services and facilities of the incumbent
would require the essential facilities doctrine to be stretched beyond even the
generous—and much criticised—limits of the Aspen Skiing case.[5]

The Australian telecommunications access requirements have applied, and
continue to apply, more broadly than 'bottlenecks'. The Telecommunications Act
1991 required the access provider (usually the incumbent) to supply access to those
services and facilities which were 'necessary or desirable' for the access seeker to

---

[1] See Bork (1978: 149).

[2] The recoupment test suggests that predation is not a rational strategy to engage in
unless the predator will be able subsequently to raise prices sufficiently to recoup profits foregone during the period of price-cutting. See, *Matsushita Electric Industrial Co.
Ltd.* v. *Zenith Radio Corporation* 475 US 574 (1986).

[3] Areeda and Turner (1975).

[4] See, *Twin Laboratories, Inc.* v *Weider Health & Fitness* 900 F.2d 566 (2nd Cir.
1990).

[5] *Aspen Skiing Co v Aspen Highlands Skiing Corp.* 472 US 585 (1985).

supply its services to customers.[6] Similarly, Part XIC of the Trade Practices A
(TPA), which now regulates access, requires access to a particular service or fac
ity (to be open) if it is in the long-term interests of end users. Statutory criteria f
this test include promoting competition, the interests of the access seeker, a»
encouraging the efficient use of infrastructure. Other counterbalancing facto
examine the legitimate business interests provider and the need to preserve inves
ment incentives. These criteria will reach to access services which would not [
caught by the most liberal application of the essential facilities doctrine.

Secondly, general competition law tends to be slow and expensive to app
successfully to abuses in telecommunications markets. The availability of
swift remedy for anti-competitive conduct is important to entrants, as they ma
rapidly lose hard-won market share to the incumbent if the latter is able to pe
severe with anti-competitive conduct whilst the entrant gathers informatio
and builds a case to meet the high evidentiary standards of general prohibitioi
on anti-competitive conduct. In Australia, contravention of the general TP,
prohibitions against anti-competitive conduct may result in a pecuniar
penalty of up to AU$10 million, but a sizeable antitrust case is likely to tak
several years to mount, will take up great deal of executive time, and preser
significant evidentiary problems to entrants affected by information asymm
tries that favour the incumbent. A direction by a regulator pursuant to specifi
regulatory powers, by contrast, can be issued by the regulator in a matter c
days and cost relatively little in terms of time or money to the entrant anc
though it does not give rise to any liability directly, is *prima facie* evidence c
the matters set out in it and provides a clear signal of the regulator's view of th
conduct in issue.

Thirdly, even if general competition laws are successfully invoked, a suit
able remedy may not be available. For example, a court may be able to deter
mine that a high price for interconnection is imposed by abuse of a dominan
position but be unable to set a price or act as a *de facto* regulator supervisin
interconnection pricing. After protracted litigation on interconnection term:
the parties in *Clear Communications Ltd.* v *Telecom Corporation of Ne*
Zealand Ltd[7] were obliged to resume negotiations.

General competition law, thus, needs to be backed up by pro-competitiv
regulation specific to the telecommunications industry, although it still has a»

---

    [6] Telecommunications Act 1991 §137.

    [7] *Clear Communications Ltd.* v *Telecom Corporation of New Zealand Ltd.* (1992) :
TCLR 166 (HC); *Clear Communications Ltd.* v *Telecom Corporation of New Zealan*
Ltd. (1993) 4 NZBLC 99–321 (NZCA); *Telecom Corporation of New Zealand Ltd.* ▾
Clear Communications Ltd. [1995] 1 NZLR 385 (PC).

important role to play, and the principles of competition analysis should underpin industry-specific safeguards for competition. For example, it would be extremely costly for both the regulatory agency and new entrants were access regulation and cost-based pricing to be imposed on all telecommunications providers. Competition analysis indicates that there is no economic justification for making entrants subject to access obligations or access price regulation or for regulating wholesale markets if there is adequate competition in supplying downstream operators.

General competition principles should therefore inform industry-specific regulation, for example in determining the appropriate thresholds for triggering regulatory mechanisms. Australia has developed a hybrid model between industry-specific regulation and general competition law, or rather, separate models for regulating access and retail behaviour which try to strike a different balance appropriate to the type of conduct being regulated and the state of competition at that level of the market.

2. Anti-competitive Conduct in Telecommunications Markets: Part XIB

Part XIB sets out the 'competition rule', which states that '[a] carrier or carriage service provider must not engage in 'anti-competitive conduct'.[8] 'Anti-competitive conduct' is defined as a contravention of specified provisions of Part IV in relation to a telecommunications market, or taking advantage of 'a substantial degree of power in a telecommunications market' with the effect, or likely effect, of substantially lessening competition in that or any other telecommunications market.[9] A 'telecommunications market' is defined as a market in which carriage services, goods or services for use in connection with a carriage service, or access to facilities are supplied or acquired.[10]

Whereas the general prohibition on anti-competitive conduct in TPA prohibits taking advantage of a substantial degree of market power for any of three proscribed purposes, engaging in anti-competitive conduct is defined, for the purposes of the competition rule, with reference to the 'effect, or likely effect, of substantially lessening competition' in a telecommunications market.[11] Thus, unlike under general competition law, it is not necessary to prove that an operator with market power had an anti-competitive purpose in engaging in the anti-competitive conduct.

[8] TPA §151AK.
[9] TPA 1974 §151AJ.
[10] TPA 1974 §151AF.
[11] TPA 1974 §151AJ.

An 'effects test' is considerably superior to a 'purpose requirement' as a threshold for regulatory action. If the purpose required is an 'objective' purpose, to be inferred from effects, it adds little to 'likely effect'. If the purpose required is 'subjective purpose'[12] the applicant is faced with real difficulties in providing proof. Subjective purpose may be evidenced by documents showing the anti-competitive intentions of officers of the accused firm. Identifying such documents is, however, a slow and expensive process and documentation may equally be used strategically, to establish a paper record of legitimate business reasons as camouflage for conduct actually engaged in for anti-competitive purposes. The effect, or likely effect, of censured conduct is more readily and reliably identifiable by direct evidence of the impact of that conduct in the market or by expert economic analysis of the likely consequences of that conduct. An 'effects' test also helps confine enforcers' attention to the economic consequences, rather than perceived moral implications, of business behaviour.[13]

However, because of the lower threshold of the 'effects test', a contravention of the competition rule, unlike a contravention of Part IV of the TPA, originally did not give rise to an immediate right of action by those suffering loss or damage as a result of that anti-competitive conduct. Instead, the ACCC was empowered to issue a 'competition notice', stating that the carrier or carriage service provider has contravened the competition rule and setting out particulars of that contravention.[14] The notice of itself does not impose liability, but gives rise to rights of action. A party other than the ACCC could seek an injunction in relation to anti-competitive conduct or bring an action for damages or compensation for breach of the competition rule if the conduct complained of was of a kind dealt with in a competition notice that was in force at the time of the conduct.[15] In court proceedings, the notice would serve as

---

[12] The purpose required under TPA 1974 §46 is subjective: *ASX Operations Pty Ltd* v *Pont Data Australia Pty Ltd.* (1991) ATPR 41–069 at 52,060 per Lockhart, Gummow and Von Doussa JJ: *Dowling* v *Dalgety Australia Ltd.* (1992) ATPR 41–165 at 40,276 per Lockhart, J.

[13] 'Intent does not help to separate competition from attempted monopolisation and invites juries to penalise hard competition. It also complicates litigation. Lawyers rummage through business records seeking to discover titbits that will sound impressive (or aggressive) when read to a jury. Traipsing through the warehouses of business in search of misleading evidence both increases the costs of litigation and reduces the accuracy of decisions. Stripping intent away brings the real economic questions to the fore at the same time as it streamlines antitrust litigation.' *AA Poultry Farms Inc.* v *Rose Acre Farms Inc.* 881 F2d 1396 (7th Cir. 1989) Easterbrook, J.

[14] TPA 1974 §151AL.

[15] TPA 1974 §§151CA, 151CC, 151CE.

rima facie evidence of the anti-competitive conduct disclosed in the notice,[16] reversing the burden of proof which usually applies in proceedings for breach of the general competition law prohibitions in Part IV.

From legislative commentary on Part XIB at the time of enactment, it appears that the government intended the 'competition notice' provisions to provide a more rapid administrative remedy to anti-competitive conduct by parties having market power than could be obtained by bringing a Federal Court action under Part IV. The competition notice procedure was also designed to mitigate some concerns of industry participants regarding the move from *ex ante* prescriptive regulation under the Telecommunications Act 1991 to *ex post* proscriptive regulation under the Telecommunications Act 1997 and TPA Part XIB.

However, the first Part XIB complaint, dealing with Telstra's refusal to provide Optus and other Internet 'backbone' operators with reciprocal interconnection (e.g. peering) to its Internet network, took the ACCC nearly one year to investigate and its competition notice was immediately challenged by Telstra in the Federal Court. The experience has been no better with subsequent notices dealing with Telstra's supply of local call resale services on discriminatory terms. Telstra alleged that competition notices must contain full and extensive particulars of the kind usually required in Anglo-American civil litigation. Were the ACCC required to state extensive particulars it could be anticipated that competition notices would become bogged down in the type of 'nit-picking' pre-trial skirmishes over the accuracy and adequacy of the particulars, so commonplace in civil litigation.

The ACCC's investigation and the issuing of the competition notice are also administrative processes subject to Australia's extensive administrative law requirements, and threats of administrative law challenge by Telstra have considerably slowed the ACCC's investigatory processes and left the Commission open to allegations of timidity. As a result, the experience with competition notice soon proved to be at odds with the need for a swift regulatory reaction to anti-competitive conduct.

3. Access Regulation: Part XIC

The telecommunications access provisions of Part XIC show the influence of the general access regime in Part IIIA, but enactment of Part XIC recognises

---

[16] TPA 1974 §151AN.

that general access provisions do not adequately reflect the particular charac teristics of the telecommunications industry.[17]

In the case of telecommunications, the industry-specific access regime under Part XIC provides for the 'declaration' of particular services (e.g. 'cal termination over the PSTN'), and imposes a series of standard access obliga tions on network operators or service providers supplying those services to themselves or others.[18] Part XIC also provides that such access providers may stipulate the terms on which they will give third parties access, in an 'access undertaking', which must be assessed by the ACCC to determine whether the proposed terms and conditions are 'reasonable' having regard to defined crite ria.[19] Finally, Part XIC provides that where an access provider and an access seeker cannot reach agreement on the terms and conditions for the provision of a declared service, the ACCC will arbitrate that dispute, with the power to impose a binding arbitrational decision on access arrangements.[20]

A fundamental issue of access regulation is the scope of application of the access regime. The essential facilities doctrine, at least as traditionally under-stood, is too narrow to capture access to many of the carriage services and sup-plementary facilities which have become accepted elements of interconnection regimes. Conversely, the interconnection net would be cast too broadly if all owners of infrastructure or all providers of services could be made equally sub-ject to mandatory access obligations. Such general application would dispense with the need for inquiry into whether access should be mandated in respect of individual facilities or services, but would greatly increase the administrative costs of the relevant agency and impose compliance costs on a great many more firms. Imposing compliance costs on more firms would, in turn, be likely to impact on investment and innovation, to the detriment of consumers. Moreover, the increased administrative and compliance costs would almost certainly not be justified by a corresponding increase in industry competitive-ness.

Access regulation need only apply to entities enjoying market power, as the object of access regulation is to provide a remedy to the anti-competitive 'mis-chief' of a powerful firm withholding or restricting access with the purpose or

---

[17] '[T]he Government's philosophy in preparing the telecommunications access regime has been to follow an approach based on Part IIIA of the TPA as far as practi-cable, but nevertheless introduce some additional refinements to ensure that the arrangements will work effectively for the telecommunications industry.' Hansard Parliamentary Debates, Senate, Tuesday 25 February 1997 at 895.

[18] TPA §152AR.

[19] TPA §152AH.

[20] TPA §152CP.

effect of inhibiting or eliminating competition. If there are competitive sources of upstream supply in wholesale services, regulation is not only unnecessary, but also accompanied by a high risk of regulatory failure which will undermine the development of vigorous wholesale competition.

If access regulation is not to apply generally, however, it is necessary to identify the appropriate threshold at which access should be mandated. The question of the appropriate threshold for mandating access demonstrates the importance of infusing industry-specific regulation with fundamental principles of competition law and economics. Unfortunately, there is a risk that this threshold issue will be obscured by the technical issues of network interoperability and that competition policy-makers will withdraw in favour of technical regulators or industry self-regulatory bodies, which may distort the development of competition.

Part XIC applies a threshold test which 'filters' out competitive wholesale services, but which applies more broadly than traditional bottleneck tests. Under Part XIC, a service may be declared as a regulated access service, if, after conducting a public enquiry, the ACCC is satisfied that validation 'will promote the long-term interests of end-users of carriage services or of services provided by means of carriage services'.[21] Declaration of an access service will be in the long-term interests of end users if it promotes competition, achieves any-to-any connectivity, or encourages the economically efficient use of, and economically efficient investment in, infrastructure.[22] Examples of the types of services which have been declared include: 'traditional' interconnection services, such as call termination and origination over a variety of network platforms, such as analogue and digital voice telephony systems (i.e. the PSTN and ISDN) and mobile networks such as GSM or AMPS networks; services considered by the regulator to be necessary for the conduct of a carrier's business, such as inter-city transmission (i.e. interLATA transmission between gateway exchanges), where those services cannot be provided competitively; or access technologies used to deliver services, such as tail-end transmission capacity from the switch or router to customer sites over particular data networks (such as Telstra's digital data network).

The workings of Part XIC are also demonstrated by the access services which the ACCC has refused to declare, with the effect that supply of those services is left to commercial negotiation between access providers and access seekers. After an extensive public inquiry, the ACCC decided not to declare domestic roaming on digital mobile networks because the ACCC believed that

---

[21] Trade Practices Act 1974 subss 152AL(2), (3).
[22] Trade Practices Act 1974 subs 152AB(2).

the three existing national mobile operators, Telstra, Vodafone and Optu
would have an economic incentive to compete against each other to attra
traffic from the new regional mobile operators.[23] Similarly, the ACC
excluded fixed-network transmission services between Sydney and Melbourn
from Part XIC because it concluded that there could be three or more compe
ing networks on that route and regulated access (e.g. cost-based charges) migl
deprive the new network operators of the economic incentives to build the
facilities.[24] No international switched or leased capacity services have bee
declared because there is vigorous competition between Australian and inte
national carriers in supplying those services.

The basis on which an access service is declared under Part XIC can hav
different regulatory consequences. The grounds for declaration can be divide
into a 'traditional' competition test (e.g. whether the access service is a 'bo
tleneck'), and an interoperability or 'any-to-any connectivity' requirement. I
has been argued that each access line (and presumably each mobile telephone
fulfils the general competition law definition of a 'bottleneck' for terminatio
service because a network is useless unless it can offer its customers ubiqu
tous termination to each other network. This leads to some rather remarkabl
conclusions. In a country such as the UK, for example, there would be 22 mil
lion individual fixed-line bottlenecks and 8 million individual mobile tele
phone bottlenecks. An individual householder may have chosen to connec
their telephone line to the BT network, a modem line to a cable telephony net
work, their employer may have supplied a work mobile phone connected t
the Colt network, and they may have decided to have a One2One mobile fo
personal use, in which case there would be four bottlenecks in a single house

Clearly, the interoperability of networks is a key requirement and a uniqu
feature of telecommunications, but using the essential facilities doctrine t
ensure interoperability can muddle views about market power and the appro
priateness and nature of the market intervention. In traditional antitrust law
possession of a bottleneck is seen as an indicator or attribute of market o
monopoly power. From the demand side, the bottleneck can indicate th

---

[23] ACCC Public Inquiry into Declaration of Domestic Intercarrier Roaming unde
Part XIC of the Trade Practices Act 1974 March 1997. ACCC Public Inquiry into
Declaration of Domestic Intercarrier Roaming under Part XIC of the Trade Practices
Act 1974 March 1997. The ACCC approach starkly contrasts to OFTEL's approach
OFTEL, Access to Second General Mobile Networks for New Entrant Third
Generation Mobile Operators, 1999, discussed in Waters, Dunroamin'
www.gtlaw.com.au.

[24] Australian Competition and Consumer Commission Competition in Data
Markets (final report) October 1998.

boundaries of the market. Measuring power on a house-by-house basis gives a distorted perspective of the relative power of each operator, with a small carrier controlling a few hundred lines in one city potentially being regulated in the same way as the incumbent accounting for 90% of lines nationwide. Carried to its logical conclusion, treating each access line as a bottleneck could mean each house should be treated as a separate market in which the access network owner is dominant at both the wholesale and retail levels. The absurdity of such a result was recognised in *Power New Zealand Ltd.* v *Mercury Energy Ltd.*, which concerned a merger between two local electricity companies:

> If the basis for market definition is taken to be substitutability, then for the local distribution function, each customer connection (e.g. a house) is a market, and the Mercury and PNZ distribution areas would consist of hundreds of local monopolies.[25]

Describing the terminating access as a bottleneck is a dangerously loose use of the term. Ubiquitous termination is a unique requirement of the telecommunication industry, but was not apparent until alternative providers of infrastructure were permitted. Although the search for analogous concepts in other areas to describe this unique feature in this one is understandable, the term 'bottleneck' is a very specific legal concept with an entire body of case law, and particular implications for market power and market definition. The bottleneck concept cannot be applied to address the need for ubiquitous termination in isolation from this body of law and these consequences.

Part XIC recognises any-to-any connectivity as being a separate basis for declaration from whether or not the service is a bottleneck. This allows the ACCC to decide that although there is competing infrastructure and the owners of the facilities do not have market power, declaration nonetheless is still required to ensure interoperability. So, for example, the ACCC considered that termination access on the three competing mobile networks should be declared so that each mobile operator and the fixed operators can be sure of being able to terminate calls to mobiles.[26] The different basis on which GSM terminating access was declared may flow through to the extent of regulatory control by the ACCC of the terms of access. The ACCC, following the FCC's lead, has adopted a total service long-run incremental cost (TSLRIC) approach to the

---

[25] *Power New Zealand Ltd.* v *Mercury Energy Ltd.* (1996) 5 NZBLC 99–369 at 104, per Barker J and Dr. Brunt. The Court further noted that: '[t]he 'disembodied' approach, relying solely upon substitutability, can not be said to follow the statute's command that [the] market is to be distinguished by substitutability 'as a matter of fact and commercial common sense' at 104.015.

[26] ACCC, Deeming of Declared Services, July 1997.

pricing of interconnection and access but the ACCC stated that TSLRIC would only apply to those declared services in respect of which competitive ser vices were weak.[27] The ACCC would arbitrate dispute over other access ser vices on a 'commercial basis'. As GSM terminating access was declared on the basis of any-to-any connectivity a strict TSLRIC approach may not be applied by the ACCC.

This creates a dual level approach to access regulation. At a minimum commercial arbitration is always available between any operators, incumbent and new entrant, or new entrant and new entrant, to ensure interoperability However, where one operator derives market power from its control of facili ties, additional and more intrusive regulation can be invoked to protect com petitors against that operator affecting competition across the market by control of essential inputs. While the ACCC performs both functions, the two layers could be made more distinct, and the separation of regulatory principles more apparent and enduring, if the commercial arbitration role is carried out by the private arbitration and mediation services which are commercially avail able or by any industry-organised and industry-sponsored service. The only necessary regulatory requirement would be that parties submit to binding arbi tration for those services which are required for any-to-any connectivity, and that the regulator have the power to intervene and assume responsibility in those cases where one party possesses market power. While there can be ambi guities and uncertainties in this approach, the regulatory risks appear lower than those arising if antitrust principles are stretched in an attempt to address interoperability between operators without market power.

V. Evaluating the Australian Regulatory Environment

Although the 1997 regime is still relatively new, we can nonetheless make a tenta tive evaluation of its performance to date. As regards its *strengths,* the combina tion of telecommunications-specific powers and responsibility for enforcing the general competition law allows for rapid uptake by the agency of regulatory 'best practice' in competition policy, while retaining a specialised body of expertise per taining to the industry. In the authors' view, neither highly general nor highly telecommunications-specific regulatory approaches are demonstrably preferable: each has its strengths and its weaknesses and both should be employed.

The ACCC's assumption of responsibility for competition safeguards in the telecommunications industry has alleviated the jurisdictional boundary disputes

---

[27] ACCC, Access Pricing Principles–Telecommunications July 1997.

which arose in the past, and which sometimes meant that neither agency acted. There are also some less obvious positive effects of integrating responsibilities for competition in telecommunications and in the economy in general within a single body. In particular, the general competition regulator has been able to accumulate expertise relevant to telecommunications that can be brought into play in the assessment of other antitrust matters, such as mergers. Given the intensity of merger activity in maturing telecommunications markets and an increasingly global marketplace, there is substantial benefit in the ability of the body responsible for assessing the competitive impact of mergers to grasp the technological and industrial features of telecommunications markets rapidly. Expertise in telecommunications is also likely to prove valuable in assessing the competitive impact of mergers and other conduct in industries dependent on communications, such as broadcasting, or when the regulator is required to deal with industries which share some economic or physical similarities to telecommunications, such as the electricity and gas pipeline industries.

Another strength of the Australian regime has been access regulation. The public inquiry process undertaken by the ACCC to determine whether access services should be declared has proven to be a much more successful forum than originally anticipated. The use of 'long-term interests of end-users' as an explicit regulatory threshold is an innovation in Australian regulatory practice but one which is workable, with the virtue of allowing reference to a greater range of considerations than do narrow economic constructions such as 'dominance' or 'substantial lessening of market power'. The threshold allows recognition of the tension between mandated access and incentives for investment in infrastructure. The public inquiry provides a means for the open and transparent exploration of the balance between regulatory intervention and the development of competition in the industry.

As regards *weaknesses*, policy-makers can underestimate the importance of regulatory procedures being practicable, workable and economical. Even where a regulatory mechanism is perfectly attuned to the economics of the industry and the mischief at which it is aimed, it will fail if it is either too slow or too costly to invoke, or if its successful invocation requires more information than the beneficiaries of the rule or regulators have ready access to. New entrants may rapidly lose market share while abuse continues. Incumbents, on the other hand, are inclined to prolong regulatory proceedings and to insist on high standards of proof of any infringement of regulation, as they are better resourced and control much of the information likely to be relevant. This is borne out by the sorry history of competition notices issued by the ACCC under Part XIB.

Australia's efforts to find a hybrid model between general competition law and industry-specific regulation to control anti-competitive behaviour of the incumbent telecommunications carrier must be judged a failure if first experiences are anything to go by. The main defect of Part XIB is that the regulator's administrative ruling on anti-competitive conduct (the competition notice) has no legally binding effect but requires the further step of litigation to enforce compliance, in which proceedings the notice has no more than an evidentiary role. The refusal to confer binding force on the ACCC's competition notice arises from the Australian Government's strict views on the requirements for separation of excecutive and judicial powers under Australia's constitution. But even accepting this limitation, the ACCC's effectiveness in promptly addressing anti-competitive conduct has been stymied by the threat of the incumbent resorting to administrative law review of the process of investigating complaints from competitors. As a result, a process which was intended to be more efficient and rapid than the ACCC or a private party bringing injunctive proceedings under the general anti-trust provisions of the TPA turned out to be precisely the opposite.

The Government, after initially blaming the ACCC for timidity, has finally recognised that there are fundamental design problems with Part XIB. The following amendments were made in 1999:

- the ACCC can issue competition notices when the ACCC has "reason to believe" a carrier or carriage service provider has engaged in anti-competitive behaviour.[28] This is meant to lower the threshold of proof the ACCC must meet, and therefore expedite its inquiries;
- the ACCC can issue competition notices which describe the anti-competitive behaviour in terms of a kind or class of behaviour, rather than specifying particular instances of anti-competitive conduct.[29] This is meant to relieve the ACCC of the burden of particularizing, in highly specific and legalistic fashion, the anti-competitive conduct in which a carrier and carriage service provider has engaged; and
- a court cannot injunct or "suspend" a competition notice during the course of any challenge by a carrier or carriage service provider.[30] The Court can injunct enforcement, but the "clock keeps ticking" on the notice so that if the notice is upheld, fines and damages will be backdated to the date the notice was issued.

---

[28] TPA, Section 151AKA(7).
[29] TPA, Section 151AKA(2)
[30] TPA, Section 151AQA.

t is yet to be seen whether these adjustments are going to cure the problems of Part XIB, but the signs are not hopeful that the fundamental problems of regulating the anti-competitive conduct of the incumbent have yet been overcome.

Australia also has not adequately addressed information asymmetries. Certain information necessary to regulate in an effective way can only be obtained from the network operators who capture that information. In particular, information on the costs of providing interconnection, which is relevant to the issue of whether the ACCC ought accept an access undertaking or impose a particular access arrangement when acting as arbitrator, is either difficult or impossible to obtain without some level of disclosure by the relevant network operator. For example, the ACCC recently experienced difficulty assessing the forward-looking costs of operating the PSTN, particularly the costs of maintaining the customer access network (CAN), for the purpose of giving (so as to give) effect to the Access Pricing Principles. That cost assessment requires information on the underlying characteristics of the PSTN, ranging from the number of traffic aggregating facilities (i.e. booths or cabinets) per local exchange, to the degree to which trenching and other installation work can be performed in an efficient manner, minimising the amount of duplication involved in developing a similar network using current best available technology. Such information could only be provided by the network operator.

The ability of regulators to test critically the allegations put to them by complainants is also essential to effective competition regulation. The ACCC has significant powers under the TPA to require the provision of information or documents which are relevant to the ACCC's decision whether to exercise its powers in relation to telecommunications matters.[31] The ACCC also has the power to require network operators with substantial market power to disclose pricing information ('tariff-filing directions'),[32] or make and retain records of certain matters ('record-keeping rules').[33] However, with the exception of the continuance of Telstra's tariff-filing obligations under the previous regime, these powers have been little used to date.

Information provided by regulated firms could be rigorously tested by exposure to critique by competing firms. Such testing is, however, constrained by the importance attached to maintaining the confidentiality of commercial information disclosed to the regulator. While protection of confidential information given to regulators is important, and a matter of concern for all

---

[31] TPA 1974 §155.
[32] TPA 1974 §151BK.
[33] TPA 1974 §151BU.

industry participants, mechanisms which intermediate between full disclosure and complete confidentiality might usefully be employed. For example, disclo sure may be made to an external panel of experts, bound to strict confidential ity and an obligation not to make commercial use of information acquired in disclosure. Amendments to the TPA now authorise the ACCC to disclose a carrier's or carriage service provider's report under the record keeping rules publicly or to specified persons on specified terms, if disclosure would be likely to promote competition or facilitate the operation of particular parts of the TPA.[34] Another TPA amendment empowers the ACCC to direct a party to access negotiations to, *inter alia,* supply relevant information to the other party and carry out research or investigations to obtain such information (section 152).

Finally, Australian policy-makers have probably placed too much faith in self-regulatory processes. While self-regulation plays an important role, it only works when all participants have an equal incentive to participate. As the mat ters being addressed in self-regulatory processes often facilitate market entry or enhance the ability of competitors to compete, the incumbent usually does not have an incentive to participate or to see self-regulatory processes move swiftly In such circumstances, industry self-regulation can result in 'deadlock', with the parties unable to reach agreement on any issues, rather than identifying common ground or distilling key issues for consideration by regulators. These problems may be exacerbated where the regulator is under-resourced, lacks the necessary expertise, or is inclined to avoid dealing with highly 'political' or oth erwise contentious issues.

This danger could be dealt with by creating a framework to monitor and control self-regulation, either legislatively, or by agreement between the regu lator and self-regulatory organisations (SROs). Such a framework could spec ify criteria to guide the decision whether to delegate a particular regulatory matter to self-regulation. In the event that a SRO fails to deal with a particular matter within a specified period, that matter should revert to the regulatory agency for resolution unless good reason exists for the industry to continue handling it. For example, OFTEL takes the view that the specification of net work interfaces is better managed by industry participants in the first instance However, OFTEL recognised that BT may not have the incentive to partici pate in the absence of a regulatory requirement, and so BT is required to give advance notice of the interfaces, or changes in existing interfaces, that it pro poses to implement. Advance notice of interface changes is intended, among other things, to give other network operators the opportunity to agree with BT

---

[34] TPA Section 151 BBA.

on the particulars of interoperability. OFTEL will not seek to impose a standard interoperable solution unless the industry cannot agree on one.[35]

VI. Conclusion

General competition law and telecommunications-specific law are often presented as stark and mutually exclusive choices, but examination of the process of liberalisation in the Australian telecommunications industry suggests that the two are instead complementary. General competition law will probably not catch all significant forms of anti-competitive behaviour insofar as it slow to react and expensive to invoke, and may not provide an appropriate remedy. It will be long time before the evolution of competition in telecommunications reaches the point where competition law alone is sufficient. The monopoly endowment of the incumbent has proved more persistent than many anticipated. Even after a decade of intensive regulatory effort, the incumbent continues to hold more than half the long-distance traffic, and 90% of the local traffic in Australia and the UK. The desire, if not impatience, of competition law policy-makers to shift telecommunications regulation onto more familiar ground may indeed cause them to disregard the time and effort required for telecommunications competition to take hold.

General competition law, on the other hand, is a effective base for industry-specific regulation. It provides a body of economic principles to guide the application of industry-specific regulation. The anchoring of industry-specific regulation to competition principles is a mechanism, if not a discipline, for adjusting regulation as competition evolves, particularly competition in wholesale services. Hence, an effective regime for the liberalisation of the telecommunications industry should use carefully targeted industry-specific regulation informed by principles of general competition law.

Furthermore, a single solution may not even be appropriate, particularly given the uneven pace with which competition is evolving across the potentially different sectors (e.g. fixed and mobile). Separate solutions may seem to produce a complex regulatory outcome, but a single approach, whilst intellectually satisfying, overlooks the more 'untidy' nature of competition in evolving markets.

Finally, institutional or administrative arrangements should not be allowed to confuse the substantive issues regarding regulatory powers. As the

---

[35] Office of Telecommunications Interconnection and Interoperability: A Framework for Competing Networks, April 1997.

Australian approach shows, industry-specific powers can be exercised by general competition regulators. The justification usually given for the assumption of telecommunications responsibilities by general competition regulators is that this will guarantee a consistent approach across different industries and avoid regulatory capture. This is a little too demeaning of the strengths and performance of industry-specific regulators. The Australian experience shows that general competition functions benefit where the general competition regulator develops a more complete understanding of the communications industries within which most of the large mergers are likely to occur in the next few years.

XI

Dieter Wolf*

Institutional Issues of Telecoms Regulation

I. Introduction

In Germany, the legal framework concerning the communication network markets is characterised by a multitude of institutions. Alongside the general competition regime of the competition authorities, that is, the German *Bundeskartellamt* and the European Commission, there are various sector-specific institutions, the most important being the Regulatory Authority for Telecommunications and Posts which emerged from the former Post Office Ministry when the telecommunications market was opened up.

The establishment of this new sector-specific regulator was controversial in Germany. Most experts warned against the creation of such a body, and demanded that the tasks involved in introducing competition to the former telecoms monopoly should be conferred on the *Bundeskartellamt*. I myself shared these concerns because I feared, and continue to fear, for the coherence of competition law. Splitting up competition law into numerous sector-specific regulations will weaken general law and give lobbyists an opportunity to push their particular concerns to the fore at the expense of the general public. The sectoral neutrality of the German antitrust law would become a thing of the past. The lawmaker, however, decided otherwise.

I do not want to rake up the past here, especially since it is becoming clear that the regulatory authority is under political pressure from those who are close to the former monopolists, and it can therefore do with some backing from all those who support the competition principle. I would like to use our discussion today to focus on technological convergence and to ask this question: What are the implications for the competition authorities of the technological convergence of information networks and services, that is, the integration of telecommunications, radio and television with computer technology and the Internet?

---

* President of the *Bundeskartellamt*, Bonn, Germany.

II. Convergence and Overregulation in the Digital Age?

Telephone calls, songs on the radio, pictures on the television, and Internet chatting, are all reduced to no more than digital impulses. At the same time, and this is easier for the consumer to see, a fusion of terminal equipment such as telephones, televisions and computers is becoming apparent. The problem we used to have with scarce frequencies and transmission stations, on the other hand, will become part of history in the digital age.

Unfortunately, this technological convergence is in no way matched by a convergence of regulatory systems, for example by a streamlining and reduction in the regulation density. The fact that the problem of managing scarce frequencies is becoming increasingly obsolete has also not yet really been reflected in the regulation system.

Let us take a look at the actual situation in Germany where in some parts overregulation which could develop into one of the most serious threats to economic development has emerged. It seems to me, however, that overregulation is not a purely German problem even if it is particularly pronounced in Germany due to the overlapping of competences arising from our federal tradition.

As far as monitoring competition is concerned, general competition law exists, as I have already said, alongside sector-specific control carried out by the newly created Regulatory Authority for Telecommunications and Posts. It goes without saying that the competences of the European Commission are unaffected by this. Broadly speaking, the tasks are allocated as follows: the regulatory authority is responsible for granting licences, and for monitoring prices and abuse pursuant to the Telecommunications Act. The *Bundeskartellamt* is responsible for monitoring cartels and for merger control pursuant to the Act against Restraints of Competition (ARC). Abuse control under the ARC is subordinated to the sector-specific abuse control under the telecommunications law, although it can be applied subsidiarily.

Under the Telecommunications Act, both authorities are obliged to co-operate with each other. To ensure that the application of the Telecommunications Act is as consistent as possible with that of general competition law, issues of market definition and determining market dominance are to be decided jointly. In practice, the first few months of our co-operation have not always been easy, but there is now clear evidence that things are running more smoothly.

That is not all, however. Market access and the control of concentration in radio and television are subject, not only to the general competition regime, but also to special media law regulation which is exercised by separate institutions.

Internet services are subject to special, but far from uniform, rules. Depending on whether they are aimed at individuals or the general public, they are subject to separate provisions, but can if necessary also be categorised as broadcasting services and are then subject to broadcasting regulations.

You will perhaps suspect that I am deliberately exaggerating here in order to confuse you with this network of regulations. I assure you, however, that the matter really is as complex and that I have in fact simplified it a little for you. I want to make clear the danger that lies in overregulating this sector, which in the future is intended to be a main driving force for growth.

III. Lean Regulation

In my opinion, the only way to resolve the problems generated by this multitude of special and sector-specific regulations is to have a radical change and pursue a course of 'lean regulation'. I could imagine the following as elements of such a lean regulation: the general competition authorities should be responsible for monitoring competition—they would probably require sharper teeth for this purpose, however. In sectors that were once monopolies, as for example telecommunications, a legislative framework is required that is geared to the active creation of competition and contains clear provisions on the joint use of 'essential facilities' and the immediate enforcement of decisions by the competition authority. Sector-specific bodies and authorities and their expertise should be brought under one roof, the roof of the general competition authority, very much like it is organised in Australia for example. Mainly national matters should be examined by this national competition authority, if necessary by means of the decentralised application of EU competition rules, and cross-border issues should be examined by the Commission. This would avoid the duplication of control measures. I do not wish to go into any more detail on this aspect of allocating tasks between the national authority and Brussels— this is not the place for that. I believe that it is important for competition authorities to have responsibility for monitoring competition in a system of lean regulation—sector-specific agencies are not really a necessity at a national or European level.

If it is considered politically as an absolute need, there could also be a national authority with the task of preserving a diversity of opinion and cultural aims. This could include for example imposing conditions on the channels with the aim of ensuring variety or protecting young viewers. Such an institution would have to go about its task with some modesty since the Internet in particular, which makes just about everything possible from telephony to television, demonstrates the limits of regulators' influence on its content. I would like to make one thing quite clear: such a control would have absolutely no economic justification, it would be exclusively based on cultural grounds. For that reason, it would probably be organised differently in the various Member States depending on the respective tradition. In Germany, something along the lines of a joint institution for all the Länder might be conceivable. Since merely cultural issues are concerned, this would also mean that no equivalent body would—at least for the time being—be required at the European level.

IV. Conclusion

To come to a close, here are just a few points to summarise what I have said:

- The technological convergence of telecommunications, computer technology and broadcasting is well underway and capacity problems are becoming less and less important.
- The regulatory framework has not yet adapted to this convergence in Germany, or in other countries. On the contrary, it is going down the wrong path by maintaining, or even creating, the artificial separation of these sectors by means of sector-specific authorities and rules.
- The way out of this regulatory labyrinth can therefore only be lean regulation. To ensure legal certainty and efficiency, we should focus on the enforcement of general competition law, reduce sector-specific regulation, and bring the latter under the roof of the general competition authority. If politically desired, one could set up another authority to monitor cultural and media aspects. But there is no need for any more institutions.

XII

Dimitri Ypsilanti*

Institutional Issues in the Regulation of Telecommunications

. Introduction

A significant new period in global telecommunications policy began in 1998 with the elimination of monopolies for the provision of telecommunication voice services across most of the European Union countries and the coming into force of the WTO agreement on basic telecommunications services. This new era is also bringing new challenges since the focus of policy debate has moved away from attaining agreement on general principles regarding market liberalisation to details of implementation of policies.

Regulators, companies and countries are now trying to impose their interpretation on principles which took so long to forge, but remained largely empty of detailed content. Despite similarity in principles, irrespective of whether they derive from the WTO Reference Paper or from EU Directives, differences are arising in terms of the interpretation of these principles through the details of implementation. Linked with differences in interpretation will be differences in rates of change in policy as regulators begin to grapple with the realities of technological and service convergence, the requirements for electronic commerce and the challenges of the Internet. In addition, differences are arising between countries in the extent to which competitive markets are emerging, as well as in terms of the evaluation by policy-makers of the potential for competition. This, in turn, impacts on the longer term policy evaluation as to how regulatory frameworks should change.

At the same time the policy agenda is in danger of distortion arising out of multi-level governance of policy-making in the communications area. There are several areas of potential difficulty here:

- first, is the question of the relative role of sector specific regulation compared to competition law;
- second, is the question of how to deal with communications convergence in terms of regulatory structures and procedures;
- third, there are complications arising out of multi-level governance and policy-making in the communications area.

* Directorate for Science, Technology and Industry, OECD, Paris.

II. Policy Divergence

There has been, as markets have opened to competition, a significant shift toward detailed regulatory prescriptions. Is this of concern? What does it imply in terms of shifting from sector specific regulation to competition law? Will the differences arising in the details of the application of broad principles matter? If so, what is the best way to ensure greater policy coherence?

The WTO Reference Paper did not try and impose *harmonisation* in terms of the details of regulatory principles implemented by Signatories but left these up to the respective countries. It is unlikely that it will be necessary to have harmonisation at this level as long as frameworks meet the criteria of non-discrimination and transparency allowing market access on fair and equal terms. However, there have been attempts to impose harmonisation to some extent. For example, in Japan-US and Japan-EU bilateral meetings on telecommunications it was strongly recommended that Japan use total long-run incremental costs, as is being adopted in the US and EU countries, to determine the incumbent's interconnection charges. Will differences in the allocation of mobile cellular licences (i.e. through a beauty contest versus through auctions) be viewed as creating unequal market access opportunities? What about differences in licensing, for example, through individual licences compared to class licences?

At the European Union level, however, objectives are quite different than at the level of the WTO agreement. The objective at the EU was to open markets and, in addition, to ensure that an European-wide economic space could be attained (Directives on Liberalisation and Directives on Harmonisation). Harmonisation in this context becomes much more important since market opportunities will differ across each market if the details of the different regulatory principles differ. It can be questioned whether a level telecommunication playing field at the EU level can be achieved where the rules of the game are different. These differences are already occurring as each country's regulator implements EU principles with different interpretations and nuances.

The differences occurring within the telecommunication sector will likely be exacerbated as regulators and policy-makers implement changes in policy frameworks to tackle technological and service convergence. This will not only create important differences between countries internationally, but at the level of the EU. For example, in the UK present indications in policy debates favour the creation of a single regulatory framework and body for the telecommunications and broadcasting sectors. Implementation of such a framework would result in quite different market access opportunities in the UK as compared to other EU countries. Another example is in Denmark which is allowing the bundling of mobile and fixed voice services using one number. Such innovative regulatory developments could lead to a further gap in market opportunities.

Countries are also responding differently to developments in Internet services, including Internet telephony and developments in electronic commerce where infrastructure plays a strong role. The following examples indicate the wide diversions in the treatment of Internet voice services in EU countries[1]: Austria, Belgium, Denmark, Germany, Italy and Sweden do not cover Internet telephony in their legal provisions for public voice telephony. However, Belgium does request a declaration and the UK believes that Internet voice services would be treated as a form of resale. In France, the law defines telephone service provided to the public in a way which is independent of the technology used so that the provider of a public telephone service is subject to the same rules whether using Internet or any other platform. Luxembourg has a similar provision. In Greece, where there is still a monopoly for voice services, it is considered that Internet telephony does not constitute voice telephony as defined in the existing legislation, whereas Portugal, also with a monopoly, states that voice over the Internet is forbidden except by the incumbent monopoly.

The fact that provision of Internet telephony may be provided by service providers who do not have physical presence in the country subjecting such services to regulation may under these circumstances cause problems within the EU. Action by one country against a service provider located in another country, where such services are allowed, could lead to jurisdictional as well as legal complications.

In addition to the different EU developments in such areas as licensing, in the structure of interconnection frameworks, in cellular mobile access and in numbering policies, it is also significant that differences are emerging in market conditions. For example, in Denmark new entrants already have 25 per cent of the international long distance market, in Sweden new entrants have 17 per cent of the national long distance market, and in Finland the incumbent has 41 per cent of the long distance market. These differences in market performance, where the market shares of incumbents have declined rapidly in some specific markets compared to most EU countries, may be important in that they can influence how the regulator evaluates market conditions. Where competition is seen to be developing, regulators are more likely to take a

---

[1] See OECD (1999).

favourable view to move away from asymmetric regulation and, in the longer term, move away from sector specific regulation.

At the same time the policy agenda is in danger of distortion arising out of multi-level governance of policy making in the communications area. There are several areas of potential difficulty here. One will be how international trade law develops in the context of the WTO and case law resulting from complaint procedures. Another area is how communication directives evolve in the EU and their relation to EU Competition Law. One other area is the difficulty many municipalities are creating in terms of rights of way and the reluctance of central governments to address these issues. As technological and service convergence develops there is a danger as well in conflicting approaches being taken in telecommunication regulation as compared to the audio-visual regulation.

III. Sector-Specific or Competition Law?

The opening of telecommunication markets to competition has begun a debate on the respective roles of sector specific regulators and competition authorities and issues of transition away from sector specific regulation to competition policy frameworks. In general, most OECD countries would agree that once effective competition has developed in communication markets that sector specific regulation should be abandoned in favour of competition law. This general principle may, in itself be quite meaningless unless clearer criteria are laid down for the transition from sector specific regulation to treating telecommunication markets equally with other industries. What criteria are necessary and how detailed should they be?

There are some general differences in the role of sector specific regulators and competition authorities. The latter are usually concerned with preserving or protecting competitive markets from abuse and anti-competitive behaviour often resulting in *ex post* reactions to market developments. Sector regulators in telecommunications are concerned essentially in promoting competition. This emphasis on pro-competitive policies, and the need to bring about a transition from former state-sanctioned monopoly markets to competitive markets, has resulted in emphasis on asymmetric regulation and regulatory safeguards. It is perhaps significant that only New Zealand, among all the OECD countries, believes that it can develop competitive telecommunication markets relying solely on competition law without the assistance of transitory sector specific regulation. Even in New Zealand the threat of imposing sector specific regulation is often used to place pressure on the different market participants to reach mutual agreements.

Forbearance

Given that there is a general understanding among policy-makers that sector specific regulation for telecommunication must be viewed as transitory, and applicable until sufficient and self—sustaining competition has been developed, then there are two challenges. First, to ensure that such competition develops. Second, to determine when competition has become self-sustaining. Meeting the first challenge depends on whether the existing tools being used by regulators are effective. To meet the second challenge it is important to have clearer notions of effective competition, but it is also dangerous to have overly rigid notions. To a large extent the concept of 'effective competition' will not depend on a mechanical determination, but on intuitive analysis of market developments.

The aftermath of liberalisation is the beginning of competition. As recognised in nearly all countries which have abolished telecommunication monopoly market structures, competition requires detailed regulatory provisions. By agreeing to the Reference Paper in the WTO agreement on basic telecommunications, WTO Members also recognised that competition in the telecommunications sector required economic and technical regulatory intervention (sector specific regulation) in addition to the elimination of existing barriers to market entry.

In particular, the Reference Paper highlighted the importance of competitive safeguards, including the need to ensure interconnection, public availability of procedures for interconnection to a major supplier, transparency of interconnection arrangements, public availability of licensing criteria, the requirement of a regulator independent of the supplier of services, and objective procedures for the allocation of scarce resources.

The regulatory objectives of most countries, while pro-competitive in nature, include other objectives, in particular universal service. This is a distributional issue rather than a competition issue and was so recognised by WTO participants in the Reference Paper where it is noted that universal service obligations 'will not be regarded as anti-competitive *per se*, provided they are administered in a transparent, non-discriminatory and competitively neutral manner. . .'.

Many telecommunication regulators do not have a specific requirement to streamline regulations or to forbear from regulation when market conditions allow this to take place. This is, however, an important requirement in order to ensure the progressive elimination of detailed regulatory requirements and to phase out asymmetric regulatory treatment of incumbents whose significant market power may decline through the competitive process. Without the requirement to forebear from regulation, and thus streamline regulatory procedures, there will be a tendency to solidify the sector specific frameworks which may even in the longer term adversely impact on the development of competition. The requirement to forebear from regulation often allows market forces to work more effectively by forcing new entrants to innovate by lifting any artificial protective barriers they may use to protect their limited market share.

The use of asymmetric regulation is one such barrier which allows new entrants to develop their market by constraining the incumbent. In the early days of competition this is a useful tool to apply, but it is difficult to determine when it should be removed. Asymmetry often constrains investment. As one example, relatively cheap access to capacity can forestall new investment in infrastructure given the profitability of resale. Another example is in the development of broadband infrastructures where incumbents have in many cases been prevented from offering content and telecommunication services bundled on the same network. Such regulation may also provide a disincentive to new entrants to invest in broadband seeking instead a cheaper solution.

IV. Concurrent Authority

The extent to which competition authorities have powers in telecommunications varies from country to country. For a number of countries there is concurrent power between the sector specific regulator and the competition authority, and market participants are not exempt from competition provisions because of sector specific requirements. In other countries the competition authority has direct responsibility for some telecommunication issues. For example, in Denmark the competition authority is responsible for monitoring all interconnection agreements. Some of the specificities for some countries are outlined below:

The Role of Competition Authorities in Telecommunications Regulation

> **Finland:** Competition authorities have full jurisdiction to apply relevant Act to telecommunications sector. Agreement between competition authority and regulatory body on how overlapping situations are addressed.

Germany: Decision taken that the task of regulating communication industry requires such a degree of specialisation and expertise over and above the simple regulation of markets that instruments of competition law were insufficient. Telecommunications Act requires regulatory provisions to be examined at regular intervals by the advisory monopoly commission. Federal Cartel Office is prevented from acting in a number of areas (interconnection, access, universal service, supervision of abuse). FCO will act when the Regulator Authority considers that it has no legal basis for intervention.

Italy: General competition authority has rights to enforce competition policy in all sectors. Communications regulatory authority has responsibilities in universal service, cost allocation, interconnection and access, and issuing licences. Antitrust Authority required to provide prior non-binding advise to communication regulator (interconnection/access, accounting separation identification of undertakings with significant market power).

United Kingdom: Director General of Fair Trading has concurrent powers with OFTEL (except where mergers are involved). No formal guidelines to ensure consistency but informal agreements. Regulator has responsibility to enforce certain licence conditions which are aimed at addressing market power.

There do not seem to have been specific cases where significant disputes have arisen between competition authorities and sector specific regulators. Co-existence is often undertaken on an informal level. However, there have been some turf battles. For example, in the Netherlands the competition authorities wanted to create a telecommunication bureau (cabinet) within the competition body. Parliament decided to create an independent regulator for telecommunications (whereas for electricity it created a bureau within the competition authority). The extent to which such informal consultation has been productive in furthering competition would be difficult to determine.

A tendency could easily emerge among sector specific regulators to take on further powers to enforce competition, much like OFTEL in the UK which incorporated fair trade provisions in licences. Such a trend would make it more unlikely that sector specific regulation is phased out in the short term.

Very little work has been undertaken to show that competition provisions

can adequately handle the strong market position of incumbent telecommunication operators. At the same time there are few examples to show regulators
when to begin diluting their powers and by default transferring them to competition authorities. There may be strong arguments, therefore to ensure that
regulators move quickly to force market change. One incentive would be to set
a fixed term mandate for the sector specific regulator, then incorporate the regulator within a competition authority as a 'bureau' with a further mandate to
reduce specific regulations over time.

V. Convergence and Regulatory Frameworks

The streamlining of specific telecommunication regulation will likely be hampered by the process of technological and service convergence taking place
between telecommunications and broadcasting. This is because there will be a
need for a further transition from service specific networks (i.e. networks dedicated to telecommunication services or dedicated to broadcasting services) to
generic networks which provide access to all services in an undifferentiated
way. Convergence will also lead to new institutional challenges for regulation.

In this context there is first and foremost the potential conflict between the
broadcasting world and their emphasis on cultural policies, their protection of
local content markets and their tendency to limit market entry to terrestrial
broadcasting markets. On the other hand there is increasing pressure from the
telecommunication side to use alternate networks as a means of creating more
competition in communication markets. In addition, there is the realisation
that in a world of electronic commerce where economic activity depends on
networks it would be inefficient to treat networks as being service specific.
Also, there is the tendency by regulators on the telecommunication side to wish
to extend their principles to cover all networks.

Pressures to deal with convergence are becoming significant, but the speed
at which these issues are dealt with is likely to vary quite radically from one EU
country to another. For the European Commission one of the greatest challenges will be to try and avoid too great a divergence in the rate at which different European markets open to competition. Those countries which rapidly
converge their communication markets are likely, as well, to shift more rapidly
to using competition law to regulate their market rather than relying on sector
specific provisions. In addition, differences in the speed at which telecommunication and broadcasting infrastructures converge across Europe will result in
different market opportunities. This will also have implications for the development of a harmonised European market.

VI. Multi-level Governance Issues

There are a number of different levels of policy-making which can influence the communications area. At the international level there is the WTO which is just emerging as a policy forum for telecommunications in addition to the International Telecommunication Union which has traditionally been a key player in terms of standardisation as well as in some policy areas.

At the regional level the European Union has been playing a key role in obtaining agreement for the principle of open markets, but national regulators still retain important powers. Additionally, in some Federal countries such as the United States, national policies are supplemented by policies at the state-level. In addition to these different vertical levels of policy making, the present convergence at the technological and service level characterising the communications area is resulting in the need for more policy co-ordination at the horizontal level, especially between the telecommunication and broadcasting areas.

The WTO agreement will have spill-over effects on the broadcasting sector. In part this will occur because important future commitments have been made by Ministers for further liberalisation of the telecommunication sector.[2]

The safeguards underlying the Reference Paper appear straightforward, but their interpretation is left open. Countries could have a free hand in the subsequent interpretation of these safeguards and/or they may be subject to an eventual dispute resolution process which will provide interpretation and provide more specific interpretation. There are already attempts by telecommunication operators to 'interpret' the Reference Paper.[3] It is fairly easy to imagine a number of areas where differences in interpretation will emerge at national and regional levels and which could result in perceived, but not necessarily intended, barriers to market entry. For example, the definition of 'cost-oriented' could be one area subject to interpretation; another would be defining universal service obligations that are no 'more burdensome than necessary'[4] to achieve stated goals. Another area where resolution may eventually be required between countries in the context of the WTO agreement is with

---

[2] The Singapore Declaration made a commitment to 'obtain a progressively higher level of liberalisation in services on a mutually advantageous basis with appropriate flexibility for individual developing country members . . . . in the continuing negotiations and those scheduled to begin no later than 1 January 2000'. (WT/MIN(96)/DEC).

[3] See, for example, 'Implementing the WTO Agreement on Trade in Telephone Services: The Requirements of the GATS Reference Paper', US West International, August 1997; AT&T presentation to the IIC Telecommunications Forum, 27–28 October 1997, mimeo.

[4] Point 3 of the Reference Paper.

respect to definitions of basic telecommunications. This can occur in particular as technological and service convergence change the menu of 'basic' services available to the public and impinge on services which may have broadcast as well as telecommunication characteristics.

The actions of individual countries will also result in differences in opinion as to principles with respect to the WTO Agreement. For example, there is already significant negative reaction to the US FCC Benchmarking Order on international settlement payments with many countries arguing that the Order goes against multilateral agreements in that it constitutes a unilateral declaration. Linked to this reaction is an informal understanding by the negotiating group at the WTO that the application of asymmetric accounting rates would not result in action by Members under dispute settlement.[5] Dispute procedures and further negotiations which may result in interpretation of the details of the Reference Paper could result in the WTO playing the unwanted role of a 'pseudo' international regulator. However, there is a possibility for some countries to shift away from sector specific regulation which will result in different landscapes in the global telecommunication economic space.

Further rounds of the WTO are likely to begin entering into more detail in fleshing-out the Reference Paper as well as examining issues on the borderline of telecommunications and broadcasting. Further detailed provisions in terms of the Reference paper have implications for the future role of competition law and its application to the communication area.

Traditionally the International Telecommunication Union (ITU) had been the international organisation responsible for discussion of international telecommunication issues. The two treaty instruments of the ITU (ITU Constitution and ITU Convention) contain several normative provisions which apply to the provision of telecommunications. Additionally, the International Telecommunications Regulations[6] have some provisions with policy implications. Perhaps the main area of 'policy' influence of the ITU is in terms of International Radiocommunication Regulations dealing with radio spectrum allocations and allotment activity. The role of the ITU was mainly in standardisation, but a number of the recommendations[7] coming out of the dif-

---

[5] It was also understood that this would be reviewed not later than the commencement of the further round of negotiations on Services Commitments due to begin not later than 1 January 2000.

[6] The International Telecommunications Regulations are treaty binding.

[7] The recommendations of the ITU are not considered as binding on the member governments.

ferent study groups have had direct or indirect policy implications. These Study Groups cover the Radiocommunication and Telecommunications areas. Part of the procedures of the ITU are the World Conferences, which are formal treaty making bodies. They exist for telecommunications (World Conference on International Telecommunications) and radio regulation (World Radiocommunication Conferences).

The ITU has also recently begun the so-called World Telecommunication Policy Forums which are aimed at making recommendations or preparing non-treaty intergovernmental agreements.[8] The first forum examined satellite-based global mobile services and agreed to a Memorandum of Understanding on terminal equipment for such satellites. The second Policy Forum examined telecommunication trade-related issues including implementation of the WTO agreement and issues of international settlements reform.

At the beginning of negotiations in the context of the WTO's Negotiating Group on Basic Telecommunications it became fairly clear (at least for WTO delegates) that agreements at the WTO would take precedence at the international level, and that the ITU in its deliberations needed to take into account any relevant WTO principles and agreements. However, there are a number of policy areas of international importance which the recent WTO Agreement has not touched on, allowing the ITU to have an 'influence' over some policy domains. The fact that the ITU will continue to have a role in standards making for new service areas will also imply some influence over some aspects of the provision of new services.

The issue of accounting rates is a specific area where the ITU, by virtue of existing international recommendations has international authority, but because of the WTO Agreement now also falls indirectly[9] within the WTO mandate. The inability in the past of the ITU to successfully reform the existing accounting rate regime also weakens that organisation's moral power to claim sole jurisdiction over this issue.

The WTO Agreement has also forced the ITU to reflect on its role in international standards setting and policy making. Much standard-setting activity takes place outside the formal bodies of the ITU; for example in informal industry groups, or in the European Telecommunications Standards Institute. The development of the Internet, and technological and service convergence

---

[8] The Resolution establishing the forum states that 'the world telecommunication policy forum shall neither produce prescriptive regulatory outcomes nor produce outputs with binding force'.

[9] 'Indirectly' because accounting rates are not mentioned specifically in national schedules or in the Reference Paper.

are resulting in much of the new and rapidly growing communications activity taking place in policy and standards areas which fall outside the traditional ITU sphere of influence. The ITU has met this challenge by increasingly trying to enter into the international telecommunications policy area. It is also trying to extend its sphere of influence to cover other areas such as Internet Governance. This was clearly evident in the Plenipotentiary conference of November 1998.

The potential for any lack of congruence in policy between ITU and WTO remains small given that most countries would tend to place their WTO commitments, which are binding, ahead of any ITU commitments. For many of the OECD countries the officials dealing with WTO issues are often closely linked with some of the key ITU areas, which facilitates policy coherence. Despite the fact that not all countries participated in the WTO negotiations, those that did constitute the bulk of the world telecommunication service market so that the relative policy weight of the other countries will be insufficient to provide the ITU with any policy clout. However, the ITU can play an important role in the development of international telecommunications by taking the WTO 'message' to the 100 or so other countries which did not participate in the WTO negotiations and by using their intermediary role in ensuring that there are adequate international concessions for telecommunications development, as well as providing guidance for the strengthening of policy frameworks in those countries.

VII. The European Challenge

In the past, commitment to liberalisation has varied across the EU. Even now, despite widespread market opening, it is not the case that commitment to open markets to competition is the same across the EU. There are still differences in the extent to which National Regulatory Authorities interpret their role, and the extent they are willing to push for further market liberalisation. In some cases this has reflected the realities of the political situation (for example, the need to provide trade unions of the incumbent operators with some guarantees). In other cases the legislative and policy formulating process moves slowly. In yet other instances, the incumbent is still viewed as a national champion requiring some protection. The feet dragging is obvious in those countries which have derogations from the 1998 market opening,[10] and by accepting this political solution the creation of an European economic space will be delayed

---

[10] In these countries the level of telecommunication development, as measured by main lines per 100 inhabitants, is at a higher level than was the UK in 1984 when it opened its market to competition and the level of network modernisation is also much higher.

significantly—directly in the telecommunication services area and indirectly in those industries relying on intensive use of telecommunication inputs.

The differences in the pace of change of policy between individual countries and the EU policy framework create problems of governance. Differences between the countries liberalising their communication markets rapidly and the slower countries may well cause more serious problems than did differences in market opening for telecommunication services. There are two reasons for this. First, once telecommunication markets are opened the potential for by-pass with new converged services will be fairly significant, including the ability to provide services without physical presence in a country. In contrast, when initial telecommunication market opening took place in the early 1980s, the potential for such by-pass was extremely limited, and the ability of existing monopolies to control entry was high. Second, convergence touches on the area of cultural policy which is a sensitive issue in some EU countries.

Differences in regulatory burdens are also likely to arise because of the relative power of different incumbents to influence the regulatory framework. The incumbents have an interest in convincing the NRAs to implement more light-handed regulation and convince regulators that the existence of market contestability should be sufficient to consider a market as competitive. The question then arises as to whether it is possible to have a trans-European market where there are differences in degrees of regulation across an ostensible single market. In that EU Directives and provisions are unclear on the treatment of trans-European networks it is likely that to develop such networks new entrants will have to negotiate on a country by country basis.

Policies will also diverge as industry structures alter through cross-border alliances, convergence between sectors and increased globalisation. This is because such developments are likely to occur first in the core EU markets where policy will need to accommodate change resulting in a two-track market framework.

Clearly, there is little guarantee that NRAs will implement directives in the same way throughout Europe, and if they do not, fragmentation will continue. Coherence and commonality can only occur through a unique Europe regulatory authority, a proposal which, while politically charged, is obtaining a better hearing now that the main agreements on liberalisation are in place.

VIII. Conclusion

As economies move in the direction of an information society, it becomes increasingly important to have global frameworks in place. Indeed, for many new services it may no longer be possible to use national frameworks since access to services is on a global basis. The Internet exemplifies these developments. National policies for the Internet are not sustainable unless supplemented through international understandings. Global co-operation is rapidly becoming the norm in such policy areas and rather than having hard and fast regulations there is a trend to move toward guidelines, frameworks and codes of conduct. These developments are also forcing industry to behave more responsibly at the global level since many governments are imposing the burden of setting standards for service provision, ensuring harmony and the balance of different objectives to the private sector rather than governments. A movement toward more industry-generated self-regulation requires quite significant changes in industry co-operation across countries as well as understandings between governments to allow this to occur. The development of global information infrastructures not only exerts pressure for the further liberalisation of communication infrastructure and service markets, but is also changing the structure of policy governance in a range of sectors and across national borders.

AFTERWORD

1999: Reviewing the Regulatory Framework

1999 marks the beginning of the EU Communications Review. 'The Review', was foreseen in the European Commission's package of telecommunications liberalisation directives adopted over the past decade (under both Articles 86 and 95 [ex 90 and 100a]). Its aim is to review and reform the current regulatory and legislative framework for the new electronic communications markets in the context of the current rapid progress and change. Thus, in light of recent and imminent structural and technological developments, the Review is supposed to re-assess telecommunications policy and to set down the main regulatory principles for the 'next phase' in the development of the regulatory framework, covering the period from about 2001 to perhaps 2006.[1]

Two related developments are commonly identified in the EU as key to this demand to move on, as soon as possible, to an advanced phase with regard to pro-competitive telecom policy. The first is simply about the progressive state of competition in the telecommunications market. The other, inherently related, factor is about technological convergence between this market and other communications networks markets.

A central, if not the central, question in the context of this Review is that of the future role and nature of sector specific regulations and regulators in relation to that of competition law and antitrust authorities.

Needless to say, many of the same basic issues that we tackled in our 1998 EU Competition Law Workshop are the key to the current discussions and issues of contention with which the Commission's Review project is currently grappling with. It seems, therefore, both timely and appropriate to relate our, essentially academic, discussions and conclusions to this real world policy process.

I. The Background to The Process and Time-Table of the 1999 Communications Review

In 1997 the Commission (DGXIII in particular) issued a 'Green Paper on Convergence'.[2] The Green Paper explored the 'convergence phenomenon' and

---

[1] Com(1999)08.
[2] COM(1997)623.

posed questions as to its implications for the telecommunications policy framework. As regards the regulation of network access and control of bottlenecks, the paper tended towards a supposition that, if sectoral distinctions between types of communication network and service were put in doubt by technological progress, so too are sector specific access regimes. The results and conclusions of the consultation process were summarised and published by the Commission at the beginning of 1999.[3] In the latter, there is still a clear tendency toward 'hammering' the view of convergence as a 'nail in the coffin' of a sector specific regulatory framework for network access rules.

As regards the regulation of network distribution, a clear message throughout the Communication is that there should be an 'increased reliance' on 'effective application of competition rules, accompanied by gradual phasing out of sector-specific regulations as the market becomes more competitive'.[4]

At the beginning of 1999 DG XIII launched a series of studies (carried out by external expert consultants and law firms) on various other aspects of the Review.[5] Subjects of study include interconnection and access (a focused review of the interconnection directive), tariff transparency in a multi-operator environment, the convergence of fixed and mobile networks (hence implications for convergence of regulatory models), and the desirability of a 'European Regulatory Agency'. The results of these studies are being presented and opened up to reactions from interested parties at public hearings throughout the year.

Alongside the conclusions of the Convergence Green Paper consultations, these Review studies' findings and the various reactions from the market and other interested parties, should be fed into the DG XIII drafting process, which will result in a Commission Communication by the end of 1999. This Communication will present the Commission's proposed framework for proposals for one, or a package of, new EU legislation. The latter would aim to be issued, as proposals for consideration and adoption by the Council and the Parliament during 2000, and to be finally adopted by end of that year. In this way, the new and reformed regulatory framework would be due for implementation by the Member States by around the beginning of 2002.

---

[3] *Results of Public Consultation on the Convergence Green Paper: Communication,* COM(1999)108.

[4] IP/99/194, Commission Press Release of 10/3/99.

[5] Website: *http://www.ispo.cec.be/infosoc/telecompolicy/en/studylist.pdf,* 1999 List of Studies at ISPO.

II. The Recognised Problems with the Current Access Regulation Framework

While the questions posed by DG XIII regarding policy solutions are, almost without exception, the subject of heated contention between policy makers, interested parties and experts, at this stage there is at least some rough consensus discernible as concerns the fact that, certainly, current policy needs to be reviewed and reformed. There is a significant amount of agreement on the existence and nature of various shortcomings (or at least foreseeable and imminent ones) within the current EU framework for network access and interconnection (i.e. on the inadequacy of the ONP model). The most common and accepted criticisms and include one or more of the following observations about the framework:

(1) It is crude and basic, applying only to the most elementary bundled carriage service for wholesale interconnection between networks;

(2) It has got hopelessly 'bogged down' in the problem of identifying and enforcing a standard, fair and efficient price for this basic service;

(3) It is inherently based on an extremely asymmetrical and static view of the nature and the rights of particular market players; that is, it is founded on an assumption of granting access rights to certain types of 'new' competitive operations (i.e. 'weak' new entrants planning to invest in long distance or value-added services, who are potentially blocked by their need to access the local loop bottlenecks for origination and termination of services); while imposing access obligations on others (i.e. the ex-monopolists still enjoying virtual monopoly market power over the final connection to the end user). Not only does this presume a certain stasis, but also a particular model of competition for the telecom market.

(4) This assumption of asymmetry and of very basic interconnect service is only appropriate and applicable to the initial and earliest stages of introducing competition to telecoms markets and to the related policy objectives of encouraging investment in long-distance networks and business services. If maintained beyond its 'use by' date it will skew the market and distort commercial investment decisions.

(5) The current ONP framework cannot cope with the range of more advanced second stage competition problems, which are now becoming apparent as competitors expand their aims and demand the opportunity to enhance services. Increasingly, for example, these occur at the retail end instead of the 'wholesale' focus of policy. This also demands a new focus

on non-price issues and the more sophisticated non-carriage elements of network access.

(6) Most importantly and specifically, the current regulatory framework does not address the competitive demand for direct access to unbundled elements of the incumbent's local loop infrastructure and resources (carriage and non-carriage elements).

(7) At the same time, the convergence phenomenon implies that the whole issue of local loop access, or direct customer access, for upstream service providers is no longer simply a straight 'telecommunications' issue (in the traditional sense of the word). Thus, even if the current EU telecom regulatory framework were advanced to address some of these 'second stage' competition issues it would still be inadequate in its traditional sectoral focus.

III. Proposals for Reform

As noted above there is, naturally enough, much less consensus apparent on how to solve these problems—that is, which way to move forward—than on the fact that there are problems. It has been noted (and lamented) by various interests in the telecoms market that there are already rather 'worrying' signs from the EU policy arena which reveal a strong 'leaning' toward solving all these complex problems in a rather simplistic way. That is, rather than focusing on how to modify and refocus the regulatory framework according to the changed and changing environment, to opt for simply abolishing it. DG XIII may be accused of a 'roll-back bias' in their Review: that is, a bias toward 'rolling back' any sector regulations wherever, and as soon as possible (and a relative neglect as concerns serious consideration of the converse solution, to advance and enhance the regulatory framework). Straight regulatory roll-back is a solution which could, at this early stage, be accused of being tantamount to 'throwing the baby out with the bath-water'.

There is much discussion, in this context, on 'stepping up' the use and role of general competition laws and safeguards in the field of competitive network access to replace the current framework specific *ex-ante* rules for particular, identified players.[6] DG XIII appears to be considering use of the concept of regulatory 'forbearance',[7] which consequently raises questions of defining triggers or

---

[6] Com (1999)108.

[7] Oral presentation by Mr Jean-Eric de Cockborne of DG XIII, at UK's Department of Trade and Industry Public Hearing on the EU Communications Review, December 1998.

thresholds for the earliest possible lifting of regulatory burdens on the incumbent operators. Alongside this is the probable assumption that the burden of proof on Significant Market Power (SMP) players should be shifted from that of having to justify the obsolescence of regulatory obligations, to that of proving their necessity. This bias is, naturally, one which is welcomed and supported by (indeed probably inspired by) the most powerful players in the EU telecom market.

There are clearly a multitude of opposing voices from contrary interests, that is, from competitors in the market who fear that their explicit regulatory rights vis-à-vis the incumbents may be whisked away prematurely. They support the position that, in many areas, their regulatory safeguards (and hence the regulatory burdens on the incumbent network) need to be advanced and enhanced, and not retracted at this critical stage in the growth of a competitive market.[8] Indeed, they do not necessarily support the presumption that sector regulation must be a transitional phase phenomenon. Rather, they argue that it has yet to be seen whether the market will develop in such a way as will allow regulatory roll-back at some point in the future.

It is of critical importance to note, in this context, that the fundamental question in the telecom policy arena as to whether the lack of a 'normal competitive market' is a transient phenomenon (stemming from a particular historical starting position of legal monopoly) or one which is fundamental to the industry, still persists.

IV. Relating the 1998 Workshop to the 1999 Review: The Key Issues of the Debate

A central theme, which has been argued both by competition lawyers and the competition players in the industry, is that competition policy, and competition concepts and principles may be being used, and abused, by the sector regulators (and their experts) in ways which are increasingly inappropriate, confusing and dangerous. It is accepted that, for the first stage of liberalisation of the telecom market and initial market entry, it was vital to have in place an immediate, basic and pragmatic regulatory framework, in order to ensure that some kind of basic interconnection is guaranteed on roughly reasonable terms and conditions. In this early stage, the use of pro-competition terms and models are inevitably pretty simplistic and crude. (this relates to 'who' has regulatory obligations, 'who' has regulatory rights, and 'what' they are). The

---

[8] Oral interventions at CEC Public Workshop on Ovum Study 'A Review of the Interconnect Directive: Initial Proposals for Discussion, 30 June 1999.

'why' issues, which would justify (legally, economically or normatively) the solution to the 'who' and 'what' access problems, are, at this early stage, not given priority. However, as we move on to adapt and fine-tune the regulatory environment to a more complex, advanced and on-going market situation, we need to come back to the foundations of our pro-competitive rules and, consequently, re-assess their application.

In the ONP environment, this involves reviewing many of the basic elements, particularly as concerns the reasoning behind the balance of access rights and access obligations, as well as what they are and when they are applied.

The key issues underlying the discussions in last year's (1998) EU Competition Workshop are of clear and significant relevance to this current discourse surrounding the EU review. Of general interest are the debates on the continuing role of sector regulations in ensuring competitive conditions in the (tele)communications market (i.e. in addition to the application of traditional competition laws and principles). Of more specific interest, are the related, particular topics which emerged under this heading—both in the Workshop and the current policy debate.

These include:

(1) The implications of 'convergence'.
(2) The use and abuse of the 'bottleneck' concept.
(3) The definition of 'significant market power' (SMP) and what this implies from a regulatory point of view.
(4) The issue of justifying 'asymmetrical' rights and obligations.
(5) The 'false dichotomy' between service-based competition and infrastructure competition.
(6) The exploration of the use of tools or concepts such as 'regulatory forbearance', 'sunset clauses', and, thus, the appropriate definition of 'thresholds' or 'triggers' in the market for applying or dis-applying special regulatory obligations or rights.
(7) The appropriate role and viability of applying structural interventions ('one off solutions' to the access bottleneck dilemma), and, related to this, 'line of business' restrictions and 'incentive regulation'.
(8) The problems of price regulation.
(9) The recognition of the challenge and the significance of addressing 'second order' access issues (which may be non-price and non-carriage elements, and often involve the entrenched retail market power of the incumbent).
(10) Direct and unbundled access to the local loop.
(11) The idea of 'virtual ring fences' around access resources.

1. The 'Janus Faced' Implications of 'Convergence'

It is useful to remember that the term 'convergence' tends to be used to address both of the following phenomena: 'intra-industry' convergence between different technologies over which traditional telecom services (mainly telephony) are provided (for instance mobile and fixed networks); and 'cross-industry' convergence between telecom and one or more adjacent industries such as computing or TV entertainment services.

In order for the policy/law/regulation implications of this 'convergence phenomenon' to be considered sensibly and realistically, the concept needs to be 'unpacked' as concerns its 'good' and 'bad' faces:

In terms of competition policy considerations, there is an optimistic view which looks at ways in which 'convergence' should represent a challenge to the traditional and entrenched dominance of the incumbent PSTN (Public Switched Telephone Network—the traditional fixed wirelines and service) network over traditional PSTN based services. This assumes (*inter alia*) that converged products—such as Internet Protocol (IP) based services and/or mobile communications —become truly 'replaceable', in terms of the consumer's perception and use, for the PSTN based product.

It is important, however, to be sufficiently wary of premature assumptions, and of any exaggerations about the regulatory implications here. It is certainly dangerous to allow the current state of, and predictions for, a certain perceived trend in technological and commercial developments to represent (already) the lynch pin for the abandonment of the regulatory focus on the dominance of the incumbent PSTN in the telecommunications market. It is not yet sufficiently apparent when, or even that, the significance of PSTN dominance will be competed out by use of alternative or parallel infrastructures. While policy makers and legal experts should be commended for avoiding 'regulatory lag' in giving due consideration to state of the art and (predicted) future market developments, we should be equally careful to avoid regulatory pre-emption and over zealous optimism. The myriad of developments caught under the label of the 'convergence' phenomenon are just beginning. They are still far from challenging the very particular structure and competition challenges of the incumbent.

In sharp contrast, we may consider the extent to which, far from being the antidote to the incumbent's dominance, convergence poses the anti-competitive risk of 'cross-market leverage' on the part of the latter. Thus, convergence may actually result in significant extension and enhancement of entrenched market power into the converging markets. An incumbent facing the prospect of more competition in a converged environment (e.g. from switched to IP based services) may seek to lever its existing power (in the PSTN environment) into the new market, before its power base dissipates. It should be noted that this might well be a form of non-price leverage based on its retail level dominance.

Incumbents in two converging markets (e.g. pay TV and telephony network services) may decide that it is in their interests to co-operate (or collude) with each other, rather than compete against each other in the converged market. While EU competition law may be applied (*ex-post*) to agreements or joint ventures in this context, this does not affect the fact that the risk of cross-market leveraging here means that the focused (*ex-ante*) regulatory control of the original source of market power needs to be emphasised, and not relaxed as a result of convergence.

Despite the above arguments and considerations there is, currently (and in particular in the context of the Review) a notable propensity for commentators and regulatory experts to overemphasise the 'good face', whilst paying insufficient attention to the 'bad' or dangerous face of convergence. Indeed, not only may the (market leverage) dangers be overlooked by many regulatory 'experts', but the convergence promises may at the same time be exaggerated or misunderstood.

'Technological convergence' (the functional possibility to provide various telecom services over non-PSTN distribution networks) does not imply that entrenched PSTN based dominance is no longer a problem for regulatory focus. It is apparent that, when the issue is handled by non-competition law experts (or at least not handled with adequate care) 'technological convergence' may be confused with 'market convergence'.

What is happening in the Commission's Review is that those outside the competition law arena proper (i.e. DG XIII) are leading an initiative for reform, which is predominantly based on competition policy concepts. In this way, there is a significant danger that confusion and blurring of principles, and their applications, may occur.

2. The Use and Abuse of the 'Bottleneck' Concept

Likewise, great care is needed in the handling and use of the 'bottleneck' concept. In the wrong hands it can be applied in a way which produces rather absurd conclusions from the point of view of competition law—most notably one which says that since every end customer line is a bottleneck, every telephone number is a market unto itself. Why does this happen?

Following on from the arguments presented in Waters/Stewarts/Simpsons'
paper for this Workshop, regulators and non-competition telecom experts may
have been guilty of slavishly transposing a very specific legal concept ('bottleneck' and/or 'essential facilities') into telecommunications policy in a way
which confuses the issue of where and when to identify significant market
power with its implications. In particular, the 'bottleneck' or essential facilities
doctrine has, clearly and conspicuously, been borrowed from the competition
law framework, but then applied (under the guise of the legitimacy carried by
its competition law origins) in order to ensure a policy objective, which, while
indisputably legitimate in its own right, is not essentially a competition law
goal: i.e. it is applied in the context of the objective of ensuring ubiquitous termination ('any-to-any' service) on and between fixed and mobile public networks. Clearly, the nature of the service of public telecommunications makes
such any-to-any access and interoperability between the networks a key
requirement of the service, and, thus, where the free market does not always
provide this, a specific 'access policy' may well be required to ensure it. Yet, this
requirement is a characteristic of the nature of the service, not a competition
requirement *per se*. Thus, the 'any-to-any bottleneck' is not necessarily a 'market bottleneck'.

In making his point, Waters reminds us that the requirement for 'any-to-
any connectivity' is pretty much unique to telecommunications. It needs, thus,
to be addressed by a unique, telecom regulatory solution as regards the necessary access and interconnect obligations. For instance, in the US and Australia
(detailed in Waters' paper) non-dominant operators have an obligation to
interconnect with other operators (i.e. to enter into commercial negotiations—
with a back up safeguard of regulatory arbitration or mediation if called for—
on terms and price).

'Bottleneck' is, on the other hand a specific legal concept which cannot be,
and is not, divorced from its generally applicable legal implications for signalling market definition and market power.

The distinction between the 'any-to-any' access issue, and the 'control-of-
market-bottlenecks' access issue is reflected in the US and Australian regime,
whereby only operators with significant market power have the special
access/interconnect obligations to provide transparent incremental cost pricing
and other standard regulated access terms.

It is implied by the arguments in the Waters' paper that, perhaps, the thinking in the EU regulatory framework needs to be a little clearer on this point, in
order to avoid confusion and blurring of the key issues—which are precisely
the issues under review in this Review process. In particular, this question is relevant to the rights and obligations as regards network access which are secured

by the ONP directives. Most specifically, this refers to the definition of Annex I operators (to all intents and purposes these have been assumed to be the incumbent PTOs), the distinction between this category and that of Annex II operators (new operators with special PTO network licences, but not significant market power) and the related balance of regulatory rights and obligations.

Unlike in the Australian environments, the EU's ONP framework does not clarify exactly what the 'access obligation' is for the non-dominant operators or, why or how it should be applied. In not clearly delineating what Annex I operators means, and how and why this definition of market power relates to the special obligations, there is growing confusion as to how this framework can apply to a current and future market where it is not so obvious that only the incumbents should be burdened with special network access obligations. This problem, once recognised, should not, however, simply lead straight to the 'throwing the baby out with the bath water' solution (basic rolling back of the regulatory framework as the demands upon it become more complex and sophisticated, instead of adapting and advancing it to meet the demand).

3. Significant Market Power (SMP) and Asymmetrical Rules

The concept of Significant Market Power relates directly to the discussions surrounding another of the concepts listed above, namely: the definition of SMP and what this implies from a regulatory point of view and the issue of justifying 'asymmetrical' rights and obligations.

Concerning the 'Annex I' versus 'Annex II' division in the ONP Interconnection Directive, we may note that when this framework was conceived, it was clear who the Annex I operators should be, so the fact that the reasoning behind the definition was somewhat loose and crude was not, immediately, a problem. As a rule of thumb, Annex I operators were public network operators with SMP. Equally, the definition of SMP, was—short of a rough market share estimate which was only indicative and not really applicable—left open. In particular, it was much easier and more practical to assume that an SMP label could be applied to a certain market player (i.e. the incumbent) across all and any of its market areas, rather than applying the SMP test to each and every access situation in the manner of a pure competition law analysis. However, now that competition in the market has developed, it is becoming much more important that the SMP or 'bottleneck control' definition becomes suitably coherent and sophisticated. It is no longer viable, or plausible, to simply label certain players (by virtue of their historical status and/or their licence type) as 'Annex I' operators. The access situation and services involved need to be explored in a more flexible manner, in order to clarify what and whether access obligations apply.

The controversy and criticisms stemming from this 'across the board' operator-related (as opposed to situation-related) SMP label have swelled the current debate about the inherent problems of 'asymmetrical regulation'. This was an issue raised in many of the papers presented to the Workshop. However, many of the complaints about the latter may be seen as a 'red herring', if the focus is shifted to a more sophisticated situation based SMP analysis.

4. Infrastructure-Based Competition versus Services-Based Competition: A False Dichotomy

Another key problem relating to the simplicity and assumptions of the current ONP framework, is the boundary between the Annex II operators (where eligibility is defined, generally, by the individual licence held by a public network operator) who have 'rights' to the regulated standard 'wholesale' interconnect terms, and 'all others' (mostly referred to as 'service providers') operating in the telecom services market who are not eligible for such wholesale terms (and must negotiate, as any other 'special' customer, for access to the relevant network resources).

The 'service providers' outside the Annex II category are, generally, those who have not (or not yet) made a decision to make a heavy and risky investment, in order to build their own public network infrastructure. Such operators have, traditionally, been regarded with mistrust in the EU regulatory arena (following from the precedent setting UK model) as 'cowboys' who seek to gain market share, simply by reselling network capacity leased from others. Thus, it follows, they should not be given too much advantage to simply make profits out of price arbitrage based on regulated prices. The idea is, rather, to promote infrastructure building in the market (again based on the UK model of telecom competition) upon the assumption that this is the best (if not only) way to create sustainable and competitive market structures. A new market structure, which is based on the achievement of parallel networks, (so the theory goes) would ultimately solve (by bypass) the bottleneck problem, and, thus, not be endlessly reliant on regulatory price intervention. Thus, regulatory price advantage (rights to cost-based network access to promote market entry) should only be granted to operators who possess the commitment and cash to build new infrastructure, and should, thus, encourage and reward their efforts. By contrast, however, so the logic of this argument follows, cost based access for 'service providers', would have the opposite effect of discouraging infrastructure investment and encouraging reliance on regulated prices.

Furthermore, according to this model, only the most basic indirect access needs to be ensured (the 'standard interconnection' service only provides switched access to a bundled package of the incumbents network facilities for call terminations). Thus, the issue of direct access (normally a leasing arrangement whereby the access user has a significant degree of discretion and control over its own use) to key network elements and resources is not addressed. Indeed, one might argue that, up until now, the ONP model of network access is based quite solidly on the 'any-to-any' policy objective, as opposed to a more 'pure' competition objective. This explains both the simple focus on how to ensure the connection and interoperability between multiple public infrastructures, and the use of the term 'bottleneck' with regard to this situation and not with regard to defining essential facilities and downstream or dependent markets.

Be that as it may, there are two key criticisms which may be levelled at the (UK inspired) competition model upon which the ONP framework appears to have been built.

The first is that it implies a false dichotomy between service-based competition and infrastructure competition and leads to simplistic assumptions about the relationship between access regulation and investment incentives. Reality is more complex. The distinction between 'service provider' and 'network operator' is increasingly unstable and blurred. Indeed, it is precisely this (assumed) 'all-or-nothing' attitude towards investment commitments and network roll-out (and consequent eligibility for rights to regulated standard access service) which may act to discourage many would-be infrastructure investors in the EU. The current environment excludes these service providers more gradual roll-out plans and the less grandiose commitments of those who require more flexibility as regards the dynamics of their decisions to buy and build some network facilities, to lease others on capacity based terms, and to opt for a per/minute (switched) bundled interconnection service for their remaining network termination needs.

Indeed, most network operators themselves are, at this stage, leasing in some areas, interconnecting in others and building out their infrastructure in still others. So, the categorisation cannot be simple or static. This leads us, once again, to the problem of making regulatory distinctions, or decisions, that are based on the attempt to identify and define the markets players, instead of the actual access situation.

5. Enhanced PSTN Services and Intelligent Networks

The second aspect of this problem, is that not all service providers who are excluded from Annex II ('network operator') category are 'cowboys' or simply 'resellers'. Whether or not they may also be planning to invest in buy or build strategies alongside their direct access demands, many service providers have strategies and ideas to gain market share by innovation or added value as regards enhancing PSTN service, and not through simple price arbitrage on the 'plain old' conveyance service. In particular, this involves Intelligent Network (IN) based services which are based on the use and connection of 'off-switch' data processing systems and software to unbundled facilities and elements of the incumbent's local loop.

Most EU consumers and businesses are not yet provided with the choice, quality and sophistication of such PSTN-based enhanced services (mainly intelligent network services, such as free-phone, local, geographic and non-geographic number portability) that have already been enjoyed for some time in the US. It may be argued that the regulatory bias in the EU (by contrast to the US) against service providers and the ensuring of flexible and unbundled local loop access for the latter, has aggravated, or even created, this current disadvantage for the EU consumer.

Thus, proponents of this argument are hoping that the Communications Review will review the 'false dichotomy model, and reconsider the regulatory distinction between 'interconnection' and 'access'. Thus, it is hoped that the EU Review will encourage policy makers to further consider: (a) regulatory frameworks addressing the demand for direct access to unbundled local loop elements (carriage and non-carriage), and (b) a more flexible attitude to the category of market players who are eligible for regulated access conditions (i.e. expansion or dissolution of the Annex II definition).

This position clearly runs contrary to both the original ONP model, as well as the focus on earliest possible regulatory roll-back in its Review.

6. The Role of Structural Interventions and Line-Of-Business Restrictions?

Perhaps a key point to reply to is the understandably strong pressure to resolve and relieve ourselves of seemingly endlessly troublesome and contentious regulatory interventions in the sector. According to the optimistic version of the ONP/UK model of encouraging infrastructure bypass, structural changes in the market would make access regulation redundant. It has been argued that, in reality, such changes are not yet sufficiently evident, and such 'redundancy' of access regulation is not likely to arise in the foreseeable future. Does that mean we are simply left with the prospect of ever more complex regulatory dilemmas (and failures)? Is there perhaps no end to the imperfect market intervention of the sector regulator?

Perhaps, in response to these questions, we might re-open (or re-phrase) the question of the relationship between behavioural remedies (which we might compare to on-going 'medicine' continuously administered to keep a chronic disease in check) and structural solutions (which might be compared to a final or 'one-off' cure for the disease). If the 'medicine' approach is so distasteful, and, if it is true that commercial market developments cannot be relied upon to bring about the structural changes needed in order to solve the network access problem (with bypass and parallel access facilities), perhaps regulation should try to provide the 'one-off' structural solution. The theory behind the latter is that, instead of dissolving the bottleneck by achieving parallel facilities, you opt for rendering the bottleneck less dangerous and much more amenable to a framework of fair and efficient access for those who need it. How? By removing the incentive for abuse of gateway control by separating the gatekeepers interests from that of the dependent markets.

This would then need to go further than the existing use of structural interventions by EU Competition Law (i.e. case by case vetting and modifying cooperative or concentrative agreements). As was recognised by many participants in this Workshop, the role and viability of enforcing divestiture obligations on existing structures in the market is an important question (and a key point of contrast between the US and the EU in this area). Alongside this is the use of 'line of business restrictions' to prevent expansions and extension of certain operations (gatekeepers) in the future.

To date, the EU, both at Commission and Member State level, has been notably reluctant to attempt to interfere with the investment and business plans of their market players in such a tough manner. Despite the bias toward increasing reliance on competition law, there is no evidence to suggest it may be an element of the Review. Meanwhile, such instruments have proved relatively effective in the US environment. Their efficacy is particularly notable as regards the possibilities they open up for the use of 'incentive regulation' to induce (instead of beating) the gatekeepers in the market to behave particularly well, without the regulator having to 'breathe down their necks'. The prime example of this, which has been noted in a few of our Workshop papers and interventions, is the use of the US 'Competitive Checklist'. Line of business restrictions—*inter alia* concerning the entry of local (Bell) operations, which were originally divested from the trunk operations of AT&T to re-enter that long distance market—may be lifted only at such a time that the FCC is satisfied that the local operator in question has fully and effectively achieved a competitive local market environment. It should be noted as an important caveat here, that many of the key elements of this list are about non-price issues and are concerned with direct access to local loop facilities (many of which are not straight carriage/conveyance infrastructure).

Of course, line-of-business restrictions are not the only way to bring in inventive regulation. Indeed, the introduction of the principle of 'regulatory forbearance' in the context of the 1999 Review is also appealing to the efficacy of this instrument. In other words, once competitive environments (or competitors) have reached (or been allowed to reach by the 'willing' of the incumbents) a 'certain state' (the actual trigger conditions being the most heated subject of debate) then the 'quid pro quo' for the incumbents is the lifting of the 'asymmetrical' controls on their behaviour. The key difference is that the US application of incentive regulations appears to be much tougher than that of the 'forbearance' idea being discussed in the EU policy arena. For instance, in the US case, local loop incumbents are the subject of local loop access regulations (at state level), as well as line-business restrictions imposed at federal level. In essence, the latter may be lifted when it is proved that the former have been effective in establishing local loop competition. By contrast, in the EU case, the incumbents are currently subject to much more basic and less detailed interconnect regulations and no line-of business restrictions. It now appears that even this rather crude, first stage, regulatory regime may be lifted, if the operators concerned can convince the authorities of the 'progress' of competitive conditions and/or the implications of technological convergence.

7. Virtual Ring Fencing

In standing back and considering the general question of organising (fair and efficient) multiple network access in communications markets, it is impossible to ignore the fact that much of the problem stems from the fact of vertical integration of the incumbent network operators into the dependent services markets. The 'bottleneck' *per se* becomes less of a problem, to the extent that it is controlled by interests which are neutral and independent of the downstream market. As Mr Barnes (amongst others) has pointed out, regulators need to recognise the overriding importance of ensuring that the right 'boundaries' are in place between the access facility and the market place (including—most importantly—the player who owns/controls the facility). If the boundaries are strong and clear enough, and if they are established in the right place (factors which should involve a hefty, but one-off regulatory effort), then the day-to-day policing of activities across the boundary (terms and conditions of access for players in the dependent market to the network facility) is a much less arduous and burdensome activity for the regulator. By contrast, where effective boundaries are not established in this context, the day-to-day policing problem is extremely frustrating and virtually impossible to get right in any sustainable and efficient way.

The complementary relationship of (or even the inverse relationship between) use of competition policy to analyse and solve structural factors of the access problem, and use of behavioural rules to regulate the access problem, was much referred to in the Workshop. It is clear that this has been applied in practice in the EU as far as the setting of regulatory 'conditions' (or behavioural remedies) for allowing structural changes in the form of mergers or agreements. However, how can this relationship be applied to the regulatory dilemma? In other words, given the fact that on-going price regulation is seen as an unpopular and increasingly non-viable option, how can structural solutions be applied to the pre-existing structural problems of vertical integrated incumbents?

As we have seen, the EU jurisdictions are reluctant to impose divestiture obligations or line-of business restrictions on operators. This would suggest that intervention in the financial and property rights of the operators is not viable. However, a compromise solution may be worth pursuing. While the 'boundaries' mentioned above are vital, it is possible that they may be established without imposing divestiture. The Commission has already recommended or imposed other types of separation of business activities on companies in this sector, in the form of legal separation and/or structural separation.[9] However, proof of the effectiveness of such solutions has yet to be established.

A more 'state-of-the-art' compromise solution is the idea of establishing 'virtual ring fences' around key access resources. If effective as a one-off solution, this should avoid both complex behavioural controls and intrusive financial interventions. This is, in essence, a technical and administrative solution which may be applied to an increasing number of access resources—in particular, as concerns intelligent network services and facilities. It involves the establishment of a neutral boundary—a 'technical fence'—to ensure fair sharing and exchange of network resources. The two key applications to date are

---

[9] For instance in the Draft Commission Directive amending Directive 98/388/EC in order to ensure that telecommunications networks and cable TV networks owned by a single operator are separate legal entities, OJ C 71/23 (1998).

centralised databases (for providing services such as local and non-geographic number portability) and electronic access gateways (for provision of local loop access facilities). These are already very effective in the US. They are currently being considered by committees and working groups in many of the Member States (and, in some cases, are actually in the process of implementation).

The key to making this solution work is 'third party management'. It is essential to lift control of the technology, service and administration of the 'fence' and 'gateway' out of the hands of the incumbent. This means that the technical gateway can and should be established 'off-switch'. But this does not imply simply shifting the burden onto the regulator. The regulator's role is rather an initially challenging, but ultimately one-off task. That is, to mandate that the technology and its management be supplied by an independent third party, and to guide and chair the process by which such a solution is selected and set up.

The general points underlined in this model are twofold. First, regulatory attention may be best refocused onto establishing the right access interface— the right type of 'fence'—instead of the day-to-day relations between parties on either side of it, or trying to interfere with the actual property rights of existing operators. New technology makes such solutions possible in a way that they were not before. Second, however, day to day management of the 'electronic gateway', and administration of key resources, may also best be entrusted to a neutral third party.

8. The Pricing Dilemma

Finally, it should be pointed out that, while the pricing issues (as recognised by the majority of our Panel I papers) has been the 'bug-bear' of the regulator and the main target of criticism of the roles and effectiveness of sector regulation, it may, in fact, be that the pricing problem (deciding what is the right price, who should provide it, how and to whom) is no longer the key (or even most appropriate) issue for regulatory focus. Indeed, as with the above discussions concerning interconnection and SMP identification, this accent on price may be relegated to being a 'bug-bear' of the first, initial phase of regulation. On the one hand, 'benchmarking' and international experience can now be used to resolve, at least roughly, the 'how much?' arguments. On the other, the current stage of competition (let us say 'second stage' in the advancement from liberalisation) demands that many non-price issues be addressed by frameworks for access regulation.

Unfortunately, while these regulatory dilemmas concerning the wholesale access level' and 'how to price it', are still extremely heated and far from being solved, this itself is only one aspect of the market power problem in these net-work markets. Addressing the incumbent's power has proved to be like 'peel-ing an onion'. Indeed, many competitors are arguing that the focus of pro-competition policy attention should be drawn to the significance of the entrenched retail market power of the incumbent, and to the related complex non-price issues and hurdles for market entrants. Even when/if the intercon-nection pricing regime is resolved, effective competition is still constrained by the next layer of the market power 'onion'. These retail issues involve, for instance, the incumbent's control of network interfaces and its discriminatory provisioning processes for services and facilities. The persistence of AT&T's market power notwithstanding its lack of control over local loop suggests that access regulation alone is not enough to address an incumbents power in this market.

9. International Experience?

The experience in the US and other countries illustrates that there is no short and simple road to a workably competitive telecom market, and that reliance on general antitrust law is not sufficient.

V. Institutional Issues and Considerations

It is important to recognise that where arguments from sector regulators (or, in this case, DG XIII) develop to support regulatory roll-back and an increased and more effective role for application of general competition law and princi-ples in the telecom sector, this does not, generally, mean that regulators are opting to simply hand-over responsibilities to 'another' institution—i.e. the anti-trust authority. Rather, it may well imply a push from regulatory institu-tions to gain an increased competence in that they themselves may gain the responsibility and powers for competition policy in the sector.

Competition authorities, on the other hand, tend to be against such initia-tives by regulators to presume to direct the use and role of competition. There is, obviously, a politico-institutional interest in avoiding the handing over of their 'exclusive rights' to apply competition laws. Slightly less cynically stated, there is often a strong argument that, in the wrong or inexperienced hands, powerful competition principles and concepts tend to get confused, abused, and hence weakened.

Conclusion

The central issues, for both the 1998 Competition Workshop and the 1999 Communications Review, are about how to regard and deal with the 'overlap' between sector regulation and competition law in the rapidly developing electronic communications sector. This involves

(i)   the legal questions – of what laws may be applied and how;

(ii) the normative questions – of what policy and rules should be implemented and why; and

(iii) the institutional questions – of who has the competence and authority to implement the rules and monitor their effects (and, where more than one institution is involved, how co-operation and co-ordination should be managed between the two.)

At the time of writing, the European Commission's Communication on the Communications Review is still being drafted, so we cannot yet comment on any official proposals for the framework for reform. This paper has commented, rather, on some of the issues and problems the Review will be tackling, and some of the informal reactions from the market and other interested parties to date. At this early stage, it would presumptuous and inappropriate to draw any firm conclusions. Thus, the attempt is simply to note some key points of contention and to emphasise some of the risks involved.

In this context, the main aim of the discussion presented is simply to draw attention to the dangers of confusing the roles of sector regulator and competition authority and, likewise, of sector regulations and competition law.

Louisa Gosling
1999

BIBLIOGRAPHY

ABA Antitrust Section (1997): *Antitrust Developments*, ABA: Washington.

Abadee, A. (1997): 'The Essential Facilities Doctrine and the National Access Regime: A Residual Role for Section 46 of the Trade Practices Act?' 5 *Trade Practices Law Journal* 27.

Ahern, (1994): 'Refusals to Deal after Aspen', 63 *Antitrust L.J.* 153, 166–82.

Albach, H. and Knieps, G. (1997): *Kosten und Preise in wettbewerblichen Ortsnetzen*, Nomos: Baden-Baden.

Alchian, A.A. (1997): *Economic Forces at Work: Selected Works by Armen A. Alchian*, Liberty Press: Indianapolis.

Amadeus/Sabre, (1992): *21st Report on Competition Policy*, Amadeus/Sabre.

Areeda, P. (1990): 'Essential Facilities: An Epithet in Need of Limiting Principles', 58 *Antitrust L.J.* 841.

Areeda, P. and Hovenkamp, H. (1992): *Antitrust Law* (Supplement to the Journal: Little Brown & Company).

Areeda, P. and Hovenkamp, H. (1996): *Antitrust.*

Areeda, P. and Turner, (1975): 'Predatory Pricing and Related Practices under Section 2 of the Sherman Act', 88 *Harvard Law Review* 697.

Areeda, P., Elhauge, E. and Hovenkamp, H. (1996): *Antitrust Law. Law* (Supplement to the Journal: Little Brown & Company).

Armstrong, M. (1998): 'Network Interconnection in Telecommunications', *Economic Journal* 545–564.

Armstrong, M. (1999): 'Competition and Collusion in the Pay-TV Market', *Journal of Japanese and International Economics* 257–280.

Arnbak, J.C. (1997): 'Technology Trends and their Implication for Telecom Regulation, in William H. Melody (ed), *Telecom Reform: Principles, Policies and Regulatory Practices*, Technical University of Denmark, 67–82.

Arnbak, J.C., Van Cuilenberg, J.J. and Dommering, E.J. (1990): *Verbinding en Ortvlechting in de Communicatie*, Cramwinckel, Amsterdam.

Atkinson, A.A. and Scott, W.R. (1982): 'Current Cost Depreciation', 9 *Journal of Business Finance and Accounting.*

Atwood, J.H. (1997): 'Competition in International Telecommunication Services', 97 *Colum. L. Rev.* 874.

Baker, D. (1993): 'Compulsory Access to Network Joint Ventures Under the Sherman Act: Rules or Roulette?', 999 *Utah. L.Rev.* 1019–1045.

Baker, D. and Brandel, R. (1996): *The Law of Electronic Funds Transfer Systems*, Warren, Gorham and Lamont: Boston.

Baumol, W.J. (1983): 'Some Subtle Issues in Railroad Regulation', 10:1/2 *International Journal of Transport Economics* 341–355.

Baumol, W.J. and Bradford, D.F. (1970): 'Optimal Departures from Marginal Cost Pricing', 60 *American Economic Review* 265–283.

Baumol, W.J. and Sidak, J.C. (1994): *Toward Competition in Local Telephony*, MIT Press and the American Enterprise Institute: Cambridge, Ma.

Baumol, W.J., Koehn, M.F., and Willig, R.D. (1987): 'How Arbitrary is Arbitrary: or, Towards the Deserved Demise of Full Cost Allocation', 3 *Public Utilities Fortnightly*.

Baumol, W.J., Panzar, J.C. and Willig, R.D. (1982): *Contestable Markets and the Theory of Industry Structure*, Harcourt Brace Janovich: New York.

Beesley, M.E. and Littlechild, S.C. (1989): 'The Regulation of Privatized Monopolies in the United Kingdom', 20:3 *Rand Journal of Economics* 454–472.

Blumenthal, (1990): 'Three Vexing Issues under the Essential Facilities Doctrine: ATM Networks as an Illustration', 58 *Antitrust L.J.* 855.

Bonbright, J.C., Danielsen, A.L. and Kamerschen, D.R. (1988): *Principles of Public Utility Rates* (2nd edition), Public Utilities Reports Inc.

Bork, R.H. (1978): *The Antitrust Paradox: A Policy at War with Itself*, Basic Books: N.J.

Brief, P. (1967): 'A Late Nineteenth Century Contribution to the Theory of Depreciation', *Journal of Accounting Research*.

Brodley, J.F. (1982): 'Joint Ventures and Antitrust Policy', 95 *Harv. L. Rev.* 1523.

Brokelmann, H. (1997): 'Las negativas de suministro en el Derecho de la competencia comunitario y español', 125 *Gaceta Jurídica de la CE*, 5–27.

Bromwich, M., (1977): 'The General Validity of Certain "Current" Value Asset Valuation Bases', 7:28 *Accounting and Business Research*.

Carroll, K.J. (1977): *Economic Studies*, Telecom Australia: Sydney.

Chambers, R.J. (1983): *Price Variation and Inflation Accounting*, Canadian Accountants Research Foundation: Vancouver.

Chambers, R.J. and Wolnizer, P.W. (1990): 'A "True and Fair" View of Financial Position', *Companies and Securities Law Journal*.

Coase, R.H. (1973): 'Business Organisation and the Accountant' in J.M. Buchanan and G.F. Thirlby (eds), *LSE Essays on Cost*, Weidenfeld and Nicolson: London.

Coates, K. (1998): 'Commission Notice on the Application of the Competition Rules to Access Agreements in the Telecommunications Sector,' *Competition Policy Newsletter*, 1998 12, European Commission.

Damus, S. (1984): 'Ramsey Pricing by U.S. Railroads: Can it Exist?', 18 *Journal of Transport Economics and Policy* 51–61.

Danielian, N.R. (1939): *AT&T*, The Vanguard Press: New York.

Department of Trade & Industry (1997): Green Paper on Regulating Communication: Approaching Convergence in the Information Age, HMSO: London.

Deringer, A. (1968): *The Competition Law of the European Community*, Commerce Clearing House: New York.

Deselaers, W. (1995): 'Die 'Essential Facilities': Doktrin im Lichte des Magill-Urteils des EuGH', *EuZW* 563.

Easterbrook (1986): 'On Identifying Exclusionary Conduct', 61 *Notre Dame L. Rev.* 972.

Economides, N. and White, N.E. (1995): 'Access and Interconnection Pricing: How Efficient is the "Efficient Component Pricing Rule"?', 40:3 *Antitrust Bulletin* 557–580.

Ehrhardt, M.C. (1994): *The Search for Value: Measuring the Company's Cost of Capital*, Harvard Business School Press: Cambridge, Ma.

Engel, C. and Knieps, G. (1998): *Die Vorschriften des Telekommunikationsgesetzes über den Zugang zu wesentlichen Leistungen: Eine juristisch-ökonomische Untersuchung*, Nomos: Baden-Baden.

Ergas, H. and Small, J. (1994): *One Way Bets on Regulated Monopolies: Theory and Evidence*, CRNEC, University of Auckland: Auckland.

European Commission (1991): *Guidelines on the Application of Competition Rules in the Telecommunications Sector* (OJC 233/2, 6.9.1991).

European Commission (1996): *Green Paper on the Development of the Common Market for Telecommunications Services and Equipment* COM(87)290.

European Commission (1996): *Towards an International Framework of Competition Rules*, COM(96)284.

European Commission (1997): *Green Paper on the Convergence of the Telecommunications, Media and Information Technology Sectors, and the Implications for Regulation*, COM(97)623.

European Commission (1997): *Results of Public Consultation on the Convergence Green Paper: Communication* , COM(1999)108.

Fabrycky, W.J., Thuesen, G.J.and Verma, D. (1998): *Economic Decision Analysis* (3rd ed.), Prentice Hall: New Jersey.

Faulhaber, G.R. (1975): 'Cross-Subsidization: Pricing in Public Enterprises', 65 *American Economic Review* 966–977.

Federal Communications Commission (1998): *Annual Assessment of the Status of Competition in Markets for the Delivery of Video Programming*, FCC: Washington.

Fisher, F.M, McGowan, J.J. and Greenwood, J.E. (1983): *Folded, Spindled and Multilated—Economic Analysis and U.S. v IBM*, A Charles River Associates Study, MIT: Cambridge, Ma.

Fox and Fox, (1999): *Corporate Acquisitions and Mergers*, Mathew Bender & Co.

Fox, E. (1981): 'The Modernization of Antitrust: A New Equilibrium', 66 *Cornell L. Rev.* 1140.

Fox, E. (1986): 'Monopolization and Dominance in the United States and the European Community: Efficiency, Opportunity, and Fairness', 61 *Notre Dame L. Rev.* 1011–17.

Fox, E. (1994): '*Eastman Kodak Co.* v *Image Technical Services*, Inc.: Information Failure as Soul or Hook?', 62 *Antitrust L.J.* 3.

Fox, E. (1996): 'Trade, Competition, and Intellectual Property: TRIPs and its Antitrust Counterparts', 29 *Vand. J. Transnat'l L.* 481.

Fox, E. (1997): 'Lessons From *Boeing*: A Modest Proposal to Keep Politics Out of Antitrust', *Antitrust Report*, Matthew Bender.

Fox, E. (1998): 'International Antitrust: Against Minimum Rules; for Cosmopolitan Principles', 43 *Antitrust Bulletin* 5.

Fox, E. (1987): 'Chairman Miller, The Federal Trade Commission, Economics and *Rashomon*', in 'Economists on the Bench', 50 *Law & Contemp. Prob.* 33.

Fox, E. and Ordover, J. (1995): 'The Harmonization of Competition and Trade Law: The Case for Modest Linkages of Law and Limits to Parochial State Action', 19 *World Competition L. & Econ. Rev.* 5.

Fox, E. and Sullivan, L., (1987): 'Antitrust–Retrospective and Prospective: Where Are We Coming From? Where Are We Going?', 62 *NYUL Rev.* 936.

Freidenfelds, J., (1981): *Capacity Expansion*, North-Holland.

Fremdling, R. and Knieps G. (1993): 'Competition, Regulation and Nationalization: The Prussian Railway System in the Nineteenth Century', XLI:2 *The Scandinavian Economic History Review* 129–154.

Gabel, D. and Kennet, D.M. (1991): 'Estimating the Cost Structure of Local Telephone Exchange Network', National Regulatory Research Institute at Ohio State University: Columbus, OH.

Gabel, D. and Kennet, D.M. (1994): 'Economies of Scope in the Local Telephone Exchange Market', 6 *Journal of Regulatory Economics* 386.

George, K. and Jacquemin H. (1990): 'Competition Policy in the European Community', in, W. Commanor (ed), *Competition Policy in Europe and North America*, Harmwood Academic Press: Harmwood, 206–245.

Glasl, D. (1994): 'Essential Facilities Doctrine in EC Anti-trust Law: A Contribution to the Current Debate', 6 *ECLR* 306–314.

Griffin, J.M. (1972): 'The Process Analysis Alternative to Statistical Cost Functions: An Application to Petroleum Refining', 62 *American Economic Review*.

Griffin, J.M. (1977): 'Long-run Production Modeling with Pseudo-data: Electric Power Generation', 125 *Bell Journal of Economics*.

Gyselen, L. (1996): 'EU Antitrust Law in the Area of Financial Services: *Capita Selecta* for a Cautious Shaping of Policy', in B. Hawk (ed), *Fordham Corporate Law Institute*, Fordham: NY.

Haag, M., Klotz, R. (1998): 'Commission Practice Concerning Excessive Pricing in Telecommunications', *Competition Policy Newsletter*, 1998/2, European Commission.

Hardin, A., (1998): *Accounting and Economic Depreciation in Forward Looking Cost Models*, at *http://www.necg.com.au*.

Hawk, B. (1996): *United States, Common Market and International Antitrust: A Comparative Guide*, Bender: New York.

Hitchings, P. (1998): 'Access to International Telecommunications Facilities, *ECLR*, 84.

Holler, M. J. (1990): 'Umstrittene Märkte und die Theorie der reinen Kosten', in: J.-M. Graf von der Schulenburg and H.-W. Sinn (eds), *Theorie der Wirtschaftspolitik: Festschrift zum fünfundsiebzigsten Geburtstag von Hans Möller*, Mohr/Siebeck: Tübingen, 146–161.

Hovenkamp, H. (1993): 'Market Power in Aftermarkets: Antritrust Policy and the Kodak Case', 40 *UCLA L. Rev.* 1447.

Hulten, C.R., and Wykoff, F.C. (1996): 'Issues in the Measurement of Economic Depreciation', 34 *Economic Inquiry* 10–23.

Hylton, (1991): 'Economic Rents and Essential Facilities', 1991 *BYUL Rev.* 1243.

Ims, L.A., (1997): 'Economics of Residential Broadband Access', 11.1 *IEEE Network*.

Independent Television Commission, *Television* (1997): *The Public's View*. ITC: London.

ITT-Belgacom, (1997): *27th Competition Policy Report*, ITT-Belgacom.

J. Seligman, (1995): *The Transformation Of Wall Street*, Northwestern University Press: Boston.

Joliet, R. (1970): *Monopolization and Abuse of a Dominant Position: A Comparative Study of the American and European Approaches to Market Power*, Collection Scientifique de la Faculté de Droit de l'Université de Liège: Liège.

Jurgens, E.C.M. (1995): in I. Baten & J. Ubacht (eds), *Een Kweslic van Toegang*, Cramwinckel, Amsterdam.

Kaplan, R.S. and Cooper, R. (1998): *Cost & Effect*, Harvard Business School Press: Cambridge, Ma.

Kerse and Cook, (1996): *EC Merger Control*, Sweet & Maxwell: London.

Kewalram, R.P. (1994): 'The Essential Facilities Doctrine and Section 46 of the Trade Practices Act: Fine-tuning the Hilmer Report on National Competition Policy', 2 *Trade Practices Law Journal* 188.

Kezsbom. A. and Goldman, A.V. (1996): 'No Shortcut to Antritrust Analysis: The Twisted Journey of the "Essential Facilities" Doctrine', 1 *Columbia Bus. L. Rev.* 1.

Knieps, G. (1993):'Competition, Coordination and Cooperation: A Disaggregated Approach to Transportation Regulation', 3:3 *Utilities Policy* 201–207.

Knieps, G. (1995): 'Die Ausgestaltung des zukünftigen Regulierungsrahmens für die Telekommunikation in Deutschland' (Diskussionsbeiträge des Instituts für Verkehrswissenschaft und Regionalpolitik Nr. 22, Universität Freiburg).

Knieps, G. (1996): *Wettbewerb in Netzen: Reformpotentiale in den Sektoren Eisenbahn und Luftverkehr*, Mohr/Siebeck: Tübingen.

Knieps, G. (1997a): 'Phasing out Sector-Specific Regulation in Competitive Telecom-munications', 50:3 *Kyklos* 325–339.

Knieps, G. (1997b): 'Costing and Pricing of Interconnection Services in a Liberalized European Telecommunications Market', *Discussion Paper, No. 39*, Institut für Verkehrswissenschaft und Regionalpolitik, Albert-Ludwigs-Universität Freiburg.

Knorr, A. (1998): 'Das Konzept der "Light-handed regulation" ', in 6 *Wirtschaft und Wettbewerb*, 541–53.

Korah, V. (1997): *An Introductory Guide to EC Competition Law and Practice*, 6th Edition, Hart Publishing: Oxford.

Laffont, J.-J. and Tirole J. (1994): 'Access Pricing and Competition', 39 *European Economic Review*, 1673–1710.

Laffont, J.-J., Rey, P. and Tirole, J. (1998): 'Network Competition: I. Overview and Nondiscriminatory Pricing', 1 *Rand Journal of Economics* 1–37.

Larson, A.C., Kovacic, W.E., Mudd, D.R. (1998): 'Competitive Access Issues and Telecommunications Regulatory Policy' 20 *J. Contemp. L.* 419.

Long, C. (1988): *Telecommunications Law and Practice*, Sweet & Maxwell: London.

Lowe, (1994): 'Telecommunications Services and Competition Law in Europe', *EBLR.*

Ma, R. and Mathews, R., (1979): *The Accounting Framework,* Longman: Cheshire.

MacNeal, K., (1939): *Truth in Accounting,* University of Pennsylvania Press: Penn.

Martínez Lage, S. (1997): 'La Comisión del Mercado de las Telecomunicaciones y el Derecho de la Competencia I y II', 136 *Gaceta Jurídica de la CE* 1–5.

Martínez Lage, S. (1997): 'Órganos sectoriales de defensa de la competencia', in 128 *Gaceta Jurídica de la CE,* 1–5.

Minoli, D. (1993): *Broadband Network Analysis and Design,* Artech House.

Montag, C. (1996): 'The Case for a Radical Reform of the Infringement Procedure under Regulation 17', 8 *ECLR* 428.

Montero, J. and Brokelmann, H. (1999): *Telecomunicaciones y Television—La nueva regulación en España.*

NERA (1998): *An Analysis of the ITC Report into Channel Bundling,* NERA: London.

NERA/OFTEL (1996): *The Methodology to Calculate Long-Run Incremental Costs, March 1996; Reconciliation and Integration of Top Down and Bottom Up Models of Incremental Costs,* NERA

Noll, R.G. (1995): 'The Role of Antitrust in Telecommunications', (Fall) *The Antitrust Bulletin,* 501.

O'Bryan, M. (1996): 'Access Pricing: Law Before Economics', 4 *Competition and Consumer Law Journal* 85.

OECD (1999): *Communications Outlook 1999,* OECD: Paris.

Office of Fair Trading (1997): *The Director General's Review of BSkyB's Position in the Wholesale Pay TV Market,* OFT: London.

OFTEL (1997): *Bundling in the Pay TV Market,* OFTEL: London.

OFTEL (1997): *OFTEL Submission to the ITC on Competition Issues Arising from the Award of Digital Terrestrial Multiplex Licences,* OFTEL: London.

OFTEL (1998): *Conditional Access Charges for Digital Television: A Statement,* OFTEL: London.

Owen, B.M. and Braeutigam H. (1978): *The Regulation Game: Strategic Use of the Administrative Process,* MIT Press: Cambridge, Ma.

Panzar, J. (1998): 'A Critique of the WIK Cost Model', University of Auckland, CRNEC: Auckland.

Parcu, P.-L (1996): 'Stato e Concorrenza, L'attività di Segnalazione dell'Autorità Antitrust: Contenuti, Efficacia e Prospettive', in *Temi e Problemi,* Autorità Garante della Concorrenza e del Mercato: Rome.

Peirson, G. and Ramsey, A. (1994): *Depreciation of Non-Current Assets,* Australian Accounting Research Foundation: Sydney.

Pheasant, J. and Weston, D. (1997): 'Vertical Restraints, Foreclosure and Article 85: Developing an Analytical Framework', 5 *ECLR* 323.

Posner, R.A. (1976): *Antitrust Law, An Economic Perspective,* University of Chicago Press: Chicago.

Ralph, E. (1998): 'Regulating an Input Monopolist With Minimal Information', *http://www.necg.com.au.*

Ratner, (1988): 'Should there be an Essential Facility Doctrine?', 21 *U. Cal. Davis L. Rev.* 327.

Rawls, J. (1971): *A Theory of Justice*, Havard University Press: Cambridge, Ma.

Ridyard, (1996): 'Essential Facilities and the Obligation to Supply Competitors under UK and EC Competition Law', 438 *ECL Rev* 446.

Riehmer, K.W. (1998): 'EG-Wettbewerbsrecht und Zugangsvereinbarungen in der Telekommunikation,' *MMR* 355.

Ryan, (1997): 'Competition in the Provision of On-line Services: the UK Approach to the Problem of Vertical Integration', 7 *ECLR* 435.

Schaub, A (1998): 'International Cooperation in Antitrust Matters: Making the Point in the Wake of the Boeing/MDD Proceedings', *Competition Policy Newsletter*, February 1998.

Scott, W.R., (1997): *Financial Accounting Theory*, Prentice Hall: New Jersey.

Shankerman, M. (1996): 'Symmetric Regulation for Competitive Telecommunications', 8 *Information Economics and Policy* 5.

Sidak, G. and Baumol, W. (1994): *Towards Competition in Local Telephony*, MIT Press: Cambridge, Ma.

Smith, Adam (1776): *The Wealth of Nations.*

Smits, J.M. (1991): *Legal Aspects of Implementing International Telecommunication Links*, Kluwer: Dordrecht.

Solomons, D. (1995): 'Criteria for Choosing an Accounting Model', IX 1 *Accounting Horizons.*

Sterling, R.R. (1982): 'The Concept of Physical Capital Maintenance', in R.R. Sterling and K.W. Lemke (eds), *Maintenance of Capital: Physical and Financial*, Scholars Book Co.

Sullivan, L. (1977): *Handbook of the Law of Antitrust*, Western Publishing Co.: St. Paul.

Sullivan, L. (1991): 'Section 2 of the Sherman Act and Vertical Strategies by Dominant Firms', 21 *Southwestern Univ. L. Rev.* 1227.

Sunder, S. (1997): *The Theory of Accounting and Control*, South Western Publishing.

Temple Lang, J. (1994): 'Defining Legitimate Competition: Companies' Duties to Supply Competitors, and Access to Essential Facilities', in, Fordham Corporate Law Institute, *International Antitrust Law & Policy*, Fordham: NY, Chapter 12.

Temple Lang, J. (1996): *European Community Antitrust Law: Innovation Markets and High Technology Industries*, Fordham: NY.

Temple Lang, J. (1997): 'European Community Antitrust Law: Innovation Markets and High Technology Industries', in B. Hawk (ed), *Fordham Corporate Law Institute*, Fordham: NY.

Temple Lang, J. (1997): 'Media, Multimedia and European Community Antitrust Law', http://europa.eu.int/en/comm/dg04/speech/seven/en/sp97070.htm, 61.

Thomas A.L. (1974): *The Allocation Problem: Part Two*, American Accounting Association.

Thomas, A.L. (1969): *The Allocation Problem in Financial Accounting Theory*, American Accounting Association.

Thuesen G.J. and Fabryky, W.J. (1993): *Engineering Economy* (8th edition), Prentice-Hall: New Jersey.

Treacy, P. (1998): 'Essential Facilities: Is the Tide Turning?', *CMLR* 501.

Tye, W.B. (1987): 'Competitive Access: a Comparative Industry Approach to the Essential Facility Doctrine', 8:2 *Energy Law Journal* 337–379.

Tye, W.B. (1993): 'Pricing Market Access for Regulated Firms', 29:1 *Logistics and Transportation Review* 39–67.

Ungerer, H. (1996): 'EC Competition Law in the Telecommunications, Media And Information Technology Sectors', in Barry Hawk (ed) *International Antitrust Law & Policy*, Fordham Corporate Law Institute: NY.

Venit, J. and Kallaugher, J. (1994): 'Essential Facilities: A Comparative Law Approach,' in, Fordham Corporate Law Institute, *International Antitrust Law & Policy*, Fordham: NY, Chapter 13.

Wallman, S.M.H. (1998): 'Competition, Innovation, and Regulation in the Securities Markets', 53 *The Business Lawyer* 341.

Weinhaus, C.L. and Oettinger, A.G. (1988): *Behind the Telephone Debates*, Ablex.

Weiss, J. R. and Stem, M.L. (1998): 'Serving Two Masters: The Dual Jurisdiction of the FCC and the Justice Department Over Telecommunications Transactions', 6 *CommLaw Conspectus* 195.

Werden, (1998): 'The Law and Economics of the Essential Facility Doctrine', 32 *St. Louis U. L.J.* 433.

Whittington, G. (1983): *Inflation Accounting: An Introduction to the Debate*, Cambridge University Press: Cambridge.

Wicksteed, P.H. (1933): *The Common Sense of Political Economy and Selected Papers and Reviews on Economic Theory*, Routledge: London.

Willig, R.D (1978): 'Pareto-superior Nonlinear Outlay Schedules', 9:1 *Bell Journal of Economics* 56–69.

Zajac, E.E. (1995): *Political Economy of Fairness*, The MIT Press: Cambridge, Ma.

INDEX

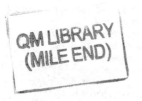